THE CANADIAN YEARBOOK OF INTERNATIONAL LAW

2001

ANNUAIRE CANADIEN DE DROIT INTERNATIONAL

The Board of Editors, the Canadian Branch of the International Law Association, the Canadian Council on International Law, and the University of British Columbia are not in any way responsible for the views expressed by contributors, whether the contributions are signed or unsigned.

Les opinions émises dans le présent *Annuaire* par nos collaborateurs, qu'il s'agisse d'articles signés ou non, ne sauraient en aucune façon engager la responsabilité du Comité de rédaction, de la Section canadienne du Conseil canadien de droit international ou de l'Université de Colombie Britannique.

Communications to the *Yearbook* should be addressed to:

Les communications destinées à l'*Annuaire* doivent être adressées à:

THE EDITOR, THE CANADIAN YEARBOOK OF INTERNATIONAL LAW
FACULTY OF LAW, COMMON LAW SECTION
UNIVERSITY OF OTTAWA
57 LOUIS PASTEUR
OTTAWA, ONTARIO K1N 6N5 CANADA

The Canadian Yearbook of International Law

VOLUME XXXIX   2001   TOME XXXIX

Annuaire canadien de Droit international

Published under the auspices of

THE CANADIAN BRANCH, INTERNATIONAL LAW ASSOCIATION

AND

THE CANADIAN COUNCIL ON INTERNATIONAL LAW

Publié sous les auspices de

LA SECTION CANADIENNE DE L'ASSOCIATION DE DROIT INTERNATIONAL

ET

LE CONSEIL CANADIEN DE DROIT INTERNATIONAL

UBC Press

VANCOUVER/TORONTO

Printed in Canada on acid-free paper ∞

ISBN 0-7748-0991-4
ISSN 0069-0058

National Library of Canada Cataloguing in Publication Data

The National Library of Canada has catalogued this
publication as follows:

*The Canadian yearbook of international law — Annuaire
canadien de droit international*

Annual.
Text in English and French.
"Published under the auspices of the Canadian
Branch, International Law Association and the
Canadian Council on International Law."
ISSN 0069-0058

1. International Law — Periodicals.
I. International Law Association. Canadian Branch.
II. Title: Annuaire canadien de droit international.
JC 21.C3   341'.05   C75-34558-6E

Données de catalogage avant publication (Canada)

*Annuaire canadien de droit international — The Canadian
yearbook of international law*

Annuel.
Textes en anglais et en français.
"Publié sous les auspices de la Branche canadienne
de l'Association de droit international et le Conseil
canadien de droit international."
ISSN 0069-0058

1. Droit international — Périodiques.
I. Association de droit international. Section canadienne.
II. Conseil canadien de droit international.
III. Titre: The Canadian yearbook of international law.
JC 21.C3   341'.05   C75-34558-6F

UBC Press
University of British Columbia
2029 West Mall
Vancouver, BC V6T 1Z2
(604) 822-3259
www.ubcpress.ca

Contents / Matière

Book Reviews / Recensions de Livres

THE CANADIAN YEARBOOK OF INTERNATIONAL LAW

2001

ANNUAIRE CANADIEN DE DROIT INTERNATIONAL

The Internet in Light of Traditional Public and Private International Law Principles and Rules Applied in Canada

J.-G. CASTEL

INTRODUCTION

In general, the jurisdiction of a state to prescribe, to adjudicate, and to enforce[1] is related to physical location. Yet, physical location is foreign to the Internet,[2] which can be defined as the electronic medium of worldwide computer networks within which

J.-G. Castel, O.C., Q.C., Professor Emeritus, Osgoode Hall Law School, York University, and Counsel, Shibley Righton L.L.P., Toronto. He is grateful to Marc Castel of Robosky; Mike Lindsay of Hewlett-Packard (Canada) Limited; and his colleagues, Peter Hogg and Janet Walker, for their valuable comments.

[1] According to para. 401 of the Restatement of the Law Third, Foreign Relations Law of the United States, (1987), vol. 1, at 232 [hereinafter Restatement of the Law Third], jurisdiction to prescribe, to adjudicate and to enforce is defined as follows:

§401. Categories of Jurisdiction

Under international law, a State is subject to limitations on

(a) jurisdiction to prescribe, *i.e.*, to make its law applicable to the activities, relations, or status of persons, or the interests of persons in things, whether by legislation, by executive act or order, by administrative rule or regulation, or by determination of a court;

(b) jurisdiction to adjudicate, *i.e.*, to subject persons or things to the process of its courts or administrative tribunals, whether in civil or in criminal proceedings, whether or not the State is a party to the proceedings;

(c) jurisdiction to enforce, *i.e.*, to induce or compel compliance or to punish non-compliance with its laws or regulations, whether through the courts or by use of executive, administrative, police, or other nonjudicial action.

With respect to jurisdiction, the Restatement of the Law Third contains rules that are accepted by Canada. See also Restatement of the Law Third, paras. 402 and 404.

[2] Also called cyberspace. Another description of this word is all media used to transmit information, either digitally or electronically.

online communication takes place. As a network of computer networks interconnected by means of telecommunications facilities using common protocols and standards to allow for the exchange of information between each connected computer, the Internet is indifferent to the physical location of the computers between which such information is routed. There is no centralized storage location, control point, or communication channel for the Internet. Although each of the networks that make up the Internet is owned by a public or private organization, no single person or entity owns the Internet. It is capable of rapidly transmitting information without direct involvement or control by the end-user. Communications can be re-routed if one or more individual links are damaged or unavailable in order to deliver the information to its destination.[3] Physical location and national boundaries are not obstacles to the ability of an individual to access websites and transact business or disseminate information anywhere in the world.[4] Since the Internet has no territorially based national boundaries, users uploading or downloading data from unknown physical locations have no knowledge of the existence of such boundaries. This absence of physical location calls into question the applicability of the traditional public and private international law principles and rules that are based primarily on territoriality, in order to delineate the jurisdiction of states and their courts over the Internet and its users.

As Judge Preska of the United States District Court in *American Library Association* v. *Pataki* explains,

Internet is wholly insensitive to geographic distinctions. In almost every case, users of the Internet neither know nor care about the physical location of the Internet resources they access. Internet protocols were designed to ignore rather than document geographic location; while

---

[3] The Internet operates by taking data, which may be an email message, a web page, a sound clip, or a video stream, and breaking it up into separate packets and sending them along different available routes to a destination computer. See *How the Internet Works, Global Internet Project*, which is available at <http://www.gip.org/gip7.htm>. In general, see D. Jackson and T.L. Taylor, *The Internet Handbook for Canadian Lawyers* (3rd ed., 2000); M. Chissick and A. Kelman, *Electronic Commerce Law and Practice* (2nd ed., 2000); J.D. Robbins, *Advising eBusiness* (2001); B.B. Sookman, *Computer, Internet and Electronic Commerce Law* (1991).

[4] The Worldwide Web, which is a component of the Internet, is a collection of documents containing text, visual images, and audio clips, that is accessible from every Internet site in the world. It is used as a method of organizing information distributed across the Internet. The information on a web page resides on a computer until it is accessed by a reader. Hyperlinks are highlighted text or images that, when selected by a user, permit the user to view another related web document.

computers on the network do have "addresses," they are logical addresses on the network rather than geographic addresses in real space. The majority of Internet addresses contain no geographic clues and, even when an Internet address provides such a clue, it may be misleading.[5]

Access to the Internet can enable users to evade national regulations in order to process information in violation of privacy laws, to avoid consumer protection laws, to obtain professional advice from persons not properly licensed, to hire persons in contravention of labour laws, to infringe intellectual property rights with impunity, to publish defamatory material, to access pornography, to disseminate hate literature, to circumvent gaming laws, to avoid security regulations, and so on.

Before examining the public and private international law principles and rules relevant to the Internet, it is necessary to understand who are the principal actors involved who may be prosecuted or sued in Canadian courts. First, there is the user who accesses and views or uses electronic content found on the Internet. For instance, the user visiting a website or posting information thereon may be a gambler, a purchaser of goods or services, a seeker of information, a seller of goods or services, or a gaming merchant.[6] Second, there is the Internet service provider (ISP), which connects the user's computer to another computer. It allows the user, who is not directly connected to the Internet, to access it and to log onto a website and access its web contents, which is hosted by that particular computer (for instance, Bell Sympatico acts as an ISP). In other words, an ISP acts as an intermediary and gatekeeper by allowing computers connected through the network to communicate, transmit, and receive information worldwide. Individuals and businesses purchase access from an ISP, which is generally privately owned. The connection is usually made through a dial-up telephone service, although faster access is available by using a connection through integrated service digital network lines or a

---

[5] *American Library Association* v. *Pataki*, 969 F. Supp. 160 (S.D.N.Y. 1997), at 170. See also *Reno* v. *American Civil Liberties Union*, 117 S. Ct. 2329, at 2334-35 (1997), aff'ing *American Civil Liberties Union* v. *Reno*, 929 F. Supp. 84, at 830 *et seq.* (E.D. Pa. 1996), *Pro-C Ltd.* v. *Computer City Inc.* (2000), 7 C.P.R. (4th) 193 (Ont. S.C.J.), rev'd, (2001) 55 O.R. (3d) 577 (C.A.) [hereinafter *Computer City*].

[6] Individuals can establish a link with the Internet by using a computer permanently connected to a computer network that is directly or indirectly connected to the Internet or by using a personal computer with a modem to connect over the telephone to a larger computer or computer network that is directly or indirectly connected to the Internet.

cable modem access. Once the connection is made, the user must communicate with the web server to download web pages or other data and view them. Web browser software is used for that purpose (for instance, Microsoft Internet Explorer). Search engines and web portals facilitate surfing the web (for instance, Yahoo).

The third actor is the author/owner[7] of the web contents. The owner (which can be a physical person or a company) who operates the website has a registered domain name, which is a website address assigned to a specific computer that can be reached by any service provider.[8] Domain names can be registered outside the jurisdiction in which the registrant resides. The author/owner of the web contents can have it hosted by a service provider in Canada or by one located anywhere else in the world (for instance, in a state where gambling is legal). The web contents (web pages),[9] which include program files, reside physically on the host computer, which is called a server. It is at this location that the website contents are recorded as electronic data. The server may be located anywhere in the world. The author/owner could also have the website contents hosted by his or her own computer, which is then connected to the Internet through an ISP.[10]

Generally, the hosting service provider requires the author/owner of the website and contents to enter into an agreement not to upload (transfer files to the ISP server's computer where the website is hosted) illegal contents (for instance, hate literature and child pornography). If this type of activity takes place, the contents will be removed and the contract will be terminated. In some countries, the service provider does not require such an undertaking. Security software may also be used to prevent unauthorized access to a website by a user (password protected).

---

[7] The author, who is also called the content provider, may not be the owner of the website or its operator.

[8] The website is an Internet address, which enables users to exchange digital content with a particular host. The user, as a web-surfer, uses a web browser (for example, Microsoft's Internet Explorer or Netscape Navigator), which incorporates the web's pointer standard or universal resource locator (URL) to find a particular website. It has been held that a domain name is not property and lacks physical existence. It is not located where it is registered: *Easthaven* v. *Nutrisystem Com. Inc.* (2001), 55 O.R. (3d) 334 (S.C.J.) [hereinafter *Easthaven*], which is discussed throughout this article.

[9] A web page is a "hypertext" document created using hypertext markup language.

[10] A website operator may be employed by the website author/owner to update the website. Note that bulletin boards may be used for posting messages.

Basically, individuals as users interact with the Internet either by putting information on the net (uploading) or by taking information from the net (downloading). Difficulties arise due to the fact that the Internet is open-ended, and a user or author/owner of a website can always move the website and its contents to a new host and redirect or re-route web traffic to that new host. What is more, a website can be a portal to other websites or an Internet operator can use a surrogate server that is located in another state to prevent others from tracking the originating point. The origin of information may therefore be disguised.

This brief description would be incomplete without a reference to privacy and the Internet. Web servers and content providers are able to obtain valuable marketing and other information about users that visit their websites through the use of an Internet "cookie" placed on the computer's hard drive. With each visit by a user, personal information supplied by the user is deposited in the cookie file about the visit. Thus, a profile of the user's interests and purchasing patterns can be obtained from this personal data. The consumer/user data is a valuable asset of the owner of the website, which can be provided to third parties for direct marketing. Security technologies, such as firewalls, anti-virus software, and encryption technology,[11] are designed to protect this valuable asset as well as other information from hackers, thieves, and malicious intruders. In order to prevent the unauthorized processing of computerized personal data, some countries have adopted comprehensive legislation to regulate databases containing online information about individuals.[12] Canada has done this to a very limited extent in the Personal Information Protection and Electronic Documents Act[13] as this legislation does not address electronic data interchange

---

[11] For example, digital signatures.

[12] In Europe, this legislation was created pursuant to EC Directive 95/46 on the Protection of Individuals with Regard to the Processing of Personal Data and on the Free Movement of Such Data, 1995, O.J.L. 281/31, esp. ch. IV, arts. 25-26, which took effect on October 24, 1998: see P.P. Swire, "Of Elephants, Mice and Privacy: International Choice of Law and the Internet" (1998) 32 Int. Lawyer 991; C. Franklin, ed., *Business Guide to Privacy and Data Protection Legislation* (1996).

[13] Personal Information Protection and Electronic Documents Act, S.C. 2000, c. 5, especially ss. 4-10 and Schedule I, as amended by S.C. 2001, c. 41. In Québec, see an Act Respecting the Protection of Personal Information in the Private Sector, R.S.Q. c. P-39.1 and an Act to Establish a Legal Framework for Information Technology, S.Q. 2001, c. 32. See also Uniform Law Conference of Canada, *Electronic Data Interchange*, Proceedings (1993), 198 at 203.

as such, but prohibits the disclosure of personal information in certain situations.

The user, as a customer, viewer, or reader visiting a website and downloading data and the ISP and its server are the actors that are most likely to be reached by laws designed to control the use of the Internet since they can usually be located physically in a particular jurisdiction. The author/owner uploading the website could also be reached if he or she can be identified and is a resident of Canada. As for transactions on the Internet, it is difficult to determine where a contract has been entered or where a tort has been committed.

The main issue is the extent to which a state can adopt and enforce laws that are effective in preventing its citizens-users from accessing websites on the Internet in order to protect them against harm that it considers important. For instance, can a foreign company executive be prosecuted in Canada for failing to filter out material that his or her company posted on its website, which is objectionable in this country? Can Canada prevent the author/owner of a website from advertising the sale of an item that is prohibited by its laws or can it prevent the publication of hate literature on the Internet? Can Canada prohibit the exchange of data between Canadian database operators and persons in other countries whether or not there exists data privacy protection? Which state can control online gambling? In other words, when can a state impose its own laws, regulations, and policies on the Internet, and how can it enforce them successfully without infringing the rights or jurisdiction of other states? At the present time, any of the Internet actors can be subjected to haphazard, uncoordinated, and often inconsistent laws, regulations, and policies by states whose citizens were not meant to be able to access a particular website and where the actors were unaware that their website was being accessed. Thus, to be successful, legal regulation and enforcement must focus on all of the actors on the Internet including, in some instances, the financial intermediaries.

In this article, an attempt will be made to answer the following questions:

- Does international law place restraints on the exercise of jurisdiction by Canada to prescribe the substantive rules of criminal and private law with respect to the use of the Internet in an international context?
- What restraints are placed upon the federal Parliament and

the provincial legislatures by the Canadian constitution in the exercise of jurisdiction to prescribe, adjudicate, and enforce laws with respect to the use of the Internet in an international context?

- How effective are present Canadian criminal and private laws that are applicable to the Internet and its actors in an international context?

RESTRAINTS PLACED BY PUBLIC INTERNATIONAL LAW ON THE EXERCISE OF JURISDICTION BY CANADA TO PRESCRIBE SUBSTANTIVE RULES OF CRIMINAL AND PRIVATE LAW WITH RESPECT TO THE USE OF THE INTERNET IN AN INTERNATIONAL CONTEXT

With the explosion of Internet use and technology and its easy access all over the world, the regulation and control of the Internet and its actors has become a priority for many states. How is this to be accomplished when the Internet is independent from geographical constraints resulting from the nature of the message transmission? Which state has the authority to regulate the Internet? In other words, what are the criteria that enable a state to prescribe rules for the Internet? Are the traditional bases of jurisdiction recognized by public international law to govern the division of legislative, judicial, and executive power among sovereign states still relevant? How can territorially based laws reach persons who operate on the Internet? If a state adopts laws applicable to the Internet in an international context, is this action improper extraterritoriality?

Traditional public international law principles that are applicable to the jurisdiction of a state to prescribe are well established. They are based primarily on territory and nationality. However, in exercising jurisdiction to prescribe, the state must not act unreasonably, especially in circumstances affecting the interests of other states. In the context of the Internet, when may Canada prescribe rules to govern persons, things, or activities that are located entirely or partially outside its territorial boundaries?

THE TERRITORIALITY PRINCIPLE

Since the Internet operates without regard for state boundaries and reaches persons located in several jurisdictions simultaneously, is territoriality still relevant as a basis for the exercise of jurisdiction in order to prescribe laws applicable to the Internet? Section 402 of the Restatement of the Law Third, Foreign Relations Law of the United States[14] declares that a state has jurisdiction to prescribe law with respect to "(i) (a) conduct that wholly or in substantial part takes place within its territory; (b) the status of persons, or interests in things, present within its territory; (c) conduct outside its territory that has or is intended to have substantial effect within its territory." The territoriality principle divides jurisdictional competence into territorial compartments over which each state has authority. It flows from the principle of the sovereign equality of states. Since territorial sovereignty enables a state to legislate freely within its own territory, equality means that no state can by its legislation infringe the sovereignty of another state. An unqualified exercise of state sovereignty in disregard of the equality of other states violates international law. Lord Macmillan succinctly declared in *The Cristina*[15] that "[i]t is an essential attribute of the sovereignty of this realm, as of all sovereign independent States, that it should possess jurisdiction over all persons and things within its territorial limits and in all causes civil and criminal arising within these limits." Within its own territory, a state is virtually supreme, and international law places few restraints upon the exercise of its authority.

With respect to users and service providers located and operating within the state where their servers are located, the strict territoriality principle (subjective territoriality) would clearly justify the application of local laws controlling the Internet and force an ISP to prevent persons within its territory from accessing certain websites. However, to maintain that the server where web pages are physically located is the situs that would justify prescriptive jurisdiction based on subjective territoriality without any other Internet contact with that situs would be unreasonable. A state could also forbid persons within its territory from uploading and downloading information that it considers to be harmful to its interests or to the interests of its citizens.

The territoriality principle, if applied literally, does not take into account the existence of a series of related acts that may be involved in an offence committed on the Internet, especially when it is difficult to ascertain the location of one of the actors or of the activities involved. In order to avoid the difficulties created by complex situations, the territorial principle has been refined to include the effects within the territory of the prescribing state as a basis for

---

[14] Restatement of the Law Third, *supra* note 1.

[15] *The Cristina*, [1938] A.C. 485, at 496 (H.L.).

jurisdiction to prescribe. The effects principle, which is also called the objective territorial principle, enables a state to prescribe laws governing persons outside its territory who by their conduct cause harmful effects within the territory. Controversy arises when the conduct creating the damaging effect is lawful where carried out. If an activity takes place on the Internet, a state can exercise jurisdiction on such an activity provided that it has, or is intended to have, a substantial effect within its territory. Thus, libellous statements, hate literature, child pornography, violence, or incitement to racial hatred and discrimination posted on the Internet by an author/owner and accessible in a particular state could subject the author/owner to the legislation of that state provided he or she can be identified, particularly if the website provides interactive contacts and targets residents of the regulating state.[16] The downloading of files in Canada, if they are intended to be accessible in this country, would make the foreign author/owner's activities subject to Canadian jurisdiction.

The application of the effects principle may give rise to conflicting claims of jurisdiction since both the state in whose territory the conduct occurs and the state in whose territory the effects are produced have jurisdiction to prescribe rules of law pertaining to the conduct. In effect, no conflict should arise where all states concerned prohibit the same conduct — for instance, hate literature — on the ground that it is detrimental to their interests. Where the effects of the foreign conduct are felt in several states, each state should be able to apply its own laws. There is no need for one state to defer to the laws of the other, since they all have suffered injury (although its nature may be different for each one of them). Furthermore, some states may only be interested in regulating certain elements of a complex situation with which other states are not interested. The effects within the territory principle does not violate the territoriality principle since the effects themselves may be considered as a domestic constituent element of the offence or

---

[16] See *Steamship Lotus (France* v. *Turkey)* (1927), P.C.I.J. Series A. no. 10 at 23 [hereinafter *Lotus*]: "the courts of many countries, even of countries which have given their criminal legislation a strictly territorial character, interpret criminal law in the sense that offences, the authors of which at the moment of commission are in the territory of another State, are nevertheless to be regarded as having been committed in the national territory, if one of the constituent elements of the offence, and more especially its effects have taken place there." The territorial principle was applied in *Québec (Procureur Général)* v. *Hyperinfo Canada Inc.* (2001), QCCQ, which is available at <http://www.canlii.org/qc/jug/qccq/2001/2001qccq12076.html> [hereinafter *Hyperinfo*].

activity sufficient to bring it within the scope of the laws and regulations of the enacting state. However, knowledge of the effects abroad or the objective ability to anticipate such effects should be present in order to attract penal liability.

In order to avoid excessive use of the effects principle, it has been suggested that jurisdiction should be claimed only by the state where the primary effects of the unlawful conduct are felt: "In order to determine whether the effects are primary or secondary, two factors should be considered: (1) are the effects felt in one State more direct than the effects felt in other States? (2) are the effects felt in one State more substantial than the effects felt in other States?"[17] This suggestion would justify jurisdiction that is exercised only by states that have a legitimate interest in applying their laws and regulations to the Internet and its actors. It could also make it easier to solve conflicting jurisdictional claims. A legitimate interest would exist if the state and its residents or citizens were specially targeted by the website author/owner. The new trend, however, is to subject the effects principle to the principles of reasonableness and fairness in accommodating the overlapping and often conflicting interests of states and individual Internet actors.[18]

THE NATIONALITY PRINCIPLE

Paragraph 2 of section 402 of the Restatement of the Law Third, which declares that a state has jurisdiction to prescribe with respect to "the activities, interests, status, or relations of its nationals outside as well as within its territory" refers to the active and passive nationality principle. The nationality of the offender or of the victim provides a good basis for the exercise of jurisdiction to prescribe with respect to all the actors involved in Internet operations, provided their identity and nationality can be ascertained. As far as Canadian citizens are concerned, it is a principle that is more effective than the territoriality principle since it does not depend upon geography. There is no need to determine the *locus delicti*. Thus, the ISP, the author/owner of a website, and Internet intermediaries, if Canadian citizens, could be subjected to Canadian law.[19]

---

[17] M. Akehurst, "Jurisdiction in International Law" (1973) 46 Br. Y.B. Int'l. L. 146 at 198.

[18] See Restatement of the Law Third, *supra* note 1 at para. 403.

[19] A.D.C. Menthe, "Jurisdiction in Cyberspace: A Theory of International Spaces" (1997-8) 4 Mich. Telecommunications and Technology L. Rev. 69, suggests that since the power to control the Internet has only the most tenuous connection to

THE PROTECTIVE PRINCIPLE

Section 402(3) of the Restatement of the Law Third refers to the protective principle when it declares that a state has jurisdiction to prescribe law with respect to "certain conduct outside its territory by persons not its nationals that is directed against the security of the State or against a limited class of other State interests." Effects within the territory of the offended state are not necessary. The protective principle is justified on the ground of self-defence since a state has a legitimate right to protect itself from the effects of harmful acts or conduct that take place abroad. Of course, if the impact of the acts or conduct abroad is within its territory, the state is therefore concerned and has the right to punish the author of such harmful acts or conduct, which brings us back to the effects principle.

The protective principle could be used by a state to regulate activities on the Internet that affect its security, for instance, preventing the disclosure of classified information, espionage, counterfeiting, falsification of documents, cyber-crime and cyber-terrorism,[20] software piracy, propaganda for the enemy in wartime, intrusion in national security systems, endangering systems with viruses, and malicious tampering with government sites, provided it is possible to identify and reach the real authors of the electronic messages.

THE UNIVERSALITY PRINCIPLE

Finally, section 404 of the Restatement of the Law Third covers the universality principle according to which "[a] State has jurisdiction to define and prescribe punishment for certain offenses recognized by the community of nations as of universal concern, such as piracy, slave trade, attacks on or hijacking of aircraft, genocide, war crimes, and perhaps certain acts of terrorism, even where none of the bases of jurisdiction indicated in §402 is present." This principle could justify the adoption of laws that would punish actors who encourage the commission of these international

---

physical location, nationality would work better as a general principle in cyberspace, which is akin to a sovereignless region, such as the high seas or Antartica, where jurisdiction to prescribe cannot be based on territoriality (at 93 *et seq.*)

[20] See Security of Information Act, R.S.C. 1985, c. O-5 as amended, s. 3; Anti-Terrorism Act, S.C. 2001, c. 41, amending the Criminal Code, R.S.C. 1985, c. C-46, s. 83.01.

crimes via the Internet, for instance, posting on the website instructions to make a bomb or to disseminate biological weapons or direct and public incitement to commit genocide, war crimes, or even crimes against humanity. Again, the difficulty would be to identify the author of the message and the actual location of that person for the purpose of enforcement.

CONFLICTS WITH RESPECT TO JURISDICTION TO PRESCRIBE LAW

Potential or actual conflicts of jurisdiction inevitably arise when two or more states claim or exercise exclusive jurisdiction or when they have concurrent jurisdiction to prescribe. In the case of exclusive jurisdiction claimed or exercised by two or more states, the question is whether the right to prescribe claimed by one state and denied by another exists under international law. Where concurrent jurisdiction to prescribe is recognized by all the states concerned, the question is one of priorities. In the absence of international law rules determining priorities, each state that has concurrent jurisdiction should be free to exercise it. Occasionally, self-judging rules of restraint will moderate the exercise of such jurisdiction in order to minimize or eliminate the conflict of jurisdiction. In appropriate situations, jurisdiction will be declined. However, the failure to do so does not constitute a violation of international law.

Today, when determining which of the several competing principles of jurisdiction has priority in a given situation, the emphasis should not be placed on rigid principles but rather on broader criteria that embrace principles of reasonableness and fairness in accommodating the overlapping or conflicting interests of states.[21] Whether customary international law considers "reasonableness" as a question of discretionary comity or a limitation on jurisdiction is not yet definitely settled. In the case of the Internet, two difficulties arise: (1) some states do not regulate the Internet at all or only allow certain files or information to be accessed or posted, whereas such accessing or posting is prohibited by other states and (2) a result of these differences is that an online actor or operator may be subject to a series of conflicting laws.

CONCLUSION

The various aspects of the Internet and its effects within the territory of each of several states should be taken into consideration

---

[21] See Restatement of the Law Third, *supra* note 1 at para. 403.

together with other factors, such as, for instance, the importance of the legitimate interests of the states concerned in order to determine whether a state has the right to apply to the Internet and its actors its own laws to the exclusion of those of another state. Traditional and functional approaches to choice of law problems, which are now well established, can be very helpful in determining the scope of a law or regulation. There should be no mechanical approach to jurisdiction to prescribe if international conflicts of jurisdiction are to be avoided.

In the *Case Concerning the Barcelona Traction, Light and Power Company, Limited (Belgium v. Spain)*, Judge Sir Gerald Fitzmaurice said:

> It is true that under present conditions, international law does not impose hard and fast rules on States delimiting spheres of national jurisdiction in such matters (and there are of course others, for instance, in the field of shipping, "antitrust" legislation, *etc.*), but leaves to States a wide discretion in the matter. It does, however:
>
> > (a) postulate the existence of limits, though in any given case it may be for the tribunal to indicate what these are with regard to the facts of that case; and (b) involve for every State an obligation to exercise moderation and restraint as to the extent of jurisdiction assumed by its courts in cases having a foreign element and to avoid undue encroachment on a jurisdiction more properly appertaining to, or more appropriately exercisable by another State.[22]

This passage, when read in connection with a passage in the *Steamship Lotus (France v. Turkey)* case, where it was declared that "all that can be required of a State is that it should not overstep the limits which international law places upon its jurisdiction,"[23] supports the view that a balancing approach based on reason, fairness, reciprocity, and a lack of arbitrariness could be used to determine the reach of laws applicable to the Internet and its actors. Since the prohibitive impact of international law upon the discretion of a state to delimit its legal competence is marginal, it is not possible to maintain that the application by a state of its national laws to the Internet and its actors on the basis of its effects within the territory constitutes a clear violation of international law. It depends upon the circumstances because effective limitations are only derived from the permissive impact of international law.

The complexity of the Internet and the difficulty in locating

---

[22] *Case Concerning the Barcelona Traction, Light and Power Company, Limited (Belgium v. Spain)*, [1970] I.C.J. Rep. 3, at 105.

[23] *Lotus, supra* note 16 at 19.

geographically its various aspects does not permit a reliance on a single element — as is the case in the criminal field — whether it be the place of occurrence of the wrongful act, the place of conduct or wrongdoing, the place of injury, or the nationality of the wrong-doer or that of the victim. A total appraisal and a flexible evalua-tion of a wide range of domestic and foreign contacts and interests are needed in order to determine whether it is reasonable to assert state control. The territoriality and nationality principles must be considered along with the relevant state policies and the signi-ficance of the Internet message to all the states concerned. The approach to jurisdiction must not be mechanical but rather be adapted to reality. Since foreign cooperation is needed for effective enforcement abroad, the degree of recognition that other states would accord to the domestic law — in other words, comity as reci-procity — should also be an important factor in deciding whether or not to take action against an Internet actor.

In fact, it may be inappropriate to speak in terms of extraterri-toriality of laws since the Internet operates without regard for state boundaries. A state should have jurisdiction to reach the actors involved in the Internet only if its contacts with any of them are close, substantial, direct, and weighty, taking into consideration the legitimate concerns and interests of other states. At the present, unless the actors involved in the Internet are present in, or resi-dents of, Canada or are Canadian citizens, the only way to access activities on the Internet is through the effects within Canada. Territoriality resurfaces since the harmful effects must take place in Canada. We are back to the principle of objective territoriality, which gives Canada jurisdiction to regulate the Internet and its actors for their activities no matter where they take place. There-fore, most traditional principles of public international law with respect to the jurisdiction of states to prescribe law are still relevant.

RESTRAINTS PLACED UPON THE FEDERAL PARLIAMENT AND THE PROVINCIAL LEGISLATURES IN THE EXERCISE OF JURISDICTION TO PRESCRIBE, ADJUDICATE, AND ENFORCE PUBLIC AND PRIVATE LAWS WITH RESPECT TO THE USE OF THE INTERNET IN AN INTERNATIONAL CONTEXT

Whether the provincial or the federal government may exercise the jurisdiction that Canada is entitled to assert under interna-tional law is a question of Canadian constitutional law. The Cana-dian constitutional framework determines the degree to which international law is applied in any given circumstance. It has now been well established that customary rules of international law are directly applicable in the Canadian domestic legal system, while conventional law must be enacted into law by the federal Parliament or the provincial Legislatures before it will affect private rights.[24] Since the federal Parliament and the provincial Legislatures enjoy equal and plenary powers to legislate within their individual spheres of competence, either one may violate international law by adopting laws that are contrary to international law whether customary or conventional. Therefore, Canadian legislative bodies are free to adopt laws governing all aspects of the Internet whether or not these laws disregard the public international law customary rules governing the jurisdiction of states to prescribe laws with extraterritorial effect, although they should try to avoid doing so.[25]

In Canada, the allocation of the authority to exercise jurisdiction to prescribe, adjudicate, and enforce laws governing the Internet in an international context is governed by the Constitution Act,[26] which includes the Canadian Charter of Rights and Freedoms.[27] Although the federal Parliament has the power to enact laws with extraterritorial effect,[28] the constitution of Canada does not confer such power on the provinces.[29] However, where legislation is in relation to a subject matter situated entirely within the province, incidental or consequential effects on extra-provincial rights will not render the enactment *ultra vires*.[30] Thus, with respect to jurisdiction to prescribe, only the federal Parliament can legislate

---

[24] H.M. Kindred et al., *International Law Chiefly as Interpreted and Applied in Canada* (6th ed., 2000), at 165 *et seq.* Also S.A. Williams and A.L.C. de Mestral, *An Introduction to International Law* (2nd ed., 1987), at 25 *et seq.*

[25] R. St. J. Macdonald, "The Relationship between International Law and Domestic Law in Canada," in Macdonald, Morris, and Johnston, eds., *Canadian Perspectives on International Law and Organization* (1974), at 88.

[26] Constitution Act, 1867 (U.K.), 30 and 31 Vict., c. 3 as amended.

[27] Canadian Charter of Rights and Freedoms, Part I of the Constitution Act, 1982, being Schedule B to the Canada Act 1982 (U.K.), 1982, c. 11 [hereinafter Charter].

[28] *Croft* v. *Dunphy*, [1933] A.C. 156, at 167; see also Statute of Westminster, 1931, s. 3, R.S.C. 1985, Appendix II, no. 27.

[29] See sections 92, 92A, 93, and 95 of Constitution Act, *supra* note 26. See also P. Hogg, *Constitutional Law of Canada* (4th student edition, 1996), ch. 13.3 and R. Tassé and M. Faille, "Online Consumer Protection in Canada: The Problem of Regulatory Jurisdiction" (2000) 2 Internet and E Commerce Law in Canada 41.

[30] *Ladore Hyperinfoe* v. *Bennett*, [1939] A.C. 468, [1939] 3 D.L.R. 1.

extraterritorially. This fact means that legislation to reach the Internet, its actors, and activities outside Canada is subject to federal law if the regulation of the Internet in all its aspects falls within the categories of subjects that come within the legislative competence of the federal Parliament under the constitution.[31]

Since the Internet is a means of inter-provincial and international communication that provides Canadians with a continuous and regular service,[32] its operation must be classified as an inter-provincial undertaking that is subject to federal jurisdiction by virtue of section 92(10)(a) of the Constitution Act.[33] This classification includes ISPs that operate inter-provincially and internationally and have network infrastructures in several provinces as well as in foreign states.[34]

The actors of the Internet, if present in Canada, and by virtue of such presence amenable to Canadian law, are entitled to the benefits of the rights guaranteed by section 2(b) of the Canadian Charter of Rights and Freedoms.[35] Since both the federal and provincial levels of government are bound by the Charter,[36] the federal Parliament and the provincial Legislatures cannot enact laws applicable to the actors of the Internet that would be inconsistent with the Charter.

---

[31] See section 91 of the Constitution Act, *supra* note 26. For instance, criminal law, intellectual property, works and undertakings beyond the province, regulation of trade and commerce, and legislation "for the peace, order and good government of Canada in relation to all matters not coming within the classes of subjects by this Act assigned exclusively to the Legislatures of the Provinces."

[32] For example, *Re Ottawa-Carleton Regional Transit Commission* (1983), 44 O.R. (2d) 560 (C.A.).

[33] Constitution Act, *supra* note 26, s. 92(10)(a): Local Works and Undertakings other than "other Works and Undertakings connecting the Province with any other or others of the Provinces, or extending beyond the Limits of the Province." See *Toronto* v. *Bell Telephone Co.,* [1905] A.C. 52; *Capital Cities Communications* v. *C.R.T.C.,* [1978] 2 S.C.R. 141.

[34] See, for example, *Communications, Energy and Paperworkers Union of Canada and CITY-TV, CHUM et al.,* [1999] CIRBD no. 22 (inter-provincial undertaking).

[35] Charter, *supra* note 27. Section 2(b) provides as follows: "Everyone has the following fundamental freedoms: (b) freedom of thought, belief, opinion and expression, including freedom of the press and *other media* of communication," "subject only to such reasonable limits prescribed by law as can be demonstrably justified in a free and democratic society" (s.1) [emphasis added]. See also ss. 7 to 15 on legal rights and equality rights. See also Hogg, *supra* note 29 at ch. 34.

[36] Section 32.

The power of Canadian courts and administrative bodies to adjudicate and enforce is also subject to constitutional limitations in the context of private international law situations involving legally relevant foreign elements. Such limitations, which apply primarily to inter-provincial situations, require a sufficient or reasonable relation with the forum state or province. In a series of cases beginning in 1990,[37] the Supreme Court of Canada held that, to be constitutionally valid, statutory or judicial private international law rules applicable to inter-provincial situations must conform to the principles of order and fairness.[38] These principles, which have their source in the notions of full faith and credit and due process, held to be implicit in the Canadian constitution, were first applied to the general rules of jurisdiction of Canadian courts and the common law rules of recognition and enforcement of sister-province judgments.

In *Morguard Investments Ltd.* v. *De Savoye*,[39] the Supreme Court of Canada was of the opinion that "[i]t hardly accords with principles of order and fairness to permit a person to sue another in any jurisdiction, without regard to the contacts that jurisdiction may have to the defendant or the subject-matter of the suit." To be fair to the defendant, the court must act through fair process and with properly restrained jurisdiction. The real issue is whether the court is exercising its jurisdiction appropriately. The principles of order and fairness mean that "permitting suit where there is a real and substantial connection with the action provides a reasonable balance between the rights of the parties. It affords some protection against being pursued in jurisdictions having little or no connection with the transaction or the parties."[40]

---

[37] *Morguard Investments Ltd.* v. *DeSavoye*, [1990] 3 S.C.R. 1077, 76 D.L.R. (4th) 256, 52 B.C.L.R. (2d) 160, [1992] 2 W.W.R. 217, 46 C.P.C. (2d) 1, 122 N.R. 81 [hereinafter *Morguard*]; *Amchem Products Inc.* v. *B.C. (W.C.B.)*, [1993] 1 S.C.R. 897 [hereinafter *Amchem Products*]; *Hunt* v. *T. & N. plc*, [1993] 4 S.C.R. 289 [hereinafter *Hunt*]; *Tolofson* v. *Jensen; Lucas* v. *Gagnon* (1994), 100 B.C.L.R. (2d) 1, [1994] 3 S.C.R. 1022, [1995] 1 W.W.R. 609 [hereinafter *Tolofson*].

[38] *Hunt, supra* note 37 at 326-7. In general, see Edinger, "The Constitutionalization of the Conflict of Laws" (1995) 25 Can Bus. J. 38.

[39] *Morguard, supra* note 37 at 1108.

[40] *Ibid.* See also *WIC Premium Television Ltd.* v. *General Instrument Corp.* (1999), 1 C.P.R. (4th) 467, aff'd., (2000), 8 C.P.R. (4th) 1 (Alta. C.A.) [hereinafter *WIC Premium Television*].

In *Hunt* v. *T. & N. plc*,[41] the Supreme Court of Canada gave constitutional status to the principles expounded in *Morguard*. Therefore, the requirement of a real and substantial connection has become the absolute constitutional limit on judicial jurisdiction of the provincial superior courts. Whenever a defendant who is an actor of the Internet is served *in juris* or *ex juris* with the process of a court of a Canadian province, he or she may challenge the proceeding on constitutional grounds if the forum province lacks a real and substantial connection with the subject matter of the proceeding or the defendant. The requirement of a real and substantial connection places a limit on the provincial rules of procedure since the provincial power to legislate with respect to service *in juris* or *ex juris* requires some serious contacts with the province. One must therefore ask the question: which electronic links or contacts have a sufficiently real and substantial connection to justify the exercise of jurisdiction on a person, thing, or entity whose connection to the forum consists of a combination of data transmission over wires or radio waves?

With respect to the recognition and enforcement of sister-province judgments, the Supreme Court of Canada declared in *Morguard*:

> Recognition in other provinces should be dependent on the fact that the court giving judgment "properly" or "appropriately" exercised jurisdiction. It may meet the demands of order and fairness to recognize a judgment given in a jurisdiction that had the greatest or at least significant contacts with the subject matter of the action. But it hardly accords with principles of order and fairness to permit a person to sue another in any jurisdiction without regard to the contacts that jurisdiction may have to the defendant or the subject matter or the suit.[42]

The Supreme Court was of the opinion that, in the past, Canadian courts had been wrong to transpose the common law rules developed for the recognition and enforcement of *foreign* money judgments to the recognition and enforcement of money judgments from sister provinces. Principles of order and fairness must prevail in this area of the conflict of laws. When present, they create a type of inter-provincial comity, which requires the recognition and enforcement of the judgments of sister provinces as it "is based on the common interest of both the jurisdiction giving the judgment and the recognizing jurisdiction. Indeed, it is in the interest of the

[41]   *Hunt, supra* note 37.

[42]   *Morguard, supra* note 37 at 1103.

whole country, an interest recognized by the Constitution itself."[43] Thus, "[i]n short the rules of comity or private international law as they apply between the provinces must be shaped to conform to the federal structure of the Constitution."[44]

The relevant test in determining the appropriate forum, which is based on the principles of order and fairness, is whether there was a real and substantial connection between the province whose court gave the judgment and the subject matter of the proceeding or the defendant.[45] The court must have had reasonable grounds for exercising jurisdiction if its judgment is to be recognized and enforced in other provinces pursuant to an implicit full faith and credit clause in the constitution of Canada.[46] At the time, *Morguard* simply modified the common law rules applicable to inter-provincial judgments by expanding the circumstances that apply when a domestic court should recognize the jurisdiction of a court from another province. Hence, when *Hunt* v. *T. & N. plc* gave constitutional status to the principles adopted in *Morguard*, it became necessary for statutory and common law rules applicable to the recognition and enforcement of judgments from sister provinces to conform to these principles.

Today, Canadian courts must, as a constitutional requirement, give full faith and credit to judgments rendered in sister provinces when the original court had reasonable grounds for exercising jurisdiction that is defined in accordance with the broad principles of order and fairness. Although there is no such constitutional requirement with respect to foreign judgments, the test of real or substantial connection has been extended to cover foreign judgments.[47] As a result, a foreign judgment rendered against one of the actors of the Internet must meet the requirements of order and fairness if it is to be recognized and enforced in Canada. The test of real and substantial connection does not violate the customary rules of international law regarding the jurisdiction of Canadian courts to adjudicate with respect to a person, thing, or entity located outside Canada since it must be based on some substantial

---

[43] *Ibid.* at 1107.

[44] *Ibid.*

[45] *Ibid.* at 1108.

[46] *Hunt, supra* note 37 at 325.

[47] See, for instance, *United States of America* v. *Ivey* (1995),16 O.R. (3d)533 (Gen. Div.) aff'd (1996), 30 O.R. (3d) 370 (C.A.), leave to appeal to S.C.C. refused, [1997] 2 S.C.R. x [hereinafter *Ivey*].

link between the forum and the person, thing, or entity over which jurisdiction is exercised.

CANADIAN CRIMINAL LAW AND PRIVATE INTERNATIONAL LAW APPLICABLE TO THE INTERNET AND ITS ACTORS IN AN INTERNATIONAL CONTEXT[48]

CRIMINAL LAW

Is Canadian criminal law capable of applying to the activities that take place on the Internet and its actors in an international context? The basic question is whether Canada can assert jurisdiction over persons not physically within its boundaries and regulate conduct that occurs in part outside these boundaries. Four major situations present themselves. First, where an offence covered by the Criminal Code[49] or other federal statutes is committed by an actor on the Internet, can such an actor be prosecuted in Canada in view of section 6(2) of the Code, which declares that no person shall be convicted or discharged of an offence committed outside Canada. Are the Internet and its actors inside or outside of Canada when committing offences on the Internet? Does this situation require the extraterritorial application of Canadian criminal law? Second, the Criminal Code or federal statutes may specifically include offences committed outside Canada. Again, are the Internet and its actors inside or outside of Canada when committing offences on the Internet ? Third, in some cases, there is no need to consider section 6(2) of the Criminal Code since, according to the Supreme Court of Canada in *Libman* v. *R.*,[50] all that is necessary to make an offence and have its perpetrator subject to Canadian law and jurisdiction is that a significant portion of the activities constituting the offence must have taken place in Canada. There must exist therefore a real and substantial link between the offence and Canada. This approach is an application of the effects principle. It solves the problem of national boundaries and extraterritoriality and the difficulties arising if the subjective territoriality principle is used. Fourth, the Criminal Code provision may apply specifically to Canadian citizens regardless of where they committed the offence.[51]

---

[48] For an earlier analysis, see C. Gosnell, "Jurisdiction on the Net: Defining Place in Cyberspace" (1998) 29 Can. Bus. L.J. 344.

[49] Criminal Code, *supra* note 20.

[50] *Libman* v. *R.*, [1985] 2 S.C.R. 178 (soliciting US residents by telephone), which was applied in *Hyperinfo, supra* note 16.

[51] Criminal Code, *supra* note 20 at s. 46(3) . This section is also extraterritorial in scope.

Whether the physical location of a server can be used as the *situs* of a criminal offence is doubtful. The problem is that, as has already been mentioned, data sent from an uploader to a server can travel around the world in data packets through randomly assigned nodes and thus be sent and received through several states on its way to the downloader. Applying *Libman*, one must concede that the realization in Canada of a particular scheme to defraud would be sufficient even if the inducement and its initiation were on the Internet somewhere in virtual space. Where the Criminal Code or another federal statutory provision contains language that gives it extraterritorial effect, activities on the Internet would be included since the scope of the provision is worldwide and is not concerned with national boundaries. Where the provision is territorial in scope and one of the actors or part of the activities on the Internet is not located in Canada, the accused, provided that he or she can be identified, would be subject to the real and substantial link test, which was developed by the Supreme Court of Canada in *Libman*. Where the offence created by the Criminal Code or other federal statute is based on Canadian citizenship, it does not matter where the offence was committed.

Should an ISP, portal, or a website author/owner be responsible under Canadian law when certain text or images that are outlawed in Canada are stored on servers somewhere else in the world where they are legal and accessible to Canadian residents? Can any of the Internet foreign actors be forced to prevent users in Canada from accessing websites containing such material through filtering or some other methods?[52] In the criminal field, the Internet is used most often for gambling, money laundering as well as the dissemination of child pornography, hate propaganda, and defamatory libel. It can also be used to circumvent securities regulations.[53] Let us examine some of these activities.

---

[52] See *La Ligue contre le Racisme et l'Antisémitisme* v. *Yahoo! Inc.*, November 20, 2000, which can be accessed at <www.cdt.org/speech/international/001120yahoo france.pdf>, where a French court ruled that Yahoo must block French users from accessing its US-based online auction sale of Nazi memorabilia in violation of French criminal law. However, in *Yahoo Inc.* v. *La Ligue contre le Racisme et l'Antisémitisme*, 169 F. Supp. 2d 1181 (N.D. Cal., 2001), the US District Court refused to defer to the injunctive order of the French court.

[53] See, for example, *In the Matter of World Stock Exchange et al.*, Alberta Securities Commission, February 15, 2000.

Online Gambling and Money Laundering

Gambling is prohibited in Canada by the Criminal Code,[54] unless specially authorized.[55] This prohibition includes online gambling on the Internet, therefore, the user and the author/owner of the gambling site who is the cyber-casino operator[56] or gaming merchant could be subjected to the provisions of the Criminal Code, provided that the alleged offences are committed in Canada as the sections of the Criminal Code prohibiting gambling have no extraterritorial effect. If the author/owner operating the online gambling site, the server for the site, and all other operations are located in a gambling-friendly state, the operator could still be committing an offence in Canada by application of the *Libman* test because a gambler residing in Canada is logging onto a site that is accessible here. The act of entering the bet and transmitting the information from Canada via the Internet would be sufficient to constitute a gambling activity in Canada, provided the operator of the gambling website targeted users who are resident in Canada.[57] However, it could be argued that receiving a bet from a gambler who is a resident of Canada is not a significant aspect of the activities constituting the offence of gambling in Canada, which would subject the foreign operator of the gambling site to criminal liability since the agreement to gamble would have been concluded on

[54] *Criminal Code, supra* note 20 at ss. 201-9.

[55] See, for instance, *ibid.* at ss. 204, 207, and 207.1 (operation of casinos on international cruise ships, which are Canadian or in Canadian waters) and the Civil Code of Quebec, Article 2629. See also An Act Respecting Lotteries, Publicity Contests and Amusement Machines, R.S.Q. c. L-6. In Ontario, see Gaming Control Act, 1992, S.O. 1992, c. 24 as amended; Ontario Casino Corporation Act, 1993, S.O. 1993, c. 25, s. 24 as amended, which repealed the Gaming Act, R.S.O. 1990, c. G.2; Alcohol and Gaming Regulation and Public Protection Act, S.O. 1996, c. 26; Ontario Lottery Corporation Act, R.S.O. 1990, c. O.25 as amended; Ontario Lottery and Gaming Corporation Act, S.O. 1999, c. 12, which has repealed and replaced the Ontario Casino Corporation Act and the Ontario Lottery Corporation Act, as amended in 1992, see Schedule L, s. 20. See also *Reference Re: Earth Furure Lottery*, 2002 PESCAD 8 (P.E.I.) (server located in Prince Edward Island, Canada). For gambling in general, see J.-G. Castel, Gambling Control Law in Ontario (2001).

[56] 3D virtual casino complete with the sights and sounds of a real casino. A virtual casino is the equivalent of placing a slot machine in every house that has a personal computer!

[57] In the United States, see *State of Minnesota* v. *Granite Gate Resorts Inc. and Kerry Rogers*, 1996 W.L. 767432 (D. Minn. 1996), aff'd 568 N.W. 2d 715 (Minn. Ct. App., 1997).

the Internet, which is delocalized or in a foreign state when the money is received by the operator of the gambling site. This question is controversial since many different opinions have been expressed as to whether the Canadian Criminal Code could be applied to foreign-based gaming operators if they are offering gambling services to Canadian residents. The *Report on Gaming Legislation and Regulation in British Columbia*, which was published in January 1999,[58] expresses the view that there exists no Canadian criminal jurisdiction over foreign gaming operators:

> The issue of jurisdiction becomes more complex where a licensed offshore Internet operator takes bets from Canadians. The question is whether Internet-based gaming operators have a "real and substantial" connection with any jurisdiction from which bets are placed. Where the Internet-based gaming operator is operating entirely offshore (*i.e.* where all contracts are concluded offshore, all banking arrangements are carried out offshore and the Internet service provider is located offshore), it is unlikely that Canadian courts will be able to exert jurisdiction over the operator.

Some gaming sites use remote servers-based software applications. Other sites require users to download proprietary software applications that must be installed on the gambler's computer before he or she can play. As for methods of payment, some sites require cash for each bet, which the user pays with a credit card or some other electronic form of payment, such as a Wells Fargo automatic teller machine and check card or bank wire transfers. More recently, digital cash is used quite often. It may be purchased with a credit card from an e-cash company and can be used for a variety of purposes, including gambling, since some credit card companies as well as the bank issuing such credit cards refuse to process gambling transactions. This restriction is due in part to the fact that online gamblers who have suffered heavy losses often refuse to pay their credit card debts or even sue the credit card companies, banks, ISPs, and gaming merchants in order to recoup their losses and/or damages for the consequences of such losses on the ground that gambling is illegal where the credit card holder is resident and where he has gambled online.

It is doubtful that an ISP or a portal providing access to online casinos would be committing the offence of conspiracy abroad or

---

[58] *Report on Gaming Legislation and Regulation in British Columbia*, January 1999, which is available at <www.gov.bc.ca/publicinfo/publications/gamingpolicy/paper/95.htm>.

in Canada to commit an indictable offence or an offence punishable on summary conviction in Canada[59] as a result of gaming activities conducted on its services, particularly if it and its servers are located in a state where gambling is lawful. Since an ISP is only an information highway or conduit that is not aware of the contents of the information and files contained or posted on the website that it is hosting and has no control over gaming activities, it would lack any *mens rea*. Nor, for the same reason, could it be a party to the offence of gambling.[60] However, it could be required to filter out gambling websites or to refuse to host them. For the same reasons, it is unlikely that parties who provide software and financial services (e-cash companies and Visa banks) that are necessary to process transactions on such sites could be held criminally liable for such activities.

Whether a gambler, who is using his or her own computer in, let us say, Toronto, at his or her place of residence and who from there places a bet online, commits an offence in Canada[61] is also a controversial question since it could be argued that gambling takes place where the bet originates[62] or where it is received, provided such places can be identified.[63] Again, in light of *Libman*, it would seem that the gambler has committed in Canada the offence listed in section 206(4) of the Criminal Code.[64] Canada is the state that, from the point of view of the gambler who is resident in Toronto, has a real and substantial link with the offence. It is also the place where the effects of gambling are felt by the gambler, win or lose. Therefore, if the gambler logging on in Toronto, assuming that he or she can be identified, is deemed to commit the offence in Canada, the fact that some elements of the gambling took place abroad does not necessarily violate international law since, as noted previously, the effects principle recognized by international law holds that a state can prescribe a rule of law governing conduct

---

[59] See Criminal Code, *supra* note 20 at s. 465(1)(c) and (d) and 465(3) and (4).

[60] See *ibid.* at s. 21(2).

[61] See *ibid.* at ss. 206(4) and 207(3)(b).

[62] Place of logging-on being Toronto.

[63] Country where the author/owner of the site accepts the bet and pays the winnings, if any.

[64] "Everyone who buys, takes or receives a lot, ticket or other device mentioned in subsection (1) is guilty of an offence punishable on summary conviction." See also Criminal Code, *supra* note 20 at section 207(3)(b) on participation in lottery scheme not authorized by section 207(1) and (2).

outside its territory that has or is intended to have substantial effect within its territory.[65]

Is visiting an Internet casino physically visiting a "common gaming house or common betting house," which is prohibited under section 201(2)(a) of the Criminal Code? And, if so, it would follow that the online gambler is a "found in" and therefore guilty of an offence punishable on summary conviction. Depending upon the circumstances, the gambler and the author/owner gaming merchant could also be charged for violating section 462.31(1)[66] of the Criminal Code, which deals with laundering the proceeds of crime, since gambling attracts organized crime and the proceeds of crime could be disguised as winnings. This section of the Code has an extraterritorial effect and could cover gaming transactions outside Canada if online gaming is used for laundering money, since the section includes: (1) the commission in Canada of an enterprise crime offence as well as (2) an act or omission anywhere that, if it had occurred in Canada, would have constituted an enterprise crime. "Enterprise crime" is defined as an offence against, *inter alia*, sections 202 (betting and so on) and 206(1)(e) (money increment schemes).

To conclude, the Canadian policy of strictly prohibiting interactive gambling on the Internet, which makes anyone criminally liable who, in Canada, places or accepts a wager online, is difficult to achieve in practice. Even if all the providers of Internet gambling services within Canada were closed down or all ISPs and servers located in Canada were prohibited from hosting gaming websites, nothing could prevent a determined gambler from dialing another server offshore. Furthermore, how could Canada secure the physical person of an accused who is not present in Canada but is a national and resident of a state where gambling is legal and therefore not an extraditable offence should a treaty of extradition exist between Canada and such a state? If those individuals involved in

---

[65] S.A. Williams and J.-G. Castel, *Canadian Criminal Law, International and Transnational Aspects* (1981), at 71 *et seq.*; J.-G. Castel, *Extraterritoriality in International Trade* (1988), at 10 *et seq.*; *People* v. *World Interactive Gaming Corp.*, New York S.C. (1999), N.Y. Misc. Lexis 425 (criminal offence in New York as a result of Internet gambling with offshore gaming merchants).

[66] See also Proceeds of Crime (Money Laundering) and Terrorist Financing Act, S.C. 2000, c. 17, as amended by the Anti-Terrorism Act, S.C. 2001, c. 41 to cover terrorist activities and terrorist groups. See also B.A.K. Rider and C.V. Nakajima, *Anti Money Laundering Guide* (2000).

the gaming business remain outside of Canada, there is little that law enforcement can do.

Other Offences Committed by Using the Internet

The dissemination of child pornography,[67] hate propaganda,[68] and defamatory libel[69] by posting it on a web page on the Internet is quite a common practice. Since the sections of the Criminal Code that make it an offence to do so are not extraterritorial in scope, it would be necessary to resort to the *Libman* test in order to reach both the author of the message and the owner of the website if they were located outside Canada, especially in a place unknown. This would not be the case with respect to the user downloading the material if he or she is a resident of Canada and physically present in that country. Should ISPs be treated as publishers and, therefore, be held criminally liable for the offensive contents that users load up on web pages residing at their sites if these online providers know or ought to know the nature of the material on their system?[70]

With respect to violations of human rights, in *Canada (Human Rights Commission)* v. *Canadian Liberty Net*,[71] the Federal Court of Canada granted an injunction to the Human Rights Commission to restrain the conduct of the defendant, which took place outside of Canada. Having violated this injunction, the defendant was found to be in contempt of court. The Supreme Court of Canada[72] supported the order since a significant part of the activities relating to the violation of the court's order took place in Canada. This

---

[67] Criminal Code, *supra* note 20 at s. 163.1 (it includes distribution, sale, and possession). See also sections 163 of the Criminal Code (corrupting morals), 172.1 (luring), and, as an example, *R.* v. *Hurtubise* (1996), B.C.S.C.; a summary can be found in *Canadian Abridgments* (2nd ed., 1997), vol. R9B, Supp. 2237 (B.C.S.C. 1996) [herinafter *Hurtubise*]; *R.* v. *Lowes*, [1998] 5 W.W.R. 147 (Man.P.C.); *R.* v. *Weir*, [1998] 8 W.W.R. 228 (Alta.Q.B.). Both sections are subject to section 2(b) of the Charter, *supra* note 27. *See R.* v. *Butler*, [1992] 1 S.C.R. 452.

[68] Criminal Code, *supra* note 20 at ss. 318-20.

[69] *Ibid.* at ss. 298-301. *R.* v. *Barret* (2000), 46 W.C.B. (2d) 368 (Ont.S.C.J.).

[70] See *R.* v. *Metro News Ltd.* (1986), 32 D.L.R. (4th) 321 (Ont.C.A.), leave to appeal to S.C.C. refused, at 321; *Hurtubise, supra* note 67.

[71] *Canada (Human Rights Commission)* v. *Canadian Liberty Net*, [1996] 1 F.C. 804 (C.A.).

[72] *Canada (Human Rights Commission)* v. *Canadian Liberty Net*, [1998] 1 S.C.R. 626, at 670.

fact constituted a substantial link between the offending conduct and Canada, pursuant to the *Libman* test.[73]

Cyber-terrorism

Cyber-terrorism, which must be distinguished from cyber-crime,[74] uses the Internet to facilitate a number of activities, for instance, soliciting and transferring funds, purchasing goods, and seeking new members. It also uses the Internet to carry out attacks against critical infrastructures that are particularly vulnerable, for instance, transportation systems, nuclear power plants, and banking and finance institutions. By infecting with a virus or other disabling method the computer networks upon which such infrastructures rely for their continued operations, cyber-terrorists are able to shut them down often causing harm to the citizens and the state relying on them.[75] Recently, Canada has adopted the Anti-Terrorism Act,[76] which is relevant to cyber-terrorism although it does not specifically address this topic. This act amends a certain number of statutes including the Criminal Code.

[73] Note that a person in Canada causes material to be communicated for the purpose of section 13(1) (hate) of the Canadian Human Rights Act, R.S.C. 1985, c. H-6, if that person effectively controls the content of the material posted on a website even if it is maintained outside Canada: *Zundel* v. *Canada (Attorney General)*, [1999] 4 F.C. 298 (F.C.T.D.) and *Zundel* v. *Canada (Attorney General)* (1998), 157 F.T.R. 59 (F.C.T.D.).

[74] See *Annual Report 2000-1: Proposal for an International Convention on Cyber Crime and Terrorism*, Center for International Security and Cooperation, Stanford University, 2000; and the Council of Europe Convention on Cybercrime, Budapest, 2001, which can be accessed at <http://conventions.coe.int./treaty/EN/Project/Finalcybercrime.htm>.

[75] K. Cesare, "Prosecuting Computer Virus Authors: The Need for an Adequate and Immediate International Solution" (2001) 14 Transnat'l Lawyer 135.

[76] Anti-Terrorism Act, S.C. 2001, c. 41. In the United States, the Patriot Act of 2001, P.L. 107-56, which, in section 814, deals specifically with the deterrence and prevention of cyber-terrorism by amending US Code, Title 18, s. 1030(a)(5). See also section 1030(e)(8), which defines damage as "any impairment to the integrity or availability of data, a program, a system or information." This provision covers acts of cyber-terrorism designed to disable a protected computer, which is defined as one that is used exclusively by a financial institution or the US government or, if not used exclusively, where the conduct constituting the offence affects them, or the computer is used in interstate or international commerce and communication, no matter where it is located, if the use affects such commerce and communication (s. 1030(e)(2)).

First, the act defines "terrorist activity" by referring to several international conventions dealing with various aspects of terrorism.[77] Second, it further defines "terrorist activity" as

(B) an act or omission, in or outside Canada,
   (i) that is committed
     (a) in whole or in part for a political, religious or ideological purpose, objective or cause, and
     (b) in whole or in part with the intention of intimidating the public, or a segment of the public, with regard to its security, including its economic security, or compelling a person, a government or a domestic or an international organization to do or refrain from doing any act, whether the public or the person, government or organization is inside or outside of Canada, and
   (ii) that intentionally
     (a) causes death or serious bodily harm to a person by the use of violence,
     (b) endangers a person's life,
     (c) causes a serious risk to the health or safety of the public or any segment of the public,
     (d) causes substantial property damage, whether to public or private property, if causing such damage is likely to result in the conduct or harm referred to in any of clauses (a) to (c), or

---

[77] Criminal Code, *supra* note 20 at section 83.01(1) on terrorist activity, para. (a). The act refers to the Convention for the Suppression of Unlawful Seizure of Aircraft, which was done at The Hague on December 16, 1970, 860 U.N.T.S. 105; the Convention for the Suppression of Unlawful Acts against the Safety of Civil Aviation, which was done in Montreal on September 23, 1971, 974 U.N.T.S. 177; the Convention on the Prevention and Punishment of Crimes against Internationally Protected Persons, including Diplomatic Agents, which was adopted by the General Assembly of the United Nations on December 14, 1973, 1977 Can. T.S. no. 43; the International Convention against the Taking of Hostages, which was adopted by the General Assembly of the United Nations on December 17, 1979, 18 I.L.M. 1456; the Convention on the Physical Protection of Nuclear Material, which was adopted in Vienna on 3 March 1980; the Protocol for the Suppression of Unlawful Acts of Violence at Airports Serving International Civil Aviation, which is supplementary to the Convention for the Suppression of Unlawful Acts against the Safety of Civil Aviation, which was done in Montreal on February 24, 1988, 27 I.L.M. 627; the Convention for the Suppression of Unlawful Acts against the Safety of Fixed Platforms Located on the Continental Shelf, which was done in Rome on March 10, 1988, 27 I.L.M. 685; the International Convention for the Suppression of Terrorist Bombings, which was adopted by the General Assembly of the United Nations on December 15, 1977; UN Doc. A/RES/52/164; and the International Convention for the Suppression of Terrorist Financing, which was adopted by the General Assembly of the United Nations on December 9, 1999, 39 I.L.M. 270.

(e) causes serious interference with or serious disruption of an essential service, facility or system, whether public or private other than as a result of advocacy, protest, dissent or stoppage of work that is not intended to result in the conduct or harm referred to in any of clauses (a) to (c) and

includes a conspiracy, attempt, or threat to commit any such act or omission or take away being an accessory after the fact or counselling in relation to any such act or omission, but, for greater certainty, does not include an act or omission that is committed during an armed conflict and that, at the time and in the place of its commission, is in accordance with customary international law or conventional international law applicable to the conflict, or the activities undertaken by military forces of a state in the exercise of their official duties, to the extent that those activities are governed by other rules of international law.[78]

Cyber-terrorism is covered by the definition of "terrorist activity" in section 83.01(1)(b) of the Criminal Code. The financing of terrorism using the Internet is covered by section 83.02 of the code[79] as well as by the Proceeds of Crime (Money Laundering) and Terrorist Financing Act[80] and Article 2 of the International Convention for the Suppression of Terrorist Financing.[81] Finally, section 3(1)(d) of the Security of Information Act,[82] in particular, covers both cyber-crime and cyber-terrorism since it includes harm caused by a terrorist group.[83] This act provides that

---

[78] Criminal Code, *supra* note 20 at section 83.01(1)(b).

[79] "Every one who, directly or indirectly, wilfully and without lawful justification or excuse, provides or collects property intending that it be used or knowing that it will be used, in whole or in part, in order to carry out

   (a) an act or omission that constitutes an offence referred to in subparagraphs (a)(i) to (ix) of the definition of "terrorist activity" in subsection 83.01(1), or

   (b) any other act or omission intended to cause death or serious bodily harm to a civilian or to any other person not taking an active part in the hostilities in a situation of armed conflict, if the purpose of that act or omission, by its nature or context, is to intimidate the public, or to compel a government or an international organization to do or refrain from doing any act,

   is guilty of an indictable offence and is liable to imprisonment for a term of not more than 10 years." See also ss. 83.03 and 83.04.

[80] Formerly the Proceeds of Crime (Money Laundering) Act, S.C. 2000, c. 17.

[81] International Convention for the Suppression of Terrorist Financing, *supra* note 77.

[82] Formerly the Official Secrets Act, R.S.C. 1985, c. o-5 as amended.

[83] *Ibid.* at section 3(2).

3(1) For the purposes of this Act, a purpose is prejudicial to the safety or interests of the State if a person ... (d) interferes with a service, facility, system or computer program whether public or private, or its operation, in a manner that has significant adverse impact on the health, safety, security or economic or financial well-being of the people of Canada or the functioning of any government in Canada.

Where cyber-terrorism is state sponsored, it constitutes an internationally wrongful act that entails the international responsibility of the state. It is also a violation of the United Nations Charter.[84] The victim state could respond in self-defence, and the Security Council could become seized of the matter.[85]

Judicial Cooperation and Extradition

The Mutual Legal Assistance in Criminal Matters Act,[86] which implements treaties on mutual legal assistance in criminal matters signed by Canada with a number of countries,[87] is also quite relevant to offences committed through the Internet since it provides, *inter alia*, for the taking of evidence in Canada to be used abroad,[88] the admissibility in Canada of evidence obtained abroad,[89] and the collection in Canada of fines imposed abroad.[90] Since the prosecution of criminal and quasi-criminal offences requires jurisdiction over the offence and over the person of the alleged offender, extradition of alleged or convicted offenders who are fugitives from justice for offences related to the use of the Internet is possible if the

---

[84] Charter of the United Nations, 26 June 1945, Can. T.S. 1945 No. 7, 59 Stat. 1031, 145 U.K.F.S. 805, art. 2(7).

[85] See, for example, Security Council Resolutions 1368, Sept. 12, 2001, 1373, Sept. 28, 2001, and 1377, Nov. 12, 2001.

[86] Mutual Legal Assistance in Criminal Matters Act, R.S.C. 1985, c. 30 (4th Supp.), as amended.

[87] For example, the Treaty between the Government of Canada and the Government of the United States of America on Mutual Legal Assistance in Criminal Matters, dated March 18, 1985, in force January 14, 1990, Can. T.S. no 19, esp. arts. II (scope), XVI (search and seizure), and XVII (proceeds of crime).

[88] Sections 17-23.

[89] Sections 36-9. What about searching databases or hard drives located abroad or checking suspicious websites? Does violation of sovereignty require acting on the territory of the violated state? See S. Wilske and T. Shiller, "International Jurisdiction in Cyberspace: Which State May Regulate the Internet?" (1997) 50 Fed. Comm. L.J. 117 (especially (C) Jurisdiction to Enforce).

[90] Section 9.

conditions of the Extradition Act[91] and the relevant provisions of a treaty of extradition between Canada and the country of refuge seeking the offender are met.[92]

Recognition and Enforcement in Canada of Foreign Judgments for Penalties

As a general rule, foreign judgments resulting in monetary penalties for the benefit of foreign states, which are imposed on the actors of the Internet, are not enforceable in Canada. To do so would constitute an infringement of local sovereignty and would involve an inquiry into the policies of the foreign state under question.[93] However, section 9 of the Mutual Legal Assistance in Criminal Matters Act[94] could be relied upon by a foreign state that is bound to Canada by a treaty of mutual legal assistance in criminal matters. The act allows the foreign state as a judgment creditor to recover the fine in civil proceedings instituted by it in Canada, as if the fine had been imposed by a Canadian court. The enforcing court would test the jurisdiction of the foreign court that imposed the fine as if it were a foreign money judgment and not a penal judgment. Provincial rules with respect to the recognition and enforcement of foreign money judgments would be applicable.[95] Moreover, the act defines "fine" as including any pecuniary penalty determined by a court of criminal jurisdiction of a foreign state to represent the value of any property, benefit, or advantage, irrespective of its location, obtained or derived directly or indirectly as a result of the commission of an offence.[96] For situations not covered by the act, the Canadian court would determine whether a foreign judgment is penal or not.[97] Characterization would be by the *lex fori*.[98]

---

[91] Extradition Act, S.C. 1999, c. 18, as amended, especially section 3.

[92] For example, the Treaty of Extradition between Canada and the United States of America and its protocols, CTS 1991/37.

[93] J.-G. Castel, *Canadian Conflict of Laws* (4th ed., 1997), at para. 95, and *Huntington v. Attrill*, [1893] A.C. 150 (P.C.). However, see *Ivey, supra* note 47.

[94] Mutual Legal Assistance in Criminal Matters Act, R.S.C. 1985, c. 30 (4th Supp.).

[95] See the recognition and enforcement of foreign and sister-provinces judgments.

[96] Mutual Legal Assistance in Criminal Matters Act, *supra* note 94 at s. 9(3).

[97] *Rosencrantz v. Union Contractors Ltd. and Thornton* (1960), 32 D.L.R. (2d) 473 (B.C.S.C.).

[98] In general, see S.A. Williams and J.-G. Castel, *Canadian Criminal Law, International and Transnational Aspects* (1981), at 436 *et seq.*

DATA PRIVACY

In a number of states, financial and personal data protection laws provide for criminal or civil liability. For instance, any local processing of online financial or personal data by a corporation established, let us say in France, would trigger the application of the French data protection law. This assertion of legislative jurisdiction accords with the subjective territorial principle. The controversial issue is whether a foreign website operator could be prosecuted for violating such privacy laws. These laws are difficult to justify and to enforce unless the accused maintains some business presence in the enacting state. Corporations not maintaining some business presence could still be subject to such laws if they used equipment located in that state for the purpose of claim processing.

Another possibility is for the privacy laws to apply to all website operators, be they foreign or domestic, who interact with domestic users. Holding foreign operators liable would be justified on the effects territorial principle. Internet intermediaries, such as ISPs or e-commerce portals, should not be held liable where they merely serve as conduits for the information and do not participate in its exchange. In 2000, Canada adopted the Personal Information Protection and Electronic Documents Act, which does not mention electronic data interchange.[99] It has no extraterritorial effect and cannot reach foreign-based organizations as defined therein. Disclosure of personal information without the consent of the person involved is restricted, which would seem to include communicating such information by any means. Canadian corporations have adopted a privacy policy and appointed a privacy officer whose duty it is to make sure that personal data is not disclosed improperly.

PRIVATE INTERNATIONAL LAW

In most situations, it is the user of the Internet who will sue those individuals maintaining a website for electronic commerce or other purposes (for example, persons or companies that advertise

---

[99] Personal Information Protection and Electronic Documents Act, S.C. 2000, c. 5, ss. 2-9 as amended and Schedule I. Sections 31 *et seq.* (electronic documents) provide for the use of electronic alternatives where federal laws contemplate the use of paper to record or communicate information or transactions (s. 32). In Québec, see an Act Respecting the Protection of Personal Information in the Private Sector, R.S.Q. c. P-39.1 and an Act to Establish a Legal Framework for Information Technology, S.Q. 2001, c. 32. See also Uniform Law Conference of Canada, 1993 Proceedings 198, Appendix G, Electronic Data Interchange.

goods for sale, which were bought and sold online; online gaming merchants; or those persons who posted defamatory statements on a Use Net site). Private international law rules become relevant in those cases where users/customers and website suppliers and wrongdoers are located in different jurisdictions.

A website established in a foreign state can easily be accessed by a Canadian Internet user, thereby enabling the actors involved to conclude all types of contracts online. Professional services such as legal or medical advice can be delivered on the Internet by individuals whose sites are hosted on ISPs in states where they are resident and licensed. Defamatory statements can be posted on a Use Net site and distributed to all other Use Net sites around the world. Copies of a song in violation of the copyright of the owner can be uploaded to an Internet site, re-transmitted by the ISPs to other sites worldwide, and then downloaded by countless users. The absence of boundaries, which characterizes the Internet, makes it difficult to determine where a contract was concluded or a wrongful act was committed. Since place elements often play a significant role in determining the jurisdiction of courts or the law to be applied to the facts of a case pending before them, some other elements that are characteristic of the Internet have to be taken into consideration, such as whether a website is passive or interactive. The residence or domicile of the defendant may also be difficult to discover for the purpose of service *ex juris* in order to establish personal jurisdiction. Addresses of the computers on the Internet are digital on the network and rarely contain geographic indications. Therefore, where a business is transacted over a computer network via a website that is accessed by a user in Ontario, one could argue that it takes place as much in Ontario as in any other province or state. Being that the location of the business transaction can occur anywhere from which the Internet can be accessed, the traditional rules of private international law applicable to offline activities may not be adequate if such activities take place online. At the outset, as in the case of the criminal law, it would seem that among all the actors involved on the Internet, an ISP or a website owner such as Yahoo, when acting as a portal, should not be held civilly liable for the activities taking place on the websites they host since they are only providing access and have no control over the contents of the electronic message. They should be treated as common carriers similar to telephone companies and should not be held responsible for the information that they carry. However, more generally, should the operators of Internet businesses be subject to the jurisdiction of the state or province where their customers are resident rather than that of the state or province where they or their servers are located? The discussion that follows is limited to contract and torts issues involving the Internet and its actors.

Jurisdiction in personam

The Internet's indifference to physical borders challenges the notion of presence by a non-resident defendant in a forum state. In addition, asserting personal jurisdiction by reason of Internet-related contacts is not always easy as persons doing business on the Internet may be subject to litigation in every jurisdiction where a web page is accessible. How can a physical person or corporation that maintains an Internet site on the worldwide web become subject to the jurisdiction of the federal and provincial courts in Canada when the site can be accessed simultaneously in many provinces or states?

In common law Canada, the exercise of adjudicative jurisdiction over the subject matter of the action and over the person of the defendant must not contravene the constitutional limitations on provincial jurisdiction that require the existence of a real and substantial connection between the forum province and the subject matter of the action or the parties. The grounds for the exercise of jurisdiction must constitute a real and substantial connection.[100] An Internet presence may have to be taken into consideration in determining the existence of a real and substantial connection.[101] However, web activity by itself should not be sufficient unless such activity was directed at persons in the forum province.

In *Easthaven Ltd.* v. *Nutrisystem.Com.Inc.*,[102] which involved a dispute over the ownership of a domain name, the Ontario Superior Court had to decide whether the fact that the registrar for the domain name of the defendant had its head office in Toronto was sufficient to constitute a real and substantial connection between

---

[100] See *Morguard, supra* note 37; *Hunt, supra* note 37; and *Craig Broadcast Systems Inc.* v. *Frank N. Magid Associates Inc.* (1998), 124 Man. R. (2d) 252 (C.A.) (real and substantial connection between the defendant and the forum province of a kind that makes it reasonable to infer that he or she had voluntarily submitted himself or herself to the risk of litigation in its courts); *WIC Premium Television, supra* note 40.

[101] *Old North State Brewing Co.* v. *Newlands Services Inc.* (1998), 58 B.C.L.R. (3d) 144 (C.A.) [hereinafter *Old North State Brewing Co.*].

[102] *Easthaven, supra* note 8.

Ontario and the subject matter of the action. The court found that there was no such connection. Since a domain name lacks physical existence, it cannot be located in Ontario: "A domain name is still simply a unique identifier for a particular internet site located on a particular computer. That computer may be located anywhere in the world and be unrelated to where the domain name is registered."[103]

In coming to this decision, the court was influenced by *Panavision International L.P. v. Toppen*,[104] in which the US Court of Appeals distinguished between general jurisdiction and specific jurisdiction. For a US court to exercise general jurisdiction, the defendant must be domiciled in the forum state, or his or her activities in that state must have been substantial or continuous and systematic. As for specific jurisdiction, it is governed by a three-part test:

(1) The nonresident defendant must do some act or consummate some transaction with the forum or perform some act by which he purposefully avails himself of the privilege of conducting activities in the forum, thereby invoking the benefits and protections of its laws; (2) the claim must be one which arises out of or results from the defendant's forum-related activities and (3) exercise of jurisdiction must be reasonable.[105]

In the present case there existed neither general nor specific jurisdiction.

The exercise of jurisdiction *in personam* by a Canadian superior court will generally accord with the Canadian constitution when it is based on the defendant's submission by agreement or attornment, or on the defendant's ordinary residence within the province, or on a real and substantial connection between the subject matter of the action or the parties and the forum province. The exercise of jurisdiction might not meet the requirements of the constitution when it is based solely on the defendant's temporary presence in the province or on the plaintiff's residence[106] or on some of the grounds for

---

[103] *Ibid.* at 341.

[104] *Panavision International L.P. v. Toppen*, 141 F. 3d 1316 (9ᵗʰ Cir. 1998) [hereinafter *Panavision International*].

[105] *Ibid.* at 1320.

[106] However, see *Dennis v. Salvation Army Grace General Hospital Board* (1996), 153 N.S.R. (2d) 211 (S.C.) (where the Chambers judge seemed to believe that the residence of the plaintiff met the constitutional standard), rev'd. 156 N.S.R. (2d) 372, 14 C.P.C. (4ᵗʰ) 207 (C.A.), which reversed the stay that had been granted on grounds of *forum non conveniens;* and Black, Comment on *Dennis v. Salvation Army Grace General Hospital Board* at 14 C.P.C. (4ᵗʰ) 222.

service *ex juris*.[107] However, a number of Canadian courts are prepared to exercise jurisdiction in situations in which the connections between the subject matter of the action and the forum are not substantial when fairness requires them to do so, particularly when the plaintiff is incapable of seeking relief in another forum.[108]

In the case of service *in juris*, the court must ascertain whether it has jurisdiction, based on a real and substantial connection, before considering the application of the doctrine of *forum non conveniens*. Jurisdiction over defendants that is based on presence, residence within the province, submission, or consent (for instance, by special agreement) poses few problems.

Where there is a real and substantial connection between the defendant or the subject matter of the action and the forum, Canadian courts may assert jurisdiction over the defendant even if he or she does not consent to the jurisdiction of the court and cannot be served within the territory. The bases for this kind of jurisdiction are set out in the legislation and regulations governing the courts' procedure, which vary somewhat among the common law provincial superior courts, the territorial courts, and the federal court.[109] This basis of jurisdiction — which is sometimes called "service *ex juris*" or "service out" or "long-arm jurisdiction" — is derived from that which was originally exercised by the English courts,[110] but it is no longer uniformly exercised by Canadian courts in the same way that it is by the English courts. Like the English courts, Canadian courts once required all plaintiffs wishing to serve a defendant outside the territory of the forum to obtain the leave of the court. It was appropriate to exercise caution in assuming jurisdiction over absent defendants who had not consented to the jurisdiction of the court because when other courts exercised jurisdiction on this basis

---

[107] *MacDonald* v. *Lasnier* (1994), 21 O.R. (3d) 177 (Gen.Div.); *Duncan (Litigation Guardian of)* v. *Neptune Corp.* (2001), 53 O.R. (3d) 754 (S.C.J.) (damage sustained in Ontario) [hereinafter *Duncan*].

[108] *Oakley* v. *Barry* (1998), 158 D.L.R. (4th) 679 (N.S.C.A.). Note that international law requires contacts between the defendant and the forum province, which may be more exacting than those necessary in domestic cases. In the United States, see G.B. Born, "Reflections on Judicial Jurisdiction in International Cases" (1987) 17 Ga. J. Int'l. & Comp. L. 1, at 33 and *Asahi Metal Indus. Co. Ltd.* v. *Superior Ct. of California*, 480 U.S. 102, at 115 (1987).

[109] For example, Alberta, Alberta Rules of Court, r. 23; Ontario, Rules of Civil Procedure, r. 17; British Columbia, Rules of Court, r. 13.

[110] See English Common Law Procedure Act of 1852 (U.K.), 15 & 16 Vict., c. 76, ss. 18 and 19.

their judgments were not recognized or enforced. As the British Columbia Court of Appeal has explained, in asserting jurisdiction the court should be "mindful of international good manners or comity" not only because absent a real and substantial connection with the matter, it is arrogant to assume jurisdiction, "but also because it cannot be in the commercial interest of Canada as a trading nation that it should acquire a reputation of enmeshing foreign merchants in lawsuits not grounded jurisdictionally on a footing generally accepted in the civilized world."[111]

Some provinces continue to require leave to serve a defendant outside the province.[112] In these provinces, the court may authorize the service of the originating process upon absent defendants, provided the subject matter of the proceeding *prima facie* falls within the scope of the relevant rule of procedure and the applicants show that they have a reasonable cause of action or a good arguable case.[113] However, in most provinces, where the subject matter of the proceeding falls within the scope of the relevant rule, leave is not required.[114] Despite the breadth of the categories of cases in which leave is not required, there is still a provision for obtaining leave where the subject matter of the proceeding falls outside the scope of the rules.[115] In Nova Scotia, the originating process may be

---

[111] *Northern Sales Co.* v. *Government Trading Corp. of Iran* (1991), 81 D.L.R. (4th) 316, at 321 (B.C.C.A.). See also *Cook* v. *Parcel, Mauro, Hultin & Spaanstra, P.C.* (1996), 136 D.L.R. (4th) 414; aff'd (1997), 143 D.L.R. (4th) 213 (B.C.C.A.), leave to appeal refused (1997), 147 D.L.R. (4th) viii (S.C.C.); *Tortel Communication Inc.* v. *Suntel Inc.* (1994), 120 D.L.R. (4th) 100, [1995] 1 W.W.R. 457 (Man. C.A.) [hereinafter *Tortel*]; *Janke* v. *Budd Canada Inc.* (1994), 28 C.P.C. (3d) 42 (Man. Q.B.); aff'd (1994), 31 C.P.C. (3d) 1 (C.A.); *Olde* v. *Capital Publishing Ltd. Partnership* (1996), 64 A.C.W.S. (3d) 1138 (Ont. Gen. Div).

[112] Alberta, Alberta Rules of Court, r. 30; and Newfoundland, Rules of the Supreme Court, r. O.XI.

[113] However, plaintiffs need not satisfy the court by proving the case as they would at trial: *Cdn. Commercial Bank* v. *McLaughlan* (1989), 38 C.P.C. (2d) 23, 70 Alta. L.R. (2d) 370 (Q.B.); *Kearney's Estate* v. *Bell Helicopter Textron Inc.* (1988), 74 Nfld. & P.E.I.R. 138 (Nfld. C.A.); *Molnlycke A.B.* v. *Kimberly-Clark of Canada Ltd.* (1991), 47 F.T.R. 161, 36 C.P.R. (3d) 493 (C.A.); *Muzak Corp.* v. *Composers Authors & Publishers Assn. of Canada Ltd.*, [1953] 2 S.C.R. 182.

[114] For example, British Columbia, Manitoba, New Brunswick, Ontario, and Saskatchewan. "Originating process" includes a counterclaim against a person who is not already a party to the main action: *Henry Grethel Apparel Inc.* v. *H.A. Imports of Canada Ltd.* (1990), 42 C.P.C. (2d) 260 (Ont. M.C.). According to the 1998 Federal Court Rules, r. 137(1): a plaintiff may serve a defendant with the statement of claim *ex juris* without leave.

[115] For example, British Columbia, Rules of Court, r. 13(3) and (4); *Ratcliffe* v. *Maj*

served anywhere in Canada or in the United states without leave and with leave elsewhere.[116]

With respect to service *ex juris* with or without leave, the subject matter of the proceeding must fall within the scope of the rules of procedure for such service.[117] The court must also consider whether a reasonable measure of fairness and justice, which is sufficient to meet the reasonable expectations of the national and international communities, would be achieved if it exercised jurisdiction.[118] Regardless of whether or not leave is required, the exercise of jurisdiction over an absent defendant lies within the discretion of the court. Defendants will not be forced to answer locally merely because the subject matter of the proceeding comes within the scope of the rules for service *ex juris* unless it is reasonable and convenient in all circumstances for them to do so. In other words, the forum selected by the plaintiff must be *forum conveniens*.[119] Any ambiguity or doubt in the application of the rules and the exercise of discretion is to be resolved in favour of the absent foreign defendant.[120]

Jurisdiction over a non-resident as a result of contacts on the Internet, including the operation of a website and the use of e-mail, raises some interesting questions. To impose traditional territorial concepts of jurisdiction on commercial users of the Internet is not always appropriate since, as has already been noted, the Internet has no geographical borders. Its websites are accessible simultaneously in many locations and, generally, the information they contain is not targeted to a particular audience. A different approach

---

(1989), 39 C.P.C. (2d) 261 (B.C.S.C.); Ontario, Rules of Civil Procedure, r. 17.03; *Upper Lakes Shipping Ltd.* v. *Foster Yeoman Ltd.* (1992), 12 C.P.C. (3d) 31 (Ont. Gen. Div.); aff'd. (1993), 14 O.R. (3d) 548; *National Bank of Canada* v. *Chance* (1996), 65 A.C.W.S. (3d) 577 (Ont. Gen. Div.); *Tortel*, 1995, *supra* note 111.

[116] Rules of Civil Procedure, r. 10.07.

[117] *McCulloch* v. *J.P.W. Investments Inc.* (1992), 68 B.C.L.R. (2d) 382, [1995] 5 W.W.R. 650 (S.C.). See also *Ell* v. *Con-Pro Industries Ltd. and Kowalski* (1992), 11 B.C.A.C. 174 (C.A.); *Canadian International Marketing Distributing Ltd.* v. *Nitsuko Ltd.* (1990), 68 D.L.R. (4th) 318 (B.C.C.A.); and *Tortel, supra* note 111.

[118] See *Quest Vitamin Supplies Ltd.* v. *Hassam* (1992), 79 B.C.L.R. (2d) 85 (B.C.S.C.); *Cool* v. *Parcel, Mauro, Hultin & Spaanstra, P.C.* (1996), 136 D.L.R. (4th) 414, at 423 (B.C.S.C.); aff'd (1997), 143 D.L.R. (4th) 213 (C.A.).

[119] See *Easthaven, supra* note 8.

[120] *Frymer* v. *Brettschneider* (1994), 19 O.R. (3d) 60 (C.A.). See also *Rudder* v. *Microsoft Corp.* (1999), 47 C.C.L.T. (2d) 168 (Ont. S.C.J.) [hereinafter *Rudder*].

may have to be devised in order to exercise jurisdiction over non-residents who are online users, whether they are suppliers or purchasers of goods or services, service providers, issuers of credit or e-cash, and so on. Should the exercise of personal jurisdiction depend upon the nature and quality of the defendant's activities in the forum province? Can online suppliers and purchasers of goods and services be considered as carrying on business in the province or state where they reside? Does jurisdiction depend upon whether the website is passive, interactive, or commercial? For instance, can a person posting a message on a website be sued in the courts of any jurisdiction where the message may be downloaded or should the website author/owner be subject only to the courts of his or her own residence or to the courts of the place where the ISP hosting the website or the portal or server is located, if such a place can be ascertained?

Where the defendant operating a website is intentionally availing himself or herself of the privilege of doing business in the province and has purposefully directed activities to persons in that province, jurisdiction would be properly exercised as the website is commercial. As a general rule, personal jurisdiction should not be asserted solely on the accessibility of a passive website that does not target persons in the province or on the location of an ISP or server. Where the place of performance or of damage is relevant with respect to an action based on a contract or tort, except perhaps with respect to a contract for services concluded and performed online, a breach of contract or damage that results from, let us say, a libel published on a passive website or bulletin board, occurs in real space and not on the Internet somewhere in virtual space, and it is therefore relatively easy to ascertain its location for the purpose of establishing jurisdiction over a non-resident defendant. The basic question is always whether the connections or contacts with the Canadian forum are real and substantial.[121]

In the United States,[122] the courts have classified Internet contacts

---

[121] *Easthaven, supra* note 8; *Kitakufe* v. *Oloya*, [1998] O.J. No. 2537 (Gen. Div.). Note that the routine use of e-mail may contribute to a finding of personal jurisdiction. In general, see F. Bachand *et al.*, "Jurisdiction and the Internet. Are Traditional Rules Enough?" which can be accessed at <http://www.law.ualberta.ca/alri/ulc/current/ejurisd.htm>.

[122] *Zippo Mfg. Co.* v. *Zippo Dot Com Inc.*, 952 F. Supp. 1119, at 1124 (W.D. Pa. 1997), which is quoted in *Braintech, Inc.* v. *Kostiuk* (1999), 171 D.L.R. (4th) 46, 120 B.C.C.A. 1 (C.A.), leave to appeal refused, [1999] S.C.C.A. no.236 (S.C.C.) [hereinafter *Braintech*] (foreign judgment: the jurisdiction of the foreign court

on a sliding scale of passive, interactive, and commercial, particularly for personal jurisdiction over non-resident defendants. Strictly
passive Internet contacts exist when a website only provides information to Internet users (for instance, merely posting information
or advertising on the Internet without targeting a particular province or state). The website operator simply provides an informational website that can be accessed by interested viewers who are
browsing in the forum province or state, but it does not serve as
a platform for soliciting business or conducting electronic commerce.[123] Interactive Internet contacts occur when an Internet user
can communicate by exchanging information with another user
(for instance, where a defendant operates an informational website
but also allows a user to exchange information with the host computer by providing an e-mail address or a toll-free number). Commercial Internet contacts exist when a defendant conducts business
over the Internet with users in the forum province or state (for
instance, where a contract is entered into on the Internet by the
defendant with a resident of the forum province or state, which
involves repeated transmission of computer files over the Internet).
In this case, the two-way online communication fosters an ongoing
business relationship. To establish jurisdiction, interactivity must
be significant.

When this sliding scale approach does not yield any results,
courts might consider resorting to the effects test, whose purpose is
to recognize that even though the defendant may not have physically entered the forum province, the effects of the contents of
the web page can be significant and felt there significantly. Thus,
passive websites that contain defamatory material, publish a company's trade secrets, or use a mark similar to a trademark could
satisfy this test, provided the plaintiff suffered harm in the forum
province and the defendant aimed his or her tortious conduct at
this province.[124] In other words, as the level of interactivity on the
Internet increases, so too does the likelihood of finding personal

---

in a case involving defamation on an internet bulletin board). See also *Panavision International, supra* note 104, with respect to jurisdictional tests: general
and specific and M. Geist , "Is There a ThereThere? Towards Greater Certainty
for Internet Jurisdiction" (2001) 16 Berkeley Tech. L. J.1345.

[123] *Cybersell, Inc.* v. *Cybersell, Inc.*, 180 F.3d 414 (9th Cir. 1997).

[124] *Panavision International, supra* note 104 at 1321, citing *Ziegler* v. *Indian River
County*, 64 F. 3d 470 (9th Cir. 1995) and *Calder* v. *Jones*, 465 U.S. 783 (1984)
[hereinafter *Calder*].

jurisdiction. On the other hand, the more passive a website is, the less likely that personal jurisdiction may be established. The registration of a domain name should not be sufficient to confer personal jurisdiction over the registrant on the courts of the province or state in which registration takes place.[125] Furthermore, where jurisdiction over the subject matter or over the defendant is based on Internet contacts, it should be limited to litigation arising from such contacts and should not give the court general jurisdiction over the defendant for actions arising from non-Internet transactions or activities. The American Bar Association in its report on *Global Jurisdiction Issues Created by the Internet*[126] clearly indicates how important targeting is to the jurisdiction to prescribe and to adjudicate:

Today, entities seeking a relationship with residents of a foreign forum need not themselves maintain a physical presence in the forum. A forum can be "targeted" by those outside it and desirous of benefiting from a connection with it via the Internet (assuming, of course, that the foreign actor is willing to confine its target to those with access to technology, a growing but still not universal subset of any forum's population). Such a chosen relationship will subject the foreign actor to both personal and prescriptive jurisdiction, so a clear understanding of what constitutes targeting is critical.

Maintenance of a web site, by itself, should not constitute targeting the world. There is no legal or practical reason why it should. At the other extreme, designing a website whose only, or at least primary, relevance is to the population of a single forum clearly does target that forum . . .

In light of fundamental jurisdictional principles, based on the premise that individuals should be able to choose whether or not they wish to become connected to any given sovereign, the critical issues are the intent of the web site sponsor and what constitutes sufficient evidence of that intent. The site itself provides the first evidence of that intent. It may contain a list of fora it intends to target and filters to block participants from other States. It may contain a list of fora it does not intend to target. But filters may be by-passed, and stated intent may not reveal reality. When transactions are involved, the best evidence of intent is the willingness to deal with persons in the forum State.

Generally, in common law Canada, service *ex juris* is permitted where relief is sought against a person domiciled, ordinarily resident, or carrying on business in the jurisdiction.[127] A defendant

---

[125] *Easthaven, supra* note 8. In the United States, see *America Online Inc.* v. *Chih-Hsien Huang,* 106 F. Supp. 2d 848 (E.D. Va. 2000).

[126] *Global Jurisdiction Issues Created by the Internet,* report of the ABA Jurisdiction in Cyberspace Project, London, 2000, s. 2.2.

[127] For example, in Alberta, Alberta Rules of Court, r. 30(c); in Ontario, Rules of Civil Procedure, r. 17.02(p).

offering goods and services for sale on a website to residents of the forum would be carrying on business in the province.

Service *ex juris* is also permitted where the proceeding is to enforce, rescind, resolve, annul, or otherwise affect a contract, to recover damages, or to obtain relief with respect to a contract[128] that is

- made in the jurisdiction;
- by its terms or implications governed by the law of the jurisdiction; or
- in which the parties agree that the local court shall have jurisdiction to entertain any proceeding in respect of the contract.[129]

Often contracts concluded online contain a forum selection and a choice of law clause.[130] If this is not the case, the provincial Rules of Court, as noted above, refer to a most relevant contract for the exercise of jurisdiction since, in the absence of an express choice, the Canadian choice of law rule calls for the application of the system of law that is most closely and really connected with the transaction.[131] Jurisdiction can also be established where the proceeding is in respect of a breach committed within the jurisdiction of a contract wherever made and irrespective of the fact (if that is the case) that the breach was preceded or accompanied by a breach committed out of the jurisdiction that rendered impossible the performance of so much of the contract as ought to have been performed in the jurisdiction.[132] This rule would cover breaches of warranties on the part of a merchant who sold goods online to residents of the forum where they were intended to be used. Where a contract is concluded online and also performed online, it is difficult to determine which court has jurisdiction unless such a contract contains a choice of jurisdiction clause or the parties to it can be localized.

---

[128] For example, in Ontario, Rules of Civil Procedure, r. 17.02(f); in Saskatchewan, Rules of Court, r. 31(1)(f).

[129] For example, in British Columbia, Rules of Court, r. 13(8) and (9).

[130] In "click wrap contracts." See *Rudder, supra* note 120 (forum selection clause valid; terms of agreement not analogous to "fine print" in written contract).

[131] Castel, *supra* note 93 at para. 452.

[132] For example, Alberta, Alberta Rules of Court, r. 30(g); Ontario, Rules of Civil Procedure, r. 17.02(f)(iv).

Service *ex juris* is possible where the proceeding is founded on a tort committed in the jurisdiction.[133] This situation poses the problem of determining the place of tort especially with respect to complex torts such as defamation on the web and consumer product liability. In the case of defamation, it would be necessary to know where the place of Internet publication is located. Does publication take place where it is manifested and comprehended by the reader — that is, at the place of downloading by subscribers[134] or at the place of uploading? Is targeting required? Finally, service *ex juris* is permitted where the proceeding is in respect of a claim for damages sustained in the jurisdiction arising from a tort[135] or a breach of contract, wherever committed.[136] This rule completes the preceding one and overcomes the difficulties involved in determining the place of the tort. It adopts the effects test.

Depending upon the circumstances, any of these rules can easily be applied to the various actors involved in online activities. Therefore, the dissemination of defamatory statements over the Internet could give jurisdiction to the court where the damage is sustained by the plaintiff, no matter where publication has taken place, especially if the defamatory material was targeted at the forum province. This fact constitutes a real and substantial connection with the forum and is an application of the effects principle.[137] Hence, where one website is within the jurisdiction of the court, will its operator be liable for defamatory statements contained in a non-resident second site that is linked to the first or does it give the court jurisdiction over the non-resident second site?

The assertion of jurisdiction over a non-resident defendant for the infringement or violation of intellectual property rights within or without Canada could be subject to the same rules. For instance, with respect to copyright, if the website is used mainly for general advertising and promotion without targeting residents of the

---

[133] For example, British Columbia, Rules of Court, r. 13(1)(h); Ontario, Rules of Civil Procedure, r. 17.02(g).

[134] See *Gutnik* v. *Dow Jones & Company Inc.*, [2001] V.S.C. 305 (Vict. S.C.) [hereinafter *Gutnik*] (publication where paid subscribers to interactive service were located).

[135] For example, Ontario, Rules of Civil Procedure, r. 17.02(h); *Duncan, supra* note 107.

[136] For example, Ontario, Rules of Civil Procedure, r. 17.02(h).

[137] In the United States, see, for example, *Calder, supra* note 124 (effects test); *Edias Software International L.L.C.* v. *Basis International Ltd.* (1996), 947 F. Supp. 413 (D.C. Ariz.).

forum state, the court should not exercise jurisdiction. The site is passive and has no real and substantial connection with the forum. On the other hand, such connection would exist if the site were interactive or commercial and allowed Internet users to download infringing material.[138]

In a recent case that involved, in part, the question of whether the territorial reach of the Copyright Act[139] extends to communications by means of telecommunications that are transmitted from host servers outside Canada, the Federal Court of Appeal held that:

[185] ... The question remains: what test for locating the communications under consideration here would be most consistent with the policy of the *Copyright Act* and other legal principles?

[186] In my view, a royalty may be made payable in Canada in respect of communications by telecommunication that have a real and substantial connection with Canada. I would also apply the real and substantial connection test to locating the infringing activity of authorizing a communication that occurs when a content provider posts copyright material on a host server ...

[191] ... The most important connecting factors will, I assume, normally be the location of the content provider, the end user and the intermediaries, in particular the host server. However, such a connection will surely exist when each of the end nodes, namely the content provider, the communicator of the material, and the end user, is in Canada.

[192] Indeed, I would go further and say that, since the policy of the Act is to protect copyright in the Canadian market, the location of the end user is a particularly important factor in determining if any Internet communication has a real and substantial connection with Canada. On the other hand, in the absence of an end user, the location of the server will be a weightier factor in determining whether the authorization of a communication has a real and substantial connection with Canada. The real and substantial connection test is also applicable to communication from caches and hyperlinks; the location of a cache or a linked site from which material is transmitted will provide an additional potentially connecting factor.[140]

---

[138] See *WIC Premium Television,* 2000, *supra* note 40; *Desktop Technologies, Inc.* v. *Color-Works Reproduction & Design Inc.* 1999 U.S. Dist. Lexis 1934 (E.D. Pa. 1999). Note that caching, which allows for greater efficiency in the transmission of information on the network by maintaining redundant copies close to those who access the information, could amount to copyright infringement.

[139] Copyright Act, R.S.C. 1985, c. C-42 as amended.

[140] *SOCAN* v. *Canadian Association of Internet Providers et al.,* 2002 FCA 166, paras. 163-92 (Issue 5), rev'g in part *Tariff* 22 (1999), 1 C.P.R. (4th) 417, esp. at 459-60.

Where websites display infringing trademarks, the infringing conduct takes place where the website is created and/or maintained and not where the trademarks can be viewed over the web. Jurisdiction can also be based on damage within the forum province if the defendant's conduct targets this province and transacted business with local residents has resulted in harmful effects there.[141]

The jurisdiction of a Canadian court to restrain non-residents from operating a foreign website where the activities at the site affect residents in Canada was considered in *Tele-Direct (Publications)* v. *Canadian Business Online Inc.*,[142] where the Federal Court of Canada issued an interlocutory injunction against the defendant to stop the use of the plaintiff's trademark. As the defendant continued to use the trademark on servers located in the United States, the court held that while it may not have jurisdiction to enforce its order, it did have jurisdiction to find the defendant guilty of contempt of court. The Federal Court of Canada also granted an injunction restraining the defendant, which was a corporation carrying on business in Canada, from providing access to its domain name to residents of Canada and the United States.[143]

In Québec, in personal actions of a patrimonial nature, Québec courts have jurisdiction where the defendant out-of-province online merchant or ISP is a legal person that has an establishment in Québec and a dispute arises partially over the activities of the establishment in Québec and partially over the activities outside Québec.[144] Even if the out-of-province actor has no establishment in Québec, there can still be jurisdiction over it on the basis of damage suffered in Québec[145] (for instance, where the user, who is a resident of Québec, takes an action in the province since the damage is presumed to have occurred at his or her residence);[146] if the place of fault or injurious act was in Québec;[147] if a contractual

---

[141] *Computer City, supra* note 5: a passive website cannot constitute a use in association with wares because no transfer is possible through that medium. The Court of Appeal stated: "It is much more sensible to apply tort principles to accommodate new technologies than to distort statutory trademark rights," at para. 16.

[142] *Tele-Direct (Publications)* v. *Canadian Business Online Inc.* (1998), 83 C.P.R. (3d) 34 (F.C.T.D.).

[143] *Bell Actimedia Inc.* v. *Puzo* (1999), 2 C.P.R. (4th) 289 (F.C.T.D.).

[144] Civil Code of Quebec, Article 3148(2).

[145] *Ibid.* at Article 3148(3).

[146] See *Morales Moving and Storage* v. *Chatigny-Britton*, [1996] R.D.J. 14 (C.A.).

[147] Civil Code of Quebec, Article 3148(3).

obligation was to be performed in Québec as determined by the law applicable to this question;[148] if there was an agreement to submit all existing or future disputes between them arising out of a specified legal relationship, such as a dispute arising from an online contract, to the jurisdiction of the Québec courts;[149] or, finally, if the defendant submitted to the jurisdiction of the Québec courts.[150] However, Québec courts have no jurisdiction "where the parties, by agreement, have chosen to submit all existing or future disputes between themselves relating to a specified legal relationship to a foreign authority or to an arbitrator, unless the defendant submits to the jurisdiction of the Québec authorities."[151]

Residence or domicile of the website author/owner in Québec is sufficient to confer jurisdiction to the Québec courts irrespective of the place where the server is located.[152] However, it should be noted that Article 3136 of the Civil Code provides for exceptional jurisdiction where the Québec courts have no ordinary jurisdiction, but the dispute has a sufficient connection with Québec and the proceedings cannot possibly be instituted outside Québec or where the institution of such proceedings outside Québec cannot reasonably be required. It is unlikely that a court will use this article to exercise jurisdiction over a foreign Internet service provider or the author/owner of the website.

As in the common law provinces, any attempt to assert jurisdiction will have to meet Canadian constitutional law principles, which require that there be a real and substantial connection between the Québec court and the defendant or the subject matter of the suit.[153] In determining whether this test has been met, the Québec courts might consider the distinction between interactive and passive activity in Québec. If the website is commercial or interactive and specially targets Québec consumers, the Québec courts would exercise jurisdiction.

In some instances, a Québec user may wish to bring a proceeding against separate entities arising out of the same online transaction

---

[148] *Ibid.*

[149] *Ibid.* at Article 3148(4).

[150] *Ibid.* at Article 3148(5).

[151] *Ibid.* at Article 3148, final para.

[152] *Ibid.* at Article 3148(1), and *Investor Group Inc.* v. *Hudson*, [1999] R.J.Q. 599 (S.C.) which relied on Article 68(1) of the Code of Civil Procedure to the same effect. See also Article 3134 of the Civil Code of Quebec.

[153] *Morguard, supra* note 37; and *Hunt, supra* note 37.

or posting, or the online defendant in the principal action may want to bring in a third party in warranty. There is no provision in the Civil Code of Québec that states that where an action is taken against a number of co-defendants, personal jurisdiction over any of them confers jurisdiction over the others, even in circumstances in which it would be preferable to have the claims against all the co-defendants decided together, so as to avoid contradictory judgments. However, if jurisdiction exists over the online merchant or author/owner of the website but not necessarily over the other participants, the action may be so related that jurisdiction over the co-defendants would be possible under Articles 3136 and 3139 of the Civil Code. The Québec courts will also exercise jurisdiction with respect to a consumer contract or a contract of employment negotiated and concluded online if the consumer or the worker has his or her domicile or residence in Québec. This rule is adequate in order to protect the consumer and the worker. A waiver of such jurisdiction by the consumer or employee is of no effect.[154]

It should be mentioned that Article 3140 of the Civil Code, which provides that "[i]n cases of emergency or serious inconvenience, Québec authorities may also take such measures as they consider necessary for the protection of the person or property of a person present in Québec," should enable Québec courts to issue injunctions against Internet actors in order to protect Québec residents. Enforcing such injunctions, however, may be difficult if the actors that are subject to them do not reside in Québec and have no assets in the province. In the contractual field, it may be advisable to distinguish between contracts negotiated and concluded online but performed, in whole or in part, offline and those contracts that are negotiated and concluded online and also performed in their totality online. In the first case, the traditional rules of jurisdiction that are applied in the common law provinces and in Québec seem to be adequate. In the second case though, it may be better to have jurisdiction depend exclusively upon a choice of forum clause.

Law Applicable to Online Contracts and Torts

Once a Canadian court has exercised jurisdiction in cases containing legally relevant foreign elements involving the use of the Internet, which law will it apply? Present Canadian choice of law rules applicable to extra-provincial or international contracts

---

[154] Civil Code of Quebec, Article 3149.

should not pose serious problems. In common law Canada, it is well established that the parties to a contract negotiated and concluded online can select the law that will be applicable to it provided that choice is *bona fide* and legal and there is no reason for avoiding the choice on the ground of public policy. The choice will be disregarded only if its purpose is to evade the mandatory provisions of the system of law with which the transaction, objectively, is most closely and really connected.[155] Anyone doing business on the Internet should use a choice of law and of forum clause. However, it may be declared to be against the public policy of the forum and ignored if there was a lack of equality of bargaining power present between the contracting parties at the time that the transaction was entered into. This scenario is possible in the case of click wrap online contracts.[156]

The choice of law may also be inferred or implied from the circumstances.[157] In the absence of an express or implied choice, the courts will apply the system of law with which the transaction has the closest and most real connection.[158] In selecting such a system of law, a number of factors will be taken into consideration, one of them being the place of contracting, which may not be easy to ascertain when contracts are concluded online. The law that is applicable to the contract will cover all of its aspects, including performance.

In Québec, a contract is governed by Article 3109, which deals with the law applicable to its form, and Articles 3111-13 of the Civil Code, which address the determination of the law applicable to its substance or contents. These articles refer to the law that is expressly designated by the parties or, in its absence, the law that is most closely connected to the contract in view of its nature and the attendant circumstances — it being presumed that a contract is most closely connected with the law of the state where the party who is to perform the prestation that is characteristic of the contract has his or her residence or, if the contract is made in the ordinary course of business of an enterprise, its establishment. Article 3127 of the Civil Code is also relevant and declares that injury from non-performance of contractual obligations is governed by the same law as the one applicable to the contract.

---

[155] Castel, *supra* note 93 at para. 449.

[156] However, see *Rudder, supra* note 120, where such a clause was upheld.

[157] Castel, *supra* note 93 at para. 450.

[158] *Ibid.* at para. 452.

Most of the time, a business-to-business contract that is concluded online and performed, in whole or in part, online or offline contains a choice of law clause. If not, it may be difficult to localize the parties and the contract. With respect to form, is the contract concluded where the server is located or at the place that is targeted by the offer posted on the web? As for the substance of the contract, in the absence of express choice, how is the presumption applied in the case of a contract concluded and performed online when the residence or the establishment of the party who is to perform the prestation that is characteristic of the contract is unknown? If the contract is to be performed offline, it is easier to determine the law of the state with which the act is most closely connected since the place of delivery of the goods or services will be identified in the contract.

With respect to the sale of goods to non-business users or gambling online, the Québec courts would likely characterize these transactions as consumer contracts governed by Article 3117 of the Civil Code, which states that

> [t]he choice by the parties of the law applicable to a consumer contract does not result in depriving the consumer of the protection to which he is entitled under the mandatory provisions of the law of the country where he has his residence if the formation of the contract was preceded by a special offer or an advertisement in that country and the consumer took all the necessary steps for the formation of the contract in that country or if the order was received from the consumer in that country.
>
> The same rule also applies where the consumer was induced by the other contracting party to travel to a foreign country for the purpose of forming the contract.
>
> If no law is designated by the parties, the law of the place where the consumer has his residence is, in the circumstances, applicable to the consumer contract.

The protection given to the consumer is the application of the law of the place of his or her residence at the time of the conclusion of the contract, a law with which he or she is presumed to be familiar, so long as the connections set forth in the article to that place are present. This law is easy to determine in the case of contracts concluded online and performed offline. The Consumer Protection Act[159] would be relevant only if applicable by virtue of Article 3117 of the Civil Code. For instance, in accordance with the first paragraph of Article 3117, in order for the law of the state of the gambler's residence to apply in an action against an online gaming

---

[159] Consumer Protection Act, R.S.Q., P-40.1 as amended.

merchant for annulment of the contract, its formation must have been preceded by a special offer or advertisement in his or her state of residence and the gambler must have taken all the necessary steps for the formation of the contract in that state or the order must have been received from the gambler in that state.[160] Information on the website by a gaming merchant does not of itself amount to publicity in every province or state where it can be read on a computer screen. Furthermore, a transaction is not concluded until the funds are approved by a financial institution and deposited into an account with the gaming merchant in a place where it is assumed that this merchant is licensed to carry on gaming operations legally. This is the case even if one has accepted the view held by some American courts that when a gambler places a bet on his or her computer, he or she creates a virtual casino in his or her home in which the gaming transaction therefore takes place. Since it is assumed that the gaming merchant has no establishment at the gambler's residence, it is difficult to see how all the necessary steps to complete the contract took place there. This scenario does not fit with the contents of Article 3117, paragraph 1. Nor could it be said that the gambler was induced by the gaming merchant to travel to a foreign country to conclude the contract by virtue of surfing the net (virtual trip).[161]

Hence, Articles 3112-3113 of the Civil Code would be applicable to a contract between a gambler and a gaming merchant. The presumption found in Article 3113 calls for the application of the law of the place of the establishment of the party who is to perform the prestation, which is characteristic of the contract. Clearly, a gaming merchant has the characteristic obligation when opening accounts, receiving deposits, paying the winnings, refunding and paying commissions, and acting under license.[162] However, the presumption in favour of the law of the place of the establishment might lead to the law of jurisdiction where gambling on the net is illegal or where the gaming merchant has no license to operate.

---

[160] Note, however, that if Québec law is applicable, a gambler, as the losing party who is an adult of sound mind, may not recover the sums paid unless there was fraud or trickery: Article 2630 of the Civil Code of Quebec. In addition, if not expressly authorized by law, the contract would be invalid: Article 2629 of the Civil Code of Quebec.

[161] See G. Goldstein and E. Groffier, *Droit international privé, Théorie générale*, vol. I (1998), para. 114, at 263; and Civil Code of Quebec, Article 3117, para. 2.

[162] It is assumed that the gaming merchant has its establishment in a jurisdiction where gaming is legal and under license.

If this is the case, the presumption under Article 3113 would be rebutted and would require the application of the law of the place where the gaming merchant is licensed. The shift to the law of the place where the merchant is authorized to act is clearly the place having the closest connection with the whole transaction and should be applied as the law governing the contract.

Where the place of the establishment coincides with the place of licensing, the law of that place governs the contract whether or not it is a consumer contract. Since gambling is not illegal in that place, the contract is valid and enforceable in Québec. Public order as understood in international relations cannot be used to set it aside.[163] Of course, a Québec court could assist a foreign country by applying its law prohibiting gambling by virtue of Article 3079 of the Civil Code, which provides that "[w]here legitimate and manifestly preponderant interests so require, effect may be given to a mandatory provision of the law of another country with which the situation is closely connected. In deciding whether to do so, consideration is given to the purpose of the provision and the consequences of its application." However, this situation is unlikely, given the strict interpretation given to this article by the Québec Court of Appeal in *Arab Bank Corporation* v. *Wightman et al.*[164] and its attitude in *Auerback* v. *Resorts International Hotels Inc.*[165]

If a sale and purchase of goods or real estate online, which is to be performed offline, is not characterized as a consumer contract, Article 3114 provides that

[i]f no law is designated by the parties, the sale of a corporeal movable is governed by the law of the country where the seller had his residence or, if the sale is made in the ordinary course of business of an enterprise, his establishment, at the time of formation of the contract. However, the sale is governed by the law of the country in which the buyer had his residence or his establishment at the time of formation of the contract in any of the following cases:

- negotiations have taken place and the contract has been formed in that country;
- the contract provides expressly that delivery shall be made in that country;

---

[163] Civil Code of Quebec, Article 3081; and *Auerbach* v. *Resorts International Hotels Inc.*, [1992] R.J.Q. 302 (C.A.) [hereinafter *Auerbach*].

[164] *Arab Bank Corporation* v. *Wightman et al.*, 21 January 1997 (C.C.) J.E. 97-306, [1996] R.J.Q. 1715 (C.S.); and G. Goldstein (1997), 76 Rev. Bar. Can. 449.

[165] *Auerback, supra* note 163.

- the contract is formed on terms determined mainly by the buyer, in response to a call for tenders.

If no law is designated by the parties, the sale of immovable property is governed by the law of the country where it is situated.

Where the sale is by auction on the Internet and no law that is applicable to it is expressly designated by the parties, Article 3115 of the Civil Code provides for the application of the law of the state where the auction takes place. This place would be difficult to find.[166] In order to avoid the problem of determining the location of some of these factors, it is always advisable to select expressly the law applicable to these types of contracts.

It should also be noted that the 1980 United Nations Convention on Contracts for the International Sale of Goods,[167] which is in force in Canada, may be applicable to some online contractual issues if both parties to a commercial transaction are from member states, unless the parties have opted out of its coverage.[168] The convention does not apply to the sale of consumer goods.

The determination of the law applicable to wrongful activities on the Internet is not easy in light of the Canadian common law position, which, as a general rule, calls for the application of the law of the place where the wrongful activity occurred.[169] Exceptions to this rule are possible with respect to wrongful activities taking place outside Canada.[170]

---

[166] With respect to contracts of employment concluded online, see Article 3118 of the Civil Code of Quebec:

> The designation by the parties of the law applicable to a contract of employment does not result in depriving the worker of the protection to which he is entitled under the mandatory provisions of the law of the country where the worker habitually carries on his work, even if he is on temporary assignment in another country or, if the worker does not habitually carry on his work in any one country, the mandatory provisions of the law of the country where his employer has his domicile or establishment.
>
> If no law is designated by the parties, the law of the country where the worker habitually carries on his work or the law of the country where his employer has his domicile or establishment is, in the same circumstances, applicable to the contract of employment.

[167] United Nations Convention on Contracts for the International Sale of Goods, C.T.S. 1992/2.

[168] See Castel, *supra* note 93 at para. 488.

[169] *Tolofson, supra* note 37.

[170] See *Hanlan* v. *Sernesky* (1997), 35 O.R. (3d) 603 (Gen. Div.), aff'd (1998), 38 O.R. (3d) 479 (C.A.). Comp. *Wong* v. *Lee* (2002), 58 O.R. (3d) 398 (C.A.).

Where is the place of wrongful activity when defamatory material is posted on a website and can be downloaded and read simultaneously in more than one province or state? Since the tort of defamation can only be committed when the defamatory material is published to someone other than the victim, simply uploading and posting such material onto a passive website does not make the author/owner of the website and the ISP where the web is hosted liable as publishers until such material has been viewed or downloaded by a user.[171] Thus, the place of viewing or downloading would be the place of publication and not the place where the ISP or website author/owner or server is located.[172] ISPs, as mere distributors or common carriers of defamatory material, should not be subject to liability provided that they do not exercise editorial control over the content of the material placed on the websites that they they are hosting and have no actual knowledge of such contents.[173] It is suggested that once the defamatory material has been viewed or downloaded by someone, the tort of defamation should be located where the victim's reputation has been most injured, generally at his or her place of residence or of work, which is not necessarily at the place of publication. The law of the victim's place of residence or of work would determine the liability of the defendant.

Where defective goods are manufactured negligently in one jurisdiction, sold online, and cause damage to the purchaser/consumer in another jurisdiction, statutory rules in some common law provinces call for the application of the *lex fori* if the consumer suffers a loss in the province because of the defect. This legislation does not contain choice of law rules for cases falling outside its territorial scope.[174] Where there is no special legislation, the application of the place of wrongful activity is not adequate. However, by analogy, relying on *Moran* v. *Pyle National (Canada) Ltd.*,[175] a Supreme Court of Canada decision dealing with jurisdiction, it could be argued

---

[171] *Reform Party of Canada* v. *Western Union Insurance Co.* (1999), 3 C.P.R. (4th) 289 (B.C.S.C.), where the website had been visited by 137 users.

[172] *Gutnick, supra* note 134 (by analogy to jurisdiction).

[173] In the United States, see *Cubby Inc.* v. *Compuserve Inc.*, 776 F. Supp. 135 (S.D.N.Y. 1991) and comp. *Godfrey* v. *Demon Internet Ltd.*, [1999] 4 All E.R. 342, [2001] Q.B. 201 (U.K.Q.B.D.).

[174] For example, Consumer Product Warranty and Liability Act, S.N.B. 1978, c. C-18.1 as amended, s. 27.

[175] *Moran* v. *Pyle National (Canada) Ltd.*, [1975] 1 S.C.R. 393.

that the place of tort is where the injury occurred, especially where the manufacturer, having advertised its goods on the Internet and targeted a particular audience, could reasonably foresee that such goods would be used or consumed where the plaintiff used or consumed them. This conclusion does not contradict *Tolofson* since, in this case, the Supreme Court of Canada admitted that where all the facts and events that constitute the wrongful activity occur in one state but the consequences of that activity are felt in another state, the place of injury is where the tort was committed.

In Québec, according to Article 3126 of the Civil Code, the law of the state where the injurious act occurred is applicable. However, if the damage was suffered in another state, the law of the latter state is applicable if the person who committed the injurious act should have foreseen that the damage would occur there. For instance, in the case of online gambling, the liability of a gaming merchant would depend upon whether or not gambling was an illegal act as determined by the law applicable to the gaming transaction. In other words, from a civil law point of view, if the gaming transaction (opening of the online gaming account with gaming merchants and betting) is legal by its proper law as determined by Québec private international law rules, the gaming merchant cannot be held civilly liable for the adverse financial consequences suffered by the gambler who has become addicted to gambling that is made easy on a computer at home. However, it is questionable whether a person who uploads defamatory information onto a site can reasonably foresee that it may be read anywhere in the world.

Where the person who committed the injurious act and the victim have their domiciles or residences in the same state, the law of that state applies.[176] Thus, with respect to a claim brought by a Québec online gambler against a Québec bank or Visa company, which enabled the gambler to open an account with a foreign gaming merchant and which resulted in losses to him or her, the law of Québec would apply. However, it is hard to see what advantage the gambler would derive from such an action since, in principle, gaming losses cannot be recovered in Québec.[177] In a class action, unless the victims are all from the same jurisdiction, there will be different places of injury for each victim. Thus, a Québec court could conclude that for each victim it is foreseeable that if the injury were to occur it would be at the victim's residence.

[176] Civil Code of Quebec, Article 3126, para. 2.

[177] *Ibid.* at Article 2630.

Article 3126 of the Civil Code is also applicable to defamation on a website as well as wrongful activities that are specific to the Internet, such as hacking. As for the liability of the manufacturer of a movable, it is governed, at the choice of the victim, by the law of the state where the manufacturer has its establishment or, failing that, its residence or by the law of the state where the movable was acquired.[178] The difficulty lies in determining the establishment or residence of the manufacturer. Furthermore, where was the movable acquired when the purchase took place online?

The determination of the law applicable to transnational infringements of intellectual property rights on the Internet is not free from controversy. Where the infringement occurs partly abroad and partly in Canada — for instance, when a copyrighted work is uploaded onto a computer in one state and then accessed and used in several other states — should the courts apply the law of the point of origin (uploading) or that of the point of reception (downloading), which corresponds to the law of the place where the plaintiff suffered injury or the law that created the right? If the infringement took place wholly in Canada, Canadian law would be relevant.[179] Applying *Tolofson* to the tort claim,[180] it would seem that in the case of infringement of foreign intellectual property rights, Canadian courts could apply Canadian law if the resulting harm to the foreign owner of the intellectual property occurred in Canada where the downloading took place.

Recognition and Enforcement of Foreign and Sister-Province Judgments

The recognition and enforcement of foreign and sister-province judgments against defendants arising out of the use of the Internet raises some important issues particularly with respect to the jurisdiction of the courts that rendered such judgments. The application by Canadian courts in the common law provinces of the principles enunciated in *Morguard*[181] means that, at common law, a judgment *in personam* rendered in a sister province or in a foreign state should be recognized and enforced if, *inter alia,* at the date of commencement of the proceeding, the original court had exercised jurisdiction over the defendant on any of the following grounds:

---

[178] *Ibid.* at Article 3128.

[179] For the infringement of trademark in Canada via the Internet, see *Computer City, supra* note 5.

[180] *Tolofson, supra* note 37.

[181] *Morguard, supra* note 37.

- the defendant was ordinarily resident or carrying on business at a permanent place within the territory over which the court exercises jurisdiction;
- the defendant had submitted to the court's jurisdiction; and
- there was a real and substantial connection between the territory over which the court exercises jurisdiction and the subject matter of the proceeding and the defendant.

When a judgment *in personam* rendered in a sister province is sought to be recognized and enforced, the exercise of jurisdiction on any of these grounds is appropriately restrained and compatible with the principles of order and fairness that have been entrenched in the Canadian constitution by the Supreme Court of Canada in *Hunt* v. *T. & N. plc.*[182] With respect to a foreign judgment, these grounds are compatible with the demands of international comity.[183]

From a practical point of view, in *inter-provincial* litigation, a defendant from a sister province should always enter an appearance and defend the Canadian action on the merits since, under *Morguard*, a default judgment would probably be enforceable throughout Canada. In *international* litigation, the decision as to whether or not a foreign defendant should enter an appearance and defend the Canadian action on the merits would depend upon the conflict of laws rules with respect to the recognition and enforcement of foreign judgments of the jurisdiction where the successful plaintiff would most likely seek to enforce the judgment. Whether a Canadian defendant, who is sued in a foreign state,

---

[182] *Hunt, supra* note 37.

[183] In *Amchem Products, supra* note 37, Justice John Sopinka, speaking for the court, adopted the following definition of comity found in the judgment of the US Supreme Court in *Hilton* v. *Guyot* (1895), 159 U.S. 113:

> "Comity" in the legal sense, is neither a matter of absolute obligation, on the one hand, nor of mere courtesy and goodwill, upon the other. But it is the recognition which one nation allows within its territory to the legislative, executive or judicial acts of another nation, having due regard both to international duty and convenience, and to the rights of its own citizens or of other persons who are under the protection of its laws.

See also *Moses* v. *Shore Boat Builders Ltd.*, [1994] 1 W.W.R. 112 (B.C.C.A.), where the Court of Appeal listed a wide variety of factors to be considered when deciding whether or not the action had a real and substantial connection with BC, for example, the place where the cause of action arose, the respective residences of the parties, whether the defendant conducted business in British Columbia, and so on (at 124).

should enter an appearance and defend the foreign action on the merits would depend upon whether there exists a real and substantial connection between the foreign state and the subject matter of the action or the Canadian defendant that would be recognized as a valid jurisdictional basis in Canada for the purpose of its recognition and enforcement in Canada, even if the foreign court exercised jurisdiction on a different basis.[184]

A real and substantial connection with the original forum province or state can be anything. It depends upon the circumstances, provided the connection used by the original court is not unfair to the parties. Certainly, the grounds for exercising jurisdiction in Canada can be used by analogy to test the jurisdiction of the original court. With respect to the Internet, in *Braintech Co. v. Kostiuk*,[185] the British Columbia Court of Appeal held that the mere posting of a defamatory statement on an otherwise passive electronic bulletin board is not sufficient to enter the foreign jurisdiction and to establish a real and substantial connection with that jurisdiction. No one within that jurisdiction had read the alleged defamatory statements. The court stated:

It is apparent the "real and substantial connection" relied upon for the assumption of jurisdiction by the Texas court is the alleged publication there of a libel which affected the interests of resident present and potential investors. This is true only if the mode of communication through the Internet supports this conclusion . . .

From what is alleged in the case at bar it is clear Kostiuk is not the operator of Silicon Investor. It is equally clear the bulletin board is "passive" as posting information volunteered by people like Kostiuk, is accessible only to users who have the means of gaining access and who exercise that means.

In these circumstances the complainant must offer better proof that the defendant has entered Texas than the mere possibility that someone in that jurisdiction might have reached out to cyberspace to bring the defamatory material to a screen in Texas. There is no allegation or evidence Kostiuk had a commercial purpose that utilized the highway provided by Internet to enter any particular jurisdiction.

It would create a crippling effect on freedom of expression if, in every jurisdiction the world over in which access to Internet could be achieved, a person who posts fair comment on a bulletin board could be hauled before the courts of each of those countries where access to this bulletin could be obtained.

---

[184] See *Beals* v. *Saldanha*, [2001] O.J. No. 3586 (C.A.) rev'ing (1998), 42 O.R. (3d) 127 (Gen. Div.), leave to appeal to the S.C.C. granted [hereinafter *Beals*].

[185] *Braintech*, *supra* note 122. See also *Old North State Brewing Co.*, *supra* note 101.

In the default judgment it is recited that the allegations of the Original and Amended Petitions "have been admitted." This simply reflects the convention in Texas that if a defendant who has been properly served does not appear the allegations in the petition are admitted as proven. This is a deemed admission which does not assist the respondent in establishing a real and substantial connection between the appellant and the Texas court.

In the circumstance of no purposeful commercial activity alleged on the part of Kostiuk and the equally material absence of any person in that jurisdiction having "read" the alleged libel all that has been deemed to have been demonstrated was Kostiuk's passive use of an out of State electronic bulletin. The allegation of publication fails as it rests on the mere transitory, passive presence in cyberspace of the alleged defamatory material. Such a contact does not constitute a real and substantial presence. On the American authorities this is an insufficient basis for the exercise of an *in personam* jurisdiction over a non-resident.[186]

In order to be recognized and enforced in Québec, a foreign money judgment must meet the conditions found in Articles 3155-59, 3161, 3165, and 3168 of the Civil Code. As in the rest of Canada, the most important condition is that the court of the province or state where the judgment was rendered must have had jurisdiction to do so in accordance with the Québec rules of jurisdiction.[187] To ascertain the jurisdiction of the foreign court that rendered the judgment, Québec courts use what appears to be a triple test. First, the requirements of Article 3168 of the Civil Code, which deal with the jurisdiction of the foreign court in personal actions of a patrimonial nature, must be met. This article provides as follows:

3168. In personal actions of a patrimonial nature, the jurisdiction of a foreign authority is recognized only in the following cases:

- the defendant was domiciled in the country where the decision was rendered;
- the defendant possessed an establishment in the country where the decision was rendered and the dispute relates to its activities in that country;
- a prejudice was suffered in the country where the decision was rendered and it resulted from a fault which was committed in that country or from an injurious act which took place in that country;
- the obligations arising from a contract were to be performed in that country;
- the parties have submitted to the foreign authority disputes which have arisen or which may arise between them in respect of a specific legal

---

[186] *Braintech, supra* note 122 at 60-2 (D.L.R.). Compare with *Gutnik, supra* note 134.

[187] See Civil Code of Quebec, Articles 3155(1), 3164, 3165, and 3168.

relationship; however, renunciation by a consumer or a worker of the jurisdiction of the authority of his place of domicile may not be set up against him;
• the defendant has recognized the jurisdiction of the foreign authority.

Second, it is necessary to fulfill the substantial connection test of Article 3164 of the Civil Code, which declares: "3164. The jurisdiction of foreign authorities is established in accordance with the rules on jurisdiction applicable to Québec authorities under Title Three of this Book, to the extent that the dispute is substantially connected with the country whose authority is seized of the case." This test is consistent with the constitutional requirements of a "real and substantial connection," which are contained in *Morguard*, although it may be more demanding.[188] The jurisdiction of foreign courts is established in accordance with the rules on jurisdiction applicable to Québec courts under Title Three of Book Ten of the Civil Code, which is devoted to the international jurisdiction of Québec authorities, to the extent that the dispute is substantially connected with the state whose court is seized of the case.[189]

Third, the Québec court must determine whether the foreign court exercised its jurisdiction appropriately in light of the general dispositions of the Civil Code.[190] For instance, a Québec court could refuse recognition of the jurisdiction of a foreign court that is otherwise competent, where, under identical circumstances, it would have declined jurisdiction on the basis of *forum non conveniens*.[191] If the exercise of jurisdiction by the foreign court over an Internet user defendant meets these tests, it will be recognized in Québec.

With respect to delictual liability, where a resident of Québec does something on the Internet that causes prejudice to a user in a foreign state, it will be difficult for the foreign resident plaintiff who obtained a judgment in that state to enforce it in Québec since Article 3168(3) of the Civil Code declares that for the jurisdiction of the foreign court to be recognized, the prejudice must have resulted from a fault or injurious act that took place in that state. It is hard to imagine such a situation. However, where the prejudice

---

[188] *Morguard, supra* note 37; and *Hunt, supra* note 37.

[189] This has been called the mirror principle. See H.P. Glenn, *Droit international privé* in *La Réforme du Code Civil* (1993), vol. 3, 769-71, paras. 116-18.

[190] Civil Code of Quebec, Articles 3134 and 3140.

[191] *Ibid.* at Article 3135. *Cortas Canning and Refrigerating Co. v. Suidan Bros. Inc./ Suidan Frères Inc.*, [1999] R.J.Q. 1227 (S.C.) [hereinafter *Cortas Canning*].

and the fault or injurious act causing it all took place in the state of the original court, such contracts would be sufficient to pass successfully the first two Québec tests of jurisdiction of the foreign court. The jurisdiction of the court of residence of the consumer could also be recognized in the context of an online consumer contract by virtue of Articles 3149 and 3164 of the Civil Code, provided there is a substantial connection with the foreign state even where the contract provides for a selection of another forum.[192] Whether the doctrine of *forum non conveniens* can be used in this context is improbable.

With respect to class actions resulting in a foreign judgment against, for instance, an online merchant or provider of services, what matters is the jurisdiction over the defendant and not the residence of the members of the class unless it is a class action based on consumer contracts. Thus, where a class action against an online merchant or provider of services is transnational, including customers from many different provinces or states, it is likely that the decision of the court of the province or state where most customers reside would be binding on customers resident elsewhere by virtue of Articles 3136 and 3164 of the Civil Code.

What constitutes submission to the jurisdiction of a foreign court is determined according to Québec law. The test is subjective.[193] As in the common law provinces, in the absence of a forum selection clause, a Québec or foreign online merchant with assets in Québec, if sued outside Québec, will have to decide whether or not to appear and defend the action on the merits, since if the merchant does appear, the foreign court may acquire jurisdiction over it in the eyes of Québec law. If the Québec or foreign online merchant does not appear and defend the action, a judgment by default would be given against it which may be enforceable in Québec,[194] provided the foreign court had jurisdiction over the merchant, according to Québec law.

Recognition and Enforcement of Foreign Judgments
Based on Foreign Public Laws

In the United States, some judgments involving activities on the Internet could be based on public laws, such as the Racketeer

---

[192] Civil Code of Quebec, Article 3168(5).

[193] See *Cortas Canning, supra* note 191.

[194] Civil Code of Quebec, Article 3156.

Influenced and Corrupt Organization Act,[195] which provides for civil remedies[196] enabling a plaintiff who has suffered injury to obtain relief in the form of treble damages. If the foreign judgment granting such damages meets the conditions of recognition and enforcement of foreign money judgments in the common law provinces or in Québec,[197] such judgment is enforceable anywhere in Canada.[198] The treble damages aspect (which is close to exemplary or punitive damages) is not necessarily against Canadian public policy nor is it penal since these damages are for the benefit of a private litigant.[199]

Recognition and Enforcement of Foreign Arbitral Awards

In the common law provinces[200] and at the federal level,[201] the conditions for recognizing and enforcing foreign arbitral awards settling claims of a civil or commercial nature arising from the use of the Internet are to be found in special legislation that incorporates the 1958 New York Convention on the Recognition and Enforcement of Foreign Arbitral Awards (New York Convention)[202] and the 1985 UNCITRAL Model Law on International Commercial Arbitration.[203]

---

[195] Racketeer Influenced and Corrupt Organization Act, (RICO), 18 U.S.C., s. 1961 *et seq.*

[196] *Ibid.* at s. 1964 (c).

[197] By analogy to Article 3079 of the Civil Code of Quebec, which allows Québec courts to apply foreign laws of immediate application.

[198] See *Ivey, supra* note 47; *U.S.A.* v. *Levy* (1999), 45 O.R. (3d) 129.

[199] Note that in *Cortas Canning, supra* note 191 at 1239-41, in an *obiter dicta,* the Québec Superior Court was of the opinion that a foreign judgment rendered by default for an amount so disproportionate with amounts rendered in similar situations in Québec, could be said not to be in conformity with public order as understood in international relations. In *Beals, supra* note 184, a Florida default judgment based on private law which granted punitive damages to the plaintiffs was held enforceable in Ontario.

[200] For example, International Commercial Arbitration Act, R.S.O. 1990, c. I.9.

[201] United Nations Foreign Arbitral Awards Convention Act, R.S.C. 1985, c. 16 (2nd supp.); Commercial Arbitration Act, R.S.C. 1985, c. 17 (2nd supp.) as amended.

[202] New York Convention on the Recognition and Enforcement of Foreign Arbitral Awards, (1959) 330 U.N.T.S. 38.

[203] UNCITRAL Model Law on International Commercial Arbitration, (1985) 24 I.L.M. 1302.

In Québec, such recognition and enforcement is dealt with in Articles 948-951.2 of the Code of Civil Procedure,[204] which to a great extent incorporates the provision of the 1958 New York Convention.[205] Arbitration appears to be a proper method of settlement of disputes arising from business-to-business contracts that are concluded and performed online or offline between parties of equal strength. In the case of consumer contracts concluded online and performed offline, which give rise to small claims, conciliation or mediation would be a cheaper and more effective method of settling disputes.

CONCLUSION

This brief survey of the relevance to the Internet of traditional public and private international law principles and rules applied in Canada indicates that, on the whole, they are quite adequate to cope with its challenges. Public international law principles and rules still provide a solid foundation for determining the jurisdiction of Canada to prescribe law covering activities on the Internet. The objective territoriality principle or effects principle is clearly the best justification for reaching such online activities, irrespective of territorial borders. Effects within the territory is also a solid foundation for jurisdiction to adjudicate. It works well in the field of private international law since it provides a real and substantial connection or contact with the forum. In the case of conflicting jurisdictional claims, the defendant can always invoke the doctrine of *forum non conveniens*.

Canadian courts should not be tempted to take jurisdiction over Internet users based on a place of origin approach where the source of transmission is located that is favoured by business interests or on a place of destination where goods or services are received that provides greater consumer protection. They should rely on a more nuanced, real, and substantial connection approach, taking into consideration targeting as one of its elements.

In order to avoid a multiplicity of legislative assertions of prescriptive and adjudicative jurisdiction over the Internet as well as in view of the uncertainty as to the exact limits of the effects principle, it would be advisable to adopt an international convention to regulate the various aspects of the Internet, especially its international

---

[204] Code of Civil Procedure, L.R.Q. 1977, c. C-25 as am.

[205] *Ibid.* at Article 948.

aspects. Short of an all-comprehensive multilateral convention, the draft Convention on Jurisdiction and Foreign Judgments in Civil and Commercial Matters would be a good place to start since it takes into account the needs of electronic commerce.[206] Voluntary codes of conduct could also be adopted by ISPs and Internet merchants of goods and services although self-regulation is not always effective.[207]

With respect to the contents of such an international convention, prescriptive and adjudicative personal jurisdiction should not be asserted solely on the basis of accessibility in a province or state of a passive website that does not target that province or state, nor should the maintenance of a website by itself constitute targeting and subject the operator of such a site to global jurisdiction.

With respect to electronic commerce, absent fraud, forum selection, and choice of law, clauses in online contracts should be enforced in business-to-business transactions. In business-to-consumer contracts, any power imbalance between them may militate against enforcing such clauses unless the consumer bargained with the seller of the goods (which is seldom the case since most consumer contracts are drafted by the seller and are not negotiable)[208] or the provisions are reasonable although they are part of a contract of adhesion. Alternative dispute resolution, such as arbitration, should be encouraged with respect to business-to-business online transactions. It would not be an appropriate method of resolution of disputes with respect to small claims by consumers, which could be resolved by conciliation or mediation.

---

[206] A preliminary draft convention adopted by the Special Commission in October 1999 and revised in June 2001. It is available online at <http://hcch.net/doc/jdgm2001draft-e.doc>. See Articles 6-10. See also Preliminary Document no. 12, Summary of Discussions on Electronic Commerce and International Jurisdiction, Ottawa, February 28 to March 1, 2000, by C. Kessedjian (2000), and Preliminary Document no. 17, The Impact of the Internet on the Judgments Project: Thoughts for the Future by A. Haines (2002), which are available at <http://www.hcch.net/e/workprog/jdgm.html>.

[207] For instance, codes of conduct for multinational corporations have not been enforced very successfully due to their private nature.

[208] Clickwrap licence agreements. However, see *Rudder, supra* note 120. Note that in *Specht* v. *Netscape Communications Corp.*, 150 F. Supp. 2d (S.D.N.Y. 2001), the US Federal District Court for the Southern District of New York held that Netscape's "smart Download" end-user licence agreement was not enforceable because the users who downloaded the software were not required to assent to the licence agreement. Thus, browse wrap agreements commonly used on many websites may not be enforceable in the absence of an unambiguous act of assent.

Since global electronic commerce is here to stay, there is a need for uniform substantive rules to provide a solid legal infrastructure supporting commercial activities on the Internet.[209] The question is who sets the rules for the Internet and how are they to be enforced? Perhaps the Internet should develop its own regulatory structures, which, in time, would lead to a separate body of customary law, such as the law merchant.[210] Until this is done, Canadian traditional principles of criminal and private law (common law and civil law) are fairly adequate to deal with most aspects of this new technology.

Sommaire

L'Internet à la lumière des principes et règles traditionnels du droit international public et privé appliqués au Canada

Cet article traite des problèmes soulevés par l'utilisation de l'Internet dans un contexte international. Le droit international autorise-t-il le Canada à réglementer l'Internet et ses utilisateurs même si ces derniers se trouvent à l'étranger? D'après la Constitution, qui a compétence législative dans ce domaine? Dans quelles circonstances les tribunaux du Québec et ceux des provinces de common law sont-ils compétents pour connaître des actions personnelles à caractère patrimonial lorsque les personnes concernées utilisent l'Internet dans un contexte international et quelles lois doivent-ils appliquer? Dans quels cas ces tribunaux reconnaissent-ils et exécutent-ils les jugements étrangers se rapportant à l'Internet et à ses utilisateurs? L'auteur traite de ces questions et conclut que dans la plupart des cas le Parlement fédéral peut réglementer l'utilisation de l'Internet et que les tribunaux canadiens sont compétents en la matière sans pour cela violer les principes et règles du droit international en vigueur. Cependant, afin d'éviter les conflits de compétence, il serait préférable d'adopter une convention internationale consacrée aux différents aspects de l'Internet.

[209] Unidroit or UNCITRAL are the proper agencies for preparing such uniform laws. For minimalist legislation, see, for example, UN Model Law on Electronic Commerce, 1996, which is available at <http://www.uncitral.org/en-index. htm>; 1999 Uniform Law Commission of Canada, Uniform Electronic Commerce Act, 1999 Proceedings 380; US Uniform Electronic Transactions Act, 1999, which is available at <http://www.law.upenn.edu/library/ulc/ulc.htm>. These model laws are not comprehensive and do not address private international law issues. However, in the field of contracts, they indicate the time and place of sending and receipt of electronic documents (Can. Uniform Law, s. 23).

[210] See D.R. Johnson and D. Post, "Law and Borders: The Rise of Law in Cyberspace" (1996) 48 Stanford L. Rev. 1367 at 1387 *et seq.*

Summary

The Internet in Light of Traditional Public and Private International Law Principles and Rules Applied in Canada

This article addresses the problems related to the use of the Internet in Canada in an international context. Does international law allow Canada to regulate the Internet and its actors even if they are located abroad? Under the constitution, which level of government has the authority to do so? In which circumstances have the courts in Québec and in the common law provinces personal jurisdiction over persons using the Internet in an international context and which law do these courts apply? When are Canadian courts prepared to recognize and enforce foreign judgments involving the Internet and its actors? The author deals with these questions and is of the opinion that in most situations the federal Parliament has the jurisdiction to prescribe and the Canadian courts have the jurisdiction to adjudicate with respect to the Internet and its actors in an international context without violating international law. However, to avoid conflicts of jurisdiction, it would be better to adopt an international convention covering the various aspects of the Internet.

La structure constitutionnelle du droit international public

ROBERT KOLB

I POSITION DU PROBLÈME

Quand on affirme l'existence d'une constitution au sein du droit international, deux choses différentes peuvent être visées.

A DE 1919 À 1945: L'ÉXISTENCE D'UN DROIT INTERNATIONAL OBJECTIF

Entre 1919 et 1945, quand ce terme eut ses premières éclosions au sein de la société internationale, il s'agissait d'un moyen de s'opposer aux enseignements positivistes encore prédominants. Le nouveau constitutionnalisme était l'une des expressions majeures de la réaction anti-positiviste au sein de la doctrine.[1] Le positivisme avait subordonné toute la création du droit à une expression de volonté. Sans consentement, pas d'obligation. Poussée à bout, cette conception avait mené à un fractionnement, à une véritable archipélisation du droit international. Selon cet enseignement il n'y avait aucun droit international général, liant tous les États au sein de la communauté juridique. Il n'y avait au contraire que du droit international particulier, liant un cercle déterminé d'États,

Robert Kolb est Docteur en droit international, L.L.M., en droit de la mer, Professeur assistant à l'Université de Berne, Chargé de cours au Centre universitaire de droit international humanitaire, précédemment Chargé d'enseignement à l'Institut universitaire de hautes études internationales, Genève.

[1] Quatre grandes orientations critiques furent avancées: la théorie du droit pur de l'Ecole de Vienne, la théorie de l'objectivisme social (Duguit, Scelle, Politis), la théorie ressuscitée du droit naturel (Pillet, Le Fur, Salvioli, Verdross) et enfin la théorie de l'institution, défendue avec force particulière en Italie à la suite de S. Romano. Voir à ce propos A. Truyol Y Serra, "Cours général de droit international public," RCADI, vol. 173, 1981-IV, p. 104 et s.

ceux qui avaient consenti à se placer sous l'empire d'une norme.[2] Il faut rappeler que même la coutume était réduite à un pacte. Contrairement aux traités qui forment des accords exprès, la coutume était considérée comme un pacte tacite.[3] La conséquence de ce qui précède est qu'il n'existe aucun véritable ordre juridique international, aucun système de normes ordonnées à un bien qui leur serait extérieur. Il n'y a pas d'unité: où que l'on regarde, on ne trouve qu'une poussière de règles de détail, assumées par les États selon leur bon-vouloir et leurs intérêts momentanés, et qu'aucun lien issu d'une architecture plus générale ne relie. Ce caractère erratique (outre qu'inorganique) du droit international a bien été mis en exergue par Sir Alfred Zimmern: "International law in fact is a law without constitution ... Unconnected with a society, it cannot adjust itself to its needs ... There is in fact, whatever the names used in the books no *system* of international law ... What is to be found in the treatises is simply a collection of rules which, when looked at closely, appear to have been thrown together or to have been accumulated, almost at haphazard. Many of them would seem to be more appropriately described as materials for an etiquette book for the conduct of sovereigns and their representatives than as elements of a true legal system."[4]

À une époque où la découverte des solidarités sur les grands problèmes mondiaux, notamment la paix, mène aux premiers efforts d'établir des organisations qui en aient la charge au nom de la collectivité toute entière, il était naturel que l'enseignement positiviste dont il a été question fut ressenti par nombre d'auteurs comme un vêtement trop étroit. L'une des réactions était de postuler une Constitution internationale, telle qu'elle était connue

[2] Cf. p. ex. H. Triepel, *Völkerrecht und Landesrecht*, Leipzig, 1899, pp. 83-84: "Da nun Völkerrecht nur aus Vereinbarung entstehen kann und eine Vereinbarung, bei der sich sämtliche existierende Staaten beteiligt hätten, nicht nachzuweisen ist, so kann es ein allgemeines Völkerrecht im Sinne eines alle vorhandenen Staaten gleichmässig beherrschenden nicht geben. Vielmehr hat jeder einzelne Völkerrechtssatz eine nach der Zahl der bei seiner Bildung betheiligten Staaten bemessene ... beschränkte Geltung. Es giebt, wenn man so sagen darf, nur partikulares Völkerrecht ..." Voir aussi A. Cavaglieri, "Règles générales du droit de la paix," RCADI, vol. 26, 1929-I, pp. 322-23; K. Strupp, "Les règles générales du droit de la paix," RCADI, vol. 47, 1934-I, p. 318.

[3] Cf. p. ex. Strupp, *supra* note 2 aux pp. 303-4, 319. Sur cette construction de la coutume, cf. H. Günther, *Zur Entstehung von Völkergewohnheitsrecht*, Berlin, 1970, p. 22 et s.; M. Mendelson, "The Formation of Customary International Law," RCADI, vol. 272, 1998, p. 253 et s. Pour de nombreux autres renvois, cf. R. Kolb, *La bonne foi en droit international public*, Paris, 2000, p. 316.

[4] *The League of Nations and the Rule of Law* (*1918-1935*), Londres, 1936, p. 98

depuis des siècles dans les sociétés internes.[5] Cette Constitution aurait pour mission d'organiser les fonctions sociales essentielles selon l'idée du droit. Elle serait capable de consolider le droit international en un système fondé sur l'ordonnancement objectif des compétences. La finalité principale de ce modèle constitutionnel est d'assurer au droit international cette unité de fondement et de fonctions qui en fasse un vrai ordre juridique objectif, et non seulement un ensemble non coordonné d'actes juridiques subjectifs, portés chacun par l'autonomie de la volonté d'un sujet divers. Le droit international fait un pas vers un système de droit public. Il n'est plus simplement un ensemble de droits privés hasardeusement juxtaposées. Par cela, il devient en même temps susceptible de contempler le bien commun de la communauté internationale en tant que telle.

B   DE 1945 À NOS JOURS: L'ÉMERGENCE DE LA
     COMMUNAUTÉ INTERNATIONALE

Entre 1945 et aujourd'hui, une autre notion de Constitution internationale se fit jour. Elle prolonge les efforts dont il a été précédemment question. Cependant, il ne s'agit désormais plus en premier lieu de fonder un droit international objectif et unitaire, s'ordonnant en système. Face aux périls communs qui commandent de s'unir ou de périr — la guerre et la paix à une période de l'arme nucléaire, la menace écologique, mais aussi la découverte des interdépendances croissantes en matière économique et sociale, la progression de valeurs communes telles que les droits fondamentaux de la personne — c'est au renforcement de l'aspect communautaire du droit international que se voue une partie toujours plus importante de la doctrine. Le droit international n'est plus configuré comme un droit au service des seuls intérêts des États

---

[5] Ce n'est pas un hasard que ce fut en Italie et en Allemagne, États où le positivisme avait le plus prévalu, que cette orientation eut le plus de succès. Cfr. p. ex. A. Verdross, *Die Verfassung der Völkerrechtsgemeinschaft,* Vienne / Berlin, 1926; S. Romano, *L'ordinamento giuridico,* Pise, 1917 et S. Romano, *Corso di diritto internazionale,* 4ᵉ éd., Padoue, 1939, p. 1 et s. Voir aussi P. Ziccardi, *La costituzione dell'ordinamento internazionale,* Milan, 1943; G. Sperduti, *La fonte suprema dell'ordinamento internazionale,* Milan, 1946. M. Giuliano, *La comunità internazionale e il diritto,* Padoue, 1950. Comme Verdross l'écrivait (*op. cit.,* p. 2), en faisant appel à Kant, un fondement purement empirique du droit, comme le positivisme le postulait, n'est pas imaginable: "So gelangt die positivistische Doktrin, von ihren eigenen Voraussetzungen aus zur Selbstauflösung, da sie Kants Warnung missachtet hat: 'Eine bloss empirische Rechtslehre ist (wie der hölzerne Kopf in Phädrus Fabel) ein Kopf, der schön sein mag, nur schade, dass er kein Gehirn hat.'"

uti singuli, détenteurs de la souveraineté. Le droit international est aussi et peut-être surtout un droit cherchant à protéger et à promouvoir les besoins et intérêts essentiels de la communauté internationale dans son ensemble (dont peut dépendre la survie de l'homme sur terre).[6] Dès lors, l'aspect bilatéraliste du droit international, centré sur la souveraineté, recule au bénéfice d'intérêts communs qui cherchent à se doter d'une priorité normative et d'un appareil d'institutions capables d'articuler et de mettre en oeuvre ce nouveau volet communautaire. À côté de l'*utilitas singulorum* vient émerger une *utilitas publica,* un droit public au sens strict. Comme l'a dit de manière très frappante A. Carrillo Salcedo: "Cette nouvelle dimension du droit international, qui n'est autre que l'ordre juridique de la communauté internationale, est venue s'ajouter aux dimensions traditionnelles de l'ordre juridique régulateur des relations inter-étatiques de coexistence et de coopération."[7] Une nuée de concepts juridiques — nouveaux ou renouvelés — traduit ces visées communautaires. C'est le cas du *ius cogens,* des obligations *erga omnes,* des crimes internationaux, de l'ordre public international, du concept de *world order treaties,*[8] de la prééminence du droit des droits de l'homme, du concept d'hiérarchisation du droit international, etc. Toute communauté s'intègre d'abord autour des valeurs et règles tenues pour essentielles pour le bon déroulement de la vie en commun. Dès lors, en droit international aussi, c'est certaines "valeurs fondamentales de la Communauté internationale" qui sont placées au sommet de la hiérarchie juridique et qui forment le vecteur pour une transformation progressive du droit international positif reçu dans la direction souhaitée. Les normes qui expriment ces valeurs suprêmes sont volontiers qualifiées d'ordre public international.[9] Cet aréopage normatif a aussi été qualifié de Constitution de l'ordre juridique

---

[6] Voir l'aperçu chez B. Simma, "From Bilateralism to Community Interest in International Law," RCADI, vol. 250, 1994-VI, p. 299 et s.

[7] A. Carrillo Salcedo, "Droit international et souveraineté des États, Cours général de droit international public," RCADI, vol. 257, 1996, p. 146. Voir en général, *ibid.,* p. 115 et s.; C. Tomuschat, "International Law: Ensuring the Survival of Mankind on the Eve of a New Century," RCADI, vol. 281, 1999, p. 72 et s.

[8] Sur cette notion, voir B. Simma, "From Bilateralism to Community Interest in International Law," RCADI, vol. 250, 1994-VI, pp. 322 et s., 331 et s.

[9] Sur la notion d'ordre public, cf. G. Jaenicke, "International Public Order," EPIL, vol. 7 (1984), pp. 314-18; H. Mosler, "General Course on Public International Law," RCADI, vol. 140, 1974-IV, p. 33 et s. Voir aussi R. Kolb, *Théorie du ius cogens international,* Paris, 2001, p. 68 et s., avec d'autres renvois.

international.[10] Si, avant 1945, la Constitution avait surtout été une notion systématique (garant de l'existence d'un système juridique international plutôt que d'un ensemble émietté de positions juridiques subjectives), dans les temps récents elle devint une notion matérielle exprimant les valeurs juridiques suprêmes qui, représentant un intérêt collectif pressant, cherchent à s'assurer une priorité dans l'application du droit.

C STRUCTURE CONSTITUTIONNELLE: UN DROIT DOMINÉ PAR DES PRINCIPES

Dans la présente note, le terme "constitution" ne sera pris ni dans l'une ni dans l'autre des acceptions présentées. Par "structure constitutionnelle," nous visons à qualifier le droit international comme un droit essentiellement de grands principes, s'opposant par cela au type du droit administratif qui enserre les phénomènes sociaux qu'il adresse dans les mailles d'une réglementation beaucoup plus capillaire.[11] En effet, le droit international est un droit en permanence "constitutionnel." Il manque d'élaboration dans de nombreux domaines. Derrière chaque argumentation, derrière chaque règle, on voit se dessiner l'ombre de quelque grand principe par rapport auquel l'énoncé de détail ne réussit guère à creuser l'écart.[12] C'est tantôt la souveraineté,[13] l'égalité, la non-ingérence;

---

[10] Cf. l'aperçu chez Simma, *supra* note 6 à la p. 256 et s. ou B. Fassbender, *United Nations Security Council Reform and the Right of Veto,* La Haye / Londres / Boston, 1998, pp. 63 et s., 89 et s.

[11] Cette notion de Constitution est donc structurelle, contrairement à celle discutée sous b) qui se voue aux valeurs communautaires et est donc matérielle. La notion de Constitution ici retenue se borne à affirmer que le droit international est avant tout un droit de principes, sans dire quels sont ces principes. Ils peuvent aller dans le sens de la Constitution de type communautaire (et alors notre acception de Constitution se recoupe avec celle évoquée sous b)), comme ils peuvent aussi ne pas aller dans ce sens (et alors notre acception de Constitution diffère de celle dont il a été question sous b)). Le lien entre les deux n'est par conséquent pas nécessaire. Quant à la notion de Constitution présentée sous a), elle n'a pas non plus de lien direct avec celle sous b) ou sous c). Elle concerne simplement l'existence d'un droit international fondé sur une base objective et s'échappant au vêtement trop étroit de la seule volonté changeante des États. Cette Constitution touche au caractère juridique et au caractère contraignant du droit international plus qu'à sa structure ou à ses contenus. C'est en quelque sorte une question préliminaire.

[12] Cf. aussi les remarques dans Kolb, *supra* note 3 à la p. 168.

[13] Y compris p. ex. la "souveraineté permanente sur les ressources naturelles." Sur ce principe, voir l'ouvrage récent de N. Schrijver, *Sovereignty over Natural Resources, Balancing Rights and Duties,* Cambridge, 1997. D'autres renvois chez L. Oppenheim, *International Law,* 9e éd. (par R. Jennings / A. Watts), Londres, 1992, p. 923.

tantôt la bonne foi, l'équité ou la proportionnalité; tantôt la stabilité des frontières, l'*uti possidetis, pacta sunt servanda;* tantôt la non-appropriation, le patrimoine commun de l'humanité, le développement durable, etc. Comme l'a dit P. Reuter: "[L]e droit international énonce un nombre important de règles sous une forme très abstraite, c'est-à-dire sous la forme de principes généraux."[14] Caractère constitutionnel signifie ici le type de droit fondé sur des préceptes à haut niveau de généralité, alors que caractère administratif désigne le type du droit fondé sur des règles ponctuelles et détaillées. Le premier est un droit flexible et malléable, d'ordre plus politique. Le second est un droit plus fixe et plus rigide, d'ordre plus technique. L'objet des quelques lignes qui suivent est d'éclairer les origines du caractère constitutionnel du droit international, ses raisons, ses conséquences les plus saillantes au niveau de l'expérience juridique et enfin les exceptions et tendances récentes vers des plages plus "administratives." Afin de rester dans le cadre d'une note, nous procéderons par illustration plutôt que par analyse.

II   ORIGINES HISTORIQUES DU CARACTÈRE "CONSTITUTIONNEL"
     DU DROIT INTERNATIONAL

Toute recherche historique en matière de droit international se décompose en deux branches.

A   HISTOIRE DU DROIT PUBLIC DE L'EUROPE

En premier lieu, la recherche historique peut chercher à expliquer les racines du droit international positif en vigueur aujourd'hui en remontant le fil des événements dans le temps. Cette perspective amène à faire l'histoire du droit public de l'Europe, car c'est de là qu'est issu le droit international contemporain.[15] En second lieu, elle peut viser à embrasser tous les phénomènes juridiques qui ont eu lieu où que ce soit et qui ont mis en contact des peuples organisés sur une base territoriale, qui entretenaient des rapports d'un certain suivi et qui étaient relativement indépendants les uns des

---

[14] P. Reuter, "Quelques réflexions sur l'équité en droit international," RBDI, vol. 15, 1980, p. 168. Voir aussi M. Virally, "Le rôle des principes dans le développement du droit international," dans: M. Virally, *Le droit international en devenir,* Paris, 1990, p. 195 et s.

[15] Cf. W. Grewe, "Vom europäischen zum universellen Völkerrecht," ZaöRV, vol. 42, 1982, p. 449 et s.

autres. Cette perspective amène à connaître tous les droits internationaux qui ont pu se former à des lieux et temps les plus divers. En fait, elle revient à s'interroger sur les institutions internationales qui ont pu exister chez les peuples autochtones avant l'arrivée des colonisateurs européens.[16] Il s'agit ici d'une perspective de *ius inter potestates* universel.

À cette distinction, il faut ajouter une autre. Dans beaucoup de cas, les contacts entre des peuples anciens étaient clairsemés et sporadiques. Le droit international se contractait alors à quelques phénomènes et situations isolés, sans former un corps apte à se consolider en véritable ordre juridique. Ce droit international fragmentaire ne dépassait guère quelques principes, enracinés souvent plutôt dans les droits internes respectifs que dans l'idée d'un droit commun: c'est le cas par exemple du principe *pacta sunt servanda*.[17] D'un autre côté, dans certaines zones et à certains moments, les échanges et les interdépendances s'accrurent à tel point qu'un véritable ordre juridique international "régional" naquit. Ce fut le cas notamment entre les Cinq Empires de l'Orient méditérannéen et d'Asie mineure entre le XVe et le XIIe siècle avant Jésus-Christ (Babylone, Egypte, Royaume hittite, Mitanni, Assyrie);[18] en Chine, au moins depuis le VIIe siècle avant Jésus-Christ;[19] et en Europe, à partir du IIIe siècle avant Jésus-Christ, à travers l'Empire romain.[20] Le droit public de l'Europe y commence sa carrière surtout comme droit transnational,[21] visant les rapports

---

[16] Cf. W. Preiser, *Frühe völkerrechtliche Ordnungen der aussereuropäischen Welt*, Wiesbaden, 1976, et W. Preiser, "History of International Law," EPIL, vol. 7 (1984), p. 126 et s. Sur ces deux histoires du droit international, voir aussi R. Kolb, *Réflexions de philosophie et de théorie du droit international public*, Bruxelles, 2003, à paraître.

[17] Chaque partie jurait la fidélité aux engagements à ses propres Dieux. Voir D.J. Bederman, "Religion and the Sources of International Law in the Antiquity," dans: M.W. Janis (dir.), *The Influence of Religion on the Development of International Law*, Dordrecht / Boston / Londres, 1991, p. 14 et s.

[18] Cf. A. Truyol Y Serra, *Histoire du droit international public*, Paris, 1995, pp. 6-7.

[19] Truyol Y Serra, *op. cit.*, p. 8; Preiser, *supra* note 16 à la p. 153 et s.

[20] Sur le droit international romain, cf. les sources et les textes indiqués dans K.H. Ziegler, *Völkerrechtsgeschichte*, Munich, 1994, pp. 43-44, 54-55, 62. Voir aussi K.H. Ziegler, "Die römischen Grundlagen des europäischen Völkerrechts," dans: *Ius commune*, vol. 4, 1972, p. 1 et s.

[21] À côté de ce droit privé entre personnes de nationalité différente, il y avait un droit proprement public pour les relations internationales. Il concernait surtout la guerre *(ius fetiale)*, les ambassades, la conclusion des traités: M. Kaser, *Ius gentium*, Cologne / Weimar / Vienne, 1993, p. 23 et s. Ce droit public s'incorpora

entre citoyens romains et étrangers. C'est le phénomène du *ius gentium*. C'est vers lui qu'il convient désormais de se tourner.

2   *Le droit romain*

Comme tout droit dans les premières phases de son évolution, le droit romain était initialement limité aux citoyens romains. C'était le principe de personnalité du droit (le *ius quiritium*). L'étranger ne jouissait pas d'une protection juridique. Il était censé être hors des sphères du droit local romain *ratione personae*. Quand l'Empire s'étendit à de nombreux autres peuples qui n'obtinrent pas la nationalité romaine et quand, après les guerres puniques, le commerce méditérannéen se développa fortement, cette stricte limitation personnelle du droit devint intenable. Sa rénovation fut confiée à des magistrats spéciaux dotés de pouvoirs considérables *(praetor peregrinus)*. Ils donnèrent corps à des règles juridiques applicables entre tous les hommes, quelle que fût leur nationalité: c'était le *ius gentium*.[22] Afin d'élaborer un droit valable pour tous les

---

peu à peu au *ius gentium* qui finit par devenir le corps juridique des relations internationales tant privées que publiques. C'est le cas dès l'époque du Code de Hermogénien à la fin du IIIᵉ siècle après J.C., avec la définition donnée par Pomponius et plus tard par St. Isidore de Séville (VIIᵉ siècle, *Etymologiae*, lib. V, cap. VI). Voir A. Truyol Y Serra, "Cours général de droit international public," RCADI, vol. 173, 1981-IV, p. 35. D'autres renvois chez Kolb, *supra* note 3 à la p. 8, note 18.

[22]   Sur le *ius gentium*: M. Voigt, *Das ius naturale, aequum et bonum und ius gentium der Römer*, 4 vol., Aalen, réimpression 1966 (1ʳᵉ éd., Leipzig, 1856-1875, vol. I-IV); P. Bonfante, *Histoire du droit romain*, t. I, Paris, 1928, p. 261 et s.; G. May, *Eléments de droit romain*, 18ᵉ éd., Paris, 1935, p. 39 et s.; J. Bryce, "The Law of Nature," dans: J. Bryce, *Studies in History and Jurisprudence*, vol. II, Londres, 1910, p. 586 et s.; G. Grosso, *Lezioni di storia del diritto romano*, 5ᵉ éd., Turin, 1965, pp. 272 et s., 290 et s.; S. Riccobono, *Lineamenti della storia delle fonti e del diritto romano*, Milan, 1949, p. 22 et s.; A. Guarino, *Diritto privato romano*, 9 éd. Naples, 1992, p. 161 et s.; M. Lauria, "Ius gentium," *Mélanges P. Koschaker*, t. I, Weimar, 1939, p. 258 et s.; P. Frezza, "Ius gentium," *Revue internationale des droits de l'Antiquité*, 1949 (2), p. 259 et s.; G. Lombardi, *Sul concetto di ius gentium*, Milan, 1974. G. Lombardi, *Ricerche in tema di ius gentium*, Milan, 1946. Kaser, *Römische Rechtsgeschichte*, 2ᵉ éd., Göttingen, 1982, p. 134 et s.; M. Kaser, *Ius gentium*, Cologne/Weimar, 1993. Sur la notion de *ius gentium* chez Grotius, cf. P. Haggenmacher, "Genèse et signification du concept de 'ius gentium' chez Grotius," *Grotiana* 1981 (2), p. 44 et s.

Cette conception n'est pas exclusivement occidentale. Ibn Khaldun, auteur arabe du XIVᵉ siècle, dans son ouvrage '*Muqaddimah*' explique l'émergence et la consolidation des États sur la base d'un processus qu'il appelle '*asabiyah*,' c.-à-d. de solidarité sociale; cfr. F. Baali, *Ibn Khaldun's Sociological Thought*, New York, 1988, partic., p. 43 et s.

hommes dans leurs contacts réciproques, le préteur écarta les règles de l'ancien droit civil romain, imprégnées de formalisme. Il forgea à leur place un corps de règles fondé sur la raison commune à tous les hommes, car à un tel droit purement rationnel, tous les hommes devraient pouvoir obéir sans limite de nationalité. Le préteur s'inspira des idées de justice naturelle, de la nature des choses, de l'utilité, de l'équité. Dépouillant les institutions juridiques de leurs accidents locaux et de leurs vêtements contingents, cherchant l'analogie des situations au-delà des limites nationales, le droit gagne en généralité, s'universalise. Par cela même, le *ius gentium* se manifeste en une série de principes généraux communs aux peuples. Le droit international de l'Europe est bien né comme un droit de principes. La similitude des processus dirigés à dégager le *ius gentium* et de ceux décrits comme étant à la base des principes généraux de droit au sens de l'article 38(1,c) du Statut[23] de la Cour saute aux yeux.[24] Il est clair que la formulation de règles communes suppose une réduction par voie d'abstraction, car ce qui est commun l'est toujours dans l'essence (ou la fonction et le but), non dans les accidents ou le vêtement concret. Le mouvement est donc nettement un mouvement d'ascension vers un droit de principes[25] avec à sa base ceux de la bonne foi (obligatoriété de la parole donnée) et de l'équité. La vocation du *ius gentium* à l'universalité, la place faite à la nature des choses ou à la raison, ont d'ailleurs depuis toujours rapproché le *ius gentium* du droit naturel.[26] On sait

[23] Principes communs dans leurs aspects fondamentaux à travers les divers ordres juridiques internes ou pour le moins à travers les grandes traditions juridiques. Cfr. B. Vitanyi, "Les positions doctrinales concernant le sens de la notion de 'principes généraux de droit reconnus par les nations civilisées,'" RGDIP, vol. 86, 1982, p. 48 et s.; Kolb, *supra* note 3 à la p. 24 et s., avec de nombreux renvois.

[24] Comparez à cet égard la définition de Gaius, *Dig.* 1, 1, 9: "Naturalis ratio inter omnes homines constituit, id apud omnes peraeque custoditur vocaturque ius gentium, quasi quo iure omnes gentes utuntur" (ce que la raison naturelle a établi entre tous les hommes et est observé également par tous ou presque tous les peuples) et Ch. De Visscher, *Théories et réalités en droit international public,* 4e éd., Paris, 1970, p. 419 et s., sur les principes généraux de droit.

[25] Cf. B. Paradisi, *Storia del diritto internazionale nel medio evo,* vol. I, Milan, 1940, p. 108.

[26] Sur les rapports du *ius gentium* avec le *ius naturale,* cfr. R. Voggensperger, *Der Begriff des ius naturale im römischen Recht,* Bâle, 1952, p. 61 et s.; Kaser, *Ius gentium,* p. 54 et s.; M. Voigt, *Das ius naturale, aequum et bonum und ius gentium der Römer,* Leipzig, 1856 (réimprimé en 1966), vol. I, p. 54 et s.; C. Phillipson, *The International Law and Custom of Ancient Greece and Rome,* vol. I, Londres, 1911, p. 67 et s.; F. Von Holtzendorff, *Handbuch des Völkerrechts,* t. I, Berlin, 1885, p. 280 et s.; R. Marcic, "Sklaverei als 'Beweis' gegen Naturrecht und Naturrechtslehre," ÖZÖR,

que le droit naturel sera un vecteur essentiel pour le développement du droit international et constituera une source première pour la formulation des règles du droit international "moderne" dès l'époque de Salamanque, puis de Grotius.[27] Le droit international

---

1964-65, pp. 190-91; A. Truyol Y Serra, *Histoire du droit international public,* Paris, 1995, pp. 15-16. Voir déjà St. Thomas d'Aquin, *Summa theologica,* II,I, q. 95, a. 2, 4; G. d'Occham, *Dialogus,* III, tr. 2, lib. I, cap. IX (*ius naturae per modum conclusionis*). Cfr. F.A. Von Der Heydte, *Die Geburtsstunde des souveränen Staates,* Regensburg, 1952, p. 141 et s.

[27] Il s'agit d'un droit naturel mélangé à des préceptes de droit romain et notamment de *ius gentium,* qui représentaient aux yeux des juristes dès le moyen âge (et au moins jusqu'au XVIIIe siècle) la *ratio scripta.* Cf. Giuliano, *supra* note 5 à la p. 11 et s. Sur le droit romain comme *ratio scripta,* cf. A. Guzmán, *Ratio scripta, Ius commune, cahier spécial n° 14,* 1981. Sur la contribution du droit romain au droit international, cf. K.H. Ziegler, "Die römischen Grundlagen des europäischen Völkerrechts," *Ius commune,* t. IV, Francfort-sur-le-Main, 1972, p. 1 et s.; B. Paradisi, *I fondamenti storici della comunità giuridica internazionale,* Sienne, 1944 (publié aussi dans *Studi Senesi,* 1944, vol. 58); B. Paradisi, *Storia del diritto internazionale nel medio evo,* t. I, Milan, 1940, p. 99 et s.; M. Müller-Jochmus, *Geschichte des Völkerrechts im Altertum,* Leipzig, 1848, p. 136 et s.; H. Kipp, *Völkerrechtsordnung und Völkerrecht im Mittelalter,* Cologne, 1950, p. 99 et s.; H. Lauterpacht, *Private Law Sources and Analogies of International Law,* Londres, 1927, p. 10 et s. Voir aussi: E.S. Creasey, *First Platform of International Law,* Londres, 1876, p. 83 et s.; R. Phillimore, *Commentaries Upon International Law,* vol. I, Londres, 1879, p. 34.; J. Kosters, "Les fondements du droit des gens," *Biblioteca Visseriana,* t. IV, Leyden, 1925, p. 156 et s.; A. Miaja De La Muela, "Aportaciónes históricas y actuales del derecho romano al orden internacional," *Mélanges Santa Cruz Teijeiro,* Valence, 1974, p. 531 et s.; A.D. McNair, "The Debt of International Law in Britain to the Civil Law and the Civilians," *Transactions of the Grotius Society* 1953 (39), p. 183 et s.; U. Scheuner, "L'influence du droit interne sur la formation du droit international," RCADI, 1939-II (68), p. 151; W. Bishop, "General Course of Public International Law," RCADI, 1965-II (115), p. 236.; J.P.A. François, "Règles générales du droit de la paix," RCADI, 1938-IV (66), p. 176; M. Sœrensen, *Les sources du droit international,* Copenhague, 1946, p. 141 et s.; G. Balladore Pallieri, *Diritto internazionale pubblico,* 8e éd., Milan, 1962, p. 96; G. Barile, "La rilevazione e l'integrazione del diritto internazionale non scritto e la libertà di apprezzamento del giudice," *Comunicazioni e studi,* 1953 (5), p. 177 et s.; H. Waldock, "General Course on Public International Law," RCADI, 1962-II (106), p. 54; C. Rousseau, "Principes de droit international public," RCADI, 1958-I (93), p. 378. Dans le contexte des principes généraux de droit, J. Spiropoulos, *Die allgemeinen Rechtsgrundsätze im Völkerrecht,* kiel, 1928, p. 46 et s. En général, voir déjà R. Wiseman, *The Law of Nations: Or the Excellency of the Civil Law above all other Human Laws whatsoever. Showing of how Great the Use and Necessity the Civil Law is to the Nation* (1656), cité par H. Lauterpacht, *Private,* p. 25; S. Cocceius (1679-1755), *Elementa iustitiae naturalis et romanae* (1740) et G.W. Leibniz (1646-1716), *Nova methodus discendae docendaeque jurisprudentiae* (1667) déjà avaient insisté sur le fait que le droit romain était la plus fidèle expression historique du droit naturel.

actuel, en tant que droit oecuménique, est donc né et s'est développé comme droit de principes jalonnant de disciplines juridiques ponctuelles les larges espaces vierges de la vie politique entre les collectivités publiques. Malgré toutes ses évolutions, il en porte encore la marque.[28]

III LES RAISONS DU CARACTÈRE "CONSTITUTIONNEL" DU DROIT INTERNATIONAL

Parmi les multiples raisons qui expliquent le caractère constitutionnel du droit international, il est important d'en relever trois.

A LES EXIGENCES DE FLEXIBILITÉ DU DROIT INTERNATIONAL

C'est d'abord l'exigence de flexibilité du droit, très vivement ressentie dans l'ordre juridique international. Il en est ainsi en premier lieu à cause du caractère politique du droit international et des Puissances qui en sont les sujets, tout comme du caractère politique de ses finalités.[29] Le droit international est sous cet angle de vue un droit public par excellence: il touche au cœur irréductible des prérogatives de puissance publique. Montesquieu avait raison d'écrire que le droit des gens "est la loi politique des nations, considérées dans le rapport qu'elles ont les unes avec les autres."[30] Le droit international est en bonne partie une espèce de rationalisation des politiques étrangères ayant le but de rendre possible leur

---

[28] On le voit dans des aspects parfois subordonnés. Ainsi, nombre de manuels ou de cours consacrent une place importante de l'exposé du droit international à ses principes fondamentaux. La tendance à consacrer une place capitale aux grands principes est reflétée p. ex. dans les cours généraux de droit international tenus à l'Académie de droit international de La Haye. Cfr. G. Abi-Saab, "Cours général de droit international public," RCADI, vol. 207, 1987-VII, p. 328 et s.; C. Tomuschat, "International Law: Ensuring the Survival of Mankind on the Eve of A New Century," RCADI, vol. 281, 1999, p. 161 et s. Voir aussi G. Cansacchi, *I principî informatori delle relazioni internazionali*, 2ᵉ éd., Turin, 1969 (principes juridiques et politiques). De même, les principes généraux ont joué un rôle essentiel dans la question du fondement ultime du droit international public. Il suffit de penser à cet égard aux sollicitations du principe *pacta sunt servanda* (D. Anzilotti, *Corso di diritto internazionale*, Rome, 1928, p. 42), de l'idée d'un ensemble de principes généraux suprêmes (Sperduti, *supra* note 5), ou de l'idée de principes constitutionnels éthiques ou structurels (Verdross, Romano, *supra*, note 5). Voir aussi Kolb, *supra* note 3 à la p. 71 et s.

[29] Cf. les renvois chez Kolb, *supra* note 3, p. 172, note 451.

[30] *De l'esprit des lois*, liv. X, c. I.

coexistence réciproque.[31] Tout droit politique tend à être un droit constitutionnel, un droit de principes. La politique exige une marge de flexibilité pour réagir aux situations les plus diverses, les plus inattendues, les plus particulières. Elle doit pouvoir répondre aux situations nouvelles en adaptant ses moyens à ce que demande une bonne défense de l'intérêt de la collectivité étatique dont l'opérateur relève. Elle doit accommoder des intérêts divergents, dont celui de la paix sociale interne, avec ce degré d'opportunisme et d'utilité qui sont l'essence du flair de l'homme d'État. Par cela même, le droit destiné à encadrer une telle action politique ne peut guère trop creuser l'écart entre ses préceptes et la vie sociale spontanée. Il ne peut pas se doter de ce formalisme juridique qui imprègne les disciplines presque complètement apolitiques du droit privé. À un niveau plus technique, la règle juridique se voue à une certaine généralité, typicité, prévisibilité. Elle est orientée à l'égalité de traitement et à la réciprocité. Elle privilégie la stabilité et la sécurité. Elle cherche à établir le juste à travers une réglementation précise, préalable au contentieux, afin de garantir à la fois l'égalité et la légalité. Tout cela ne peut convenir au domaine du politique (et encore moins du hautement politique), qui est dominé par le dynamisme, la flexibilité, l'imprévisibilité et une tendance à la contingence et aux fluctuations, dus à la nécessité de réagir et de s'adapter rapidement aux changements permanents des situations sociales et des constellations politiques. C'est pourquoi le droit qui régit ces activités n'est qu'un droit qui encadre et qui indique des finalités que l'action politique peut ou doit poursuivre selon ses propres moyens. Dès lors, c'est un droit fragmentaire de principes généraux qui correspond le plus à la structure du domaine politique.[32]

Une deuxième raison qui explique l'exigence particulièrement prononcée de flexibilité au niveau du droit international tient à la difficulté de modifier le droit. Dans une société sans législateur institutionnel, décidant sur l'adaptation du droit aux besoins nouveaux par voie de majorité, le droit risque d'accuser un retard toujours plus grand sur l'événement. Tout particulièrement en période de transformations rapides, quand les repères traditionnels se

---

[31] Il ne s'agit pas de la coopération ou des besoins de la communauté internationale en tant que telle. Sur la relation réciproque entre ces volets du droit international, voir les réflexions de R-J. Dupuy, "Communauté internationale et disparités de développement," RCADI, vol. 165, 1979-IV, p. 1 et s.

[32] Voir p. ex. H. Henkel, *Einführung in die Rechtsphilosophie*, 2ᵉ éd., Munich, 1977, p. 125 et s.

perdent, cette modification sera la plus difficile à réaliser. Il en est ainsi parce que les époques de rapides bouleversements sont aussi des périodes de crise et de divergence d'intérêts. Dès lors, un droit qui repose sur le principe du consensualisme trouvera les plus grands obstacles à son adaptation précisément aux moments où celle-ci sera la plus urgente. Dans un tel environnement, les principes généraux jouent un rôle vital dans le métabolisme normatif du système.[33] Par leur généralité et leur caractère ouvert, ils permettent d'accueillir le droit nouveau par touches successives, en s'inspirant d'interprétations nouvelles, en postulant de nouveaux équilibres. Les principes sont un vecteur de transformation silencieux: ils remplacent la législation manquante par la petite monnaie de projections normatives changeantes auxquelles les principes s'offrent comme fondement. Leur flexibilité leur permet d'opérer au service d'idées nouvelles, d'être lancés comme têtes de pont d'une nouvelle *opinio iuris* ou de simplement servir de support à de nouvelles argumentations juridiques (parfois par voie de modification des poids respectifs de certains principes, par exemple la non utilisation de la force et la légitime défense). Par leur malléabilité, les principes généraux sont autant de véhicules de dynamisme juridique.

À cet égard, il faut mettre en garde contre l'opinion que l'abstraction des principes généraux ne convient pas à un ordre juridique techniquement aussi peu développé que le droit international.[34] Le contraire est vrai. Ce que le droit international souffre peu, c'est un nombre trop élevé de normes vouées à des situations typiques et donc relativement inflexibles. Ce n'est pas le cas des principes généraux dont c'est précisément l'indétermination qui permet la prise en compte des multiples spécificités des espèces. Il n'est paradoxal qu'à première vue que plus une norme est concrète et précise dans ses contenus, plus elle exclut la prise en compte des éléments individualisants propres à une espèce; alors que plus la norme est générale et indéterminée, plus elle permet ou requiert de tenir compte des circonstances particulières constitutives de l'espèce.[35] Le droit international est par conséquent un droit particulièrement propice aux principes généraux et aux

---

[33] Voir les réflexions de Virally, *supra* note 14, p. 201 et s.

[34] Ainsi Ch. De Visscher, *supra* note 24, pp. 421-22, voit dans le caractère particulariste du droit international (sur ce point, *infra*, в) une limite au rôle des principes généraux dans le droit international.

[35] Cf. Henkel, *supra* note 32, pp. 476-77.

maximes juridiques,[36] à cause même de son besoin de flexibilité et de concrétion.

B   LE PARTICULARISME DU DROIT INTERNATIONAL

Il y a ensuite le caractère particulariste du droit international, savoir le niveau modeste de typicité des situations juridiques qu'il régente.[37] Tout droit et toute branche du droit oscillent en permanence entre valeurs au respect égal desquelles ils se préposent idéalement: entre généralité, typicité, sécurité juridique, égalité, normativité d'un côté, et particularité, individualité, équité, prise en compte des différences, factualité (respect des circonstances de l'espèce) de l'autre. Moins un ordre juridique est développé, plus l'emprise du politique y est grand et plus les rapports qu'il régit sont irréguliers, et plus il tendra vers le spectre de l'individualisation. Ainsi, le droit international est un droit concret et individualisant; il est peu typique, peu formaliste.[38] C'est le reflet de

[36] Cf. R. Kolb, "Les maximes juridiques en droit international public: questions historiques et théoriques," RBDI, vol. 35, 1999, p. 407 et s.

[37] Sur le caractère particulariste du droit international, cf. Ch. De Visscher, *supra* note 24, pp. 165-66 et aussi pp. 421-22. Cfr. aussi F. Berber, *Lehrbuch des Völkerrechts*, t. I, Munich, 1975, p. 22 et s.; J.L. Brierly, "Les règles générales du droit de la paix," RCADI, vol. 58, 1936-IV, p. 16; J.L. Brierly, *The Outlook for International Law*, Oxford, 1944, p. 40; A.P. Sereni, *Diritto internazionale*, t. I, Milan, 1956, p. 97; A. Hold-Ferneck, *Lehrbuch des Völkerrechts*, t. I, Vienne, 1930, p. 82 et s.; H. Mosler, "Völkerrecht als Rechtsordnung," ZaöRV, vol. 36, 1976, p. 27; M. Virally, "Panorama du droit international contemporain," RCADI, vol. 183, 1983-V, pp. 39, 169-70; D. Schindler, "Contribution à l'étude des facteurs sociologiques et psychologiques du droit international," RCADI, 1933-IV (46), p. 265; A Ross, *A Textbook of International Law*, Londres / New York / Toronto, 1947, pp. 58-59. J. Stone, *Legal Controls of International Conflict*, New York, 1954, p. 330; A. Verdross, "Abstrakte und konkrete Regelungen im Völkerrecht," *Völkerrecht und Völkerbund* 1937/8 (4), p. 212 et s. Voir la synthèse dans Kolb, *supra* note 3, pp. 169-71.

[38] Ch. De Visscher l'a très bien formulé, "ces différenciations profondes qui procèdent de l'individualité ethnique et historique propre des nations, des inégalités de leur constitution physique et de leurs ressources économiques, du nombre réduit des États par comparaison avec celui des individus, du caractère éminemment politique de leurs fins propres, de l'irrégularité et de la moindre fréquence de leurs rapports mutuels, conduisent ici à la prédominance des situations particulières sur les situations générales" (*Théories ...*, *supra* note 24, pp. 165-66). L'abstraction propre à des rapports indifféremment interchangeables si connus en droit interne fait presque entièrement défaut au droit international. Jamais la cession d'un territoire ne pourra acquérir la typicité du contrat achat et vente du droit interne. Diverses conséquences s'attachent à ce qui précède: un moindre poids de la sécurité juridique, une difficulté relative à fixer et à développer le

son caractère politique et de la contingence des situations qu'il envisage. Souvent, ces situations ont une portée historique hautement propre et non fongible.[39] On peut songer à des cas de succession d'États. Dans un tel contexte, il est difficile d'élaborer des règles générales détaillées, visant à régenter tous les événements d'un même "type." C'est précisément ce "type" qui fait défaut ou dont l'expression est trop faible. Dès lors, le droit international privilégie l'opération avec des principes généraux, infiniment plus adaptables aux circonstances particulières d'espèces souvent atypiques.

C   L'ABSENCE D'ORGANES INTERNATIONAUX DE GOUVERNANCE

Il faut mentionner en troisième lieu l'absence d'organes internationaux de gouvernance (*governance*). C'est là un prolongement du caractère inorganique du droit international. En effet, malgré la floraison de multiples organisations internationales à compétences limitées, il manque un appareil intégré d'organes techniques à compétence obligatoire, susceptible de secréter par sa pratique un réel droit "administratif" dense et capillaire. Certes, des progrès considérables ont été accomplis en ce domaine depuis 1945.

---

droit par voie de codification, une place plus importante faite aux moyens politiques de solution des différends. Le droit de la mer est un domaine qui a été particulièrement marqué par cette individualisation du droit. Un rôle tout à fait prépondérant y est joué par des considérations historiques, économiques ou autrement locales; la délimitation maritime a même été dominée pendant longtemps par la doctrine de l'*unicum* du donné circonstanciel de chaque espèce, aboutissant ainsi à une fragmentation dramatique du droit. Le droit international public peut être considéré comme droit particulier ou équitable aussi sous un aspect évolutif. Selon R-J. Dupuy, *supra* note 31, p. 115 et s., le droit international classique était formel et positiviste, considérant les États de manière abstraitement égalitaire parce que censés appartenir à une catégorie homogène. Ce droit reposait sur la notion de loi générale et impersonnelle. Avec l'indépendance des pays en voie de développement, cet édifice formaliste aurait été ébranlé; ces États ont revendiqué une égalité matérielle, faite de règles spécifiques fondées sur la prise en compte de leur situation particulière et notamment des disparités économiques et sociales. Le droit actuel se composerait ainsi davantage de normes redistributives, individualisantes, différenciées et concrètes (p. ex. ressources, États sans littoral, États géographiquement désavantagés, États insulaires, etc.). Dupuy parle de droit "situationnel" (*ibid.*, p. 120).

[39] Cela a souvent été relevé pour le droit de la succession d'États; cf. p. ex. A. Verdross / B. Simma, *Universelles Völkerrecht*, 3ᵉ éd., Berlin, 1984, p. 608. Voir aussi G. Abi-Saab, "Cours général de droit international public," RCADI, vol. 207, 1987-VII, p. 423. Plus sceptique encore, entre autres, J. H.W. Verzijl, *International Law in Historical Perspective, State Succession*, vol. VII, Leyden, 1974, p. 2.

Il n'en demeure pas moins que les États ne sont pas prêts à se soumettre de manière générale à des organes internationaux à compétences contraignante, car ils se dévêtiraient ainsi de leur pouvoir de décider souverainement. Sans de tels organes, du droit "constitutionnel" est parfaitement possible, car les principes vivent du normatif est non de l'institutionnel. Cependant, sans de tels organes, un droit "administratif" est difficilement imaginable, car la réglementation capillaire qui en est la marque propre suppose l'activité régulière de l'institutionnel.

IV   Exemples du caractère "constitutionnel" du droit international

Des illustrations du droit international comme droit de principes peuvent être trouvées partout. Le rôle et les incidences que peut avoir cette structure particulière du droit international varient toutefois de branche en branche. Parfois, les principes ont un rôle nettement "progressif." Il s'agit alors de principes féconds, de têtes de pont du droit, voués à servir de base à une juridification progressive de certaines matières. D'autres fois, les principes ont un rôle plus "conservateur." Le but est ici de maintenir un maximum de marge de manœuvre politique en résistant à une pénétration plus capillaire des disciplines juridiques dans un domaine donné. Voici quelques exemples.

A   LES PRINCIPES GÉNÉRAUX "PROGRESSISTES"

I   *Patrimoine commun de l'humanité*

Le droit des espaces non soumis à souveraineté étatique, c'est-à-dire la mer (y compris la haute mer et son sous-sol), l'espace extra-atmosphérique, et à un certain degré aussi l'Antarctique, a été transformé sous la bannière d'une série de principes généraux. Il est possible de les résumer en bonne partie sous la bannière unificatrice de patrimoine commun de l'humanité.[40] Ce concept a été

---

[40] Sur ce concept, cf. K. Baslar, *The Concept of the Common Heritage of Mankind in International Law*, La Haye / Boston / Londres, 1998; A. Blanc Altemir, *Patrimonio Común de la Humanidad*, Barcelone, 1992; A. Cassese, *International Law in a Divided World*, Oxford, 1986, p. 376 et s. R-J. Dupuy, "La notion de patrimoine commun de l'humanité appliquée aux fonds marins," dans: *Mélanges C.A. Colliard*, Paris, 1984, 197 et s.; R. Goy, "The International Protection of the Cultural and Natural Heritage," NYIL, vol. 4, 1973, p. 117 et s. C. Joyner, "Legal Implications of the Concept of the Common Heritage of Mankind," ICLQ, vol. 35, 1986,p. 190 et s.; A.C. Kiss, "La notion de patrimoine commun de l'humanité,"

lancé dans le droit de la mer. Il s'agissait, vers la fin des années 1960, d'éviter que les États les plus industrialisés s'approprient l'ensemble des fonds marins au titre de plateau continental. Ils auraient pu en effet invoquer à leur bénéfice le critère vague d'exploitabilité dont fait état la Convention de Genève de 1958 sur le plateau continental pour ce qui est de la limite extérieure de ce plateau.[41] La Résolution 2749 (XXV) de l'Assemblée générale des Nations Unies proclama dès 1970 le principe du patrimoine commun, repris depuis par une série de textes, dont le Traité sur la lune et les corps célestes (1979).[42] Le principe du patrimoine commun peut se décomposer en une série de principes plus concrets qui forment en quelque sorte sa congrégation. En même temps, ils fixent le droit constitutionnel moderne des espaces situés en dehors de la souveraineté nationale (sauf la colonne d'eau de la haute mer). Il s'agit: (1) de la non-appropriation; (2) de l'utilisation au bénéfice de tous les États et de tous les peuples; (3) de l'utilisation exclusivement pacifique et de l'interdiction de stationnement d'armes, notamment de destruction massive; (4) de la liberté de la recherche scientifique; (5) des devoirs de conservation et de protection de l'environnement; (6) de la non discrimination et de la prise en compte adéquate (*due regard*) des activités et intérêts des autres États. Ces principes ont opéré une unification normative du droit des espaces.[43] Parfois des conventions ont tenté de préciser le régime

---

RCADI, vol. 175, 1982-II, p. 99 et s.; V. Postyshev, *The Common Heritage of Mankind: From New Thinking to New Practice*, Moscou, 1990; W. Stocker, *Das Prinzip des Common Heritage of Mankind als Ausdruck des Staatengemeinschaftsinteresses im Völkerrecht*, Zurich, 1993; S. Sucharitkul, "Evolution continue d'une notion nouvelle: le patrimoine commun de l'humanité," dans: *Mélanges S. Rosenne*, Dordrecht / Boston / Londres, 1989, p. 887 et s.; R. Wolfrum, *Die Internationalisierung staatsfreier Räume*, Berlin, 1984, p. 328 et s.; R. Wolfrum, "The Principle of the Common Heritage of Mankind," ZaöRV, vol. 43, 1983, p. 312 et s.

[41] Sur la limite extérieure du plateau continental selon le régime de la Convention de 1958, cf. C. Vallée, *Le plateau continental dans le droit positif actuel*, Paris, 1971, p. 115 et s.; E.D. Brown, "The Outer Limit of the Continental Shelf," *Juridical Review*, vol. 2, 1968, p. 111 et s.

[42] Article 11 du Traité.

[43] Voir Wolfrum, *Internationalisierung* ..., *supra* note 40. Voir aussi J.A. Pastor Ridruejo, "Le droit international à la veille du 21ème siècle: normes, faits et valeurs," RCADI, vol. 274, 1998, pp. 257 et s., 265 et s. On peut aussi citer la cristallisation du droit de la délimitation maritime moderne à partir du principe général de l'équité et des principes équitables. Voir à ce propos, entre tant d'autres, V.D. Degan, "Equitable Principles in Maritime Delimitation," *Mélanges R. Ago*, Vol. II, Milan, 1987, p. 107 et s.; P. Bravender-Coyle, "The Emerging Legal Principles and Equitable Criteria Governing the Delimitation of Maritime

balisé par ces principes, notamment pour ce qui est de l'espace extra-atmosphérique[44] et de la mer.[45] Les principes mentionnés, régissant les *global commons*, ont eu tendance à butiner aussi ailleurs, quand se posait le problème d'une ressource commune.[46] Ainsi, par exemple, s'agissant des données recueillies par télédétection satellitaire (*remote sensing*), l'Assemblée générale des Nations Unies a insisté dans sa Résolution 41/65 du 3 décembre 1986 que l'observation de la terre par satellite est licite, mais qu'elle doit se plier à quinze principes. Ces principes correspondent *grosso modo* à ceux du patrimoine commun de l'humanité.[47] En termes analytiques, les principes dont il a été question forment un premier point d'attache juridique et axiologique en terre encore largement vierge. À travers une argumentation répétée, fondée sur ces préceptes, dans une série de contextes concrets et pour trouver des solutions à des

---

Boundaries between States," *Ocean Development and International Law*, vol. 19 1988, p. 171 et s.; M.D. Blecher, "Equitable Delimitation of Continental Shelf," AJIL, vol. 73, 1979, p. 60 et s.; R. Jennings, "The Principles Governing Maritime Boundaries," *Mélanges K. Doehring*, Berlin, 1989, p. 397 et s.; L.D.M. Nelson, "The Roles of Equity in the Delimitation of Maritime Boundaries," AJIL, vol. 84, 1990, p. 837 et s.; B. Kwiatkowska, " Equitable Maritime Boundary Delimitation—A Legal Perspective," *International Journal of Estuarine and Coastal Law*, vol. 3, 1988, p. 287 et s.; J.I. Charney, "Ocean Boundaries between Nations," AJIL, vol. 78, 1984, p. 582 et s.

[44] Voir L. Oppenheim (dir. R. Jennings / A. Watts), *International Law*, 9ᵉ éd., Londres, 1992, p. 828 et s.

[45] Partie XI de la Convention de Montego Bay sur le droit de la mer. Cf. F. Paolillo, "The Institutional Arrangements for the International Sea-Bed Authority and their Impact on the Evolution of International Organisations," RCADI, vol. 188, 1984-V, p. 145 et s. Pour les évolutions ultérieures: D.H. Anderson, "Resolution and Agreement Relating to the Implementation of Part XI of the United Nations Convention on the Law of the Sea: A General Assessment," ZaöRV, vol. 55, 1995, p. 275 et s.

[46] W. Graf Vitzthum (dir.), *Völkerrecht*, Berlin / New York, 1997, p. 466 et s.

[47] Voici les principes fondamentaux contenus dans ce document: (1) les activités de télédétection sont menées pour le bien et dans l'intérêt de tous les pays; (2) elles sont menées conformément au droit international; (3) les États doivent encourager la coopération internationale en la matière; (4) un système d'assistance technique doit être encouragé; (5) l'échange d'informations doit avoir lieu; (6) l'accès aux données recueillies doit être assuré à des conditions raisonnables; (7) la télédétection doit servir aussi à la protection de l'environnement et à la prévention des catastrophes. Sur cette Résolution, cf. C.A. Colliard, dans: AFDI, vol. 32, 1986, p. 697 et s.; C.A. Christol, dans: Journal of Space Law, vol. 16, 1988, p. 21 et s.; R. Szafarz, dans: PolYIL, vol. 17, 1988, p. 229 et s. Pour un ouvrage plus ancien sur la télédétection, cf. N. Matteesco Matte / H. De Saussure (dir.), *Legal Implications of Remote Sensing from Outer Space*, Leyden 1976.

problèmes précis, les principes gagnent un champ d'application toujours plus commensurable. Sur la carte encore largement blanche du début viennent ainsi se placer des reliefs, des localités, des chemins. En un mot, les principes sont le vecteur d'une pénétration progressive de la règle et de la technique juridiques.

2 Principe d'équité inter-générationnelle

Parfois, les principes lancés sont encore plus vagues et à connotation encore plus incertaine. Il en est ainsi par exemple du principe d'équité inter-générationnelle. Cependant, même de tels principes peuvent générer un développement proprement juridique, plus ou moins inattendu. Pour l'équité inter- ou trans-générationnelle, les arrêts de juridictions internes commencent à lui donner des contenus partiels juridiques *(juristische Teilgehalte)*.[48]

---

[48] Ainsi, la Cour constitutionnelle fédérale d'Allemagne a fondé son arrêt sur les quote-part aux assurances de soins-vieillesse en partie sur la notion d'équité trans-générationnelle. Selon la Cour, les personnes sans enfants profitent de la prestation des parents d'enfants, car le financement de leurs soins à l'avenir repose sur les cotisations des jeunes générations. Dès lors, le législateur doit prendre en compte le principe d'équité trans-générationnelle ainsi que le principe d'égalité afin de moduler les prestations, en particulier en permettant à des personnes avec enfant à charge de déduire de leurs cotisations à ces caisses un certain montant (restant à déterminer). Cf. BVerfGer., arrêt du 3.4.2001, 1 BVR 1629/94, communication à la presse:

3. Der Erste Senat stellt jedoch eine verfassungswidrige Benachteiligung von Eltern auf der Beitragsseite der sozialen Pflegeversicherung fest. Er geht dabei davon aus, dass das Risiko, pflegebedürftig zu werden, jenseits der 60 deutlich und jenseits der 80 sprunghaft ansteigt. Pflegebedürftige sind deshalb auf die Pflegeversicherungsbeiträge der nachwachsenden Generation angewiesen. Auf Grund dieses Umlagesystems profitieren die Kinderlosen von de Erziehungsleistung der Eltern. Beide sind darauf angewiesen, dass genug Kinder nachwachsen, die in der Zukunft Beiträge zahlen und ihre Pflege finanzieren. Dies ist unabhängig davon, ob sie selbst Kinder erzogen und damit zum Erhalt des Beitragszahlerbestandes beigetragen haben oder nicht. Kinderlosen, die lediglich Beiträge gezahlt, zum Erhalt des Beitragszahlerbestandes aber nichts beigetragen haben, erwächst daher ein Vorteil. Zwar finanzieren sie mit ihren Beiträgen auch die Abdeckung des Pflegerisikos der beitragsfrei versicherten Ehegatten und Kinder mit. Insgesamt wird der Vorteil, den Kinderlose durch das Aufziehen der nächsten Generation erlangen, durch die Umlage für die Familienversicherten aber nicht aufgezehrt. Allerdings kann der Gesetzgeber die Benachteiligung von Eltern solange vernachlässigen, wie eine deutliche Mehrheit der Versicherten Kinder bekommt und betreut. Dies folgt aus dem Recht des Gesetzgebers zur Generalisierung. Trägt die große Mehrheit der Beitragszahler daneben durch Erziehung und Betreuung von

On peut citer à cet effet l'affaire *Mineurs Oposa* c. *Secrétaire du Dépar-tement de l'environnement et des ressources naturelles* (1993), tranchée par la Cour suprême des Philippines.[49] Les demandeurs, tous des mineurs représentés par leurs parents, avaient requis que les tribu-naux philippins ordonnent au gouvernement de ne pas renouveler des licences concédant l'exploitation du bois de forêts vierges. Ils se fondèrent sur l'article 16, paragraphe 2, de la Constitution de 1987 qui prévoit que l'État doit protéger et développer le droit de chacun à un environnement sain, conformément aux textes internationaux. Les plaignants firent aussi valoir les concepts de "inter-generational responsibility" et de "inter-generational jus-tice." Ils rappelèrent que les forêts tropicales dont les Philippines sont riches contiennent un patrimoine génétique et biologique ir-remplaçable. De plus, la déforestation excessive aurait pour consé-quence des tragédies environnementales majeures, dont une longue liste d'échantillons est fournie.[50] La Cour suprême des Philippines cassa l'arrêt de première instance en admettant que les allégations des plaignants avaient un corps pleinement juridique. Les deman-deurs avaient qualité pour agir au nom des générations futures sur la base du principe de la responsabilité inter-générationnelle.[51] La Cour ajoute: "[E]very generation has a responsibility to the next to preserve that rhythm and harmony [of nature] for the full enjoyment of a balanced and healthful ecology."[52] Ce droit à un environnement sain emporte un devoir corrélatif de s'abstenir de

---

Kindern zum System bei, ist das System im Großen und Ganzen im genera-tiven Gleichgewicht. Solange liegt es auch innerhalb des gesetzgeberischen Gestaltungsspielraums, die Beiträge nicht danach zu differenzieren, ob Kinder erzogen werden oder nicht. Die Einführung des SGB XI im Jahr 1994 ohne Kindererziehungskomponente überschreitet jedoch den geset-zgeberischen Gestaltungsspielraum. Denn schon 1994 war bekannt, dass die Zahl der Kinderlosen in der Gesellschaft drastisch ansteigt. Der Gesetz-geber konnte nicht davon ausgehen, dass die große Mehrheit der Versich-erten sowohl Beiträge zahlen als auch Kinder erziehen würde. Insgesamt müssen weniger Beitragszahler die Pflege der älteren Generation finan-zieren und die Kosten der Kindererziehung tragen. Ein gleicher Versich-erungsbeitrag führt damit zu erkennbarem Ungleichgewicht zwischen dem Gesamtbeitrag der Eltern (Kindererziehung und Geldbeitrag) und dem Geldbeitrag der Kinderlosen. Die hieraus resultierende Benachteiligung von Eltern ist im Beitragsrecht auszugleichen.

[49] Cf. ILM, vol. 33, 1994, p. 173 et s.

[50] *Ibid.*, pp. 177-78.

[51] *Ibid.*, p. 185.

[52] *Ibid.*, p. 185.

détériorer l'environnement, ce qui implique à son tour un devoir de protéger les forêts.[53] Eu égard à l'ampleur de l'exploitation prévue, les licences accordées par le gouvernement ne sauraient être maintenues sans donner aux demandeurs la possibilité de les contester.[54] On peut ajouter que cette décision a été rendue à l'unanimité des quatorze juges signataires.

B   LES PRINCIPES GÉNÉRAUX "CONSERVATEURS"

Dans certains domaines, les principes servent davantage à empêcher une capillarisation juridique plus poussée qu'à la favoriser. Les États s'accommodent des seuls principes malléables pour maintenir délibérément la matière dont il s'agit dans l'espace politique.

I   *Principe d'autodétermination des peuples*

C'est le cas, par exemple, du principe d'autodétermination des peuples,[55] qui jusqu'à récemment a été laissé dans un clair-obscur

---

[53] *Ibid.*, p. 188.

[54] *Ibid.*, p. 198.

[55] Pour des contributions récentes sur ce droit, cf. A. Cassese, *Self-Determination of Peoples: A Legal Reappraisal,* Cambridge, 1995; C. Tomuschat, "International Law: Ensuring the Survival of Mankind on the Eve of a New Century," RCADI, vol. 281, 1999, p. 239 et s. Pour une bibliographie plus complète, cf. J.P. Müller / L. Wildhaber, Praxis des Völkerrechts, 3ᵉ éd., Berne, 2001, pp. 234-35. Originairement, ce concept n'avait qu'une portée politique dépourvue de tout statut juridique. Il en était à son égard un peu comme du principe des nationalités au XIXᵉ siècle. L'idée de droits octroyés à des peuples apparaît déjà dans le Projet de Déclaration du droit des gens de l'abbé Grégoire du 23 avril 1795, notamment à l'art. 17 qui dit qu'un peuple peut entreprendre la guerre pour défendre sa souveraineté, sa liberté, sa propriété. Un essor supplémentaire est donné à cette idée dans les 14 points du Président Wilson et dans la doctrine issue de la Révolution d'Octobre de 1917. Lié souvent à des idéologies révolutionnaires, le concept finit par prendre une tournure anti-colonialiste. C'est à ce titre qu'on le retrouve dans les Résolutions 1514(XV), 1541(XV) ou 2625(XXV) de l'Assemblée générale des Nations Unies. Le point de référence de la doctrine d'autodétermination a donc constamment changé, tout en se maintenant à la pointe des transformations et des luttes politiques quant aux statuts territoriaux de la société internationale: (1) lien avec l'idéologie de la Révolution française, souveraineté populaire; (2) lien avec les nationalismes et le droit des minorités à l'époque de la Société des Nations; (3) lien avec la décolonisation dès 1960; (4) lien avec les mouvements minoritaires ethniques, religieux ou autres, prétendant à la sécession dès les années 1990. Il n'est guère étonnant que des aspirations politiques ayant une telle vigueur finissent par se doter d'une doctrine juridique apte à répondre sur le plan normatif à leurs besoins. Il n'est guère

remarquable. En particulier, aucune définition suffisante du "peuple" détenteur du droit n'a pu être donnée. Il n'y a pas là qu'une difficulté issue de la nature des choses, sachant qu'un peuple n'est pas qu'une donnée objective, culturelle, d'ethnie ou de langue, mais surtout un construit subjectif, fondé sur une volonté de communauté. C'est de surcroît que les États, non peu d'entre eux étant menacés par des sécessionnismes potentiels,[56] préfèrent opérer au cas par cas la qualification du peuple attitré à exercer l'autodétermination, soit individuellement,[57] soit collectivement, notamment au sein des Nations Unies.[58] Ils maintiennent ainsi un meilleur contrôle sur des événements qui par leurs implications relèvent de la haute politique et ne se laissent pas réduire à une simple technique disciplinée par le droit.

étonnant non plus que cette doctrine juridique reste largement tributaire du politique avec toutes ses fluctuations, sélectivités et incertitudes.

[56] Voir déjà la Résolution 2625 (de 1970) de l'Assemblée générale qui réserve l'intégrité territoriale des États: "Rien dans les paragraphes précédents ne sera interprété comme autorisant ou encourageant une action, quelle qu'elle soit, qui démembrerait ou menacerait, totalement ou partiellement, l'intégrité territoriale ou l'unité politique de tout État souverain et indépendant se conduisant conformément au principe de l'égalité des droits des peuples à disposer d'eux-mêmes énoncé ci-dessus ..."

[57] Cf. p. ex. la Turquie et la République de Chypre du Nord, non reconnue par aucun autre État. Sur le conflit de Chypre et les activités des organes internationaux en général, voir V. Coussirat-Coustere, "La crise chypriote de l'été 1974 et les Nations Unies," AFDI, vol. 20, 1974, p. 437 et s.; G. Tornatiris, *The Turkish Invasion of Cyprus and Legal Problems Arising Therefrom*, Nicosia, 1975; C. Papalekas, *Die Zypenfrage: Problematik und Perspektiven eines Dauerkonflikts*, Frankfurt am Main /Berne, 1987; G. Von Laffert, *Die völkerrechtliche Lage des geteilten Zypern und Fragen seiner staatlichen Reorganisation*, Frankfurt am Main /Berne, 1995 (avec des renvois bibliographiques). Cfr. aussi J. Dugard, *Recognition and the United Nations*, Cambridge, 1987, pp. 108-11; M. El Kouhenne, *Les garanties fondamentales de la personne en droit humanitaire et droits de l'homme*, Dordecht/Boston/Lancaster, 1986, p. 230 et s. Pour la position turque, cf. Z.M. Necatigil, *The Cyprus Question and the Turkish Position in International Law*, Oxford, 1989. Pour un résumé de l'activité devant les organes de la Convention européenne des droits de l'homme, voir G. Cohen-Joanthan / J.P. Jacque, "Activité de la Commission européenne des droits de l'homme," AFDI, vol. 25, 1979, p. 383 et s.

[58] Cf. G. Abi-Saab, "Cours général de droit international public," RCADI, vol. 207, 1987-VII, p. 407 et s.; I. Brownlie, "International Law at the Fiftieth Anniversary of the United Nations," RCADI, vol. 255, 1995, p. 56 et s. Selon W. Friedmann, "General Course on Public International Law," RCADI, vol. 127, 1969-II, p. 185 et s., l'autodétermination est un principe uniquement politique et non juridique, précisément à cause de l'indétermination de ses titulaires.

La littérature juridique et la pratique ont bien essayé de dégager les contenus essentiels de l'autodétermination. La systématisation suivante est la plus communément acceptée: (1) il y a une autodétermination intérieure et extérieure; (2) l'autodétermination intérieure concerne les relations du peuple et de l'État au sein de celui-ci. Elle se décompose en: (a) la non-intervention dans les affaires intérieures dont jouit le peuple constitué en État; (b) un régime de protection des minorités ou un droit à la démocratie et au bon gouvernement (*good governance*) dont jouit le peuple à l'égard de son État. Dans ce cadre l'autodétermination est respectueuse du cadre étatique constitué: (3) l'autodétermination extérieure concerne la faculté donnée à un peuple de résister par la force à une domination et/ou de chercher à exercer un droit à la sécession. Cette autodétermination est en conflit avec le principe de l'intégrité territoriale des États constitués. Il a été dit qu'un tel droit d'autodétermination séparatiste peut être exercé: (a) dans le cas de colonies; (b) quand un peuple est opprimé par des occupants étrangers ou des régimes racistes; (c) quand un groupe défini de la population est exclu de tout accès raisonnable au gouvernement de l'État on se voit l'objet de persécutions massives.[59] Les minorités sont exclues du droit de demander la sécession si elles ne tombent pas sous le coup de l'une des situations mentionnées.

Là s'arrête l'objectivisation opérée par le droit. Le problème demeure toujours celui de la définition du "peuple" doté de ces droits. À cet égard la politique reste maîtresse. Il a souvent été dit qu'à défaut de critères objectivisables préétablis, il fallait s'en remettre à la reconnaissance d'un mouvement par l'organisation régionale ou par l'Assemblée générale des Nations Unies (par

---

[59] Cf. désormais aussi l'avis relatif à la *Sécession du Québec*, Cour suprême du Canada, 20.8.1998, ILM, vol. 37, 1998, p. 1373, § 138: "En résumé, le droit à l'autodétermination en droit international donne tout au plus ouverture au droit à l'autodétermination externe dans le cas des anciennes colonies; dans le cas des peuples opprimés, comme les peuples soumis à une occupation militaire étrangère; ou encore dans le cas où un groupe défini se voit refuser un accès réel au gouvernement pour assurer son développement politique, économique, social et culturel. Dans ces trois situations, le peuple en cause jouit du droit à l'autodétermination externe parce qu'on lui refuse la faculté d'exercer, à l'interne, son droit à l'autodétermination. Ces circonstances exceptionnelles ne s'appliquent manifestement pas au cas du Québec dans les conditions actuelles. Par conséquent, ni la population du Québec, même si elle était qualifiée de 'peuple' ou de 'peuples,' ni ses institutions représentatives, l'Assemblée nationale, la législature ou le gouvernement du Québec ne possèdent, en vertu du droit international, le droit de faire sécession unilatéralement du Canada."

exemple l'OLP, plus récemment les Kosovars, etc.). Le droit reste dès lors largement subordonné à la politique, ce qui, dans de tels domaines, n'est pas en soi illégitime, ni incompréhensible. La politique se dote, jusqu'à un certain point, de l'habit et de l'appui du droit. Mais il répugne à se laisser complètement objectiviser. De là ce régime juridique flexible, servant de support à une politique d'émancipation individuelle, mais placé sous l'aile d'une volonté politique véhiculée par les grandes enceintes internationales.

2   Compétences extraterritoriales de l'État

Un autre domaine où dominent des principes à défaut de règles précises est celui des compétences extraterritoriales de l'État.[60] Domaine sensible s'il en est, car il met aux prises les compétences souveraines de deux ou plusieurs États (le plus souvent l'une territoriale, l'autre extraterritoriale) non rarement dans ce qui à un moment donné est censé participer d'intérêts importants de la nation. On ne peut qu'être frappé par l'absence d'une réglementation véritable au niveau du droit international d'un domaine présentant une telle importance pour la vie internationale. En effet, le droit international se borne à renvoyer à une série de principes d'un vague évocateur. Selon le droit, il faut l'existence d'un lien raisonnable fondant une compétence ou son exercice; il faut tenir compte des intérêts en présence; il faut aussi soupeser les effets d'une mesure sur l'État qui la subit, voire sur des États tiers.[61]

[60] Cf. F.A. Mann, "The Doctrine of Jurisdiction in International Law," RCADI, vol. 111, 1964-I, pp. 43 et s., 82 et s.; M. Bos, "The Extraterritorial Jurisdiction of States," Annuaire de l'IDI, vol. 65-I, 1993, p. 13 et s.; F. Rigaux, "The Extraterritorial Jurisdiction of States (Rapport provisoire)," Annuaire de l'IDI, vol. 68-I, 1999, p. 507 et s. Voir aussi les quelques remarques dans Tomuschat, *supra* note 55, p. 196 et s.

[61] Cf. les auteurs cités à la note précédente. Une tentative de concrétisation de ces principes, et surtout de l'étoile polaire du "raisonnable," peut être trouvée dans le *Restatement Third of the Foreign Relations Law of the United States* (1986), § 402 et 403. L'application de ces règles-principes par les juridictions américaines montre cependant le degré de leur perméabilité à des considérations d'espèce explicables seulement par une perception unilatérale des intérêts en cause. Voici le texte des deux dispositions célèbres:

   402. Bases of Jurisdiction to Prescribe

   Subject to § 403, a state has jurisdiction to prescribe law with respect to

   (1) (a) conduct that, wholly or in substantial part, takes place within its territory;

      (b) the status of persons, or interests in things, present within its territory;

C'est déraisonnablement vague, d'autant plus que les intérêts susceptibles d'entrer en compte ainsi que leur poids respectif sont laissés à l'auto-appréciation des États. On comprend que chaque État tende à surévaluer ses intérêts propres (qui sont toujours raisonnables!) et à faire bon marché des intérêts d'autrui. Car tout

---

    (c) conduct outside its territory that has or is intended to have substantial effect within its territory;

  (2) the activities, interests, status or relations of its nationals outside as well as within its territory; and

  (3) certain conduct outside its territory by persons not its nationals that is directed against the security of the state or against a limited class of other state interests.

403. Limitations on Jurisdiction to Prescribe

  (1) Even when one of the bases for jurisdiction under § 402 is present, a state may not exercise jurisdiction to prescribe law with respect to a person or activity having connections with another state when the exercise of such jurisdiction is unreasonable.

  (2) Whether exercise of jurisdiction over a person or activity is unreasonable is determined by evaluating all relevant factors, including, where appropriate:
    (a) the link of the activity of the regulating state, i.e., the extent to which the activity takes place within the territory, or has substantial, direct, and forseeable effect upon or in the territory;
    (b) the connections, such as nationality, residence, or economic activity, between the regulating state and the person principally responsible for the activity to be regulated, or between that state and those whom the regulation is designed to protect;
    (c) the character of the activity to be regulated, the importance of regulation to the regulating state, the extent to which other states regulate such activities, and the degree to which the desirablity of such regulation is generally accepted;
    (d) the existence of justified expectations that might be protected or hurt by the regulation;
    (e) the importance of the regulation to the international political, legal or economic system;
    (f) the extent to which the regulation is consistent with the traditions of the international system;
    (g) the extent to which another state may have an interest in regulating the activity; and
    (h) the likelihood of conflict with regulation by another state.

  (3) When it would not be unreasonable for each of two states to exercise jurisdiction over a person or activity, but the prescriptions by the two states are in conflict, each state has an obligation to evaluate its own as well as the other state's interest in exercising jurisdiction in light of all the relevant factors, Subsection 2; a state should defer to the other state if that state's interest is clearly greater.

repose en dernière analyse sur une pesée des intérêts concurrents, la pesée étant bien entendu entreprise par chaque État *uti singuli*. Dès lors, un unilatéralisme remarquable domine l'ensemble de cette branche du droit. La loi Helms-Burton (1996)[62] n'en est qu'un exemple caricatural. Mais il en est d'autres. On peut évoquer l'affaire *Marc Rich* (contentieux diplomatique Suisse/US, 1987)[63] ou l'affaire *Hartford Fire Insurance* c. *Californie* (Cour suprême des États-Unis, 1993).[64] Dans la première, un ordre judiciaire américain enjoignait de produire des documents aux États-Unis à une entreprise suisse domiciliée en Suisse (et ayant une filiale aux

[62] Sur la législation Helms-Burton, cf. M. Cosnard, "Les lois Helms-Burton et d'Amato-Kennedy, interdiction de commerce avec et d'investir dans certains pays," AFDI, vol. 42, 1996, p. 33 et s.; W.F. Fairey, "The Helms-Burton Act: The Effect of International Law on Domestic Implementation," *American University Law Review*, vol. 46, 1997, p. 1289 et s.; H.S. Fairley, "Exceeding the Limits of Territorial Bounds: The Helms-Burton Act," CYIL, vol. 34, 1996, p. 161 et s.; C. Kress, "Der Helms-Burton-Act aus völkerrechtlicher Sicht," dans: *Recht der internationalen Wirtschaft*, vol. 43, 1997, p. 630 et s.; V. Lowe, "US Extraterritorial Jurisdiction: The Helms-Burton and D'Amato Acts," ICLQ, vol. 46, 1997, p. 378 et s.; W. Meng, "Extraterritoriale Jurisdiktion in der US-amerikanischen Sanktionsgesetzgebung," *Europäische Zeitschrift für Wirtschaftsrecht*, vol. 8, 1997, p. 423 et s.; A. Reinisch, "Widening the US Embargo against Cuba Extraterritorially," EJIL, vol. 7, 1996, p. 545 et s.; B. Stern, "Vers la mondialisation juridique? Les lois Helms-Burton et d'Amato-Kennedy," RGDIP, vol. 100, 1996, p. 979 et s. D'autres renvois chez Tomuschat, *supra* note 55, p. 199.

[63] Voir ASDI, vol. 40, 1984, p. 160 et s.

[64] Cf. l'Op. diss. Scalia, dans: ILR, vol. 100, p. 600: "Under the Restatement, a nation having some "basis" for jurisdiction to prescribe law should nonetheless refrain from exercising that jurisdiction "with respect to a person or activity having connections with another state when the exercise of such jurisdiction is unreasonable." Restatement (Third) § 403 (1). The "reasonableness" inquiry turns on a number of factors including, but not limited to: "the extent to which the activity takes place within the territory [of the regulating state];" "the connections, such as nationality, residence, or economic activity, between the regulating state and the person principally responsible for the activity to be regulated;" "the character of the activity to be regulated, the importance of regulation to the regulating state, the extent to which other states regulate such activities, and the degree to which the desirability of such regulation is generally accepted;" "the extent to which another state may have an interest in regulating the activity;" and "the likelihood of conflict with regulation by another state." Rarely would these factors point more clearly against application of United States law. The activity relevant to the counts at issue here took place primarily in the United Kingdom, and the defendants in these counts are British corporations and British subjects having their principal place of business or residence outside the United States. Great Britain has established a comprehensive regulatory scheme governing the London reinsurance markets, and clearly has a heavy "interest in regulating the activity."

États-Unis), alors que le droit suisse interdisait la remise de ces documents. L'ordre était muni d'une astreinte *(subpoena)* de 50 000 dollars par jour en cas de non-exécution. Les intérêts suisses se voyaient ignorés de manière flagrante, d'autant plus que la mesure visait à obliger des individus suisses, sur sol Suisse, à agir d'une manière contraire au droit suisse. Le contentieux s'étendit dès lors vers les ministères des affaires étrangères. Dans la seconde affaire, il s'agissait d'appliquer la fameuse législation américaine *anti-trust* à un marché étranger, réglementé par la loi d'un État étranger, en l'occurrence le marché des assurances anglais. La Cour suprême estima que les effets des activités londoniennes le sol américain étaient suffisants pour justifier l'application de la loi américaine. Elle estima que les entreprises britanniques visées auraient parfaitement pu respecter la loi américaine sans contrevenir à la loi du sol britannique. Dès lors, selon la Cour, il n'est pas nécessaire de procéder à la pesée des intérêts pour voir lequel des deux États en cause avait un lien plus intime avec les transactions en question. Ce constat, qui fait bon marché du devoir de peser des intérêts et donc de tenir compte de ceux de l'autre partie de manière adéquate, marque bien l'ampleur de l'impérialisme juridique que le droit international tolère en la matière à cause de l'absence de règles plus capillaires.

Un autre exemple instructif est le récent contentieux diplomatique entre la Hongrie et la Roumanie sur les minorités hongroises en Roumanie.[65] Par une loi, la Hongrie décida d'octroyer des droits et des avantages financiers aux membres de ses minorités sur divers territoires, dont celui de la Roumanie. Certains de ces avantages devaient revenir à ces ressortissants étrangers hongrois lors d'un séjour de leur part en Hongrie. L'élément extraterritorial est ici atténué. D'autres avantages devaient au contraire être octroyés directement aux ressortissants à l'étranger, par exemple sur le sol roumain. La Roumanie s'est élevée contre cette loi en arguant de son caractère extra-territorial, de l'interférence massive avec son ordre public et sa souveraineté territoriale, et du danger d'une discrimination entre ses citoyens, sur son territoire, pouvant être la source de tensions. On connaît les troubles violents qui eurent lieu dans le passé, y compris récent, entre les Roumains et les Hongrois dans certaines régions du pays. Pourtant, cette loi a été mise en vigueur cet été, malgré les protestations répétées de la Roumanie.

---

[65] Voir dans *Neue Zürcher Zeitung (NZZ)* du 23 juillet 2001, n° 168, p. 4. Voir aussi la *NZZ* du 27 avril 2001, n° 97, p. 7 et la *NZZ* du 23/4 juin 2001, n° 143, p. 7.

En tenant compte de ce qui précède, il est difficile de dire que le domaine soit réellement discipliné par le droit. En fait, il demeure très largement dominé par des pesées politiques.

V CONSÉQUENCES DU CARACTÈRE CONSTITUTIONNEL DU DROIT INTERNATIONAL

Le caractère constitutionnel du droit international emporte une série de conséquences auxquelles il serait bon de consacrer une analyse beaucoup plus serrée que cela ne pourra être le cas ici. À cette place, il faut se borner à en mentionner quelques-unes parmi les plus marquantes.

A ACTION POLITIQUE DES ÉTATS

Une conséquence évidente du caractère constitutionnel du droit international est qu'il laisse beaucoup d'espace à l'action politique des États. Par ses réglementations capillaires, le droit administratif enserre davantage la capacité d'action des sujets dans les mailles de l'ordre juridique en leur assignant des droits et des devoirs assez strictement définis. Par cela même, la portée de l'appréciation politique et donc les marges d'action se trouvent diminuées. Un droit de principes, au contraire, n'offre aux disciplines juridiques qu'une pénétration limitée dans la chair de ce qui demeure un corps étranger. Il laisse une grande flexibilité aux acteurs de système. Ceux-ci peuvent utiliser ces marges de manœuvre pour faire ce qui bon leur semble.

Pour ce qui est du droit international, on peut évoquer l'accommodation des effectivités, la place modeste du règlement juridique des différends comparé à celui politique, l'importance de droits discrétionnaires (notamment la reconnaissance, les pouvoirs du Conseil de Sécurité des Nations Unies), l'indétermination de concepts tels que la continuité ou la succession d'États (dominés dès lors par des reconnaissances subjectives selon les intérêts propres),[66] les débats autour de la configuration de droits essentiels comme la légitime défense ou l'autodétermination, etc. D'où d'ailleurs aussi le danger permanent d'un détournement de la "légalité" internationale à des fins politiques particulières, car l'espace laissé par les principes est tout désigné pour l'action relativement incontrôlée

---

[66] K. Zemanek, "The Legal Foundation of the International System, General Course on Public International Law," RCADI, vol. 266, 1997, p. 78 et s.

des puissances, surtout des grandes.[67] C'est contre cette toile de fond qu'il faut également apprécier l'auto-interprétation. Elle constitue la règle en droit international.[68] En droit interne, l'auto-interprétation n'est jamais qu'un premier échelon de la mise en oeuvre du droit, sujet au contrôle d'organes de la collectivité supérieurs. En droit international, c'est en règle générale le point de départ et le point d'arrivée dans l'exécution du droit. Les principes généraux sont particulièrement inadaptés à la seule auto-interprétation.[69] Leur texture ouverte permet aux États de trop facilement embrigader les contenus substantiels qu'ils véhiculent au service de leurs fins politiques particulières. Le principe de légitime défense, avec toutes ses interprétations extensives, en est un exemple parlant.[70]

---

[67] Selon Ch. De Visscher, *Théories . . .* , *supra* note 24, p. 112 et s., c'est l'une des raisons pour lesquelles il n'y a pas de véritable communauté internationale: "Que l'on compare à ce sujet l'action de la contrainte dans le milieu international à la coercition au sein de l'État. Celle-ci est conçue et acceptée comme l'émanation impersonnelle du droit dans un ordre de subordination. Dans l'ordre de juxtaposition, qui est actuellement celui des rapports internationaux, l'action collective internationale n'est pas réellement dépolitisée; au mieux, elle apparaît encore comme celle d'une majorité contre une minorité, exposée par conséquent à être détournée vers des fins particulières. Il en sera ainsi tant que l'idée d'un bien commun supranational n'aura pas implanté dans les consciences un sens nouveau des solidarités humaines et des disciplines qu'elles imposent."

[68] Cf. G. Abi-Saab, "'Interprétation' et 'auto-interprétation': quelques réflexions sur leur rôle dans la formation et la résolution du différend international," *Mélanges R. Bernhardt,* Berlin e.a, 1995, p. 9 et s.

[69] Cf. Kolb, *supra note 3,* pp. 164-66: pour une partie de la doctrine, les principes normatifs pallient tant bien que mal aux faiblesses structurelles du droit international, car sans eux il n'y aurait même plus ce minimum de devoir juridique indispensable pour pouvoir parler d'un ordre juridique (p. ex. H. Lauterpacht); pour d'autres, les concepts vagues ne peuvent qu'augmenter l'anarchie dans une société traversée d'antagonismes politiques et non dotée de moyens juridictionnels obligatoires (p. ex. Zoller). D'autres tentent une synthèse selon une équation précise: la carence institutionnelle impose des limites aux règles primaires (matérielles), leur densité normative ne pouvant dépasser la limite de rupture de charge que représente l'infrastructure de règles secondaires (institutionnelles). Donc: du normatif oui, mais pas plus que le système ne peut absorber. Cf. Abi-Saab, *supra* note 58, p. 125.

[70] Cf. A. Randelzhofer, "Article 51," dans: B. Simma (dir.), *The Charter of the United Nations—A Commentary,* Oxford, 1995, p. 661 et s. Pour des interprétations très différentes de l'extension de la légitime défense, voir p. ex. les ouvrages de Brownlie et de Bowett, cités en bibliographie chez Randelzhofer (*op. cit*).

B   PAUVRETÉ NORMATIVE EN DROIT INTERNATIONAL

Une autre conséquence est une certaine pauvreté normative (voire des lacunes) en droit international. Virtuellement, le droit international est un ordre complet, non pas tant parce qu'on peut appliquer une règle résiduelle de liberté,[71] mais parce que des

---

[71] La règle a la teneur suivante: tout ce qui n'est pas interdit est permis. Sur cette règle, voir l'affaire du *Lotus* (1927), CPJI, sér. A, n° 10, p. 19: "Il ne s'ensuit pas que le droit international défend à un État d'exercer, dans son propre territoire, sa juridiction dans toute affaire où il s'agit de faits qui se sont passés à l'étranger et où il ne peut s'appuyer sur une règle permissive du droit international. Pareille thèse ne saurait être soutenue que si le droit international défendait, d'une manière générale, aux États d'atteindre par leurs lois et de soumettre à la juridiction de leurs tribunaux des personnes, des biens et des actes hors du territoire, et si, par dérogation à cette règle générale prohibitive, il permettait aux États de ce faire dans des cas spécialement déterminés. Or, tel n'est certainement pas l'état actuel du droit international. Loin de défendre d'une manière générale aux États d'étendre leurs lois et leur juridiction à des personnes, des biens et des actes hors du territoire, *il leur laisse à cet égard une large liberté, qui n'est limitée que dans quelques cas par des règles prohibitives;* pour les autres cas, chaque État reste libre d'adopter les principes qu'il juge les meilleurs et les plus convenables ... Dans ces conditions, tout ce qu'on peut demander à un État, c'est de ne pas dépasser les limites que le droit international trace à sa compétence; en deça de ces limites, le titre à la juridiction qu'il exerce se trouve dans la souveraineté." La question a été soulevée à de nombreuses reprises depuis, que ce soit en droit international général (cf. l'affaire relative à la *Légalité de la menace ou de l'utilisation d'armes nucléaires,* CIJ, Rec., 1996, pp. 238-39, 247) ou dans des droits plus intégrés, comme celui des Communautés européennes (cf. l'opinion de l'avocat général Darmon à la CJCE en l'affaire *Ahlström* (1988), ILR, vol. 96, p. 179). À propos de l'avis des armes nucléaires, voir J. Salmon, "Le problème des lacunes à la lumière de l'avis 'licéité de la menace ou de l'emploi d'armes nucléaires' rendu le 8 juillet 1996 par la CIJ," *Mélanges N. Valticos,* Paris, 1999, p. 197 et s. Sur la règle résiduelle de liberté, voir aussi les réflexions intéressantes dans les textes suivants: H. Lauterpacht, *The Development of International Law by the International Court,* Londres, 1958, p. 359 et s.; H. Lauterpacht, "Some Observations on the Prohibition of 'non liquet' and the Completeness of the Law," *Mélanges J.H.W. Verzijl,* La Haye, 1958, p. 196 et s.; J. Stone, "Non Liquet and the Function of Law in the International Community," BYIL, vol. 35, 1959, p. 124 et s.; J. Stone, "Non Liquet and the Judicial Function," dans: C. Perelman (dir.), *Le problème des lacunes en droit,* Bruxelles, 1968, p. 305 et s.; J. Salmon, "Quelques observations sur les lacunes en droit international public," dans: C. Perelman (dir.), *Le problème des lacunes en droit,* Bruxelles, 1968, pp. 316-17; A. Bleckmann, "Die Handlungsfreiheit der Staaten," *Österreichische Zeitschrift für öffentliches Recht und Völkerrecht,* vol. 29, 1978, p. 173 et s.; A. Bleckmann, "Die Völkerrechtsordnung als System von Rechtsvermutungen," dans: *Mélanges H.U. Scupin,* Berlin, 1983, p. 407 et s.; U. Fastenrath, *Lücken im Völkerrecht, Schriften zum Völkerrecht,* vol. 93, Berlin, 1991, p. 239 et s. Des remarques intéressantes sur la "règle du Lotus" peuvent être trouvées notamment chez M. Bourquin, "Règles générales du droit

principes généraux s'offrent toujours comme points susceptibles d'une extension à des cas non réglementés ou nouveaux. Toutefois, au-dessous de ce niveau très général, l'élaboration normative du droit international accuse de graves faiblesses. La raison formelle est l'absence d'un processus de législation centralisé, régulier et permettant les prises de décision par voie majoritaire. La raison matérielle réside dans le fait que la société internationale reste encore très largement une société dominée par des rapports de puissance et de politique. Ce n'est pas toujours qu'une règle précise soit absente, par exemple par manque de pratique pertinente pour établir la règle coutumière.[72] D'autres fois, c'est parce que la règle se trouve en conflit avec une nouvelle doctrine juridico-politique qu'elle vacillera.[73] Ou alors, c'est qu'il y a une pratique trop discordante, trop marquée par des intérêts politiques contingents, qu'une règle juridique précise ne peut en résulter. Pendant les années 70 et 80, la question cruciale des expropriations et de la

---

de la paix," RCADI 1931-I (35), p. 101 et s.; F. Castberg, "La méthodologie du droit international public," RCADI 1933-I (43), p. 342 et s.; G. Salvioli, "Les règles générales de la paix," RCADI 1933-IV (46), pp. 21 et s., 62; L. Le Fur, "Règles générales du droit de la paix," RCADI 1935-IV (54), p. 302; Basdevant, "Règles générales du droit de la paix," RCADI 1936-IV (58), p. 593 et s.; J.L Brierly, "The Lotus Case," dans: J.L. Brierly, *The Basis of Obligation in International Law*, Oxford, 1968, pp. 143-44; G.G. Fitzmaurice, "The General Principles of International Law Considered from the Standpoint of the Rule of Law," RCADI 1957-II (92), p. 50 et s.; G.G. Fitzmaurice, "The Law and Procedure of the ICJ, 1951-54: General Principles and Sources of Law," BYIL, vol. 30, 1953, p. 8 et s.; H. Mosler, "Völkerrecht als Rechtsordnung," ZaöRV, vol. 36, 1976, p. 37 et s.; A. Verdross / B. Simma, *Universelles Völkerrecht*, 3ᵉ éd., Berlin, 1984, p. 388. Il faut noter que la règle ne sert guère lorsqu'il s'agit de droits concurrents ou d'une délimitation, car alors il n'y a pas de "liberté résiduelle;" cf. C. Rousseau, "L'aménagement des compétences en droit international," RGDIP, vol. 37, 1930, pp. 423-24; L. Le Fur, "Règles générales du droit de la paix," RCADI, vol. 54, 1935-IV, p. 302; J. Salmon, "Quelques observations sur les lacunes en droit international public," dans: C. Perelman (dir.), *Le problème des lacunes en droit*, Bruxelles, 1968, p. 317.

[72] Comme p. ex. pour la question de l'existence d'une règle sur l'admissibilité des preuves indirectes; cf. l'affaire du *Détroit de Corfou*, CIJ, Rec., 1949, p. 18.

[73] Cf. p. ex. la collision du principe de la liberté des mers avec l'idée des grands fonds marins comme patrimoine commun de l'humanité, collision ayant été résolue par une restriction de la portée de la liberté des mers. Cf. le plaidoyer de F. Orrego Vicuna, "Les législations nationales pour l'exploitation des fonds des mers et leur incompatibilité avec le droit international," AFDI, vol. 24, 1978, p. 810 et s. Voir aussi G. Jaenicke, "The Legal Status of the International Seabed—The Controversy about the Legality of National Legislation on Deep Sea Mining," *Mélanges H. Mosler*, Berlin e.a., 1983, p. 429 et s.; R. Young, "The Legal Régime of the Deep Sea Floor," AJIL, vol. 62, 1968, p. 641 et s.

compensation nécessaire donna lieu à des interprétations telle-
ment divergentes entre les États occidentaux et les États impor-
tateurs de capitaux que certains auteurs refusaient d'admettre
qu'une quelconque règle s'était fixée.[74] La formule consacrée de
la "compensation adéquate" masquait ces divergences sans les surmonter d'aucune façon. Le principe de "l'adéquat" était en effet
d'une malléabilité telle qu'il permettait de fonder une réclamation
inverse de l'État expropriateur en lieu et place d'un paiement
vers l'exproprié. L'enrichissement excessif en fournissait le pivot.
Il s'agissait de mettre en balance des profits "excessifs" tirés par
l'entreprise étrangère lors des ses activités passées (par exemple
en profitant d'une législation sociale permissive) et sa valeur au
moment de la saisie. Si la pratique s'était fixée sur la pleine compensation réciproque de l'enrichissement, et si elle avait précisé
les données à prendre en compte, on aurait eu un standard objectif. Il est compréhensible qu'une telle pratique clarificatrice n'eut
jamais lieu, vu les résistances mutuelles des deux blocs en cause.

Par ailleurs, cette pauvreté normative au niveau des règles (non
des principes) explique en bonne partie les difficultés et les obstacles que rencontre en droit international toute tentative de
codification.[75] Elle rend plus compréhensible aussi la tendance à
l'hypertrophie de normes de *soft law,* si caractérisée en droit international.[76] Le *soft law* a la fonction d'un palliatif. À défaut d'un
nombre suffisant de règles "administratives," le *soft law* vient former
un pont entre les principes généraux et les applications concrètes, tentant d'influencer dans un sens voulu ces dernières. C'est
fréquemment le cas dans des matières nouvelles ou hautement

---

[74] Voir R. Dolzer, "Expropriation and Nationalization," EPIL, vol. II (E-I) (1995),
p. 322. Voir aussi A. Cassese, *International Law,* Oxford, 2001, p. 416. Alterna-
tivement, il faut analyser la situation comme étant dominée par deux coutumes
régionales distinctes, applicables chacune au groupe d'États qui y adhèrent. Sur
ce conflit entre coutumes particulières, voir M. Akehurst, "Custom As a Source
of International Law," BYIL, vol. 47, 1974/5, p. 31. Sur l'état du droit en
matière d'expropriation, voir aussi O. Schachter, "Compensation for Expropriation," AJIL, vol. 78, 1984, p. 121 et s.

[75] Voir déjà J.L. Brierly, "Les règles générales du droit de la paix," RCADI, vol. 58,
1936-IV, p. 21.

[76] En sens critique, voir P. Weil, "Cours général: le droit international en quête de
son identité," RCADI, vol. 237, 1992-VI, p. 215 et s. En sens plus favorable, voir
Abi-Saab, *supra* note 58, p. 205 et s.; G. Abi-Saab, "Eloge du droit assourdi.
Quelques réflexions sur le rôle de la soft law en droit international contemporain," *Mélanges F. Rigaux,* Bruxelles, 1993, p. 59 et s.; A. Pellet, "Le bon droit et
l'ivraie, plaidoyer pour l'ivraie," *Mélanges C. Chaumont,* Paris, 1984, p. 465 et s.

politiques, parce que les défauts du processus de législation internationale s'y font le plus évidemment sentir et que les États y exercent le plus de résistance à concrétiser les principes par des règles détaillées de *hard law*. On peut évoquer le droit de l'environnement ou le droit des droits de l'homme.

C   SÉQUENCE DE LA CRÉATION DU DROIT

En troisième lieu, il s'établit souvent en droit international une séquence assez spéciale de la création du droit. D'abord, un ou plusieurs principes sont postulés comme têtes de pont à la fois juridiques et axiologiques. Le rôle des principes est ici avant tout dynamique: à travers eux, l'idée du droit s'installe dans des espaces nouveaux tandis que la technique juridique n'y pénètre que plus tard. Ces principes sont les campements premiers du droit en terre étrangère. Ce n'est que dans un second temps qu'une élaboration plus détaillée du droit suit à travers une pratique opérant par à-coups selon les contingences multiples de la vie internationale. Un élément empirique vient alors enrichir les postulats généraux des principes qui s'offraient dans un premier temps comme autant de points de déduction féconds pour l'argumentation juridique. Le droit de l'espace extra-atmosphérique ou le droit de la mer, déjà évoqués, offrent des exemples où ce processus a pu se déployer sans obstacles. Le droit du nouvel ordre économique mondial est une illustration où l'évolution de la société internationale vers des modèles plus libéraux a arrêté, puis interverti le processus qui avait été lancé.

Pour ce qui est du droit de l'espace, c'est l'Assemblée générale des Nations Unies, après le lancement du Spoutnik en 1957, qui se saisit de la question. Par sa Résolution 1962 (de l'année 1963), elle proclame une série de principes qui devraient régir le droit de l'espace. Ces principes seront repris et développés quelques années plus tard par le Traité sur l'Espace (1967) qui forme une espèce de traité-cadre. Une étape ultérieure de concrétisation suivra avec une série de conventions plus spécifiques, par exemple la Convention de 1968 sur le sauvetage des astronautes, la Convention de 1972 sur la responsabilité pour les objets spatiaux, la Convention de 1979 sur la lune et les autres corps célestes, etc.[77] Le droit de la délimitation maritime est un autre exemple évocateur. En se fondant sur la Proclamation Truman de 1945, la Cour internationale

---

[77] Voir le bref aperçu dans Pastor Ridruejo, *supra* note 43, p. 265 et s.

de Justice a estimé que la règle coutumière pour ces délimitations est celle qui prescrit le recours à des principes équitables, en un mot à l'équité.[78] Dans sa jurisprudence postérieure et dans la pratique des États, les implications les plus diverses ont été tirées de ces principes équitables. Elles donnèrent corps à un droit détaillé des délimitations maritimes. Il s'agit par exemple du respect dû aux circonstances pertinentes, du non-empiétement, du partage égal des chevauchements, du respect de la géographie ("ne pas refaire totalement la géographie"), de la proportionnalité entre la longueur des côtes et les espaces maritimes obtenus par chaque État, de l'effort d'éviter les répercussions catastrophiques pour la subsistance de la population locale, etc. Tous ces préceptes ont été tirés de manière prétorienne du principe général de l'équité. L'aspect remarquable des délimitations maritimes, c'est que le développement du droit a été confié au juge plus que dans tout autre domaine. Alors que le droit international est généralement un droit prétorien sans préteur, dans les délimitations maritimes c'est un droit prétorien avec préteur.

Le décalage de la formation juridique entre une phase axée sur des principes et une phase plus prétorienne se manifeste également dans le fait que dans peu d'autres ordres juridiques le pas entre l'interprétation de la norme et son application est aussi grand. Etant donné que la base d'induction ou de déduction du raisonnement juridique international fait souvent appel à des principes ou des normes assez indéterminés, l'"interprétation" re-créatrice d'un sens prédéterminé par le législateur laisse davantage qu'ailleurs la place à une "concrétisation" créatrice dans un contexte juridique variable. La mise en œuvre du droit se fait donc plus par la paire concrétisation/application que par celle plus technique d'interprétation/application.[79] Le pas est double: à un sens inhérent à la norme, il faut ajouter un sens supplémentaire par voie de *law-making* partiel et contextuel. Cet état des choses rend compte de la difficulté accrue du travail judiciaire en droit international. Le juge est en fait souvent appelé à développer le droit

---

[78] Affaires du *Plateau continental de la mer du Nord,* CIJ, Rec., 1969, pp. 3 et s., 46 et s.

[79] Le *policy-oriented-approach* du droit international n'est qu'une conceptualisation extrême de cette tendance du droit international. Pour une adoption de cette approche au-delà du cercle de l'École de New Haven, cf. R. Higgins, "General Course on Public International Law: International Law and the Avoidance, Containment and Resolution of Disputes," RCADI, vol. 230, 1991-V, p. 23 et s. Pour une critique, cf. Abi-Saab, *supra* note 58, p. 35 et s. ou Tomuschat, *supra* note 55, pp. 25 et s., 53-55.

en s'arrogeant de micro-pouvoirs législatifs, car il ne trouve pas les règles internationales suffisamment concrètes et adaptées à l'espèce qu'il traite. Paradoxalement, c'est au niveau international qu'a cours avec le plus de virulence la fiction d'un juge particulièrement lié aux expressions de volonté des États. Cette fiction volontariste sert à protéger le juge international, assez faible face aux unités de puissance que sont les États (qui ne consentent qu'exceptionnellement à renoncer un tant soit peu au pouvoir souverain de qualification juridique).[80] Elle lui permet de faire passer pour des conséquences de leur accord ce qui en réalité n'est que le fruit de sa propre élaboration juridique. En fait, comment ne pas voir les apports largement constitutifs d'une norme plus concrète et plus opérationnelle que le juge pétrit dans le corps souvent hésitant du droit international? Dans les matières les plus diverses, les exemples de *judicial legislation* ne se comptent plus, que ce soit en matière de responsabilité internationale,[81] d'utilisation de la force,[82] de délimitation terrestre et maritime,[83] en matière de compétences,[84] etc. Le plus souvent, ce n'est pas le droit qui fixe les règles que la pratique ne fera qu'appliquer; c'est au contraire la pratique qui concrétise le droit en lui donnant un corps juridique plus précis.

D   PROBLÈMES TERMINOLOGIQUES ET CONCEPTUEL

Ensuite, on peut faire mention des fréquentes incertitudes, confusions, voire contradictions terminologiques et conceptuelles qu'un

---

[80] Cf. J. Stone, "Fictional Elements in Treaty Interpretation," dans: J. Stone, *Of Law and Nations—Between Power Politics and Human Hopes,* New York, 1974, p. 194 et s.; H. Waldock, "General Course on Public International Law," RCADI, vol. 106, 1962-II, p. 104; L. Gross, "The International Court of Justice: Consideration of Requirements for Enhancing its Role in the International Legal Order," AJIL, vol. 65, 1971, partic. p. 268. Voir aussi H. Lauterpacht, *The Development of International Law by the International Court,* Londres, 1958, p. 75 et s.

[81] Cf. p. ex. l'affaire de *L'Usine de Chorzów,* CPJI, sér. A, n° 17; l'affaire des *Phosphates du Maroc,* CPJI, sér. A/B, n° 74 (et les plaidoiries); l'affaire de la *Fonderie du Trail,* RSA, vol. III, p. 1905 et s.; l'affaire *Nottebohm,* CIJ, Rec., 1955, p. 4 et s.

[82] Cf. p. ex. l'affaire des *Activités militaires et paramilitaires au Nicaragua et contre celui-ci,* CIJ, Rec., 1986, p. 14 et s. ou les affaires pendantes entre la Yougoslavie et les États de l'OTAN qui posent le problème de l'intervention humanitaire. Voir aussi l'affaire *Tadic* (1997) du TPY, § 584s et s.; *Tadic* (1999), § 68 et s., etc.

[83] Cf. p. ex. l'affaire du *Temple de Préah Vihéar,* CIJ, Rec., 1962, p. 6 et s. (applicabilité de l'acquiescement et de l'estoppel) ou les affaires du *Plateau continental de la mer du Nord,* CIJ, Rec., 1969, p. 3 et s.

[84] Cf. p. ex. l'affaire du *Lotus,* CPJI, sér. A, n° 10.

corps juridique peu concrétisé ne manque pas de susciter.[85] En effet, la clarté terminologique et conceptuelle est le plus souvent fonction de l'existence de règles précises de type "administratif." Plus ces dernières sont clairsemées et plus la terminologie a aussi tendance à flotter. Un exemple évocateur de ce cas de figure est fourni par les deux termes *"saisie"* et *"réquisition"* dans le droit de la guerre.[86] Le sens de ces termes varie déjà selon les contextes: occupation de guerre, opérations militaires, droit des prises sur mer. L'opinion la plus répandue distingue de surcroît les deux termes selon la nature des biens appropriés: ceux susceptibles d'une utilisation militaire sont saisis, les autres sont réquisitionnés, pour autant toutefois qu'ils peuvent être utiles aux besoins de l'armée qui progresse ou à la force d'occupation.[87] Pour d'autres auteurs, la saisie est limitée à la guerre sur mer, la réquisition à la guerre sur terre.[88] Ou alors, la saisie est reliée à la propriété publique, la réquisition à la propriété privée.[89] D'autres encore considèrent que la réquisition couvre tous les actes d'appropriation de biens pour les besoins de l'armée, alors que la saisie ne s'appliquerait qu'aux biens meubles pris comme butin de guerre.[90] Encore, certains auteurs estiment que les deux termes se recouvrent partiellement et ne peuvent être distingués qu'au regard de deux éléments: d'abord, *ratione materiae*, la réquisition tendant à couvrir aussi les biens immeubles, contrairement à la saisie; ensuite, *ratione personae*, la réquisition se bornant à la propriété privée ou aux biens des

---

[85] Cf. R. Kolb, "Des problèmes conceptuels, systématiques et terminologiques en droit international public," ZöR, vol. 56, 2001 pp. 501 et s.

[86] Cf. p. ex. les art. 23(g) et 52 du Règlement annexé à la Convention IV de La Haye (1907) sur les lois et coutumes de la guerre sur terre. Pour le texte de la Convention, cf. D. Schindler / J. Toman, *Droit des conflits armés*, Genève, 1996, pp. 84, 91.

[87] Cf. M. Greenspan, *The Modern Law of Land Warfare*, Berkeley / Los Angeles, 1959, pp. 293 et s., 296, 300. Voir aussi F.A. Von Der Heydte, *Völkerrecht*, t. II, Cologne / Berlin, 1960, pp. 324-25; P. Jessup, "A Belligerent Occupant's Power Over Property," AJIL, vol. 38, 1944, pp. 458-59; A.D. McNair / A. Watts, *The Legal Effects of War*, Cambridge, 1966, pp. 394-95.

[88] Cf. L. Oppenheim / H. Lauterpacht, *International Law*, vol. II, *Disputes, War and Neutrality*, 7e éd., Londres / New York / Toronto, 1952, pp. 474-76.

[89] Cf. P. Fauchille, *Traité de droit international public*, t. II, *Guerre et neutralité*, Paris, 1921, pp. 254 et s., 281 et s. La réquisition est un terme plus étroit que la saisie, car il y a le principe du respect de la propriété privée. Dès lors les conditions pour une réquisition sont plus exigeantes.

[90] Cf. L.H. Woolsey, "The Forced Transfer of Property in Enemy Occupied Territories," AJIL, vol. 37, 1943, p. 285.

autorités locales en zone occupée, la saisie s'étendant à la propriété publique et privée.[91] Enfin, il est des auteurs qui estiment que la réquisition est un terme d'art signifiant un régime juridique, tandis que la saisie n'est que l'acte matériel d'appropriation, en d'autres termes un simple fait juridique.[92] Quelques sentences arbitrales semblent s'inspirer de cette dernière conception. C'est le cas de l'affaire *Tesdorpf* c. *Allemagne* (1923) où les arbitres affirment que la saisie n'opère pas le transfert de propriété.[93] Chaque auteur fait comme si le sens qu'il attribue lui-même au terme était généralement admis. Immanquablement, cette impression est créée chez le lecteur. On tend alors à donner des certitudes, sources de mésententes qu'il n'est pas malaisé d'imaginer.

E   RULE OF LAW

Il faut dire aussi que la société internationale n'est pas ordonnée au droit au sens de l'existence d'une véritable *rule of law*.[94] C'est vrai dans un double sens. D'abord, du point de vue formel, le juge, qui est l'organe par excellence du droit, n'a qu'une position faible dans les relations internationales.[95] Les États privilégient le règlement par des moyens politiques, à la fois plus flexibles et plus respectueux de leur souveraineté. De plus, à l'intérieur du cadre des moyens politiques, les normes de référence ne sont pas simplement celles du droit international (que celles-ci confèrent une large marge d'action ou non). Au contraire, c'est le plus souvent la transaction ou d'autres règlements particuliers, parfois instables dans le temps, que les États préfèrent. Ensuite, du point de vue matériel, le droit international n'offre guère une vraie prise à une *rule of law* strictement entendue. Il lui présente des parois de mollusque sur lesquelles la *rule* n'arrive pas à se greffer. Les principes

---

[91] Cf. G. Schwarzenberger, *International Law—As Applied by International Courts and Tribunals*, vol. II, *The Law of Armed Conflict*, Londres, 1968, p. 269. Voir aussi *ibid.*, p. 291 et s., avec des développements détaillés.

[92] Cf. C. Rousseau, *Le droit des conflits armés*, Paris, 1983, pp. 166-70, 167.

[93] RSA, vol. I, p. 107 et s.

[94] Cf. Pastor Ridruejo, *supra* note 43, pp. 32-33. Sur la *rule of law* internationale, cf. A. Watts, "The International Rule of Law," GYIL, vol. 36, 1993, p. 15 et s.; J.Y. Morin, "L'État de droit: émergence d'un principe du droit international," RCADI, vol. 254, 1995, p. 9 et s.

[95] Voir *supra*, note 80. Selon Tomuschat, *supra* note 55, p. 424, les avis consultatifs de la Cour internationale ont été un moyen privilégié d'instiller une certaine *rule of law* dans des matières hautement politiques au sein des Nations Unies.

dont se compose le droit international laissent trop d'interstices et ne commandent guère assez l'action concrète pour que les exigences d'une véritable *rule of law* soient satisfaites. Le droit international n'est souvent qu'un droit-cadre. D'où certaines faiblesses de son expression formelle (théorie des sources) dont le revers est l'affaiblissement de la *rule*. En droit interne, c'est bien le droit administratif qui au sein du droit public est censé garantir les exigences de la *rule*. Le droit constitutionnel, trop général et ponctuel, n'y est pas perçu comme étant suffisant pour assurer les citoyens contre l'arbitraire.

F   CONFLIT DE PRINCIPES

Ce qui vient d'être dit explique aussi que les grands problèmes du droit international se résument souvent à un conflit de principes. Par exemple: souveraineté / droits de l'homme;[96] non-utilisation de la force / légitime défense *lato sensu* ou intervention humanitaire,[97] etc.; respect des droits acquis ou *pacta sunt servanda* / souveraineté permanente sur les ressources naturelles;[98] intégrité territoriale ou *uti possidetis* / autodétermination des peuples;[99] principe du

---

[96] Cf. p. ex. le Rapport du Conseil fédéral à l'Assemblée fédérale du 2 juin 1982, dans l'ASDI, vol. 39, 1983, pp. 206-8. Voir aussi la Résolution de l'Institut de droit international à la Session de St. Jacques de Compostelle, "La protection des droits de l'homme et le principe de non-intervention dans les affaires intérieures des États," Ann. IDI, Résolutions, 1957-1991, Paris, 1992, p. 206 et s. Voir en général, F. Ermacora, "Article 2(7) of the Charter," dans: Simma, *supra* note 70, p. 139 et s., avec une bibliographie.

[97] Voir *supra*, note 70. Sur le problème de l'intervention humanitaire, voir p. ex. les deux contributions récentes de B. Simma, "NATO, the UN and the Use of Force: Legal Aspects," EJIL, vol. 10, 1999, p. 1 et s. et de A. Cassese, *"Ex iniuria ius non oritur:* Are We Moving Towards International Legitimation of Forcible Humanitarian Countermeasures in the World Community?" EJIL, vol. 10, 1999, p. 23 et s. Pour des renvois plus nourris à la littérature récente sur le sujet, cf. Tomuschat, *supra* note 55, p. 218 et s.

[98] Voir *supra*, note 13.

[99] Cf. O. Corten, "Droit des peuples à disposer d'eux-mêmes et *uti possidetis*: deux faces d'une même médaille?" dans: O. Corten *e.a* (dir.), *Démembrements d'États et délimitations territoriales: l'uti possidetis en question(s),* Bruxelles, 1999, p. 403 et s.; G. Nesi, *L'uti possidetis nel diritto internazionale,* Padoue, 1996, p. 250 et s.; Pastor Ridruejo, *supra* note 43, pp. 225-26, estime que l'*uti possidetis* doit être limité au contexte colonial, car sinon il cimenterait nombre d'injustices en contradiction avec le principe de l'autodétermination des peuples. Plus favorable à l'*uti possidetis,* cf. M. Kohen, "Le problème des frontières en cas de dissolution et de séparation d'États: quelles alternatives?" dans: Corten, *op. cit.,* p.365 et s.

consensualisme / bonne foi;[100] effectivité / légitimité,[101] etc.[102] Peut-être nul autre droit n'a le don d'autant faire coaguler ses conflits essentiels en des oppositions entre les grands principes qui captivent en un point unique les faisceaux épars du différend concret. Celui-ci subit dès lors souvent une transformation: il gagne en généralité. Cet état des choses ne facilite pas toujours sa solution. Au niveau des divinités que sont les grands principes, l'aspect d'opposition ressort clairement et parfois s'accuse au point de rendre plus difficile sa solution juridique. Le soubassement concret qui tisse des liens aussi divers que discrets tend au niveau suprême à être éclipsé par l'implacable antagonisme des deux impératifs généraux. De surcroît, ceux-ci expriment alors le plus souvent la position et les intérêts d'un groupe déterminé d'États. L'opposition entre principes souligne encore une fois la dimension plus politique que technique de nombre de différends internationaux.

---

[100] Cf. R. Kolb, *La bonne foi en droit international public,* Paris, 2000; R. Kolb, "La bonne foi en droit international public," RBDI, vol. 34, 1998, p. 661 et s.

[101] En droit international en général, cf. A. Verdross / B. Simma, *Universelles Völkerrecht,* 3ᵉ éd., Berlin, 1984, pp. 51-53. Pour les litiges territoriaux, cf. R. Pinto, "La prescription en droit international," RCADI, vol. 87, 1955-I, p. 391 et s. En philosophie du droit, ce problème s'approche de celui cardinal de toute jurisprudence, le rapport entre l'être et le devoir être (*Sein / Sollen*). Cfr. sur ce dernier, l'aperçu dans: P. Schneider (dir.), *Sein und Sollen im Erfahrungsbereich des Rechtes: Vorträge des Weltkongresses für Rechts- und Sozialphilosophie,* Milan — Gardone Riviera, 9.IX.-13.IX, 1967; F. Achermann, *Das Verhältnis von Sein und Sollen, als ein Grundproblem des Rechts,* Winterthur, 1955. Voir aussi G. Schurz, *The Is—Ought Problem,* Dordrecht e.a, 1997; R. Stuhlmann-Laeisz, *Das Sein-Sollen-Problem,* Stuttgart, 1983; B. Celano, *Dialettica della giustificazione pratica: saggio sulla legge di Hume,* Turin, 1994.

[102] Cette technique de la mise en balance de principes en conflit est bien connue du droit interne. En effet, elle constitue l'essence du droit constitutionnel et garde de l'importance au sein du droit administratif. Cfr. B. Schlink, *Abwägung im Verfassungsrecht,* Berlin, 1976; *Mélanges W. Hoppe, Abwägung im Recht,* Cologne / Berlin, 1996; K-H. Ladeur, '*Abwägung*' — *Ein neues Paradigma des Verwaltungsrechts,* Francfort-sur-le-Main, 1984; T.A. Aleinikoff, "Constitutional Law in the Age of Balancing," Yale Law Journal, vol. 96, 1987, p. 943 et s. Voir aussi W. Leisner, *Der Abwägungsstaat: Verhältnismässigkeit als Gerechtigkeit?,* Berlin, 1997; W. Enderlein, *Abwägung in Recht und Moral,* Freiburg i.B. / Munich, 1992. Voir encore M. Buergisser, *La pesée des intérêts comme méthode: bref aperçu historique,* Bâle / Francfort-sur-le-Main, 1996. Pour le droit international, P. Hector, *Das völkerrechtliche Abwägungsgebot,* Berlin, 1992.

VI Tendances (récentes) à densifier
    le droit international

Parmi les nombreuses tendances récentes ou moins récentes de
conférer un corps plus précis au droit international, il sera ici question de trois aspects.

A   LE HARD ET LE SOFT LAW "ADMINISTRATIF"

1   Le hard law administratif

Depuis toujours, certaines matières supposaient des règles administratives au-delà des principes si une application raisonnable
du droit devait être garantie. Le droit des conflits armés en est un
exemple. Ce droit repose certes sur une série de principes généraux (appelés aussi principes humanitaires) absolument domi-
nants en la matière.[103] C'est le cas notamment des principes de
distinction (objectifs militaires/civils), de proportionnalité, de protection, de non-discrimination, jusqu'au principe d'humanité (y
compris la Clause Martens)[104] d'un côté; et celui de nécessité

---

[103] Cf. J. Pictet, *Les principes du droit international humanitaire*, Genève, 1966. Voir
aussi les principes du droit humanitaire invoqués par la Cour internationale,
affaire des *activités militaires et paramilitaires au Nicaragua et contre celui-ci*, CIJ,
Rec., 1986, pp. 113-15, § 217 et s.; affaire de la licéité de la *menace ou de l'emploi
d'armes nucléaires* (AGNU), CIJ, Rec., 1996, p. 257, § 79. Sur le rôle des
principes généraux en droit humanitaire, cfr. I.P. Blishchenko, "Les principes
du droit international humanitaire," *Mélanges J. Pictet*, Genève, 1984, p. 291 et
s.; R. Abi-Saab, "Les principes généraux du droit humanitaire selon la Cour
internationale de Justice," RICR, vol. 69, 1987, p. 381 et s.; D.W. Greig, "The
Underlying Principles of International Humanitarian Law," Austr.Y.B.I.L., vol.
9, 1985, p. 46 et s.; M. Lachs, "The Unwritten Laws of Warfare," *Tulane Law
Review*, vol. 20, 1945, p. 120 et s. Cfr. aussi J. Pictet, "The Principles of International Humanitarian Law," RICR, vol. 48, 1966, pp. 411 et s., 461 et s., 513 et s.;
A.P. Sereni, "Ragione di guerra e principi di umanità nel diritto internazionale
bellico," RDI, vol. 47, 1974, p. 169 et s.; G. Moynier, *Essai sur les caractères
généraux des lois de la guerre*, Genève, 1985.

[104] Sur le principe d'humanité, cf. Truyol Y Serra, *supra* note 1, p. 88 et s.; I.
Schoebel, *Das Humanitätsprinzip im völkerrechtlichen Kriegsrecht und sein Nieder-
schlag in Hugonis Grotii 'De iure belli ac pacis,'* thèse, Innsbruck, 1954; M. Huber,
"Le droit des gens et l'humanité," *Revue internationale de la Croix-Rouge*, vol. 34,
1952, p. 646 et s.; A.P. Sereni, "Ragione di guerra e principi di umanità nel
diritto internazionale bellico," RDI, vol. 47, 1974, p. 169 et s.; H. Knackstedt,
"Humanität und Völkerrecht: Der Einfluss der humanitären Idee auf die
Entwicklung des Völkerrechts," dans: *Deutsches Rotes Kreuz* (éd), *Schriftenreihe no.
27/4*, Bonn, 1962, p. 99 et s. Cfr. aussi G. Del Vecchio, *Humanité et unité du droit*,
Paris, 1963. Sur la Clause Martens, cf. H. Strebel, "Martens Clause," EPIL, vol.

militaire[105] de l'autre. Il a cependant été ressenti très tôt que le droit des conflits armés, précisément parce qu'il régit des situations extrêmes marquées par l'effondrement de l'ordre social et la lutte pour la survie, ne pourrait atteindre à un minimum d'effectivité[106] que pour autant que ses prescriptions fussent traduites dans des règles de détail. Le personnel militaire sur le terrain doit savoir avec précision quelle conduite est permise et quelle conduite est interdite. Il ne peut s'adonner à des exercices de mise en balance contextuelle de grands principes sur de trop nombreux aspects. D'où le corps du droit des conflits armés qui représente un ensemble étonnamment dense et réglementé, proche d'un type de droit "administratif" international.[107] Il en va de même pour des structures institutionnelles complexes, comme celle mise sur pied pour l'exploitation des grands fonds marins (Zone).[108] Les dispositions de la Partie XI de la Convention de Montego Bay se lisent comme du vrai droit "administratif," détaillé et presque pédant.

3, pp. 252-53; F. Münch, "Die Martens'sche Klausel und die Grundlagen des Völkerrechts," ZaöRV, vol. 36, 1976, p. 347 et s.; S. Miyazaki, "The Martens Clause and International Humanitarian Law," *Mélanges J. Pictet*, Genève, 1984, p. 433 et s.; A. Cassese, "The Martens Clause: Half A Loaf or Simply Pie in the Sky?," EJIL, vol. 11, 2000, p. 187 et s.; T. Meron, "The Martens Clause, Principles of Humanity, and Dictates of Public Conscience," AJIL, vol. 94, 2000, p. 78 et s.

[105] Sur la nécessité militaire, cf. Y. Dinstein, "Military Necessity," EPIL, vol. III (J-P) (1997), pp. 395-97, avec quelques renvois. Voir W.G. Downey, "The Law of War and Military Necessity," AJIL, 1953, vol. 47, p. 251 et s.; G. Schwarzenberger, "Military Necessity: A Misnomer," *Mélanges S. Séfériadès*, vol. I, Athènes, 1961, p. 17 et s.; H. McCoubrey, "The Nature of the Modern Doctrine of Military Necessity," *Revue de droit militaire et de droit de la guerre*, vol. 30, 1991, p. 237 et s.; D. Fleck (dir.), *The Handbook of Humanitarian Law in Armed Conflicts*, Oxford, 1995, p. 30 et s.; P.A. Pillitu, *Lo stato di necessità nel diritto internazionale*, Pérouse, 1981, pp. 347-410. Pour la pratique, cf. M.M. Whiteman, *Digest of International Law*, vol. 10, Washington, 1963, p. 298 et s.

[106] Voir la remarque de Holland, reprise par H. Lauterpacht, et qui trouve une application particulièrement pertinente en matière de droit de la guerre: "International law is the vanishing point of jurisprudence ..." Cf. T.E. Holland, *Elements of Jurisprudence*, 6ᵉ éd. (1893), p. 339, cité par H. Lauterpacht, dans: Collected Papers de H. Lauterpacht (E. Lauterpacht, dir.), *International Law*, vol. I, Cambridge, 1970, p. 207.

[107] Cf. R. Kolb, "Aspects historiques de la relation entre le droit international humanitaire et les droits de l'homme," CYIL, vol. 37, 1999, pp. 94-95. Pour un aperçu des textes, cf. D. Schindler / J. Toman, *Droit des conflits armés*, Genève, 1996.

[108] Voir *supra* note 45.

2   *Phénomène du soft law international "administratif"*

Dans les années 1990, un nouveau phénomène est venu s'ad-
joindre à celui à peine décrit. C'est celui du *soft law* international
"administratif."[109] Des organes internationaux ou des conférences
mondiales consacrées à un sujet particulier n'hésitent pas à
édicter des textes extrêmement détaillés, prescrivant la conduite
attendue de la part des États. Ainsi, l'Agenda 21 adoptée dans
le cadre de la Conférence internationale de Rio sur l'environnement et le développement (1992)[110] est un document de 400
pages rempli de dispositions de détail. Le Sommet mondial pour le
développement social tenu à Copenhague en 1994 ou la quatrième
Conférence sur les femmes tenue à Pékin en 1995 ont produit des
textes similaires.[111] Dans une période d'interdépendances croissantes, ces textes remplacent des textes "administratifs" durs dont
l'absence de gouvernement international prive la société internationale. S'ils ne sont que des textes de *soft law,* ils tendent à produire
une pression normative et se présentent comme modèles pour s'attaquer aux problèmes dont ils traitent. En ce sens, ils offrent à la
communauté internationale un droit international "administratif"
de rechange.

B   LA PROLIFÉRATION DE TRIBUNAUX ET
     D'AUTRES INSTANCES DE RECOURS[112]

Depuis deux décennies, les tribunaux et autres instances de
recours se sont considérablement multipliés au niveau international. Par leur pratique, ces tribunaux secrètent un droit international toujours plus capillaire. Organes du droit plus que de la
politique, ils cherchent à fixer plus objectivement les conditions
d'application des règles générales en opérant ce pas de concrétisation dont il a été question plus haut. Toute jurisprudence tend à
préciser les notions plus ou moins vagues soumises à son attention
en les baignant dans le relief concret des espèces. Il s'en ensuit une
capillarisation progressive du corps normatif par une définition

---

[109] Voir l'aperçu chez Tomuschat, *supra* note 55, p. 68 et s. et C. Tomuschat, "The
Concluding Documents of World Order Conferences," *Mélanges K. Skubiszewski,*
La Haye e.a., 1996, p. 563 et s.

[110] Doc. N.U. A/CONF. 151/26I, Rev. 1.

[111] Cf. Tomuschat, Concluding . . . , *supra* note 109, pp. 564-67, avec les références.

[112] Cf. J. I. Charney, "Is International Law Threatened by Multiple International
Tribunals?" RCADI, vol. 271, 1998, p. 101 et s., avec des renvois.

plus précise des champs et des conditions d'application, des priorités et concurrences entre les normes, des rapports de règles et d'exception. Ainsi, des notions qui par leur généralité s'ouvraient au début à la subjectivité des représentations personnelles sont peu à peu objectivisées; elles sont enserrées dans des critères d'application déterminables *a priori*; elles finissent parfois par avoir dans le langage juridique un sens technique différent du langage commun. Cette objectivisation progressive des notions n'est rien d'autre qu'une juridification progressive de la matière. Un écart se creuse entre la norme et les activités sociales spontanées, entre la règle et les représentations des valeurs; la technique juridique s'y engouffre. Ce mouvement vers le droit est le propre de toute jurisprudence prétorienne.

Dans certaines branches du droit, l'institution du juge obligatoire et le recul des moyens de *self-help* sont déjà très avancés. On peut évoquer l'exemple de l'OMC et de son système de règlement des différends.[113] Par ailleurs, on peut faire état de la Cour internationale de Justice, de la Cour permanente d'arbitrage, du Tribunal irano-américain des réclamations, du Tribunal du droit de la mer, des Tribunaux pénaux internationaux *ad hoc,* des tribunaux administratifs internationaux, des Panels au sein de zones de libre échange (par exemple l'ALÉNA), des juridictions des droits de l'homme (Cour européenne des droits de l'homme, Cour interaméricaine des droits de l'homme, la future Cour africaine des droits de l'homme), etc. Dans certaines matières, la capillarisation offerte par la jurisprudence est remarquable. De fait, il est impossible de connaître le droit sans y avoir recours. C'est le cas notamment en matière de droits de l'homme,[114] d'interprétation ou de réserves aux traités,[115] de principes généraux de droit,[116] de

---

[113] Cf. H.U. Petersman, *The GATT/WTO Dispute Settlement System,* Londres / La Haye / Boston, 1996.

[114] Pour le système européen, cf. L.E. Pettiti / E. Decaux / P.H. Imbert (dir.), *La Convention européenne des droits de l'homme: commentaire article par article,* 2ᵉ éd., Paris, 1999; J.A. Frowein / W. Peukert, *Europäische Menschenrechtskonvention: EMRK-Kommentar,* 2ᵉ éd., Kehl / Strasbourg, 1996; D.J. Harris / M. O'Boyle / C. Warbrick, *Law of the European Convention on Human Rights,* London / Dublin / Edinburgh, 1995. Pour le Pacte des droits civils et politiques, cf. M. Nowak, *United Nations Covenant on Civil and Political Rights, Commentary,* Kehl / Strasbourg / Arlington, 1993.

[115] Cf. Charney, *supra* note 112, p. 139 et s.

[116] *Ibid.,* p. 189 et s.

responsabilité internationale[117] et des règles de compensation du dommage,[118] de l'épuisement des voies de recours internes,[119] des règles sur la nationalité d'individus et d'entreprises,[120] de délimitations terrestres et maritimes,[121] etc.

C   LA MULTIPLICATION DES INSTITUTIONS INTERNATIONALES

Les organisations internationales et autres organes internationaux se sont remarquablement multipliés depuis le début du XXᵉ siècle. Un peu comme les tribunaux, ces organes internationaux secrètent par leur pratique des règles détaillées dans leurs sphères d'action respectives. L'apport au droit international par des organisations internationales n'est pas négligeable.[122] Nombre de domaines du droit ont été façonnés soit par l'action normative, soit par l'action exécutive des organisations internationales, soit par les deux à la fois. Le droit international de coopération dont elles sont le gardien s'est intégré au sein même du droit international général.[123] Les organisations d'intégration comme les Communautés européennes sont allées plus loin: l'élément "administratif" et supranational y est prédominant. Dans les deux cas, qu'il s'agisse de coopération ou d'intégration, les Organisations forment des unités de "gouvernance" internationale. Comme tout exécutif, les normes et décisions qu'elles aident à forger relèvent en règle générale de ce niveau intermédiaire de type technique ou administratif. Il suffira ici d'évoquer les exemples de l'OMC en matière

---

[117] *Ibid.*, p. 237 et s.

[118] *Ibid.*, p. 265 et s.

[119] *Ibid.*, p. 285 et s.

[120] *Ibid.*, p. 303 et s.

[121] Pour les délimitations maritimes, *ibid.*, p. 315 et s. Pour les délimitations terrestres, cf. R. Kolb, dans: J.P. Müller / L. Wildhaber, *Praxis des Völkerrechts*, 3ᵉ éd., Berne, 2001, p. 317 et s.

[122] Cf. F.B. Sloan, *United Nations General Assembly Resolutions in Our Changing World*, New York, 1991; Abi-Saab, *supra* note 58, p. 154 et s.; E. McWhinney, *United Nations Law Making*, New York, 1984; I. Detter, *Law-Making By International Organizations*, Stockholm, 1965. Sur le droit des organisations internationales, voir p. ex. deux ouvrages récents: H.G. Schermers / N.M. Blokker, *International Institutional Law*, 3ᵉ éd., La Haye / Londres / Boston, 1999; M. Panebianco / G. Martino, *Elementi di diritto dell'organizzazione internazionale*, Milan, 1997.

[123] Cf. W. Friedmann, *The Changing Structure of International Law*, Londres, 1964, p. 60 et s.; M. Virally, "Panorama du droit international contemporain," RCADI, vol. 183, 1983-V, p. 247 et s.

de commerce international,[124] du Conseil de l'Europe en matière de démocratie et d'état de droit (allant du *standard setting* jusqu'aux visites dans les prisons),[125] des Commissions fluviales ou autres unions administratives dans leurs domaines respectifs, de l'OIT en matière de travail. L'OIT, par exemple, a codifié la matière du travail sous une perspective qui révèle une sensibilité certaine pour les droits de l'homme en se dotant d'un arsenal de 183 Conventions et 191 Recommandations.[126] Des questions telles que celle du travail forcé, du travail des femmes et des enfants, de la protection de la liberté syndicale, de l'élimination des discriminations au travail ou de la sécurité au travail ont été adressées.[127] Il est difficile de ne pas y voir une capillarisation "administrative" de cette branche du droit.

---

[124] Il convient d'ailleurs d'ajouter que le droit économique international (et désormais le droit de l'OMC) a été présenté par quelques auteurs comme un nouvel embryon de droit constitutionnel international. Cfr. E.U. Petersmann, *Constitutional Functions and Constitutional Problems of International Economic Law*, Fribourg, 1991; M. Hilf (dir.), *National Constitutions and International Economic Law*, Deventer / Boston, 1993; E.U. Petersmann, "Constitutionalism and International Adjudication: How to Constitutionalize the U.N. Dispute Settlement System," *New York University Journal of International Law and Politics*, vol. 31, 1999, p. 753 et s.; G. Evans, *Law-Making under the Trade Constitution—A Study in Legislating by World Trade Organization*, La Haye / Boston / Londres, 2000. Voir aussi J.H.H. Weiler, *The EU, the WTO and NAFTA: Towards a Common Law of International Trade*, Oxford, 2000. Outre la croissance d'un corps de règles d'une plus grande densité et précision, c'est parfois d'une Constitution matérielle, centrée sur un ordre économique libéral pourvu de ses propres mécanismes de régulation, qu'il est question. Ainsi, E.U. Petersmann (*Constitutional Functions ...*, *op. cit.*), p. XLI, écrit: "The self-imposed liberal international economic obligations can therefore serve 'constitutional functions' for a more liberal interpretation, application and agreed extension to foreign trade of the corresponding constitutional principles of democratic societies such as: transparent policy-making ('government by discussion'), non-discriminatory market access, separation and only limited delegation of government powers, public choice of proportionate policy instruments, 'due process' and judicial protection of equal freedoms, of competition and property rights in transnational economic transactions."

[125] Voir les publications du Conseil dès 1993, "Le Conseil de l'Europe, Activités et réalisations." Voir aussi *La Documentation française, Le Conseil de l'Europe, 50 ans au service de l'homme et du progrès social*, Paris, 1999; J.L. Burban, *Le Conseil de l'Europe*, 3ᵉ éd., Paris, 1996.

[126] État en août 2001. Ces textes peuvent être consultés sur Internet, à l'adresse suivante: <www.ilo.org/public/english/sitemap.htm>.

[127] Voir le bref aperçu dans Müller / Wildhaber, *supra* note 121, pp. 593-94.

VII CONCLUSION

Lors de sa longue histoire, le droit international public s'est présenté surtout comme un droit de principes plutôt que comme un droit de règles détaillées, nombreuses et ordonnées de manière cohérente. Avec les progrès de l'institutionnel, la fonction exécutive internationale prend forme et figure. Il s'établit un substratum encore bien mince de gouvernance internationale, tendant à s'orienter aux besoins de la société internationale. L'une des conséquences remarquables de cette évolution est l'émergence d'un nouveau type de droit international venant se placer au-dessous des grands principes du droit. Il s'agit d'un droit international de type "administratif," relativement dense et précis, axé sur les moyens plutôt que sur les buts. Ce droit est le revers normatif des organes de gouvernance internationale: l'institutionnel génère toujours du droit de type "administratif," alors que le relationnel[128] s'accommode parfaitement du seul "constitutionnel." Si ces tendances se poursuivent, la structure du droit international pourrait changer. À côté, et en partie à la place, du droit international de coexistence ou de coopération, pourrait venir s'ériger un droit international de gouvernance internationale (ou de la communauté internationale), s'inspirant davantage d'un modèle fédéral que d'un modèle de juxtaposition de pouvoirs. L'expression normative en serait "l'administrativisation" du droit international et le progrès parallèle de la *rule of law*. Il va de soi que les pas dans cette direction seront tout graduels et peut-être même très lents. Mais il serait bon de ne pas perdre de vue cette nouvelle dimension.

---

[128] Les termes "institutionnel" et "relationnel" comme paire opposée sont repris de R.-J. Dupuy, "Communauté internationale et disparités de développement," RCADI, vol. 165, 1979-IV, p. 46 et s. L'institutionnel correspond au droit international de coopération (organisation internationale), le relationnel au droit international de coexistence (inter-étatique).

Summary

The Constitutional Structure of Public International Law

This article focuses on international law as a law of principle ("constitutional law") much more than a law of detailed regulation ("administrative law"). After reviewing the history of, and reasons for, this characteristic, examples are provided to illustrate how the development of norms around basic principles sometimes allows for progressive flexibility (for example, through the common heritage principle) but sometimes strands an issue in the political realm, subject to the discretion of states (for example, self-determination). There follows a discussion of the consequences of this characteristic, namely, the significant role of politics in international law, its modest normative content, obstacles to its codification, its character as law-after-the-fact (principles generate state practice), its often imprecise concepts and terminology, and the lack of rule of law. Finally, the author explores the recent trend towards clarifying the corpus of international law, from the normative standpoint as well as that of international institutions, likely in due course to exude new law.

Sommaire

La structure constitutionnelle de droit international public

Cet article traite du droit international comme un droit de principes ("droit constitutionnel") bien plus qu'un droit de réglementation détaillée ("droit administratif"). Après un survol de l'origine historique et de la raison d'être de cette caractéristique du droit international, des exemples sont donnés pour illustrer comment le développement de normes autour de grands principes sert parfois les fins de la flexibilité progressive (par exemple à travers le principe du patrimoine commun), parfois en revanche vise à laisser une matière dans l'espace politique, à la discrétion des États (par exemple l'autodétermination). Puis sont abordées les conséquences de cette caractéristique, notamment, la place importante de l'action politique en droit international, la pauvreté normative du droit international, sa codification difficile, la création différée du droit (les principes génèrent la pratique des États), les flottements conceptuels et terminologiques fréquents, l'absence d'une rule of law. *Enfin est explorée la tendance récente à préciser le corpus de droit international, à la fois sur le plan normatif et celui des institutions internationales, aptes à formuler en temps et lieu du droit nouveau.*

In the Name of the International: The Supreme Court of Canada and the Internationalist Transformation of Canadian Private International Law

ROBERT WAI

PART 1: INTRODUCTION

Globalization and internationalization are pervasive in contemporary cultural, political, and economic policy discourses. Not surprisingly, a concern with internationalization and globalization increasingly characterizes the policy discourses of law. While the law often operates at a lag to broader social trends, it is sometimes more active in constituting such trends. This article is concerned with a striking episode of legal change oriented towards the perceived new realities of the international system, which occurred in the unlikely venue of private international law in Canada.

In a tetralogy of four cases released from 1990 to 1994,[1] the Supreme Court of Canada transformed the subject of private international law in terms of doctrine, policy, and overall approach. The speed and comprehensiveness of reform, change of direction in

Robert Wai, Associate Professor, Osgoode Hall Law School, York University, Toronto. This article is based on parts of an LL.M. thesis, which was submitted in 1995, and an S.J.D. dissertation, which was submitted in 2000, to Harvard Law School. My thanks for funding for graduate work that was provided by a Social Sciences and Humanities Research Council Doctoral Fellowship, a Law Foundation of British Columbia Graduate Fellowship, a Canada-US Fulbright Scholarship, and the Addison Brown Prize in Private International Law at Harvard Law School. I gratefully acknowledge the comments on relevant chapters of the dissertation by Bill Alford, Robert Howse, Kerry Rittich, and Anne-Marie Slaughter. Particular thanks to David Kennedy for his comments and for his supervision of my doctoral work at Harvard.

[1] *Morguard Investments Ltd.* v. *De Savoye*, [1990] 3 S.C.R. 1077 [hereinafter *Morguard*]; *Amchem Products Inc.* v. *British Columbia (WCB)*, [1993] 1 S.C.R. 897 [hereinafter *Amchem*]; *Hunt* v. *T & N plc*, [1993] 4 S.C.R. 289 [hereinafter *Hunt*]; and *Tolofson* v. *Jensen; Lucas (Litigation Guardian of)* v. *Gagnon*, [1994] 3 S.C.R. 1022 [hereinafter *Tolofson*].

policy orientation, and significance for related fields such as constitutional federalism are exceptional for common law reform in Canada. While not dramatic in comparison with, for example, the promulgation of the Canadian Charter of Rights and Freedoms in 1982,[2] the changes are significant given that they occurred in a legal subject that is dominated by judicial rather than legislative reform and one that has tended to change incrementally, if at all. As Peter North observed just before the tetralogy was released, change in private international law in Commonwealth jurisdictions was based on "reform, but not revolution."[3]

As notable as the doctrinal changes for the particular field of private international law are the multiple ways in which the tetralogy of Supreme Court of Canada judgments are connected to larger forces that are crucial for legal decision-making in Canada, in particular, the forces of internationalization and globalization. The effort of law-makers, including judges, to grapple with the consequences of significant levels of political, economic, cultural, and personal connections that cross national borders is a defining aspect of Canadian law-making today. The tetralogy is an excellent chance to examine the ways in which judges have responded to, and helped to shape, the processes of globalization. In particular, the tetralogy offers a striking study in judicial activism in reforming laws in the name of the international.[4]

The tetralogy of cases in Canada has not gone unnoticed. Both commentators and lower courts have wrestled with the significant issues broached by these cases. Moreover, there is a strong sense that the judgments constitute an unusual break in the normal activity in the field. Commentaries have proliferated, both critical and supportive, focusing on a number of angles, including the constitutional issues.[5] However, less attention has been paid to the study of the role of the Supreme Court of Canada in actively instituting legal reform that responds to, and helps to construct, Canadian law in an era of globalization.[6]

---

[2] Canadian Charter of Rights and Freedoms, Part 1 of the Constitution Act, 1982, being Schedule B to the Canada Act 1982 (U.K.), 1982, c. 11.

[3] P. North, "Reform but Not Revolution" (1990) 220 Rec. des Cours 1.

[4] For a critical assessment of Canadian policy reform instituted "in the name of globalization," see J. Laxer, *False God: How the Globalization Myth Has Imperiled Canada* (Toronto: Lester, 1993) at 3.

[5] See, for example, E. Edinger, "The Constitutionalization of the Conflict of Laws" (1995) 25 Can. Bus. L. J. 38.

[6] For a model examination of the crucial role of the European Court of Justice in

The judgments of the tetralogy show how the global becomes the local in Canadian legal life. Public international lawyers and international policymakers have often overlooked private law as an important venue for diplomacy and legislation. Yet private international law cases are an example of how international concerns can "touch down" in the lives and practice of lawyers and citizens who do not specialize in international relations. Almost all practising lawyers must have some familiarity with the conflict of laws — something that is still largely untrue of subjects of public international law, such as the laws of war or the laws of international trade regulation. In addition, an understanding of the arguments concerning the international realm in the tetralogy provides useful insight to those persons who face similar international considerations in subjects such as trade law, immigration, or criminal law.[7] At the most general level, the understanding of the international in the tetralogy feeds into, and evidences the importance in a particular legal field of, the debate about how Canadian society should respond to globalization and internationalization.

For scholars interested more generally in globalization, the Canadian tetralogy provides a concrete and particular study of the importance of ideas and beliefs to the reception and shaping of globalization processes.[8] As common law judgments, the tetralogy

---

actively constructing the process of European integration, see J.H.H. Weiler, "The Transformation of Europe" (1991) 100 Yale L. J. 2403. I explore the activist role of the Supreme Court of Canada under the leadership of Justice Gérard La Forest in internationalist reform in private international law as well as in other areas of Canadian law in R. Wai, "Justice Gérard La Forest and the Internationalist Turn in Canadian Jurisprudence," in R. Johnson and J. McEvoy, eds., *Gérard V. La Forest at the Supreme Court of Canada 1985-1997* (Winnipeg: Supreme Court of Canada Historical Society by the Canadian Legal History Project, 2000) 421.

[7] The connection of the judgments in private international law to decisions in other areas of Canadian law is explored in Wai, *supra* note 6.

[8] Legal studies of globalization can offer helpful detail to more amorphous and abstract studies of globalization and internationalization. From this perspective, this article is an effort to provide a "thick" description of a particular episode in the processes of globalization and internationalization, showing one venue where that process is reflected and instituted, and showing as well the connection of this episode to some of the larger social contexts and policy issues at stake in globalization. This is the approach invoked by many as the way forward for studies of globalization; see, for example, P. Cheah and B. Robbins, eds., *Cosmopolitics: Thinking and Feeling beyond the Nation* (Minneapolis: University of Minnesota Press, 1998). The concept of thick description is associated with the cultural anthropologist Clifford Geertz; see, for example, C. Geertz, *Local Knowledge: Further Essays in Interpretive Anthropology* (New York: Basic Books, 1983).

provides the opportunity to study texts that record the ideational character of globalization as the judges attempt to provide public reasons for their decisions. These judgments therefore provide an opportunity that is not available to more general, abstract, or macro-oriented studies of globalization.[9] A more detailed examination of the policy argumentation in the tetralogy with respect to international matters will hopefully bring out more clearly the manner in which the law both responds to and constructs the processes of globalization. It will also highlight some of the significant dangers and biases that might operate when internationalist reform occurs with inadequate attention to specific conditions.

To this end, the article proceeds in six stages. This introduction constitutes the first part. In the second part, the tetralogy of cases is described and the underlying policy views of the international are identified in key passages of the judgments. The third part of the article then compares two "modes" of internationalization in law — internationalization by international treaty and internationalization by "policy consciousness" — arguing that the tetralogy is a good example of the latter. The fourth part describes the main features of the overall approach to international matters contained in the tetralogy, identifying three strands of policy argumentation related to (1) an economic objective of facilitating international commerce; (2) a political objective of aiding interstate cooperation; and (3) a moral objective of promoting cosmopolitan fairness. It is then suggested that this vision of the international is similar to the vision found in three traditions of internationalism. The first tradition is the intellectual tradition of liberal internationalism, with its commitment to free trade, peaceful interstate cooperation, and cosmopolitan individualism. The second tradition is the national tradition of Canadian internationalism in

[9] A sense of the peculiar opportunity offered to study both the ideational and material aspects of globalization and its construction might explain the interest in fields related to private international law and international business law recently evidenced by leading figures from other disciplines who specialize in globalization such as the sociologists Pierre Bourdieu and Yves Dezalay (see, for example, P. Bourdieu, "Foreword," in Y. Dezalay and B. Garth, eds., *Dealing in Virtue: International Commercial Arbitration and the Construction of a Transnational Legal Order* (Chicago: Chicago University Press, 1996)), the systems theorist Gunther Teubner (see, for example, G. Teubner, ed., *Global Law without a State* (Aldershot, UK: Dartmouth, 1997)), and the political economist Saskia Sassen (see, for example, S. Sassen, *Losing Control? Sovereignty in an Age of Globalization* (New York: Columbia University Press, 1996); S. Sassen, *Globalization and Its Discontents: Essays on the New Mobility of People and Money* (New York: New Press, 1998)).

national identity, foreign policy, and legal culture. The third tradition is the disciplinary tradition of international lawyers committed to the expansion of international law and institutions to preserve international order and to achieve mutually beneficial objectives such as liberal international trade.

The fifth part critically analyzes the international public policy arguments that inform the legal reforms in the cases and identifies five general dangers in the tetralogy's approach to internationalist policy argumentation. It is argued that the internationalist public policy arguments used in the tetralogy are often misunderstood and naively applied by legal decision-makers, such as lower courts who must wrestle with the legacy of the tetralogy while lacking significant experience in addressing international affairs. At certain points in the tetralogy, the Supreme Court of Canada may have itself overstated the nature of the policy arguments for internationalization and reached decisions that contain contestable analyses of internationalization. I will attempt to show how countervailing or alternative considerations are relevant to each of the political, economic, and moral objectives that inform the legal reforms of the tetralogy.

A focus on the Supreme Court of Canada judgments demonstrates how a particular understanding and version of internationalism can occupy the space of "the" internationalist understanding of legal reform. Internationalism, like justice or fairness or the right, is contestable discursive terrain. There are in fact many internationalisms, each consisting of distinctive visions and priorities. It will be argued that the internationalist commitments in the tetralogy have controversial features, including a narrow commitment to transnational commerce, a naive understanding of interstate cooperation, and a shallow sense of cosmopolitan fairness to individuals. Although the Supreme Court of Canada judgments themselves may have used these internationalist objectives effectively in the tetralogy, in other cases these goals may be overstated and conflict with other legitimate goals, such as justice to individual parties and effective social regulation. The continuing development and usage of these cases requires a careful understanding of the nature and the limits of the vision of the international expressed in these cases. I conclude the fifth section of this article, therefore, by articulating several general cautions about using the internationalist reasoning in the tetralogy.

The article closes in its sixth section with a discussion of two specific issues in private international law in order to demonstrate what it would mean to have a richer discourse about international public policy in the development of Canadian private international law. While some key issues have been decided, many doctrinal issues remain to be resolved and the room for argumentation, even within seemingly settled doctrinal areas, remains very broad. A more critical approach to internationalist economic, political, and moral argumentation will hopefully encourage judges, legislators, practitioners, and commentators to deploy a more sophisticated understanding of the international system and its demands — an approach that rejects both naive internationalism and naive anti-internationalism. A legacy of sophisticated arguments about Canadian law in an international age would be still more significant than the already substantial reforms achieved by the tetralogy.

PART 2: THE TETRALOGY OF JUDGMENTS IN PRIVATE
           INTERNATIONAL LAW AT THE SUPREME COURT
           OF CANADA

It is widely acknowledged that the field of conflict of laws in Canada, which has traditionally been very stable, is now undergoing dramatic changes.[10] Legal change in this area is clearly identified with several decisions of the Supreme Court of Canada after years of limited jurisprudence from the court on conflict of laws. In particular, basic change was accomplished in a tetralogy of cases that include *Morguard Investments Ltd.* v. *De Savoye, Amchem Products Inc.* v. *British Columbia (WCB), Hunt* v. *T&N plc,* and *Tolofson* v. *Jensen.*[11] In these cases, the Supreme Court of Canada effected dramatic reform in each of the main subjects of the conflict of laws: recognition and enforcement, jurisdiction, and choice of law. It also made a crucial ruling concerning the conduct of discovery in inter-jurisdictional litigation. At the same time, the court instituted two fundamental changes in approach to the subject: first, it gave constitutional status to at least some of the rules of private international law and, second, it forcefully emphasized the importance of international public policy arguments in reasoning about private international law in Canada.

The following summary of the four judgments of the Supreme Court of Canada is not focused on the doctrinal implications of the

[10] See, for example, J-G. Castel, *Canadian Conflict of Laws,* 4th ed. (Toronto: Butterworths, 1997) c. 2; M. Baer, *et al.,* eds., *Private International Law in Common Law Canada* (Toronto: Emond Montgomery, 1997) at 4.

[11] All of these cases are cited in note 1.

decisions.[12] Rather, I focus on the language used in the decisions and observe that the judgments share a common vision of the international realm, which is argued to necessitate reform of the rules of private international law, both within the Canadian federation and at the international level.

MORGUARD INVESTMENTS LTD. V. DE SAVOYE [13]

The Supreme Court of Canada's judgment in *Morguard* is the foundational judgment for contemporary private international law in Canada, and it has become one of the most-cited and influential decisions in the theory and practice of Canadian law of the last decade. *Morguard* addressed the common law rules for recognition and enforcement of foreign judgments in Canada. The case concerned a default judgment rendered against a British Columbia defendant in an Alberta court. The plaintiff sought recognition and enforcement of the judgment in British Columbia, while the defendant relied on the lack of jurisdiction of the Alberta court, given his lack of presence or submission. A unanimous Supreme Court of Canada rejected the defence and held that Canadian common law courts should consider only whether the other state has a "real and substantial connection" to the action.[14] *Morguard*, thus, substantially increases the risk to defendants of following the common strategy of refusing to appear in the courts of a jurisdiction in which a plaintiff has commenced an action, thus permitting a default judgment to be made against them.[15]

---

[12] This is admirably done in a number of case comments and articles, some of which are referred to in the notes following; more generally, see Castel, *supra* note 10, especially c. 2.

[13] *Morguard*, *supra* note 1. For case commentary, see "Symposium: Recognition of Extraprovincial and Foreign Judgments" (1993) 22 Can. Bus. L. J. 1; J. Blom, "Conflict of Laws — Enforcement of Extraprovincial Default Judgments — Real and Substantial Connection: *Morguard Investments Ltd.* v. *De Savoye*" (1991) 70 Can. Bar Rev. 733; P. Glenn, "Foreign Judgments, the Common Law and the Constitution: *De Savoye* v. *Morguard Investments Ltd.*" (1992) 37 McGill L. J. 537.

[14] *Morguard*, *supra* note 1 at 1104-10.

[15] The uncertainty generated and the lowered standard meant that it would be very difficult for counsel to advise a client not to defend abroad. Moreover, once defence was begun, it is arguable that the party could be said to have voluntarily submitted. See Blom, *supra* note 13. The United States faced a similar situation at the International Court of Justice [hereinafter ICJ] in *Military and Paramilitary Activities in and against Nicaragua*, [1986] I.C.J. Rep. 14. The United States, by arguing on the jurisdiction point, was taken by some of the judges to have voluntarily submitted on the merits. This questionable interpretation of the nature

The reasoning in the judgment is of special interest because the court identified some of the general policy issues that it perceived to be at stake in the area of conflict of laws. The language used has often been cited by both lower courts[16] and by the Supreme Court of Canada itself in subsequent cases.[17] Justice Gérard La Forest, writing for the unanimous court, observed that

> [t]he common law regarding the recognition and enforcement of foreign judgments is firmly anchored in the principle of territoriality as interpreted and applied by the English courts in the 19th Century ... This principle reflects the fact, one of the basic tenets of international law, that sovereign states have exclusive jurisdiction in their own territory. As a concomitant to this, states are hesitant to exercise jurisdiction over matters that may take place in the territory of other states ... The English approach, we saw, was unthinkingly adopted by the courts of this country, even in relation to judgments given in sister provinces.[18]

Justice La Forest expressed serious doubts that the common law rules based on the English rules concerning recognition and enforcement of foreign judgments remained appropriate for the Canadian federation. However, he went much further by undertaking an analysis of the traditional rules of recognition and enforcement under contemporary international conditions:

> Modern states, however, cannot live in splendid isolation and do give effect to judgments given in other countries in certain circumstances ... This, it was thought, was in conformity with the requirements of comity, the informing principle of private international law, which has been stated to be the deference and respect due by other states to the actions of a state legitimately taken within its territory ...

> ... the real nature of the idea of comity, an idea based not simply on respect for the dictates of a foreign sovereign, but on the convenience, nay necessity, in a world where legal authority is divided among sovereign states of adopting a doctrine of this kind ...

> For my part, I much prefer the more complete formulation of the idea of comity adopted by the Supreme Court of the United States in *Hilton* v. *Guiyot*, 159 U.S. 113 (1895), at pp.163-4:

---

of ICJ jurisdiction has been severely criticized: see, for example, M. Reisman, *Systems of Control in International Adjudication and Arbitration* (Durham, NC: Duke University Press, 1992) c. 2.

[16] See "Symposium: Recognition of Extraprovincial and Foreign Judgments," *supra* note 13; J. Sullivan, "The Enforcement of Foreign Judgments in B.C. — Ten Years after Morguard" (2001) 59 The Advocate 399.

[17] For example, in *Amchem, supra* note 1 at 913-14; *Hunt, supra* note 1 at 321-28; *Tolofson, supra* note 1 at 1048-49.

[18] *Morguard, supra* note 1 at 1095.

... "Comity" in the legal sense, is neither a matter of absolute obligation, on the one hand, nor of mere courtesy and good will, upon the other. But it is the recognition which one nation allows within its territory to the legislative, executive or judicial acts of another nation, having due regard both to international duty and convenience, and to the rights of its own citizens or of other persons who are under the protection of its laws.[19]

Having invoked comity as the underlying international policy behind the traditional rules concerning recognition and enforcement, Justice La Forest signalled how the policy of comity and the rules connected with it must be adapted to a new international society in which the normative, economic, and political conditions of sovereignty have changed:

The world has changed since the above rules were developed in 19th century England. Modern means of travel and communications have made many of these 19th century concerns appear parochial. The business community operates in a world economy and we correctly speak of a world community even in the face of decentralized political and legal power. Accommodating the flow of wealth, skills and people across state lines has now become imperative. Under these circumstances, our approach to the recognition and enforcement of foreign judgments would appear ripe for reappraisal. Certainly, other countries, notably the United States and members of the European Economic Community, have adopted more generous rules for the recognition and enforcement of foreign judgments to the general advantage of litigants.[20]

These extraordinary passages are among the most important statements made by Canadian courts about the nature of contemporary international society. In addition, Justice La Forest's judgment posits a strong connection between the reform of particular rules on recognition and enforcement and this vision of new international realities. Specifically, he indicates that recognition and enforcement of foreign judgments by common law courts should occur so long as there is a "real and substantial connection" between the foreign court that has given the judgment and the action.[21] This test effects a more generous approach because "the *most* real and substantial connection is not required."[22]

Since the case involved two common law provinces of Canada, Justice La Forest also surveyed a range of issues related to federalism.

---

[19]   *Ibid.* at 1095-96.

[20]   *Ibid.* at 1098.

[21]   *Ibid.* at 1108-09. For a cautious critique of some ambiguities of this approach, see Blom, *supra* note 13.

[22]   Castel, *supra* note 10 at 44.

First, he signalled that the conditions of an international society are at least as present in the federal context, namely that the movement of wealth, skills, and peoples is a social reality and an accepted objective in Canada.[23] Second, he signalled that the reform of these rules would be consistent with the constitution of Canada. He cited an assortment of constitutional provisions, including mobility rights under section 6 of the Charter and the little-used federal customs union provision, section 121 of the Constitution Act, 1867.[24] These passages of the judgment suggested to many observers that the court was indicating that the Canadian constitution might require certain rules in the conflict of laws.[25] In the recognition and enforcement context, the judgment in *Morguard* seems to accept that the Canadian constitution contained provisions not unlike the US constitution's "full faith and credit" clause.[26]

The judgment left open several key issues. First, the exact contours of the real and substantial test were vague and were left to be developed gradually by lower courts.[27] Second, it was unclear whether the more generous approach to judgments from other Canadian provinces should also apply to the recognition and enforcement of foreign judgments from outside Canada.[28] Third, it was unclear whether the private international law rules were constitutionalized, given that it was unnecessary for the court to determine that issue in order to reach its decision on the case.

For the purposes of this article, however, what is central is the nature of the influential policy arguments about the international

---

[23] J. McEvoy, "Federalism, Territorialism and Justice La Forest," in Johnson and McEvoy, *supra* note 6 at 345.

[24] *Morguard, supra* note 1 at 1099. Constitution Act, 1867 (U.K.), 30 & 31 Vict., c. 3, reprinted in R.S.C. 1985, App. II, No. 5.

[25] Scholars of Canadian constitutional law and conflict of laws had been speculating on this possibility in the years preceeding *Morguard*. In particular, see J. Swan, "The Canadian Constitution, Federalism and the Conflict of Laws" (1985) 63 Can. Bar Rev. 271 and V. Black, "Enforcement of Judgments and the Conflict of Laws" (1989) 9 Oxford J. Leg. Studies 547, cited by the court in *Morguard, supra* note 1 at 1094.

[26] Article IV.1 of the US constitution provides that "[f]ull faith and Credit shall be given in each State to the public Acts, Records and Judicial Proceedings of every other State."

[27] See Blom, *supra* note 13.

[28] Lower courts have subsequently applied *Morguard* with respect to non-Canadian judgments; see J. Blom, "The Enforcement of Foreign Judgments: Morguard Goes Forth into the World" (1997) 28 Can. Bus. L. J. 373.

that were expressed in *Morguard* — policy arguments whose influence I will track in the succeeding judgments.

AMCHEM PRODUCTS INC. V. BRITISH COLUMBIA (WORKERS' COMPENSATION BOARD)[29]

The decision of the Supreme Court of Canada in *Amchem* is a crucial decision in a relatively discrete area of conflict of laws, namely the standards for issuance of anti-suit injunctions. In addition, the judgment has implications for the subject of jurisdiction more generally. The case concerned asbestos litigation in which a number of plaintiffs, most of whom were resident in British Columbia at the time of injury, brought suit in the state of Texas against a number of corporate defendants. The plaintiffs included the Workers' Compensation Board of British Columbia, which had subrogated interests by virtue of having paid disability or death benefits to workers whose health had allegedly been adversely affected by asbestos. On a motion by the defendants, the British Columbia Supreme Court in chambers issued an anti-suit injunction restraining the plaintiffs from continuing the US tort litigation.

In contrast to *Morguard,* the Supreme Court of Canada was dealing with an international dispute rather than a federal dispute. Moreover, Texas has been one of the most aggressive jurisdictions in the United States in assuming jurisdiction and has become a forum of choice for plaintiffs from all over North America and the world. The British Columbia courts and the Supreme Court of Canada, then, were wrestling with a jurisdiction that was perceived to be one of the most assertive in the world.

The history of asbestos litigation, of which this case was a part, made the outcome in *Amchem* that much more striking. Through the 1980s and 1990s, the proceedings on the tort claims had been dominated by complicated procedural strategies. Indeed, the procedural complexity of the litigation has generated a number of leading rulings on civil procedure and litigation practice, including two of the core decisions of the tetralogy.[30] The procedural

---

[29] *Amchem, supra* note 1. For commentary, see E. Edinger, "Conflict of Laws — Discretionary Principles — Forum Non Conveniens — Anti-Suit Injunctions: *Amchem Products Inc.* v. *British Columbia (Workers Compensation Board)*" (1993) 72 Can. Bar Rev. 366.

[30] In Canada, litigation and legislation related to asbestos has been the source of many leading decisions testing the limits of the rules of civil procedure, including the conflict of laws. The Supreme Court of Canada had heard only a few

manoeuvring at times rivalled that of such famous jurisdictional battles between United States and Commonwealth judges as the *Laker Airways* v. *Sabena* litigation.[31] In the background to the *Amchem* case were a series of injunctions by the British Columbia and the Texas courts that included anti-suit injunctions, anti-anti suit injunctions, and, arguably, an anti-anti-anti suit injunction.[32]

The issue directly before the court was the appropriate standard for the granting of an anti-suit injunction. The unanimous judgment of the five-member court, written by Justice John Sopinka but with Justice La Forest notable among the concurring members of the court, sets a very high standard for the granting of anti-suit injunctions. The test to be used has two stages. First, a court should consider whether the foreign court "could reasonably have concluded that there was no alternative forum that was clearly more appropriate."[33] In the second stage, a court should consider whether the injunction would "deprive the plaintiff of advantages in the foreign forum of which it would be unjust to deprive him."[34] Justice Sopinka noted that the result of these principles would be that no anti-suit injunction would be granted in situations where the "foreign court assumes jurisdiction on a basis that generally conforms to our rule of private international law relating to the *forum non conveniens.*"[35]

Among the identified policy reasons for this restrictive standard for granting anti-suit injunctions were concerns of comity. Justice Sopinka quoted the definition of comity from Justice La Forest's

---

years earlier an asbestos litigation case on the standard for dismissal of an action for failure to state a cause of action; *Hunt* v. *Carey Canada Inc.*, [1990] 2 S.C.R. 959. *Hunt, supra* note 1 arose out of the same asbestos litigation. Asbestos even plays a role in Canadian litigiousness at the interstate level of the World Trade Organization [hereinafter WTO]; see, for example, *European Communities — Measures Affecting Asbestos and Asbestos-Containing Products*, 18 September 2000, Doc. WT/DS135/R (Panel Report), 12 March 2001, Doc. WT/DS135/AB/R (Appellate Body Report), in which Canada unsuccessfully challenged French restrictions on the import of asbestos and asbestos products.

[31] *Laker Airways* v. *Sabena, Belgian World Airlines*, 731 F.2d 909 (1984). For a description of the *Laker Airways* litigation, see L. Collins, *Essays in International Litigation and the Conflict of Laws* (Oxford: Oxford University Press, 1994) at 110-16. The reaction of the US court in the *Laker Airways* litigation is mentioned in *Amchem, supra* note 1 at 913.

[32] *Amchem, supra* note 1 at 905-08.

[33] *Ibid.* at 932.

[34] *Ibid.*, quoting from *SNI Aérospatiale* v. *Lee Kui Jak*, [1987] 1 A.C. 871 (H.L) [hereinafter *Aérospatiale*].

[35] *Ibid.* at 934.

judgment in *Morguard*[36] and observed that anti-suit injunctions are generally considered to be inconsistent with comity. Although anti-suit injunctions are still needed because of the injustice that might be caused by courts of other jurisdictions inappropriately assuming jurisdiction, Justice Sopinka observed that Canadian courts should only entertain such applications where a "serious injustice will be occasioned as a result of the failure of a foreign court to decline jurisdiction."[37]

In the course of its judgment, the court confirmed the use of the *forum non conveniens* doctrine in Canada. Under the test for *forum non conveniens*, a court should grant a stay of proceedings if "the existence of a more appropriate forum" is clearly established.[38] The status of this doctrine had been unclear. An earlier Supreme Court of Canada case had signalled that it might be applicable in Canada, and many lower courts and academic commentators had supported it.[39] In *Amchem*, the Supreme Court of Canada approved of the use of the doctrine both in situations of service *ex juris* and in applications for a stay of proceedings. In its judgment, the court cited two House of Lords decisions of Lord Goff, *Spiliada Maritime Corp.* v. *Cansulex Ltd.* and *SNI Aérospatiale* v. *Lee Kui Jak*, which reformed the English rules with respect to *forum non conveniens* and to anti-suit injunctions.[40] In citing the House of Lords and Privy Council decisions so closely, as well as in its detailed survey of the English, United States, and Australian laws on anti-suit injunctions, the Supreme Court of Canada evidenced its comfort with continuing the well-established Canadian practice of judicial borrowing from foreign courts.[41]

The judgments in this case are less notable than the combination of the doctrines and the application in this particular case. The House of Lords decision in *Spiliada* and the Privy Council decision in *Aérospatiale* changed the English tests, but, in their application to the facts, the House of Lords signalled a much less deferential attitude. Ironically, the House of Lords in *Spiliada* refused to

---

[36] *Ibid.* at 914-15.

[37] *Ibid.* at 915.

[38] *Ibid.* at 921.

[39] *Antares Shipping Corp.* v. *The Ship "Capricorn,"* [1977] 2 S.C.R. 422.

[40] *Spiliada Maritime Corp.* v. *Cansulex Ltd.*, [1987] 1 A.C. 460 (H.L.) [hereinafter *Spiliada*]; *Aérospatiale, supra* note 34.

[41] See G.V. La Forest, "The Use of International and Foreign Material in the Supreme Court of Canada," in *Proceedings of the 1988 Conference of the Canadian Council of International Law* (Ottawa: Canadian Council on International Law, 1988) 230.

grant a stay of proceedings in England on *forum non conveniens* grounds in which British Columbia was the other jurisdiction with strong connections to the litigation.[42] Moreover, in *Aérospatiale*, the Privy Council held that an anti-suit injunction should be granted against a Texas court, which was the same jurisdiction that was involved in the *Amchem* case.

In the *Amchem* case, the Supreme Court of Canada was dealing with the courts of Texas, but, unlike the Privy Council in *Aérospatiale*, it applied the highly deferential standard it set out as the rule. The Supreme Court of Canada did so even though the Texas courts did not have at the time a doctrine of *forum non conveniens*,[43] a fact that seemed significant to the granting of the anti-suit injunction by both the trial court and the British Columbia Court of Appeal.[44] The trial court also seemed troubled by the anti-anti suit injunction that had been granted by the Texas court. In contrast, the Supreme Court of Canada, acting in a magnanimous fashion, focused on the issue of whether the Texas court had, on the particular facts at stake, acted in an unjust way. It concluded that while Texas did not have a *forum non conveniens* doctrine, it was not a clearly inappropriate forum in this case. There was enough of a connection that the court, while it may not have agreed that Texas was the best forum for the trial of these claims, gave the Texas court significant deference and refused to grant the anti-suit injunction.

Amchem carried the logic of the *Morguard* decision into the area of jurisdiction. By approving a lower standard for *forum non conveniens* and a high standard for anti-suit injunctions, the judgment set Canadian courts on a path wherein the assumption of jurisdiction was to be much more deferential towards foreign courts. Moreover, the *Amchem* decision suggested that the new generous, cooperative attitude of Canadian courts, which was developed in the *Morguard* decision, would apply *vis-à-vis* non-Canadian courts, including courts from even the most aggressive foreign jurisdictions.[45]

---

[42] See *Spiliada, supra* note 40 at 485-88.

[43] See L. Silberman, "Developments in Jurisdiction and *Forum Non Conveniens* in International Litigation: Thoughts on Reform and a Proposal for a Uniform Standard" (1993) 28 Tex. Int'l L. J. 501.

[44] See the discussion of the lower court judgments, *Amchem, supra* note 1 at 910-11.

[45] The willingness of the Canadian courts to accept *forum non conveniens* and to restrict anti-suit injunctions without seeking reciprocity generated favourable, if surprised, commentary in the United States; see, for example, A. Lowenfeld, "Forum Shopping, Antisuit Injunctions, Negative Declarations, and Related Tools of International Litigation" (1997) 91 Am. J. Int'l L. 314 at 323-24.

HUNT V. *T & N PLC*[46]

In *Hunt*, the Supreme Court of Canada addressed the procedural barriers to the conduct of cross-border civil litigation placed by a blocking statute. Provisions of the Quebec Business Concerns Records Act[47] prohibited the removal of documents from Québec for purposes of discovery in asbestos litigation proceedings in British Columbia. The case therefore concerned a procedural statute that could act as an effective barrier to litigation in a forum that had valid connections to the suit as well as being the forum chosen by the plaintiff. The British Columbia courts, on motions of the plaintiff for orders of discovery against the Québec defendants, ruled that the blocking statute of the sister province had to be respected. In order to avoid putting the defendants in an untenable position, no discovery order would be made by the British Columbia court.

In the Supreme Court of Canada, the majority concluded that the Quebec Business Concerns Records Act was constitutionally inapplicable with respect to litigation in another Canadian province. It left unclear whether these constitutional limits would also apply with respect to litigation in a non-Canadian jurisdiction. The judgment of the court, again written by Justice La Forest, observed that the clear purpose of the blocking statute was a decision by a provincial legislature to prevent the successful litigation of claims against asbestos companies in foreign jurisdictions, particularly suits in US courts. The fact that the legislature had a clear public purpose did not seem to argue for deference on the part of the court. Rather, the court focused on how this purpose was clearly problematic for international and federal comity:

The whole purpose of a blocking statute is to impede successful litigation or prosecution in other jurisdictions by refusing recognition and compliance with orders issued there. Everybody realizes that the whole point of blocking statutes is not to keep documents in the province, but rather to prevent compliance, and so the success of litigation outside the province that that province finds objectionable. This is no doubt part of sovereign

---

[46] *Hunt, supra* note 1. For commentary, see V. Black and W. MacKay, "Constitutional Alchemy in the Supreme Court: *Hunt* v. *T & N plc*" (1994) 5 N.J.C.L. 79; C. Walsh, "Conflict of Laws — Enforcement of Extra Provincial Judgments and *In Personam* Jurisdiction of Canadian Courts: *Hunt v. T & N plc*" (1994) 73 Can. Bar Rev. 394; Edinger, *supra* note 5; R. Wisner, "Uniformity, Diversity and Provincial Extraterritoriality" (1995) 40 McGill L. J. 759.

[47] Quebec Business Concerns Records Act, R.S.Q., c. D-12.

right, but it certainly runs counter to comity. In the political realm it leads to strict retaliatory laws and power struggles. And it discourages international commerce and efficient allocation and conduct of litigation. It has similar effects on the interprovincial level, effects that offend against the basic structure of the Canadian federation.[48]

The blocking statute ran counter to the values of comity, order, and fairness that had been central to the judgments in *Morguard* and *Amchem* and that had justified reform of the relevant common law rules. In this appeal, however, statutory provisions passed by a legislature were at stake rather than common law rules. The court's decision, therefore, rested on Canadian constitutional provisions of the federal division of powers, including the interpretation of provincial powers under section 92, in particular, section 92(13), which concerns "property and civil rights in the Province." Beyond a "pith and substance" analysis of section 92(13), Justice La Forest further invoked the diverse set of constitutional provisions that he had identified in *Morguard* and that, for him, provided the basic structure of the Canadian federation and demonstrated the "obvious intention of the Constitution to create a single country."[49] These diverse constitutional provisions included common citizenship, inter-provincial mobility (reflected in section 6 of the Charter), the Canadian common market (reflected in sections 91(2), 91(10), 121 and the peace, order, and good government clause), and the "unitary structure of the Canadian judicial system with the Supreme Court of Canada at its apex."[50]

Justice La Forest emphasized, seemingly more than any specific provision of the constitution, how the use of blocking statutes ran counter to the basic policies of economic efficiency and equality of treatment in a federal state:

It is inconceivable that in devising a scheme of union comprising a common market stretching from sea to sea, the Fathers of Confederation would have contemplated a situation where citizens would be effectively deprived of access to the ordinary courts in their jurisdiction in respect of transactions flowing from the existence of that common market. The resultant higher transactional costs for interprovincial transactions constitute an infringement on the unity and efficiency of the Canadian marketplace . . . as well as unfairness to the citizen.[51]

---

[48] *Hunt, supra* note 1 at 327.

[49] *Morguard, supra* note 1 at 1099, cited in *Hunt, supra* note 1 at 322.

[50] *Hunt, supra* note 1 at 322.

[51] *Ibid.* at 330.

For the court, the lack of order and fairness of provincial blocking statutes was highlighted by the fact that the basic rules of civil procedure were the same in the different provinces of Canada. Discovery would be available to a plaintiff if he or she brought an action in Québec or if both parties to the action had been from British Columbia, "[b]ut somehow, because of the fortuitous combination of litigation in British Columbia involving a defendant from Quebec or Ontario, the discovery process is barred."[52]

TOLOFSON V. *JENSEN; LUCAS (LITIGATION GUARDIAN OF)* V. *GAGNON* [53]

The Supreme Court of Canada's judgment in *Tolofson* completed the tetralogy by instituting reform in the area of choice of law. In turning to choice of law, the court addressed perhaps the most vexed area in conflict of laws: choice of law in tort. Choice of law in tort poses special difficulties partly because in contrast to cross-border contractual situations there is usually no opportunity for parties to indicate clearly that their legal relation is connected to the governing law of a particular jurisdiction.[54] Yet, choice of law rules in tort are important in private international relations because of the numerous situations where non-contractually related parties with connections to different jurisdictions will find themselves involved in a tort dispute. Moreover, international tort litigation is frequently large in scale and complex in its international connections. Environmental accidents and defective products, for example, can cause damage that spreads across many jurisdictional borders, especially given contemporary technology and the scope of the international market. Finally, tort law is the subject of private law that is most closely associated with broader public policy purposes, including deterrence and punishment.[55]

---

[52] *Ibid.* at 331.

[53] *Tolofson, supra* note 1. For commentary, see J.-G. Castel, "Back to the Future! Is the New 'Rigid' Choice of Law Rule for Interprovincial Torts Constitutionally Mandated?" (1995) 33 Osgoode Hall L. J. 35; P. Kincaid, "*Jensen* v. *Tolofson* and the Revolution in Tort Choice of Law" (1995) 74 Can. Bar Rev. 537.

[54] The tort/contract distinction can be overstated. Many disputes involve overlapping claims in contract and tort. Moreover, some tort claims involve situations with a transactional character where there are possibilities of bilateral bargaining and negotiation; see, for example, M. Whincop and M. Keyes, "The Market Tort in Private International Law" (1999) 19 Northwestern J. Int'l L. and Bus. 215.

[55] It is therefore not surprising that choice of law in tort was central to the development of the "governmental-interest analysis" approach in the United States; see,

In the United Kingdom and in many Commonwealth jurisdictions, a restrictive "double actionability" rule had prevailed with respect to choice of law in tort. The rule required that the accident be actionable under the rules of both the forum state (*lex fora*) and the state where the accident occurred *(lex loci delicti)*. The result was a two-pronged rule that effectively erected two barriers to recovery by plaintiffs. It was widely believed that this rule had to be reformed. In the judgment in *Tolofson,* Justice La Forest clearly signalled his dislike for the old rules:

> What strikes me about the Anglo-Canadian choice of law rules as developed over the past century is that they appear to have been applied with insufficient reference to the underlying reality in which they operate and to general principles that should apply in responding to that reality. Often the rules are mechanistically applied. At other times, they seem to be based on the expectations of the parties, a somewhat fictional concept, or a sense of "fairness" about the specific case, a reaction that is not subjected to analysis, but which seems to be born of disapproval of the rule adopted by a particular jurisdiction. The truth is that a system of law built on what a particular court considers to be the expectations of the parties or what it thinks is fair, without engaging in further probing about what it means by this, does not bear the hallmarks of a rational system of law.[56]

What is notable about the majority judgment that follows is not that the court chose reform but rather its choice of reform that was extreme in its simplicity. Following a decision of the Australian High Court,[57] the Supreme Court of Canada radically moved from the double actionability rule to a rigid *lex loci delicti* rule. The return to the rule for choice of law in tort that had applied in the early twentieth century was a surprising turn to many scholars of Canadian conflict of laws.[58] A number of less rigid alternatives to the *lex*

---

for example, *Babcock* v. *Jackson,* 12 N.Y. 2d 473 (1963); B. Currie, *Selected Essays on the Conflict of Laws* (Durham, NC: Duke University Press, 1963); L. Brilmayer, *Conflict of Laws,* 2nd ed. (Boston: Little, Brown, 1995) c. 2.

[56] *Tolofson, supra* note 1 at 1046-47. For commentary, see, for example, N. Guthrie, "'A Good Place to Shop': Choice of Forum and the Conflict of Laws" (1995) 27 Ottawa L. Rev. 201.

[57] In particular, the minority concurring opinion of Chief Justice Mason in *Breavington* v. *Godleman,* (1988), 80 A.L.R. 362 (Australia H.C.). The ratio of this case is almost unascertainable given the multiple judgments pulling in various directions. It is interesting that an equally muddy decision is also a leading case in English choice of law in tort; *Boys* v. *Chaplin,* [1971] A.C. 356 (H.L.). For a discussion of this case and its background in English choice of law in tort, see J. Morris, *The Conflict of Laws,* 4th ed. by J.D. McClean (London: Sweet and Maxwell, 1993) at 280-91.

[58] See, for example, Castel, *supra* note 53.

loci delicti rule existed. The idea of the "proper law of the tort," for example, as developed by John Morris, attempted to avoid rigidity and arbitrariness by assessing the various connecting factors of the tort to the different jurisdictions.[59] British legislation, which is based on proposals of the English and Scottish Law Commissions, implements rules based on a "place of the accident plus" formulation, which chooses the law of the place of the tort, but with a number of limited exceptions.[60]

The court's reasons for choosing the rigid rule evidences the priority of certain policy values for contemporary private international law, most of which had already been articulated in earlier cases of the court. Justice La Forest evoked the reforms in *Morguard* and *Hunt* for the idea that, with respect to rules of recognition and enforcement and jurisdiction of courts in transactions with ties to more than a single state, a plaintiff should generally be able to choose the jurisdiction most convenient to it, because such choice "fosters mobility and a world economy."[61] However, Justice La Forest also noted that courts have developed rules to restrict "overreaching," such as the "real and substantial connection" test with respect to recognition and enforcement of judgments and *forum non conveniens* analysis for refusal to exercise jurisdiction.[62]

What choice of law rule in tort is consistent with the view of the international system that was developed in *Morguard*, *Amchem*, and *Hunt*? Justice La Forest reasoned that

[f]rom the general principle that a state has exclusive jurisdiction within its own territory and that other states must under principles of comity respect the exercise of its jurisdiction within its own territory, it seems axiomatic to me that, at least as a general rule, the law to be applied in torts is the law of the place where the activity occurred, i.e., the *lex loci delicti.*[63]

The majority judgment of Justice La Forest cites a number of "practical considerations" for the choice of the *lex loci delicti* rule. First, he argues that the rule "has the advantage of certainty, ease of application and predictability."[64] Second, he argues that the territorial

---

[59] J. Morris, "The Proper Law of A Tort" (1951) 64 Harv. L. Rev. 881.

[60] Part III of the Private International Law (Miscellaneous Provisions) Act (U.K.) 1995. For a discussion of the Law Commission work that informed the new laws, see P. North, *Essays in Private International Law* (Oxford: Clarendon Press, 1993), c. 4.

[61] *Tolofson, supra* note 1 at 1049.

[62] *Ibid.*

[63] *Ibid.* at 1049-50.

[64] *Ibid.* at 1050.

rule accords with normal expectations of people. Third, he invokes the idea of international order in a world where no rule exists to single out the appropriate jurisdiction:

> If other states routinely applied their laws to activities taking place elsewhere, confusion would be the result. In our modern world of easy travel and with the emergence of a global economic order, chaotic situations would often result if the principle of territorial jurisdiction were not, at least generally, respected. Stability of transactions and well grounded legal expectations must be respected. Many activities within one state necessarily have impact in another, but a multiplicity of competing exercises of state power in respect of such activities must be avoided.[65]

Although the *lex loci delicti* rule would ensure that Canadian courts encouraged an orderly choice of law, the rule is controversial where many or all of the parties' connections, other than to their physical location at the time of the accident, are to jurisdictions other than the place of the accident and where the laws of the other relevant jurisdictions would lead to very different outcomes. This was the situation in the *Tolofson* case itself, in which the plaintiff infant passenger and the defendant driver (and, in the background, the driver's insurer) were both from British Columbia. Under the laws of Saskatchewan, which was the place of the accident, the plaintiff's claim would have been defeated by a guest passenger statute and a limitations period provision on suits by minors, while the same claim could have succeeded under the laws of British Columbia. In the face of such arguments, Justice La Forest maintained the importance of the *lex loci delicti* rule:

> I remain unconvinced by these arguments. These "public policy" arguments simply mean that the court does not approve of the law that the legislature having power to enact it within its territory has chosen to adopt. These laws are usually enacted on the basis of what are often perceived by those who make them as reasonable, though they may turn out to be unwise. The residents of the jurisdiction must put up with them until they are modified, and one does not ordinarily ignore the law of the land in favour of those who visit. True, it may be unfortunate for a plaintiff that he or she was a victim of a tort in one jurisdiction rather than another and so be unable to claim as much compensation as if it had occurred in another jurisdiction. But such differences are a concomitant of the territoriality principle. While, no doubt, as was observed in *Morguard*, the underlying principles of private international law are order and fairness, order comes first. Order is a precondition to justice.[66]

---

[65]   *Ibid.* at 1051.

[66]   *Ibid.* at 1058.

The majority invoked the idea of convergence in the underlying laws of different jurisdictions as a reason why the emphasis on order and certainty would not constitute significant injustice or defeated expectations:

I should add that the "public policy" problems, particularly between the provinces, tend to disappear over time. Ever since the launching of the *Tolofson* case, Saskatchewan has repealed its guest passenger statute and has changed the rule regarding the limitation period of minors. The biggest difference between provinces now is in insurance schemes, and this only creates problems of quantum, not of liability.[67]

Although such concerns would offer little comfort to the plaintiffs in the particular case, it seems that Justice La Forest and the court were focused on the broader issues of international and federal public policy.

PART 3: THE INTERNATIONALIZATION OF CANADIAN PRIVATE INTERNATIONAL LAW: TWO CONTRASTING MODES

The tetralogy has much to say about the need for the internationalist reform of traditional rules, and one way to understand the tetralogy is to view it as part of a process of the "internationalization" of Canadian private international law through the mechanisms of public international law. I will argue in the proceeding text that values that are important in public international law have much to do with the kinds of reforms and policy justifications made in the tetralogy. However, these values play an indirect role. What the tetralogy is not is the traditional use of public international law processes — whether customary or conventional international law — to reform private international law. Instead, in Canada, as in most non-European jurisdictions, private international law remains largely municipal in its sources and venues. What the tetralogy does involve is the triumph of a substantive vision and a set of policy objectives that are identifiably associated with the goals of public international law.

INTERNATIONALIZATION THROUGH INTERNATIONAL AGREEMENTS

International conventions have not traditionally been significant sources of the rules of private international law in common law jurisdictions, and the Supreme Court of Canada in the tetralogy does not institute legal reform of specific rules because the court

---

[67] *Ibid.* at 1059.

believed reforms were necessitated by binding international treaty commitments on the part of Canada. However, the decisions of the court do draw on, parallel, and augment some limited reforms instituted through the implementation of international conventions on related subjects.

Like most other common law jurisdictions, Canada has signed few of the conventions developed through the Hague Conference on Private International Law (Hague Conference).[68] The Hague conventions to which Canada is a party, such as the Convention on Service Abroad of Judicial and Extrajudicial Documents in Civil and Commercial Matters and the Convention on the Taking of Evidence Abroad in Civil and Commercial Matters,[69] concern matters of minor practical importance compared with the reforms instituted through the tetralogy. However, they can be viewed as precursors in their approach to facilitating mutually beneficial objectives through the use of cooperation among courts and diplomatic offices.[70]

International treaties and institutions have had their greatest impact in Canadian private international law with respect to arbitration. In 1986, Canada signed the Convention on the Recognition and Enforcement of Foreign Arbitral Awards (New York Convention), which both eased procedures for, and limited grounds for refusal of, the recognition and enforcement of foreign arbitral awards.[71] Federal and provincial legislation subsequently

---

[68] There are, in addition, the private international law provisions of specialized conventions such as the Convention for the Unification of Certain Rules Relating to International Carriage by Air, October 12, 1929, 137 L.N.T.S. 13, Can. T.S. 1947 No. 15, as amended by the Protocol to Amend the Convention for the Unification of Certain Rules Relating to International Carriage by Air, September 28, 1955, 478 U.N.T.S. 371, Can. T.S. 1964, No. 29.

[69] Convention on Service Abroad of Judicial and Extrajudicial Documents in Civil and Commercial Matters, November 15, 1965, 658 U.N.T.S. 163; Convention on the Taking of Evidence Abroad in Civil and Commercial Matters, March 18, 1970, 847 U.N.T.S. 241. See generally, G. Droz, "A Comment on the Role of the Hague Conference on Private International Law" (1994) 57 Law and Contemp. Probs. 3.

[70] For a sense of this hopeful cosmopolitan and internationalist sentiment, see, for example, T.M.C. Asser Institute, *The Influence of the Hague Conference on Private International Law: Selected Essays to Celebrate the 100th Anniversary of the Hague Conference on Private International Law* (Dordrecht: Martinus Nijhoff, 1993); Hague Conference on Private International Law, *Proceedings of the Seventeenth Session*, Tome 1 — Second Part, "Centenary" (La Haye: SDU Publishers, 1994-95).

[71] Convention on the Recognition and Enforcement of Foreign Arbitral Awards, June 10, 1958, 330 U.N.T.S. 38, Can. T.S. 1986 No. 43 [hereinafter New York Convention]. See J.-G. Castel *et al.*, eds., *The Canadian Law and Practice of*

implemented the New York Convention.[72] Canadian jurisdictions have since implemented legislation based on the 1985 United Nations Commission on International Trade Law (UNCITRAL) Model Law on International Commercial Arbitration.[73] The Canadian reforms were part of a broader international movement towards acceptance and promotion of international commercial arbitration.[74] The legislative acceptance of international commercial arbitration paralleled and, in important senses, anticipated the policy outlook that the Supreme Court of Canada adopted in the tetralogy.

The nature of the reforms in the Canadian law related to international commercial arbitration and the policy justifications for the reforms share many of the characteristics of the reforms and policy justifications in the tetralogy. The judicial acceptance of similar values is in some sense unsurprising. No arbitration system is self-executing. National courts are needed both to enforce arbitration clauses and to recognize and enforce arbitral awards.[75] Although the Supreme Court of Canada has not issued a judgment concerning the New York Convention and the UNCITRAL Model Law, lower courts in Canada have been very supportive of the relevant legislation and the use of arbitration. For example, lower courts have generally supported the arbitration legislation by staying court proceedings and enforcing arbitration clauses, restricting court interference with arbitration procedures, and limiting the judicial review of arbitral awards made in Canadian jurisdictions and of foreign arbitral awards.[76] This approach contrasts

---

International Trade with Particular Emphasis on Export and Import of Goods and Services, 2nd ed. (Toronto: Emond Montgomery, 1997) at 724-25.

[72] See J.B. Casey, *International and Domestic Commercial Arbitration* (Scarborough, ON: Carswell, 1992) (updated 1999), c. 2, for a review of the federal and provincial legislation.

[73] United Nations Commission on International Trade Law Model Law on International Commercial Arbitration, June 21, 1985, (1985) 24 I.L.M. 1302. For commentary on relevant Canadian law and practice, see Castel *et al., supra* note 71 at c. 21.

[74] Dezalay and Garth, *supra* note 9, provide a sophisticated sociological analysis of the establishment of international commercial arbitration in a number of different jurisdictions.

[75] The failure to fully attend to the role of national courts is one of the principal weaknesses of the account by Dezalay and Garth, *supra* note 9, of the establishment of the arbitration regime.

[76] For example, see the review of the legislative provisions and judicial interpretation related to international commercial arbitration in R. Pepper, "Why

with the greater suspicion that traditionally characterized the common law attitude towards international commercial arbitration. In *Burlington Northern Railroad Co.* v. *Canadian National Railway Co.*,[77] the Supreme Court of Canada, with Justice La Forest writing for the court, reinstated a trial decision enforcing an arbitration clause, adopting the reasons of a dissenting judge in the appellate court who adopted the view that it was

the very strong public policy of this jurisdiction that where parties have agreed by contract that they will have the arbitrators decide their claims, instead of resorting to Courts, the parties should be held to their contract.[78]

The fact that a similarly supportive stance towards international conventions and implementing legislation in private international law would probably have been adopted by the Supreme Court of Canada is demonstrated by its approach to the Convention on the Civil Aspects of International Child Abduction (Child Abduction Convention).[79] In *Thomson* v. *Thomson*,[80] a majority of the court interpreted the laws of Manitoba that implemented the Child Abduction Convention and held that a court deciding on the return of a child should not simply consider the best interests of the particular child as it would in a domestic custody hearing.[81] The majority also indicated that it would consider that an application for the return of a child under the convention would pre-empt a local custody application — in this case, a transitory order giving

---

Arbitrate?: Ontario's Recent Experience with Commercial Arbitration" (1998) 36 Osgoode Hall L. J. 807; Castel *et al.*, *supra* note 71 at c. 21; *Quintette Coal Ltd.* v. *Nippon Steel Corp.*, [1991] 1 W.W.R. 219 (B.C.C.A.), leave to appeal to S.C.C. refused [1990] 2 S.C.R. x.

[77] *Burlington Northern Railroad Co.* v. *Canadian National Railway Co.*, [1997] 1 S.C.R. 5.

[78] *Burlington Northern Railroad Co.* v. *Canadian National Railway* (1995), 7 B.C.L.R. (3d) 80 at 94 (B.C.C.A.), quoting from *Boart Weden AB* v. *NYA Stomnes AB* (1988), 41 B.L.R. 295 at 302-03 (Ont. H.C.).

[79] Convention on the Civil Aspects of International Child Abduction, October 25, 1980, Can. T.S. 1983 No. 35. This convention was also considered in *W.(V.)* v. *S.(D.)*, [1996] 2 S.C.R. 108; and briefly in *Gordon* v. *Goertz*, [1996] 2 S.C.R. 27 at 76-77, L'Heureux-Dubé J.

[80] *Thomson* v. *Thomson*, [1994] 3 S.C.R. 551 at 578-80, La Forest J. [hereinafter *Thomson*]. For commentary, see V. Black and C. Jones, Case Comment (1994) 12 C.F.L.Q. 321.

[81] Justices Claire L'Heureux-Dubé and Beverley McLachlin dissented on this point.

the mother interim custody while she proceeded with a custody application in Scotland. Rather, the court used its remedial flexibility to advance the "purpose and spirit" of the Child Abduction Convention by ordering the return of the child to Scotland from Canada under an undertaking from the Scottish father to commence custody proceedings expeditiously before a Scottish court and not to take physical custody of the child until a Scottish court permitted such custody.[82]

The New York Convention, the UNCITRAL Model Law on International Commercial Arbitration, and other important conventions on private international law that have been reached among various European jurisdictions,[83] as well as the Hague conventions, suggest to some commentators that private international law is shifting from development and reform focused on state courts to reform negotiated through international conventions and implemented through state legislation. The most recent effort for the internationalization of private international law through international conventions is the negotiation under the auspices of the Hague Conference to reach a multilateral convention on recognition and enforcement of judgments.[84] Unlike the earlier Hague conventions, this treaty would cover a core topic of private international law. However, a number of barriers exist to the successful completion of such a convention.[85] Furthermore, it is quite likely

---

[82] *Thomson, supra* note 80 at 605, La Forest J.

[83] Convention on Jurisdiction and the Enforcement of Judgments in Civil and Commercial Matters, September 27, 1968, 1262 U.N.T.S. 1653 [hereinafter Brussels Convention]; Convention on Jurisdiction and the Enforcement of Judgments in Civil and Commercial Matters, September 16, 1988, 1659 U.N.T.S. 13 [hereinafter Lugano Convention]; Convention on the Law Applicable to Contractual Obligations, June 19, 1980, 1605 U.N.T.S. 59 [hereinafter Rome Convention].

[84] For a useful discussion of the Hague Conference on Private International Law negotiations concerning a treaty for recognition and enforcement of judgments, see "Symposium Enforcing Judgments Abroad: The Global Challenge" (1998) 24 Brooklyn J. Int'l L. 1; A. von Mehren, "Recognition and Enforcement of Foreign Judgments: A New Approach For the Hague Conference?" (1994) 57 Law and Contemp. Probs. 271.

[85] V. Black, "Commodifying Justice for Global Free Trade: The Proposed Hague Judgments Convention" (2000) 38 Osgoode Hall L. J. 267. The Preliminary Draft Convention on Jurisdiction and Foreign Judgments in Civil and Commercial Matters was adopted by the Special Commission of the Hague Conference on October 30, 1999; text can be found online at <http://www.hcch.net/e/conventions/draft36e.html> (last modified: October 30, 1999).

that any such convention will include substantial room for variation with respect to municipal rules among different signatories.[86]

In addition to the practical difficulties of negotiating new international conventions, some further limits on the use of public international law as a mode for reform in private international law are demonstrated by the somewhat undisciplined use of international law materials by the Supreme Court of Canada in the tetralogy. The court's judgments frequently refer to international and comparative materials. For example, Justice La Forest's judgment in *Morguard* contrasted Canadian rules on recognition and enforcement with developments under the European conventions on recognition and enforcement of judgments.[87] One reading might be that the Canadian courts are engaged in a process of harmonization through dialogue with foreign and international legal systems[88] and incorporation of international law norms into Canadian law. However, as Stephen Toope has observed, the court has not developed a clear understanding of its use of either international conventions or customary international law.[89] At the same time, the court repeatedly invokes international materials as useful supports for interpreting and developing Canadian law. Such engagement with international materials permits some harmonization of rules, where the court feels inclined in that direction, but not where it disagrees with, or is uninformed about, customary or conventional international law. A lack of clarity with respect to the use of customary and conventional international law may partly be related to an effort by Canadian courts to bracket contentious issues of federalism, such as the status of the treaty implementation power, which is an issue to which I will return later in this article. For the

---

[86] R. Weintraub, "How Substantial Is Our Need for a Judgments-Recognition Convention and What Should We Bargain Away to Get It?" (1998) 24 Brooklyn J. Int'l L. 167.

[87] *Morguard*, *supra* note 1 at 1098 and 1100.

[88] See, for example, A. Bayefsky, *International Human Rights Law: Use in Canadian Charter of Rights and Freedoms Litigation* (Toronto: Butterworths, 1992); A.-M. Slaughter, "A Typology of Transjudicial Communication" (1994) 29 U. Richmond L. Rev. 99. The judges of the court frequently discuss this subject in speeches and articles; for example, La Forest, *supra* note 41; G.V. La Forest, "The Expanding Role of the Supreme Court of Canada in International Law Issues" (1996) 34 Can. Y.B. Int'l L. 89 at 97-100. Given the limited range of "appropriate" topics for judicial speeches, the prominence of this subject is suggestive of the consensus behind internationalism in Canada.

[89] S. Toope, "Canada and International Law," in *The Impact of International Law on the Practice of Law in Canada* (The Hague: Kluwer, 1999) 33 at 34-38.

purposes of this section, however, the undisciplined approach of Canadian courts to the use of international law sources supports the view that internationalization in private international law has not been primarily a matter of formally binding international law but, instead, more a matter of courts accepting and promoting internationalist policy values. This is reform through the mode of internationalist "consciousness."

INTERNATIONALIZATION BY INTERNATIONALIST "CONSCIOUSNESS"

The tetralogy evidences another, arguably more important, mode of internationalization of Canadian private international law — an internationalization of the "consciousness" of Canadian legal decision-makers at the level of overall approach and policy orientation.[90] Law operates as a link between norms and material consequences in various state apparatuses. In this sense, the tetralogy demonstrates the importance of "internationalism" as a set of beliefs that can have material effects both at the international level and at the municipal level. The judgments in the tetralogy repeatedly refer to the need to update traditional rules to meet the demands of contemporary international society.[91]

I believe that the tetralogy evidences a particular set of policy goals associated with internationalism. The facilitation of international commerce, the emphasis on comity and cooperation among state systems and courts, and the invocations against parochialism echo economic, political, and moral arguments familiar from other kinds of policy discourses concerning international relations and international society. In particular, I argue that significant characteristics of the policy vision found in the tetralogy track the economic, political, and moral aspirations of traditions of liberal internationalism. Focusing on the policy discussion in these four judgments offers an unusually salient opportunity to explore the different policy planks of liberal internationalist policy argumentation in law.

Even if the trend towards formal internationalization continues, I believe that a focus on internationalist policy consciousness in

90 For a related analysis, see H. Arthurs, "Globalization of the Mind: Canadian Elites and the Restructuring of Legal Fields" (1998) 12 Can. J. Law and Soc. 219.

91 This trope of reform is a constant in international law; see D. Kennedy, "A New World Order: Yesterday, Today and Tomorrow" (1994) 4 Transnat'l L. and Contemp. Probs. 329.

private international law is useful. This utility is partially due to the fact that the courts will continue to play a large role in addressing the many legal issues not subject to international conventions or national legislation.[92] In addition, the interpretation of treaties and legislation and the application of provisions to particular disputes is often not a mechanical exercise but rather a creative process that involves courts inevitably in policy analysis. Moreover, the legislators, negotiators, academics, and policymakers who formulate, negotiate, and implement international conventions in this area share many of the same conceptions of the international that were articulated by the court in the tetralogy. A critical assessment of these policy justifications should therefore be useful to legal actors involved in the internationalization trend, regardless of whether law reform in private international law remains in the hands of municipal courts or becomes the subject of international agreements.

Intellectual Contexts

Since law is both a material and ideational social phenomenon, the role of general ideas, outlooks, and sentiments in generating particular legal regimes is obvious. Precise connections are very difficult to track. One approach is to look towards a shared legal "consciousness" of a particular group or society at a particular time.[93] Something like a common "vision" or "sentiment" concerning the international system can be shared by a number of different legal actors in a legal system, including judges, diplomats, bureaucrats, legislators, practitioners, and business actors.

Other accounts utilize the idea of legal "cultures" to illuminate the importance of background norms and beliefs in international law.[94]

---

[92] The current situation in Britain is a good example of the continuing relevance of both traditions — international and municipal. One instance of the tensions generated by efforts to incorporate international conventions into a traditional common law subject are recent editions of the leading UK treatise; L. Collins, ed., *Dicey & Morris on the Conflict of Laws,* 12th ed. (London: Sweet and Maxwell, 1993) [hereinafter *Dicey & Morris*]. On this tension, see R. Wai, "Book Review of *Dicey & Morris on the Conflict of Laws,* edited by L. Collins" (1997) 8 Eur. J. Int'l L. 386.

[93] See, for example, D. Kennedy, "Toward an Historical Understanding of Legal Consciousness: The Case of *Classical* Legal Thought in America, 1850-1940" (1980) 3 Research in Law and Society.

[94] See, for example, O. Korhonen, *International Law Situated: An Analysis of the Lawyer's Stance towards Culture, History and Community* (The Hague: Kluwer, 2000), c. 2.

Some of this scholarship has emphasized that to understand why arguments about internationalist reform have such a ready audience one must have an understanding of the international law elite as sharing a disciplinary "culture," which disposes them towards a fundamental, basic commitment to "the simple idea that things go better when they go internationally."[95] Some recent work in international law, for example, has turned towards the biographical and professional class characteristics of legal decision-makers in order to illuminate some overlooked aspects of the discipline.[96] This approach to international law seems appropriate because so many of its leading figures have similar backgrounds and similar values. Indeed, public international lawyers have been famously described by Oscar Schachter as an "invisible college" whose members share certain subject interests and outlooks.[97]

Other scholarship traces the connections of the belief systems of international lawyers to the more general intellectual and cultural currents of their time.[98] An illustrative study that explores the ideas of disciplinary and broader cultures of internationalism is the

[95] D. Kennedy, "The Disciplines of International Law and Policy" (1999) 12 Leiden J. Int'l L. 9 at 23.

[96] See, for example, "The Academic as Cosmopolite: Legal Visions of International Governance in the Twentieth Century," in *On Violence, Money, Power and Culture: Reviewing the Internationalist Legacy: Proceedings of the 93rd Annual Meeting* (Washington DC: American Society of International Law, 2000), 325-31. In previous work, I attempted to provide some focus for this important aspect of international law by tracking the influence of the policy vision of the international system in the work and background of Justice La Forest, the leading judge on international law matters at the Supreme Court of Canada; Wai, *supra* note 6. Justice La Forest was the leading figure in the tetralogy as well. He wrote the majority judgment in three of the cases and was on the panel of five that decided the fourth. In the *Amchem* case, Justice Sopinka identifies his judgment as being consistent with the judgment and approach in *Morguard*; and in the later *Hunt* and *Tolofson* judgments, Justice La Forest in turn interprets the judgment in *Amchem* to be consistent with, and indeed an integrated component of, his vision for private international law in Canada.

[97] O. Schachter, "The Invisible College of International Lawyers" (1977) 72 Northwestern U. L. Rev. 217.

[98] Nathaniel Berman pioneered this approach in his studies of the connections between the international law of the inter-war period and concurrent ideas of modernism in culture and politics. See, for example, N. Berman, "Modernism, Nationalism, and the Rhetoric of Reconstruction" (1992) 4 Yale J. L. and Humanities 351; N. Berman, "'But the Alternative is Despair': European Nationalism and the Modernist Renewal of International Law" (1993) 106 Harv. L. Rev. 1792.

recent study of Sir Hersch Lauterpacht by Martti Koskenniemi.[99] Koskenniemi describes Lauterpacht's disciplinary efforts in international law as originating in a nineteenth-century "Victorian tradition," with "its liberal rationalism and its ideal of the rule of law, its belief in progress, its certainty about the sense and direction of history,"[100] and coming "to rest in a pragmatism of the 1960s, a pragmatism which by now may have spent whatever creative force it once had."[101] Koskenniemi's study demonstrates how the biographical and national contexts of Lauterpacht's position as a Jew in Austria help to explain Lauterpacht's "assimilation" strategy of support for the Victorian tradition and for legal cosmopolitanism.[102]

In what follows, I try to elaborate on some of the disciplinary and national contexts for the internationalism of the Supreme Court of Canada's judgments in private international law. I will then focus on how the judgments rely on a contemporary version of an internationalist vision that is a manifestation of the "liberal rationalism" that Koskenniemi attributes to Lauterpacht and to an important strand of the discipline of public international law.

Internationalist Consciousness and the Cosmopolitan Style
in International Law

In order to understand the policy vision of the international that was advanced in the tetralogy, it seems useful to explore the strong affinities of the internationalist values contained in the judgments with the belief-systems of a group of "cosmopolitan" post-Second World War public international lawyers. The Supreme Court of Canada's approach to the international system in many ways seems more familiar to public international lawyers than private international lawyers. Was the tetralogy, in effect, a diffuse conquest of private international law by the values, if not the processes, of public international law?

Recent analyses observe that many public international lawyers define their role to be part of a "project" of building international order through international law. Most international lawyers are engaged and committed to the project of expanding the domain of

---

[99] M. Koskenniemi, "Lauterpacht: The Victorian Tradition in International Law" (1997) 8 European J. Int'l L. 215.

[100] *Ibid.* at 216.

[101] *Ibid.* at 262.

[102] *Ibid.* at 228-33.

international law and institutions against the disorder of *realpolitik* and narrow national interests.[103] For this group, international law and institutions are without question better than a world of conflict and anarchy. Especially in the twentieth century, this grouping of international lawyers and policymakers have seen their role as an attempt to minimize the possibility of the descent of the anarchic international system into war and economic depression. International lawyers, no doubt, have understood the importance of sovereignty and national polities. From the perspective of maintaining a peaceful international order, however, the problem has never seemed to be excessive constraint of national sovereignty by international law and institutions.

The focus on the idea of a single set of values shared by international lawyers can obscure the fact that there are different approaches to the achievement of international law and order. A useful map for understanding the tetralogy is suggested by David Kennedy's analysis of the "international style" in post-Second World War law and policy. Kennedy considers that the post-Second World War debate on international law and policy has involved two distinct "styles," each committed to building the international order and to countering state sovereignty, but with different emphases.[104] On the one hand, "metropolitans" favour supranational institutional remedies modelled on those of the traditional nation-state, whether through the reassertion or revival of domestic institutions or, more likely, through the construction of parallel structures — regulatory boards, administrators, technocracies, courts — at the international level. On the other hand, "cosmopolitans" are less concerned with looking for such "traditional" institutional remedies and, instead, believe that international order and objectives can be achieved through the operation of a diffuse regime of policymakers with a shared internationalist policy outlook. As Kennedy observes of John Jackson, a leading US international trade lawyer, the concern of cosmopolitans was less with the establishment of strong international-level institutions and more with the goal of a "widespread and vigorous liberal spirit."[105]

The variation in styles does not affect the basic commitment of both cosmopolitans and metropolitans to the general idea that

---

[103] Kennedy, *supra* note 95.

[104] D. Kennedy, "The International Style in Postwar Law and Policy" (1994) Utah L. Rev. 7 at 28-29.

[105] *Ibid.* at 13.

there should be an "internationalist" solution that advances international-level goals. Such a commitment to the building of international institutions and international law can blind internationalists to some of the concomitant dangers of their solutions and marginalize certain types of alternative policies. The consequence is that for both cosmopolitans and metropolitans, "the sense of having rejected or replaced sovereignty works, perhaps ironically, to insulate the text from actual political conflict."[106]

The tetralogy of the Supreme Court of Canada demonstrates well the way in which a national court could effect internationalist reform through "cosmopolitan" means. This kind of reform shows how an internationalist-minded set of national legislators, bureaucrats, and judges worldwide could effect reform that would forward internationalist objectives through a "widespread and vigorous liberal spirit."[107]

A more metropolitan strand in private international law is perhaps best represented by the reform work of the Hague Conference. The conference is a good example of the eclectic mix of individuals that populate the world of policymaking in the field of private international law. The conference demonstrates a common culture of international lawyers and scholars, with similar backgrounds, training, and interests, but committed to the development of international treaties in the field of private international law. The conference has drafted numerous draft conventions, although few have significant numbers of signatories.[108] Currently, the Hague Conference is the negotiating venue for efforts to reach an international convention on recognition and enforcement of judgments.[109] In this process, the Hague Conference has itself been changing as it becomes subject to the hard-nosed world of trade law diplomacy and commercial interest bargaining.[110]

Metropolitan international law strategies such as the treaties of the Hague Conference have, so far, had limited impact on actual

---

[106] *Ibid.* at 29.

[107] *Ibid.* at 13.

[108] The only two conventions related to commercial matters that have been widely accepted concern relatively minor subjects: see discussion in note 69.

[109] See von Mehren, *supra* note 84.

[110] Black, *supra* note 85, observes that representation at these meetings is shifting from the grand old men of private international law to international trade diplomats. The latter may be more interested in the give-and-take of international negotiations than the search for common principles or issues of justice of older unification projects.

national rules of private international law. Much more important to internationalist reform have been the decisions of particular national courts. The private international law judgments of the Supreme Court of Canada fit well into the mode of the cosmopolitan internationalist national lawmaker, attempting to promote international values even in the absence of an international legal architecture. Unlike in fields such as public international law or international trade law, it is the courts that have been the most significant source of reform in Canadian private international law. In this sense, the tetralogy provides stronger examples of legal activism in the name of the international than the work of most public international law judges or scholars, as these municipal judges are law-makers in a way that most public international lawyers are not. The private international law context also demonstrates how a decentralized process of reform can lead to similar results across jurisdictions because of the prevalence of certain types of policy arguments in the mindset of key decision-makers — a kind of harmonization by shared vision and spirit.

What does this cosmopolitan spirit consist of? It continues to identify nationalism and statism as the values that pose the most serious threats of disorder.[111] In particular, the internationalist professional and disciplinary class often views itself as fighting tendencies within domestic governments and populations towards parochialism and narrow self-interest.[112] A lapse into parochialism jeopardizes mutually beneficial cooperation and public goods, including the benefits of international peace and a functioning international economy. The nightmare scenarios for the discipline of international lawyers are those of the interwar period, in which increasing militarism led to constant violent conflicts and eventually to world war, and economic nationalism led to the complete collapse of the trading system and economic depression. Avoiding such downward spirals is the key concern of cosmopolitan internationalists in public international law. In the tetralogy, we see the spread of these sentiments into a realm of law more removed from high politics.

One general danger of adopting the goals of public international law in private international law is that private international lawyers and most national judges hearing disputes in private international

---

[111] See, for example, T. Franck, "Clan and Superclan: Loyalty, Identity and Community in Law and Practice" (1996) 90 Am. J. Int'l L. 359.

[112] Kennedy, *supra* note 95.

law are not experts in the challenges of international conflicts and negotiations of state interests. Although gently cosmopolitan, private international lawyers and judges focus more specifically on rules justified by "lower" level concerns, such as fairness to the parties and the development of a workable scheme for domestic courts, rather than large-scale state concerns, such as peace and interstate trade. Few private international scholars and judges are familiar with the experience of public international lawyers or governmental officials engaged in security negotiations. Nor are they typically familiar with the hard-bargaining and unhappy compromises of trade law practitioners or negotiators. Many private international lawyers and judges have experienced the international as a realm of peaceful cooperation, economic exchange, cosmopolitan education, and multinational values. Ironically, this perspective may prepare the way for an uncritical embrace of internationalist values. Such an uncritical reception of internationalism is a particular danger in the Canadian context.

Canadian Legal Internationalism and Canadian International Legalism

The importance of traditions of internationalism and multilateralism in Canadian policymaking and identity-formation is also relevant to Canadian legal institutions and legal values. Contemporary Canadian lawmakers, including the judges of the tetralogy at the Supreme Court of Canada, operate in a national context that is marked by a commitment to internationalism and multilateralism. National context matters to internationalism. In the United States, international lawyers and cosmopolitan liberals, more generally, while being crucial in defining the academic discipline of international law, are largely marginal players in the mainstream of US politics and law-making.[113] In contrast, what was marginal in the United States has, especially in the post-Second World War period, become more the mainstream in Canada. Internationalist policy argumentation is much more positively received in Canada. Indeed, I will argue that this more favourable view of the international lapses, at times, into a naively simple support for the international.

Foreign and international elements are pervasive in Canadian law.[114] The imperial and commonwealth legacy remains very strong.

---

[113] *Ibid.* at 17-29.

[114] For a critical commentary on the sociology of a legal profession that has diminished ties to Canada, see Arthurs, *supra* note 90.

The availability of appeals to the Judicial Committee of the Privy Council from the Supreme Court of Canada was not formally discontinued until 1949.[115] More importantly, recourse by Canadian courts, lawyers, and scholars to British and Commonwealth court decisions and scholarly writings has continued to this day. Canadian law schools include an unusual amount of foreign materials in their teaching, and many Canadian legal academics are immigrants from Britain or other Commonwealth jurisdictions or are Canadians who have studied or worked abroad.[116]

A number of the judges of the Supreme Court of Canada have international experience through study or work abroad. Justice La Forest, the leading judge in the tetralogy, was raised in a bilingual, bicultural environment, completed graduate work at Oxford and Yale,[117] and was the author of the leading Canadian treatise on extradition.[118] Justice Frank Iacobucci did graduate work in England and worked in private practice in New York. Justice Louise Arbour, recently appointed to the court, was the former chief prosecutor for the International Criminal Tribunal for the Former Yugoslavia.[119] The Canadian judges participate actively in the

---

[115] See P. Hogg, *Constitutional Law of Canada*, 4th ed. (Toronto: Carswell, 1997) at section 8.2.

[116] For example, fourteen of the fifty-two full-time faculty at Osgoode Hall Law School in Toronto in the 1997-98 academic year received their legal training entirely outside of Canada. These included Peter Hogg, the current dean of the school and the author of the leading treatise on Canadian constitutional law, who is originally from New Zealand and was educated there and in Australia. In addition, forty-five of the fifty-two full-time faculty had at least one university degree from a non-Canadian university; *Osgoode Hall Law School of York University 1997-1998 Calendar* at 11-12.

[117] See, generally, Johnson and McEvoy, *supra* note 6.

[118] G.V. La Forest, *Extradition to and from Canada* (New Orleans: Hauser Press, 1961). The most recent edition is edited by Anne Warner La Forest, *La Forest's Extradition to and from Canada*, 3rd ed. (Aurora, ON: Canada Law Books, 1991). Justice La Forest was the leading authority at the court on extradition, and he wrote the court's judgments in a series of significant extradition cases; for example, *Canada* v. *Schmidt*, [1987] 1 S.C.R. 500; *McVey (Re)*; *McVey* v. *United States*, [1992] 3 S.C.R. 475; *Kindler* v. *Canada (Minister of Justice)*, [1991] 2 S.C.R. 779 [hereinafter *Kindler*]; *Reference Re Ng Extradition (Can.)*, [1991] 2 S.C.R. 858 [hereinafter *Re Ng Extradition*]. These cases offer an interesting parallel to the private international law judgments; see Wai, *supra* note 6.

[119] It is interesting to note the change in Justice Louise Arbour's approach to international matters as she moved from being a leading judge of Canadian criminal law to being the chief prosecutor for the International Criminal Tribunal for the Former Yugoslavia. As a domestic judge, Justice Arbour was a strong

formal and informal networks among courts and lawyers, which one commentator has variously labelled "transjudicial dialogue," "transgovernmentalism," and "judicial foreign policy."[120] The judges travel frequently and meet with judicial counterparts from other jurisdictions.[121]

This personal experience of the judges of the Supreme Court of Canada may contribute to internationalist trends in the court's judgments. At the level of sources, for example, Canadian courts now regularly cite US materials[122] and frequently discuss provisions of international law,[123] although in a fashion that is at times haphazard.[124] The tetralogy is filled with references to foreign and international materials. For example, the judgment in *Morguard* invokes the examples of the "full faith and credit" provisions in the United States and Australia constitutions, the European conventions on the recognition and enforcement of judgments, and the doctrine of comity in the United States.[125] The judgment in *Amchem*

---

defender of the rights of the accused. For example, in the decision of the Ontario Court of Appeal in *R.* v. *Finta* (1992), 92 D.L.R. 4th 1, she sided with a three-justice majority, which acquitted the accused war criminal. The failure of the appeal of that judgment at a deeply divided Supreme Court of Canada effectively emasculated Canadian domestic prosecution of accused war criminals from the Second World War; *R.* v. *Finta*, [1994] 1 S.C.R. 701. As chief prosecutor, the much less settled terrain of the war crimes prosecutions led to her development and advocacy of tools such as sealed indictments that it seems unlikely she would have accepted in a domestic context. Her return to Canada in 1999 as a member of the Supreme Court of Canada may see the pendulum switch back, as she may become a leading figure in a return to emphasis on underlying domestic values. For example, the Supreme Court of Canada effectively overruled *Kindler* and *Re Ng Extradition, supra* note 118, in finding that the Canadian Charter of Rights and Freedoms did not permit extradition of Canadian suspects to a US jurisdiction without assurances that they would not face the death penalty; *United States* v. *Burns*, [2001] 1 S.C.R. 283. This is a dramatic change and reflects a quite different conception of international criminal matters than that which the court, under Justice La Forest's lead, had been pursuing just one decade earlier; see Wai, *supra* note 6; E. Morgan, "In the Penal Colony: Internationalism and the Canadian Constitution" (1999) 49 U.T.L.J. 447.

[120] See A.-M. Slaughter, "The Real New World Order" (1997) 76 Foreign Affairs 183 at 186-89. See also Slaughter, *supra* note 88.

[121] Slaughter, *supra* note 120 at 188-89.

[122] G.V. La Forest, "The Use of American Precedent in Canadian Courts" (1994) 46 Maine L. Rev. 211.

[123] See, for example, Bayefsky, *supra* note 88; La Forest, *supra* note 41.

[124] See Toope, *supra* note 89.

[125] *Morguard, supra* note 1 at 1096, 1098, and 1100.

cites and discusses the important House of Lords decisions with respect to both *forum non conveniens* and anti-suit injunctions.[126] In contrast, even the most internationalist of US decisions[127] rarely cite, let alone seriously consider, international or comparative materials. The parochialism of US courts with respect to foreign and international law has been the source of comment both outside[128] and within the United States.[129]

The tetralogy and other international law decisions of the Supreme Court of Canada may simply reflect the significant traditions of internationalism in general Canadian policy discourse. This notion is partly due to the political and economic reality of a small national economy, which was formerly part of larger empires and more recently is highly integrated into the international economy, particularly with the United States.[130] Canadian political and cultural identities have also been bound up with foreign and international matters because of significant and continuing migration. As a consequence of immigration and Canadian policies of multiculturalism, many Canadians retain strong identifications with other national cultures.[131] Canadian foreign policy has involved a significant focus on multilateralism, with a strongly favourable view of international organizations and law as a place for Canada to play a "middle power" role.[132] In international law, Canadian legal

---

[126] *Amchem*, *supra* note 1 at 922-25.

[127] For example, the decision of the US Supreme Court in *Mitsubishi Motors Corp. v. Soler-Chrysler Plymouth Inc.*, 473 U.S. 614 (1985) [hereinafter *Mitsubishi Motors*].

[128] See La Forest, *supra* note 122 at 218-20.

[129] See H. Blackmun, "The Supreme Court and the Law of Nations" (1994) 104 Yale L. J. 39. For a critique of the common perception that US courts are xenophobic, see K. Clermont and T. Eisenberg, "Commentary: Xenophilia in American Courts" (1996) 109 Harv. L. Rev. 1120.

[130] See, for example, H. Innis, *The Fur Trade in Canada* (New Haven: Yale University Press, 1930); H. Innis, *Essays in Canadian Economic History* (Toronto: University of Toronto Press, 1956); R. Naylor, *Canada in the European Age 1453-1919* (Vancouver: New Star Books, 1987); K.R. Nossal, *The Politics of Canadian Foreign Policy*, 3d ed., (Scarborough, ON: Prentice Hall, 1997) at 29-31.

[131] See J. Holmes, *The Better Part of Valour: Essays on Canadian Diplomacy* (Toronto: McClelland and Stewart, 1970); for a skeptical view, see Nossal, *supra* note 130 at 57.

[132] See, for example, W. Kymlicka, *Multicultural Citizenship* (Oxford: Clarendon Press, 1995); C. Taylor, "The Politics of Recognition," in A. Gutmann, ed., *Multiculturalism* (Princeton, N.J.: Princeton University Press, 1994); C. Taylor, *Reconciling the Solitudes: Essays on Canadian Federalism and Nationalism* (Montreal: McGill-Queen's University Press, 1993).

academics have been significant advocates of multilateralism and the international cooperative approach.[133] David Kennedy's description of international lawyers in the difficult climate of the post-Second World War United States seems even more appropriate with respect to Canadian international lawyers:

> [L]egal internationalists in the United States tend to be humanist and liberal in the European sense; overwhelmingly committed to the idea that international law is a good thing, both inevitable and worth working quite hard for even against formidable odds. Their most significant disciplinary commitment is less to the politics of American liberalism than to the single idea that things go better when they go internationally.[134]

The strong traditions of internationalism in Canadian legal culture and in the policy community more generally do not automatically translate into internationalist legal reforms. It may be that on international matters, as in other areas, the Canadian courts operate at a lag to other Canadian institutions and to changes in Canadian social values. In *Morguard*, the court itself invoked this sense of law being at a lag to internationalizing tendencies in the broader society in order to bolster the case for the legal reforms undertaken in the judgment.

Hence, in the tetralogy, the court may simply be reflecting more general Canadian social values. However, courts also sometimes move in advance of broader opinion and can play a role in shaping policies and attitudes. Arguably, the Supreme Court of Canada judgments in private international law are an example of a court playing a leading role in constituting an internationalist system in both rules and values. In this role, the court can be compared to the role of the European Court of Justice in promoting the process of European integration.[135] The Supreme Court of Canada's role in promoting internationalist reform is perhaps more unexpected in that this was a national court rather than an international court.

---

[133] See, for example, R. St. J. Macdonald, G. Morris, and D. Johnston, "Canadian Approaches to International Law," in R. St. J. Macdonald, G. Morris, and D. Johnston, eds., *Canadian Perspectives on International Law and Organization* (Toronto: University of Toronto Press, 1974) 940 at 950-54. Canadian lawyers have been prominent in international institutions; for example, John Humphrey's role in the first years of the United Nations. More recently, Canadians have figured prominently in the operation of the war crimes tribunals for Rwanda and the Former Yugoslavia; see, for example, P. Knox, "Canadian Key Players at Hague Tribunal," *Globe and Mail* (July 17, 2001), A10.

[134] Kennedy, *supra* note 95 at 23.

[135] See, for example, Weiler, *supra* note 6.

No doubt, the Supreme Court of Canada in the tetralogy was both reflecting and deploying an internationalist vision in a national and disciplinary context in which these values already had some resonance. In doing so, the court instituted national legal reform by deploying a powerful, but a particular, internationalist vision. In addition to many benefits thereby achieved, there are clearly dangers in this mode of internationalization. Specifically, reform in the name of the international can fail to acknowledge that there are many internationalist goals and visions. Being for the international, even in Canada, should not be a simple matter.

PART 4: THE STRUCTURE OF INTERNATIONALIST POLICY ARGUMENTATION IN THE TETRALOGY

The previous section explained the modes of internationalism that were operating in the tetralogy of private international law cases of the Supreme Court of Canada. The following section describes in more detail the content of the particular internationalist visions advanced in the tetralogy. In the "cosmopolitan" internationalization in private international law, common structures of policy argumentation are more important than whether a decision-maker points to binding international law treaties or institutions to explain their decisions. While imperfectly articulated sentiments towards the international might form the bulk of internationalism in "a vigorously liberal spirit,"[136] I believe that this internationalist "spirit" can be described with somewhat more precision as involving a policy commitment towards some basic international values. Ultimately, these policy commitments may involve many indeterminacies and irrationalities, but they also provide the language and structure for the recognition and analysis of such indeterminacies and irrationalities.

STRUCTURES OF POLICY ARGUMENT

The policy argumentation behind the internationalist reform in the tetralogy powerfully invokes a set of political, economic, and moral arguments for an internationalist order. I believe that the policy concerns identified are associated with liberal internationalism and, in particular, policies related to international commerce, international cooperation, and cosmopolitan fairness.[137]

---

[136] Kennedy, *supra* note 104 at 13.

[137] Each of these policy objectives is discussed in detail in R. Wai, *Commerce, Cooperation, Cosmopolitanism: Private International Law and the Public Policy Structure of*

When combined, these policy concerns provide reinforcing justifications for particular legal reforms. They have special pull when the argumentation is deployed in contexts such as a cosmopolitan disciplinary consciousness or an internationalist national tradition such as those already described.

These types of policy justification for internationalist reforms have a heritage. All three can be traced back to the traditions of liberal internationalism and can be found in the work of liberal theorists such as John Stuart Mill and Immanuel Kant.[138] Liberal internationalist theorists have generated a system of reasoning about political and economic interests in which ideals of non-intervention and cooperative interaction achieved an underlying normative harmony of interests. At the political level, the ideal of non-intervention, perhaps backed up by either international institutions or the policies of powerful states, provides a means for sovereign states to achieve peace.[139] In the international economy, the ideal of a liberalized trading order replaced the mercantilist idea of conflict over a fixed set of economic goods with the liberal ideal of cooperative gains in worldwide production through international exchange and specialization based on principles of comparative advantage.[140] Even imperial relations were understood through the lens of a potential harmony of interests, although rife with problematic claims about the "needs" of barbarian peoples for the political, economic, and moral resources and guidance of the West.[141] Informing

---

Internationalism (S.J.D. dissertation, Harvard Law School, 2000) (on file at Harvard Law School Library).

[138] I track these arguments in John Stuart Mill's theories of international politics, international economics, and empire in R. Wai, *John Stuart Mill and International Relations* (M.Phil. thesis, Oxford University, 1990) [unpublished]. On liberal traditions of international relations and law, see A.-M. Slaughter, "International Law in a World of Liberal States" (1995) 6 European J. Int'l L. 503; T. Nardin and D. Mapel, *Traditions of International Ethics* (Cambridge: Cambridge University Press, 1992), chapters 7, 8, 10, and 12.

[139] See, for example, J.S. Mill, "A Few Words on Non-Intervention" (1859) in J.M. Robson, ed., *Collected Works of John Stuart Mill* (Toronto: University of Toronto Press, 1963-91), vol. XXI, *Essays on Law, Equality, and Education*, 109.

[140] See, for example, J.S. Mill, *The Principles of Political Economy*, 7th ed. (London: Longmans, Green and Company, 1909), Book III, chapters 17 and 18.

[141] See, for example, J.S. Mill, *Considerations on Representative Government* (1861) chapter XVIII ("Of the Government of Dependencies by a Free State"), in Robson, *supra* note 139, vol. XIX, *Essays on Politics and Society*; J.S. Mill, "Wakefield's The New British Province of South Australia," in Robson, *supra* note 139, vol. XXII, *Newspaper Writings*, 738; J.S. Mill, "England and Ireland," in Robson, *supra*

all of these concerns was a moral cosmopolitanism linked to a liberal individualism, which prioritized the rights or at least the interests of the individual over claims of nation, community, or the collective.[142]

As discussed earlier in this article, these liberal internationalist values of international commerce, cooperation, and cosmopolitanism have deep foundations in the discipline of public international law. Joseph Weiler observes that similar objectives of "prosperity, peace and supranationalism" were at work as "foundational ideals" in the building of the European Union.[143] For a Europe devastated by the political and economic catastrophes of the world wars, European integration was oriented towards the basic ideals of peace and prosperity. As to "supranationalism," Weiler means less a commitment to any particular institutional structure and more a sense, consistent with Enlightenment liberalism, in which the treatment of individuals would not depend on their state citizenship.[144]

CHARACTERIZING INTERNATIONALIST REFORM: COMMON FEATURES
OF INTERNATIONALIST REFORM

Although each of the doctrinal reforms in the tetralogy has distinctive features, some common characteristics do emerge. The connections between these doctrinal reforms have been observed by both supporters and critics.[145] At least four common characteristics of the reforms can be identified: an emphasis on greater certainty and predictability in rules (certainty), the promotion of

---

note 139, vol. VI, *Essays on England, Ireland, and the Empire*, 505; Mill, *supra* note 140, Book II, c. 13.

[142] The state or community instead is justified as instrumental to the interests or rights of individuals, rather than as an end in itself; see Wai, *supra* note 138 at c. 1.

[143] J. Weiler, *The Constitution of Europe* (Cambridge: Cambridge University Press, 1999) at 238-46.

[144] *Ibid.* at 252.

[145] See, for example, J.J. Fawcett, ed., *Declining Jurisdiction in Private International Law* (Oxford: Clarendon Press, 1995); T. Carbonneau, "Mitsubishi: the Folly of Quixotic Internationalism" (1986) 2 Arbitration Int'l 116 at 125; A. Lowenfeld, *International Litigation and the Quest for Reasonableness* (Oxford: Clarendon Press, 1996); J. Paul, "Comity in International Law" (1991) 32 Harv. Int'l L. J. 1. Paul groups many of these reforms under his more expansive definition of "comity." I believe that comity is more narrowly concerned with interstate cooperation, and so I prefer the term "internationalist policy" for the range of economic, political, and moral arguments required to support a practice of comity.

common standards across jurisdictions (uniformity), an increased deference to foreign laws and processes (comity), and a greater enforcement of party autonomy (autonomy).

First, a number of the reforms are intended to increase certainty and predictability in the rules and processes of private international law. For example, the move in *Tolofson* to choice of law rules based on the *lex loci delicti* arguably has the virtue of setting a rule that is simpler than one based on multiple different considerations and exceptions. Regular enforcement of foreign judgments as envisaged by *Morguard* is thought to assist parties to understand that they should defend foreign suits unless there is very clearly a lack of connection of the foreign jurisdiction to the action. Multilateral conventions, such as the Convention on Jurisdiction and the Enforcement of Judgments in Civil and Commercial Matters (Brussels Convention),[146] increase certainty by setting uniform grounds for jurisdiction and recognition and enforcement, and by reducing judicial discretion to stay actions or to refuse to recognize and enforce.

Second, the tetralogy's efforts to reform Canadian private international law in accordance with foreign practices can promote the objective of increasing the uniformity of private international law rules. Existing conventions, such as the New York Convention, as well as proposed conventions, such as the Hague Conference discussions with respect to recognition and enforcement of judgments, would clearly increase uniformity of private international law rules across jurisdictions. In *Tolofson*, the Supreme Court seemed to consider that a common rigid rule of choice of law in tort would help to control for variations in applicable laws that would invite forum shopping and cause uncertainty.[147] The turn to constitutionalization, which is suggested in *Morguard* and expressly decided in *Hunt*, places limits on the ability of provincial courts and legislatures to adopt completely different rules.

Third, the reforms share a policy of comity, in the sense of a greater respect and deference for the jurisdiction, the substantive laws, and the judgments of foreign jurisdictions. The eased standards for stays of actions based on *forum non conveniens*, the greater facility of recognition and enforcement, the discouragement of anti-suit injunctions, the use of choice of law rules based on factors other than the interest-analysis of the forum state, all involve municipal

---

[146] Brussels Convention, *supra* note 83.

[147] *Tolofson, supra* note 1 at 1052.

courts revising their approach to international cases in order to better recognize the laws and the courts of other jurisdictions.

Fourth, the reforms in the tetralogy reinforce party autonomy in dispute resolution. The restrictions on anti-suit injunctions set out in *Amchem* and the emphasis on comity in recognition and enforcement of foreign judgments articulated in *Morguard* increase the effectiveness of the choice by plaintiffs as to where to proceed with litigation. The tetralogy also occurs against a backdrop, most pronounced with respect to international arbitration, in which Canadian courts are increasingly reluctant to interfere with dispute-resolution processes that are agreed to by parties. Choice of law, forum selection, and arbitration clauses are increasingly supported by national courts.[148]

These general characteristics of internationalist reform in private international law are not very compelling as ends in themselves. For example, neither deference to foreign courts nor predictability of rules would seem to be worthwhile on their own. Rather, laws with such characteristics are justified because they serve more fundamental normative objectives. While the ultimate justification or motivation for any actual legal decision or legal reform is complex and can always be disputed, I posit significant explanatory power in background political, economic, and moral objectives related to the international system. An understanding of internationalist policy argumentation is an important part of contemporary policy debate in private international law and a significant concern and challenge for effective advocacy in the field.

COSMOPOLITANISM AND ANTI-PAROCHIALISM

The judgments of the tetralogy argue strongly for a cosmopolitan spirit in common law adjudication with respect to matters that cross provincial and national borders. In *Morguard*,[149] for example, the court stated that contemporary private international law should reject a parochial inclination to act only as if in a bounded world.

Traditional private international law is an easy target for a cosmopolitan critique because in its sources and orientation it is clearly a kind of municipal law. In terms of sources, issues of private international law are not, as has been discussed earlier, the subject

---

[148] See J-G. Castel and J. Walker, eds., *Canadian Conflict of Laws*, 5th ed. (Toronto: Butterworths, 2002) at sections 13.7 (forum selection), 31.2(a) (express choice of law in contract), 15.3-15.4 (arbitration clauses).

[149] *Morguard, supra* note 1 at 1098.

of either customary public international law or conventional public international law. Rather, domestic legislatures, and, in common law jurisdictions, the courts, have been the source of relevant laws.[150] In addition, in terms of policy orientation, private international law has focused on the policy concerns of the jurisdictions in which the courts or legislatures are situated. For example, the limited "public policy" exception in the common law rules on recognition and enforcement has been oriented towards the public policy of the court considering recognition, not the public policy concerns of foreign jurisdictions.[151]

Non-domestic concerns have played an indirect role in traditional private international law. Sometimes this role has been played through doctrines, such as the comity concerns of Joseph Story, which are thought to also be in the long-term self-interest of the jurisdiction in question.[152] At other times, cosmopolitan interests have, intentionally or not, been protected through rules, such as the vested rights approach of A.V. Dicey, which shift the focus away from domestic interests and onto the formal characteristics of different legal relations.[153] As often, cosmopolitanism has been a form of critique that has hovered over policy debate in private international law, calling on legislators and adjudicators to act in a non-parochial "spirit." It is this kind of reforming spirit that is brought to the fore in the tetralogy.

Cosmopolitanism argues that policymakers take a normative standpoint that includes the interests and values of individuals and societies outside of a defined state jurisdiction.[154] The cosmopolitan view argues that it is improper to restrict one's normative judgments to a consideration of the interests and values of the home jurisdiction. This normative approach, which has been associated with moral and political theories from natural law through global liberalism, rejects the identification of normative boundaries with juridical boundaries. A liberal theory of rights, for example, would

[150] *Dicey & Morris, supra* note 92 at 1-2; Castel, *supra* note 10 at 4-5.

[151] See, for example, *Dicey & Morris, supra* note 92 at 88-91.

[152] In J. Story, *Commentaries on the Conflict of Laws* (Boston: Hilliard, Gray and Company, 1834) at 34, Joseph Story notes that comity was based on the idea of laws which arise from mutual interest and utility, from a sense of the inconveniences that would result from a contrary doctrine, and from a sort of moral necessity to do justice in order that justice may be done to us in return.

[153] A.V. Dicey, *A Digest of the Law of England with Reference to the Conflict of Laws* (London: Stevens and Sons, 1896).

[154] T. Pogge, "Cosmopolitanism and Sovereignty" (1992) 103 Ethics 48.

question whether an individual with weak connections to the jurisdiction of a court and, hence, who is unable to vote or otherwise participate in the polity, is properly subject to the authority of the state's legal institutions.[155]

Such general theories of morality are sometimes useful in legal debate. They act as a reminder to state actors, such as common law judges, to consider more broadly the way in which moral obligations do not end at the border. To use Justice La Forest's phrase from the international criminal law context, "we are all our brother's keeper."[156] The claims of cosmopolitan concern are especially powerful as the number of social, political, economic, and cultural ties that cross borders increase due to the dramatic changes in communications, transportation, migration, and markets that we associate with globalization.[157]

Obviously, there is a limit to what cosmopolitanism can offer in terms of legal decision-making. The basic problem is simply that moral arguments of cosmopolitanism provide limited institutional guidance. As Thomas Pogge observes, moral cosmopolitanism does not equate to legal cosmopolitanism.[158] Moral cosmopolitanism is concerned with the belief "that all persons stand in certain moral relations to one another: we are required to respect one another's status as ultimate units of moral concern — a requirement that imposes limits on our conduct and, in particular, upon our efforts to construct institutional schemes."[159] This moral position may or may not support legal cosmopolitanism, which Pogge defines as involving "a concrete political ideal of a global order under which all persons have equivalent legal rights and duties, that is, are fellow citizens of a universal republic."[160] It seems clear that various

---

[155] Brilmayer, *supra* note 55 at 206.

[156] *R.* v. *Libman*, [1985] 2 S.C.R. 178 at 213-14.

[157] See, for example, A. von Mehren and D. Trautman, "Recognition of Foreign Adjudications: A Survey and A Suggested Approach" (1968) 81 Harv. L. Rev. 1601 at 1603:

> The ultimate justification for affording some degree of recognition is that if in our highly complex and interrelated world each community exhausted every possibility of insisting on its parochial interests, injustice would result and the normal patterns of life would be disrupted.

The court in *Morguard* quotes this passage, *supra* note 1 at 1097.

[158] Pogge, *supra* note 154 at 48-49.

[159] *Ibid.*

[160] *Ibid.* at 49.

kinds of institutional arrangements are consistent with moral cosmopolitanism. For example, instead of supranational government, cosmopolitans might also support the growth of international organizations or transnational processes such as the international market, telecommunications, and transportation, each of which seems to bypass governance through traditional forms of government.[161] Alternatively, some cosmopolitans believe that the creative use of international markets and transnational civil society networks can be combined with the preservation of the nation-state system to present an alternative to the need for supranational institutions or law.[162]

It follows that it is difficult to determine the implications of moral cosmopolitanism for specific doctrines of private international law. In order to generate more specific institutional recommendations, it seems that the cosmopolitanism expressed in the tetralogy is linked to, and identified with, two other general policy goals that are central commitments of liberal internationalism: on the economic level, support for international commerce and trade and, on the political level, support for interstate cooperation and comity.

TRADE AND COMMERCE

The internationalist reform in the tetralogy brings the discourse of international commerce into the area of private international law. In *Morguard*, for example, Justice La Forest, in a key passage, writes that "[t]he business community operates in a world economy even in the face of decentralized political and legal power. Accommodating the flow of wealth, skills and peoples across state lines has become imperative."[163] In *Tolofson*, Justice La Forest again invokes contemporary international economic order, and observes that "[s]tability of transactions and well grounded legal expectations must be respected."[164] The choice of a rigid choice of law rule of *lex loci delicti* was informed by the supposed value of a predictable and clear rule for the purposes of economic planning. Similarly, in *Hunt*, Justice La Forest observed that one of the problems of a

---

[161] This corresponds to the cosmopolitans identified by Kennedy, *supra* note 104 at 13.

[162] See, for example, Slaughter, *supra* note 120.

[163] *Morguard, supra* note 1 at 1096.

[164] *Tolofson, supra* note 1 at 1051.

blocking statute was that "it discourages international commerce and efficient allocation and conduct of litigation."[165]

The view that reform of traditional private international law is needed to promote international commerce is found in other internationalist reform venues, such as in the support for the Brussels Convention and the Convention on the Law Applicable to Contractual Obligations (Rome Convention) in Europe,[166] and in the push at the Hague Conference for a multilateral convention on jurisdiction and recognition and the enforcement of judgments.[167] The policy objective of promoting international commerce has registered as a powerful rhetorical tool even in jurisdictions where internationalist arguments normally are not persuasive.[168] The objective clearly impacts on other areas of law as well, such as with respect to doctrines concerning the commercial activity exception to sovereign immunity.[169]

International commerce is also increasingly advocated as an important policy objective among scholars and theorists of private international law. Although commercial concerns were often considered of secondary significance, the objective of facilitating international commerce was a long-established public policy goal in the foundational scholarship in private international law, for example,

---

[165] *Hunt, supra* note 1 at 327.

[166] Brussels and Rome Conventions, *supra* note 83. See, for example, *Report on the Convention on the Law Applicable to Contractual Obligations*, 1979 O.J. (C59) 1, 4-5 (*Giuliano-Lagarde Report*), reprinted in R. Plender, *The European Contracts Convention: The Rome Convention on the Choice of Law for Contracts*, Annex V (London: Sweet and Maxwell, 1991); *Dicey & Morris, supra* note 92 at 1195. For this view of the European regime, see R. Brand, "Recognition of Foreign Judgments as a Trade Law Issue: The Economics of Private International Law," in J. Bhandari and A. Sykes, eds., *Economic Dimensions in International Law: Comparative and Empirical Perspectives* (Cambridge: Cambridge University Press, 1997) 592.

[167] See, for example, Black, *supra* note 85.

[168] See, for example, the United States Supreme Court decision in *Mitsubishi Motors, supra* note 127 at 629-39 (per Blackmun J.). For a discussion of this case, *Morguard,* and the policy discourses of liberal internationalism, see R. Wai, "Transnational Liftoff and Juridical Touchdown: The Regulatory Function of Private International Law in an Era of Globalization" (2002) 40 Colum. J. Transnat'l Law 209 at 224-29.

[169] See R. Wai, "The Commercial Activity Exception to Sovereign Immunity and the Boundaries of Contemporary International Legalism," in C. Scott, ed., *Torture as Tort: Comparative Perspectives on the Development of Transnational Human Rights Litigation* (Oxford: Hart, 2001) 213.

in the work of Ulrik Huber[170]and Joseph Story.[171] Nonetheless, traditional private international law regimes have often been described by contemporary scholars as commercially dysfunctional.[172] Such writers criticize the system of national court adjudication as an archaic process that is based on sovereigntist conceptions that do not attend to the realities and the needs of the contemporary international economy.[173]

In contemporary policy discourse, the concern for international commerce connects two well-established sets of theoretical ideas, which are familiar policy objectives in other fields of law such as international trade regulation and the laws of international business transactions.[174] First, theorists concerned with international trade fear that national courts act as protectionist actors who use the play in the laws to advance national interests rather than the mutually beneficial objective of facilitating international transactions according to theories of comparative advantage.[175] Second, efficiency analysis and transaction cost analysis suggest that the patchwork of national conflict of laws regimes, in addition to the disparities in the underlying substantive laws of states, generate costly uncertainty,[176] lead to overlapping litigation processes that waste resources, and permit forum-shopping and other kinds of strategic behaviour by individual parties.[177]

---

[170] U. Huber, *De Conflictu Legum,* translated in D.J. Llewelyn Davies, "The Influence of Huber's *De Conflictu Legum* on English Private International Law" (1937) 18 Brit. Y.B. Int'l L. 49 at 65-66.

[171] Story, *supra* note 152 at 34. See more generally, D. Bederman, "Compulsory Pilotage, Public Policy and the Early Private International Law of Torts" (1990) 64 Tulane L.Rev. 1033.

[172] See, for example, Brand, *supra* note 166; M. Pryles, "Tort and Related Obligations in Private International Law" (1991) 227 Rec. des Cours 9.

[173] See, for example, Pryles, *supra* note 172 at 28.

[174] Brand, *supra* note 166, pairs these two kinds of arguments in advocating liberalized rules on recognition of judgments.

[175] See, for example, Brand, *supra* note 166 at 613-26.

[176] This concern is, of course, connected to the perpetual debate in most areas of law concerning the value of rules versus standards and certainty versus flexibility. See, for example, P. Hay, "Flexibility versus Predictability and Uniformity in Choice of Law: Reflections on Current European and United States Conflict Law" (1991) 226 Rec. des Cours 281.

[177] See, for example, M. Whincop and M. Keyes, *Policy and Pragmatism in the Conflict of Laws* (Aldershot UK: Ashgate, 2001) c. 8.

Transaction Costs

Theoretical support for internationalist reform of private international law is partly based on economic arguments that aggregate economic benefits are maximized by rules that promote predictability and uniformity and that thereby reduce transaction costs.[178] Reforms that increase uniformity and predictability are also thought to control the wasteful litigation costs associated with forum-shopping by plaintiffs.

Uncertainty makes it difficult to assess risk accurately, and, therefore, uncertainty increases transaction costs.[179] When risks are ascertainable, it is claimed, parties are able to allocate risks between themselves and undertake planning in that light, for example, through insurance, diversification, or reserve provisions.[180] However, an adequate assessment of risk is not always possible because of imperfect information. Uncertainty may prevent parties from allocating risks between themselves or to third parties in an optimal way.[181] In any event, risk assessment and allocation is not costless. Complex or unascertainable risk increases the cost of most transactions (for example, through the amount of an insurance premium), and it may prevent altogether some marginal transactions.

The objective of reducing transaction costs is served, it is claimed, by doctrinal reforms such as the clear international allocation of jurisdiction. In one such view, jurisdiction should be assumed only by the courts with the most significant connections to the dispute, a goal that is served by treaties such as the Brussels Convention and by doctrines such as *forum non conveniens*. Restraint by courts in assuming jurisdiction would restrict suits proceeding in multiple

---

[178] Transactions costs analysis in law builds from the foundational work of Ronald Coase; see, for example, R. Coase, *The Firm, the Market, and the Law* (Chicago: University of Chicago Press, 1988).

[179] See, for example, D.C. North, *Institutions, Institutional Change and Economic Performance* (Cambridge: Cambridge University Press, 1990) at 126.

[180] The importance and complexity of insurance for risk in international commerce is discussed in V. Haufler, *Dangerous Commerce: Insurance and the Management of International Risk* (Ithaca, NY: Cornell University Press, 1997).

[181] This could be done through contractual allocation between the parties, diversification, or insurance. The idea that parties cannot and do not allocate unknown risks has been disputed; see, for example, G. Triantis, "Contractual Allocations of Unknown Risks: A Critique of the Doctrine of Commercial Impracticability" (1992) 42 Univ. Toronto. L. J. 450; for a compromise view, see M. Trebilcock, *The Limits on Freedom of Contract*, (Cambridge, MA: Harvard University Press, 1993) at 127-28, 138, and 144.

jurisdictions or in jurisdictions with weak connections to the dispute and, thereby, would reduce litigation costs such as lawyers fees, travel costs, and time lost for witnesses and parties to attend process. Furthermore, both clear rules allocating jurisdiction and restraint through doctrines such as *forum non conveniens* would reduce the costs associated with the strategic behaviour related to the determination of the most appropriate jurisdiction.

Efficiency is also arguably served by respect for party choice of law and forum selection clauses, clear rules concerning choice of law, and easy recognition and enforcement of foreign judgments and arbitral awards across state borders. These reforms increase predictability and permit parties to formulate expectations and plan for contingencies arising out of potential legal disputes.[182] In addition, greater predictability will act as an incentive for parties to make rational assessments of the likelihood of success of different jurisdictional strategies and, hence, deter frivolous suits with limited likelihood of success.

Uniformity of rules across jurisdictions is also thought to reduce transaction costs by reducing the range of possible outcomes and easing the assessment of risks. The ideal would be the standardization of rules promoted by the implementation of international conventions, such as the New York Convention with respect to foreign arbitral awards or the Brussels or Rome Conventions in Europe. However, convergence on doctrines such as *forum non conveniens* would also serve this purpose.

Finally, granting parties to business transactions the autonomy and flexibility to structure their relations through contractual provisions such as choice of law and forum selection clauses might permit them to increase predictability and also to allocate risks optimally. Enforcing party choice as to private international law issues allows parties to make more predictable their potential liabilities, to reduce costly and inconvenient uncertainty, and to plan transactions and insurance accordingly.[183] More generally, reformist writers identify arbitration and other forms of alternative dispute resolution as a superior mode for resolution of international private disputes.[184] They link such forms to the *lex mercatoria* that

---

[182] P. Nygh, "The Reasonable Expectations of the Parties as a Guide to Choice of Law in Contract and Tort" (1995) 251 Rec. des Cours 268.

[183] North, *supra* note 60 at 183.

[184] J. Jackson, W. Davey, and A. Sykes, eds., *Legal Problems of International Economic Relations*, 3rd ed. (St. Paul, MN: West Publishing, 1995) at 73-81.

was developed in the period before the rise of the modern nation-state.[185] Party autonomy over dispute resolution is argued to limit defects of national court systems such as unpredictability over the applicable laws, the possibility of bias, and uncertainty over the quality and expertise of adjudicators.

Promoting International Trade

In addition to the objective of minimizing transaction costs in international commerce, internationalist reform to private international law rules also draws on the concern in international trade theory of achieving the aggregate benefits of international trade based on comparative economic advantage rather than trade dictated by the narrow interests protected by juridical boundaries of states. Rules of private international law and private law can be argued to operate as barriers to trade according to comparative advantage. International trade regulation has traditionally been most concerned with trade barriers involving border measures such as tariffs and quotas. However, as the international trade regulation regime has extended in scope and depth, regulation has become increasingly concerned with domestic policies that have either the aim or the effect of obstructing international trade such as internal taxes, intellectual property laws, technical standards, and health and safety regulations.[186]

The concern with domestic policies plausibly extends to private law and private international law. Private law and civil procedures may be governmental measures that have the purpose or the effect of discriminating against foreign producers in order to protect domestic producers. State legislatures and courts may favour domestic economic interests in a way that is harmful not just to particular foreign interests but also to global economic welfare.[187]

---

[185] See, for example, L. Trakman, *The Law Merchant: The Evolution of Commercial Law* (Littleton, CO: Fred B. Rothman, 1983).

[186] See, for example, J. Jackson, *The World Trading System: Law and Policy of International Economic Relations*, 2nd ed. (Cambridge, MA: MIT Press, 1997) at 130; F. Roessler, "Diverging Domestic Policies and Multilateral Trade Integration," in J. Bhagwati and R. Hudec, *Fair Trade and Harmonization: Prerequisites for Free Trade?* vol. 2 (Cambridge, MA: MIT Press 1996) 21.

[187] The potential links of private law and international trade are raised by the challenge in *Loewen Group Inc. and Raymond Loewen v. United States of America*, ICSID Case No. ARB(AF)/98/3, Notice of Claim, October 30, 1998 [hereinafter *Loewen v. United States*] under Chapter 11 of the North American Free Trade Agreement, December 17, 1992, Can T.S. 1994 No.2, (1993) 32 I.L.M. 605

Protectionism through private international law could come in various forms. For example, a court might decide whether or not to assume jurisdiction based on whether a plaintiff or defendant is from the jurisdiction. A court may be motivated to protect domestic interests in applying a choice of law rule rather than by attempting to figure out which substantive rule would be the most appropriate from an efficiency or regulatory perspective. Similarly, a jurisdiction might restrict recognition and enforcement of foreign judgments against defendants from its own jurisdiction, either through a blanket rule or through biased application of a discretionary standard.

The Québec legislation considered in the *Hunt* case seems, from an international trade perspective, to have been enacted for a protectionist purpose. As the Supreme Court of Canada noted, blocking statutes of this kind are intended to discourage suits in foreign jurisdictions against domestic defendants by making it procedurally more difficult for the foreign suit to proceed by, for example, impeding discovery or document production.[188] A more familiar example is found in the disputes between the United States and other jurisdictions concerning the enforcement of judgments obtained under the private litigation of antitrust suits. Many foreign jurisdictions have refused to enforce such judgments and, indeed, have legislated "clawback" provisions that permit defendants to recover any damages awarded to the plaintiffs in foreign antitrust litigation.[189] While genuine differences concerning antitrust policy are at stake, at least part of the concern of foreign governments is the effect of foreign antitrust laws on the economic welfare of businesses and industries based in their jurisdictions. Internationalist reforms can be partly viewed as attempts to ensure that such strategic behaviour does not occur through the mechanisms of private international law.

The most effective discipline on economic protectionism through private international law would be a binding international treaty among states such as the Brussels Convention. Short of such conventions, reforms with the characteristics of the tetralogy might

---

[hereinafter NAFTA]. This case is discussed later in this article under the heading "Recognition and Enforcement of Judgments: The Example of US Punitive Damage Awards."

[188] *Hunt, supra* note 1 at 327-28.

[189] See, for example, Protection of Trading Interests Act 1980, s. 6 (U.K.); Foreign Extraterritorial Measures Act, R.S.C. 1985, c. F-29, s. 9.

be justified as a partial control against protectionism. For example, protectionism could be discouraged through predictable rules such as the rigid *lex loci delicti* rule from *Tolofson* and through the use of *forum non conveniens* restraints as in *Amchem*. Similarly, respect for the choices of parties with respect to choice of law, forum-selection, and arbitration are thought to limit the potential biases of national courts to engage in *sub rosa* favouritism towards parties with domestic connections.

INTERSTATE COOPERATION

The objective of international trade according to comparative advantage is connected to perhaps the central internationalist policy objective of promoting interstate cooperation. The goal of cooperative interstate relations has figured less prominently in private international law, but the tetralogy has re-emphasized orderly and friendly inter-jurisdictional relations.

Cooperation in public international law is commonly used to support various forms of international institutions or treaties. In private international law, this awareness of inter-jurisdictional relations has been more associated with the spirit of comity. Comity would serve the purpose of promoting interstate cooperation through increased deference to foreign laws, through more restraint in assumption of jurisdiction, and through greater willingness to recognize foreign judgments. It is also reflected in the restrictions on the use of pre-emptive procedural tactics such as anti-suit injunctions, as in *Amchem*, or blocking statutes, as in *Hunt*.

Comity, which had not featured prominently in Canadian law, was elevated to a key principle of private international law in the *Morguard* decision.[190] Subsequently, the comity principle, and often the same quote from *Morguard*, has been repeated in lower court judgments and in other Supreme Court of Canada judgments, including the tetralogy. For example, in *Amchem*, Justice Sopinka quoted from *Morguard* for the proposition that comity would limit the use of anti-suit injunctions,[191] and he proceeded to conclude that the failure to respect comity was what might invite an anti-suit injunction from a Canadian court.[192] The constitutional analysis

---

[190] *Morguard, supra* note 1 at 1096-97.

[191] *Amchem, supra* note 1 at 913-14.

[192] *Ibid.* at 934.

of the blocking statute in *Hunt* also fixes on the "central" idea of comity from *Morguard*.[193]

The concerns for comity and cooperation are partly a concern with rationalizing unseemly and dangerous battles between different state courts. More importantly, it is based on a sense that cooperation is to the mutual benefit of all jurisdictions involved. Among these cooperative benefits would be the benefits of international commerce described earlier, but they also extend beyond commercial interests.

Regulating Interstate Dispute Settlement

Nothing is as central to public international law as the objective of an international process that will avoid recourse to armed conflict for settlement of international disputes. The concern with cooperative international process is also central to the effort of international trade law regimes to develop a multilateral process to replace the harmful spiral of unilateral tit-for-tat retaliation that undermines the cooperative benefits of liberal free trade.

There is a tendency to uncritically identify expanding legalistic process, even in fields such as private international law, with the greater achievement of interstate peace. A focus on legalistic court adjudication may distract attention from alternative international dispute settlement processes. Support for international legal process also has the tendency to abstract from the substantive justice of the underlying dispute. Nonetheless, the conduct of international relations through peaceful means remains a powerful basic justification for international law.[194]

Realizing Cooperative Benefits

The basic concern that interstate disputes be resolved by peaceful means is further augmented by the idea that cooperative institutions and binding rules assist the achievement of uncontroversial, mutually beneficial objectives. The challenge of international

---

[193] *Hunt, supra* note 1 at 321-27.

[194] It is arguably the achievement of this effect that informs all the obfuscation of doctrine, process, and institutions that David Kennedy has identified as being central to international law; D. Kennedy, *International Legal Structures* (Baden-Baden: Nomos Verl.-Ges., 1987). The important objective is that states, for all the obscurities introduced by international law doctrine and process, are at least arguing about their concerns in terms of law and in legal institutions, rather than in terms of, and using the instruments of, pure power.

anarchy, in which there is no overarching authority over states, is that sovereign states may fail to realize cooperative benefits, such as the productive gains of liberal free trade or international peace. A common way to explain the cooperative benefits objective in private international law is to use game theory models that have been widely applied in international relations.[195] For example, Larry Kramer and Lea Brilmayer deploy classic game theory models, such as Prisoner's Dilemma, the Stag Hunt, and the Game of Chicken, to illuminate choice of law problems.[196] These simple games are intended to model situations where short-term self-interest will lead participants towards outcomes that are less favourable to each of them than if they cooperate. Cooperation is impeded by the lack of trust and the absence of a coordinating authority to ensure that the other side does not cheat. In this context, parties are not able to make and enforce credible commitments to each other.

In the choice of law situation, for example, a game theoretic model suggests that autonomous states, through their own courts and perhaps under the instruction of legislatures, will define their own interest. Following the many choice of law approaches that lead them to prefer their own self-interest, they will apply forum law. If each jurisdiction makes this decision, however, there may be situations where all sides do less well than they would if each was less rigid in guarding its particular interest in every case. If appropriate institutions were developed, a court in State A might apply the law of State B in some situations in order that, in other situations, State B might apply the law of State A where State A may have a greater interest.

The best institutional solution would be a binding arrangement, such as an international treaty like the Brussels Convention, which

---

195 L. Kramer, "Rethinking Choice of Law" (1990) 90 Columbia L. Rev. 277 at 339-45; Brilmayer, *supra* note 55 at c. 4. For an early example of the use in international law of game theory models taken from international relations, see K. Abbott, "Modern International Relations Theory: A Prospectus for International Lawyers" (1989) 14 Yale J. Int'l L. 335.

196 Brilmayer, *supra* note 55 at 156. Modern game theory builds from the work of J. Von Neumann and O. Morgenstern, *Theory of Games and Economic Behavior* (Princeton, NJ: Princeton University Press, 1944). For the classic expositions of game theory and international relations and the texts most influential in international law, see T. Schelling, *The Strategy of Conflict* (Cambridge, MA: Harvard University Press, 1960) and R. Axelrod, *The Evolution of Cooperation* (New York: Basic Books, 1984). More generally on the use of game theory in law, see D. Baird, R. Gertner, and R. Picker, *Game Theory and the Law* (Cambridge, MA: Harvard University Press, 1994).

commits each state to act in a cooperative fashion. Similarly, federal constitutional provisions, such as the United States "full faith and credit" clause, permit parties to act cooperatively since states are committed to act in less parochial ways and other states can rely on such constrained behaviour. This kind of discipline is arguably what the Supreme Court of Canada is achieving through the constitutionalization of some limits on conflict of laws rules in *Morguard* and in *Hunt.*

Without such treaty-based or constitutional disciplines, principles of comity might encourage a rough form of reciprocity and cooperation.[197] Reciprocity is especially useful where there are repeated interactions and different states can get a better sense of which other states can be relied on to cooperate.[198] However, the difficulties for this sort of reciprocity are numerous, including insufficient iterations of the game, inadequate information on each state's interests or preferences, free rider problems, difficulties in monitoring defection, and complexities in coordinating judges within each state.[199] Nonetheless, cooperative benefits can be achieved in a "diffuse" manner and, over time, courts may genuinely take better account of the interests of foreign parties and jurisdictions, whether through notions of comity or doctrines that focus more on neutral factors such as vested rights.[200] In addition, emerging norms of cooperation, such as the comity doctrine or a rigid *lex loci delicti* rule with respect to tort, might provide "focal point solutions" for coordination.[201] This kind of rough reciprocity may be what the court was looking for in *Amchem* before granting an anti-suit injunction when it explored whether the foreign court had failed to observe the principles of comity with which Canadian courts were concerned.[202]

---

[197] Brilmayer, *supra* note 55 at 184-87; Axelrod, *supra* note 196.

[198] Kramer, *supra* note 195 at 342-44.

[199] *Ibid.* at 343, n. 228.

[200] Brilmayer, *supra* note 55 at 188-89 (contrasting "diffuse reciprocity" to "specific reciprocity"); Kramer, *supra* note 195 at 344, discusses the interesting example of the development of rules with respect to the recognition of foreign judgments in the pre-revolutionary era in the United States.

[201] Brilmayer, *supra* note 55 at 185. The concept is developed by Schelling in *The Strategy of Conflict, supra* note 196; Kramer, *supra* note 195. See also L. Kramer, "More Notes on Methods and Objectives in the Conflict of Laws" (1991) 24 Cornell Int'l L. J. 245.

[202] *Amchem, supra* note 1 at 934.

Convergence

The argument for achieving cooperative benefits even without binding international or constitutional laws is reinforced by a belief in the convergence in both the underlying private laws and the private international law rules of different jurisdictions around the world. Convergence in the laws and values of different jurisdictions seems to make it empirically more likely and morally more justified for courts to engage in a practice such as comity. In *Tolofson*, for example, the notion of convergence in applicable laws suggested to Justice La Forest that plaintiffs and defendants would not have much at stake in the different choice of laws.[203] In *Morguard*, a faith in shared basic values helps to explain why, with respect to rules of jurisdiction and recognition and enforcement, it would not really matter which court considered a claim so long as it had a real and substantial connection to the dispute.[204]

Such arguments recall theories of international relations that argue that a fundamental underlying convergence of values among states should make a difference to interstate relations. In particular, theorists developing insights from Kant have argued that liberal states infrequently go to war with other liberal states.[205] With respect to law, it is argued that, similarly, a convergence in domestic laws and values should lead to a distinctive pattern of international legal relations. Anne-Marie Slaughter, for example, contends that among liberal states there is more room for transnational dialogue among courts, with increased borrowing, cooperation, and comity.[206] Slaughter characterizes conflict of laws and choice of law in this situation of basic convergence of liberal values as a "reciprocal dialogue in which courts of different States engaged in a common

---

[203] *Tolofson, supra* note 1 at 1059.

[204] *Morguard, supra* note 1.

[205] The concept of the liberal peace is taken from I. Kant, "Perpetual Peace," in T. Humphrey, ed., *Perpetual Peace and Other Essays* (Indianapolis: Hackett Publishing Company, 1983). The modern restatement of the concept as an empirical claim concerning contemporary international relations is found in M. Doyle, "Kant, Liberal Legacies, and Foreign Affairs: Parts One and Two" (1983) 12 Philosophy and Public Affairs 205 and 325. See also B. Russett, *Grasping the Democratic Peace: Principles for a Post Cold-War World* (Princeton, NJ: Princeton University Press, 1993); A. Moravscik, "Taking Preferences Seriously: A Liberal Theory of International Politics" (1997) 51 International Organization 513.

[206] Slaughter, *supra* note 138.

endeavor to make transnational relations among individuals more certain and predictable while taking account of multiple State interests."[207] From this conception, it follows that (1) courts will face fewer constraints on their application of foreign law, (2) within a "zone of legitimate difference," courts will "presume the legitimacy of a wide range of different means to achieve similar ends" and will only refuse to apply a foreign law where "the potentially applicable laws reflect different choices as to which of those values should trump";[208] and (3) courts will recognize "a common core of political and economic values that will preserve roughly the same boundary between 'political' and 'legal' questions as would exist in domestic cases."[209] The process of transjudicial dialogue among the courts of liberal states will be reinforced by the "density and velocity of transnational transactions among liberal states," such as trade, which are leading to convergence in the underlying range of state laws.[210]

Convergence is thought to operate with respect to both rules of private international law and underlying substantive laws. For example, the Supreme Court of Canada in *Amchem* seemed to think it was presumptuous with respect to anti-suit injunctions to assume that a Texas court would not exercise appropriate restraint in its decision of whether to assume jurisdiction. However, both on the face of Texas laws and with respect to the conduct of the Texas court in the particular case, it was clear that the rules of private international law in Texas were very different from the Canadian rules being applied by the Supreme Court of Canada in its decision. In particular, the Canadian *forum non conveniens* analysis that the court approved in *Amchem* was specifically not part of the Texas law at that time.[211]

THE RELATIONSHIP AMONG INTERNATIONALIST POLICY VALUES

Each internationalist policy value has a separate logic and justification. In addition, internationalist policy values are often presented and understood as providing reinforcing, mutual support for the same kinds of reforms. For example, reforms that promote

---

[207] *Ibid.* at 524.

[208] *Ibid.* at 525.

[209] *Ibid.*

[210] *Ibid.* at 521.

[211] Silberman, *supra* note 43.

common and uniform rules are defended as aiding economic efficiency through increasing certainty and predictability, promoting cooperative behaviour through limits on strategic manipulation by different jurisdictions, and achieving cosmopolitan fairness by avoiding parochial application of local rules and standards. The sense of reciprocal support among goals as general as commerce, cooperation, and cosmopolitanism, however, permits two kinds of bootstrapping.

First, internationalist reforms are often presented as an overall package, which is then justified as the best available overall package of reforms. For example, reforms intended to strengthen the protection of contractual enforcement are lumped together with reforms geared to controlling the *de novo* review of recognition and enforcement of judgments, as if these two reforms were necessary to each other.

Second, reforms that are not fully sustainable under one of the policy goals are given additional, incremental support through the belief that they are at least partly consistent with the other policy goals. The linkage of economic arguments for free trade to arguments concerning the cosmopolitan case for free trade has a particularly strong rhetorical effect. The rhetoric of non-discrimination is central to the trade disciplines of the World Trade Organization (WTO) and the General Agreement on Tariffs and Trade (GATT), including, for example, the most-favoured-nation principle (non-discrimination among different trading partners) and the national treatment principle (non-discrimination between foreign and domestic parties).[212] Free traders often wrap the arguments for free movement of goods into a general claim that only this position is consistent with a moral cosmopolitanism that does not discriminate against foreigners.[213] It has been argued earlier in this article

---

[212] For example, Articles I and III of the General Agreement on Tariffs and Trade, October 30, 1947, 55 U.N.T.S 194, T.I.A.S. No. 1700 [hereinafter GATT].

[213] See, for example, Trebilcock, *supra* note 181 at c. 9. In that chapter, Trebilcock groups together as "discrimination," human rights discrimination, immigration policy, and restrictions on free trade. The connection between liberal attitudes towards free trade and to migration are also evoked in M. Trebilcock and R. Howse, *The Regulation of International Trade*, 2nd ed. (London: Routledge, 1999) at 1, 13, and 14. There are, however, arguably as many differences as similarities between these topics from a discrimination perspective. For example, the "discrimination" contained in trade restrictions often has less serious consequences for disadvantaged groups and such restrictions are also often justifiable in a way that the other kinds of discrimination are not.

that this connection is questionable if moral cosmopolitanism is properly distinguished from institutional or legal cosmopolitanism.[214] More generally, this approach fails to acknowledge that the three internationalist policy goals often do not each provide support for a particular internationalist reform. Indeed, sometimes the three internationalist goals can be in tension with each other. The examination of internationalist public policy values at high levels of generality and abstraction obscures the lack of mutual support and potential conflicts among the three values.

The linkage among international commerce, international cooperation, and cosmopolitanism has deep foundations in traditions of international liberalism. For example, the belief in the "civilizing" force of commerce on international affairs was an important part of liberal arguments for the virtues of a capitalist economic system. In early versions of this hypothesis, a growth in international commerce would create a sense of "interests" that would overcome irrational dynastic and imperial "passions."[215] Later British liberals, such as Jeremy Bentham, John Stuart Mill, Richard Cobden, and Norman Angell, argued that free trade would assist peace in a number of ways, including through a recognition that national economic self-interest was not served by military conflict and through the creation of a transnational class of cooperative interests whose self-interests would demand international peace.[216] In turn, webs of economic self-interest should reinforce the inclination against wasteful international political conflict.[217] Such

---

[214] See the section entitled "Cosmopolitanism and Anti-Parochialism" earlier in this article.

[215] See A.O. Hirschman, *The Passions and the Interests: Political Arguments for Capitalism before Its Triumph* (Princeton, NJ: Princeton University Press, 1977) at 79-82. Hirschman is mainly concerned with seventeenth- and eighteenth-century writers, such as Montesquieu and James Steuart. The idea of the *doux commerce* as a civilizing function continued on in liberal writings on international trade. For example, Mill ends his influential chapter on international trade with the observation that "the economical advantages of commerce are surpassed in importance by those of its effects which are intellectual and moral"; Mill, *supra* note 140 at 581-82.

[216] Joseph Nye labels these two categories of liberal internationalists as "commercial/trade" liberals and "sociological/transnational" liberals; see J. Nye, "Neorealism and Neoliberalism" (1988) 40 World Politics 235 at 245-47. More generally, see M. Ceadel, *Thinking about Peace and War* (Oxford: Oxford University Press, 1989) especially chapters 6 and 7.

[217] See, for example, R. Cobden, *Russia, 1836*, in R. Cobden, *Political Writings of Richard Cobden* (London: Unwin, 1903) 122 at 222-25.

historical conceptions of the interlocking importance of commerce, peace, and cosmopolitanism reinforce the sense that policy reforms directed towards any one of these objectives are also supported by the other policy objectives.

The grouping together of internationalist reform proposals as one overall package and the lumping together of the three internationalist policy goals to provide one overall justification of the reform package obscures careful consideration of internationalist reforms. Internationalist reform in private international law and more generally should not be understood simply as a package deal. Both the set of internationalist reforms and the package of internationalist policy justifications for such reform need to be disaggregated.

PART 5: THE HAZARDS OF NAIVE INTERNATIONALISM

As with many dramatic reforms, the Supreme Court of Canada's general approach to international issues and its application in private international law has limits and dangers. Two general kinds of problems with policy argumentation — false necessity and excluded objectives — also characterize the internationalist policy argumentation in the tetralogy. These concerns do not invalidate the kinds of policy concerns identified in the tetralogy, but they do complicate the policy analysis or reform prescriptions. The result is that rarely are there simple, general prescriptions that apply across fact situations without regard to particular circumstances. This section of the article will identify several kinds of complicating considerations for the international analysis of reform in private international law.

THE APPEAL OF THE COOPERATIVE VISION

I have described the power of policy justification in international affairs based on consent and cooperative benefit elsewhere.[218] The specific idea of building an international order that would ensure cooperation rather than conflict is central to the project of public international law. Somehow, through the right combination of laws and institutions, an international order can be achieved that will ensure that the potential harmony of interests among states will be realized. Modern western international law was to play a role

---

[218] See Wai, *supra* note 169.

analogous to that of law in the domestic context — to resolve conflicts among sovereign equals and to realize cooperative benefits.[219]

The ideal of cooperative benefit accords with popular welfare criteria in economics and in international relations. Internationalist law reform is argued to satisfy Pareto optimality in that such reforms make no party any worse off than it was before the reform.[220] Similarly, game theoretic models of international behaviour suggest that in some situations positive-sum gains to both sides are possible through cooperation.[221]

In international relations, the emphasis on cooperative benefit is especially important because it offers a normative stance that suggests potentially beneficial controls on state sovereignty, without requiring sacrifice by any state that would render such reform proposals seemingly unrealistic. This is especially important in international law because, as Martti Koskenniemi has argued, international law argumentation operates in the difficult terrain between apology and utopia.[222] International law discourse must constantly straddle between the realistic condition of an international system without a supranational sovereign entity and normative requirements to control sovereign behaviour in the name of global justice and order.

While the focus on inter-jurisdictional cooperative benefit seems convincing in realms such as the laws of war, there are clearly limits to what can be addressed and resolved under this rubric. The welfare criterion of cooperative benefit has the drawback of being unable to address more generally issues of distributive fairness. For example, baseline distributions between parties are not questioned nor are the relative shares of cooperative gains. Cooperative benefit brackets some of the most pressing problems by not taking on difficult issues of distributive justice, regulation, and human rights.[223]

---

[219] M. Koskenniemi, *From Apology to Utopia: The Structure of International Legal Argument* (Helsinki: Finnish Lawyers' Publishing Company, 1989) at 55-73. Koskenniemi considers the view of the Westphalian Peace as a form of "social contract" in which the liberal structure of politics was adopted into international relations in Europe (at 73).

[220] On the Pareto criteria in welfare economics, see, for example, Trebilcock, *supra* note 181 at 7-8.

[221] For a survey of rational cooperation models and international law, see D. Snidal, "Political Economy and International Institutions" (1996) 16 Int'l Rev. L. and Econ. 121.

[222] Koskenniemi, *supra* note 219.

[223] See Wai, *supra* note 169 at 235-39 (limits on arguments from cooperative benefit).

TWO KINDS OF ERRORS

Partially because of the powerful pull of the cooperative internationalist vision, there is a danger in the tetralogy of a kind of naive internationalism. Internationalism is too often misunderstood as a single coherent position. Although internationalist policy objectives such as facilitating international commerce or interstate cooperation are worthwhile goals, there are identifiable gaps between the policy objectives and particular legal consequences in any particular subject of private international law. In addition, these policy objectives do not exhaust the range of policy concerns that seem consistent with an internationalist or cosmopolitan viewpoint in private international law.

False Necessity

The first kind of critique made in dealing with each of the arguments from commerce, cooperation, and cosmopolitanism focuses on the gap that exists between such general policy objectives and the particular institutional or doctrinal reforms that have been advocated.[224] Inattention to the gap between general internationalist policy goals and particular legal reforms also obscures the possibility that arguments for commerce, cooperation, and cosmopolitanism may be in conflict with each other rather than being mutually supportive, as advocates of internationalist reform in private international law tend to assume.

For example, the goal of promoting international cooperation, with its ideal of cooperation for mutual benefit, is not that useful to private international law because most of the key issues in private international law involve situations of what Joseph Singer has

---

[224] This, of course, is a version of the Holmesian dictum from *Lochner* v. *New York*, 198 U.S. 45 at 76 (1905), Holmes J., dissenting, that "[g]eneral propositions do not decide concrete cases." This general critique of formalist legal reasoning was a key plank of legal realism. Here, I follow critical legal studies scholars in applying the dictum to policy reasoning in law; see, for example, D. Kennedy, "Form and Substance in Private Law Adjudication" (1976) 89 Harv. L. Rev. 1685; D. Kennedy, "A Semiotics of Legal Argumentation" (1991) 42 Syracuse L. Rev. 75; M. Kelman, *A Guide to Critical Legal Studies* (Cambridge, MA: Harvard University Press, 1987), c. 4 and 5; J. Singer, "Legal Realism Now" (1988) 76 Cal. L. Rev. 465. For the development of this theme more generally in social theory, see R. Unger, *False Necessity* (London: Verso, 1987).

labeled "real conflicts,"[225] or what economists would view as situations of choice among Pareto-optimal alternatives.[226]

Similarly, the ideal of cosmopolitan fairness may be convincing as a general frame for reasoning and judgment in private international law, but the ethical ideal of cosmopolitan justice differs from, and cannot justify incontrovertibly, an internationalist institutional orientation. It seems clear that moral cosmopolitanism would reject rules that absolutely refused enforcement of foreign judgments or that always favoured the forum on questions of jurisdiction or choice of law. However, forum-oriented rules can actually favour foreign interests, for example, when foreign laws or processes are disadvantageous to foreign plaintiffs, or where a domestic plaintiff seeks to enforce a foreign judgment against the domestic assets of a foreign defendant. What would a cosmopolitan perspective demand where a court must consider whether to decline jurisdiction over a tort claim by a foreign plaintiff against a domestic business defendant? From one view, anti-parochialism would seem to require that a domestic court should not presumptuously take jurisdiction in a belief that it offers better legal process than a foreign jurisdiction. In this connection, cosmopolitanism would demand that assumptions concerning the inferiority, inadequacy, or absence of foreign laws and processes be carefully examined.[227] From another view, however, cosmopolitan concern and anti-protectionism suggests that the court should take jurisdiction given that it is a foreign plaintiff who has chosen to make the claim against a domestic defendant, especially where there are weaknesses in the foreign jurisdiction's ability or willingness to protect that plaintiff's interests.

Again, the supposed connection between the goal of promoting international commerce and particular policies, such as rules promoting certainty and predictability, may be contingent on specific fact configurations. The indeterminacy of policy recommendations based on efficiency criteria is often underestimated in

---

[225] J. Singer, "Real Conflicts" (1989) 69 Boston Univ. L. Rev. 1.

[226] See, for example, G. Calabresi, "Pointlessness of Pareto: Carrying Coase Further" (1991) 100 Yale L. J. 1211; D. Snidal, "International Political Economy Approaches to International Institutions," in Bhandari and Sykes, *supra* note 166 at 485.

[227] A danger especially with respect to developing countries; see, for example, M. Sornarajah, "The Myth of International Contract Law" (1981) J. World Trade 187 at 200-01.

internationalist reform in law.[228] For example, international exchange may not be served by instituting clear and predictable rules concerning jurisdiction and the recognition and enforcement of judgments. What efficiency advocates of clear and predictable rules fail to consider is that greater enforcement may be a disincentive for some international transactions. *Ex post*, it is clear, for example, that a party that is being sued for breach of contract does not consider greater recognition and enforcement to be in its interest. As Duncan Kennedy and Frank Michelman observe in the case of enforcement of contract, "as of the time of the lawsuit, the enforcement of a contract *cannot* be said to make both parties better off. If performance was in the interest of both parties it would normally occur without enforcement."[229] An analysis based on transaction costs might hold that from an *ex ante* viewpoint both sides would favour a regime that ensures clear and credible commitments. However, the *ex ante* appeal of a regime of clear and predictable enforcement might very much depend on what each party believes the future will hold, in particular, whether the party is the promisor or the promisee on a commitment and what the likelihood of breach of the promise is.[230] In some situations, strict enforcement and clear rules may actually deter transactions.

Excluded International Objectives

In addition to false necessity with respect to particular legal reforms, a second general problem with internationalist policy reasoning is that concerns about commerce, interstate cooperation, and cosmopolitan fairness do not capture the full range of defensible international objectives. For example, despite the enthusiastic

---

[228] In *Bank of Nova Scotia* v. *Angelica Whitewear Ltd.*, [1987] 1 S.C.R. 59, the Supreme Court of Canada signalled its awareness of this problem in an international commercial context involving letters of credit. Justice Le Dain for the court considered whether the use of letters of credit as an important payment mechanism in international commerce would be advanced by expanding or restricting the fraud exception to a bank's obligation to pay under a letter of credit. Justice Le Dain described how, on the one hand, the international commercial use of letters of credit would be harmed by a broad fraud exception that "created serious uncertainty and lack of confidence in the operation of letter of credit operations," but that, on the other hand, the principle of autonomy of the letter of credit should not be used to "encourage or facilitate fraud" in international transactions (at 72).

[229] D. Kennedy and F. Michelman, "Are Contract and Property Efficient?" (1980) 8 Hofstra L. Rev. 711 at 741.

[230] *Ibid.*

support for facilitating international commerce in *Morguard*, the question of whether commerce should be promoted and in what form can be queried for defensible cosmopolitan as well as for domestic reasons. These reasons include considerations of distribution, environmental degradation, and regulatory control.[231] Moreover, in some contexts, the cosmopolitan or internationalist position may embrace local control and diversity of domestic regimes. In the international realm, a commitment to simple international cooperation or to facilitating commerce may not be possible where real conflicts exist in values and interests among states and among sub-state and transnational interests.

Similarly, the goals of facilitating international commerce and interstate cooperation suffer from various limits related to their economistic reasoning. These problems include a state-centric focus, an under appreciation of non-economic interests, and the difficulty of defining interests where there are substantial transnational connections and identities.[232] Once broader conceptions of interest are used, the reform implications of internationalization for doctrinal reform become complex and particularistic.

SIX DANGERS IN THINKING ABOUT THE INTERNATIONAL

A sophisticated understanding of the international requires recognition of complexity. The international rarely simplifies; it usually adds complexity to analysis. Arguably the Supreme Court of Canada was engaged, in the tetralogy, in a sophisticated area-by-area focus on reforms informed by, but not overwhelmed by, its internationalist vision. However, a naive interpretation of the judgments may lead lower courts and some commentators to incorrectly conclude that there is a single internationalist policy that can be routinely or automatically applied to dispose of individual cases.[233] The next section describes several kinds of errors that seem to result from the failure to recognize that many internationalist policies do not lead to obvious particular reforms and that there are a number of different kinds of policy objectives, all of which are international in their orientation.

---

[231] I elaborate on the goal of transnational regulation in private international law in Wai, *supra* note 168.

[232] See Wai, *supra* note 169 at 236-39.

[233] It may be that the expansive application of *Morguard, supra* note 1, to recognition and enforcement of default judgments from non-Canadian jurisdictions may be an example of this kind of misperception; see Blom, *supra* note 28.

International Relations 101: The Consequences of Anarchy

The theme of comity among courts and among societies is invoked repeatedly in the court's judgments in the tetralogy, as in its judgments in other areas of law related to international matters, such as criminal law, extradition, and sovereign immunity.[234] Informing the principle of comity is the idea that national courts should give proper respect and deference to foreign interests, values, and institutions so as to promote a better international order. Canadian courts should adopt a proper respect for the institutions and interests of foreign jurisdictions in order to encourage cooperative behaviour more generally in the international system. In addition, the presumptively shared benefits of greater efficiency in dispute resolution require that deference be shown to foreign courts and to the choices of parties with respect to forum selection, arbitration, and choice of law.

From an international relations perspective, however, this view ignores the basic structure of an anarchic international system: the lack of an overarching authority that can ensure compliance and reciprocity on the part of individual participants in that system.[235] The game theory models described earlier have as their descriptive purpose an explanation of how, even in situations of potential cooperative benefit, it is rational for a state not to cooperate with others given the lack of a compliance mechanism. In some accounts, forms of unilateralism and retaliation are sometimes required in order to get an imperfect form of compliance. In such a realm, one-sided voluntary internationalism may reward the parochialism of others and, perversely, harm the long-run benefits of an international order.[236] Thus, for example, the willingness of Canadian courts to be restrained in granting anti-suit injunctions, to decline jurisdiction for *forum non conveniens,* and to recognize and enforce foreign judgments including default judgments may actually encourage jurisdictions such as Texas to refuse to adopt similar restraints.[237]

---

[234] I discuss these similarities in Wai, *supra* note 6.

[235] H. Bull, *The Anarchical Society* (London: Macmillan, 1977).

[236] See, for example, Trebilcock and Howse, *supra* note 213 at 7-9, for a discussion of this argument in the context of international trade regulation.

[237] Effectively, non-reciprocity means abandonment of a "tit-for-tat" strategy that may actually serve the strategic purpose of achieving a rough form of international cooperation; see Brilmayer, *supra* note 55 at 184-87.

To the extent that it addresses the international anarchy at all, the court in the tetralogy seems to anticipate a strategy of "leading by example" so as to build up trust and reciprocity and to achieve cooperative benefits even without effective international institutions. In addition, it seems to rely on the presence of similar values among foreign adjudicators and legislators, with respect to the laws and principles of private international law such as comity.

This approach is connected to the tendency in the tetralogy to elide the federal and the international levels in policy analysis. It is revealing that three of the cases in the tetralogy involve conflicts among Canadian jurisdictions. In *Hunt*, indeed, the court specifically excluded consideration of the international aspect. However, the underlying policy logic of the cases, and the nature of the fourth case, *Amchem*, have suggested to many commentators and lower courts that the same kinds of reforms were required with respect to non-Canadian jurisdictions. For example, a large number of cases have applied *Morguard* to the recognition and enforcement of judgments from non-Canadian jurisdictions, predominantly from the United States.[238] The principle of comity, which is seen to be central to *Morguard* and the other cases, has also led courts to creatively change other doctrines, such as easing the rule against enforcement of foreign public laws.[239]

There are several difficulties with too closely analogizing international relations and federal systems. Most serious is that there are substantial and fundamental differences in the political and legal contexts of international and federal systems. Most obviously, without an effective international convention, Canadian courts have limited ability to directly control or reliably predict the behaviour of foreign courts or legislatures. In the Canadian federal context, in contrast, the Supreme Court of Canada, the federal government, and the other political institutions of the federation permit some direct control. Therefore, it seems foolish to simply analogize interprovincial and international disputes in the context of controlling aggressive assumptions of jurisdiction by foreign courts, part of

---

[238] Some lower courts have applied *Morguard* to international cases of recognition and enforcement; see, for example, *Moses v. Shore Boat Builders Ltd.* (1993), [1994] 106 D.L.R. (4th) 654 (B.C.C.A.), leave to appeal to S.C.C. refused, [1994] 1 S.C.R. xi [hereinafter *Moses*]; *Arrowmaster Incorporated v. Unique Forming Ltd.* (1993) 17 O.R. (3d) 407 (Gen.Div.). See, generally, Blom, *supra* note 28; Sullivan, *supra* note 16.

[239] For example, *United States v. Ivey*, (1995) 26 O.R. (3d) 533 at 549, citing the principle of comity from *Morguard* in support of reform of the rule.

the function of both restrictions on recognition and enforcement of judgments as in *Morguard* and anti-suit injunctions as in *Amchem*. A basic understanding of international relations would highlight this point. In the absence of any overarching authority, there is only an indirect hope for comity and reciprocal restraint by foreign jurisdictions.

Furthermore, the assumptions about convergence in values among different jurisdictions that inform the tetralogy and that are most evident in the *Tolofson* judgment may apply very differently within the Canadian federation as compared to between Canadian and foreign jurisdictions. A liberal theory of international relations might argue that a private international law among liberal jurisdictions should be much more harmonious and comitious because the underlying values represented in both the substance and processes of law should be similar.[240] This assumption, however, is less than determinative for the purposes of private international law. Convergence on some basic political values does not obviously or necessarily translate into greater convergence in legal regimes nor greater accommodation in practice. After all, many conflict of laws disputes are generated by disputes between Canadian provinces, which share nearly identical liberal political values, and yet legal differences that matter to private law disputes continue, as in the differences over the passenger laws of Saskatchewan and British Columbia in the *Tolofson* case. The divergences are still greater with many of our liberal neighbours in the United States — the source of most of the private international law disputes that Canadian courts will face. Significant differences in societal values and legal rules exist between Canadian and US jurisdictions on major issues such as gun control, affirmative action, and the death penalty.[241] These differences extend to private law and private procedure, especially in so far as private law performs functions of social regulation. The final part of this article contains a more

---

[240] Slaughter, *supra* note 138.

[241] In this connection, it is interesting in this respect to compare the majority Supreme Court of Canada judgments with respect to extradition to the United States to face the potential death penalties in *Kindler, supra* note 118, and *Re Ng Extradition, supra* note 118, which were written by a court contemporaneously generating the tetralogy in private international law. In contrast, the recent judgment in *United States* v. *Burns, supra* note 119, may indicate a rethinking at the court concerning the nature of its internationalism in the criminal law area. For an argument concerning some of the shared characteristics of the extradition cases and the tetralogy in private international law, see Wai, *supra* note 6.

extended discussion of this concern using the example of punitive damages.

Real Conflicts and the Sacrifice of Domestic State Interests

A weak appreciation of the consequences for cooperation of a fundamentally different structure of an international anarchy is worsened when an internationalist approach fails to appreciate that significant jurisdictional interests may sometimes be at stake in private litigation across borders. For example, a policy of comity with respect to foreign state processes and laws is a potential problem if domestic interests are too readily sacrificed. While the US governmental-interest analysis of choice of law problems may often overstate the state legislative interest in private law disputes, there are occasions when a state's interests in having the level of regulatory protection of, for example, its tort laws could be jeopardized by deference to a foreign court's assumption of jurisdiction or through a decision to apply foreign law rather than forum law. This is especially a concern if regulatory preferences are understood to include not only the decision to set a high standard of regulatory protection but also to set a lower standard based on balancing a number of different interests and policies.[242] Comity in this situation may undermine the complex political and normative settlements that underpin the regulatory structure of a Canadian jurisdiction.

The *Hunt* decision evidences the manner in which private international law disputes may raise issues that are of significant legislative and social concern. The Québec blocking statute, which was held to be inapplicable, was legislation that specifically identified out-of-province and outside-of-Canada asbestos litigation as being problematic for the public policy of Québec. With respect to this issue, the Québec National Assembly presumably was concerned with a range of interests, including those of the workers in the Québec asbestos industry. To prioritize international system objectives, such as the promotion of international trade or the cosmopolitan fairness to litigants, is to overturn this legislative determination.

Similarly, the liberal recognition and enforcement of foreign judgments rendered against Canadian defendants might constitute a significant additional cost for Canadian businesses. This is a problem if the assessment of the quality of the connection of the foreign

---

[242] Singer, *supra* note 225 at 41.

court to the dispute is too deferential. Moreover, since comity and cooperation, not reciprocity or a binding international treaty, are the guiding principles, there is no way to ensure that the foreign jurisdictions are treating Canadian judgments in the same way. Similar concerns exist with respect to the policy set out in *Amchem* of discouraging the use of anti-suit injunctions.

Unfairness to Individuals

A further concern about the internationalist approach in the tetralogy is that in adopting an international focus, the court both overstated the importance of private international law to interstate cooperation and understated the importance of private international law to individual parties. The consequence is an approach that departs from the traditional focus of Canadian private international law on fairness to the parties and moves instead towards the protection of systemic goals such as ensuring cooperative interstate order and facilitating interstate commerce.

Traditional private international law in Canada, in contrast to US governmental-interest analysis, has not emphasized the significance to state interests of most kinds of private international law disputes. Private international legal disputes are often relatively minor from the point of view of states, and military conflict or trade wars are not real consequences of private international law disputes. As Max Rheinstein notes, "[n]ever in private law is there a conflict between states in the sense in which states clash on questions of boundary, treatment of foreign nationals or property, or spheres of interest."[243] One view would be, therefore, that the court's internationalist approach is a sensible trade-off of some limited state interests for the benefits of encouraging the state interests in international order, international commerce, and anti-parochialism.

This emphasis on international system concerns and objectives would not be a problem if state interests were the only matter at hand. Private international law in the Commonwealth traditions, however, has traditionally focused on the conflicts between the interests and preferences of individual parties. A significant danger in promoting international system objectives is that the interests and values of individual parties are dealt with unfairly. This concern about the consequences of focusing away from individuals

[243] M. Rheinstein, "How to Review a Festschrift" (1962) 11 Am. J. Comp. L. 632 at 664, quoted in F. Juenger, *Choice of Law and Multistate Justice* (Boston: Martinus Nijhoff, 1993) at 161, n. 997.

and onto states is what has undermined English support for the doctrine of comity.[244] Before the tetralogy, Canadian courts followed the English courts in de-emphasizing state interests and attempting to develop private international law rules based on the characteristics of different categories of relations among individual litigants.

The sacrifice of individual fairness is a major problem in a liberal interpretation of the rules from the tetralogy. Generous and liberal recognition and enforcement of foreign judgments may assist in predictability and in interstate relations, but it may be unfair to a defendant who has formulated expectations of justice based on its various connections to a Canadian jurisdiction and a foreign jurisdiction. Similarly, the use of a rigid *lex loci delicti* rule assists in promoting predictability and in protecting against parochialism in choice of law in tort. However, the unfairness to individual litigants can be very high, and it can be argued that in *Tolofson,* Justice La Forest and the court may have become too focused on systemic objectives at the cost of fairness to the plaintiffs whose substantive claim failed because of the ruling. The idea that as between order and fairness "order comes first"[245] is to overstate the importance of certainty to order and the importance of order itself. Some degree of conflict can be managed in transnational civil litigation without serious losses to the system; in comparison, unfairness to individuals caused by false suppression of conflict can be substantial. It is for this reason that Jean-Gabriel Castel, reasserting the values of the traditional private international law approach, argues that "[i]f a choice must be made, fairness should prevail over order."[246]

Disturbing the Laws and Politics of Federalism

I noted earlier that the tetralogy evidences a strong and dangerous tendency to analogize the international to the federal, even

---

[244] See *Dicey & Morris, supra* note 92 at 5-6:

> [I]t is clear that English courts apply *e.g.* French law in order to do justice between the parties, and not from any desire to show courtesy to the French Republic, nor even in the hope that if English courts apply French law in appropriate cases, French courts will be encouraged in appropriate cases to apply English law.

The authors' choice of France for their example is of interest.

[245] *Tolofson, supra* note 1 at 1058.

[246] Castel, *supra* note 10 at 67.

where the basic institutional features of the two levels are different. There is a further danger connected with too closely identifying the international and the federal in policy reasoning: the disturbance of established and functioning federal systems of governance. The tetralogy demonstrates a fascinating connection between changing international realities and issues of Canadian federalism. Justice La Forest, for example, the leading judge at the court in the tetralogy and in international law more generally, was also a leading expert on federalism, both as an academic[247]and as a judge.[248] The tetralogy — particularly its ideas about the constitutional limits on provincial jurisdiction, the Canadian common market, and the significance of mobility rights — provides a powerful vision of a federation in need of reform to suit both Canadian and international realities.[249] At the policy level, the tetralogy emphasizes the close connection between federal and international analyses in that the Supreme Court of Canada and lower courts have almost interchangeably identified a process of increasing commerce, mobility, and convergence in values in both federal and international societies and argued for similar legal responses in both venues. The potential hazards of reforms to federalism posed by the tetralogy have been somewhat obscured because the effective mode of internationalization has been by policy consciousness rather than by formal implementation of international treaties.

Internationalization through the mode of international treaties can pose serious challenges for the division of powers in federal states. In the law and politics of Canadian federalism, the federal treaty implementation power has been a frequent source of contention between those who advocate the need for a federal state to act in a unified way on the international plane and those who believe that an expansive federal treaty implementation power

---

[247] G.V. La Forest, *The Allocation of the Taxing Power under the Canadian Constitution*, 2nd ed. (Toronto: Canadian Tax Foundation, 1981); G.V. La Forest, *Natural Resources and Public Property under the Canadian Constitution* (Toronto: University of Toronto Press, 1969). In an early article, Justice La Forest made the connection between the constitutional law of federalism and international law; G.V. La Forest, "May the Provinces Legislate in Violation of International Law?" (1961) 39 Can. Bar Rev. 78.

[248] See, for example, *R. v. Crown Zellerbach Canada Ltd.*, [1988] 1 S.C.R. 401, La Forest J. dissenting; *Air Canada v. B.C.*, [1989] 1 S.C.R. 1161; *Friends of the Oldman River Society v. Canada*, [1992] 1 S.C.R. 3; *Ontario Hydro v. Ontario (Labour Relations)*, [1993] 3 S.C.R. 327.

[249] See McEvoy, *supra* note 23.

effectively undermines provincial powers.[250] More recently, international trade treaties, such as the WTO agreements[251] and the North American Free Trade Agreement (NAFTA),[252] create complex issues related to the law and politics of federal states.[253] The tetralogy never directly addresses the issue of the treaty implementation power, but the judgments do effectively constrain provincial jurisdiction since most private law and, consequently, most private international law is within provincial jurisdiction. In *Morguard*, the court found constraints on courts applying provincial common law with respect to the recognition and enforcement of judgments from other provinces; lower courts have extended this reasoning to judgments from non-Canadian jurisdictions. In *Hunt*, the court prevented provincial legislatures from impeding trans-provincial litigation by constitutionalizing certain limits on provincial jurisdiction in the area of private international law. The court did not elaborate on these limits and expressly did not rule on whether there are any limits on provincial legislatures on private international law matters with respect to non-Canadian jurisdictions,[254] but it seems clear that this decision amounts to a constitutional limit on provincial legislative jurisdiction, which had not formerly been articulated and which has almost as much impact as the implementation of a formal international treaty.[255]

---

[250] *A.G. Can.* v. *A.G. Ont. (Labour Conventions)*, [1937] A.C. 326. For the debates about the treaty implementation power, see Hogg, *supra* note 115 at c. 11; G.V. La Forest and Associates, *Water Law in Canada: The Atlantic Provinces* (Ottawa: Information Canada, 1973) at 63-68.

[251] For example, GATT, *supra* note 212 at Article XXIV(12).

[252] NAFTA, *supra* note 187.

[253] See, for example, D. Wirth, "Government by Trade Agreement," in D. Dallmeyer, ed., *Joining Together, Standing Apart: National Identities after NAFTA* (The Hague: Kluwer, 1997) 111 at 124-25. The impact of international trade treaties on not only issues of federal-state relations but also municipal government is demonstrated clearly by the recent arbitral award of the tribunal constituted pursuant to Chapter 11 of the NAFTA in *Metalclad Corp.* v. *Mexico* (Arbitration Award, August 30, 2000) and the judicial review of that award, *Mexico* v. *Metalclad Corp.*, [2001] B.C.J. 950 (BC Supreme Court, May 2, 2001).

[254] *Hunt, supra* note 1.

[255] Another example of the indirect impact of internationalization on federal relations is seen in the recent decision of the Supreme Court of Canada in *Ward* v. *Canada (Attorney General)*, 2002 S.C.C. 17, where the court considered whether federal legislation restricting the trade in seal and seal products fell within the federal fisheries power under section 91(12) of the Constitution Act, 1867, *supra* note 24, or fell instead within provincial powers over property and civil

There are several points to make about these increased constraints placed on provincial legislatures and courts. First, many of the other concerns about the reforms in the name of the international also apply with respect to reforms done in the name of the federal in an era of the international. There are significant differences between the two levels; for example, the federal government and the Supreme Court of Canada have an oversight role that differs from the formally anarchic relations between sovereign states. However, as with the international context, there remain significant differences in social and legal values among provinces, provincial laws often reflect policy compromises developed to suit local communities, and reform to suit federal relations may overlook fairness to individuals whose expectations may be linked to provincial laws and processes.

Second, it is important to remember the central concern of the difficult debate over the treaty implementation power, which is that merely because a matter has international dimensions does not mean that legislative jurisdiction should be automatically removed from the local levels of government. Within Europe, the debates about subsidiarity have emphasized the costs associated with removing policy-making to higher and more distant levels of government. This lesson, of course, is a major theme of the Canadian constitutional law on the federal division of powers.

Finally, the rules that should apply to the conflict of laws among Canadian jurisdictions might be different from the rules that should apply with respect to non-Canadian jurisdictions. It seems clear that Canadian jurisdictions should be careful in simply extending the same treatment given to other Canadian jurisdictions to foreign jurisdictions under principles such as those provided in *Morguard*. Still more clearly, the unanswered question in *Hunt*, concerning whether there are constitutional limitations on the power of provincial legislatures with respect to non-Canadian jurisdictions, should be answered so as to permit provincial legislatures significant room to choose their private international law rules with respect to non-Canadian jurisdictions. This flexibility

---

rights under section 92(13). In characterizing the legislation, the court referred to the desire of the federal government to respond to concerns about international sales boycotts of seal and other fisheries products as relevant to its characterization of the federal legislation as being in pith and substance concerned with matters of management and control of the fisheries. *Ibid.* at paras. 2, 8, and 21.

concerning constitutional limits is needed to temper the existing effects of internationalist reform on the federal division of powers, to account for the problem of oversight and divergence in values with non-Canadian jurisdictions, and for reasons of deference to legislatures in international matters — a matter that will be discussed in the next section.

Constitutionalization and Legislatures, Executives, and the Courts

As was noted earlier, the lack of an effective overarching institutional authority in international matters means that real conflicts develop between sovereign entities that cannot be resolved in a determinative fashion. Instead, many international disputes are resolved, if at all, through extended processes of international negotiation and compromise.[256] While similar kinds of enforcement difficulties arise in domestic disputes, there are still substantial differences in degree between the two contexts.

An awareness of workable political process in international relations requires an awareness of the relative strengths and drawbacks of various institutional alternatives. National courts without enforcement power outside their jurisdiction are usually not the best political institutions for dealing with international conflict. For example, national courts are neither authorized nor able to directly negotiate with foreign jurisdictions, to engage in ongoing negotiation and monitoring, to link issues to create the possibility of larger compromises, and to engage in broader consultations with affected domestic constituencies as negotiations proceed. All of these arguments are familiar policy concerns, which inform the traditional deference of common law courts to the executive branch on international matters, which is evident in doctrines such as sovereign immunity[257] and in the Crown prerogative to conduct international relations.[258]

---

[256] Even within the more "legalistic" processes established in international institutions such as the WTO, dispute resolution retains significant "pragmatic" elements; see, generally, G. R. Shell, "Trade Legalism and International Relations Theory: An Analysis of the World Trade Organization" (1995) 44 Duke L. J. 829.

[257] See S. Williams and A.L.C. de Mestral, *An Introduction to International Law: Chiefly as Interpreted and Applied in Canada*, 2nd ed. (Toronto: Butterworths, 1987) c. 8.

[258] See Hogg, *supra* note 115 at sections 1.8, 11.2, and 11.3.

In the tetralogy, the court seems to move away from this deference in the realm of private international law. In this respect,
Canadian courts should take a lesson from Justice La Forest's work
in other areas, which emphasizes the limits of national courts as
an effective institution in the international context.[259] This sense
of limits of national courts has led him to argue, for example, for
deference to the executive and legislative branches in the application of the Charter in almost all international matters. First, some
Charter rights were modified for the international context. For
example, Justice La Forest emphasized that the scope of Charter
review does not extend to the review of foreign proceedings for
problems such as unreasonable delay or inadequate counsel.[260] Second, Justice La Forest's approach to the justification of infringement under section 1 of the Charter gave significant discretion to
the political and executive branches of the Canadian government
to take into account the numerous considerations that might be at
play in legal disputes with an international aspect.[261]

The deferential approach adopted by Justice La Forest in the
Charter context seems to contrast sharply with the constitutional
limits on provincial courts and legislatures in private international
law articulated in the tetralogy. Particularly in the *Hunt* decision,
Justice La Forest seemed to signal that the room for provincial legislatures to set private international law rules that are not in keeping with the basic norms of comity will be tightly controlled. While
the degree of deference to the legislative and executive branch in
the Charter context might be too statist and deferential on some
international matters, such as extradition, the degree of internationalist activism demonstrated in the tetralogy at times seems too
interventionist.

It may be that since private international law is an area predominantly developed by common law courts, Justice La Forest was less
concerned with the problems of a lack of institutional competence.
Given little evidence that legislatures were intending to legislate in

[259] In Wai, *supra* note 6, I compare and contrast the lack of deference in the tetralogy with (1) Justice La Forest's legal realist take on the limited effectiveness of
adjudication in comparison to legislative, executive and administrative
processes; (2) his generally deferential attitude towards the legislative and executive branches in the application of the Charter; and (3) his restricted idea of
the role of national courts in other international areas, such as in extradition.

[260] *Canada* v. *Schmidt, supra* note 118; *R.* v. *Harrer,* [1995] 3 S.C.R. 562.

[261] *United States* v. *Cotroni; United States* v. *El Zein,* [1989] 1 S.C.R. 1469 at 1487-90.

private international law to institute international reforms, it fell to the courts to promote such reform. None of these arguments, however, overcomes the concern that with respect to international reform more recognition is needed of the traditional limits of common law courts in international matters.

This concern is most problematic in the implications of constitutionalization for the ability of provincial courts and legislatures to tailor their reforms to the complex process of policy involving foreign jurisdictions. In some areas, such as in the blocking statute deliberately constructed by the provincial legislature with respect to asbestos litigation in *Hunt* or in legislation such as clawback statutes in antitrust, it seems clear that the legislative branch has spoken and should be given wide discretion to tailor domestic laws for political exigencies, including extended or failed international negotiations. In light of the institutional disadvantages of the common law courts, it makes some sense to restrictively interpret the constitutionalization of the rules of the tetralogy at least with respect to non-Canadian jurisdictions. In *Hunt,* for example, the court expressly did not address the issue of whether the blocking statute would be constitutionally inapplicable with respect to litigation proceeding in non-Canadian jurisdictions. Given the different institutional structures, as well as the lack of relative institutional competence of the courts in foreign affairs,[262] the constitutional limits on provincial legislatures should be less restrictive with respect to non-Canadian jurisdictions than with respect to other Canadian provinces.[263] In *Tolofson,* Justice La Forest signalled that the rigid *lex loci delicti* rule might permit exceptions for "injustice, in certain circumstances," although he thought they would be few.[264] It may be that significant differences in the underlying tort law and the choice of law rules in tort between Canadian and non-Canadian jurisdictions, including US jurisdictions, might mean that Canadian courts and particularly Canadian legislatures should be permitted to vary the rule.

---

[262] Justice La Forest notes in *Hunt, supra* note 1 at 328, that the federal Parliament is expressly permitted by the constitution to legislate with international extraterritorial effect; see *Statute of Westminster, 1931* (U.K.), 22 Geo.V, c.4, s. 3: "It is hereby declared and enacted that the Parliament of a Dominion has full power to make laws having extra-territorial operation."

[263] *Hunt, supra* note 1 at 331.

[264] *Tolofson, supra* note 1 at 1054.

Overlooked International Objectives

In addition to harms to individual, local, and federal interests and policies, the concern to promote international commerce and interstate relations may lead Canadian courts to ignore other important international objectives, such as effective international regulation or distributive justice across state borders. For example, internationalist reform may overlook the function of private international law in assisting the regulatory oversight of transnational businesses.[265] Internationalist policy argumentation tends to promote court respect for party autonomy in the choice of dispute-resolution by forum selection, choice of law, and arbitration clauses. However, this approach may fail to identify appropriately the regulatory challenges posed by this "lift-off" of transnational business from state-based private law regulation. As in the domestic realm, the courts are part of a complex mix of institutional processes, both governmental and non-governmental. Courts may provide a more accessible point of access for groups or individuals than either legislative or executive processes. In view of the increasing concern that key areas of social control are slipping away into international bureaucracies and global markets, it may be necessary to critically and creatively re-evaluate or limit the institutional deference of national courts to other domestic, foreign, and international institutions.

In the final part of this article, I will attempt to explore how concerns such as effective transnational regulation can be better incorporated into a policy approach to private international law that acknowledges complexity and the existence of plural objectives.

PART 6: TWO EXAMPLES OF PARTICULARISTIC AND CONTEXTUAL INTERNATIONALIST POLICY ANALYSIS

It has been argued that considerations of the international rarely simplify, and frequently make more complex, legal determinations in private international law. The response must be that general policy concerns such as international commerce, interstate cooperation, and cosmopolitan fairness identify valuable concerns, but that other international and domestic policy goals must be considered. Particularism and context will therefore matter very much.[266]

---

[265] I argue this in Wai, *supra* note 168.

[266] For example, in Wai, *supra* note 169, I argue that the commercial activity exception to sovereign immunity lacks necessary particularism. This is particularly

This need not lead to hopelessly fact-specific determinations. The internationalist policy objectives, together with others, help to identify dimensions of concern that will help to structure argumentation and decision in particular cases.[267] In this respect, private international law already contains complex doctrines such as *dépeçage*, under which different national laws might apply to different aspects of one relation or transaction.[268] In a pragmatic or eclectic framework, this principle might extend as well to tailoring applicable laws and procedures for the structural features of different kinds of disputes, such as the nature of the foreign jurisdiction involved in the problem. The ability to address complexity and real conflicts with an orderly framework for argumentation and decision-making is key to private international law. In order to show how this kind of contextual analysis might operate in Canadian private international law, this section concludes the article with some international policy analysis of two contrasting examples: jurisdiction over Canadian corporations conducting business in developing economies, and the recognition and enforcement of US punitive damages awards.

JURISDICTION, *FORUM NON CONVENIENS*, CANADIAN COURTS, AND CANADIAN CORPORATIONS IN THE DEVELOPING WORLD

In *Amchem*, the Supreme Court of Canada promoted the use of *forum non conveniens* as a vehicle for the rational allocation of jurisdiction and the promotion of comity in inter-jurisdictional relations. There are many virtues to the doctrine, and it has been adopted in a number of non-Canadian jurisdictions as well. However, there are also dangers. In particular, there is a danger in considering whether there is *forum non conveniens* of a lapse into naive internationalism through an excessive concern with comity and procedural efficiency. Such concern with comity and efficiency may be inappropriate in a context where the litigation is directed

---

problematic when, on the one hand, a broad exception to sovereign immunity has been taken with respect to commercial activity and, on the other hand, the immunity rule has been applied broadly with respect to almost all other kinds of activity, including activity involving human rights abuses.

[267] For a model of this "pragmatic" approach in the US conflict of laws, see J. Singer, "A Pragmatic Guide to Conflicts" (1990) 70 Boston Univ. L. Rev. 731.

[268] Under *dépeçage*, various state laws may govern different aspects of a "single" business relationship, for example, different laws may apply sales, transportation, and credit aspects. See, for example, Rome Convention, *supra* note 83, articles 3(1) and 4(1); Castel *et al.*, *supra* note 71 at 171.

against a Canadian corporation conducting business abroad in a developing country. In this context, a Canadian court may require a more nuanced sense of (1) the problem of effective transnational regulation where the other potential jurisdictions for the litigation have weak or non-existent regulatory protection and (2) the need to protect justice and fairness for the foreign plaintiff.

A more sophisticated and contextual understanding of the international system would recognize the need to assess differentially jurisdictional issues related to attempts to sue Western multinational enterprises in their home jurisdictions for claims related to their operation abroad in developing economies. Canadian courts that focus narrowly on the convenience of litigation may decline jurisdiction with the consequence of injustice to foreign plaintiffs, under-regulation in the transnational system, and even a form of inadvertent parochialism. In the most prominent example of such a case since the tetralogy, a Québec court used *forum non conveniens* analysis to grant a stay of proceedings in Québec courts against a Québec-based mining company accused of causing environmental damage in a cyanide spill at one of its mines in Guyana.[269] The case recalled the decision of the New York courts to decline jurisdiction for reasons of *forum non conveniens* in litigation by Indian plaintiffs against Union Carbide for the Bhopal chemical factory accident in India.[270]

The Québec court in *Recherches Internationales Québec v. Cambior Inc.*[271] seemed especially concerned to emphasize the need for

---

[269] *Recherches Internationales Québec v. Cambior Inc.*, [1998] Q.J. No. 2554 (Quebec Superior Court, August 14, 1998) [hereinafter *Cambior*]. For an extended commentary, see S. Seck, "Environmental Harm in Developing Countries Caused by Subsidiaries of Canadian Mining Corporations: The Interface of Public and Private International Law" (1999) 37 Can. Y.B. Int'l L. 139.

[270] *Re Union Carbide Corporation Gas Plant Disaster at Bhopal, India in December, 1984,* 634 F. Supp. 842 (S.D.N.Y. 1986), aff'd 809 F.2d 195 (2d Cir. 1987) [hereinafter *Union Carbide*]. The Second Circuit ruled that a suit against Union Carbide by Indian victims and the Indian government of the Bhopal chemical disaster was *forum non conveniens* in the New York courts and should be heard in the courts of India. This conclusion was reached in spite of the submissions of the Indian government who agreed that the suit was better heard in the US court. The court did impose a number of conditions on its stay, including that Union Carbide consent to submit to the broad discovery under the US Federal Rules of Civil Procedure. For critical commentary, see U. Baxi, *Inconvenient Forum and Convenient Catastrophe: The Bhopal Case* (Delhi and Bombay: Indian Law Institute and N.M. Tripathi, 1986); Paul, *supra* note 145 at 61-2.

[271] *Cambior, supra* note 269.

comity and due respect for the courts of Guyana, focusing on evidence as to the procedural effectiveness of the Guyanese courts. This reinforced the other main concern of its analysis, namely issues of procedural advantage such as proximity to the accident site and to relevant witnesses.

While the relative connections of the action to Québec and Guyana can be debated, the court might have factored in a concern with effective transnational regulation as an international policy objective, which is as important as interstate cooperation and comity or procedural efficiencies. These regulatory concerns arise both at the international level and the domestic level. At the international level, it may be that there are systemic problems of under-regulation of transnational business conduct. With weak international-level regulatory authorities, regulatory gaps with respect to externalities created by transnational business actors often fail to be regulated by an imperfectly coordinated set of sovereign authorities. In some cases, a process of regulatory competition may worsen the regulatory problem as states compete to attract economic production by mobile transnational business actors through reductions of domestic regulatory levels below levels that would otherwise be chosen by those societies.[272]

There may also be substantial reasons for a Canadian court to consider the challenges for developing countries in creating and implementing an effective regime of domestic regulation of business conduct. In the *Cambior* case, there was little sign that effective environmental regulation was in place. Likewise, the tort laws related to environmental damage were weak and not well suited to the scale of the mining or to the size and resources of the transnational defendant. In contrast, Canadian courts are very familiar with both the public and private law regulation of mining companies and their operations. Moreover, in the surrounding support for such litigation, the Canadian jurisdiction may offer significant advantages, including better support services, better access to experts, and superior non-governmental organization support. This is not to argue that developing economies always lack effective legal systems, only to argue that a court may need to consider more broadly what effectiveness would amount to in a particular litigation.[273]

---

[272] I discuss regulatory gaps and regulatory competition as problems of international cooperation in private international law in Wai, *supra* note 168 at 250-58.

[273] The recent House of Lords decision in *Lubbe* v. *Cape plc*, [2000] 4 All E.R. 268 (H.L.), considered *forum non conveniens*, but in its application permitted South

In both *Re Union Carbide Corporation Gas Plant Disaster at Bhopal, India in December,* 1984[274] and *Cambior,* the courts used an internationalist rhetoric of comity where arguably no real issue of comity was present and where substantial policy goals would have been served by the assumption of jurisdiction. In *Union Carbide,* comity concerns seemed especially improbable given that the Indian government expressly did not object to the assumption of jurisdiction by the New York court over the litigation. In *Cambior,* the Guyanese government neither objected nor promoted the litigation.[275] This should not be surprising given that governments may want to appear neutral so as not to alarm current or future foreign investors or to invite more general incursions of foreign courts into other domestic matters.[276]

Policy arguments related to cosmopolitan fairness and anti-parochialism in the *Cambior* case would seem to operate against, rather than for, applying *forum non conveniens* in this case. It is hard to see how it can be anti-parochial to reject the preferences of foreign plaintiffs and instead observe the preferences of a defendant with strong Canadian connections. Indeed, by declining jurisdiction, the court is open to the accusation that it fed into perceived Canadian economic interests.

Neither do arguments based on individual fairness to the Canadian defendant seem especially strong. Canadian corporations and their legal advisors are familiar with the Canadian legal process — even more so than with the processes of a foreign jurisdiction. While such corporations will not necessarily be held to the same standards as at home, they should have some expectation of possible legal challenges based in Canadian courts. Moreover, as assumption of jurisdiction is not the same as choice of law, a Canadian court may still choose to apply the foreign law even after

---

African plaintiffs to continue with their litigation in English courts against an English parent company for personal injuries related to exposure to asbestos. This decision may be an example of greater sensitivity to the particular procedural problems that may impede litigants in the legal systems of some developing countries.

[274] *Union Carbide, supra* note 270.

[275] Comity concerns make more sense where governments take a position that domestic processes are sufficient.

[276] On the difficult position of developing countries with respect to international legalism in a global context of neoliberalism and neoimperialism, see Wai, *supra* note 169 at 241-45.

assuming jurisdiction. And, in any event, the foreign plaintiff must still overcome the substantial challenges and costs of proving its case in a Canadian trial. Most important, as Sara Seck argues, Canada should take some responsibility for the action abroad of the significant number of leading multinational mining and oil and gas corporations based in Canada.[277] These kinds of operations generate significant environmental and health risks and frequently operate in developing economies that often lack significant experience with such operations. A Canadian commitment to responsible internationalism and governance is challenged if there is no effort to take some responsibility in sectors where Canadian business actors are among the most important transnational actors. The allegations against the Talisman oil company of human rights problems related to its oil operations in Sudan are another high-profile example where a Canadian court, faced with a private suit, might be tempted to use *forum non conveniens* analysis without consideration of broader international contexts.[278]

Transnational tort actions involving developing economies may require a different analysis of questions of jurisdiction. In contrast, there may be no reason to be concerned about effective regulation or legal protections with respect to a transnational tort action relating to the United States for reasons such as the basic public regulatory structures in place, the generally protective purpose of US tort law, the highly developed tort-litigation process, and the economic and political power of the United States in Canada. Indeed, such differences in context might argue for a very different treatment of some Canadian private international law rules with respect to American jurisdictions, as I will attempt to illustrate in the next section.

RECOGNITION AND ENFORCEMENT OF JUDGMENTS:
THE EXAMPLE OF US PUNITIVE DAMAGE AWARDS

A developing and important issue in the recognition and enforcement of judgments concerns punitive damage awards from the United States. This issue is an example where a Canadian court, following the internationalist policy orientation in the tetralogy, may

---

[277] Seck, *supra* note 269.

[278] With respect to the complaints concerning Talisman, see, for example, *Human Security in Sudan: The Report of a Canadian Assessment Mission*, prepared by John Harker for the Minister of Foreign Affairs (Ottawa, January 2000).

miss important specific concerns of state interests and individual fairness.[279]

The *Morguard* case involved two Canadian jurisdictions. Although the court identified some distinctively Canadian factors to reinforce its judgment, the basic rationale for the decision was the functional needs of an increasingly interdependent international system and the guiding principle of comity. A number of lower courts have followed this reasoning and applied the *Morguard* principles to permit recognition and enforcement of judgments from non-Canadian judgments.[280] In *Moses v. Shore Boat Builders Ltd.*, for example, the British Columbia Court of Appeal applied the *Morguard* rule to a default judgment of an Alaskan court against a British Columbia defendant.[281] This approach has been supported by some academic commentators who have observed that the comity arguments in the *Morguard* case would apply internationally as well as interprovincially and that: "[a]ll aspects of international or interprovincial conflict of laws should be subjected to the same limitation: that there must exist a real and substantial connection to the forum for it to take jurisdiction or to apply its own law, and to have its judgments recognized elsewhere."[282] Yet with respect to US judgments, a number of concerns arise. Lord Denning expressed these concerns most colourfully in his observation that "[a]s a moth to the light, so a litigant is drawn to the United States. If he can only get his case into their courts, he stands to win a fortune."[283] Among the many concerns expressed by Lord Denning with respect to US civil litigation, the availability of punitive damages in

---

[279] A significant recent example of a related debate in the Canada-US context concerns the willingness of Canadian courts perhaps too readily to "complement, coordinate and where appropriate accommodate the proceedings" of US courts in cross-border insolvencies; see *Re Babcock & Wilcox Canada Ltd.*, (2000) 18 C.B.R. (4th) 157 (Ont. S.C.J. [Commercial List]) at para 9. It evidences the importance of the tetralogy in Canadian law that Justice Farley, the leading judge in Ontario on matters related to cross-border insolvencies, invoked *Morguard* in his judgment in *Babcock* and in previous judgments as providing a strong policy support for extending the practice of comity to the international context and to the context of cross-border insolvencies. For critical commentary, see, for example, J. Ziegel, "Corporate Groups and Canada-US Cross-border Insolvencies: Contrasting Judicial Visions" (2000) 25 C.B.R. (4th) 161.

[280] See Blom, *supra* note 28, for a survey of cases.

[281] *Moses, supra* note 238.

[282] Castel, *supra* note 10 at 66.

[283] *Smith Kline & French Laboratories Ltd.* v. *Bloch* (1983), 2 All E.R. 72 at 74 (C.A.).

combination with jury trials and contingent fee agreements seems to figure foremost.

Under the internationalist interpretation of the *Morguard* ruling, it would seem that because of the concerns of comity, Canadian courts have little basis on which to conduct detailed reviews of the punitive damages components of US judgments so long as the jurisdiction in question has a real and substantial connection to the matter in dispute. Moreover, such refusals would seem to be an unacceptable parochialism given that Canadian courts also award punitive damages.[284] However, the argument for liberalized recognition and enforcement of judgments is based on a general convergence in underlying substantive regimes, and the need for international cooperation ignores the degree to which genuine, and relevant, private law conflicts regularly occur between jurisdictions that have similar underlying laws. More attention must be paid to the particular kind of conflict typically in dispute in private international law. Most private international law disputes are not a threat to international system-level concerns. For individual litigants, however, such disputes do involve serious issues of distributive fairness.

The broad emphasis on international cooperation inadequately captures what practically speaking amounts to a substantial policy disagreement between Canadian and American jurisdictions concerning punitive damages policy. The mere shared classification of damages as punitive damages disguises the degree to which substantial differences exist in Canada on the quantum of such damages. For most practical purposes, substantial disputes about differences in quantum are as important as disputes about liability.[285] The

---

[284] Canadian courts may award exemplary damages in tort law and, more rarely, in contract; see S. Waddams, *The Law of Damages* (Toronto: Canada Law Book, 1997) at paras. 11.250-11.260. The recent decision of the Supreme Court of Canada in *Whiten* v. *Pilot Insurance Co.*, 2002 S.C.C. 18, signals that substantial punitive damages may be available, although "very much the exception rather than the rule" (para. 94), in breach of contract cases in Canada. It is interesting that the court considered submissions concerning the excesses of the US experience with punitive damages in the course of its evaluation of what Canadian law on the issue should be (paras. 60-65).

[285] The court in *Tolofson, supra* note 1 at 1059 did not seem to appreciate this; it considered that general convergence in liability principles with respect to guest passenger statutes had diminished public policy problems because only differences in quantum remained. In *Kidron* v. *Grean*, (1999) 48 O.R. (3d) 775 (Gen.Div.), leave to appeal refused 48 O.R. (3d) 784, Justice Brennan suggested a more cautious approach to the recognition and enforcement of a

significant differences in damage awards could amount to a transfer of resources from one jurisdiction to another. More importantly, the differences may cause hardship to particular defendants who may have acted in reliance on reasonable expectations that did not include potential exposure to such punitive damage awards enforceable in their home jurisdictions.

The quantum of punitive damages in the United States has raised concerns among many of the states engaged in negotiations for a multilateral convention on recognition and enforcement of judgments.[286] National courts have also been reluctant to give recognition and enforcement to such awards. In an important 1992 decision, for example, the German Bundesgerichtshof recognized and enforced a judgment of a California court with respect to damages under a number of heads but refused to enforce the punitive damages part of the judgment, citing reasons of "public policy."[287] Similar approaches have been taken with respect to punitive damages by courts in jurisdictions such as Japan.[288]

The use of a public policy exception with respect to punitive damage awards would be an expansion from the very restricted use of the exception in contemporary conflict of laws in common law jurisdictions,[289] and would seem to run counter to a regime of expanding international policy values. However, such expansion is a potentially sensible change to accompany a more liberalized regime of recognition and enforcement of judgments.

A good example of the significance of the differences in punitive damages is found in the 1995 judgment of a Mississippi state court

---

California judgment that included a substantial award for emotional distress damages. The judge seemed particularly concerned about the quantum of the damages awarded in comparison to the caps on recovery of such damages in Canada.

[286] See Weintraub, *supra* note 86 at 203-05.

[287] Judgment of June 4, 1992, 13 ZIP 1256 (1992), (1993) 32 I.L.M. 1320. See H. Bungert, "Enforcing U.S. Excessive and Punitive Damages Awards in Germany" (1993) 27 Int'l Lawyer 1075; P. Hay, "The Recognition and Enforcement of American Money-Judgments in Germany — The 1992 Decision of the German Supreme Court" (1992) 40 Am. J. Comp. L. 729; Brand, *supra* note 166 at 608-13.

[288] See, for example, *An Oregon Partnership, Northcon I* v. *Yoshitaka Katayama; Mansei Kogyo Kabushiki Kaisha, H.J.* (1376) 79 [1991], H.T. (760) 250 [1991] (Tokyo District Court, 18 February 1991) reported at (1992) 35 Japanese Annual Int'l L. 177; see Brand, *supra* note 166 at 612.

[289] Castel, *supra* note 10 at 171-74.

in *O'Keefe* v. *Loewen Group, Inc., et al.*[290] In a jury trial, the Loewen Group, a funeral home company based in Burnaby, Canada, was found to have been in breach of contract in a commercial dispute concerning licenses and negotiations connected to the takeover by Loewen of some funeral homes in Mississippi. The property in dispute involved three contracts valued at US $1 million and an exchange of funeral homes worth US $2.5 million for an insurance property valued at US $4 million. The jury awarded US $100 million in compensatory damages and US $400 million in punitive damages. Faced with this award, Loewen sought to appeal. Partly based on a Mississippi rule that required posting of a 125 per cent bond, which in this case would have totalled US $625 million, Loewen eventually settled for approximately $175 million. Loewen subsequently went into reorganization under bankruptcy laws. In an interesting indication of the convergence of private law and international trade law, Loewen and its founder Ray Loewen have also filed a complaint under the NAFTA investment chapter seeking damages.[291] Whatever the merits of the Mississippi judgment as the basis for a claim in international trade law, the refusal by a Canadian court of enforcement of some part of the judgment in the *Loewen* case might have been an appropriate expression of the differences in views between Canada and Mississippi as to the size of awards and the purpose of punishment served by punitive damage awards.

The different scale of punitive damages between the United States and Canada reflects different underlying views of the uses of civil litigation as a tool of regulatory policy and of the purposes of deterrence and punishment. In the United States, civil litigation is an important part of the regulatory framework through a system of countervailing power. The system of "private attorneys general"

---

[290] *O'Keefe* v. *The Loewen Group Inc. et al.*, 91-67-423 (Cir.Ct, Hinds Co., Miss. 1995).

[291] *Loewen* v. *United States, supra* note 187. The claim was filed under the private-party investor dispute settlement provisions of Section B, Chapter 11 of NAFTA, *supra* note 187. The substantive claim is based on Articles 1102, 1105, and 1110 of NAFTA. See "NAFTA Panel Expected to be Constituted Soon in Canadian Firm's $725 Million NAFTA Claim" January 20, 1999, BNA Int'l Trade Reporter 81; M. Krauss, "NAFTA Meets the American Torts Process: *O'Keefe v. Loewen*" (2000) 9 George Mason. L. Rev. 69. An initial ruling of the panel rejected arguments by the United States on matters of competence and jurisdiction; see *The Loewen Group, Inc. and Raymond L. Loewen* v. *United States of America* (ICSID Case No. ARB (AF)/98/3), Decision of the Arbitral Tribunal on Hearing of Respondent's Objection to Competence and Jurisdiction (January 5, 2001).

in areas such as securities regulation and antitrust demonstrate the significance of regulation through private actions in the United States. The US system of antitrust litigation mixes government regulation and private litigation. The award of treble damages is an important part of this system. Treble damages are also available for certain kinds of private actions under the Securities Exchange Act.[292] The degree to which Canada and US legislators have different views of private litigation and the quantum of damages is reflected in Canadian legislation that permits the "clawback" of such treble damage awards.[293]

From an international trade perspective, the punitive damage awards may themselves be as suspect as the refusal of a foreign court to recognize and enforce such awards. The punitive damage awards may be motivated by parochial dislike of foreigners who conduct business in a jurisdiction. The scale of such awards may also amount to *de facto* discrimination, in that foreign competitors may either be dissuaded from entry into the local market or forced to take out expensive forms of liability insurance, especially given that they already face public law regulation in their home jurisdictions. More generally, such awards may be economically inefficient in providing over-deterrence, in particular, where they serve a purely punitive, rather than a deterrent, function. Indeed, even within the United States, substantial debate exists as to the utility of punitive damages beyond a certain quantum.[294]

Even under ideas of international cooperation among liberal states, it is not clear that a Canadian jurisdiction should necessarily recognize and enforce judgments with which it disagrees. Slaughter, for example, has written that with respect to the Act of State doctrine national courts should feel less worried about deference

---

[292] Securities Exchange Act of 1934, 15 U.S.C. §78 (1934).

[293] See, for example, Foreign Extraterritorial Measures Act, *supra* note 189; Castel *et al.*, *supra* note 71 at 645-46.

[294] Substantial disagreement about punitive damages is reflected in debates within the United States itself. Weintraub observes that in international negotiations concerning the recognition and enforcement of US judgments, "[d]efense of punitive damages will not be helped by the fact that most states have, by statute or decision, placed limits on punitive awards and that the U.S. Supreme Court has held that a 'grossly excessive' award of punitive damages violates due process"; Weintraub, *supra* note 86 at 182-83 [notes omitted]. The Mississippi judgment against Loewen features prominently as a chapter in a conservative journalist's book severely criticizing the legal system in the United States; M. Boot, *Out of Order: Arrogance, Corruption, and Incompetence on the Bench* (New York: Basic Books, 1998) at 158-60; see also Krauss, *supra* note 291.

to foreign courts of jurisdictions that share common basic values and institutions because there is less risk of ideologically motivated interference with the foreign jurisdiction.[295] Transjudicial dialogue among the courts of liberal jurisdictions should include the ability to engage in more critical dialogue concerning judgments.

With this understanding, the approach of refusing to enforce some part of a foreign punitive damages award seems like a tailored, compromise solution. A plaintiff is not left with a useless judgment. Most of the other heads of damages, which may be substantial, will be recognized against Canadian assets of the defendant. Often, defendants, especially corporate defendants, have assets in other jurisdictions against which the plaintiff may be able to enforce even the punitive damages component of the judgment. Finally, the plaintiff always has the option of commencing an action in the Canadian jurisdiction if most of the assets are in Canada. The judgment will be enforceable to the full extent in the forum jurisdiction and partly enforceable in the foreign jurisdiction. This seems to be a rough compromise reflecting the fact that both jurisdictions have connections to the matter but disagree as to the applicable results in the dispute. It may also best reflect the legitimate expectations of fairness of both parties to the litigation.

PART 7: CONCLUSION

The judgments of the tetralogy have brought the policy dimensions of internationalization clearly into the centre of law-making and adjudication in Canadian private international law. It seems clear that legal actors — including legislators, judges, and practitioners — must master the features of this internationalist discourse in order to make good decisions and to be effective advocates in today's terrain of private international law and other aspects of law, which are impacted by globalization and internationalization.

The danger is that the new discourse of internationalism will be misunderstood as a narrow apology for only a limited kind of doctrinal reform and a narrow definition of the policy purposes of private international law in an era of globalization. There is nothing about any one of the international policy objectives – international commerce, interstate cooperation, or cosmopolitan fairness — that compels ignoring other policy objectives in the field. Indeed, general

---

[295] A-M. Burley, "Law among Liberal States: Liberal Internationalism and the Act of State Doctrine" (1992) 92 Columbia L. Rev. 1907 at 1975-85 and 1993.

policy objectives such as international commerce, interstate cooperation, and cosmopolitan fairness often are indeterminate with
respect to particular doctrinal reforms. In order to understand the
nature and the limits of internationalist reform better, it is necessary to examine some of the personal, national and historical contexts for such reforms. This article situated the internationalist
policy discourse of the tetralogy in the contexts of traditions of
liberal internationalism, Canadian internationalism, and the disciplinary internationalism of public international law. By situating
the policy discourse in this way, the article attempted to give a better sense of how the openness of internationalist policy justifications can become narrow and be misused to exclude valid policy
concerns.

The tetralogy also shows how courts play an active role in constituting the legal terrain of the international system. The judgments
show how concepts and ideational orientations about the international realm can lead to concrete results. Hopefully, a critical
understanding of the tetralogy will provide a sense of how debates
about internationalism can be productively used in debates about
private international law and other fields impacted by internationalization. The strengths and limits of the policy argumentation in
the tetralogy are symptomatic of other policy debates concerning
the global and the international in Canada as elsewhere. For example, recent controversies concerning international trade regulation,
such as the defeat of the proposed Multilateral Agreement on Investment, the failures of the 1999 Seattle Ministerial Meeting of the
World Trade Organization, and the protests at the 2001 Québec
meetings concerning the proposed Free Trade Area of the Americas, indicate substantial resistance to further expansion of the international trading order. This resistance is at least partly a response
to a policy focus in international trade regulation on a narrow set
of liberal internationalist objectives centred on promoting international commerce, facilitating inter-state relations, and promoting a
shallow and economistic conception of non-discrimination.[296] Moreover, the willingness on the part of governments to suppress critical
policy discussion at the APEC meetings in Vancouver in 1997[297]
and at the FTAA meetings in Québec may be symptomatic of a

---

[296] Unfortunately, some such resistance tends toward equally naive anti-
internationalist positions rather than carefully articulated policy analysis and
response.

[297] See W. Pue, *Pepper in Our Eyes: The APEC Affair* (Vancouver: UBC Press, 2000).

narrow policy concept of internationalism. The policy aspects of the internationalist reform of private international law in Canada suggests that being for the international must also be about debating the international.

Sommaire

Au nom de l'international: La Cour suprême du Canada et la métamorphose internationaliste du droit international privé canadien

Cet article examine quatre arrêts de la Cour suprême du Canada qui ont eu pour effet de transformer le droit international privé au Canada, les présentant comme un épisode remarquable dans l'internationalisation du droit, un genre d'activisme judiciaire au nom de l'international. Selon l'auteur, ces arrêts révèlent un modèle d'internationalisation fondé sur la conscience politique internationaliste, distinct mais souvent complémentaire de l'internationalisation au moyen de traités internationaux et de changements au droit international coutumier. Les traits saillants de cette approche semblent présenter des ressemblances avec les traditions de l'internationalisme libéral, de l'internationalisme canadien et du droit international public. L'article fait une mise en garde contre plusieurs dangers d'ordre général que soulève le recours à cette approche pour la réforme du droit et le raisonnement judiciaire. L'auteur mentionne en particulier deux questions de doctrine en droit international privé afin d'illustrer une approche plus sophistiquée à une politique d'internationalisme.

Summary

In the Name of the International: The Supreme Court of Canada and the Internationalist Transformation of Canadian Private International Law

This article discusses four judgments of the Supreme Court of Canada that transformed private international law in Canada and represent a striking episode in the internationalization of law — a form of judicial activism in the name of the international. It is argued that these cases evidence a mode of internationalization by internationalist policy consciousness that is distinct from, although often complementary to, internationalization via the mechanism of international treaties or changes in customary international law. The key features of this approach suggest some resemblances to the vision found in the traditions of liberal internationalism, Canadian internationalism, and public international law. The article cautions against several general dangers in the use of this approach in law reform and adjudication and uses two specific doctrinal issues in private international law to demonstrate what a richer policy discourse concerning internationalism would be.

La "guerre contre le terrorisme," le droit international humanitaire et le statut de prisonnier de guerre

MARCO SASSÒLI

I INTRODUCTION

Ceux qui ont commis les crimes inexcusables du 11 septembre 2001 les ont certainement considérés comme faisant partie de leur "guerre." Le Président des États-Unis les a également immédiatement désignés comme des actes de "guerre." La réaction américaine, souvent qualifiée de "guerre contre le terrorisme," n'a pas seulement pris la forme de poursuites pénales nationales et internationales, mais également, depuis le 6 octobre 2001, celle d'une "guerre" en Afghanistan. Dans son discours sur l'état de l'Union du 29 janvier 2002, le Président a utilisé le mot "guerre" à douze reprises, et a laissé entrevoir qu'après la victoire en Afghanistan, la "guerre" allait continuer contre des États comme l'Iran, l'Iraq et la Corée du Nord.[1] Si on a beaucoup parlé de "guerre," on n'a, en revanche, pas beaucoup entendu parler de droit, et encore moins de droit international suite à ces événements, et ceci, bien que la réaction des États-Unis ait porté, le temps d'une journée, le nom de "justice immuable." Pourtant, la "guerre" est un phénomène régi par le droit international, et ce à deux titres: les règles du *jus ad bellum* déterminant les situations dans lesquelles il est licite de recourir à la "guerre" et celles du *jus in bello*, réglementant la conduite d'une "guerre." Ces dernières comprennent en

Marco Sassòli est professeur de droit international public à l'Université du Québec à Montréal. Il aimerait remercier ses assistants de recherche, Mme Marie-Louise Tougas et M. Alexis Demirdjian, d'avoir révisé un premier projet de cet article.

[1] White House, President George Bush, "President Delivers State of the Union Address," en ligne: White House, <http://www.whitehouse.gov/news/releases/2002/01/20020129-11.html> (date d'accès: 30 janvier 2002).

particulier le droit international humanitaire, protégeant les victimes de la "guerre." Ce droit est aujourd'hui largement codifié dans les quatre Conventions de Genève du 12 août 1949,[2] auxquelles tous les États de la planète sont parties, et dans leurs deux Protocoles additionnels de 1977,[3] qui comptent 159 et 153 États Parties, respectivement, mais qui sont rejetés par les États-Unis et auxquels l'Afghanistan n'est pas partie.

Il est donc justifié de vérifier si ce droit international humanitaire s'applique aux attaques contre New York et Washington et à leurs suites et comment il les qualifie. Ceci est d'autant plus indiqué que l'applicabilité et l'application de ce droit dans la "guerre contre le terrorisme" sont controversées, particulièrement en ce qui a trait au statut des personnes arrêtées par les États-Unis en Afghanistan et transférées sur leur base militaire de Guantánamo (Cuba).

Certains ont soutenu que le droit international humanitaire était dépassé (outdated) dans cette "guerre contre le terrorisme" et qu'il méritait d'être révisé.[4] Une éminente internationaliste fait valoir

[2] *Convention de Genève pour l'amélioration du sort des blessés et des malades dans les forces armées en campagne,* 12 août 1949, 75 R.T.N.U. 31, R.T. Can. 1965 n°20 (entrée en vigueur: 14 novembre 1965) (ci-après Iᵉ Convention); *Convention de Genève pour l'amélioration du sort des blessés, des malades et des naufragés des forces armées sur mer,* 12 août 1949, 75 R.T.N.U. 85, R.T. Can. 1965 n°20 (ci-après IIᵉ Convention); *Convention de Genève relative au traitement des prisonniers de guerre,* 12 août 1949, 75 R.T.N.U. 135, R.T. Can. 1965 n°20 (entrée en vigueur: 14 novembre 1965) (ci-après IIIᵉ Convention); *Convention de Genève relative à la protection des personnes civiles en temps de guerre,* 12 août 1949, 75 R.T.N.U. 287, R.T. Can. 1965 n°20 (entrée en vigueur: 14 novembre 1965) (ci-après IVᵉ Convention).

[3] *Protocole additionnel aux Conventions de Genève du 12 août 1949 relatif à la protection des victimes des conflits armés internationaux (Protocole I),* 8 juin 1977, 1125 R.T.N.U. 3, R.T. Can. 1991 n°2 (entrée en vigueur: 20 mai 1991) (ci-après Protocole I), et *Protocole additionnel aux Conventions de Genève du 12 août 1949 relatif à la protection des victimes des conflits armés non internationaux (Protocole II),* 8 juin 1977, 1125 R.T.N.U. 609, R.T. Can. 1991 n°2 (entrée en vigueur: 20 mai 1991) (ci-après Protocole II).

[4] Voir, par exemple, C. Rosett, "POWs. CUBA: The Red Cross needs to get real," Wall Street Journal (23 janvier 2002) A33; H. Kamer, "Gulliver auf Guantánamo?," Neue Zürcher Zeitung (26/27 janvier 2002) 3; D. Montgomery, "Geneva Convention's Gentility, Treaty Stresses Civil Treatment of Prisoners," Washington Post (17 février 2002) F01, et certaines remarques du secrétaire américain à la défense D. Rumsfeld lors d'une conférence de presse du 8 février 2002, en ligne: U.S. Department of Defence, <http://www.defenselink.mil/news/Feb2002/t02082002_t0208sd.html> (date d'accès: 12 février 2002) ainsi que du porte-parole de la Maison blanche, Ari Fleischer, dans White House, "Press Briefing by Ari Fleischer" du 28 janvier 2002, en ligne: The White House

que les Conventions de Genève n'ont pas été négociées pour s'appliquer à de tels conflits.[5] Plus nuancés, des membres du gouvernement canadien ont affirmé, devant la Chambre des communes, que ces conventions ont été écrites à une époque antérieure et qu'elles ne s'appliquaient pas si facilement aux conditions actuelles.[6] Même des dirigeants du Comité international de la Croix-Rouge (CICR), qui est pourtant le gardien des Conventions de Genève,[7] avancent que celles-ci "ne sont pas des tables de la loi faites pour l'éternité . . . Avec Al-Qaeda, nous sommes en train d'entrer dans une zone grise du droit international humanitaire. Le droit devra s'ajuster à cette évolution de la nature de la guerre."[8] Le Président G.W. Bush, quant à lui, a répondu à un journaliste qui lui posait la question, que les Conventions de Genève n'étaient pas dépassées.[9] Il a toutefois confirmé les dires de son secrétaire à la défense D. Rumsfeld, qui avait dès le début affirmé que les personnes détenues à Guantánamo n'étaient pas des prisonniers de guerre, mais des "combattants illégaux," tout en promettant que les Conventions de Genève

---

<http://www.whitehouse.gov/news/releases/2002/01/20020128-11.html> (date d'accès: 29 janvier 2002).

[5] R. Wedgewood, "Personal View: Prisoners of a different war: The Geneva convention applies to conventional soldiers, not to the terrorists being held at Camp X-Ray," Financial Times, (30 janvier 2002), en ligne: <http://globalarchive.ft.com/globalarchive/article.html?id=020130001411&query=camp+x-> ("were not negotiated to govern wars against piratical groups that operate internationally.)"

[6] Comme par exemple Art Eggleton, ministre de la Défense, et Bill Graham, ministre des Affaires étrangères; voir R. Fife, "Ottawa proposes detainee deal," *National Post*, (5 février 2002), en ligne <http://www.nationalpost.com>, (date d'accès: 5 février 2002).

[7] Voir Y. Sandoz, *The International Committee of the Red Cross as Guardian of International Humanitarian Law,* Genève, CICR, 1998.

[8] P. Hazan, "Pour Paul Grossrieder [qui est directeur général du CICR], il faut compléter les Conventions de Genève. 'Le droit humanitaire doit s'adapter'," *Libération*, (30 janvier 2002), en ligne: <http://www.liberation.fr/quotidien/semaine/020130-010009106MOND.html> (date d'accès: 1er février 2002). Le Président du CICR, J. Kellenberger, ne semble pourtant pas avoir de tels doutes sur l'adéquation du droit international humanitaire; voir Y. Monge, "A los talibanes detenidos se les trata como prisioneros de guerra — Jakob Kellenberger, Presidente del CICR," El Pais, (31 janvier 2002), en ligne: <http://www.elpais.es/diario/internacional/index.html?d_date=20020131> (date d'accès: 13 février 2002).

[9] White House, "President Meets with Afghan Interim Authority Chairman," en ligne: The White House <http://www.whitehouse.gov/news/releases/2002/01/20020128-13.html> (date d'accès: 29 janvier 2002).

seraient, dans les faits, respectées.[10] Après certaines hésitations et divergences de vue au sein de son administration, le Président a finalement décidé, le 7 février 2002, que les Conventions de Genève s'appliquaient aux Talibans détenus, mais non pas aux membres d'Al-Qaïda. Malgré cette applicabilité des Conventions, les Talibans qui se trouvent sur la base de Guantánamo ne seraient, néanmoins, pas des prisonniers de guerre.[11]

Nous sommes donc confrontés à un problème d'interprétation du droit existant (de la *lex lata*) et à la question de savoir si ce droit doit être modifié et dans quel sens il doit l'être (question relevant de la *lex ferenda*). Dans un ordre juridique comme le droit international, qui s'applique à une société décentralisée, dans laquelle les sujets sont en même temps les législateurs, la distinction entre *lex lata* et *lex ferenda* est moins stricte qu'en droit interne. Si tous les États estiment ou veulent que le droit soit changé, il est changé. Ceci est évident pour le droit international coutumier, mais cette affirmation est également valable pour des dispositions conventionnelles comme celles des Conventions de Genève. Une disposition conventionnelle peut tomber en désuétude ou recevoir une interprétation nouvelle en fonction de la pratique ultérieure des parties.[12] Les mêmes considérations liées au but, à l'objet et au

---

[10] Conférences de presse du secrétaire à la défense des États-Unis du 11 et 22 janvier 2002, D. Rumsfeld, "DoD News Briefing — Secretary Rumsfeld and Gen. Pace — Tuesday, Jan. 22, 2002," en ligne: U.S. Department of Defense <http://www.defenselink.mil/news/Jan2002/t01222002_t0122sd.html> (date d'accès 23 janvier 2002) et D. Rumsfeld, "DoD News Briefing — Secretary Rumsfeld and Gen. Myers — Friday, Jan. 11, 2002," en ligne: U.S. Department of Defense <http://www.defenselink.mil/news/Jan2002/t01112002_t0111sd. html> (date d'accès 13 janvier 2002); témoignage du secrétaire D. Rumsfeld devant le Sénat américain le 5 février 2002, D.Rumsfeld, "Fiscal Year 2003 Department of Defense Budget Testimony," en ligne: <http://www.defenselink. mil/speeches/2002/s20020205-secdef2.html> (date d'accès: 6 février 2002).

[11] Voir "Geneva Convention Applies to Taliban, not Al Qaeda," dans American Forces Information Service News Articles, 7 février 2002, en ligne: U.S. Department of Defence <http://www.defenselink.mil/news/Feb2002/n02072002_ 200202074.html> (date d'accès: 8 février 2002); conférence de presse du Secrétaire à la Défense D. Rumsfeld du 7 février 2002, en ligne: *ibid.*, <http://www. defenselink.mil/news/Feb2002/t02072002_t0207sd.html> (date d'accès: 8 février 2002), ainsi que conférence de presse par le porte-parole de la Maison blanche, A. Fleischer, du même jour, en ligne: The White House <http://www. whitehouse.gov/news/releases/2002/02/20020207-6.html> (date d'accès: 8 février 2002).

[12] *Convention de Vienne sur le droit des traités*, 23 mai 1969, 1155 R.T.N.U. 331, art. 31(3)(b).

contexte qui sont invoquées en faveur d'une révision du droit servent également à interpréter le droit existant.[13] Malgré ce qui précède, nous déterminerons, dans un premier temps, si le droit international humanitaire existant s'applique aux attaques du 11 septembre 2001 et au conflit mené par les États-Unis et leurs alliés en Afghanistan. Nous analyserons ensuite les conséquences d'une telle applicabilité, vu l'actualité, à l'exemple des personnes détenues à Guantánamo. Dans un deuxième temps, nous aborderons la question plus fondamentale de savoir si le résultat de notre analyse du droit applicable démontre que les Conventions de Genève doivent être adaptées à la "guerre contre le terrorisme." Dans cet article, nous traiterons le droit, mais nous ne pourrons pas trancher sur les faits. Nous ne sommes ni dans le secret des dieux ni dans celui des services secrets (qui n'ont d'ailleurs pas donné l'impression d'être très au courant de la réalité dans toute cette affaire). Nous devons simplement assumer, pour les fins de cet article, qui est consacré à une discussion du *droit,* certains faits ou alors discuter les conséquences juridiques de quelques situations factuelles possibles. De plus, comme c'est toujours le cas lorsque l'on traite de problèmes d'actualité, des faits et arguments supplémentaires risquent de s'être ajoutés au moment où ces lignes sortiront de presse.

II Le droit international humanitaire et son
    indépendance absolue des règles relatives
    à la légalité du recours à la force

Le droit international humanitaire s'applique aux conflits armés et non seulement aux guerres, institution tombée en désuétude — dans la terminologie juridique tout au moins — depuis la seconde guerre mondiale.[14] Il limite l'usage de la violence dans ces conflits armés à ce qui est indispensable pour atteindre le but du conflit. Ce dernier peut être — indépendamment des causes au nom desquelles il est mené — uniquement celui d'affaiblir le potentiel militaire de l'ennemi. Le droit international humanitaire protège en particulier celles et ceux qui ne participent pas — ou ne participent plus — directement aux hostilités. La plupart de ses règles, y compris les quatre Conventions de Genève et le Protocole I, ne s'appliquent qu'aux conflits armés internationaux. Les conflits armés non internationaux sont couverts uniquement par des règles plus sommaires,

---

[13] *Ibid.*, art. 31(1).

[14] Art. 2(1) commun aux quatre Conventions de Genève; E. David, *Principes de droit des conflits armés,* 2ᵉ éd., Bruxelles, Bruylant, 1999, pp. 96-100.

prévues en particulier dans l'art. 3 commun aux Conventions et le Protocole II.

Le droit international humanitaire des conflits armés internationaux s'applique à une situation qui ne devrait pas exister si le droit international était respecté. En effet, le recours à la force armée dans les relations internationales est interdit par une règle impérative du droit international[15] (le *jus ad bellum* s'est transformé en un *jus contra bellum*). Des exceptions à cette interdiction sont admises en cas de légitime défense individuelle ou collective[16] et de mesures prises ou autorisées par le Conseil de sécurité.[17] Au moins l'une des parties viole donc le droit international du seul fait de l'usage de la force, même si elle respecte le droit international humanitaire. Même s'ils sont interdits, les conflits armés surviennent et le droit international doit faire face à cette réalité de la vie internationale, non seulement en la combattant, mais aussi en la réglementant pour garantir un minimum d'humanité dans une situation inhumaine. Pour des raisons pratiques, politiques et humanitaires, le droit international humanitaire doit être identique pour les deux belligérants: celui qui a recours légalement à la force et celui qui viole le *jus contra bellum*. Convaincre les belligérants de respecter le droit international humanitaire serait impossible sinon, car, au moins entre les belligérants, la question de savoir qui a eu recours à la force en conformité avec le *jus ad bellum* et qui l'a violé est toujours controversée. Or, le droit international humanitaire doit être appliqué pendant le conflit par ces belligérants. De plus, d'un point de vue humanitaire, les victimes du conflit nécessitent, de chaque côté, une protection identique. Ce ne sont d'ailleurs généralement pas elles qui sont responsables pour les éventuelles violations du *jus ad bellum* commises par "leur" partie.

Le droit international humanitaire doit donc être respecté indépendamment de tout argument de *jus ad bellum*. Toutes les théories, passées, présentes ou futures de "guerre juste" ne peuvent concerner que le *jus ad bellum* et ne peuvent pas justifier (mais sont en fait souvent utilisées pour suggérer) que ceux qui se battent pour une cause juste aient plus de droits ou moins d'obligations que leurs ennemis. Cette séparation totale entre *jus ad bellum* et *jus in bello* a été reconnue par des dispositions conventionnelles, la

---

[15] *Charte des Nations-Unies,* 26 juin 1945, R.T. Can. 1945 n° 7, par. 4 de l'art. 2.

[16] Reconnue *ibid.,* art. 51.

[17] Dans les formes prévues *ibid.* au c. VII.

jurisprudence et la doctrine.[18] Elle signifie que le droit international humanitaire s'applique à chaque fois qu'il y a *de facto* un conflit armé, quelle que soit sa qualification en termes de *jus ad bellum*. Elle implique également qu'un argument de *jus ad bellum* ne puisse pas être utilisé pour interpréter le droit international humanitaire. Ceci est particulièrement difficile, nous le verrons, lorsqu'il faut qualifier les parties d'un conflit pour déterminer s'il est international.

III Le droit international humanitaire s'applique-t-il aux attaques du 11 septembre 2001 et à la réaction des États-Unis?

Un conflit armé est international s'il se déroule entre des "Hautes Parties contractantes."[19] Les États-Unis et l'Afghanistan sont des États Parties aux Conventions de Genève. Il faut donc déterminer si les attaques du 11 septembre 2001 peuvent être considérées comme ayant été perpétrées par l'Afghanistan et si la réaction armée des États-Unis est dirigée contre cet État. Ce sont évidemment deux questions différentes par rapport aux faits, mais les réponses sont régies par certaines règles juridiques communes. En ce qui concerne les faits pertinents pour la première question, nous partirons de l'hypothèse que les attaques ont été exécutées par des membres du réseau Al-Qaïda qui se trouvaient aux États-Unis, mais dont le chef, Oussama Bin Laden, se trouvait en Afghanistan. C'est lui qui dirigeait ces attaques. Les Talibans étaient au courant de la présence de Oussama Bin Laden sur le sol afghan et du type d'activités de son groupe,[20] mais pas nécessairement du plan des attaques du 11 septembre. Constatons qu'ils n'ont rien fait pour empêcher les activités de Oussama Bin Laden, bien qu'ils aient eu la possibilité de le faire. D'un point de vue juridique, il

---

[18] Protocole I, par. 5 du préambule; US Military Tribunal at Nuremberg dans le procès contre *Wilhelm List et autres,* The United Nations War Crimes Commission, *Law Reports of Trials of War Criminals,* vol. VIII, 34-76 (voir pour ce cas et d'autres références M. Sassòli et A. Bouvier, *How Does Law Protect in War?,* Genève, CICR, 1999, pp. 83-87, 665, 681 et 682); C. Greenwood, "The Relationship Between *jus ad bellum* and *jus in bello,*" (1983) 9 Review of International Studies 221-34; R. Kolb, "Sur l'origine du couple terminologique *jus ad bellum/jus in bello,*" (1997) 827 RICR 593; H. Meyrowitz, *Le principe de l'égalité des belligérants devant le droit de la guerre,* Paris, Pedone, 1970.

[19] Art. 2 commun des quatre Conventions.

[20] Voir *Résolution 1267* Doc. off. CS NU, 4051e séance, Doc. NU S/RES/1267 (1999), citée *infra* note 38.

faut donc déterminer si le comportement d'Al-Qaïda peut être attribué aux Talibans, et si le comportement de ces derniers peut être attribué à l'Afghanistan. Ces questions d'attribution d'un acte illicite à un État sont régies par les règles concernant la responsabilité internationale de l'État, qui définissent les modalités et les conséquences d'une violation du droit international. Après quarante ans de délibérations, la Commission du droit international (CDI) a adopté, le 26 juillet 2001, un Projet d'articles codifiant ce domaine des règles dites secondaires.[21] Selon la jurisprudence, ce sont également ces règles d'attribution d'un acte illicite qui déterminent si c'est le droit international humanitaire des conflits armés internationaux ou celui des conflits armés non internationaux qui s'applique aux actes commis lors d'un conflit donné.[22]

A   LES TALIBANS ÉTAIENT-ILS UN ORGANE DE L'AFGHANISTAN?

Traditionnellement, un État ne répond que du comportement de ses organes.[23] Il n'est pas responsable du comportement d'acteurs non étatiques qui agissent sous sa juridiction et sur son territoire,[24] sauf si ces acteurs sont habilités, par le droit de cet État, "à exercer des prérogatives de la puissance publique."[25] En principe et sous réserve des exceptions discutées ci-après, l'Afghanistan n'est donc pas responsable des actions d'Al-Qaïda. Se pose en revanche la question de savoir s'il est responsable de celles des Talibans, malgré que ceux-ci n'aient été reconnus comme gouvernement de l'Afghanistan que par le Pakistan et les Émirats arabes unis. La plupart des

---

[21] *Projet d'articles sur la responsabilité de l'État pour fait internationalement illicite* et commentaires relatifs (ci-après *Projet d'articles*), dans *Rapport sur les travaux de sa cinquante-troisième session*, Doc. off. CDI NU, 53ᵉ sess., Doc. NU A/56/10 (2001), aux pp. 60-391, en ligne: Organisation des Nations Unies <http://www.un.org/law/ilc/reports/2001/2001report.htm> (date d'accès: 2 décembre 2001) (ci-après *Rapport de la CDI*). L'Assemblée générale de l'ONU a pris note de ce Projet dans sa résolution A/RES/56/83 du 12 décembre 2001.

[22] *Procureur* c. *Dusko Tadic* (1999), Affaire nᵒ IT-94-A (Tribunal Pénal International pour l'ex-Yougoslavie, Chambre d'appel), aux par. 103-104, en ligne: Nations Unies <http://www.un.org/icty/jugements-f.htm> (date d'accès: 2 décembre 2001).

[23] *Projet d'articles, supra* note 21, art. 4(1).

[24] *Rapport de la CDI, supra* note 21 aux pp. 83-84. Pour une revue exhaustive de la pratique, voir R. Ago, "Quatrième Rapport sur la responsabilité des États" dans *Annuaire de la Commission du droit international 1971*, vol. 2, New York, NU, aux pp. 103-38.

[25] *Projet d'articles, supra* note 21, art. 5.

autres États reconnaissaient encore comme gouvernement légitime celui du président Rabbani, chassé de Kaboul en 1996, et l'Alliance du Nord à laquelle il appartient. Ce gouvernement représentait également l'Afghanistan à l'ONU. Les forces qui lui étaient loyales ne contrôlaient toutefois plus que 10 % du territoire afghan, alors que les Talibans en contrôlaient 90 %. Ces derniers formaient donc le gouvernement *de facto* de l'Afghanistan. En droit international, un État est responsable pour le comportement d'un tel gouvernement *de facto*.[26]

B   LES MEMBRES D'AL-QAÏDA ÉTAIENT-ILS DES AGENTS *DE FACTO* DES TALIBANS?

Quant aux membres d'Al-Qaïda, le droit afghan ne leur donnait, à notre connaissance, pas un statut d'organe. L'Afghanistan pourrait toutefois répondre de leur comportement s'ils agissaient, en fait, suivant les instructions ou les directives ou sous le contrôle de cet État, donc, en l'occurrence, des Talibans.[27] Pour que cette exigence soit remplie, la Cour internationale de Justice requiert, dans l'affaire *Nicaragua* c. *États-Unis*, un contrôle *in concreto* du comportement contraire au droit international. Elle y écrit, à propos des *contras*, un mouvement insurrectionnel ayant commis des actes terroristes, qui était soutenu par les États-Unis, que:

même prépondérante ou décisive, la participation des États-Unis à l'organisation, à la formation, à l'équipement, au financement et à l'approvisionnement des *contras*, à la sélection de leurs objectifs militaires ou paramilitaires et à la planification de toutes leurs opérations demeure insuffisante en elle-même, d'après les informations dont la Cour dispose, pour que puissent être attribués aux États-Unis les actes commis par les contras au cours de leurs opérations militaires ou paramilitaires au Nicaragua ... [M]ême le contrôle général exercé par eux sur une force extrêmement dépendante à leur égard, ne signifierait pas ... sans preuve complémentaire, que les États-Unis aient ordonné ou imposé la perpétration des actes ... allégués ... Ces actes auraient fort bien pu être commis par des membres de la force *contra* en dehors du contrôle des États-Unis.

[26] *Rapport de la CDI, supra* note 21 aux pp. 170-71; Pour la pratique, voir J.A. Frowein, *Das de facto-Regime im Völkerrecht*, Cologne, Heymanns, 1968 aux pp. 70-71; A. C. Bundu, "Recognition of Revolutionary Authorities: Law and Practice of States," (1978) 27 I.C.L.Q. 18 aux pp. 36-45, en particulier par exemple, les sentences arbitrales rendue dans les affaires *Aguilar-Amory and Royal Bank of Canada Claims* (affaire Tinoco), (1923) Recueil des sentences arbitrales vol. I., 355 à la p. 386 (Nations Unies), et *G. W. Hopkins,* (1927) 21 AJIL aux pp. 164-65.

[27] *Projet d'articles, supra* note 21, art. 8.

Pour que la responsabilité juridique de ces derniers soit engagée, il devrait en principe être établi qu'ils avaient le contrôle effectif des opérations militaires et paramilitaires au cours desquelles les violations en question se seraient produites.[28]

En conséquence, la Cour a par la suite jugé les violations du droit international humanitaire commises par les *contras* selon les règles applicables aux conflits armés non internationaux.[29] Il est peu probable que les attaques du 11 septembre 2001 avaient été exécutées sous le contrôle effectif des Talibans. Selon l'arrêt *Tadic* du Tribunal pénal international pour l'ex-Yougoslavie (TPIY), il suffirait toutefois qu'un État dispose d'un contrôle global sur une entité non étatique pour lui attribuer les comportements de cette dernière.

[I]l faut établir que [l'État] exerce un contrôle global sur le groupe, non seulement en l'équipant et le finançant, mais également en coordonnant ou en prêtant son concours à la planification d'ensemble de ses activités militaires. Ce n'est qu'à cette condition que la responsabilité internationale de l'État pourra être engagée à raison des agissements illégaux du groupe. Il n'est cependant pas nécessaire d'exiger de plus que l'État ait donné, soit au chef du groupe soit à ses membres, des instructions ou directives pour commettre certains actes spécifiques contraires au droit international.[30]

Le TPIY a, en conséquence, jugé selon le droit international humanitaire des conflits armés internationaux des actes commis par des Serbes de Bosnie qui se trouvaient sous un contrôle global de la République fédérale de Yougoslavie. À notre connaissance, les Talibans avaient des objectifs qui se limitaient à l'Afghanistan et ne s'intéressaient pas à la lutte planétaire contre les États-Unis et l'Occident, qui était celle d'Al-Qaïda. Dans ce cas, il est peu probable qu'ils aient coordonné ou prêté concours à l'ensemble des activités d'Al-Qaïda.

C   LES TALIBANS ONT-ILS ENTÉRINÉ LES ATTAQUES?

Ajoutons que selon les règles sur la responsabilité des États adoptées par la CDI, un État peut se voir attribuer ultérieurement

---

[28] *Affaire des activités militaires et paramilitaires au Nicaragua et contre celui-ci (Nicaragua c. États-Unis d'Amérique),* [1986] C.I.J. Rec. 1 au par. 115.

[29] *Ibid.,* par. 219.

[30] *Supra* note 22, par. 116-44, par. 131. Voir également notre critique dans M. Sassòli et L. Olson, "Case Report, Judgment, *The Prosecutor* v. *Dusko Tadic,* Case No. IT-94-A, ICTY Appeals Chamber, 15 July 1999," (2000) 94 AJIL 571 à la p. 575.

un comportement d'une entité non étatique, dont il n'était pas responsable au moment de la commission, s'il le reconnaît et l'adopte comme étant le sien par la suite.[31] On peut douter qu'une telle responsabilité rétroactive corresponde effectivement à la pratique internationale. Le seul précédent pertinent est celui d'un État qui avait approuvé, suite à une succession territoriale, un comportement, en l'occurrence la rupture d'un accord de concession, des autorités antérieures et qui avait continué à profiter de ses conséquences, alors qu'il aurait dû rétablir la situation antérieure.[32] En tout état de cause, un simple appui, entérinement ou une approbation d'un comportement ne sont pas suffisants pour engager une telle responsabilité. Il faut que l'État "identifie et fasse sien le comportement en question."[33] Or, les Talibans se sont tout au plus réjouis des attaques du 11 septembre 2001.

D   LES ATTAQUES SONT-ELLES ATTRIBUABLES AUX TALIBANS EN RAISON DE LEUR VIOLATION DU DEVOIR DE DILIGENCE?

Si nous partons des hypothèses factuelles qui précèdent, les attaques du 11 septembre 2001 ne peuvent pas être attribuées à l'Afghanistan et elles ne sont, en conséquence, pas régies par le droit des conflits armés internationaux. Pour éviter tout malentendu sur la responsabilité des Talibans, nous nous empressons d'ajouter quelques précisions sur la responsabilité de ceux-ci par rapport à ces attentats. Les comportements des Talibans, dont l'Afghanistan répond, comprennent les actions et les omissions de ceux-ci.[34] L'État est responsable de veiller à ce que ses organes exercent la diligence voulue (la "due diligence") par rapport à des comportements non étatiques violant des droits ou des biens protégés par le droit international.[35] Ce devoir a été précisé pour la

---

[31] *Projet d'articles, supra* note 21, art. 11.

[32] *Concession des Phares de l'Empire ottoman* (1956), Recueil des sentences arbitrales, vol. XII 155 aux pp. 197-98 (Nations Unies). Dans l'*Affaire relative au personnel diplomatique et consulaire des États-Unis à Téhéran*, [1980] C.I.J. Rec. 3 au par. 74, également citée par la CDI pour appuyer la règle, la République islamique de l'Iran avait déjà été responsable par rapport au comportement non étatique en raison d'une violation du devoir de diligence, le comportement, une prise d'otages, constituait une violation continue, et l'attribution du comportement à l'Iran après qu'il l'avait entériné n'avait donc pas nécessairement, pour la Cour, un effet rétroactif.

[33] *Rapport de la CDI, supra* note 21, à la p. 128.

[34] *Projet d'articles, supra* note 21, art. 2.

[35] Pour de nombreuses références à la doctrine, voir dans *Annuaire de la Commission*

première fois dans l'affaire de l'*Alabama* en 1871. Le Royaume-Uni a été tenu responsable d'avoir permis, sur son territoire, à des acteurs privés d'équiper des navires de guerre sudistes pendant la guerre de Sécession américaine. Ces navires ont ensuite coulé ceux des États-Unis.[36] Corollaire de sa souveraineté territoriale, interdisant à d'autres États d'y agir pour défendre leurs droits, chaque État a l'obligation de veiller avec la diligence voulue à ce que son territoire ne soit pas utilisé aux fins d'actes contraires aux droits d'autres États.[37] En découle l'obligation de prendre des mesures raisonnables pour prévenir de tels actes et de punir ou d'extrader ceux qui les commettent. Les Talibans étaient prévenus du type d'activités d'Al-Qaïda par une résolution du Conseil de Sécurité qui avait condamné, en 1999 déjà, "le fait que des terroristes continuent d'être accueillis et entraînés, et que des actes de terrorisme soient préparés, en territoire afghan" et déploré "que les Talibans continuent de donner refuge à Oussama Bin Laden et de lui permettre … de se servir de l'Afghanistan comme base."[38] Or, les Talibans n'ont rien fait.

---

de droit international 1975, vol. 2, New York, NU, à la p. 87; L. Condorelli, "L'imputation à l'État d'un fait internationalement illicite," (1984) 188 Recueil des Cours de l'Académie de droit international de la Haye 10 aux pp. 105-16; R. Pisillo-Mazzeschi, "The Due Diligence Rule and the Nature of the International Responsibility of States," (1992) 35 German Yearbook of International Law 9 et R. Pisillo-Mazzeschi, *'Due diligence' e responsabilità internazionale degli stati*, Milan, Giuffrè, 1989. Notons que G.A. Christensen, "Attribution issues in State Responsibility" (Panel Discussion) dans American Society of International Law, *Proceedings, 83rd Annual Meeting*, Washington, ASIL, 1989, pp. 51-59, estime que la jurisprudence devient de plus en plus réticente à reprocher à un État d'avoir manqué à son devoir de diligence par rapport à des acteurs privés, ce qui semble effectivement être le cas pour le "U.S.-Iran Claims Tribunal."

[36] A. De la Pradelle et N. Politis, *Recueil des arbitrages internationaux*, 2ᵉ éd., Paris, Éditions internationales, 1957, vol. II, pp. 713 et s. et 965 et s.

[37] Voir dans ce sens la Cour internationale de justice dans l'*Affaire du détroit de Corfou, Fond*, [1949] C.I.J. Rec. 4 à la p. 22, et M. Huber en tant qu'arbitre dans l'*Affaire de l'Île de Palmas* (1949), 2 Recueil des sentences arbitrales 829 à la p. 839 (Nations Unies).

[38] *Supra* note 20. Elle poursuit en notant "qu'Oussama bin Laden et ses associés sont poursuivis par la justice des États-Unis d'Amérique," notamment pour les attentats de Nairobi et Dar es-Salaam et pour complot visant à tuer des citoyens américains se trouvant à l'étranger, et demande que les Taliban remettent Oussama Bin Laden "aux autorités compétentes soit d'un pays où il a été inculpé, soit d'un pays qui le remettra à un pays où il a été inculpé, soit d'un pays où il sera arrêté et effectivement traduit en justice."

L'Afghanistan a donc violé le droit international en hébergeant Oussama Bin Laden et son groupe. À notre avis, cette violation flagrante du devoir de diligence ne constitue toutefois pas des hostilités qui, elles seules, peuvent déclencher l'applicabilité du droit international humanitaire des conflits armés internationaux. Personne n'a estimé que le Royaume-Uni était en guerre contre les États-Unis en raison de l'affaire de l'*Alabama*. Les attaques du 11 septembre 2001 ne pourraient être considérées comme des hostilités entre l'Afghanistan et les États-Unis uniquement si Oussama Bin Laden agissait sous la direction ou le contrôle de cet État, étant ainsi son organe *de facto*.[39] Un manque délibéré de la part de l'Afghanistan à son devoir de diligence concernant Oussama Bin Laden ne suffit pas. Considérer ce manque de diligence comme des hostilités déclenchant l'applicabilité du droit des conflits armés internationaux équivaudrait à un retour à une théorie prévalant dans la pratique arbitrale du 19ᵉ siècle, qui estimait que l'État ne remplissant pas son devoir de diligence par rapport à des actes privés commis sur son territoire en était complice.[40] Aujourd'hui, la pratique et la doctrine considèrent que l'État "est responsable d'avoir enfreint, non pas l'obligation internationale avec laquelle l'action de la personne privée pouvait être en contradiction, mais l'obligation générale ou spéciale mettant à la charge de ses organes un devoir de protection."[41] L'État qui n'a pas empêché un privé de tuer un diplomate ne contrevient pas à l'inviolabilité de la personne du diplomate, mais à son devoir de protéger le diplomate. L'Afghanistan, en n'empêchant pas Oussama Bin Laden de planifier, sur son territoire, des attaques contre les États-Unis, ne s'est pas engagé dans des hostilités, mais a violé son devoir de diligence.

E   LES ATTAQUES CONSTITUENT-ELLES UN CONFLIT ARMÉ NON INTERNATIONAL SUR LE TERRITOIRE DES ÉTATS-UNIS?

Si les attaques ne s'inscrivent pas dans un conflit armé international, elles peuvent constituer un conflit armé non international.

---

[39] Voir la partie III(B) ci-dessus, et I. Brownlie, *International Law and the Use of Force by States,* Oxford, Clarendon Press, 1963, pp. 370-72.

[40] *Annuaire de la Commission du droit international 1975,* vol. 2, New York, NU, aux pp. 79-80, et R. Ago, "Quatrième Rapport sur la responsabilité des États" dans *Annuaire de la Commission du droit international 1972,* vol. 2, New York, NU, aux pp. 109-14.

[41] *Annuaire de la Commission du droit international 1975,* vol. 2, New York, NU, à la p. 87, avec références.

Elles sont sans aucun doute marquées d'un degré de violence suffisant pour les qualifier d'hostilités. On peut toutefois se demander
si un seul acte concerté de très grande violence constitue à lui seul
un conflit armé. Le *Commentaire* publié par le CICR, qui plaide
pourtant en faveur d'un champ d'application très large de l'art. 3
commun aux quatre Conventions de Genève exige "des 'hostilités'
mettant aux prises des 'forces armées'."[42] Même si Al-Qaïda pouvait être considéré comme une force armée, nous avons de grandes
réticences à considérer les dix-neuf membres suicidaires impliqués
dans ces attaques comme agissant en tant que "force armée."[43]

F   LES ATTAQUES AURAIENT VIOLÉ LE DROIT INTERNATIONAL
     HUMANITAIRE S'IL AVAIT ÉTÉ APPLICABLE

Si on estimait que le droit international humanitaire s'appliquait
aux attaques du 11 septembre 2001, celles-ci le violeraient à tous les
égards. Même dans une lutte pour la cause la plus légitime, le droit
international humanitaire des conflits armés internationaux et des
conflits armés non internationaux interdit des attaques contre des
civils ainsi que des actes ou menaces dont le but principal est de
répandre la terreur parmi la population civile.[44] Il oblige, en outre,
les combattants à se distinguer de la population civile lorsqu'ils
prennent part à une attaque.[45] Même le Pentagone, qui peut être
considéré comme un objectif militaire, ne peut pas être attaqué
par un acte de perfidie, en feignant d'être des civils, en utilisant
un avion civil et en tuant inévitablement les civils passagers de
l'avion.[46] C'est d'ailleurs une définition possible de l'acte terroriste
qui évite la vieille critique selon laquelle les terroristes des uns
sont les héros des autres: est terroriste tout acte, commis en temps
de guerre ou de paix, qui serait interdit par les règles du droit

---

[42] J.S. Pictet, dir., *Les Conventions de Genève du 12 août 1949, Commentaire*, vol. 3,
Genève, CICR, 1958 à la p. 43.

[43] A. Roberts, "Counterterrorism, Armed Force and the Laws of War," (2002) 44
Survival 7 aux pp. 11-12, est également très sceptique.

[44] Art. 51(2) du Protocole I et 13(2) du Protocole II, qui correspondent à des
règles coutumières; voir M. Sassòli, *Bedeutung einer Kodifikation für das allgemeine
Völkerrecht — mit besonderer Betrachtung der Regeln zum Schutze der Zivilbevölkerung
vor den Auswirkungen von Feindseligkeiten*, Basel, Helbing & Lichtenhahn, 1990,
pp. 387-92, 396-402.

[45] Art. 44 du Protocole I et, pour plus de détails, voir ci-dessous la partie IV(E).

[46] Voir, outre les dispositions citées, art. 37(1)(c) du Protocole I.

international humanitaire protégeant les civils, même à des combattants en temps de guerre.[47]

G LA RÉACTION DES ÉTATS-UNIS AUX ATTAQUES DU 11 SEPTEMBRE 2001 CONSTITUE-T-ELLE UN CONFLIT ARMÉ INTERNATIONAL?

Depuis le 6 octobre 2001, la réaction des États-Unis aux attaques du 11 septembre 2001 n'est pas uniquement pénale, mais également militaire. Les forces armées américaines ont commencé un conflit armé sur le sol afghan, dirigé non seulement contre des cibles d'Al-Qaïda, mais également contre les Talibans. Pour cette dernière raison, tout au moins, ces hostilités doivent être qualifiées de conflit armé international.[48] Le fait que les États-Unis n'aient pas reconnu les Talibans comme gouvernement de l'Afghanistan n'a pas d'importance, aussi longtemps, du moins, que les Talibans luttent pour un État, l'Afghanistan, dont ils étaient le gouvernement *de facto*. Les États-Unis ont d'ailleurs justifié ces hostilités sous le *jus ad bellum* à titre de légitime défense, justification qui est nécessaire uniquement s'ils font usage de la force contre un État sans l'accord du gouvernement de ce dernier. Ils n'ont jamais fait valoir qu'ils avaient l'accord du gouvernement Rabbani et de l'Alliance du Nord, accord qui pourrait justifier une participation à un conflit armé non international qui se déroule dans un pays tiers. Étant donné que les Talibans constituaient le gouvernement effectif de l'Afghanistan, non seulement ils engageaient la responsabilité de cet État,[49] mais étaient les seuls qui auraient pu donner un consentement valable à une intervention militaire.[50] Notons que, dans

---

[47] M. Sassòli, "International Humanitarian Law and Terrorism," dans: Wilkinson et Steward (dir.), *Contemporary Research on Terrorism*, Aberdeen, Aberdeen University Press, 1987, 466 aux pp. 469-70; The International Law Association, "Report of the Committee on International Terrorism at the 1984 Paris Conference of the International Law Association," Report of the Sixty-fifth Conference, Paris, 1984, 313 à la p. 317.

[48] Roberts, *supra* note 43 à la p. 20. E. David, *supra* note 14 aux pp. 120 et 124-25, estime à juste titre que même des hostilités contre un groupe non étatique comme Al-Qaïda déclenchent l'applicabilité du droit des conflits armés internationaux si l'État territorial ne donne pas son accord. Voir dans ce sens également l'arrêt *Al Nawar c. Minister of Defence* de la Cour suprême d'Israël (dans Sassòli et Bouvier, *supra* note 18 aux pp. 819-23).

[49] Voir *supra* note 26.

[50] Voir pour l'intervention des États-Unis à Grenade D.F. Vagts, "International Law under Time Pressure: Grading the Grenada Take-Home Examination," (1984) 78 AJIL 169 à la p. 171; O. Schachter, *International Law in Theory and Practice*,

l'intérêt de leurs forces armées, le gouvernement et les tribunaux des États-Unis ont traditionnellement adopté une interprétation extensive de la notion de conflit armé international déclenchant l'applicabilité de la IIIe Convention de Genève. C'est ainsi que le général Manuel Antonio Noriega, évincé du pouvoir au Panama par une intervention militaire des États-Unis en 1989, accusé et condamné pour trafic de drogues, a été reconnu comme prisonnier de guerre, malgré le fait que les États-Unis ne l'aient nullement considéré comme un représentant légitime du Panama.[51]

Considérant ce qui précède, c'est donc à juste titre que le Président Bush reconnaît, par sa décision du 7 février 2002, l'applicabilité des Conventions de Genève aux hostilités en Afghanistan. Selon des sources canadiennes, depuis le début de l'engagement en Afghanistan, il n'y aurait d'ailleurs eu aucun doute sur cette question entre les forces américaines, britanniques et canadiennes.[52] Au commencement des hostilités, le CICR a rappelé aux parties du conflit, y compris aux États-Unis, leurs obligations en vertu du droit international humanitaire. Selon son communiqué de presse, il a, à cette occasion, affirmé: "Les combattants capturés par les forces ennemies dans le conflit armé international entre les Taliban et la coalition dirigée par les États-Unis doivent être traités conformément aux dispositions de la IIIe Convention de Genève et les civils détenus par une partie dont ils ne sont pas des ressortissants doivent être traités en conformité avec la IVe Convention de Genève."[53]

Dordrecht, Nijhoff, 1991, p. 115.; E. Gordon *et al.*, "International Law and the United States Action in Grenada, A Report," (1984) 18 Int'l Lawyer 331 aux pp. 369-70, et la position du conseiller juridique du Département de l'État des États-Unis, D. R. Robinson, *ibid.* 381 aux pp. 382-83. Tous ces auteurs discutent l'aspect de la légitimité d'un usage de la force sous le *jus ad bellum* en cas d'invitation par les autorités locales, mais il nous semble que si une invitation n'est pas valable en *jus ad bellum,* le droit des conflits armés internationaux est nécessairement applicable.

[51] *U.S.* v. *Manuel Antonio Noriega,* United States District Court for the Southern District of Florida, 808 F. Supp. 791 (1992), partiellement reproduit dans Sassòli et Bouvier, *supra* note 18 aux pp. 932-42.

[52] Voir S. Thorne, "Canada, Allies Press Americans to Explain PoW Process in Afghanistan," *National Post* (6 février 2002), en ligne: <http://www.nationalpost. com> (date d'accès: 6 février 2002).

[53] Comité international de la Croix-Rouge, *Afghanistan: le CICR demande à toutes les parties au conflit de respecter le droit international humanitaire,* Communication à la presse 01/47 du 24 octobre 2001, en ligne: <http://www.icrc.org/icrcfre.nsf/> (date d'accès: 30 janvier 2002), également reproduite dans (2001) 844 RICR aux pp. 1178-79.

Il semble que les États-Unis aient refusé d'accepter ce rappel, mais non pas parce qu'ils ont estimé que le droit international humanitaire des conflits armés internationaux n'était pas applicable. Leur refus était plutôt dû au fait que le CICR avait mentionné que l'emploi d'armes nucléaires serait incompatible avec le droit international humanitaire, ce que les États-Unis contestent. Les États-Unis ont par conséquent accepté une nouvelle version de l'appel qui ne fait pas référence aux armes nucléaires.[54]

IV Quel est le statut et le traitement, selon le droit international humanitaire, des personnes détenues à Guantánamo?

Au cours des opérations militaires en Afghanistan, un grand nombre d'Afghans, un certain nombre de nationaux de pays tiers et un ressortissant des États-Unis ayant rejoint le groupe Al-Qaïda sont tombés au pouvoir des États-Unis. Certains ont été arrêtés et transférés sur la base militaire de Guantánamo, où se trouvent également des personnes arrêtées dans des pays tiers. Le secrétaire à la défense D. Rumsfeld a indiqué qu'il s'agissait de Talibans et de membres d'Al-Qaïda et que toutes ces personnes n'étaient pas des prisonniers de guerre, mais des "combattants illégaux."[55] Cette qualification a été confirmée par le Président Bush, malgré le fait qu'il ait décidé que les Conventions de Genève s'appliquaient aux Talibans.[56]

A Arguments invoqués pour ne pas accorder le statut de prisonnier de guerre aux personnes détenues à Guantánamo

Ceux qui s'opposent à la qualification des personnes détenues à Guantánamo de prisonniers de guerre, invoquent deux ordres d'arguments.[57] Tout d'abord, ils expliquent pourquoi ce statut ne

---

[54] Voir pour cet épisode Roberts, *supra* note 43 à la p. 16; L. Condorelli, "Éditorial, Les attentats du 11 septembre et leurs suites: où va le droit international?" (2001) 105:4 R.G.D.I.P. 829, aux pp. 847 et 848.

[55] Voir *supra* note 10.

[56] Voir *supra* note 11.

[57] Nous tirons les arguments qui suivent de conférences de presse données le 28 janvier 2002 par le Président Bush (*supra* note 9), le même jour par son porte-parole (*supra* note 4) ainsi que par le secrétaire à la défense des États-Unis D. Rumsfeld les 11 et 22 janvier 2002 (*supra* note 10), le 7 février 2002 (*supra* note 11) et le 8 février 2002 (*supra* note 4), du témoignage de ce dernier du 5

serait pas applicable en faisant valoir qu'Al-Qaïda n'est pas un État, que les Talibans n'étaient pas reconnus par les États-Unis comme gouvernement légitime de l'Afghanistan, que les détenus sont des assassins et des terroristes, qu'ils auraient violé le droit international humanitaire et qu'il s'agirait d'une nouvelle forme de guerre. Aucun détenu n'aurait la nationalité d'un pays contre lequel les États-Unis seraient en guerre. L'administration américaine prétend, en outre, que les personnes détenues à Guantánamo n'auraient porté ni d'uniformes ni d'armes ouvertement, mais confirme qu'ils auraient tiré avec des armes à feu en Afghanistan.

Dans un deuxième ordre d'idées, on énumère les conséquences fâcheuses d'une qualification de prisonniers de guerre de ces personnes. On a affirmé que s'ils avaient ce statut, il deviendrait plus difficile de les poursuivre pour des attaques contre des objectifs militaires comme le navire de guerre "USS Cole" et des baraquements militaires des États-Unis en Arabie saoudite. En tant que prisonniers de guerre, ils devraient être rapatriés à la fin des hostilités ou poursuivis pour un crime. Ils ne pourraient pas être interrogés sur les réseaux terroristes. Le détenteur serait obligé de respecter leurs convictions et leurs droits personnels. On invoque ensuite de possibles problèmes de sécurité. Ils ne pourraient pas être enfermés. Ils auraient le droit de correspondre librement avec leurs familles et d'avoir en leur possession certains objets comme des ciseaux, des peignes, des rasoirs, des aiguilles et des canifs. Dans un esprit plus pointilleux, on fait valoir qu'en tant que prisonniers de guerre, les détenus de Guantánamo auraient droit à des rations de tabac, à des instruments musicaux et à des avances de solde.

Quant aux arguments niant l'applicabilité du droit international humanitaire, nous avons déjà traité de celui voulant que les Talibans n'aient pas la qualité de partie d'un conflit armé international avec les États-Unis. Il nous reste à discuter ceux qui se rapportent au statut de prisonnier de guerre et au traitement qui serait réservé aux détenus s'ils avaient ce statut.

---

février 2002 devant le Sénat (*supra* note 10), tout comme des articles de Rosett, Kamer et Montgomery (*supra* note 4) ainsi que de Wedgewood (*supra* note 5). Roberts, *supra* note 43 aux pp. 11, 24 et 25, mentionne également certains arguments, mais reste très nuancé et insiste, en particulier dans sa conclusion, *ibid.*, à la p. 27, sur l'applicabilité du droit international humanitaire à la "guerre contre le terrorisme."

B   LE DROIT INTERNATIONAL HUMANITAIRE S'APPLIQUE
     ÉGALEMENT AUX CONFLITS ARMÉS DIRIGÉS CONTRE DES
     ÉTATS "TERRORISTES"

Il y a cinquante ans déjà, un auteur nous expliquait que le statut de prisonnier de guerre était en danger dans toute "guerre-croisade."[58] Pourtant, en raison de la séparation absolue entre *jus ad bellum* et *jus in bello,* tout argument lié à la légitimité de la cause des États-Unis et à l'illégitimité de celle de leurs ennemis n'a pas d'incidence juridique sur la qualification et la protection des individus en droit international humanitaire.[59] Quant à l'argument selon lequel il s'agirait d'une nouvelle forme de guerre, il n'implique pas nécessairement que le droit existant ne s'y applique pas, si ce droit la couvre selon son texte, but, objet et contexte.[60] Adolf Hitler et Oussama Bin Laden estimaient tous deux s'être engagés dans une nouvelle forme de guerre à laquelle les vieilles règles ne s'appliquaient pas. Le "terrorisme" n'est d'ailleurs pas un concept juridique utile en droit international.[61] Celui-ci interdit plutôt les actes de terrorisme[62] et il organise et prescrit leur poursuite.[63] Il faudra revenir sur la question de savoir si une personne perd la protection offerte par le droit international humanitaire en raison de violations de ce droit commises par elle-même ou par les forces armées auxquelles elle appartient. Au-delà de cette question technique, l'on peut écarter tout argument lié aux crimes, non pas des personnes détenues elles-mêmes, mais directement ou indirectement attribués à leur groupe ou l'entité à laquelle elles appartiennent. Fort heureusement, les Alliés de la seconde guerre mondiale n'ont jamais estimé que les soldats allemands n'avaient pas droit au statut de prisonniers de guerre. Ces derniers appartenaient

---

[58] W. Flory, "Vers une nouvelle conception du prisonnier de guerre," (1954) 58 R.G.D.I.P. 53 à la p. 56.

[59] *Voir* ci-dessus, partie II.

[60] C'est ce qu'a affirmé à juste titre le ministre des Affaires étrangères canadien B. Graham, *supra* note 6, qui est également professeur de droit international.

[61] L. Henkin, "General Course on Public International Law," (1989) 216:4 Recueil des Cours 9 à la p. 159.

[62] Voir ci-dessus, partie III(F).

[63] Voir M. Henzelin, *Le principe de l'universalité en droit pénal international,* Genève, Helbing & Lichtenhahn, 2000, pp. 287-88, 294-98, 314-21, ainsi que la *Résolution 1373,* Doc.off. CS, 4385ᵉ séance, Doc. NU S/RES/1373 (2001), du 28 septembre 2001 qui décrète un petit code pénal international de la lutte contre le terrorisme.

pourtant à une "Wehrmacht" violant systématiquement le droit international humanitaire dans les territoires qu'elle occupait. Ils défendaient en outre un régime qui a tué six millions de Juifs en raison de leur seule appartenance raciale. À cause de leur lutte acharnée, le génocide a pu perdurer. Al-Qaïda, les Talibans et leurs membres sont-ils vraiment plus assassins et terroristes que ne l'étaient le régime nazi et ses soldats pendant la Seconde Guerre mondiale? Étant donné que les parties des conflits actuels se considèrent souvent mutuellement comme criminelles, il est essentiel pour la survie du droit international humanitaire et conforme à sa lettre et à son esprit de reconnaître son applicabilité juridique dans un tel cas. Des soldats américains risquent également de tomber un jour au pouvoir de forces armées qui considèrent les États-Unis et leur politique comme "criminels." Il est primordial pour eux qu'ils soient qualifiés de prisonniers de guerre et non pas de "combattants illégaux."

C   TOUTES LES PERSONNES QUI TOMBENT AU POUVOIR DE L'ENNEMI AU COURS D'UN CONFLIT ARMÉ INTERNATIONAL SONT PROTÉGÉES PAR LE DROIT INTERNATIONAL HUMANITAIRE

Des personnes qui tombent pendant un conflit armé international au pouvoir de la partie adverse sont ou bien des combattants — et elles deviennent des prisonniers de guerre protégés par la IIIe Convention — ou elles ne le sont pas — et elles deviennent des civils protégés selon la IVe Convention.[64] Ainsi que le résume le *Commentaire* publié par le CICR: "Il n'y a pas de statut intermédiaire; aucune personne se trouvant aux mains de l'ennemi ne peut être en dehors du droit."[65] Des civils qui participeraient directement aux hostilités perdent toutefois la protection prévue par le droit humanitaire *pendant la durée* de cette participation.[66]

---

[64] Art. 4(4) de la IVe Convention. C'est peut-être en vue de cette disposition que le Président Bush affirme dans sa déclaration du 7 février 2002 (*supra* note 11) que les Talibans détenus de Guantánamo ne sont pas des prisonniers de guerre, mais que les Conventions de Genève s'appliquent. Le secrétaire D. Rumsfeld mentionne toutefois trois catégories possibles: les combattants, les civils et les "combattants illégaux" (Témoignage du secrétaire D. Rumsfeld devant le Sénat américain, *supra* note 10).

[65] J.S. Pictet, dir., *Les Conventions de Genève du 12 août 1949, Commentaire, Convention de Genève relative à la protection des personnes civiles en temps de guerre*, vol. 4, Genève, CICR, 1956, p. 58.

[66] Art. 51(3) du Protocole I, qui correspond à une règle coutumière (voir Sassòli, *supra* note 44 aux pp. 393-96).

Traditionnellement, de telles personnes qui n'étaient pas des combattants, mais qui participaient néanmoins — et donc illégalement — aux hostilités ont été qualifiées de "combattants illégaux."[67] Même si on continue à utiliser ce terme, ces personnes sont aujourd'hui protégées par la IVᵉ Convention[68] dès qu'elles tombent au pouvoir de l'ennemi, ce qui n'exclut pas qu'elles puissent être punies pour leur participation directe aux hostilités, pour des crimes de guerre ou d'autres crimes. Mentionnons pour terminer qu'une des premières réactions du Président Bush aux attaques du 11 septembre 2001, celle de déclarer Oussama Bin Laden "wanted dead or alive" est difficilement compatible avec le droit international humanitaire. Comme le reconnaît le Manuel militaire des États-Unis, même en temps de guerre, il est interdit d'offrir une récompense pour la capture d'un ennemi "mort ou vivant."[69]

D   QUI A DROIT AU STATUT DE PRISONNIER DE GUERRE?

Sont considérés commes combattants, les membres des forces armées d'une partie à un conflit international. L'article 43(1) du Protocole I a adopté une notion large de "forces armées," en y incluant "toutes les forces, tous les groupes et toutes les unités armés et organisés qui sont placés sous un commandement responsable de la conduite de ses subordonnés devant cette Partie, même si celle-ci est représentée par un gouvernement ou une autorité non reconnus par une Partie adverse." La disposition précise que "ces forces armées doivent être soumises à un régime de discipline

---

[67] Voir Roberts, *supra* note 43 aux pp. 22-23;

[68] Roberts, *ibid.*, ne remarque pas cette conséquence. R.R. Baxter, "So-called 'Unprivileged Belligerency': Spies, Guerillas, and Saboteurs," (1951) 28 British Yearbook of International Law 323 aux pp. 328 et 344 mentionne la protection par la IVᵉ Convention, mais il donne, *ibid.* aux pp. 328, 336-38 et 343, tout comme Roberts, *ibid.*, et Rumsfeld, *supra* note 64, l'impression que les "combattants illégaux" constituent, à côté des prisonniers de guerre et des civils protégés, une troisième catégorie.

[69] L'art. 23(b) du Règlement de La Haye concernant les lois et coutumes de la guerre sur terre annexé à la Convention IV de 1907, interdit "de tuer ou blesser par trahison des individus appartenant à la nation ou à l'armée ennemie" (J.B. Scott (dir.), *Les Conventions et déclarations de la Haye de 1899 et 1907*, New York, Oxford University Press, 1918, p. 100). Cette disposition est interprétée par les États-Unis de la façon suivante: "This article is construed as prohibiting ... putting a price upon an enemy's head, as well as offering a reward for an enemy 'dead or alive'" (FM 27-10, Department of the Army Field Manual, The Law of Land Warfare, Washington D.C., Department of the Army, 1956, règle 31).

interne qui assure, notamment, le respect des règles du droit international applicable dans les conflits armés." La IIIe Convention utilise, dans son article 4(A)(1), une notion plus restrictive de "membres des forces armées d'une Partie au conflit, de même que ... membres des milices et des corps de volontaires faisant partie de ces forces armées," auxquels elle accorde le statut de prisonnier de guerre sans autre exigence quant à leur comportement.[70] Elle étend toutefois, par son article 4(A)(2), le statut de combattant à des membres d'autres groupes armés appartenant à une partie au conflit, à condition qu'un tel groupe soit soumis à une personne responsable pour ses subordonnés, porte un signe distinctif fixe et reconnaissable à distance et ses armes ouvertement et se conforme aux lois et coutumes de la guerre. Son article 4(A)(3) précise que "les membres des forces armées régulières qui se réclament d'un gouvernement ou d'une autorité non reconnus par la Puissance détentrice" bénéficient également du statut de prisonnier de guerre. Si les Talibans étaient, comme nous l'avons vu, le gouvernement de fait de l'Afghanistan, nous ne voyons pas comment l'on pourrait soutenir que leurs combattants n'appartenaient pas à leurs "forces armées" ou à des "milices et des corps de volontaires faisant partie de ces forces armées."

En tout état de cause, si l'on voulait appliquer les exigences du Protocole I[71] ou de l'art. 4(A)(2) de la IIIe Convention, il faudrait prendre en considération le fait que les Talibans étaient suffisamment organisés et disciplinés pour contrôler pendant des années la majorité du territoire afghan et pour mener efficacement le conflit contre l'Alliance du Nord. À notre connaissance, ni les États-Unis ni l'Alliance du Nord ne leur reprochent de ne pas s'être suffisamment distingués de la population civile. Cette condition fait référence à la situation de la guerre de guérilla. Les hostilités menées par les Talibans n'étaient pas une guerre de guérilla, vu qu'ils contrôlaient le territoire. Quant à la condition de respecter le droit international humanitaire, il est certain que beaucoup de ses règles ont été violées pendant des années en Afghanistan, tout autant par les Talibans que par l'Alliance du Nord. Les États-Unis n'ont, en revanche, à notre connaissance, jamais reproché aux Talibans un

---

[70] Voir toutefois Y. Sandoz, C. Swinarski et B. Zimmermann, dir., *Commentaire des Protocoles additionnels du 8 juin 1977 aux Conventions de Genève du 12 août 1949*, Genève, CICR, 1986, pp. 519-20.

[71] Qui réserve, en tout état de cause, à son art. 44(6) le droit de tous ceux qui auraient été considérés comme prisonniers de guerre sous la IIIe Convention.

non-respect généralisé du droit international humanitaire à leur égard, pendant les hostilités en Afghanistan. L'exigence du respect ne doit pas faire réapparaître, en droit international humanitaire, la condition de réciprocité, selon laquelle son respect ne serait pas dû à un ennemi qui ne le respecte pas. Cette réciprocité n'est pas applicable aux engagements de droit international humanitaire.[72] La pratique des États, y compris des États-Unis, est d'ailleurs à juste titre réticente à priver des prisonniers de guerre de leur statut pour la seule raison des violations commises par leurs forces ou leur partie. C'est ainsi que les États-Unis n'ont, à notre connaissance, jamais contesté ce statut pendant la Seconde Guerre mondiale aux soldats allemands, dont les forces armées étaient pourtant responsables d'exactions inouïes contre les populations civiles. La Commission internationale de Juristes mentionne dans une lettre adressée aux autorités américaines les manuels militaires d'États comme l'Argentine, la Hongrie, l'Italie, le Kenya, les Pays-Bas, la Nouvelle-Zélande, la Russie, l'Espagne et la Suisse comme preuves d'une pratique générale consistant à considérer tous ceux qui luttent en faveur d'une partie à un conflit international comme combattants, sans faire de distinction entre des forces armées régulières et irrégulières.[73] Précisons enfin que la nationalité d'un combattant n'a pas d'importance pour sa qualification de prisonnier de guerre, qui dépend uniquement de son appartenance aux forces armées ennemies. C'est seulement s'il a la nationalité du capteur qu'il ne bénéficie pas, de l'avis de la doctrine dominante, du statut de prisonnier de guerre.[74]

En ce qui concerne les membres d'Al-Qaïda, les États-Unis les rattachent apparemment à l'Afghanistan. Autrement, ils n'auraient pas pu, suite aux attaques effectuées par des membres de ce groupement, diriger leur légitime défense contre l'Afghanistan.

---

[72] Voir art. 60(5) de la *Convention de Vienne sur le droit des traités, supra* note 12; art. 1 commun aux quatre Conventions (l'obligation de respecter "en toutes circonstances," voir *infra* note 142); J. De Preux, "Les Conventions de Genève et la réciprocité," (1985) 751 RICR 24.

[73] Voir lettre de la Commission internationale de Juristes au Secrétaire d'État américain du 7 février 2002, en ligne: Commission internationale de Juristes <http://www.icj.org/press/press02/English/powel102.htm.> (date d'accès: 12 février 2002).

[74] H. Lauterpacht, dir., *Oppenheim's International Law, Disputes, War and Neutrality,* 7ᵉ éd., London, Longmans, vol. 2, 1952, à la p. 268; Flory, *supra* note 58 à la p. 81; R.C. Hingorani, *Prisoners of War,* 2ᵉ éd., New Delhi, 1982, aux pp. 31-32. *Contra:* R.-J. Wilhelm, "Peut-on modifier le statut des prisonniers de guerre?," (1953) 35 RICR 516 aux pp. 685-88.

Objectivement et considérant les faits, il peut tout de même être difficile de qualifier Al-Qaïda de force armée afghane, même au sens large. Nous ignorons si les membres de ce groupe qui agissaient en Afghanistan avaient été intégrés aux forces talibanes[75] ou s'ils étaient tout au moins subordonnés à l'Afghanistan, comme l'exigent les dispositions précitées de la IIIe Convention pour qu'ils soient des prisonniers de guerre.[76] Vu les déclarations de leur chef, on peut exprimer de sérieux doutes quant à savoir s'ils disposent du minimum de volonté de respecter le droit international humanitaire qu'on doit exiger malgré tout ce qui précède.[77] Ses membres seraient alors plutôt des civils protégés par la IVe Convention, mais ayant participé illégalement au conflit. Dans ce sens uniquement, ils pourraient être considérés comme "combattants illégaux." La distinction faite par le Président Bush dans sa décision du 7 février 2002, entre les Talibans et les membres d'Al-Qaïda, est donc tout à fait soutenable. Il est, en revanche, étonnant que le Président n'explique pas pourquoi ces derniers ne seraient pas protégés par la IVe Convention, même lorsqu'ils ont été capturés en Afghanistan.

E   DANS QUELLES CIRCONSTANCES ET SELON QUELLE PROCÉDURE PERD-ON LE STATUT DE COMBATTANT ET DE PRISONNIER DE GUERRE?

Les combattants des Talibans, tout au moins, sont donc, à notre avis, protégés par la IIIe Convention. Même s'ils avaient commis des crimes de guerre ou d'autres crimes, ils garderaient leur statut de prisonniers de guerre, y compris en cas de condamnation.[78] Seuls les combattants qui tombent au pouvoir de l'ennemi *alors* qu'ils ne se distinguent pas de la population civile, bien qu'ils prennent part à une attaque ou à une opération militaire préparatoire d'une attaque, perdent leur statut.[79] C'est dans ce contexte que la Cour

---

[75] Ce n'est pas exactement la question que nous avons analysée ci-dessus, soit si les membres d'Al-Qaïda impliqués dans les attentats du 11 septembre 2001 étaient en droit ou de fait des organes des Talibans (voir ci-dessus, partie III(B)). En effet, on pourrait imaginer que les combattants à l'intérieur de l'Afghanistan étaient contrôlés par les Talibans, mais non pas ceux qui se trouvaient à l'extérieur du pays. Les considérations que nous y avons faites nous amènent toutefois ici également à de forts doutes quant à leur "attribution" à l'Afghanistan.

[76] Art. 4(A)(1) et (2) de la IIIe Convention.

[77] *Supra* note 68.

[78] Art. 85 de la IIIe Convention.

[79] Art. 44(4) et (5) du Protocole I. Le Protocole I a relâché les exigences quant à la

suprême des États-Unis a utilisé en 1942 la qualification de "combattants illégaux" et refusé le traitement de prisonniers de guerre à des saboteurs, membres des forces armées allemandes, qui s'étaient déguisés en civils aux États-Unis.[80] Il est peu probable que *tous* les membres des Talibans transférés à Guantánamo avaient été capturés dans une telle situation.

En tout état de cause, ce n'est pas au Président des États-Unis de faire cette détermination collectivement pour tous les prisonniers, mais à un tribunal de le faire individuellement pour chacun. En effet, la IIIe Convention prescrit que "s'il y a doute sur l'appartenance à l'une des catégories énumérées à l'article 4 des personnes qui ont commis un acte de belligérance et qui sont tombées aux mains de l'ennemi, lesdites personnes bénéficieront de la protection de la présente Convention en attendant que leur statut ait été déterminé par un tribunal compétent."[81] Le Protocole I statue, qui plus est, qu'il y a doute dès qu'une personne revendique elle-même le statut de prisonnier de guerre.[82] La notion d'acte de belligérance ne fait d'ailleurs pas référence à la légitimité de l'acte (en *jus ad bellum* ou même en *jus in bello*), mais vise "le principe au nom duquel les intéressés ont agi."[83] Pendant la guerre du Vietnam, les États-Unis ont institué de tels tribunaux.[84] Dans le cas du général Manuel Antonio Noriega, arrêté par les États-Unis lors de leur invasion du Panama en 1989, un juge de district américain s'est déjà reconnu compétent pour reconnaître à une personne le statut de prisonnier de guerre contre l'avis du gouvernement.[85]

---

manière de se distinguer (*cf.* art. 44(3)), par rapport à celles de l'art. 4(A)(2) de la IIIe Convention, ce qui fut une des raisons majeures du rejet du Protocole I par les États-Unis (voir *infra* note 129 et Roberts, *supra* note 43 aux pp. 12-13). Sur les exigences du Protocole I, voir David, *supra* note 14 aux pp. 388-403.

[80] *Ex Parte Quirin et al.*, 317 U.S. 1 (1942), reproduit dans Sassòli et Bouvier, *supra* note 18 aux pp. 689-91.

[81] Art. 5(2). Voir également Baxter, *supra* note 68 aux pp. 343-44. Cette règle est confirmée dans le règlement 190-8 de l'armée américaine (voir témoignage du secrétaire D. Rumsfeld devant le Sénat américain du 5 février 2002, *supra* note 10).

[82] Art. 45(1) du Protocole I.

[83] Pictet, vol. 3, *supra* note 42 à la p. 86.

[84] David, *supra* note 14 à la p. 414, et *United States Military Assistance Command, Vietnam. Directives No. 381-46, Military Intelligence: Combined Screening of Detainees, 27 December 1967*, dans: Sassòli et Bouvier, *supra* note 18 aux pp. 780-83.

[85] *U.S. v. Manuel Antonio Noriega, supra* note 51.

Les États-Unis faisaient dans un premier temps valoir que concernant les détenus à Guantánamo, il n'existait pas de doute.[86] Vu ce qui précède et le fait que plusieurs États, le CICR et de nombreux experts soient d'un autre avis, nous croyons qu'il y a doute. Plus récemment, les États-Unis ont prétendu que l'exigence d'une décision par un tribunal est satisfaite par l'enquête que des agents du département de la défense, de la justice et de la CIA feraient sur place, en Afghanistan, avant d'envoyer un détenu à Guantánamo.[87] Il est vrai que la Convention ne spécifie pas la nature du "tribunal" et les travaux préparatoires nous indiquent que par ce terme, les États ne voulaient pas désigner exclusivement le tribunal pénal compétent pour juger une participation directe aux hostilités,[88] chef d'accusation inadmissible dans les cas où l'accusé bénéficie du statut du prisonnier de guerre.[89] Il nous semble tout de même que le terme "tribunal" fait référence à un organe judiciaire, qui doit avoir un minimum d'indépendance et être distinct des fonctionnaires ou soldats qui font le premier tri lorsque des personnes tombent au pouvoir d'un État. Si ces derniers pouvaient être considérés comme un tribunal, l'exigence que seul un tribunal peut trancher en cas de doute perdrait son effet utile. C'est donc à juste titre que le CICR a mentionné, suite à la décision rendue par le Président Bush le 7 février 2002, que la seule divergence qui subsistait entre les États-Unis et lui était la question relative aux procédures à appliquer pour déterminer que les personnes détenues n'ont pas droit au statut de prisonnier de guerre.[90] Notons enfin que ce n'est pas parce que le gouvernement actuel de l'Afghanistan semble être d'accord qu'il ne s'agit pas de prisonniers de guerre, que les Talibans perdent leur statut.[91]

[86] Voir témoignage du secrétaire D. Rumsfeld devant le Sénat américain du 5 février 2002, *supra* note 10.

[87] Voir les affirmations du secrétaire à la défense D. Rumsfeld lors de sa conférence de presse du 8 février 2002, *supra* note 4.

[88] Pictet, vol. 3, *supra* note 42 à la p. 86.

[89] Voir ci-dessous, partie IV(F).

[90] CICR, Communication à la presse n° 02/11, du 9 février 2002, en ligne: CICR, <http://www.icrc.org/icrcfre.nsf/c1256212004ce24e4125621200524882/c9 1ae8379fb6e215c1256b5b0036e3e9?OpenDocument> (date d'accès: 9 février 2002).

[91] Voir "Afghan Agrees With Bush on Prisoners," New York Times, 30 janvier 2002, en ligne: <http://www.nytimes.com/2002/01/30/international/asia/30 DETA.html> (date d'accès: 30 janvier 2002) et art. 6 de la IIIᵉ Convention: "Aucun accord spécial ne pourra porter préjudice à la situation des prisonniers,

F DES PRISONNIERS DE GUERRE PEUVENT ÊTRE POURSUIVIS POUR
DES CRIMES QU'ILS AURAIENT COMMIS

Si on reproche à des prisonniers de guerre des crimes individuellement commis (et non simplement leur appartenance à un
groupe dont d'autres membres auraient commis des crimes),[92] ils
peuvent être jugés devant les tribunaux militaires de la puissance
détentrice.[93] En vertu du principe de la compétence universelle,
des poursuites pour des crimes de guerre et des crimes contre l'humanité sont certainement admissibles.[94] La question de savoir si les
attaques du 11 septembre 2001 peuvent être qualifiées de crimes
contre l'humanité, ce qui serait le cas si elles constituaient une
attaque systématique ou généralisée contre une population civile,[95]
est controversée. Une telle qualification n'aurait toutefois pas de
conséquences pour les personnes détenues à Guantánamo, car la
Cour pénale internationale (CPI) n'est de toute façon pas compétente pour les attaques de New York et Washington.[96] Les États-Unis,
de leur côté, peuvent sans aucun doute poursuivre des personnes
soupçonnées d'être impliquées dans ces attaques en vertu de
leur compétence territoriale ordinaire. Concernant d'autres délits

---

telle qu'elle est réglée par la présente Convention, ni restreindre les droits que
celle-ci leur accorde."

[92] Voir dans ce sens déjà Baxter, *supra* note 68 à la p. 338.

[93] Art. 84 de la IIIᵉ Convention.

[94] Art. 49(2), 50(2), 129(2) et 146(2), respectivement, des quatre Conventions et
art. 85(1) du Protocole I; Henzelin, *supra* note 63.

[95] Voir pour la définition des crimes contre l'humanité, *Statut de la Cour pénale internationale*, adopté à Rome le 17 juillet 1998, art. 7, Doc. NU A/CONF/183.9, en
ligne: <http://www.un.org/law/icc/statute/romefra.htm> (date d'accès: 10
février 2002). Une telle qualification est, par exemple, proposée par la Haut
Commissaire des Nations Unies pour les droits de l'homme, M. Robinson, dans
une déclaration du 25 septembre 2001, en ligne: <http://www.un.org/News/
dh/20010925.htm#28> (date d'accès: 15 février 2002) et Roberts, *supra* note
43, à la p. 8; *De lege lata* plutôt sceptique A. Cassese, "Terrorism is also Disrupting
some Crucial Legal Categories of International Law," (2001) 12 EJIL 993 aux
pp. 994-95.

[96] En effet, le Statut de la CPI n'était, premièrement, pas encore en vigueur, n'ayant
reçu, au 15 février 2002, que 52 des 60 ratifications ou adhésions nécessaires.
Les États-Unis sont, deuxièmement, opposés à ce Statut (voir *infra* note 131) et
la poursuite par les États-Unis aurait, troisièmement, la priorité même si la CPI
était compétente (art. 17 du Statut, *supra* note 95). Ceux qui souhaitent une
poursuite des auteurs des attaques du 11 septembre 2001 devant la CPI pro-
posent donc une révision de son Statut (voir Cassese, *supra* note 95 à la p. 1000).

commis en Afghanistan, ils ne sont, en revanche, pas nécessairement compétents. Les poursuites se déroulent selon la même procédure que celle qui serait applicable à des soldats américains.[97] Le
cas du général Manuel Antonio Noriega constitue un précédant
lors duquel les États-Unis ont poursuivi une personne qu'ils reconnaissaient comme prisonnier de guerre, même pour des crimes
non liés au conflit armé au cours duquel elle a été capturée.[98] En
revanche, puisqu'il est un combattant, un prisonnier de guerre
ne peut pas être poursuivi pour le seul fait d'avoir participé aux
hostilités contre les États-Unis, s'il a respecté le droit international
humanitaire. Des hostilités contre les forces des États-Unis en
Afghanistan ne seraient donc pas punissables. Les attaques contre
le navire "USS Cole" et les baraquements en Arabie saoudite ne
se sont, en revanche, pas produites pendant un conflit armé entre
l'Afghanistan et les États-Unis. Si le droit international humanitaire avait été applicable, elles l'auraient violé, même si elles
visaient des objectifs militaires. En effet, les attaquants ont feint
d'avoir le statut de civils, ce qui est un acte de perfidie.[99] Des prisonniers de guerre pourraient, en conséquence, être poursuivis
pour avoir pris part à ces attaques.[100]

Contrairement à ce que certains ont cru comprendre, la règle
générale selon laquelle un prisonnier de guerre n'est tenu de
déclarer que ses nom, prénoms et grade, sa date de naissance et son
numéro matricule[101] n'interdit pas qu'on lui pose d'autres questions et ne s'applique pas à une enquête pénale. Lors d'une telle
enquête, toutes les questions qui pourraient être posées à un soldat
américain sont admissibles,[102] mais aucune contrainte physique ou
morale ne peut être exercée sur le prévenu pour qu'il se recon-
naisse coupable.[103]

---

[97] Art. 102 de la III⁰ Convention.

[98] *U.S. v. Manuel Antonio Noriega et al.*, United States District Court for the Southern District of Florida, 746 F. Supp. 1506 (1990), partiellement reproduit dans
Sassòli et Bouvier, *supra* note 18 aux pp. 923-32.

[99] Art. 37(1)(c) du Protocole I.

[100] Contrairement à ce que craint R. Wedgewood, *supra* note 5.

[101] Art. 17 de la III⁰ Convention.

[102] *Ibid.*, art. 102.

[103] *Ibid.*, art. 99(2). Notons que le 5⁰ amendement de la Constitution des États-Unis
et l'art. 14(3)(g) du *Pacte international relatif aux droits civils et politiques*, 19 décembre 1966, 999 R.T.N.U. 171, [1976] R.T. Can. 1976 n° 47 (entrée en vigueur:
19 août 1976), vont bien plus loin en ce qui concerne ce droit de se taire.

G   LE TRAITEMENT DES PRISONNIERS DE GUERRE

Les prisonniers de guerre peuvent être internés en dehors de l'Afghanistan. Il est normal de les interner en pays ennemi, mais l'ennemi peut établir un camp de prisonniers de guerre sur tout autre territoire qu'il contrôle. Il est vrai que les prisonniers de guerre doivent avoir une certaine liberté de mouvement dans leur camp et qu'ils ne peuvent pas être détenus dans des pénitenciers ni enfermés, à l'exception de ceux qui sont soumis à des poursuites pénales.[104] Les règles très détaillées sur leur traitement sont différentes pour les prisonniers de guerre ordinaires[105] et pour ceux qui se trouvent en détention préventive.[106] Elles ont été élaborées par des experts militaires, tenant compte des besoins de sécurité de la puissance détentrice. Cette dernière établit en particulier les règlements, donne les ordres et assure la discipline.[107] Le CICR a le droit de visiter les prisonniers de guerre dans leur lieu d'internement selon ses modalités de visite traditionnelles pour vérifier leurs conditions de détention.[108]

Les prisonniers doivent être autorisés à correspondre avec leur famille, mais la censure et des limitations s'appliquent à cette correspondance.[109] Ils doivent également être autorisés à recevoir des instruments musicaux dans le cadre d'envois de secours,[110] mais il est clair que de tels envois peuvent faire l'objet de tous les contrôles de sécurité nécessaires. Le tabac doit être autorisé, mais non fourni.[111] Les ciseaux, les peignes, les rasoirs, les aiguilles et les canifs ne sont pas mentionnés dans la IIIe Convention, mais il est vrai que le *Commentaire* du CICR énumère ces articles parmi ceux qui devraient pouvoir être achetés par des prisonniers de guerre dans leur cantine.[112]

---

[104] Art. 21 et 22 de la IIIe Convention.

[105] *Ibid.*, art. 25-29.

[106] *Ibid.*, art. 103(3), 97 et 98.

[107] *Ibid.*, art. 39-42.

[108] *Ibid.*, art. 126(4).

[109] *Ibid.*, art. 71.

[110] *Ibid.*, art. 72(1).

[111] *Ibid.*, art. 26(3).

[112] Pictet, *supra* note 42 à la p. 203, concernant l'art. 28 de la IIIe Convention. R. Wedgewood, *supra* note 5, écrit: "The treaty guarantees them utensils including "razors, combs (and) nail scissors," as well as "needles" and "pen-knives." Elle énumère ces objets entre guillemets comme s'ils apparaissaient dans le texte de la Convention et comme si la puissance détentrice devait les fournir aux prisonniers de guerre.

À notre avis une puissance détentrice est, malgré ce passage du *Commentaire*, en droit d'interdire, pour des raisons de sécurité, la vente, dans la cantine, d'objets qui sont interdits aujourd'hui à tout passager de l'aviation civile, mais elle doit évidemment garantir autrement que les prisonniers puissent satisfaire leurs besoins hygiéniques. Il est en revanche vrai qu'une puissance détentrice doit verser à des prisonniers de guerre une avance de solde équivalant à huit Francs suisses (ce qui correspond à environ huit dollars canadiens) par mois.[113] Finalement, les prisonniers de guerre doivent être rapatriés à la fin des hostilités actives, à l'exception de ceux qui seraient sous le coup d'une poursuite pénale ou qui purgeraient une peine.[114] Pour l'instant, la fin des hostilités entre les États-Unis et les Talibans n'est pas encore arrivée. On ne pourra toutefois pas attendre jusqu'à la fin de la "guerre contre le terrorisme," qui peut être longue, surtout si on assimile au terrorisme tout ce que les États-Unis perçoivent comme les maux du monde.

H   DES CIVILS PROTÉGÉS PAR LE DROIT INTERNATIONAL
    HUMANITAIRE NE POURRAIENT PAS ÊTRE DÉTENUS
    À GUANTÁNAMO

Toutes les personnes capturées par les États-Unis en Afghanistan, qui ne sont pas des combattants selon ce qui précède, sont des civils tombés au pouvoir de l'ennemi dans un territoire occupé.[115] À l'exception de nationaux des États-Unis, elles sont protégées par la IVe Convention, indépendamment de ce qu'on leur reproche.[116] Leur détention n'est admissible qu'en vue d'un procès régulier ou pour d'impérieuses raisons de sécurité.[117] Si elles sont appréhendées en tant qu'espion ou saboteur ou parce qu'elles ont fait individuellement l'objet d'une suspicion légitime de s'être livrées à une activité préjudiciable à la sécurité des États-Unis, elles peuvent, dans les cas où la sécurité militaire l'exige absolument, être privées des droits de communication prévus par la IVe Convention.[118] Elles

---

[113] Art. 60 de la IIIe Convention.

[114] *Ibid.*, art. 118 et 119(5).

[115] Voir ci-dessus, partie IV(B).

[116] Art. 4(1) de la IVe Convention: "Sont protégées par la Convention les personnes qui, à un moment quelconque et de quelque manière que ce soit, se trouvent, en cas de conflit ou d'occupation, au pouvoir d'une Partie au conflit ou d'une Puissance occupante dont elles ne sont pas ressortissantes."

[117] *Ibid.*, art. 76 et 78, respectivement.

[118] *Ibid.*, art. 5(2).

aussi peuvent être visitées par le CICR en vue de vérifier leurs conditions de détention.[119] Des tribunaux militaires peuvent être constitués par les États-Unis afin de les juger pour des violations du droit international, par exemple en cas de participation (illégale pour des civils) à des hostilités, mais uniquement en Afghanistan.[120] Quant à leur lieu de détention, la Convention prescrit que les personnes protégées inculpées, condamnées ou internées pour des raisons de sécurité doivent être détenues dans le pays occupé.[121] C'est ainsi que le Conseil de Sécurité et des États tiers ont régulièrement condamné Israël pour la déportation de Palestiniens en dehors des territoires palestiniens occupés.[122] Le CICR a également qualifié de déportation violant la IVe Convention le fait que l'Iraq transféra sur son propre territoire des Iraniens qu'il avait arrêtés dans des territoires iraniens qu'il occupait.[123] Plus spécifiquement, fut condamné par le CICR comme violation de la IVe Convention, le fait qu'Israël transféra, sur son propre territoire, des détenus qu'il avait arrêtés pour des actes terroristes au Sud du Liban et qu'il avait dans un premier temps détenus sur ce territoire occupé.[124]

Des personnes arrêtées en Afghanistan qui ne seraient pas des prisonniers de guerre ne pourraient donc pas être détenues à Guantánamo. Il est étonnant que ni les États-Unis ni le CICR n'abordent publiquement ce problème. Pour l'administration américaine, la question du respect de la IVe Convention de Genève se pose toutefois inévitablement en ce qui concerne les Talibans, étant donné qu'elle reconnaît que les Conventions les protègent, mais leur nie le statut de prisonnier de guerre. Nous avons vu qu'elle prétend que le tri par un "tribunal compétent" se fait déjà en Afghanistan.[125]

---

[119] *Ibid.*, art. 143(5).

[120] *Ibid.*, art. 66.

[121] *Ibid.*, art. 76(1) et 49(1).

[122] Voir *Résolution* 607, Doc. off. CS, 2780[e] séance, Doc. NU S/RES/607 (1988), du 5 janvier 1988, et *Résolution* 681 Doc. off. CS, 2970[e] séance, Doc. NU S/RES/681 (1990), du 20 décembre 1990, ainsi que *Note de la Direction du droit international public du Département [suisse] des affaires étrangères,* du 20 janvier 1988, dans: (1989) 46 Annuaire suisse de droit international 247.

[123] Voir Memorandum adressé par le CICR le 7 mai 1983 à tous les États parties des Conventions de Genève, dans: Sassòli et Bouvier, *supra* note 18 aux pp. 978, 981-82.

[124] Voir communiqué de presse du CICR sur la fermeture du camp de détention d'Insar au Sud du Liban, CICR, *Communiqué de presse n° 1504,* du 4 avril 1985, dans Sassòli et Bouvier, *ibid.*, pp. 889-90.

[125] Voir *supra* note 87.

Or, si cette enquête avait déterminé qu'une personne n'est pas un prisonnier de guerre, cette personne ne pouvait pas être transférée à Guantánamo. Si la décision du "tribunal" ne survient qu'à Cuba, la personne concernée doit être renvoyée en Afghanistan, pour rétablir la situation antérieure au transfert qui s'est révélé contraire au droit international.[126]

V   Le droit international humanitaire devrait-il être révisé pour tenir compte de la "guerre contre le terrorisme"?

Après chaque guerre majeure, le droit international humanitaire a été révisé pour l'adapter aux réalités militaires et technologiques changeantes et surtout pour couvrir de nouveaux problèmes humanitaires et de nouvelles catégories de victimes.[127] Ces dernières années, on a en particulier tenté de renforcer les mécanismes de mise en œuvre par l'établissement de tribunaux pénaux internationaux *ad hoc* et d'une Cour pénale internationale (CPI), à interdire complètement certaines armes et à rapprocher, par la jurisprudence et dans certains traités, le droit des conflits non internationaux de celui des conflits armés internationaux.[128] Tout processus de révision implique toutefois le risque que les États en profitent pour élargir leur liberté d'action au lieu de renforcer la protection des victimes. Le résultat en forme de traité doit ensuite être accepté par chaque État pour le lier. Les États-Unis ne sont pas très coopératifs dans ce domaine. Ils n'ont même pas encore accepté la dernière grande vague de révisions, celle des Protocoles additionnels de 1977,[129] ils rejettent l'interdiction des mines anti-personnelles[130] et s'opposent farouchement à l'établissement d'une Cour pénale internationale.[131] Considérant cette réticence du membre le plus

---

[126]   Voir *Projet d'articles, supra* note 21, art. 35.

[127]   T. Meron, "The Humanization of Humanitarian Law," (2000) 94 AJIL 239.

[128]   Pour un panorama des développements récents du droit international humanitaire et des principales questions ouvertes voir Y. Sandoz, "Le demi-siècle des Conventions de Genève," (1999) 834 RICR 241.

[129]   G. Roberts, "The New Rules for Waging War: The Case Against Ratification of Additional Protocol I" (1985) 26 Virg. JIL 109; A. Sofaer, "Agora: The US Decision not to Ratify Protocol I to the Geneva Conventions on the Protection of War Victims, The Rationale for the United States Decision," (1988) 82 AJIL 784.

[130]   Sandoz, *supra* note 128 aux pp. 251-53.

[131]   M. Leigh, "The United States and the Statute of Rome," (2001) 95 AJIL 124.

influent du Conseil de sécurité, on ne pourra pas non plus utiliser ce qui semble être devenu la nouvelle voie rapide de législation internationale, celle d'une résolution du Conseil de Sécurité qui vient de révolutionner, par exemple, le droit international pénal en matière de lutte contre le terrorisme.[132] Abstraction faite des difficultés liées à l'élaboration et à l'acceptation de nouvelles règles dans la société internationale actuelle, reste la question de fond à savoir si et comment le droit pouvait être adapté pour mieux couvrir une attaque terroriste comme celle du 11 septembre 2001 et la "guerre contre le terrorisme" que les États-Unis ont déclenchée en réaction.

A DES RÈGLES POUR "HUMANISER" LA "GUERRE" D'AL-QAÏDA?

Les attaques terroristes, nous l'avons vu, sont clairement interdites dans la mesure où le droit international humanitaire s'applique. Pourrait-on imaginer des règles de ce droit qui s'adapteraient à cette "nouvelle forme de guerre"? Pour ce faire, elles devraient, comme le fait le droit international humanitaire traditionnel, permettre aux protagonistes d'atteindre leur objectif, à Al-Qaïda donc d'attaquer les États-Unis, tout en leur imposant un minimum d'humanité, en évitant des souffrances "non nécessaires" ou "collatérales." Nous ne croyons pas que de telles règles puissent être élaborées tout en restant humanitaires. Si elles prévoyaient un minimum d'humanité, il est peu probable qu'elles seront acceptées et encore moins imaginable qu'elles seront respectées par de tels groupes. Une possibilité d'"adhésion" de la part de tels groupes à ces règles rencontrerait d'ailleurs une réticence de la part des États craignant certainement qu'elle puisse donner un certain statut et une certaine légitimité à ces groupes. Certes, on pourrait imaginer un "code de conduite" adopté par les États ou des organisations humanitaires pour de tels groupes, mais il est peu probable que ces derniers se sentiraient liés par un tel document. On créerait d'ailleurs inévitablement une nouvelle catégorie, avec un seuil d'application et un contenu différents de ceux que le droit actuel prévoit pour les conflits internationaux et non internationaux, avec tous les risques d'abus et toutes les controverses de qualification que cela implique.

---

[132] *Résolution 1373*, *supra* note 63, qui décrète un petit code pénal international de la lutte contre le terrorisme. Pour quelques questions concernant cette étonnante nouvelle forme de législation, voir Condorelli, *supra* note 54 aux pp. 834 et 835.

B   LE DROIT INTERNATIONAL EST-IL INADÉQUAT POUR LA
      "GUERRE CONTRE LE TERRORISME"?

La "guerre contre le terrorisme," quant à elle, doit se traduire surtout en la recherche, la poursuite et la punition des responsables, mais également en toutes sortes de mesures de défense sociale destinées à éradiquer les injustices, les inégalités, la pauvreté, les souffrances et les frustrations qui constituent un terrain fertile, parfois même la cause, mais jamais une justification pour des actes terroristes. Ce n'est pas le droit international humanitaire, mais les droits de la personne civils, politiques, économiques, sociaux et culturels, qui s'appliquent et qui facilitent une telle défense sociale. Notons toutefois qu'un respect scrupuleux de la IVᵉ Convention de Genève par l'Israël dans les territoires qu'il occupe serait certainement une contribution à faire tarir les sources dont des groupes tels qu'Al-Qaïda se nourrissent.

Si la "guerre au terrorisme" prend la forme d'hostilités avec des groupes armés organisés, nous l'avons vu, le droit international humanitaire s'applique. Si ces groupes contrôlent et représentent, légitimement ou non, un État, c'est même le droit des conflits armés internationaux qui doit être respecté — par les deux parties. Notre analyse n'a révélé aucune disposition de la IIIᵉ ou de la IVᵉ Convention de Genève qui ne pourrait pas être respectée dans une telle "guerre." L'ennemi peut être défait, les responsables peuvent être traduits en justice, les terroristes peuvent être détenus et la sécurité à Guantánamo peut être garantie. Après analyse des différents arguments pratiques contre un respect intégral de la IIIᵉ Convention de Genève, seule l'obligation de payer des avances de solde apparaît comme une conséquence fâcheuse d'une applicabilité de la IIIᵉ Convention. Une telle dépense de huit Francs suisses par détenu et par mois nous semble toutefois être un inconvénient mineur dans une guerre qui coûte un milliard de dollars américains par mois.

C   COMMENT DÉFINIR LE CHAMP D'APPLICATION DE NOUVELLES
      RÈGLES POUR LA "GUERRE CONTRE LE TERRORISME"?

Si on voulait élaborer de nouvelles règles pour une nouvelle forme de guerre, il faudrait également définir les situations auxquelles elles s'appliqueraient. Selon les États-Unis, ce n'est pas seulement la "guerre" contre Al-Qaïda, mais aussi celle contre les Talibans qui tombe dans cette catégorie. Les États-Unis ont annoncé qu'ils ne feraient pas de distinction entre les terroristes et ceux qui les hébergent ou les soutiennent.[133] Est-ce également vrai pour les règles humanitaires qui devraient être applicables? La poursuite de la guerre contre l'Iraq, l'Iran et la Corée du Nord est annoncée.[134] Ces conflits tomberont-ils également sous les nouvelles règles? Ou alors considérera-t-on que le régime de Saddam Hussein est plus légitime que celui des Talibans? Il est sûr que dans les faits, le régime iraquien ne contrôle pas une portion supérieure du territoire iraquien à celle que les Talibans contrôlaient, le 11 septembre 2001, du territoire afghan. Et si la Russie de Putin ne s'était pas démonstrativement ralliée aux États-Unis après le 11 septembre, mais opposée à toute opération en Asie centrale, une guerre contre la Russie serait-elle également tombée sous ces nouvelles règles? Certes, une ligne de partage peut être trouvée. Encore doit-elle être acceptée, y compris par ceux contre qui la guerre tombera sous des règles révisées. Les nouvelles règles qui offriront, par hypothèse, une protection moindre aux prisonniers, s'appliqueront-elles des deux côtés d'une "guerre contre le terrorisme" ou propose-t-on d'abandonner le principe de l'égalité des belligérants devant le droit international humanitaire? Dans ce dernier cas, qui croît que ces règles seront respectées par ceux qui sont qualifiés de "terroristes"?

D   QUELLES NOUVELLES RÈGLES HUMANITAIRES POUR LA "GUERRE CONTRE LE TERRORISME"?

Une fois le domaine d'application du nouveau droit défini, il faudra se mettre d'accord sur son contenu. Faut-il créer une brèche entre la IIIe et la IVe Convention de Genève avec une catégorie de "combattants illégaux" qui bénéficieraient de moindres garanties humanitaires? Qui procéderait à la qualification nécessaire? Comment éviter que dorénavant chaque belligérant considère son adversaire comme "terroriste" et qualifie les prisonniers qu'il détient

---

[133] Voir Public Law 107-40, 107th Congress, Joint Resolution to authorize the use of United States Armed Forces against those responsible for the recent attacks launched against the United States, 18 septembre 2001, S.J. Res. 23, en ligne: <http://thomas.loc.gov/cgi-bin/bdquery/z?d107:s.j.res.00023> (date d'accès: 4 février 2002): "That the President is authorized to use all necessary and appropriate force against those nations, organizations, or persons he determines planned, authorized, committed, or aided the terrorist attacks that occurred on September 11, 2001, or harbored such organizations or persons, in order to prevent any future acts of international terrorism against the United States by such nations, organizations or persons."

[134] Voir *supra* note 1.

de "combattants illégaux"? Ceux qui risquent de devenir des "combattants illégaux" aux mains de l'ennemi respecteront-ils encore moins le droit international humanitaire qu'ils ne le font actuellement? Qui veut permettre la torture pour démanteler des réseaux terroristes? Interdire toute correspondance entre des "terroristes" et leurs familles? Faut-il rendre des Talibans luttant en Afghanistan en portant leurs armes ouvertement punissables s'ils attaquent un char américain? Est-ce indispensable dans la "guerre contre le terrorisme" que des civils accusés de terrorisme puissent être détenus et jugés sur une île des Caraïbes et non pas là où ils ont été arrêtés pendant la guerre?

Certes, théoriquement, les États peuvent adopter de nouvelles réponses à toutes les questions qui précèdent. Un nouvel ensemble de règles du droit international humanitaire serait né. Constituerait-il vraiment un progrès pour toutes les victimes des nombreux conflits armés dans le monde ou tout au moins pour la plupart d'entre elles? Le nouveau droit devra inévitablement s'appliquer à tous les conflits. Vu les difficultés de qualification, il serait pratiquement impossible de garder les vieilles règles pour les conflits qui ne tomberaient pas dans la catégorie des "nouveaux conflits." À l'image de la société des États à laquelle il s'applique, le droit international reste marqué par la décentralisation, la coordination et, surtout, *l'auto-application* des règles. Les quelques éléments précurseurs d'un ordre international de subordination et d'institutionnalisation, tels que l'organisation des Nations Unies et la Cour pénale internationale n'ont pas la faveur des États-Unis. Une résolution du Conseil de Sécurité décidant qu'un certain conflit tombe sous les nouvelles règles n'impressionnera pas beaucoup la partie adverse. Le Conseil de Sécurité devrait d'ailleurs être utilisé pour décider, légitimer et conduire la guerre contre le terrorisme, mais il serait alors partie et donc mal placé pour émettre une qualification. La Cour pénale internationale, quant à elle, n'interviendra qu'après le conflit, tandis que les règles applicables du droit international humanitaire devraient être claires et respectées *pendant* le conflit.

E   FAUT-IL ATTENDRE UN MONDE MEILLEUR AVANT D'ADOPTER
     UN DROIT HUMANITAIRE POUR LES "ACTIONS DE POLICE
     INTERNATIONALE"?

Précisons, pour terminer, que nous aussi souhaitons ardemment qu'un jour un nouveau droit international humanitaire, complètement différent de celui que nous connaissons, puisse être adopté, parce qu'il correspondra, ce jour-là, à la réalité d'une société internationale de 200 États qui sera devenue une communauté internationale de six milliards d'êtres humains. D'autres ont souhaité, dans le même esprit, "la fin du droit international humanitaire."[135] Ce jour-là, le monde sera régi par la primauté du droit, il disposera d'une police internationale qui la met en œuvre et les États (même Unis) ne seront plus souverains. Ce jour-là, la séparation entre *jus ad bellum* et *jus in bello* n'aura plus de raison d'être et l'égalité des belligérants devant le droit international humanitaire pourra finalement prendre sa retraite bien méritée dans l'histoire du droit international. Les guerres seront alors effectivement devenues des actions d'application de la loi, dans lesquelles il faudra prescrire des *"temperamenta belli,"* des restrictions allant bien au-delà de celles du droit international humanitaire actuel et qui s'adresseront à la police internationale.[136] Comme le droit international des droits de la personne le prescrit actuellement pour les opérations de police, l'usage de la force devra être proportionnel et une mesure subsidiaire même à l'égard de ceux qui prendraient part à des hostilités et qu'on pourra qualifier de "criminels internationaux." Il est vrai que ces derniers ne pourront plus être liés aux mêmes règles (ou même par n'importe quelle règle). Comme dans les droits internes, il n'y aura plus de règles qui statueront comment ceux qui s'opposent à la police peuvent lutter contre la police. Il est évident que ce jour-là, les statuts de combattant et de prisonnier de guerre n'auront plus de raison d'être. Tous ceux qui s'opposeront à la légalité internationale seront des "combattants illégaux" qui devront faire face à la justice.

De ce nouveau monde qui exige un nouveau droit international humanitaire, nous en sommes encore bien loin. Le soussigné se demande même si nous ne nous sommes pas éloignés de ce monde meilleur depuis le 11 septembre 2001. En effet, ce monde nécessitera des institutions fortes et crédibles et ne pourra tolérer l'unilatéralisme, l'autoprotection et la légitime défense qu'en dernier ressort. Or, indépendamment de la question de savoir si les États-Unis pouvaient invoquer la légitime défense contre un acteur non étatique et pour justifier une opération militaire contre des États

---

[135] Sandoz, *supra* note 128 aux pp. 258-59.

[136] Pour Grotius, les restrictions des *"temperamenta belli"* s'adressaient également uniquement à la partie qui mène une guerre juste, et non pas à leur ennemi; voir P. Haggenmacher, *Grotius et la doctrine de la guerre juste,* Paris, Presses Universitaires de France, 1983, en particulier pp. 597-605.

hébergeant cet acteur,[137] nous regrettons que les États-Unis aient préféré cette voie unilatérale à la voie institutionnelle de mesures contre des menaces à la paix et la sécurité internationales décidées par le Conseil de Sécurité. C'est d'autant plus regrettable que les États-Unis avaient main libre dans cet organe et qu'ils auraient pu prendre toutes les mesures effectivement prises jusqu'à fin janvier 2002 à titre de réponse institutionnelle des Nations Unies (ou avec une autorisation des Nations Unies).[138] Les Nations Unies et leur Conseil de sécurité en particulier peuvent certes être critiqués à maints égards. Leur composition, leur réglementation juridique, leur pratique sélective et leur faiblesse sont loin de ce qu'on souhaiterait d'un organe pour faire prévaloir la primauté du droit international. Il s'agit toutefois du seul embryon fragile représentant la communauté internationale institutionnalisée dont nous disposons. Même les États-Unis, seule superpuissance, auraient un intérêt à renforcer la crédibilité de ces institutions au lieu de montrer, sans réelle nécessité, qu'elles n'ont pas de véritable importance dans le domaine pour lequel elles ont été créées: le maintien de la paix.[139]

[137] Voir à ce sujet quelques réflexions de Condorelli, *supra* note 54, aux pp. 838 et 839; des remarques critiques lors d'un débat sur le site Internet de l'*European Journal of International Law*, en ligne: <http://www.ejil.org/forum_WTC/index.html> (date d'accès: 5 février 2002) auquel ont participé les Professeurs A. Pellet, P.-M. Dupuy, G. Gaja et A. Cassese; voir aussi J.I. Charney, "The Use of Force Against Terrorism and International Law, Editorial Comment," (2001) 95 AJIL 835 à la p. 836; Cassese, *supra* note 95 aux pp. 995-99. Dans la doctrine antérieure, voir les vues restrictives de A. Cassese, "Article 51," dans J.P. Cot et A. Pellet, *La Charte des Nations Unies,* 2ᵉ éd., Paris, Économica, 1991, 771 aux pp. 780-84; Schachter, *supra* note 50 aux pp. 164-69; Henkin, *supra* note 61 aux pp. 161-62. Pour une défense de la légalité des actions américaines, voir W.M. Reisman "In Defense of World Public Order, Editorial Comment," *ibid.,* pp. 833-35, et T.M. Franck, "Terrorism and the Right of Self-Defense, Editorial Comment," *ibid.,* pp. 839-43.

[138] Suivant les constatations de Condorelli, *supra* note 54, aux pp. 840-44, les différentes résolutions adoptées par le Conseil de Sécurité depuis le 11 septembre 2001 (voir en particulier la *Résolution 1368,* Doc. off. CS, 4370ᵉ séance, Doc. NU S/RES/1368 (2001) et la *Résolution 1373, supra* note 63) et les débats à l'Assemblée générale et au Conseil de Sécurité peuvent être considérées comme exprimant une *opinio juris* des États sur l'admissibilité de l'invocation de la légitime défense par les États-Unis. Voir dans le même sens Cassese, *supra* note 95 aux pp. 996-97. Cette attitude presque générale des autres États ne modifie toutefois pas la nature unilatérale et non institutionnelle de la réaction américaine.

[139] Voir dans ce sens également A. Pellet, "Malaise dans la guerre: à quoi sert l'ONU?," *Le Monde,* 15 novembre 2001, et Charney, *supra* note 137 aux pp. 836-39.

En attendant ce monde meilleur, dont certains craignent qu'il ne s'éloigne, gardons le droit international humanitaire qui est adapté aux réalités du monde actuel. Malgré les débuts fragiles d'institutionnalisation à travers les Nations Unies, notre monde consiste encore en une société d'États souverains et égaux. Le droit international humanitaire actuel traitant les belligérants d'un conflit international sur un pied d'égalité et prévoyant les statuts de combattant et de prisonnier de guerre (tout en exigeant la punition des individus qui commettent des crimes) correspond à cette réalité.

VI CONCLUSION

Nous n'avons pas de soucis quant au traitement des personnes détenues à Guantánamo. Nous sommes convaincus que les États-Unis les traitent humainement et le CICR est présent pour le vérifier. D'autres, en particulier les personnes détenues dans le conflit entre forces afghanes, auxquel le droit des conflits armés internationaux ne s'applique pas, courent sans aucun doute des risques bien supérieurs à cet égard. Notre souci est la survie du droit international humanitaire, et donc le traitement des victimes des conflits futurs. Est-ce "devenir les défenseurs des terroristes?"[140] Faisons-nous partie de "poches isolées *d'hyperventilation internationale*?"[141] Si un État de droit comme les États-Unis invoquait largement des arguments liés à la légitimité de sa lutte pour qualifier ses ennemis de "combattants illégaux," un précédant dangereux serait créé. Nous nous réjouissons donc de la décision du Président américain du 7 février 2002 qui reconnaît l'applicabilité des Conventions de Genève. Le Canada, engagé aux côtés des États-Unis, était en droit de leur rappeler leurs obligations, allant dans ce sens, en vertu du droit international humanitaire. C'est ainsi qu'il a rempli, premièrement, son obligation, prévue à l'article 1 commun aux quatre Conventions de Genève, de non seulement respecter, mais

---

[140] Comme le Premier ministre Chrétien l'a reproché, le 6 février 2002 à la Chambre des Communes, aux députés du Bloc québécois qui posaient des questions sur le statut et le destin des personnes capturées par les forces canadiennes en Afghanistan (voir M. Cornellier, "Le Bloc défend les terroristes, dit Chrétien," Le Devoir, 7 février 2002, pp. 1 et 8).

[141] Le secrétaire à la défense D. Rumsfeld a parlé lors de sa conférence de presse du 8 février 2002, *supra* note 4, de "isolated pockets of international hyperventilation."

également "faire respecter" ces Conventions "en toutes circonstances."[142] Un tel rappel était, deuxièmement, dans l'intérêt des soldats canadiens, qui eux aussi ont tout intérêt à ce qu'aucun ennemi ne puisse jamais les qualifier de "combattants illégaux" pour les priver de certaines protections. Troisièmement, lorsque des personnes protégées par la IIIe Convention tombent au pouvoir des forces canadiennes déployées en Afghanistan, le Canada est responsable de leur traitement. Il ne peut les transférer aux États-Unis qu'après s'être assuré que ceux-ci sont "désireu[x] et à même d'appliquer la Convention."[143]

Nous espérons qu'au moment où ces lignes sortiront de presse, les États-Unis auront également mesuré les conséquences, décrites dans cet article, de l'applicabilité des Conventions de Genève. Pour les personnes détenues à Guantánamo et tombées au pouvoir des États-Unis en *Afghanistan,* l'applicabilité du droit international humanitaire implique qu'elles doivent ou bien être reconnues comme prisonniers de guerre ou alors des arguments liés au comportement de chacune d'elles au moment de leur capture doivent les faire apparaître, à un tribunal institué par les États-Unis, comme n'ayant pas droit au statut de prisonnier de guerre. Elles seront alors protégées par la IVe Convention de Genève et devront être détenues en Afghanistan. Dans les deux cas, l'applicabilité du droit international humanitaire à la "guerre contre le terrorisme" serait réaffirmée et les voix réclamant une révision du droit à cet effet seront reléguées à l'oubli. Ce droit s'applique à cette "guerre." Il n'empêche pas, nous l'avons vu, de la poursuivre. Certains estimeront, qui plus est, que son respect facilitera la victoire, étant donné qu'il montrera à l'ennemi et surtout à ses sympathisants potentiels la nature véritable des sociétés occidentales. La primauté

---

[142] L. Condorelli et L. Boisson De Chazournes, "Quelques remarques à propos de l'obligation des États de 'respecter et faire respecter' le droit international humanitaire en toutes circonstances," *Studies and Essays on International Humanitarian Law and Red Cross Principles in Honour of Jean Pictet,* The Hague, ICRC, Martinus Nijhoff Publishers, 1984, pp. 17-35; L. Condorelli et L. Boisson De Chazournes, "Common Article 1 of the Geneva Conventions Revisited: Protecting Collective Interests," (2000) 837 RICR, pp. 67-87; N. Levrat, "Les conséquences de l'engagement pris par le H.P.C. de 'faire respecter' les conventions humanitaires" dans F. Kalshoven et Y. Sandoz, dir., *Implementation of International Humanitarian Law,* Dordrecht, Martinus Nijhoff Publishers, 1989, pp. 263-96; U. Palwankar, "Mesures auxquelles peuvent recourir les États pour remplir leur obligation de faire respecter le droit international humanitaire," (1994) 805 RICR 11.

[143] Art. 12(2) de la IIIe Convention.

du droit se manifeste toujours par le fait qu'elle s'applique surtout et particulièrement dans la lutte contre ceux qui s'y opposent. Nous comprenons que, pour les victimes des attaques du 11 septembre 2001, l'idée que les soldats américains et les Talibans sont égaux devant le droit international humanitaire est choquante. À notre avis, la séparation stricte entre *jus ad bellum* et *jus in bello* et l'égalité des belligérants devant le droit international humanitaire reste toutefois la clef de voûte de cette branche face aux réalités de notre monde, et sa seule chance de survie.

Summary

The "War against Terrorism": International Humanitarian Law and the Status of Prisoners of War

The United States qualifies the attacks of September 11, 2001, and its reaction as "war." The author reviews the applicability and application of international humanitarian law to those events. He concludes that this law did not apply to the attacks of New York and Washington, but applies to the conflict in Afghanistan, independently of the legitimacy of that war and of the causes espoused by the parties. Hence, Taliban and possibly some Al-Qaïda fighters captured by the United States and coalition forces are, in principle and until individual decision to the contrary, prisoners of war protected by the third Geneva Convention. Its provisions are not inappropriate for the treatment of such persons, some of whom are held in Guantánamo Bay. All other persons arrested by the United States in Afghanistan are protected civilians under the fourth Geneva Convention. Such persons may not be held in Guantánamo. Finally, the author reviews different arguments recently brought forward to deny that the Geneva Conventions are adapted to the "war against terrorism." He comes to the conclusion that they largely are and that, in any case, it would be impossible to adopt new, more appropriate rules of international law.

Sommaire

La "guerre contre le terrorisme," le droit international humanitaire et le statut de prisonnier de guerre

Les États-Unis ont qualifié les attaques du 11 septembre 2001 ainsi que leur lutte contre le terrorisme de "guerre." L'auteur analyse l'applicabilité et

l'application du droit international humanitaire à ces événements. Il arrive à la conclusion que ce droit ne régit pas les attaques contre New York et Washington, mais la guerre en Afghanistan, indépendamment de la légitimité de celle-ci et des causes soutenues par les parties. En conséquence, tout au moins les membres des forces armées talibanes — et possiblement certains membres d'Al-Qaeda, qui sont tombés, en Afghanistan, au pouvoir des forces américaines, sont en principe et jusqu'à ce qu'une décision individuelle statuant le contraire soit rendue, des prisonniers de guerre protégés par la IIIe Convention de Genève. Les dispositions de celle-ci sont appropriées pour régir le traitement de ces personnes en partie détenues à Guantánamo Bay. Toutes les autres personnes arrêtées par les États-Unis et leurs alliés en Afghanistan sont des civils protégés par la IVe Convention de Genève. En tant que tels, elles ne peuvent pas être détenues à Guantánamo. Pour terminer, l'auteur revoit les différents arguments avancés ces derniers temps selon lesquels les Conventions de Genève ne sont pas adaptées à la "guerre contre le terrorisme." Selon l'auteur, cette thèse n'est pas justifiée et il serait en tout état de cause impossible d'adopter de nouvelles règles mieux adaptées.

Use of Economic Sanctions under International Law: A Contemporary Assessment

M. SHERVIN MAJLESSI

And as the law of humanity prescribes to nations no less than to individuals, the mildest measures, when they are sufficient to obtain justice; whenever a sovereign can, by the way of reprisals, procure a just recompence, or a proper satisfaction, he ought to make use of this method, which is less violent, and less fatal than war.[1]

Emerich de Vattel (1714-67)

INTRODUCTION

In the past few years, economic sanctions have been in the international news almost every day.[2] From Haiti to Iraq and from

---

M. Shervin Majlessi, Doctor of Civil Law Candidate, McGill University, Montreal, Canada. Certain sections of the present article form part of a chapter by the author appearing in a forthcoming special volume collecting the work of a group of researchers. It is entitled *International Economic Sanctions in International Law* and is the result of extensive research carried out at the Centre for Studies and Research in International Law and International Relations at the Hague Academy of International Law. The volume is co-edited by L. Picchio Forlati and L.A. Sicilianos and published by Kluwer Law International in the series Law Books of the Academy. I would like to thank S.J. Toope, C. Greenwood, and L. Picchio Forlati for their remarks, and L.A. Sicilianos and participants of the summer 2000 session of the Research Centre of the Hague Academy of International Law for their helpful discussions on the subject of sanctions. Parts of this article are also based on a thesis submitted in partial fulfillment of the requirements of an LL.M. degree at McGill University.

[1] *The Law of Nations; or Principles of the Law of Nature: Applied to the Conduct and Affairs of Nations and Sovereigns: A Work Tending to Display the True Interest of Powers*, trans. from French, new edition (London: G.C.J and J. Robinson, and Whieldon and Butterworth, 1793) at 267, para. 354.

[2] Of course, economic sanctions have been used for centuries in international relations. There are a myriad of historical examples of situations in which sanctions have been used. See E.S. Colbert, *Retaliation in International Law* (New York: King's Crown Press, 1948) at 10; B.E. Carter, *International Economic Sanctions: Improving the Haphazard U.S. Legal Regime* (Cambridge: Cambridge University Press, 1988) at 8, note 2; C. Phillipson, *The International Law and Custom of Ancient*

South Africa to Norway, countries have been subjected to economic sanctions by other states or groups of states. The common feature of all of these cases of economic sanction is that they all have been controversial. The controversy surrounding the use of economic sanctions has traditionally focused on three main issues: the economic impact of sanctions on the sanctioned and sanctioning countries, the effectiveness of such sanctions, and their legality. In studying economic sanctions, the political scientist's aim is to measure the effectiveness of sanctions in compelling compliance; the economist is concerned with the economic consequences of the sanctions; while the lawyer's quest is to determine whether such sanctions are legal and whether they conform to the framework of international relations. The present article will examine the issue from the lawyer's perspective.[3]

In 1931, J.L. Brierly noted on the subject of sanctions: "The true problem for consideration is ... not whether we should try to *create* sanctions for international law, but whether we should try to organize them in a system."[4] Today, the problem remains the same. There is no doubt about the importance of sanctions as a means of enforcing international law. However, the question is whether they should be *reorganized* systematically. To answer this question, the traditional theory of sanctions will be scrutinized and reassessed, taking into account the developments of international law in the past decades. The second part of this article presents an analysis of the relevant provisions of the Charter of the United Nations (Charter)[5] and the practice of their implementation during the past fifty years. In addition, a new category of collective sanctions for breach of *erga omnes* obligations, which can be justified on the basis of the theory of retaliation, will be proposed. Drawing on the

---

Greece and Rome, vol. 2 (London: McMillan and Company, 1911) at 383; M.P. Doxey, *Economic Sanctions and International Enforcement,* 2nd edition (New York: Oxford University Press, 1980) at 10.

[3] Such a study will necessarily take into account the economic and political implications of imposing sanctions.

[4] J.L. Brierly, "Sanctions," in H. Lauterpacht and C.H.M. Waldock, eds., *The Basis of Obligation in International Law and Other Papers by the Late James Leslie Brierly* (Oxford: Clarendon Press, 1958) 201 at 202 [emphasis in original]. For the difference between sanctions in international law and sanctions in general, see G. Scelle, *Droit international* (Manuel de droit international public) (Paris: Éditions Domat-Moncherstien, 1948) at 865.

[5] Charter of the United Nations, June 26, 1945, Can. T.S. 1945 No. 7 [hereinafter Charter].

cases of implementation of sanctions, which are referred to in the second part, and the development of international law since the drafting of the Charter, further limitations on the use of economic sanctions will be examined in the third part. The main conclusion of this part is that the *lex lata* in the field of sanctions does not correspond to international law developments in the last fifty years. Moreover, traditional conditions for the legality of sanctions and the lawful use of enforcement actions should be subject to additional norms of international humanitarian law. In the fourth part, an attempt is made to determine the position of sanctions in contemporary international law, and proposals for the legitimate use of economic sanctions under international law are suggested.

Finally, in the conclusion, it is submitted that international law has become more humane over the course of the last five decades. While at the dawn of the twentieth century, resort to war was not prohibited but subject to certain modalities, today, use of armed force is permissible only in exceptional circumstances. The increasing popularity of economic sanctions is, in part, the result of states being deprived of other important means of enforcement. Still, if economic sanctions result in pain and suffering, which is comparable to the pain and suffering that results from the use of force, they should be subject to similar restrictions. It is not suggested that the use of economic sanctions should be banned. In fact, sanctions are one of the only means of enforcement at the international level. However, they should be applied in a more refined manner, which would avoid severe consequences for innocent civilians. This article, thus, supports a more institutionalized application of collective sanctions. In the search for a *lex ferenda* in the field of sanctions, this article touches upon other important issues. These include morality and international law and their relationship with one and other; constitutional questions within the United Nations; and proposals for reform in that organization. Each of these issues is a topic for an article in its own right and, thus, will only be discussed briefly.

The Legal Basis of Collective Sanctions: Chapter VII and Beyond

A systematic legal study of economic sanctions must first deal with the different types of sanctions.[6] Sanctions may be categorized

---

[6] At the outset, the meaning of the term "sanction" in the context of this article should be clarified. The following text will examine "economic sanctions" as

on the basis of the reasons for which they are imposed[7] or on the basis of the means by which they are implemented (unilateral and collective). In the context of this study, a means-based categorization is of primary importance since unilateral and collective sanctions are based on different legal premises, and this article only deals with collective sanctions.[8] Collective sanctions[9] are centralized

---

opposed to other types of non-violent sanctions. For different types of non-violent sanctions, see M.P. Doxey, *International Sanctions in Contemporary Perspective* (New York: St. Martin's Press, 1996) at 11-15. The term "economic sanction" can refer to "boycott," "embargo," and "countermeasure." These terms are often used interchangeably. However, in most cases, they refer to unilateral sanctions. See M.S. Daoudi and M.S. Dajani, *Economic Sanctions* (London: Routledge, 1983) at 2; T.M. Holland, *Lectures on International Law,* edited by T.A. Walker and W.L. Walker (London: Sweet and Maxwell, 1933) at 239; P.J. Kuyper, *The Implementation of International Sanctions* (Alphen aan den Rijn: Sijthoff and Noordhoff International Publishers, 1978) at 1. The International Law Commission's [hereinafter ILC] commentary entitled *Draft Articles on Responsibility of States for Internationally Wrongful Acts* clarifies the terminology in the field. It is contained in the *Report of the International Law Commission on the Work of Its Fifty-Third Session,* UN GAOR, 51st Sess., Supp. No. 10, UN Doc. A/56/10 (2001), which is available online at <http://www.un.org/law/ilc/reports/2001/english/a_56_10e.pdf> (date accessed: October 14, 2001) at 181, para. 3 [hereinafter *ILC's Report on Fifty-Third Session*].

[7] Implementation of economic sanctions may have different objectives. Any evaluation of the effectiveness of sanctions as well as the decision to terminate their application depends on the attainment of their objectives. These issues are not dealt with in detail in this article. See Daoudi and Dajani, *supra* note 6 at 161; M. Miyagawa, *Do Economic Sanctions Work?* (New York: St. Martin's Press, 1992) at 89, 91-93; C.C. Joyner, "Sanctions and International Law," in D. Cortright and G.A. Lopez, eds., *Economic Sanctions, Panacea or Peacebuilding in a Post-Cold War World* (Boulder: Westview Press, 1995) 73 at 74; C.C. Joyner, "Sanctions, Compliance and International Law: Reflections on the United Nations' Experience against Iraq" (1991) 32 Va. J. Int'l L. 1 at 3; G.C. Hufbauer, J.J. Schott, and K.A. Elliott, *Economic Sanctions Reconsidered: History and Current Policy,* vol. 1, 2nd ed. (Washington, DC: Institute for International Economics, 1990) at 163; Doxey, *supra* note 6 at 54-65.

[8] According to some writers, the above-mentioned sanctions and embargoes are *negative sanctions,* as opposed to *positive sanctions* or incentives (P.J. Kuyper, "International Legal Aspects of Economic Sanctions," in P. Sarcevic, H. van Houtte, eds., *Legal Issues in International Trade* (London: Graham and Trotman, 1990) 145 at 145.

[9] Unilateral sanctions — unlike collective sanctions, which are treaty-based — are based on the theory of retaliation and are usually imposed by an individual state. For the theory of retaliation, and the conditions for its application (prior breach, prior demand for redress, and proportionality), see O. Schachter, *International Law in Theory and Practice* (Dordrecht: Martinus Nijhoff Publishers, 1991) at 185; D.W. Bowett, "International Law and Economic Coercion" (1976) 16:2 Va. J.

sanctions that are decided upon within the institutional framework of the organization that implements them. They are "concerned fundamentally with matters pertaining to international peace."[10] Therefore, the legal basis for this category of sanctions must be sought within the legal framework of their organization. In fact, the international organizations that can implement collective sanctions

---

Int'l L. 245 at 252; I. Brownlie, *System of the Law of Nations: State Responsibility*, part 1 (Oxford: Clarendon Press, 1983) at 60. These conditions are confirmed in several cases, see, for example, *S.S. Wimbledon Case* (1923), P.C.I.J. (Ser. A) No. 1, 15 at 30 and 33; *The Spanish Zone of Morocco Claims (Great Britain v. Spain)* (1925), II R.I.A.A. 615 at 641; *Case Concerning the Factory at Chorzów (Claim for Indemnity Merits) (Germany v. Poland)* (1928), P.C.I.J. (Ser. A) No. 17, 3 at 29; *Reparation for Injuries Suffered in the Service of the United Nations*, Advisory Opinion, [1949] I.C.J. Rep. 174 at 184; *Corfu Channel Case (United Kingdom v. Albania)*, [1949] I.C.J. Rep. 4 at 23; the *Naulilaa Case (Portugal-Germany)* (1928), II R.I.A.A. 1013 at 1025-26); *North Sea Continental Shelf Cases (Federal Republic of Germany v. Denmark; Federal Republic of Germany v. Netherlands)*, [1969] I.C.J. Rep. 3; *Cases Concerning the Delimitation of the Continental Shelf between the United Kingdom of Great Britain and Northern Ireland, and French Republic* (1977), XVIII R.I.A.A. 3; *Case Concerning the Continental Shelf (Tunisia v. Libyan Arab Jamahiria)*, [1982] I.C.J. Rep. 18. For more on the further division of unilateral sanctions to reprisals and retorsion, see D.W. Bowett, "Economic Coercion and Reprisals by States," in R.B. Lillich, ed., *Economic Coercion and the New International Economic Order* (Charlottesville: Michie Company, 1976) 7 at 14-15; O.Y. Elagab, *The Legality of Non-Forcible Countermeasures in International Law* (New York: Oxford University Press, 1988); Schachter, *supra* note 9 at 185-86; *ILC's Report on Fifty-Third Session, supra* note 6 at 325, para. 3. See also the *Declaration of Principles of International Law Concerning Friendly Relations and Co-operation among States in accordance with the Charter of the United Nations*, October 24, 1970, GA Res. 2625 (XXV), UN GAOR, 25th Sess., Supp. No. 28, UN Doc. A/8028 (1970) 121.

10 C.L. Brown-John, *Multilateral Sanctions in International Law: A Comparative Analysis* (New York: Praeger Publishers, 1975) at 45. Other criteria suggested for this category of sanctions — which distinguish them from other types of sanctions imposed by a group of states — are: (1) the decision-making body must be universally or regionally international; (2) its membership should normally encompass all states within the universal or regional system; (3) the organization must have a formally constituted body with express powers to make mandatory decisions; (4) the organization must have a procedure for formally reaching an obligatory decision; and (5) the organization must be considered as definitive or authoritative in its sphere of international activity (at 46).

Applying such criteria, sanctions imposed by the European Economic Community (which serves the economic and political interests of its European members), the activities of the North Atlantic Treaty Organization, and the Arab League are unilateral sanctions. Sanctions imposed under the auspices of the Security Council, the Organization of American States [hereinafter OAS], and the United Nations specialized agencies — if they are oriented towards international peace through legal processes — are collective sanctions.

are not numerous.[11] Among them, undoubtedly, the United Nations is the most important as it has the largest membership of any one organization.[12] In view of the dominant role that the United Nations plays on the international scene and the importance of sanctions in the UN system, the focus of my study of collective sanctions will be the UN's economic sanctions.

In the first four sections of this article, I will examine the relevant provisions of the Charter (that is, Chapter VII of the Charter) as the legal basis of implementation of collective economic sanctions. In the second section, emphasis will be placed on the expansion of the notion of threat to the peace. Since the existing provisions of the Charter are not sufficient to justify all of the potential impositions of collective sanctions, I will propose, in the fifth section, an alternative legal basis for collective economic sanctions under the general rules of international law.

It is clear that, "in framing the Charter of the United Nations, special attention was given to the use of economic sanctions as part of a more sophisticated system of collective security."[13] The key article in Chapter VII of the Charter — the chapter that is dedicated to the system of collective security — is Article 39, which provides that

[11] International organizations should meet the criteria mentioned in note 10 for their actions to be considered to be collective sanctions.

[12] Another important example of collective sanctions are those imposed by the OAS on its member-states. However, in the case of the OAS, it is doubtful whether the organization is entitled to determine that the economic sanctions are compulsory or recommendatory. According to Article 8 of the Inter-American Treaty of Reciprocal Assistance, September 2, 1947, 21 U.N.T.S. 77 (comprising the Dominican Republic, Guatemala, Costa Rica, Peru, El Salvador, and so on):

> For the purposes of this Treaty, [in case of a conflict between two or more American States] the measure on which the Organ of Consultation may agree will comprise one or more of the following ... partial or complete interruption of economic relations or of rail, sea, air, postal, telegraphic, telephonic, and radiotelephonic or radiotelegraphic communications; and use of armed force.

In the case of the Dominican Republic, in 1960, the organization applied compulsory economic measures against that state, but in the case of Haiti, the action was recommendatory (see D.E. Acevedo, "The Haitian Crisis and the OAS Response: A Test of Effectiveness in Protecting Democracy," in L.F. Damrosch, ed., *Enforcing Restraint: Collective Intervention in Internal Conflicts* (New York: Council on Foreign Relations Press, 1993) 119 at 135-37.

[13] C.C. Joyner, "Collective Sanctions as Peaceful Coercion: Lessons from the United Nations Experience" (1995) 16 Aus. Y.B. Int'l L. 241.

[t]he Security Council shall determine the existence of any threat to the peace, breach of the peace, or act of aggression and shall make recommendations, or decide what measures shall be taken in accordance with Articles 41 and 42, to maintain or restore international peace and security.

In order to understand the scope of Article 39 better and to analyze the underlying principles of this article properly, the historical origins of the article, the intent of its drafters, and the ways in which it has been applied over the course of the last fifty years[14] must be understood.

Under the League of Nations system, the prerequisite for the use of economic and military sanctions (as stipulated in Article XVI of the Covenant of the League[15]) was that a member of the League of Nations had gone to war in violation of Articles XII, XIII, and XV of the Covenant of the League.[16] Unlike the Charter, the Covenant of the League did not provide for binding decisions of the League's organs in this area. It was up to each member to decide whether or not to apply sanctions.[17] Implementation of economic sanctions was the only instance in which the implementation of sanctions was not considered to be a collective decision of the League of Nations. Rather, economic sanctions were deemed to reflect "the

---

[14] There are few instances of actions taken under Article 39 since 1945. However, the end of the Cold War provided the Security Council with the opportunity to play the role that the Charter envisioned for it. There were only two cases of centralized sanctions in the first forty-five years of the United Nation's existence, South Africa and Rhodesia. Since the 1990s, there has been a dramatic increase in the number of such sanctions.

[15] Article XVI of the Covenant of the League of Nations, June 28, 1919, 2 U.S.B.C. 48 (entered into force January 10, 1920) Part 1: Treaty of Peace between the Allied and Associated Powers and Germany [hereinafter Covenant of the League of Nations].

[16] See Simma et al., eds., *The Charter of the United Nations: A Commentary* (Oxford: Oxford University Press, 1994) at 606. See also E. Clark, ed., *Boycotts and Peace, a Report by the Committee on Economic Sanctions* (New York and London: Harper and Brothers Publications, 1932) at xiii; Joyner, "Sanctions and International Law," *supra* note 7 at 80; T.E. Førland, "The History of Economic Warfare: International Law, Effectiveness, Strategies" (1993) 30:2 J. Peace Research 151; Daoudi and Dajani, *supra* note 6 at 59; Doxey, *supra* note 2 at 45; R. Renwick, *Economic Sanctions* (Cambridge, MA: Center for International Affairs, Harvard University, 1981) at 16; Hufbauer, Schott, and Elliott, *supra* note 7 at 124-31.

[17] See L.M. Goodrich, E. Hambro, and A.P. Simons, *Charter of the United Nations: Commentary and Documents*, 3rd rev. ed. (New York: Columbia University Press, 1969) at 311.

coexistence of corresponding but independently taken decisions of the member states."[18]

Unlike under the League, the Security Council has been vested with a broad competence to impose economic sanctions. This fact is made manifest by the *travaux préparatoires* for Article 39 of the Charter and the text of the article. Wide discretion was given to the Council "to avoid, on the one hand, the possibility that the aggressor might turn any detailed definition to his advantage and, on the other, the danger of premature action."[19] The Dumbarton Oaks Proposals[20] were finally adopted. Other proposals, which attempted to enlarge the competence of the General Assembly, limit the freedom of choice of the Security Council, and restrict the discretion of the Security Council, were turned down.[21] Consequently, Chapter VII of the Charter enables the Security Council to employ military force and economic measures against any member state that is breaking the "peace" or committing an "act of aggression."[22]

[18] Simma et al., *supra* note 16 at 607: "This is also confirmed by the fact that the Italian government protested directly to the various states involved in the imposition of sanctions rather than to the organs of the League of Nations."

[19] L.M. Goodrich and A.P. Simons, *The United Nations and the Maintenance of International Peace and Security* (Washington DC: Brookings Institution, 1955) at 352.

[20] Proposals for the Establishment of a General International Organization, the text can be accessed online at <http://www.ibiblio.org/pha/policy/1944/441007a.html> (last accessed August 6, 2002).

[21] For different proposals, see Simma et al., *supra* note 16 at 607-8.

[22] Furthermore, economic sanctions may be implemented in different ways. In the framework of the United Nations, the Security Council enjoys great discretion in implementing different forms of sanctions. The Charter details "an illustrative, non-exhaustive enumeration" of forms of implementation of sanctions (not only economic) and gives the Security Council the discretion to apply any combination of the measures that it considers appropriate (*ibid.* at 624). Article 41 of the Charter states that

> [t]he Security Council may decide what measures not involving the use of armed force are to be employed to give effect to its decisions, and it may call upon the Members of the United Nations to apply such measures. These may include complete or partial interruption of economic relations and of rail, sea, air, postal, telegraphic, radio, and other means of communication, and the severance of diplomatic relations.

The measures enumerated in Article 41 are only by way of example, and the Security Council can take measures that are not mentioned in Article 41. According to Simma et al.'s commentary on the Charter, "[t]he most far-reaching use of Art. 41 ordering measures not listed was made by Resolution 827 (1993) of May 25 1993 setting up the international tribunal for prosecuting persons responsible for serious violations of international humanitarian law committed in the territory of former Yugoslavia" (at 626).

Article 41 of the Charter entitles the Security Council to impose mandatory economic sanctions.[23] The Charter has further anticipated the possible conflict between the obligations imposed by it and other obligations of member states by providing that the obligations under the Charter prevail over any other international agreement.[24] Considering these provisions and the obligation of states to carry out the decisions of the Security Council, it is obvious that the Security Council is competent to impose sanctions on states and that its decisions are binding on all the members of the United Nations.[25] The Security Council's decision to impose sanctions, which is usually in the form of a resolution based on a draft submitted by one or more members, "rests on a factual finding, as well as on an interpretation of Charter provisions and a weighing of political considerations, procedures for clarifying the facts have assumed special importance."[26] It is generally accepted that the responsibility for the decision, "is solely that of the Council, that no commission could receive authority to make the finding or to bind the Council, and that the determination had to be made with respect to an actual situation."[27] The Charter also provides that decisions of the Council in such matters "shall be made by an affirmative vote of nine members including the concurring votes of the permanent members."[28]

Accordingly, it is also suggested that there is both a procedural and a substantive standard that the Council should observe when applying enforcement measures under Chapter VII of the Charter.[29] There is little controversy and debate over the procedural requirement (that is, the Council's decision by concurrence of nine members, including the votes of the permanent members to enforce its will against a state). Therefore, the substantive standard

---

[23] The text of Article 41 of the Charter can be found at note 22. However, no resolution of the Security Council has expressly referred to Article 41 of the Charter (Goodrich, Hambro, and Simons, *supra* note 17 at 313).

[24] Article 103 of the Charter stipulates that, "[i]n the event of a conflict between the obligations of the members of the United Nations under the present Charter and their obligations under any other international agreement, their obligations under the present Charter prevail."

[25] See J.L. Kunz, "Sanctions in International Law" (1960) 54 A.J.I.L. 324.

[26] Goodrich and Simons, *supra* note 19 at 351.

[27] *Ibid.* at 348.

[28] Article 27(3) of the Charter, *supra* note 5.

[29] T.M. Franck, *Fairness in International Law and Institutions* (New York: Oxford University Press, 1995) at 220.

(that is, the determining "breach of the peace," "threat to the peace," or "act of aggression") is of great importance. According to L.M. Goodrich and A.P. Simmons, "[t]he determination of the existence of a threat to the peace, breach of the peace, or act of aggression is a decision of great significance because it is a condition to the exercise by the Security Council of power of an exceptional nature under Article 41 and 42 of the Charter."[30] During the past fifty years, the Security Council and the General Assembly, as well as complainant states, have used the terms "threat to the peace," "breach of the peace," and "act of aggression" on different occasions, sometimes "loosely" and at other times "exaggeratedly."[31] Nevertheless, there have been some serious and thoughtful efforts to define the meaning of these terms so as to provide useful guidance to action.[32] In an attempt to define the meaning of the terms used in Article 39 of the Charter in the light of the Council's practice, I will now examine the provisions that the Security Council must interpret in deciding whether or not it should act.

THREAT TO THE PEACE

The concept of "peace" can be defined narrowly — as the absence of an organized use of force between states — or broadly — requiring the existence of friendly relations.[33] Apparently, "peace," according to the Charter, means the absence of the organized use of force.[34] However, "the express incorporation of the threat to the peace shows that Article 39 can come into play long before a breach of the peace occurs."[35] "Threat to the peace" is the broadest and most vague concept in Article 39.[36] It is submitted that the legitimate assertion of the Security Council's Article 39 jurisdiction

[30] Goodrich and Simons, *supra* note 19 at 346.

[31] *Ibid.* at 354.

[32] *Ibid.*

[33] Simma et al., *supra* note 16 at 608.

[34] At the same time, the statement read at the conclusion of the meeting of the Security Council held at the level of heads of state and government on January 21, 1992, stated that "[t]he absence of war and military conflicts amongst States does not in itself ensure international peace and security. The non-military sources of instability in the economic, social, humanitarian and ecological fields have become threats to peace and security" (*Note by the President of the Security Council,* UN Doc. S/23500 (1992), reprinted in 31 I.L.M. 759).

[35] Simma et al., *supra* note 16 at 608.

[36] *Ibid.* at 610.

requires a threat to *international* peace.[37] The Security Council's practice, however, demonstrates that it has not accepted this limitation, but, rather, it has read the article in a much wider manner.[38]

In one case, in 1946, the representative of Poland in the Security Council raised the issue of the existence of the fascist regime in Spain before the Council.[39] He submitted a draft resolution, which asked the Council to take measures under Article 39 and 41 because the situation in Spain had "endangered international peace and security." A subcommittee that was appointed by the Security Council concluded that the situation in Spain "constitutes a situation likely to endanger the maintenance of international peace and security, [and does not] constitute an existing threat to international peace and security."[40] The Polish representative criticized this conclusion, arguing that "[a]ny threat to the peace is potential by nature. It may mature tomorrow, after tomorrow, or in five years. It is a question of time."[41] The French representative defended the report of the subcommittee. While agreeing that "threat to the peace" clearly implied a state of affairs in which there was a situation of potential danger, "he asserted the steps to be taken by the Council, whether under Article 39 or Article 34 [of the Charter[42]],

---

[37] The reason is that Article 2(4) of the Charter, which prohibits the use of force, applies only to the international relations of states and not to internal situations, which belong to states' domestic jurisdiction. As a result, the first part of Article 39 does not refer to the use of force in the international realm of states. However, a civil war can lead to a threat to international peace (*ibid.* at 608-9). For the discussions on this subject during the Palestine question, see Goodrich and Simons, *supra* note 19 at 355-6.

[38] D.J. Harris, *Cases and Materials on International Law*, 4th ed. (London: Sweet and Maxwell, 1991) at 876. See also P.H. Kooijmans, "The Enlargement of the Concept 'Threat to the Peace,'" in R.-J. Dupuy, ed., *The Development of the Role of the Security Council; Workshop of the Hague Academy of International Law, 21-23 July 1992* (Dordrecht: Martinus Nijhoff Publishers, 1993) 111.

[39] Poland invoked Articles 2(6) (ensuring that non-member states act in accordance with the UN principles), 34 (Security Council's investigation of situation that may give rise to dispute), and 35 (bringing matters to the attention of the Security Council) of the Charter, *supra* note 5, regarding the activities of the Franco regime.

[40] *Report of the Sub-Committee on the Spanish Question*, UN SCOR, 1st Year, 1st Series, Spec. Supp. (1946) at 5, cited in Harris, *supra* note 38 at 874.

[41] *Report of the Sub-Committee on the Spanish Question, supra* note 40 at 10, cited in E. Jimenez de Arechaga, *Voting and the Handling of Disputes in the Security Council* (New York: Carnegie Endowment for International Peace, 1950) at 163.

[42] Charter, *supra* note 5.

might depend on whether the threat to the peace was immediate or remote."[43]

In the case of the Greek complaint of December 1946, following the frontier accidents in which Greek guerrillas were supported by Albania, Bulgaria, and Yugoslavia,

[t]he majority of the members of the commission, appointed by the Security Council to investigate and to report [on the issue], were of the opinion that support of armed bands, formed in the territory of one state and crossing into the territory of another, or the refusal of a government, in spite of the demands of the state concerned, to take all possible measures in its own territory to deprive such bands of any aid or protection should be considered by the Council as the threat to the peace within the meaning of the Charter. All the members of the Council except Poland[44] and the Soviet Union were prepared to accept this view.[45]

In another instance in 1950, the Soviet government argued that the Korean conflict was a civil war. The United Kingdom's representative, in response, claimed that

a civil war in certain circumstances might well, under Article 39 of the Charter, constitute a "threat to the peace," or even a "breach of the peace," and if the Security Council so decided, there would be nothing whatever to prevent its taking any action it liked in order to put an end to the incident, *even if it should involve two or more portions of the same international entity.*[46]

The United States's representative, in another case, defined "threat to the peace" with the following words:

[43] Goodrich and Simons, *supra* note 19 at 355; on Article 34 of the Charter, see the discussion in note 48 of this article.

[44] Compare Poland's position on this issue with her position on the Spanish case. This change of position in a few months shows how political considerations have an impact on the interpretation of the Charter by members.

[45] Goodrich and Simons, *supra* note 19 at 355. It is interesting to note the similarity of the view of this commission to that of the International Court of Justice [hereinafter ICJ] in the *Case Concerning Military and Paramilitary Activities in and against Nicaragua (Nicaragua v. United States),* [1986] I.C.J. Rep. 14 at 103, para. 195 [hereinafter *Nicaragua* case], in which the court stated that,

   [i]n particular, it may be considered to be agreed that an armed attack must be understood as including not merely action by regular armed forces across an international border, but also the "sending by or on behalf"of a State of armed bands, groups, irregulars or mercenaries, which carry out acts of armed force against another State of such gravity as to amount to (*inter alia*) an actual armed attack conducted by regular forces, or its substantial involvement therein.

[46] UN SCOR, 5th Year, No. 28, 486th Mtg. (1950) at 6, cited in Goodrich and Simons, *supra* note 19 at 356 [emphasis added].

What constitutes a "threat to the peace" as that term is used in Article 39 of the Charter? A threat to the peace is created when a State uses force or the threat of force to secure compliance with its demands. The acts of the Government of the USSR in illegally obstructing by threat of force the access of the three Western Powers to Berlin creates a threat to the peace.[47]

In many resolutions, the Security Council has spoken of a threat to the peace,[48] and, in some cases, "the Council has adopted measures of the kind expressly authorized by Article 40 without any previous determination under Article 39."[49] In 1965, following the unilateral declaration of independence by the racist minority regime of Rhodesia from the United Kingdom, the Security Council, in Resolution 217, determined that the continuation of the regime "in time constitutes a threat to the peace."[50] Later, in 1966, the council expressly "determine[d] that the resulting situation constitutes a threat to the peace."[51] However, there is no explanation as to why such a situation constituted a threat to the peace.[52]

---

[47] This occurred when the Berlin situation was being discussed in the Security Council. UN SCOR, 3rd Year, No. 115, 363rd Mtg. (1948) at 4, cited in Goodrich and Simons, *supra* note 19 at 356.

[48] Another issue in this regard is the distinction between a threat to the peace and endangering peace. The relationship between the concept of endangering the maintenance of international peace and security, as expressed in Articles 34 and 37 of the Charter, with the concept of threat to the peace is not clear. Article 34 of the Charter, *supra* note 5, states that, "[t]he Security Council may investigate any dispute, or any situation which might lead to international friction or give rise to a dispute, in order to determine whether the continuance of the dispute or situation is likely to endanger the maintenance of international peace and security;" and, according to Article 37:2 of the Charter, "[i]f the Security Council deems that the continuance of the dispute is in fact likely to endanger the maintenance of international peace and security, it shall decide whether to take action under Article 36 or to recommend such terms of settlement as it may consider appropriate."

In some cases, the Security Council, in its resolution, has spoken of a threat to the peace or a danger to peace without a clear differentiation between them. For instance, in Resolution 567 (SC Res. 567, June 20, 1985, UN Doc. S/RES/567 in (1985) 39 Y.B.U.N. 182), South Africa was condemned because of an act of aggression against Angola, and it was determined that international peace and security were seriously "endangered" (see Simma et al., *supra* note 16 at 611).

[49] Goodrich and Simons, *supra* note 19 at 346.

[50] SC Res. 217, November 20, 1965.

[51] SC Res. 221, April 9, 1966.

[52] For a criticism of designation of that situation as a threat to the peace, see C.G. Fenwick, "When is There a Threat to the Peace? — Rhodesia," editorial comment (1967) 61 A.J.I.L. 753.

According to B. Simma et al., "[t]he members of the Security Council were apparently convinced that the danger of armed conflicts in southern Africa would be brought about by the racist minority regime."[53] Although it is assumed, on the basis of this case, that the internal conditions of a state alone can be considered as a threat to the peace, "one may not overlook the particular situation in southern Africa, including the danger of violent involvement with neighboring states."[54]

EXPANSION OF THE NOTION OF THREAT TO THE PEACE

The end of the Cold War and the beginning of the 1990s marked the turning point in the activities of the Security Council. In light of the practice of the Council, it can be concluded that the following situations, under certain circumstances, can be considered to to be threats to international peace:[55] massive violations of human rights in specific situations or serious violations of international law that may provoke armed countermeasures; extreme violence within a state; non-compliance with international obligations; concerns about future conduct of a state (measures with regard to armament);[56] and the massive flow of refugees across international borders.[57]

---

[53] Simma et al., *supra* note 16 at 612.

[54] *Ibid.*

[55] Alternatively, Schweigman proposes the following categories for causes of Chapter VII actions of the Security Council: humanitarian concerns; extradition of alleged terrorists; preventive measures; quasi-judicial measures. See *The Authority of the Security Council under Chapter VII of the U.N. Charter : Legal Limits and the Role of the International Court of Justice* (The Hague: Kluwer Law International, 2001) at 150-55.

[56] See Resolution 825 concerning North Korea (SC Res. 825, May 11, 1993).

[57] In my analysis of the recent practice, I have relied, in part, on the categorization of "hard cases" by Thomas Franck: cases that did not involve actual or imminent international military hostilities, but were nonetheless treated by the United Nations as constituting a threat to the peace by Thomas Franck (See Franck, *supra* note 29 at 222-24). Examples of "easy cases" — where, as opposed to hard cases, the legitimacy of Security Council's decisions was beyond dispute — are: the Security Council's intervention in 1948 in Palestine, armed attack by North Korea on South Korea on June 25, 1950, and the 1990-91 crisis following Iraq's conquest of Kuwait. While Franck uses this categorization to support his arguments about fairness in the Security Council actions, I am using the same categorization to support the conclusion that, in certain cases, the alternative base for imposing collective sanctions — that of sanctions for breach of *erga omnes* obligations — can be a more compelling justification for imposing sanctions.

Massive Violations of Human Rights That May Provoke Armed Countermeasures

Cases of massive violations of human rights do not expand the notion of a threat to international peace. In the cases of Rhodesia[58] and South Africa,[59] the Security Council has already taken action on this basis. It can thus be inferred from these two cases that violations of human rights or the rules of international law by a government, which may eventually lead to war, can create a threat to the peace: "Not every violation of international human rights law, however, would necessarily constitute that threat."[60] In the recent practices of the Security Council, there is no similar case of imposing sanctions.[61] However, in cases of extreme violence within a state (which may overlap with cases of massive violations of human rights), situations have been designated as a threat to the peace.[62]

Extreme Violence within a State (Civil War)

In certain cases, civil wars have been deemed to be threats to the international peace. The case of the former Yugoslavia reinforces

---

For another example of categorization of threats to the peace, see L.E. Fielding, "Taking a Closer Look at Threats to Peace: The Power of the Security Council to Address Humanitarian Crises" (1996) 73 U. Det. Mercy L. Rev. at 551.

[58] In Rhodesia, the Security Council decided that the situation constituted a threat to international peace and focused on "the inalienable rights of the people of Southern Rhodesia to freedom and independence." SC Res. 232, December 16, 1966, para. 4.

[59] In the case of South Africa, the Council determined "that acquisition by South Africa of arms and related material constitute[d] a threat to the maintenance of international peace and security." SC Res. 418, November 4, 1977. In addition to "the military build-up by South Africa and its persistent acts of aggression against the neighboring States," the decision of the Security Council was taken to react to the violent suppression of segments of the South African people by the government. The preamble of Resolution 418 "strongly condemn[ed] the racist regime of South Africa for its resort to massive violence against and wanton killings of the African people" and "Consider[ed] that the *policies* and acts of the South African Government [were] fraught with danger to international peace and security" [emphasis added].

[60] Franck, *supra* note 29 at 231.

[61] Boutros Boutros-Ghali in his 1992 report states that "[r]espect for human rights is clearly important in order to maintain international peace and security and to achieve social and economic development." *Report of the Secretary-General on the Work of the Organization*, UN Doc. GA/47/407 (1992).

[62] D. Sarooshi, "The United Nations Collective Security System and the Establishment of Peace" (2000) 53 Current Legal Problems at 626-27.

this view. Under Resolution 713,[63] sanctions were imposed on Serbia because the continuation of the situation constituted a threat to international peace and security:

Sanctions were imposed despite the fact that the conflict in Yugoslavia initially involved parties *within* what was still a member state of the UN. This made the decision to find a "threat to international peace and security" and the invocation of Chapter VII an important indicator of the Council's view of its powers. The resolution sought to soften the edge of this precedent by noting in its opening preambular paragraph "that Yugoslavia has welcomed the convening of a Security Council meeting."[64]

A few months later, due to fighting between Somalia's different factions in the absence of a central government, the Security Council again decided that the situation constituted a threat to international peace.[65] The council authorized military intervention in the civil war there because "the magnitude of the human tragedy caused by the conflict ... constitute[d] a threat to international peace and security."[66] In November 1992, the Security Council decided that the civil war in Liberia was a threat to the peace in West Africa.[67] In September 1993, the Security Council determined that, as a result of National Union for the Total Independence of Angola (UNITA) military action, the situation in Angola constituted a threat to international peace and security, and an arms and oil embargo was imposed on UNITA.[68] In May 1994, the ongoing violence in Rwanda, which resulted in the widespread killing of civilians, the internal displacement of the Rwandan population, and numerous violations of international humanitarian law, was considered to constitute "a threat to peace and security in the region."[69] Moreover, in the case of the more recent fighting in Kosovo, after noting its concern over "the excessive and indiscriminate use of

---

[63] SC Res. 713, September 25, 1991. In Resolution 713, the Security Council determined that the situation in the former Yugoslavia, where war had broken out between forces of the federal government and the states of Slovenia and Croatia (which had declared themselves independent) constituted a threat to the peace.

[64] Franck, *supra* note 29 at 237 [emphasis in original].

[65] SC Res. 733, January 23, 1992. See also SC Res. 751, April 24, 1992, SC Res.767, July 24, 1992.

[66] SC Res. 794, December 3, 1992.

[67] SC Res. 788, November 19, 1992.

[68] SC Res. 864, September 15, 1993. See also SC Res. 1127, August 28, 1997.

[69] SC Res. 918, May 17, 1994. See also SC Res. 997, June 9, 1995 and SC Res. 1013, September 7, 1995.

force" by Serbian forces and "reports of increasing violations of human rights and of international humanitarian law," the Security Council decided that the situation in Kosovo constituted a threat to peace and security in the region and acted under Chapter VII of the Charter.[70] However, it cannot be concluded from these examples that the Council can, or is willing to, intervene in all cases of civil war. It is clear that the circumstances surrounding each case — and especially the "magnitude of the human tragedy" — are important factors in the Security Council's decisions.

Non-Compliance with International Obligations

In the case of Iraq, the Security Council continued its Chapter VII action after the act of aggression was terminated. In Resolution 687, the Council invoked Iraq's non-compliance with different treaties to which it is a party in order to justify its reaction.[71] More precisely, it grounded this reaction on the fact that "egregious violations of treaties imposing duties of major importance to the preservation of peace may be deemed to be threats to the peace, inviting recourse to remedies under Chapter VII."[72] In addition, the Security Council has usurped a role traditionally performed by the judiciary, namely the act of deciding whether or not a treaty has been violated. From the Security Council's decisions in the case of Iraq, some authors draw the conclusion that the failure of a state to ratify major international conventions, combined with past behaviour, could justify Chapter VII actions against such a state.[73]

---

[70] SC Res. 1199, September 23, 1998. See also SC Res. 1160, March 31, 1998.

[71] The following treaties were mentioned: Agreed Minutes between the State of Kuwait and the Republic of Iraq Regarding the Restoration of Friendly Relations, Recognition and Related Matters, October 4, 1963, 485 U.N.T.S. 321; Protocol for the Prohibition of the Use in War of Asphyxiating, Poisonous or Other Gases, and of Bacteriological Methods of Warfare, June 17, 1925, XCIV L.N.T.S. (1929) 65 (Germany, United States, Austria, Belgium, Brazil, and so on); Convention on the Prohibition of the Development, Production and Stockpiling of Bacteriological (Biological) and Toxin Weapons and on Their Destruction April 10, 1972, 1015 U.N.T.S. 163, 26 U.S.T. 583; Treaty on the Non Proliferation of Nuclear Weapons, July 1, 1968, 729 U.N.T.S. 161; International Convention against the Taking of Hostages, December 18, 1979, GA Res. 34/146, UN GAOR 34 Sess., Supp. No. 46, UN Doc. A/34/46 (1979) 245.

[72] Franck, *supra* note 29 at 232.

[73] In the case of Iraq, this country's failure to ratify the convention on biological weapons was deemed to contribute to the threat that it posed to international peace and security.

In Resolution 707, the Security Council relied on an extension of its powers in another sense. In this resolution, the Security Council threatened Iraq that, if it did not comply with its obligations flowing from an agreement with the International Atomic Energy Agency, further collective measures might be used.[74] In 1992, the Security Council, "reaffirm[ing] that, in accordance with the principle in Article 2(4), of the Charter of the United Nations, every State has the duty to refrain from organizing, instigating, assisting or participating in terrorist action in another State," decided that the Libyan refusal to implement Resolution 731[75] constituted "a threat to international peace and security."[76] Similarly, following the attempted assassination of President Hosni Mubarak of Egypt in Addis Ababa and after the terrorists sought asylum in Sudan, the situation was deemed to constitute a threat to international peace and security in the region.[77] In October 1999, the Council determined that "the failure of the Taliban authorities to respond to the demands [to bring the terrorists to justice] constitutes a threat to international peace and security."[78] This trend was unequivocally confirmed by Resolution 1373, which deemed the 11 September attacks in New York and Washington, DC, as a threat to international peace and security. Acting under Chapter VII, the Security Council adopted measures against terrorists.[79]

Concerns about the Future Conduct of a State
(Measures with Respect to Armament)

According to this interpretation of threats to the peace, the Security Council has considered concerns about the future conduct of a state as justifying Chapter VII enforcement measures:

[74] In SC Res. 707, August 15, 1991, the Council took action under Chapter VII of the Charter and "condemn(ed) non-compliance by the Government of Iraq with its obligation under its safeguard agreement with the International Atomic Energy," and "[r]equire[d] the Government of Iraq ... to comply fully and without delay with all its international obligations."

[75] SC Res. 731, January 21, 1992.

[76] SC Res. 748, March 31, 1992. This case was considered by some authors as "[t]he most far-reaching use of the notion of threat to the peace" (Simma et al., *supra* note 16 at 611).

[77] SC Res. 1054, April 26, 1996. Resolution 1070 (SC Res. 1070, August 16, 1996) imposed aerial embargo. See also SC Res. 1044, January 31, 1996).

[78] SC Res. 1267, October 15, 1999.

[79] SC Res. 1373, September 28, 2001; See also SC Res. 1377, November 12, 2001.

If this is a correct interpretation of the Council's actions under Security Council Resolution 687, ending the military hostilities against Iraq and imposing a loser's regime, it suggests a new interpretation of the scope of Articles 2(7), 39, and 41, with significant implications in other situations where a "threat to the peace" might be deduced from collateral evidence of a government's "tendencies," even in the absence of ongoing aggressive behavior.[80]

The Security Council's actions in this case have significantly broadened the notion of "threat to the peace." The termination of acts of aggression by Iraq, which had given rise to Chapter VII enforcement actions, did not prevent the Security Council from dealing with matters normally considered to be essentially domestic. Apparently, the reason for the continued intervention of the Security Council was because it was deemed to be necessary to ensure that the threat to the peace did not recur.

Massive Flow of Refugees

The massive flow of refugees has been considered to be a threat to international peace in several cases. With respect to Iraq, Resolution 688[81] referred to the situation as a threat to international peace and security and recognized that the "repression of the civilian population by its own government were thought not to be primarily within the domestic jurisdiction of Iraq."[82] In order to legitimize this assumption, the Security Council stated that a massive flow of refugees caused by Iraqi government actions contributed to the threat to the peace and security in the region. A similar justification was used in the case of Haiti when the military regime refrained from relinquishing power to the government of legally elected president Jean-Bertrand Aristide, causing a massive flow of refugees.[83] In 1997, following the military coup and the massive violations of human rights by the junta in Sierra Leone —

---

[80] Franck, *supra* note 29 at 232.

[81] SC Res. 688, April 5, 1991. In 1991, in the aftermath of the Persian Gulf War, the Security Council decided that the Iraqi government's repression of the Kurdish population threatened international peace and security in the region, because it resulted in the movement of refugees across international borders, but Chapter VII measures were not invoked.

[82] Franck, *supra* note 29 at 235-36.

[83] SC Res. 841, June 16, 1993. See also SC Res. 861, August 27, 1993, SC Res. 867, September 23, 1993, SC Res. 873, October 13, 1993, SC Res. 917, May 6, 1994, SC Res. 940, July 31, 1994, SC Res. 944, September 29, 1994, SC Res. 975, January 30, 1995, SC Res. 1048, February 29, 1996, SC Res. 1063, June 28, 1996.

apparently due to the refugee problem caused by the situation in that country — the Security Council decided that a threat to international peace and security in the region existed.[84] However, in the case of Iraq's repression of its Kurd population, Chapter VII measures were not invoked. This is an interesting contrast with the aforementioned cases in which civil war and the repression of the civil population resulted in the Council taking enforcement measures.

BREACH OF THE PEACE

L.M. Goodrich, E. Hambro, and A.P. Simons, assert that

[f]rom the Council's discussion, it would appear to be generally accepted that a determination of a breach of the peace is less serious than a finding of aggression, in so far as the positions of the parties are concerned, but more serious than a determination of a "threat to the peace" in terms of implications for further Council action.[85]

Breach of the peace should include any use of armed force.[86] Conversely, only a few of the many armed conflicts that have occurred since the Second World War have been considered to be breaches of the peace by the Security Council.[87] In 1982, following Argentina's invasion of the Falklands/Malvinas, the Security Council considered the situation there to be a breach of the peace.[88] It is submitted that a breach of the peace also exists when armed forces "are applied by or against an effective independent *de facto* regime which is not recognized as a state."[89] In the case of Korea, after North Korean forces attacked South Korea, the Security Council considered the situation to be a breach of the peace.[90] In the cases of the Iran-Iraq war,[91] Kuwait,[92] and the former Yugoslavia crisis,[93]

[84] SC Res. 1132, October 8, 1997. See also SC Res. 1156, March 16, 1998, SC Res. 1171, June 5, 1998, SC Res. 1181, July 13, 1998, SC Res. 1270, October 22, 1999, SC Res. 1299, May 19, 2000, and SC Res. 11306, July 5, 2000.

[85] Goodrich, Hambro, and Simons, *supra* note 17 at 297.

[86] *Ibid.* at 298.

[87] Harris, *supra* note 38 at 876-77.

[88] SC Res. 502, April 3, 1982.

[89] Simma et al., *supra* note 16 at 609.

[90] SC Res. 82, June 25, 1950.

[91] SC Res. 598, July 20, 1987.

[92] SC Res. 660, August 2, 1990.

[93] SC Res. 713, *supra* note 63.

the Security Council also found that breaches of the peace had existed.

In some cases, the Council has refrained from defining a situation as a breach of the peace.[94] It was proposed, for instance, that South Africa's continued illegal occupation of Namibia be considered a breach of the peace. The resolution, however, was vetoed. Simma states that "the situation involving an illegal occupation of territory through the continuation of an originally legal administration must be distinguished from a breach of the peace in the sense of Article 39."[95] The hostilities between India and Pakistan in 1971 were deemed to be a threat to international peace, and the American draft resolution on this subject reflected this interpretation of the situation.[96]

ACT OF AGGRESSION

"Aggression presumes the direct or indirect application of the use of force."[97] Even though the term "breach of the peace" was broad enough to cover aggression, the latter was included by way of a proposal by the Soviet Union.[98] The attempt to define aggression has a long history,[99] and there are two useful sources regarding acts of aggression: the General Assembly Resolution on the Definition

---

[94] The more recent case of Ethiopia-Eritrea conflict is one example. It can be considered a "manifest breach of ... international peace and security" (Schweigman, *supra* note 55 at 150). However, the council determined that it is a threat to regional peace and security and imposed a weapons embargo on both countries. SC Res. 1298, May 17, 2000.

[95] Simma et al., *supra* note 16 at 610.

[96] *Ibid.* at 611; The draft resolution read in part: "Gravely concerned that hostilities continue between India and Pakistan which constitute an immediate threat to international peace and security" (*ibid.*).

[97] *Ibid.* at 610.

[98] Goodrich, Hambro, and Simons, *supra* note 17 at 298.

[99] Much scholarly work has been devoted to the subject of the definition of aggression. The quest dates back to the era of League of Nations. Only in Article X does the Covenant of the League of Nations, *supra* note 15, expressly refer to aggression (see J. Stone, *Aggression and World Order* (Berkeley: University of California Press, 1958) at 27-40). For more information on the history of attempts to define "aggression," see generally A.V.W. Thomas and A.J. Thomas, Jr. *The Concept of Aggression in International Law* (Dallas: Southern Methodist University Press, 1972) at 14-45; and, for a general discussion on aggression, see E. Aroneanu, *La Définition de l'agression* (Paris: Les éditions internationales, 1958).

of Aggression[100] and the *Case Concerning Military and Paramilitary Activities in and against Nicaragua (Nicaragua v. United States).*[101] The definition of acts of aggression has been the subject of debate at the United Nations for many years,[102] and the General Assembly passed a resolution on the definition of aggression in 1974. This resolution contains seven articles, which define aggression in the following way: "Aggression is the use of armed forces by a State against the sovereignty, territorial integrity or political independence of another State, or in any other manner inconsistent with the Charter of the United Nations, as set out in this Definition."[103] Furthermore, the use of armed force by a state in contravention of the Charter shall constitute *prima facie* evidence of an act of aggression.[104] However, in light of other relevant circumstances, the Security Council may conclude that an act of aggression has not been committed.[105] A list of acts considered to be acts of aggression is given in the resolution,[106] but according to Article 4 this list is not exhaustive. Of course, a General Assembly resolution is not binding upon the Security Council. However, the General Assembly's definition of aggression has influenced the Council's practice, and it has been referred to in the drafting of Security Council resolutions.[107]

---

[100] Resolution on the Definition of Aggression, January 14, 1975, GA Res. 3314 (XXIX), UN GAOR, 29th Sess., Supp. No. 31, UN Doc. A/RES/3314(XXIX) (1974), 142; UN GAOR, 29th Sess., Supp. No. 31, at 142, UN Doc. A/9631 (1974).

[101] *Nicaragua* case, *supra* note 45.

[102] Harris, *supra* note 38 at 879.

[103] Resolution on the Definition of Aggression, *supra* note 100 at Article 1.

[104] "Act of aggression" should be distinguished from "war of aggression." According to Y. Dinstein, *War, Aggression and Self-Defence,* 2nd ed. (Cambridge: Grotius Publications, 1994) at 125, "[a]n act of aggression may trigger war. However, this is not a foregone conclusion, since aggression may also take the form of an act short of war. When an aggressive act short of war is committed, although a violation of international law occurs, no crime against peace is perpetrated."

[105] Resolution on the Definition of Aggression, *supra* note 100 at Article 2. According to this article, such circumstances include lack of sufficient gravity.

[106] *Ibid.* at Article 3, which states that among others "invasion or attack by the armed forces," "any military occupation," "[b]ombardment by the armed forces of a State against the territory of another State," and "[t]he blockage of the ports or coasts of a State by the armed forces of another State" are acts of aggression.

[107] Harris, *supra* note 38 at 880.

The second relevant source is the *Nicaragua* case,[108] in which the International Court of Justice (ICJ) examined the questions of the use of force and acts of aggression. The case presented an exceptional opportunity for the court to explore in detail the customary law governing the use of armed forces. The decision is especially significant, as it recognizes that an "act of aggression" includes cases of indirect military intervention of one state in another state. In this sense, the decision of the court affirms that Article 3(g) of Resolution 3314,[109] which reflects customary international law on the use of force. The court stated that

[t]his description, contained in Article 3, paragraph (g), of the Definition of Aggression annexed to General Assembly resolution 3314 (XXIX), may be taken to reflect customary international law. The Court sees no reason to deny that, in customary law, the prohibition of armed attacks may apply to the sending by a State of armed bands to the territory of another State.[110]

South Africa's aggression against Angola in 1976 was the first time that the Security Council found that "aggression" had occurred.[111] In many cases, military actions by South Africa or Israel have been seen as acts of aggression by the Council.[112] Examples include Resolution 407 (1977),[113] condemning an act of armed aggression perpetrated against the People's Republic of Benin on January 16, 1977, Resolution 573 (1985),[114] condemning Israel's air raid on Palestinian Liberation Organization targets in Tunisia, and Resolution 577 (1985),[115] which demanded that South Africa cease all acts of aggression against Angola.[116]

---

[108] *Nicaragua* case, *supra* note 45.

[109] See text of article in note 106.

[110] *Nicaragua* case, *supra* note 45 at 103, para. 195.

[111] SC Res. 387, March 31, 1976.

[112] Simma et al., *supra* note 16 at 610.

[113] SC Res. 407, April 14, 1977.

[114] SC Res. 573, October 4, 1985.

[115] SC Res. 577, December 6, 1985.

[116] Following Israel's raid on Iraq's nuclear installations on June 7, 1981, Resolution 487 of the Security Council condemned the military attack by Israel as a clear violation of the Charter and the norms of international conduct, and expressed its concern about the danger to international peace and security created by the Israeli air attack. However, the Council did not designate Israel's act as an act of aggression (see SC Res. 487, June 19, 1981).

COLLECTIVE SANCTIONS IN RESPONSE TO BREACHES
OF *ERGA OMNES* OBLIGATIONS

The earlier categorization clarifies the practice of the Security
Council regarding Chapter VII of the Charter and, more specifically, the situations that it has designated as threats to international
peace. The Security Council's exercise of its enforcement powers
under Chapter VII is often criticized, but, even in the debatable
cases, the Council can use the *erga omnes* justification as the basis
for its actions. Although the Security Council has, in the past few
years, extended its definition of a threat to the peace, Article 39 of
the Charter, in my view, is not capable of supporting such broad
interpretations. Even if we accept that the Council's decisions under
Chapter VII have been justifiable under the Charter,[117] situations
may arise that will not justify enforcement actions under Chapter
VII, despite the international community's concerns.[118] In such
cases, collective action can be legitimized on a different legal basis.
In the extreme case of breaches of *erga omnes* obligations (including international crimes), there is an alternative legal justification
for collective action.[119] If breach of an *erga omnes* obligation is a
ground for the imposition of unilateral sanctions by all other states
(because an obligation towards all states has been breached), then
it can be a ground for collective sanctions in the framework of an
international organization.[120]

---

[117] The argument would be that in all the cases of Security Council enforcement
actions there has been some *international* repercussions.

[118] The example of the Kosovo crisis was one such situation.

[119] See also P.M. Dupuy, "Observations sur la pratique récente des "sanctions" de
l'illicite" (1983) 87 R.G.D.I.P. 533-42.

[120] This view is reinforced by Articles 40 and 41 (particular consequences of a serious breach of an obligation under this chapter) of Chapter III (serious
breaches of obligations under peremptory norms of general international law)
of Part 2, as well as Articles 48 (invocation of responsibility by a state other than
an injured state) and 54 (measures taken by states other than an injured state)
of the *Draft Articles on State Responsibility*, which is contained in the *ILC's Report
on Fifty-Third Session, supra* note 6. However, it should be noted that the subject
of serious breaches of obligation to the international community as a whole
(Part 2, chapter III), and especially Article 54, have been among the outstanding issues in the commission and different views were expressed on these articles (at 33-37). It was even recommended by the open-ended working group
on outstanding issues that Article 54 be deleted and replaced by a saving clause
(at 36).

Even if the breach of *erga omnes* obligations does not amount to a "threat to the peace," "breach of the peace," or an "act of aggression," collective sanctions can be imposed, or at least recommended, by the Security Council.[121] No provision of the Charter stops the Security Council from administering and harmonizing collective actions in the case of a breach of *erga omnes* obligations.[122] It should be noted that, in these cases, the legal basis for sanctions would be different from the first category of collective sanctions. The theory of retaliation will be the basis of sanctions. As a result, these sanctions will be subject to the same limitations as unilateral sanctions.[123] Whether this decision will be binding to the same

[121] As D.W. Bowett states, "although in principle these obligations rest on states whenever a crime is committed, and the decision that a crime has been committed is for each state to reach, in practice it is likely that the Security Council will both take the decision and coordinate the sanctions." D.W. Bowett, "Crimes of State and the 1996 Report of the International Law Commission on State Responsibility" (1998) 9 Eur. J. Int'l L. 173.

[122] According to a report prepared by a Committee of the American Branch of the International Law Association,

> it is unclear whether the imposition of mandatory economic sanctions requires a determination by the United Nations Security Council, under Chapter VII of the Charter, of a threat to the peace. The uniform practice of the Council, however, has been to make such a determination before imposing mandatory economic sanctions. The authority of the Council, as well as that of such other UN organs as the General Assembly, to recommend economic sanctions is much broader.

See "Report of the Committee on Economic Sanctions: Economic Sanctions and Internal Armed Conflict, Some Salient Problems," in *Proceedings of the American Branch of the International Law Association* (New York: International Law Association, American Branch, 1993-94) 45 at 65. Note should also be taken of Article 94(b) of the Charter, *supra* note 5, which states that "[i]f any party to a case fails to perform the obligations incumbent upon it under a judgment rendered by the Court, the other party may have recourse to the Security Council, which may, if it deems necessary, make recommendations or decide upon measures to be taken to give effect to the judgment." A situation may arise in which the ICJ finds a state party to litigation in breach of an *erga omnes* obligation, and would ask for the Security Council's action after that party's failure to comply with the court's ruling.

[123] So far, the Security Council has never attempted to impose sanctions on this basis. It has always used Article 39 to justify collective actions. In the case of the Tehran hostage crisis, the United States attempted to impose sanctions through a Security Council resolution, but failed to do so because of the Soviet veto. The draft resolution would have provided for mandatory sanctions against Iran in accordance with Articles 39 and 41 of the Charter, *supra* note 5. *United States of America: Draft Resolution*, UN SCOR, 35th year, Supp. for Jan, Feb., Mar., 1982, UN Doc. S/13735 (1982) at 10. In my view, in this case, an alternative

degree as enforcement measures under Article 39 is, however, also arguable. The question of binding force of non-Chapter VII decisions of the Security Council turns around different interpretations of Article 25 of the Charter. Some authors argue that under Article 25 of the Charter — which concerns the obligation to carry out decisions of the Council[124] — resolutions that are not issued on the basis of Chapter VII are also binding.[125]

---

    justification for the imposition of sanctions could have been the breach of an *erga omnes* obligation by Iran.

[124] According to Article 25, "[t]he members of the United Nations agree to accept and carry out the decision of the Security Council in accordance with the present Charter."

[125] According to Simma et al.'s commentary, *supra* note 16 at 410, on the Charter:

    [a] closer analysis reveals that the opinion according to which Article 25 declares only those decisions to be binding which are taken by the Security Council under Chapter VII, i.e. decisions on enforcement measures, is not tenable. If one followed such a narrow interpretation of Article 25, the whole system set up for the maintenance of peace and within it the position of the Security Council as the organ charged with the primary responsibility for the maintenance of peace ... would be weakened, which would clearly run counter to the overall concept of the Charter.

    This view is supported by Kelsen, *The Law of the United Nations* (New York: Frederick A. Praeger, 1951) at 97-98; see also S.D. Bailey, *The Procedure of the UN Security Council* (Oxford: Clarendon Press, 1975), at 206-10) and the ICJ's advisory opinion on *Namibia* (*Legal Consequences for States of the Continued Presence of South Africa in Namibia (South West Africa) notwithstanding Security Council Resolution 276 (1970)*, [1971] I.C.J. Rep. 16, at 53-54, paras. 114-16 [hereinafter *Namibia* case]). The court states that, "[i]f Article 25 had reference solely to decisions of the Security Council concerning enforcement action under Article 41 and 42 of the Charter, that is to say, if it were only such decisions that had binding effect, then Article 25 would be superfluous, since this effect is secured by Articles 48 and 49 of the Charter" (at 53).

    The court has reached the same conclusion as Kelsen and uses the exact same words as him (only three words differ). However, the court has authoritatively omitted any citation! Yet, this majority opinion of the ICJ judges was not shared by several leading ICJ judges (compare with the dissenting opinions by Judges Fitzmaurice at 292-5, and Gros at 340-1, and separate opinions by Judges Petrén at 136, and Dillard at 165-6). Judge Fitzmaurice states: "If the effect of [Article 25] were automatically to make *all* decisions of the Security Council binding, then the words 'in accordance with the present Charter' would be quite superfluous. They would add nothing to the preceding and only other phrase in the Article, namely: 'The Members of the United Nations agree to accept and carry out the decisions of the Security Council,' which they are clearly intended to qualify (at 292) [emphasis in original]. In the view of some, this approach does not appear appropriate in the light of the overall structure of the Charter.

Even if we accept that such collective actions under the Charter will not have the binding force of decisions based on a determination by the Security Council under Article 39, such actions may have extensive moral authority and may receive wide support from members.[126] However, it should be added that the issue of action by states other than the injured state, as evidenced by different opinions in the International Law Commission (ILC), is certainly far from being resolved.[127]

Constraints on the Use of Economic Sanctions[128]

In this part, I analyze the current practice regarding sanctions and revisit the legal basis of sanctions with a more critical approach. Application of sanctions by the United Nations has been criticized on several grounds. First, the legitimacy of the Security Council itself has been called into question. When one examines the issue closely, it becomes evident that there exists, in fact, three inter-related problems regarding the decisions of the Security Council: (1) a general problem regarding the legitimacy of the collective

---

See further Simma et al., *supra* note 16 at 613-14. The view of the majority of the court has not found support in practice. During the discussion of the advisory opinion in the Security Council, many permanent members rejected that view (UN SCOR, 26th Year, 1588th Mtg., UN Doc. S/PV.1588 (1971) para. 18 (Mr. Koscinsko-Morizet, France); UN SCOR, 26th Year, 1589th Mtg., UN Doc. S/PV.1589 (1971) para. 50-53. (Sir Colin Crowe, United Kingdom)); see also T. Mori, "Namibia Opinion Revisited: A Gap in the Current Arguments on the Power of the Security Council" (1997) 4 I.L.S.A. J. Int'l and Comp. L. at 121 and, more recently, G. Arangio-Ruiz, "On the Security Council's 'Law Making'" and "Article 39 of the ILC First Reading Draft Articles on State Responsibility" (2000) Rivista di diritto internazionale at 609 and 747, respectively. Notwithstanding these opposing views, I find the majority opinion of the court persuasive.

[126] Judge Petrén in his separate opinion has stated that "it is quite out of the question that in this case the Court is confronted with Security Council decisions invested with binding force for States. They cannot be anything other than recommendations which, as such, obviously have great moral force but which cannot be regarded as embodying legal obligations" (*Namibia* case, *supra* note 125 at 136).

[127] See the entire discussion in note 120. For a comprehensive study of this issue, see J.A. Frowein, "Reactions by Not Directly Affected States to Breaches of Public International Law" (1994) 248 Rec. des Cours at 345.

[128] In addition to the restraints on use of economic sanctions, there are certain problems associated with the enforcement and effectiveness of sanctions. These questions are more relevant in the political analysis of sanctions. See Doxey, *supra* note 2 at 80-105 and Doxey, *supra* note 6 at 82-93 and at 91.

authority of the council;[129] (2) if one assumes that the Security Council's collective authority is legitimate, there is the problem of the broad interpretation of Article 39 by the Council and its limitations; and (3) if there are limitations to the power of the Council, there remains the question of how these limitations are to be enforced and who the body will be that will oversee this enforcement. Other controversial issues include the negative humanitarian consequences, the effects on third states, and the politicization of the practice of implementing sanctions, which will be surveyed in the following part.

LEGITIMACY OF THE COLLECTIVE AUTHORITY OF THE SECURITY
COUNCIL: THE TERMINATION OF THE SECURITY COUNCIL'S ACTIONS
AND THE PROBLEM OF THE "REVERSE VETO"

The collective authority of the Security Council has been challenged on two grounds. The fact that the Council is dominated by a few states is cited by those who challenge the legitimacy of the Council. It is also claimed that "the veto held by the permanent members is unfair."[130] In addition, there is the problem of terminating Security Council actions, which is also known as the reverse veto problem. For the purposes of this study, only the latter problem will be examined in more detail.

---

[129] For a detailed study of this problem, see D.D. Caron, "The Legitimacy of the Collective Authority of the Security Council" (1993) 87 A.J.I.L. 552.

[130] *Ibid.* at 562. On justifications of the veto power of permanent members, see W.M. Reisman, "The Constitutional Crisis in the United Nations" (1993) 87 A.J.I.L. 83 at 83-84 and 98; Goodrich, Hambro, and Simons, *supra* note 17 at 291. In contrast, see Caron, *supra* note 129 at 566-68. See also B. Fassbender, *UN Security Council Reform and the Right of Veto: A Constitutional Perspective* (Hague: Kluwer Law International, 1998) at 197-207; *Resolutions 1991 Adopted by the General Assembly*, GA Res. 1991A (XVIII), UN GAOR, 18th Sess., Supp. No. 15, UN Doc. A/5515 (1963) 21. On other questions related to voting and veto in the Security Council, see Simma et al., *supra* note 16 at 443; S.D. Bailey, *Voting in the Security Council* (Bloomington: Indiana University Press, 1969) at 18-25; A.W. Rudzinski, "The So-Called Double Veto" (1951) 45 A.J.I.L. 443; M. Ewing, *Justifying Humanitarian Intervention* (LL.M. thesis, McGill University, Institute of Comparative Law, 1993) [unpublished] at 83.

It is in response to these challenges that proposals for reform in the UN system and the Security Council have been submitted. Such proposals, including reform of the veto, increasing the membership of the Security Council and increasing the involvement of the General Assembly, will be evaluated in the final section of this article. These challenges are, however, directed at the composition and practice of the Security Council in general and not merely at the enforcement powers of the Council.

The question of terminating economic sanctions imposed by the Security Council has become a serious problem in the Council. As the former secretary-general of the United Nations has pointed out in the *Supplement to an Agenda for Peace*:

[t]he objectives for which specific sanctions regimes were imposed have not always been clearly defined. Indeed they sometimes seem to change over time. This combination of imprecision and mutability makes it difficult for the Security Council to agree on when the objectives can be considered to have been achieved and sanctions can be lifted.[131]

The Charter has no provisions regarding the means by which actions taken by the Security Council should be terminated. In the absence of such provisions, it can be concluded that "it is for the Council itself to end or modify its actions."[132] The case of Rhodesia is often cited in support of this interpretation. The sanctions against Rhodesia were terminated by a Security Council Resolution.[133] Currently, the United Kingdom and the United States support the view that it is the Council that has the power to terminate. Nonetheless, in the case of Rhodesia, the position of these two countries was the source of debate and controversy. Since the United Kingdom and the United States are two permanent members of the Security Council, it is interesting and important to examine their position in this regard.

In the case of Rhodesia, after the Smith regime accepted the resumption of full legislative and executive authority over Southern Rhodesia by a British governor, the United Kingdom informed the Council that

[t]he state of rebellion in the Territory has been brought to an end ... in these circumstances, the obligations of Member States under Article 25 of the Charter in relation to [the sanctions] are, in the view of the Government of the United Kingdom, to be regarded as having been discharged. This being so, the United Kingdom is terminating the measures which were taken by it pursuant to the decisions adopted by the Council in regard to the then situation of illegality.[134]

---

[131] *Supplement to an Agenda for Peace: Position Paper of the Secretary-General on the Occasion of the Fiftieth Anniversary of the United Nations*, UN Doc. A/50/60; S/1995/1, 25 (1995), para. 68 [hereinafter *Supplement to an Agenda for Peace*].

[132] Caron, *supra* note 129 at 578.

[133] SC Res. 460, December 21, 1979.

[134] Letter dated December 12, 1979, from the representative of the United Kingdom of Great Britain and Northern Ireland to the President of the Security Council, UN SCOR, 34th Sess., Supp. for Oct.-Dec. 1979 at 119, 120, cited in Caron, *supra* note 129 at 581.

Many African states and the Soviet Bloc opposed the United Kingdom's position and asserted that the Security Council's resolutions could only be revoked by a decision of the Security Council.[135] However, after considering the matter, the Security Council decided to terminate the sanctions without much debate.[136] The United Kingdom's statement following the vote is interesting: "Our view remains that the obligation to impose those sanctions fell away automatically with the return to legality of the colony. But we have been very conscious that many countries have attached great importance to the adoption by the Council of a resolution on this subject."[137] However, as D.D. Caron asserts, today there is no doubt that the Rhodesian case confirms the view that the council has the authority to terminate its own action.[138] Any ambiguity caused by the statements of the United Kingdom and the United States regarding Rhodesia were resolved by their statements towards the end of the Persian Gulf war.[139]

The fact that the Security Council has the exclusive power to terminate actions that it initiated paves the way for the permanent members of the Security Council to exercise what is called a *reverse* veto. A reverse veto is the veto of a permanent member of the Security Council on the question of the termination of a Council action. Such veto can be criticized on the grounds that it "increases the

---

[135] Letter dated December 14, 1979 from the representative of Madagascar to the President of the Security Council and letter dated December 21, 1979 from the representative of the Union of Soviet Socialist Republics to the President of the Security Council, UN SCOR, 34th Sess., Supp. For Oct.-Dec. 1979, at 119, 120, and 138, cited in Caron, *supra* note 129 at 581.

[136] SC Res. 460, UN SCOR, 34th Sess., Res. and Dec., 2181st Mtg., UN Doc. S/PV.2181 at 2, cited in Caron, *supra* note 129 at 582.

[137] *Ibid.* The United States position, however, was not exactly the same. It expressed its pleasure that the Council was terminating its measures and stated that "it was in recognition of that fact that the United States made its recent announcement regarding [termination] of sanctions." Tanzania, on the other hand, emphasized that any individual interpretation concerning sanctions should not be accepted (at 582).

[138] See Caron, *supra* note 129.

[139] See statements of Mr. Pickering, representative of the United States: "It is only here in the Security Council that we could agree to lift sanctions against Iraq" (UN SCOR, 34th Sess., 2977 Mtg., UN Doc. S/PV.2977 (1991) (part II) (closed-Resumption 3) at 301 [provisional]); and statement of Sir David Hannay, representative of the United Kingdom: "[O]nly the Security Council itself can make that judgement" (*ibid.* at 313).

dominance of the permanent members in Council deliberations that revisit action already taken, [and] it curtails the already limited ability of actors within and without the Council to end a crisis by negotiation."[140] This reverse veto problem became manifest in the case of Iraq. While, today, it may be difficult to find the consensus that existed in 1990 to impose sanctions on Iraq, it has become impossible to lift or modify the sanctions due to the veto of the permanent members of the Council.

THE LEGITIMACY OF THE COUNCIL'S ACTIONS
UNDER CHAPTER VII

In examining the legal basis of collective sanctions, it becomes clear that "[t]he Security Council has potentially far-reaching enforcement powers."[141] Nevertheless, "to assert the legitimacy of its actions and to pull members towards compliance with its decisions, the Council must be seen to be acting in accordance with established procedures and limitations."[142] In the words of Judge Shahabuddeen, the relevant questions are "whether there are any limitations on the power of the Council to characterize a situation as one justifying the making of a decision entailing such consequences ... [and] [i]f there are any limits, what are those limits and what body, if other than the Security Council, is competent to say what those limits are?"[143] The application of sanctions by the Security Council has been criticized and challenged — one instance being the *Case Concerning Questions of Interpretation and Application of the 1971 Montreal Convention Arising from the Aerial Incident at Lockerbie (Libyan Arab Jamahiryia* v. *United Kingdom)* (*Lockerbie* case). Even if it is accepted that the Security Council's decisions were political, there is still room to examine the legitimacy of the Security Council's actions under Chapter VII of the Charter. The underlying purpose of Chapter VII powers is to provide an incentive for peaceful

---

[140] Caron, *supra* note 129 at 582-83.

[141] Franck, *supra* note 29 at 218.

[142] *Ibid.*

[143] *Case Concerning Questions of Interpretation and Application of the 1971 Montreal Convention Arising from the Aerial Incident at Lockerbie (Libyan Arab Jamahiryia* v. *United Kingdom)*, Provisional Measures, Order of 14 April 1992, [1992] I.C.J. Rep 3; *Questions of Interpretation and Application of the 1971 Montreal Convention arising from the Aerial Incident at Lockerbie (Libyan Arab Jamahiryia* v. *United States)*, Provisional Measures, Order of 14 April 1992, [1992] I.C.J. Rep 114 at 142 (separate opinion of Judge Shahabuddeen) [hereinafter *Lockerbie* case].

settlement of the disputes.[144] However, the language used by the Security Council in its resolutions is not always clear:

A problem with Security Council resolutions is that they speak in the covered language of diplomacy, sometimes out of political necessity, sometimes out of the drafters' professional habit. They often fail to address issues of fairness, which leaves Council actions vulnerable to attack as exercises in unprincipled power. This adversely affects the resolution, its capacity to garner voluntary compliance, and perceptions of the process' legitimacy.[145]

The Council's discretion in taking decisions under Chapter VII and the two contrary positions regarding limits on the Security Council's discretion should be examined before the question of the legitimacy of the Council's actions is addressed.

There Is No Limit on the Security Council's Discretion

According to one view, which is supported by eminent scholars such as Hans Kelsen, there is virtually no limit to the Security Council's discretion under Article 39.[146] Kelsen's argument is summarized later in this article[147] and relies on provisions that are found in Chapter V of the Charter. This chapter is dedicated to the Security Council, and, more specifically, Article 24 stipulates the functions and powers of the Council and provides:

1. In order to ensure prompt and effective action by the United Nations, its members confer on the Security Council primary responsibility for the maintenance of international peace and security, and agree that in carrying out its duties under this responsibility the Security Council acts on their behalf.

---

[144] See R.F. Kennedy, "*Libya v. United States*: The International Court of Justice and the Power of Judicial Review" (1993) 33 Va. J. Int'l L. 903.

[145] Franck, *supra* note 29 at 230.

[146] The extreme version of this position is best stated by former US Secretary of State, John Foster Dulles, *War or Peace* (New York: MacMillan, 1950) at 194-95:

The Security Council is not a body that merely enforces agreed law, it is a law unto itself. If it considers any situation as a threat to the peace, it may decide what measures shall be taken. No principles of law are laid down to guide it; it can decide in accordance with what it thinks is expedient. It could be a tool enabling certain powers to advance their selfish interests at the expense of another power.

[147] Kelsen, *supra* note 125 at 287-95; compare with M. Bedjaoui, "Du Contrôle de Légalité des Actes du Conseil de Sécurité" in *Nouveaux Itinéraires en Droit: Hommage à François Rigaux* (Bruxelles: Bruylant, 1993) at 83-87.

2. In discharging these duties the Security Council shall act in accordance with the *Purposes and Principles of the United Nations.* The specific powers granted to the Security Council for the discharge of these duties are laid down in Chapters VI, VII, VIII and XII.[148]

According to this article, actions of the Security Council should be in accordance with the "Purposes and Principles of the United Nations." Article 1 of the Charter articulates the "purposes" of the United Nations, the first of which is

[t]o maintain international peace and security, and to that end: *to take effective collective measures* for the prevention and removal of threats to the peace, and for the suppression of acts of aggression or other breaches of the peace, and to bring about by peaceful means, and *in conformity with the principles of justice* and international law, *adjustment or settlement of international disputes* or situations which might lead to a breach of the peace.[149]

This statement contains two elements. The first deals with the maintenance of peace and security by taking *effective collective measures,* and the second relates to the *peaceful settlement of disputes.* Since "conformity with the principles of justice and international law" is only mentioned in the latter case, some writers assert that "the Security Council is not legally bound by the Charter to respect principles of international law when acting under Chapter VII."[150] Similarly, the Charter does not provide that the decisions of the Security Council must be in conformity with the law that exists at the time they are adopted in order for them to be enforceable. Further, "[t]he purpose of the enforcement action under Article 39 is not to maintain or restore the law, but to maintain or restore peace, which is not necessarily identical with the law."[151]

Other provisions of the Charter do not place any limitations on the Security Council's powers. According to Kelsen, "[t]he statement in the preamble, providing that the peoples of the United Nations are determined 'to establish conditions under which justice and respect for the obligations arising from treaties and other sources of international law can be maintained' is hardly applicable to an enforcement action under article 39."[152] Kelsen argues that, even if one assumes that the principles of the preamble (which

---

[148] [emphasis added].

[149] Article 1 (1) [emphasis added].

[150] See Kennedy, *supra* note 144 at 906.

[151] Kelsen, *supra* note 125 at 294.

[152] *Ibid.* at 295.

is cited earlier in this article) are applicable to Article 39 enforcement actions, and were the council bound to act "in conformity with the principles of justice and international law,"[153] the power of the Security Council would not be restricted. In his words, "[t]he Council would be empowered to establish justice if it considered the existing law as not satisfactory, and hence to enforce a decision which it considered to be just though not in conformity with existing law. The decision enforced by the Security Council may create new law for the concrete case."[154]

The Security Council Should Exercise Its Power Justly

A contrary view holds that "[t]here is no real peace and security if these are achieved only at the sacrifice of justice."[155] In the case, *Namibia (Legal Consequences for States of the Continued Presence of South Africa in Namibia (South West Africa) notwithstanding Security Council Resolution 276 (1970)),* some of the judges of the ICJ criticized the Security Council for acting in cases in which the perceived threat did not constitute a threat to the peace.[156] Judge Gerald Fitzmaurice, in his dissenting opinion, explored the limitations on the power of the Security Council under Chapter VII and then stated that

limitations on the powers of the Security Council are necessary because of the all too great ease with which any acutely controversial international situation can be represented as involving a latent threat to international peace and security, even where it is really too remote genuinely to constitute one. Without these limitations, the function of the Security Council could be used for purposes never originally intended.[157]

Accordingly, even if we presume that the collective authority of the Security Council is legitimate, and that the enforcement powers of the council are *political,* the council must also persuade states that it is exercising its powers justly.[158] In practical terms, the actions taken by the council should correspond to the "standards of legitimacy

---

[153] As stated in Article 1(1) of the Charter, *supra* note 5.

[154] Kelsen, *supra* note 125 at 295.

[155] Goodrich, Hambro, and Simons, *supra* note 17.

[156] *Namibia* case, *supra* note 125 at 294 (dissenting opinion of Judge Sir Gerald Fitzmaurice) and 340 (dissenting opinion of Judge Gros).

[157] *Ibid.* at 294.

[158] Bedjaoui, *supra* note 147 at 87.

and fairness" in order to gain the support and compliance of the states.[159]

The treaty basis of the United Nations (and, consequently, its political organs) is emphasized by those who see limits to the power of the Security Council. Put more eloquently, Thomas Franck writes:

The United Nations is the creature of a treaty, and as such it exercises authority legitimately only insofar as it deploys powers which the treaty parties have assigned to it ... [t]hese may be modestly augmented by a "penumbra" of other powers which are necessarily incidental to the effective implementation of the enumerated ones.[160]

Accordingly, the criterion for the legitimacy of actions by the Security Council should be sought in the Charter: "[I]f the organization decides to exceed powers [delegated to it] then its decisions cease to be legitimate."[161] Article 2(7) of the Charter defines the limits of the power of the United Nations and, thus, the limits of the Security Council's power. Article 2(7) provides:

Nothing contained in the ... Charter shall authorize the United Nations to intervene in matters which are essentially within the domestic jurisdiction of any state or shall require the Members to submit such matters to settlement under the ... Charter; but this principle shall not prejudice the application of enforcement measures under Chapter VII.

Thus, the general rule is that the United Nations cannot intervene in matters within the domestic jurisdiction of a state. This rule is subject to two caveats. First, the notion of what is "essentially domestic" has changed over the past fifty years. Multinational corporations have emerged as major players on the world scene, and civil wars are no longer considered to be exclusively within the realm of a country's domestic affairs. Second, there is a crucial exception to the Article 2(7) rule: it does not apply when the Security Council has authorized, or resorted to, enforcement measures under Chapter VII. Earlier in this article, it was submitted that the application of enforcement measures by the Security Council was subject to fulfillment of a "substantive" and a "procedural" condition. The determination of a threat to the peace, breach of the peace, or act of aggression are substantive conditions and not merely formal declarations.

---

[159] Franck, *supra* note 29 at 219.

[160] *Ibid.* at 219.

[161] *Ibid.* at 220.

Practically speaking, however, as evidenced by the cases studied earlier in this article, the "open-textured"[162] quality of Chapter VII has enabled the Council to redefine international peace and security according to its perceptions and policies (and to the needs of its permanent members). Even the proponents of restricting the Security Council's powers admit this point. Former president of the ICJ, Mohammed Bedjaoui, after examining recent resolutions of the Security Council and stating that their legality ought to be subject to verification,[163] stated that "[i]ndeed, whether one is in favour of it or not, the Council's freedom of appraisal finds clear textual warrant in the Charter. For that reason it could not, as such, very well be the object of legality-control."[164] However, he then goes on to say:

> On the other hand ... the same degree of immunity can surely not apply in the domain of the more concrete activities that the Council is led to deploy as a result, in particular, of its qualification of a given situation under Article 39 of the Charter. It is in this area of action undertaken, or of the ways and means decided for having them carried out, that the need may arise and a proper place be found for testing the legality of Security Council resolutions.[165]

Bedjaoui then rejects Kelsen's position that the Council can enforce decisions that are not in conformity with law and create new law for the concrete cases. His rejection of Kelsen's analysis is based on several grounds.[166] According to Bedjaoui, the Security Council is

---

[162] H.L.A. Hart, *The Concept of Law* (Oxford: Clarendon Press, 1960) at 120.

[163] These resolutions include: SC Res. 687, April 3, 1991, concerning Iraq, which established an observer mission for Iraq and Kuwait, a UN Special Commission for supervising neutralization of Iraq's chemical or biological weapons, a UN Compensation Commission, and a Sanctions Committee; SC Res. 731, January 21, 1992, and 748, March 31, 1992, concerning Libya; SC Res. 808, February 22, 1993, and 827, May 25, 1993, on the establishment of an international criminal tribunal; SC Res. 837, June 6, 1993, concerning Somalia; and SC Res. 713, September 25, 1991, concerning the arms embargo on Bosnia and Herzegovina. Thomas Franck has also referred to these resolutions when he reached the conclusion that, in certain cases, the Security Council "has significantly extend[ed] its Chapter VII jurisdiction" (Franck, *supra* note 29 at 241).

[164] M. Bedjaoui, *The New World Order and the Security Council: Testing the Legality of Its Acts* (Dordrecht: Martinus Nijhoff Publishers, 1994) at 52.

[165] *Ibid.* at 52-53.

[166] See *ibid.* at 32-35. Bedjaoui presents a long list of arguments. Among others, he points out that the organs of the United Nations are not empowered to create new customs through their concordant, consistent, and undisputed practice according to the Charter. Even a plenary and representative organ such as the

bound to respect the Charter and international law. This view is reinforced by the fact that, since the Persian Gulf war, the Council has resumed the practice of citing the chapter and verse that form the basis for its decisions, thereby grounding them in the law.[167] In sum, even though the decisions of the Security Council are essentially political, it is limited in its exercise of power by the Charter and by the given rules of general international law.[168]

General Assembly can, at most, make "recommendations" to encourage progressive development of international law (Article 13 of the Charter, *supra* note 5). On the subject of the rule making power of international organizations, Bedjaoui shares the view according to which, "having been created by states, international organizations themselves create legal rules addressed to various entities, all of whose provisions, however, even if they have their due place within the particular legal order of the organization concerned, are subjected to international law" (P.-M. Dupuy, *Droit international public* (Paris: Dalloz-Sirey, 1992) at 127, cited in Bedjaoui, *supra* note 164 at 32-33). Bedjaoui also points out that if, like any other international treaty, the Charter may contradict rules of international law, at the very least, it cannot contradict imperative norms of international law. Kelsen, *supra* note 125 at 294-95, holds that, in order to restore international peace and security, the Security Council may in some cases not be able to act in accordance with international law (use of force under Chapter VII being an example). Bedjaoui, on the other hand, deems it to be impossible for the Security Council to brush aside, when it resorts to use of force, fundamental norms of the law of war (humanitarian law), or on human rights and self-determination of peoples: norms which express principles rooted in the "universal conscience of mankind." Finally, Bedjaoui believes that today it is no longer possible to draw a distinction between peace and law: "The restoration of peace can only be illusory without the observance of international law." Bedjaoui, *supra* note 164 at 35.

[167] Bedjaoui, *supra* note 164 at 35. On the other hand, in 1988, Sonnenfeld wrote, "in its practice the Security Council has adopted only a few resolutions referring *expressis verbis* to Article 39 ... This proves that the content of resolutions negotiated in the Security Council rarely reflects the real situations." R. Sonnenfeld, *Resolutions of the United Nations Security Council* (Dordrecht: Martinus Nijhoff Publishers, 1988) at 89-91.

[168] This is also reflected in the following words of Sir Gerald Fitzmaurice: "This is a principle of international law that is as well-established as any there can be — and the Security Council is as much subject to it (for the United Nations is itself a subject of international law) as any of its individual members are" (*Namibia* case, *supra* note 125 at 294 (dissenting opinion of Judge Sir Gerald Fitzmaurice)). As for M. Bothe, he states that "Les Nations Unies sont basées sur le respect du droit, et il serait inconcevable d'exclure le droit comme facteur déterminant d'un élément clé de leurs activités. Le Conseil de sécurité n'est pas une sorte de pape du droit international : 'Roma locuta, causa finita'"("Les limites des pouvoirs du Conseil de sécurité," in R.-J. Dupuy, ed., *supra* note 38 at 69). Such limits should also be borne in mind in connection with the proposal for an alternative legal basis for collective sanctions (for breach of *erga omnes* obligations).

Control over the Activities of the Security Council: The Lockerbie *Case*

The conclusion that there is a limit to the actions of the Security Council leads to another question: who will exercise control over the activities of the Council? If there are limits to the Council's powers, which body is competent to oversee its actions? During the Cold War, the reciprocal operation of the veto created a system that was a "functional equivalent" of a "constitutional theory of checks and balances." However, the Charter did not explicitly provide for anything of this kind.[169] As a result, when, with the end of the Cold War, the Security Council became more effective, the said informal system of checks and balances ceased to function. I shall, therefore, examine the recent developments in this respect.

In recent years, the Security Council has become more "secretive."[170] There are many "mini-councils" within the Council, which meet behind closed doors and do not keep minutes of their meetings. Often, the final decisions of the Security Council are taken in accordance with the recommendations of these secretive meetings.[171] Such decision-making by the Security Council may have been acceptable in the case of indisputable acts of aggression, such as Kuwait's invasion by Iraq, but in a case such as the one involving sanctions against Libya for the alleged export of state terrorism, it may be considered to be acting like "a world directorate for *anything* they determine to be a 'threat to the peace.'"[172] Would the ICJ, as the principal judicial organ of the United Nations, be the appropriate body to review the actions of the Security Council and check on the legality of its actions? According to the Charter, there is no doubt that the court does not have the power to review the actions of other organs of the United Nations. However, the Charter also provides that the court can exercise its own jurisdiction and reach its own conclusion in a case, even if the matter is simultaneously before another organ of the United Nations.[173]

---

[169] Reisman, *supra* note 130 at 84.

[170] *Ibid.* at 85.

[171] *Ibid.* at 85-86.

[172] *Ibid.* at 86 [emphasis in original].

[173] See Kennedy, *supra* note 144 at 910. There have been cases of concurrent jurisdiction of the court and the Council over the same issue; The *Case Concerning United States Diplomatic and Consular Staff in Tehran (United States v. Iran)*, [1980] I.C.J. Rep. 3, and the *Nicaragua* case, *supra* note 45, are two examples of such a situation. I should also mention Article 36 of the Charter, *supra* note 5, according to which the Security Council should, as a general rule, refer legal questions

In dealing with Libya's request for interim measures in the *Lockerbie* case, the ICJ confronted serious constitutional debates regarding the legal framework governing the United Nations.[174] By bringing this matter in front of the ICJ, Libya raised the question of the jurisdictional boundary between the court and the Security Council as well as the question of whether the court has supervisory control over the Security Council's decisions. An inference can be drawn from the ICJ's decision in *Lockerbie,* namely that the court is unwilling to review a decision of the Security Council that is taken under the power conferred on the Council by Chapter VII.[175] However, before addressing this issue, the case itself needs to be examined in some detail.

---

pertaining to the pacific settlement of disputes between parties to the ICJ. This provision seems to imply that at least in the cases involving legal questions — that is, in the case of legal disputes as enumerated in Article 36(2) of the Statute of the ICJ — the court can play a role. According to Article 36(2) of the Statute of the ICJ, subject to voluntary recognition of the compulsory jurisdiction of the court by the states party to disputes, the court will in fact have jurisdiction in "all legal disputes concerning: (a) the interpretation of a treaty; (b) any question of international law; (c) the existence of any fact which, if established, would constitute a breach of an international obligation; (d) the nature or extent of the reparation to be made for the breach of an international obligation" (Statute of the International Court of Justice, June 26, 1945, Can. T.S. 1945 No. 7, at 48).

[174] The court's decision was only in response to a request for interim measures and the question will be considered again in a merits phase. After Libya filed its written pleadings, the United Kingdom and the United States raised objections to the court's jurisdiction and to the admissibility of the Libyan claims. In two separate judgments handed down on February 27, 1998, on these preliminary objections, the court declared that it had jurisdiction to deal with the merits of the disputes between Libya and the United Kingdom, and Libya and the United States. It based its jurisdiction on Article 14, paragraph 1, of the Convention for the Suppression of Unlawful Acts against the Safety of Civil Aviation (with Final Act of the International Conference on Air Law held under the auspices of the International Civil Aviation Organization at Montreal in September 1973), September 23, 1971, 974 U.N.T.S. 177 [hereinafter Montreal Convention], which concerns the settlement of disputes on the interpretation or application of the provisions of this convention. The court also found the Libyan claim admissible and stated that it was not appropriate at this stage of the proceedings to make a decision on the arguments of the United Kingdom and the United States that resolutions of the United Nations Security Council have rendered these claims without object (*Questions of Interpretation and Application of the 1971 Montreal Convention Arising from the Aerial Incident at Lockerbie (Libyan Arab Jamahiriya v. United States),* Preliminary Objections, Judgment of February 27, 1998, reprinted in I.L.M. (1998) 37 at 590. See also C. Gray "The Lockerbie Case Continues" (1998) Cambridge L. J. 57 at 433.

[175] Ewing, *supra* note 130 at 76.

Libya brought the United States and the United Kingdom to the ICJ for alleged violations of its rights under the 1971 Convention for the Suppression of Unlawful Acts against the Safety of Civil Aviation (Montreal Convention).[176] In November 1991, the authorities in the United Kingdom and the United States charged two Libyan nationals with placing a bomb aboard Pan Am flight 103 on December 21, 1988, causing the plane to explode over Lockerbie in Scotland. The two governments, in a joint declaration issued in November 1991, asked Libya to surrender the accused for trial. The subject of this declaration was later considered by the Security Council, which on January 21, 1992, adopted Resolution 731 to the same effect.[177] Libya claimed that the Montreal Convention was the only appropriate convention in force between the parties dealing with such offences, that the United Kingdom and the United States were bound by that convention, and that these two countries were acting in breach of their obligations.[178] Furthermore, Libya requested the court to grant provisional measures:

(a) to enjoin the United Kingdom [and the United States] from taking any action against Libya calculated to coerce or compel Libya to surrender the accused individuals to any jurisdiction outside of Libya; and
(b) to ensure that no steps are taken that would prejudice in any way the rights of Libya with respect to the legal proceedings that are the subject of Libya's Application.[179]

On March 31, 1992 (three days after the close of the hearing and before the ICJ's order was rendered), the Security Council adopted Resolution 748,[180] which stated that "the Libyan Government must now comply without any further delay with paragraph 3 of

---

[176] Montreal Convention, *supra* note 174.

[177] SC Res. 731, January 21, 1992.

[178] Articles 5(2), 5(3), 7, 8(2), and 11 of the Montreal Convention, *supra* note 174, were invoked by Libya. The convention has adopted the customary international law rule of *aut dedere aut judicare*, according to which the alleged offender found in the territory of a contracting state should either be extradited to the country in whose territory the offence was committed or submit the case to its competent authorities for the purpose of prosecution. Libya claimed that it has taken such measures as were necessary to establish its jurisdiction over the offences charged. Libya also claimed that the United Kingdom and the United States by their actions and threats were in breach of their obligations under the Montreal Convention.

[179] *Lockerbie* case, *supra* note 143 at 8 and 119.

[180] SC Res. 748, March 31, 1992.

Resolution 731." The last-mentioned resolution was taken under Chapter VII of the Charter. The court took this resolution into consideration[181] and stated that "whatever the situation previous to the adoption of that resolution [748], the rights claimed by Libya under the Montreal Convention cannot now be regarded as appropriate for protection by the indication of provisional measures."[182]

In the words of W.M. Reisman, "[w]hen the Security Council makes a decision under Chapter VII of the Charter that concerns a state and the decision is inconsistent with some other treaty-based right claimed by that state, the Council decision prevails."[183] The basis of the ICJ's decision, thus, is the existence of a Security Council decision under Chapter VII,[184] and I tend to agree with Reisman, who claims that the court's approach "precludes in blanket fashion, the exercise of judicial jurisdiction *whenever* and *simply because* the Council is in a Chapter VII decision mode."[185] In order to draw general conclusions in this debate, it is useful to consider the different choices available to the court:

[It] [c]ould have held that the sanctions ordered by Resolution 748 should be suspended until such time as the Court ascertained, at the merits stage, that Libya's claim was groundless. Or it could have decided that, since no sufficient case of *mala fides* or *ultra vires* had been established by Libya at this preliminary stage, there were no grounds upon which the Court could order such interim relief. Or, third, the Court could have held that no relief would be forthcoming at any stage of the proceedings if granting that relief would require the Court to make a finding that a Chapter VII decision of the Security Council exceeded its lawful authority.[186]

---

[181] Reisman, *supra* note 130 at 88.

[182] *Lockerbie* case, *supra* note 143 at 15 and 126-27. The court, by eleven votes to five, "[found] that the circumstances of the case are not such as to require the exercise of its power under Article 41 of the Statute to indicate provisional measures" (at 15 and 127).

[183] Reisman, *supra* note 130.

[184] Reisman has criticized this reference to Chapter VII as formalistic and as the result of an "unsound constitutional policy reasoning, which may prove to be troublesome in subsequent cases." In his view, it is enough for the Council to be factually in a Chapter VII mode, and, as such, even recommendations may have the effect of overriding treaty or custom-based rights (that is, Resolution 731 was enough for the court to reach this conclusion) (see *ibid.* at 87-90).

[185] *Ibid.* at 90 [emphasis in original]. I should emphasize that, according to Article 59 of the Statute of the ICJ, "[t]he decision of the Court has no binding force except between the parties and in respect of that particular case."

[186] T.M. Franck, "The 'Powers of Appreciation': Who is the Ultimate Guardian of UN Legality?" (1992) 86 A.J.I.L. at 521.

An implicit right of judicial review would result from either of the first two options, while judicial restraint or abdication would be the consequence of the third option.[187] It is important to note that the court chose not to assume "judicial restraint or abdicate."[188] In fact, it chose a variation of the second option, which can be construed as the ICJ's assertion of a power to review Security Council actions, even though it did not vote in favour of interim measures.[189] As R.F. Kennedy has pointed out, "[t]his sort of "review" does not appear to be foreclosed by the Charter, notwithstanding the potentially disastrous ramifications of the existence of two conflicting, binding decisions by coequal branches of the United Nations."[190]

Even if, in a future case, the ICJ decides to use its powers differently as the "guardian of legality for the international community" and make a decision contrary to that of the Security Council, it would have no practical effect. It would simply lead to controversy. This is because, according to the Charter, it is the Security Council that has the power to enforce the court's decisions upon its discretion.[191] Furthermore, according to Article 59 of the Statute of the ICJ, the court is barred from any *erga omnes* pronouncements.[192] Thus, it is not likely that the court would contradict the Security Council's Chapter VII decisions in the future, as doing so would be futile and the only consequence would be a weakening of the UN system.[193]

In his separate opinion in the *Lockerbie* case, Judge Lachs expresses this point of view:

---

[187] *Ibid.*

[188] Franck, *supra* note 29 at 243.

[189] Franck's conclusion from the court's decision is that

> [t]he majority and dissent opinions seem to be in agreement that there are such limits and that they can not be left exclusively to the Security Council to interpret. The legality of actions by any UN organ must be judged by reference to the Charter as the "constitution" of *delegated* powers. In extreme cases, the Court may have to be the last-resort to enjoy the adherence of its members. This seems to be tacitly acknowledged judicial common ground (Franck, *supra* note 186 at 522-23 [emphasis in original]).

[190] Kennedy, *supra* note 144 at 913.

[191] See Article 94(2) of the Charter, which is discussed in note 122.

[192] For the text of Article 59 of the Statute of the ICJ, see note 185.

[193] See also D.W. Bowett, "Judicial and Political Functions of the Security Council and the International Court of Justice," in H. Fox, ed., *The Changing Constitution of the United Nations* (London: B.I.I.C.L., 1997) at 73.

It is important for the purposes and principles of the United Nations that the two main organs with specific powers of binding decision act in harmony — though not, of course, in concert — and that each should perform its functions with respect to a situation or dispute, different aspects of which appear on the agenda of each, without prejudicing the exercise of the other's power.[194]

It can be concluded from this debate that, while the ICJ may not have the power to review and overturn the Security Council's decisions *stricto sensu,* in theory, it has the power to decide a case concurrently with the Security Council and reach a binding contradictory decision. In my view, Judge Lachs's opinion demonstrates the reluctance that rightly exists in the court to contradict the Security Council. Regardless of the opposing views of scholars on the issue,[195] the ICJ will continue to deal with this legal issue in a very political manner.[196] On the other hand, given the political and jurisdictional constraints upon the ICJ, the role that the law will play will depend largely on the self-restraint of the Council and not on the imposition of formal, legal control.

SANCTIONS VIOLATING HUMANITARIAN LAW
AND BASIC HUMAN RIGHTS

Having reached the conclusion that the Security Council is bound by the principles of international law in rendering its decisions, it is important to determine which principles of international law are relevant for sanctions — that is, which principles must be respected by the United Nations in the implementation of sanctions. Reisman and Stevick argue that the relevant principles of international

---

[194] *Lockerbie* case, *supra* note 143 at 139.

[195] See, for instance, the views expressed by two prominent scholars, Franck and Reisman: Franck claims that in its decision on provisional measures in the *Lockerbie* case, *supra* note 143, the ICJ "marked its role as the ultimate arbiter of institutional legitimacy" (Franck, *supra* note 186 at 523). Reisman states that "[h]ard substantive and procedural standards for review of Chapter VII actions are difficult to pinpoint in the Charter. Their very absence, in a context where so much power is assigned to the Council, is telling. A judicial review function, viewed in the formal Charter regime, seems somewhat difficult" (Reisman, *supra* note 130).

[196] Kennedy, in his article on this subject, *supra* note 144 at 925, has reached the same conclusion, in that he hopes that "Court and Council will continue to complement each other, as required by the spirit of the *U.N. Charter,* and will remain cognizant of their roles and capabilities, each acknowledging the distinctive competence of the other for addressing particular kinds of disagreements in the international arena."

humanitarian law[197] should be observed by the Security Council when implementing sanctions and that the enforcement actions of the council may be illegal if they do not distinguish between combatants and non-combatants.[198] In fact, as early as 1934, concern was expressed over the fact that economic sanctions, "operate against whole peoples and tend to drag millions of innocent parties into an affair not of their making."[199] The question, then, is whether economic sanctions that are designed to paralyze a nation's economic life, and which, thereby, cause suffering in a given community, are more "humane" than military actions? According to Damrosch,

some programs of collective economic sanction, begun with the best of intentions, may severely harm the very people they are intended to help. There is the perception, and possibly the reality, that *sanctions,* rather than the crises to which they respond, have created humanitarian emergencies.[200]

Likewise, A. Cassese writes: "Respect for human dignity has acquired such importance in the world community that it is no longer possible

[197] Such rules were embodied in four Geneva conventions of 1949: (1) Geneva Convention for the Amelioration of the Condition of the Wounded and Sick in Armed Forces in the Field, August 12, 1949, 75 U.N.T.S. 31 (entered into force on October 21, 1950); (2) Geneva Convention for the Amelioration of the Condition of the Wounded, Sick and Shipwrecked Members of Armed Forces at Sea, August 12, 1949, 75 U.N.T.S. 85 (entered into force on October 21, 1950); (3) Geneva Convention relative to Treatment of Prisoners of War, August 12, 1949, 75 U.N.T.S. 135 (entered into force on October 21, 1950); and (4) Geneva Convention relative to the Protection of Civilian Persons in Time of War, August 12, 1949, 75 U.N.T.S. 287 (entered into force on October 21, 1950).

[198] W.M. Reisman and D.L. Stevick, "The Applicability of International Law Standards to United Nations Economic Sanctions Programmes" (1998) 9 Euro. J. Int'l L. 86 at 94.

[199] P.S. Wild, Jr., *Sanctions and Treaty Enforcement* (Cambridge, MA: Harvard University Press, 1934) at 219. In spite of such concerns, for many years the impact of economic sanctions on the population of target states was ignored. The *First Report of the Collective Measures Committee* enumerates functions of the proposed "co-ordinating committee" for collective economic and financial measures which includes co-ordination, making specific recommendations to the Council or the Assembly regarding additions to, and amplification or modification of collective economic measures, but considering the human impact of sanctions was not mentioned. See *First Report of the Collective Measures Committee,* UN GAOR, 6th Sess., C1, 480th Mtg. (Jan. 4, 1952) at 15-16, cited in Goodrich and Simons, *supra* note 19 at 419.

[200] L.F. Damrosch, "The Civilian Impact of Economic Sanctions," in Damrosch, *supra* note 12 at 275.

to sacrifice the interests and exigencies of human beings for the sake of responding to wrongs caused by States."[201] The imposition of sanctions in certain circumstances may result in economic crises in the target states, which, in turn, result in a population's impoverishment. Often, the policymakers of the target states, who are responsible for the breaches of international law, are those who are least affected by the sanctions. Even when the formalities for the implementation of sanctions are respected, the United Nations may still ignore the socio-economic history of the target state.[202]

The human catastrophe caused by sanctions is often emphasized (in certain cases in an exaggerated manner)[203] by the target states in order to incite international public opinion against the sanctions.[204]

---

[201] A. Cassese, *International Law in a Divided World* (Oxford: Clarendon Press, 1986) at 242.

[202] In the case of Haiti for instance, "the United Nations observed the legal formalities for implementing sanctions pursuant to the framework set out in the Charter. Yet the organization virtually ignored Haiti's socio-economic history despite the obvious poverty of the country." F. Swindells, "U.N. Sanctions in Haiti: A Contradiction under Articles 41 and 55 of the U.N. Charter" (1997) 20 Fordham Int'l L. J. 1878 at 1960.

[203] Cuba has criticized economic sanctions imposed by the United States as a policy of deliberate genocide. See "Cuba Condemns US Embargo as Genocide," which can be found online at <http://news2.thls.bbc.co.uk/hi/english/world/americas/newsid_446000/446761.stm> (date accessed: September 14, 1999).

[204] For example, in the case of the UN sanctions against Iraq, the United States claims that Saddam Hussein refuses to distribute food and medicines to his people. Then State Department spokesman James Rubin said: "We often hear that sanctions are hurting the Iraqi people, but an analysis, an objective analysis of the facts reveals that Iraq has access to international markets and the money to buy food, but Saddam will not buy or distribute it to the needy." Another senior State Department official Martin Indyk said that while the mortality rate continued to rise amongst children, it was not due to a lack of food or medicine as a result of international sanctions: "Those medicines and nutritional supplements are either sitting in warehouses under Saddam Hussein's control, or he has refused to order them" ("As Iraqis Starve, U.S. Asserts Their Leaders Live in Luxury," *New York Times* (September 14, 1999) A8). Another report concerning Iraq states that Iraq is re-exporting the supplies intended for children it says are suffering because of sanctions. In August 1999, Kuwait impounded a small boat, bound for the United Arab Emirates, when it was discovered to contain two-hundred-and-fifty tonnes of baby goods and other supplies. Rubin said Iraq was showing cynical disregard for children's suffering by exporting baby supplies for hard currency in violation of international sanctions. The official Iraqi news agency said the supplies, including feeding bottles from India and baby powder from China, were of poor quality and were being returned ("Iraq: Mysterious Traffic," *New York Times* (August 18, 1999) A14).

Nonetheless, many independent studies have confirmed the claims of target states in this regard. Notably, there has been controversy surrounding the impact of sanctions against Haiti and Iraq's civil population. In the case of Haiti, it had even been claimed that "the economic situation in Haiti had reached the point where military intervention was 'the most humane solution.'"[205] The situation in Iraq provides a good example of the effect that ongoing sanctions can have. The United Nations Children's Fund (UNICEF) has revealed that infant mortality in heavily populated parts of Iraq has doubled since sanctions were imposed. From a rate of fifty-six per 1,000 in 1989, infant mortality has increased to 131 per 1,000 in the period from 1994 to 1999.[206] A survey by the World Health Organization calculated that 500,000 more children had died than would have been the case if medical conditions had been allowed to improve at the pre-sanctions rate.[207] However, the head of UNICEF, Carole Bellamy, has stated that the UN sanctions are not the only reason.[208] According to Bellamy, "[s]anctions are tools that are used, they are decided by others than UNICEF, but we would urge that in imposing them to take into account the implications for children."[209] It is also reported that malnutrition and severe health problems due to the absence of medicines and water purification systems are commonplace.[210] According to Denis Halliday, the United Nations humanitarian coordinator for Iraq, one-quarter of all Iraqi children under the age of six are malnourished.

---

[205] Letter from Rep. Robert Torricelli to President George Bush (January 10, 1992), cited in Reisman and Stevick, *supra* note 198 at note 207.

[206] B. Crossette, "Children's Death Rates Rising in Iraqi Lands, UNICEF Reports," *New York Times* (August 12, 1999) A6.

[207] "Special Report: Sanction-Breakers Risk Jail," text can be accessed online at <http://news2.thls.bbc.co.uk/hi/english/special_report/regions/wales/new sid_420000/420544.stm> (date accessed August 14, 1999).

[208] The UNICEF report sparked a controversy between Iraq and the United States over who is to blame. Baghdad claimed it proved that sanctions are killing thousands of children every month. The United States alleged that Iraqi inefficiency and obstructionism are also key factors. Carole Bellamy said she would plead the cause of Iraq's children before the UN sanctions committee ("UNICEF Chief Pleads the Cause of Iraqi Children," *Agence France Presse* (October 17, 1999), which can be accessed online at Lexis-Nexis (News. CURNWS)).

[209] *Ibid.*

[210] See the following reports: J. Dreze and H. Gazdar, "Hunger and Poverty in Iraq, 1991" (1992) 20:7 World Development and FAO Nutritional Assessment Mission to Iraq, November 1993, cited in M. Grey, "UN Sanctions against Iraq: The Human Impact" (1994) 70:11 Current Affairs Bulletin 11 at 13.

In 12 per cent of cases, chronic malnutrition is leading to stunted growth, high school drop-outs, and reduced attention spans.[211] Sanctions can also have a long-term impact on the population of a targeted country. The view that "sanctions are only temporary tools and in theory should only have short term effects"[212] is also reflected in Security Council discussions.[213] In many cases, sanctions severely affect the economic infrastructure of the target countries, which will in turn create long-term consequences for generations to come.

Concerns over the humanitarian impact of sanctions have been raised in the Security Council several times. Most importantly, the humanitarian impact was acknowledged in a letter dated April 13, 1995, from the permanent representatives of the permanent members of the Security Council to the president of the Council.[214] The letter outlined some considerations that should be taken into account in cases concerning the implementation of sanctions. In addition to the Security Council, reports from other UN bodies reflect the same concern. A 1998 report from the Committee on Economic, Social and Cultural Rights acknowledges that "sanctions often cause significant disruption in the distribution of food, pharmaceuticals and sanitation supplies, jeopardize the quality of food and the availability of clean drinking water, severely interfere with the functioning of basic health and education systems, and undermine the right to work."[215]

In practice, while the earlier resolutions of the Security Council did not address this issue, its recent practice in this regard has changed. In the case of Iraq, "supplies intended strictly for medical purposes, and, in humanitarian circumstances, foodstuffs" were

---

[211] "Sanctions 'Have Hurt People,' not Leader," which can be accessed online at <http://www.irish-times.com/irish-times/paper/1998/0225/wor5.html> (date accessed: February 28, 1998).

[212] Swindells, *supra* note 202 at 1955.

[213] UN SCOR, 49th Year, 3376th Meeting, UN Doc. SC/5841 (1994) (following the adoption of Resolution 917).

[214] Letter dated 13 April 1995 from the Permanent Representatives of China, France, the Russian Federation, the United Kingdom of Great Britain and Northern Ireland and the United States of America to the United Nations addressed to the President of the Security Council, UN Doc. S/1995/300 (1995).

[215] *General Comment 8: The Relationship between Economic Sanctions and Respect for Economic, Social and Cultural Rights*, UN ESCOR, 17th Sess., Annex V, UN Doc. E/C.12/1997/10 (1998) at 119.

exempted from the sanctions.[216] Resolution 666 delegated the task of determining what constituted "humanitarian circumstances" under Resolution 661 to the Sanctions Committee.[217] Resolution 687, in addition to restating the exception to the sanctions, authorized the Sanctions Committee to approve "material and supplies for essential civilian needs" under an accelerated no-objection procedure.[218] The UN Security Council has been concerned with the humanitarian consequences of sanctions and has "made a conscious effort to weave humanitarian concerns into its design of the economic sanctions levied against Iraq."[219] Resolutions 706 and 712 of the Security Council provided Iraq with the possibility of exporting oil to earn funds to purchase food and other humanitarian goods.[220] Following the conclusion of the Dayton Accords,[221] the sanctions were gradually lifted. During the period in which the sanctions were eased, the Security Council began to allow measures that "benefited primarily the people of the Federal Republic of Yugoslavia, not their rulers."[222]

The resolution imposing sanctions on Haiti established a sanctions committee to monitor the implementation of sanctions and approve the shipment of oil for humanitarian needs.[223] When the sanctions first began in Haiti, the Security Council did not take into account the possible disproportionate or discriminatory effects of sanctions. Later, however, the Council's president stated that it was "deeply concerned by the suffering of the Haitian people."[224]

---

[216] SC Res. 661, August 6, 1990, para. 4.

[217] SC Res. 666, September 13, 1990, paras. 6 and 8.

[218] SC Res. 687, April 3, 1991, paras 20 and 22.

[219] D.E. Reuther, "UN Sanctions against Iraq," in Cortright and Lopez, *supra* note 7 at 130.

[220] SC Res. 706, August 15, 1991; SC Res. 712, September 19, 1991.

[221] Dayton Agreement of Implementing the Federation of Bosnia and Herzegovina of 10 November 1995, Republic of Bosnia and Herzegovina and Federation of Bosnia and Herzegovina, 35 I.L.M. 172; General Framework Agreement for Peace in Bosnia and Herzegovina, Republic of Bosnia and Herzegovina, Republic of Croatia and the Federal Republic of Yugoslavia, December 14, 1995, 35 I.L.M. 89.

[222] Reisman and Stevick, *supra* note 198 at 113. For instance, according to Resolution 943, para. 12, international passenger air traffic with Serbia and Montenegro, passenger services to Bari, Italy, and Serbia's participation in international sporting and cultural exchanges were permitted (see SC Res. 943, September 23, 1994).

[223] SC Res. 841, June 16, 1993.

[224] *Report of the Secretary-General on Haiti*, UN Doc. S/26480 (1993).

The Security Council expressed its determination "to minimize the impact of the ... situation on the most vulnerable groups and call[ed] upon Member States to continue, and to intensify, their humanitarian assistance to the people of Haiti."[225] Despite the fact that some of Security Council decisions targeted the military authorities in Haiti, these measures were only complementary to the already-existing UN sanctions.[226] Other than in the aforementioned instances, the Security Council did not formally consider the humanitarian consequences of sanctions on Haiti.[227] In the case of Libya, the Security Council, for the first time, "insisted that it had considered the possible effects of the sanctions on Libyan people in designing and imposing the initial sanctions regime of Resolution 748 in March 1992."[228] Representatives of the United States, the United Kingdom, and France argued that the sanctions against Libya were precise and limited and were appropriately designed to penalize the government of Libya and not the Libyan people.[229] However, after the sanctions were tightened, the Security Council did not investigate, nor did it formally consider, the possible impacts of the sanctions on the Libyan people. Finally, in the case of sanctions against the Taliban, Resolution 1267 established a sanctions committee that, among others, was entrusted with the task of "mak[ing] periodic reports to the Council on the impact, including the humanitarian implications, of the measures imposed."[230] In the case of sanctions against the former Yugoslavia, the only exceptions were "supplies intended strictly for medical purposes and foodstuff notified to the Committee" that had been previously established.[231]

---

[225] *Note by the President of the Security Council Concerning the Situation in Haiti,* November 15, 1993, UN Doc. S/26747.

[226] For example, some measures adopted under Resolution 917, May 6, 1994.

[227] See Reisman and Stevick, *supra* note 198 at 122-23. The authors have given two reasons for the international community's failure to recognize the disproportionately harmful impact of sanctions on the Haitian people; first, the fact that Aristide strongly supported economic sanctions against his country, and second, Haiti's strategic insignificance to the great powers on the Security Council (*ibid.*).

[228] *Ibid.* at 109.

[229] UN Security Council Official Records, UN SCOR, 47th Year, 3063 Mtg., UN Doc. S/PV.3063 (1992), at 67, 69 and 74.

[230] F. Alabrune, "La pratique des comités des sanctions du Conseil de sécurité depuis 1990" (1999) 45 A.F.D.I. at 49.

[231] See B. Pisik, "The U.N. Report," *Washington Times* (August 30, 1999) A14; "Emirate Calls for Diplomatic Solution to Iraq Crisis," *Agence France Presse*

Since non-military instruments — including economic sanctions — can be destructive, it can be concluded that they "should be tested rigorously against the criteria of international law of armed conflict and other relevant norms of contemporary international law *before* a decision is made to initiate or to continue to apply them."[232] This proposition means that economic weapons are subject to principles of *jus ad bellum* and *jus in bello*.[233] The relevance of international humanitarian law and the principles of human rights[234] is not limited to situations of collective economic sanctions. Subparagraph (d) of Article 50 of the ILC's *Draft Articles on Responsibility of States for Internationally Wrongful Acts* echoes the same concern and imposes another restriction on the use of unilateral economic sanctions.[235] Even though unilateral sanctions are less likely to

---

(January 26, 1999), which can be accessed online at Lexis-Nexis (News. CURNWS); E. Bryant, "Arab Meeting Ends in Disarray," *United Press International* (January 24, 1999), which can be accessed online at Lexis-Nexis (News. CURNWS); B. Pisik, "U.S. Plan Would Ease Iraqi Pain; Unlimited Oil Sales Would Buy Food," *Washington Times* (January 15, 1999) A1; J.M. Goshko, "On Security Council, Mixed Views of Attack; Some Question Action but Also Blame Iraq," *Washington Times* (December 17, 1998) A30.

[232] Reisman and Stevick, *supra* note 198 at 95 [emphasis in original].

[233] See also the heading "Applying International Humanitarian Law Standards to Sanctions," later in this article.

[234] Regarding the relationship of international humanitarian law and human rights, H. McCoubrey, *International Humanitarian Law: Modern Developments in the Limitation of Warfare*, 2nd ed. (Darthmouth: Ashgate, 1998) at 5-6, states that

> [t]here is manifestly a significant degree of convergence between the concerns of international humanitarian law and those of the international law of human rights. However, the precise nature of the interface between these two sectors is a more controversial question. The idea of fundamental entitlements inherent in the human social condition is of ancient provenance, with long roots in the tradition of naturalist jurisprudence, and it has played a prominent role in the constitutional development of some states since the late 18th century. As a distinct sector of public international law, however, the law of human rights has taken shape largely since 1945.

For a comprehensive bibliography on the subject, see International Committee of the Red Cross, *Bibliography of International Humanitarian Law Applicable in Armed Conflicts* (Geneva: International Committee of the Red Cross and Henry Dunant Institute, 1987).

[235] According to this article, "[c]ountermeasures shall not affect ... (c) Obligations of a humanitarian character prohibiting reprisals; (d) Other obligations under peremptory norms of general international law." *ILC's Report on Fifty-Third Session*, *supra* note 6.

violate rules of humanitarian law, resort to countermeasures that lead to the violation of basic human rights is prohibited.

During the past century, the essential rules of humanity and inviolable rights have been recognized by international law, leading to the prohibition of reprisals in times of international or internal armed conflict. This development has led to similar restrictions on reprisals in times of peace.[236] In the *Naulilaa Case (Portugal-Germany)*, the tribunal stated that a lawful reprisal must be "limited by the requirements of humanity and the rules of good faith applicable in relations between States."[237] A similar statement was made by the Institut de droit international in its 1934 resolution.[238] Furthermore, in many cases of unilateral economic sanctions and even mere retorsion, states have taken humanitarian considerations into account.[239] In addition, the last subparagraph of Article 50 of the *Draft Articles on Responsibility of States for Internationally Wrongful Acts* prohibits countermeasures that are in contravention of a

---

[236] See *Report of the Commission to the General Assembly on the Work of Its Forty-Seventh Session*, UN Doc. A/50/10, in *Yearbook of the International Law Commission 1995*, vol. II, part 2 (New York, United Nations, 1996) (UN Doc. A/CN.4/SER. A/1995/Add.1(Part 2)) at 72 [hereinafter *Commission's Report on Forty-Seventh Session*].

[237] *Naulilaa* case, *supra* note 9 at 1026.

[238] Paragraph 4 of Article 6 of this resolution states that

Dans l'exercice des représailles, l'Etat doit se conformer aux règles suivantes: ... 4- S'abstenir de toute mesure de rigueur qui serait contraire aux lois de l'humanité et aux exigences de la conscience publique. "Résolutions votées par l'Institut au cours de sa XXXIXe Session" (1934) 38 Ann. inst. dr. int. 708 at 710.

[239] For example, in the case of the United Kingdom's sanctions against Argentina during the Falkland Islands crisis, funds that would normally be necessary for living, medical, and educational supplies and similar expenses of residents of the Argentine republic in the United Kingdom were not frozen. Or, in the case of United States's total blockade of trade relations with Libya, an exception was made for the publications and donations of articles intended to relieve human suffering, such as food, clothing, medicine, and medical supplies, which were intended strictly for medical purposes (see *Commission's Report on Forty-Seventh Session*, *supra* note 236 at 73). More recently the United States changed its sanctions policy in line with the concerns over the humanitarian impact of sanctions. Accordingly, humanitarian items will be exempted from future sanctions. Under-Secretary of State Stuart Eizenstat told reporters: "[S]ales of food, medicine and other humanitarian necessities do not generally enhance a nation's military capacity or support terrorism ... our purpose in applying sanctions is to influence the behavior of regimes, not to deny people their basic humanitarian needs." "U.S. Eases Policy on Some Sanctions," *New York Times* (April 21, 1999) A1 and A12.

peremptory norm of general international law.[240] This prohibition has been "widely recognized in the contemporary doctrine since the Second World War."[241] However, while there is no doubt that *jus cogens* rules may not be departed from in international law, the debate persists as to the scope of such norms.[242]

The issue of the human impact of collective sanctions and the conformity of their application with the principles of international humanitarian law and human rights is one of the most important problems of economic sanctions. The problem is, in fact, the Achilles heel of economic sanctions as an enforcement measure — it is a serious and well-founded criticism of economic sanctions and should be addressed by the states and organizations implementing such sanctions. Apparently, the Security Council has not gone any further than providing for exceptions on the import of humanitarian goods in trade embargoes, and there is no constant practice of studying the humanitarian impact of sanctions by the Council. A number of recent UN studies as well as studies by other

---

[240] This is also in line with the regime of the Vienna Convention on the Law of Treaties, May 23, 1969, 1155 U.N.T.S. 311 (entered into force January 27, 1988) in Article 53, which states that "[a] treaty is void if, at the time of its conclusion, it conflicts with a peremptory norm of general international law." Prohibition of countermeasures that are in contravention of a peremptory norm of general international law encompasses some of the prohibited countermeasures mentioned earlier in the text. The reason is that there is a certain overlap between the spheres of human rights and *jus cogens* in general. Certain general rules protecting specific human rights (including racial discrimination, apartheid, slavery, genocide, and the self determination of peoples) have been described as peremptory norms (see Cassese, *supra* note 201 at 149). See also Judge Tanaka's dissenting opinion in the *South West Africa Cases (Ethiopia* v. *South Africa; Liberia* v. *South Africa)* Second Phase, Judgement, [1966] I.C.J. Rep. 5 at 298, in which he states that "surely the law concerning the protection of human rights may be considered to belong to the *jus cogens.*"

[241] *Commission's Report on Forty-Seventh Session, supra* note 236 at 74 [footnote omitted]. See also D. Alland, "International Responsibility and Sanctions: Self-Defence and Countermeasures in the ILC Codification of Rules Governing International Responsibility," in M. Spinedi and B. Simma, eds., *United Nations Codification of State Responsibility* (New York: Oceana Publications, 1987) 143 at 185; and Elagab, *supra* note 9 at 99.

[242] For this very reason, the *Draft Articles on Responsibility of States for Internationally Wrongful Acts* do not contain a list of peremptory norms, and the commentary in the *ILC Draft Article 40* points out that the examples given in this commentary are not exhaustive (see *ILC Report on Fifty-Third Meeting , supra* note 6 at 283, paras. 4 to 6). The ambiguity exists especially as to which breaches of human rights obligations, other than slavery, genocide, and apartheid — often-cited examples — constitute international crimes.

organizations have concluded that the aforementioned exemptions have not achieved the goal of ensuring basic respect for economic, social, and cultural rights within the target states. A major study prepared for the General Assembly states that "humanitarian exemptions tend to be ambiguous and are interpreted arbitrarily and inconsistently ... Delays, confusion, and the denial of requests to import essential humanitarian goods cause resource shortages."[243] Another report concludes that the review procedure established under the various sanctions committees set up by the Security Council "remain cumbersome and aid agencies still encounter difficulties in obtaining approval for exempted supplies."[244] Furthermore, the sanctions committees of the Security Council have been criticized for operating secretively and without being monitored[245] as well as for having failed to establish a constant and coherent practice with regard to humanitarian concerns. Apparently, the Security Council has taken some actions to address these criticisms.[246]

THE EFFECTS ON THIRD STATES

In most cases in which resort is made in the UN security system to economic sanctions, "some states will suffer unduly for geographic reasons or because of their special economic and financial relationships with the victim state or the state against which measures are directed."[247] In many cases, the economies of neighbouring countries are so interdependent that the imposition of economic sanctions against one of those states inevitably has serious effects

[243] "Impact of Armed Conflict on Children: Note by the Secretary-General" (A/51/306), annex, para. 128, cited in *General Comment 8, supra* note 215 at 120.

[244] L. Minear, et al., *Toward More Humane and Effective Sanctions Management: Enhancing the Capacity of the United Nations System* (Providence: Thomas J Watson Jr. Institute for International Studies, 1998) at vii.

[245] See J.A. Paul, "Sanctions: An Analysis," text can be accessed at <http://www.globalpolicy.org/security/sanction/analysis.htm> (date accessed November 28, 1998).

[246] See, for example, *Note by the President of the Security Council on Greater Recourse to Open Meetings of the Security Council,* October 30, 1998, UN Doc. S/1998/1016. *Note by the President of the Security Council on Improvements to Make Procedures of the Sanctions Committees More Transparent,* March 29, 1995, UN Doc. S/1995/234. *Note by the President of the Security Council on Improvements to Make Procedures of the Sanctions Committees More Transparent,* January 24, 1996, UN Doc. S/1996/54. *Note by the President of the Security Council: Work of the Sanctions Committees,* January 29, 1999, UN Doc. S/1999/92.

[247] Goodrich, Hambro, and Simons, *supra* note 17 at 343.

on the economies of the others.[248] This problem may lead to the non-participation or weak participation of the targeted country's trade partners.[249] Logically, the cost of collective sanctions should not be born exclusively by the innocent members of the international community that have significant trade relations with the target states. However, in legal terms, it is very difficult to argue for the indemnification of states that bear the loss as a consequence of economic sanctions. Article 50 of the Charter may be invoked by injured states that are not the target of the sanctions.[250] This article provides that

[i]f preventive or enforcement measures against any state are taken by the Security Council, any other state, whether a Member of the United Nations or not, which finds itself confronted with special economic problems arising from the carrying out of those measures shall have the right to consult the Security Council with regard to a solution of those problems.

The above quotation does not impose any substantial obligation on the Security Council to provide specific remedies. In fact, a proposal that was made by Venezuela during the process of drafting the Charter to replace the mere right to consultations with a right to assistance was unsuccessful.[251]

In examining the practice of the Security Council, it becomes evident that until very recently, it never went beyond "an appeal to the member states to render assistance" to member states that had suffered hardship as a result of participating in the implementation of UN sanctions.[252] This practice, however, appears to have

[248] Kuyper, *supra* note 8 at 154.

[249] The case of Rhodesia is a good example. There, the economies of Zambia and Botswana were affected by the sanctions against Rhodesia and, as a result, they did not apply the sanctions. R. Renwick, *Economic Sanctions* (Cambridge, MA: Center for International Affairs, Harvard University, 1981) at 46.

[250] The problem of third states was addressed before the Charter in a report of the secretary-general of the League of Nations. See Wild, *supra* note 199 at 145.

[251] Simma et al., *supra* note 16 at 659. However, even non-member states are entitled to consultation under Article 50. Germany, in the case of sanctions against Rhodesia, and Switzerland and Korea, in the case of sanctions against Iraq, have used this right (*ibid.* at 660).

[252] See especially the following Security Council resolutions regarding sanctions against southern Rhodesia: Resolution 253 (May 29, 1968), Resolution 277 (1970), Resolution 329 (1973), in which it was mentioned that Zambia and Mozambique deserved such assistance. The Council followed up its call by sending an expert commission to Zambia to study its problems (see Simma et al., *supra* note 16 at 660).

changed, at least in the case of the sanctions imposed on Iraq. In this case, numerous states requested assistance under Article 50.[253] According to Resolution 669, the committee established under Resolution 661 was entrusted with the task of examining these requests.[254] A working group was established to consider the requests, and it recommended that the world community should support the affected countries with financial help.[255] Furthermore, the Security Council's Resolution 687 anticipated that Iraq would be "liable under international law for any direct loss, damage, including environmental damage and the depletion of natural resources, or injury to foreign Governments, nationals and corporations, as a result of Iraq's unlawful invasion and occupation of Kuwait."[256] Resolution 687 established the Compensation Commission to administer the payment of indemnities caused by damages incurred as a result of the invasion. Although the wording of Resolution 687 suggests that the injuries resulting from economic sanctions should be considered as consequences of Iraq's unlawful occupation of Kuwait, this possibility was not considered in the reports of the Compensation Commission.[257] In addition, since 1996, several requests from Turkey under Article 50 of the Charter have not been responded to.[258]

---

253 N. Schrijver, "The Use of Economic Sanctions by the UN Security Council: An International Law Perspective," in H.H.G. Post, ed., *International Economic Law and Armed Conflict* (Dordrecht: Martinus Nijhoff, 1994) at 149.

254 SC Res. 661, August 6, 1990.

255 Simma et al., *supra* note 16 at 661.

256 SC Res. 687, April 3, 1991, at 16.

257 On May 2, 1991, pursuant to paragraph 19 of Security Council Resolution 687, the secretary-general submitted a detailed report to the council on the work of the commission and the fund established under the resolution. *Report of the Secretary-General Pursuant to Paragraph 19 of Security Council Resolution 687*, UN Doc. S/ 22559 (1991), reprinted in 30 I.L.M. 1706. The exemplary categorization of the claims given in paragraph 23 of this report does not contain claims related to economic sanctions. Neither does the letter dated August 2, 1991 from the President of the Governing Council of the United Nations Compensation Commission to the President of the Security Council, UN Doc. S/ 22885 (1991), reprinted in 30 I.L.M. 1711, mention such claims. Later, the Governing Council excluded compensation for losses suffered as a result of the trade embargo and related measures. *Decision Taken by the Governing Council of the United Nations Compensation Commission during Its Third Session at the Eighteenth Meeting, Held on 28 November 1991, as Revised at the Twenty-Fourth Meeting Held on 16 March 1992*, UN Doc. S/23765, S/AC.26/1991/7/Rev.1, reprinted in 31 I.L.M. 1045 at 1046.

258 Alabrune, *supra* note 230 at 50.

Both Resolution 748 on Libya and Resolution 757 on Yugoslavia contain references to Article 50 of the Charter in the preamble.[259] In the case of Libya, the Security Council did not deal with the special economic problems due to the sanctions that it had imposed against that state. In the case of Yugoslavia, the Council received several communications under Article 50, and the Sanctions Committee made recommendations for assistance similar to those adopted in the case of Iraq.[260] In the case of Haiti, Resolution 917 entrusted the committee, which was established by Resolution 841, with this task.[261] In contrast, former secretary-general Boutros Boutros-Ghali has acknowledged the existence of the problem, stating that "there is an urgent need for action to respond to the expectations raised by Article 50 of the Charter."[262] Furthermore, this question has been constantly discussed in the General Assembly's Special Committee on the Charter and has been addressed by the General Assembly itself.[263]

POLITICIZATION, SELECTIVITY, AND DOUBLE STANDARDS

The principled application of sanctions is important in the case of *collective* sanctions. As former secretary-general Boutros Boutros-Ghali emphasized in his report, *An Agenda for Peace; Preventive Diplomacy, Peacemaking and Peace-keeping,* "the principles of the Charter must be applied consistently, not selectively, for if the perception should be of the latter, trust will wane and with it the moral authority which is the greatest and most unique quality of that instrument."[264]

---

[259] P. Butchkov, N. Kovatcheva, and R. Raytcheva, "The Economic and Political Effects of the 'Yugo-Sanctions' on Neighbouring Bulgaria," in W.J.M. Van Genugten and G.A. de Groot, eds., *United Nations Sanctions* (Antwerpen: Intersentia, 1999) at 35.

[260] Schrijver, *supra* note 253 at 150.

[261] See SC Res. 841, June 16, 1993.

[262] *Supplement to an Agenda for Peace, supra* note 131, para. 73. See also *Resolution on Implementation of the Provisions of the Charter of the United Nations Related to Assistance to Third States Affected by the Application of Sanctions,* January 25, 2000, GA Res. 54/107, UN Doc. A/RES/54/107 [hereinafter *Resolution for Assistance to Third States*].

[263] See *Report of the Special Committee on the Charter of the United Nations and on the Strengthening of the Role of the Organization: Implementation of the Provisions of the Charter of the United Nations Related to Assistance to Third States Affected by the Application of Sanctions,* September 23, 1999, UN Doc. A/54/383; and *Resolution for Assistance to Third States, supra* note 262.

[264] *An Agenda for Peace, infra* note 336 at 23.

Boutros-Ghali criticized the Security Council for paying more attention to the Yugoslavia case, when a human tragedy was occurring in Somalia.[265] This problem is, in part, related to the question of the legitimacy of the actions of the Security Council. The decision to implement collective sanctions is in the hands of a limited number of countries sitting on the Security Council, and the Security Council has a seemingly unconstrained ability to assess its own jurisdiction. Therefore, there is always a risk that the sanctions may be applied for reasons other than those provided in the Charter. Sanctions may be applied against governments for political reasons. For instance, the human rights abuses in China and the former Soviet Union, as well as the invasion of Afghanistan by the Soviet Union, were never sanctioned because the countries in question were permanent members of the Security Council and thus had a veto right.[266]

The other problem is that of selectivity or the application of double standards. It is closely related to the question of whether the application of sanctions is political. In some cases of human rights violations, sanctions are imposed, while, in other cases, these same violations are ignored. The point that has been raised by many writers is that, in most cases, the concern over the human rights situation of the target states or the concerns about international peace is not the main motive for implementing sanctions. Sometimes other factors are considered. The question, then, is how to define the categories of cases that warrant a collective response.[267] Even though the concern about double standards may have some basis, when considering the politicization of the Security Council's decisions, it should be noted that it is not a judicial body and, thus, is not expected to perform as such. In the words of Kelsen, "[s]eparation of law from politics in the presentation of national or international problems is possible in so far as law is not an end in itself, but ... a specific social technique for the achievement of ends determined by politics."[268] The reality of international relations inevitably results in politicized practices. The fact that five of the strongest states are accorded a dominant role in the Security

---

[265] L.F. Damrosch, "The Collective Enforcement of International Norms through Economic Sanctions" (1994) 8 Ethics and Int'l Affairs 59 at 62.

[266] A. Rosen, "Canada's Use of Economic Sanctions for Political Purposes" (1993) 51 U.T. Fac. L. Rev. 1 at 42.

[267] Damrosch, *supra* note 200 at 277.

[268] Kelsen, *supra* note 125 at xiii.

Council and are able to bind all the other members "on the occurrence of rather vague contingencies that they themselves are authorized to determine" simply reflects reality.[269] Politicization of the
Security Council's decisions is inevitable and can only be redressed
by the good faith of the council in taking its decisions and by the
careful balancing of the political interests of the different powers
sitting on the Council.

PROPOSALS

Although, from a classical legal perspective, the implementation of sanctions — subject to the observance of the conditions
examined earlier — can very well be justified, the practice of implementing sanctions can be modified in such a way as to avoid the
undesired consequences of sanctions and to render them more
efficient and legitimate. Before drawing some general conclusions
regarding sanctions, proposals for the modification and refinement
of sanctions practices — primarily in the context of the UN collective sanctions — will be examined. In presenting these proposals,
the following points must be taken into account: the consequences
and objective of the implementation of economic sanctions; the
developments of international law in the past decades; the past
practice regarding the imposition of sanctions; and the reaction of
international public opinion to different cases.

INCREASING THE LEGITIMACY OF THE COLLECTIVE AUTHORITY OF
THE SECURITY COUNCIL AND ITS DECISIONS: REVERSE VETO

Criticism of the legitimacy of the Security Council can be overcome by the reform of the Council, with a view to rendering decisions of the council more legitimate and acceptable. While reform
proposals will not have a direct effect on the practice of the Council
with respect to economic sanctions, they will have an impact on
decision-making as well as on the enforcement actions of the Security Council, in general. The question of reform of the Security
Council is basically a question about the appropriate balance
between "legitimacy" and "effectiveness:" "Just as it seems wrong to
gain effectiveness at too great an expense to legitimacy, so does it not
make sense to increase legitimacy at the expense of a significant

[269] Reisman, *supra* note 130 at 83.

loss of effectiveness."[270] Many feasible proposals for the reform of the Security Council aim at changing its composition.[271]

Moreover, with respect to the question of the reverse veto, specifically, in so far as the problem of termination of sanctions relates to the ambiguity of the objectives of sanctions, this problem can be solved by "defin[ing] an objective criteria for determining that their purpose has been achieved."[272] Solving the problem of the reverse veto in the Security Council, contrary to reform of the veto, in general, does not require Charter amendment.[273] The easiest solution, of course, is to address the problem at the time that resolutions under Chapter VII of the Charter are passed. This solution requires incorporating provisions regarding different voting procedures for the termination of Chapter VII actions in the relevant resolutions. There is precedent supporting this approach since this is what happened in the case of the Compensation Commission that was established following the Gulf War. According to this commission, a Governing Council composed of members of the Security Council was placed in charge of making decisions regarding the commission, and the Governing Council did not have the

---

[270] Caron, *supra* note 129 at 567.

[271] See, generally, Fassbender, *supra* note 130 at 221-75. See also *Question of Equitable Representation on and Increase in the Membership of the Security Council*, GA Res. 47/62, UN GAOR, 47th Sess., Agenda Item 40, UN Doc. A/RES/47/62 (1993); *Question of Equitable Representation on and Increase in the Membership of the Security Council: Report of the Secretary-General*, UN GAOR, 48th Sess., Agenda Item 33, UN. Doc. A/48/264 (July 20, 1993) and Add.1 (July 26, 1993), Add. 2 (July 27, 1993) and Add.2/Corr.1, Add. 3 and 4 (September 28, 1993); Resolution 48/26 of December 3, 1994, which was adopted consensually (Draft Resolution A/48/L.28); *Conference Room Paper by the Bureau of the Working Group*, UN Doc. A/AC.247/1997/CRP.8, at para. 1; S.D. Bailey, *The Procedure of the UN Security Council* (Oxford: Clarendon Press, 1975) at 167-71; Schweigman, *supra* note 55 at 288-95. Furthermore, there are some proposals that avoid the modification of the Charter. According to Caron, in order to avoid the complications of amending the Charter and adding new members to the Security Council, the demands of states seeking membership in the Security Council can be satisfied through the establishment of informal mechanisms for their involvement in the Security Council activities. See Caron, *supra* note 129 at 574. Other ways of satisfying the need for change include offering the promise of increased consultations with regional powers and placing some regional powers or representatives of certain groups of states on special Council committees on different issues (*ibid.*).

[272] *Supplement to an Agenda for Peace*, *supra* note 131 at para. 68.

[273] Caron, *supra* note 129 at 584.

right to veto the commission's decision.[274] D.D. Caron notes that, in drafting modified voting clauses to apply the above-mentioned proposal, a double veto situation should be avoided: "There should be no need to discuss whether the second resolution modifies the first or whether it creates new obligations, a categorization issue to which the veto might apply."[275] He also proposes that "the number of affirmative votes to terminate a resolution should be high so as to prevent political maneuvering by the state at which the resolution is directed."[276] Such a solution may be appealing to permanent members because it shields them from the abusive use of the veto by other permanent members. Furthermore, modified voting clauses are generally desirable because they "increase the perceived legitimacy of decision making generally by encouraging the maintenance of consensus." They are also desirable in the case of economic sanctions because "[they] enable the state targeted by the sanctions to act with a view of ending them."[277]

Another proposed solution is the incorporation of "sunset provisions" in Chapter VII resolutions, similar to those included in peacekeeping resolutions. After the lapse of a certain amount of time, the sanctions or the Security Council's actions would terminate automatically and renewing the actions would require another resolution. This solution, it is argued, is consistent with the spirit of the Charter and the principle of good faith.[278] In fact, the more recent practice of the Security Council does seem to take account of the problem of termination of sanctions and these proposed solutions. For the first time, in May 2000, the Security Council's Resolution 1298, which imposed an arms embargo on Eritrea and Ethiopia, stated that the sanctions "are established for twelve months and that, at the end of that period, the Council will decide

---

[274] SC Res. 692, May 20, 1991.

[275] Caron, *supra* note 129 at 585.

[276] *Ibid.* at 586.

[277] *Ibid.* at 587. The case of Iraq may be a good example. If the target states feel that no matter what they do the sanctions will remain in place due to the veto of a few members of the Security Council, they will see no point in trying to comply with the Security Council resolutions.

[278] *Ibid.* at 584. Similar solutions are proposed in the *Draft Report of the Working Group on General Issues of Sanctions,* February 14, 2001, text can be accessed online at <http://www.cam.ac.uk/societies/casi/info/scwgs140201.html> (date accessed: October 14, 2001) [hereinafter *Draft Report of the Working Group on Sanctions*].

whether the governments of Eritrea and Ethiopia have complied with paragraphs 2, 3 and 4 above, and accordingly, whether to extend these measures for a further period with these same conditions."[279] This new trend has been followed in subsequent Security Council resolutions imposing sanctions.[280]

AMELIORATING THE LEGITIMACY OF THE SECURITY COUNCIL'S ACTIONS UNDER CHAPTER VII

Establishing a Chapter VII Consultation Committee

Reisman's proposal addresses the problem caused by the "absence of an appropriate informational loop from Council to Assembly." He suggests that a "Chapter VII Consultation Committee [composed of] twenty-one members of the Assembly, representing a range of regions and interests, to be selected annually by the Assembly" be formed by the Security Council.[281] In cases that require a decision under Chapter VII of the Charter, the Security Council would notify the committee, and the president of the Council and the secretary-general would meet the committee to exchange views and information. According to Reisman, by doing so, "the Council would always be apprised of representative Assembly views and the Assembly, for its part, would have the full benefit of the Council's perspective."[282] In the present system, the non-permanent members are not "charged with maintaining an open line between the Council and the Assembly." Applying this proposal, he concludes, will fill this gap.[283]

Other proposals to the same effect — including "open[ing] up Council proceedings to the General Assembly and thus increas-[ing] the sense of participatory governance"[284] — would give the assembly the power to evaluate and criticize the efforts of the Security Council to maintain international peace and security and provide the secretary-general with the authorization to notify the General Assembly of disputes and situations being dealt with by

---

[279] SC Res. 1298, May 17, 2000.

[280] See, for example, SC Res. 1343, March 7, 2000.

[281] Reisman, *supra* note 130 at 99.

[282] *Ibid.* Reisman also points out the importance of consultation in international law as a practice that does not give a veto power to the party consulted but, at the same time, is more than mere notification (*ibid.*).

[283] *Ibid.*

[284] Caron, *supra* note 129 at 575.

the Security Council.[285] However, regardless of which of the earlier-mentioned proposals is adopted, the issue remains the same. In the words of Lori Damrosch, "the Security Council must be perceived as acting on a principled basis in order to continue to elicit compliance with its decisions and support from states whose interests do not coincide with those of the permanent members."[286]

Limitations on the Power of the Council: Supervisory Control over the Security Council's Actions

Earlier in this article, it was determined that the ICJ has no supervisory control over the decisions of the Security Council. Nonetheless, there are possible ways in which such a supervisory role for the ICJ may evolve.[287] In fact, in the *Lockerbie* case, the court did not overrule the possibility of pronouncing, in the future, its views on the decisions of the Security Council. The former president of the ICJ, Mohammed Bedjaoui, argues that even though no supervision of legality was introduced under the San Francisco system,

[n]ow that the United Nations has come of age, it is unthinkable that the system should not be perfected by introducing that supervision of legality, the principle advisability of which was admitted by the San Francisco Conference, though the Conference left for future decision the methods and procedures by which it might be achieved.[288]

Bedjaoui also finds it

increasingly inadmissible that international political organs should take liberties with the Charter or adopt a relaxed attitude towards international law when it is they, surely, even more than States, that have been given the duty of fortifying international law's credibility and reliability.[289]

One can suggest, by adopting a *de lege ferenda* approach, different ways in which judicial control by the ICJ or political control by the General Assembly may develop. Similar attempts have been made

---

[285] *Ibid.*

[286] Damrosch, *supra* note 265 at 62.

[287] The possible exercise of supervisory power by the ICJ in the *Lockerbie* case will be an indirect control, based on the Montreal Convention, *supra* note 175, and not on the Charter. It is suggested that if there are indirect ways for the court to exercise a judicial control on the Security Council's actions, there can be a direct control to avoid the problem of haphazard judicial control of some actions and not others (see Bothe, *supra* note 168 at 80).

[288] Bedjaoui, *supra* note 164 at 129.

[289] *Ibid.* at 130.

by, *inter alia*, the American Society of International Law, the International Law Association, the Grotius Society, and the Institut de droit international.[290] In 1950, a committee set up by the American Society of International Law proposed that the ICJ, in the framework of its advisory function, consider the cases where one or more member state challenge the United Nation's competence under the Charter in a given situation.[291] The International Law Association, on the other hand, in its forty-seventh conference in Dubrovnick, proposed an amendment to Article 96 of the Charter, according to which it would be the duty of the political organs of the United Nations to request an advisory opinion of the court on any situation in which a member state alleged that an organ had committed an excess of its powers.[292] In 1950, André Gros was entrusted by the Grotius Society to report on "the Problem of Redress against the Decisions of International Organization." He suggested that in response to the need for judicial redress for states against *ultra vires* decisions of international organizations, the court should have jurisdiction to adjudicate. The remedy before the court would be directed against the decision itself and not against the organization, and the action thus conceived would be deemed to have arisen out of a dispute between the applicant member state and one of the member states having voted for the decision impugned. The Grotius Society did not endorse the suggestion of its rapporteur because of the possibility of too many legal actions being held against political organs.[293] Finally, in 1957, the Institut de droit international, in its Amsterdam session, took up the question and acknowledged the merits of the judicial supervision of international political organs.[294]

---

[290] Bedjaoui has mentioned these efforts, and the related texts can be found in an annex to his book. See *ibid.* at 55-61 and annexed documents.

[291] J.P. Chamberlain, L.B. Sohn, and L.H. Woolsey, "Report of Special Committee on Reference to the International Court of Justice of Questions of United Nations Competence" (44th Annual Meeting of the American Society of International Law, Washington, DC, April 27-29, 1950) (1950) Am. Soc. Int'l L. Proc. 256 at 256-69.

[292] G. Schwarzenberger, "Second Report on the Review of the Charter of the United Nations" (Forty-Seventh Conference of the International Law Association, Dubrovnik, August 28, 1956) (1956) Rep. Int'l L. Assoc. 109 at 109-20.

[293] A. Gros, "The Problem of Redress against the Decisions of International Organizations" (Proceedings of the International Law Conference, Second Session, Middle Temple Hall, London, October 28, 1950) (1951) 36 Grot. Soc. 30 at 30-31.

[294] M.W. Wengler, "Recours judiciare à instituer contre les décisions d'organes internationaux" (La quarante-huitième session de l'Institut de Droit International, Septmber 24, 1957) (1957) 47:2 Ann. inst. dr. int. 274 at 275.

This question concerns the powers of the Security Council. It is subject to the same problems that surround the question of a reform of the veto. Realization of any such proposal cannot be expected in the near future.[295] Due to the seemingly insurmountable differences of opinion regarding the reform of the Security Council and the judicial control over its actions, it is more realistic to focus on other proposals for improving the practice of imposing economic sanctions.

Continuing Assessment of Sanctions and the Procedural Reform of the Sanction Committees[296]

The continuing assessment of sanctions is one way to address many of the problems related to economic sanctions: "Economic sanctions programmes must continuously update their information as the programme proceeds to ensure that they are consistent, in their effects with international law."[297] A letter dated April 13, 1995, from the representatives of the permanent members of the Security Council to the president of the Council (regarding the human impact of sanctions) recommends the objective assessment "of the short- and long-term humanitarian consequences of sanctions in the context of the overall sanctions regime, [and in appropriate situations, reviewing] the application of sanctions and tak[ing] appropriate actions." The letter also recommends that due regard be given to the humanitarian situation of the target state, that simple authorization procedures be developed in the case of essential humanitarian supplies, and that "the effectiveness of the sanctions committees [be improved], by drawing on the experience and the work of different sanctions committees."[298] Similarly, *General Comment 8* of the UN Committee on Economic, Social, and Cultural Rights gives proposals for the assessment of sanctions. The committee has noted proposals such as

---

[295] See, generally, Bedjaoui, *supra* note 147 at 93-107.

[296] For a comprehensive case study of the work of sanction committees (in the case of Iraq), see P. Conlon, *United Nations Sanctions Management: A Case Study of the Iraq Sanctions Committee, 1990-1994* (Ardsley, NY: Transnational Publishers, 2000).

[297] Reisman and Stevick, *supra* note 198 at 140.

[298] Letter dated 13 April 1995 from the Permanent Representatives of China, France, the Russian Federation, the United Kingdom of Great Britain and Northern Ireland and the United States of America to the United Nations addressed to the President of the Security Council, *supra* note 214 at 2-3.

those calling for the creation of a United Nations mechanism for anticipating and tracking sanctions impacts; the elaboration of a more transparent set of agreed principles and procedures based on respect for
human rights; the identification of a wider range of exempt goods and
services; the authorization of agreed technical agencies to determine
exemptions; the creation of a better resourced set of sanctions committees; more precise targeting of the vulnerabilities of those whose behaviour the international community wishes to change and the introduction
of greater overall flexibility.[299]

It has also been suggested that while the obligations created by
the implementation of Chapter VII sanctions are very important
and pre-empt any conflicting statutes or obligations,[300] the sanctions law or sanctions administration and procedural law are among
the least-developed areas of international law.[301] In line with the
proposals for institutionalizing sanctions, one proposal is to create
a general sanctions committee that would be a subsidiary organ
of the Security Council. This model could be varied by having several such subsidiary bodies, one for substantive political matters,
one for purely administrative tasks, and one that would be specialized in addressing humanitarian exemptions. There should also be
more accountability in the future sanction committees. They should
be required to submit periodic reports on their work to the Security
Council.[302]

APPLYING INTERNATIONAL HUMANITARIAN LAW
STANDARDS TO SANCTIONS

Several commentators have argued that the standards of international humanitarian law should be applied when implementing
economic sanctions.[303] If principles of international humanitarian
law are "an established and accepted means of evaluating the use
of one instrument of statecraft that can cause great pain, suffering

---

[299] *General Comment 8, supra* note 215 at 122.

[300] See Article 103 of the Charter, which is quoted in note 24.

[301] See P. Conlon, "Lessons from Iraq: The Functions of the Iraq Sanctions Committee as a Source of Sanctions Implementation Authority and Practice"
(1995) 35 Va. J. Int'l L. 633 at 664-65.

[302] *Ibid.* at 666-67.

[303] According to J. Pictet, *Humanitarian Law and the Protection of War Victims* (Leyden: A. W. Sijthoff, 1975) at 28, "the fundamental principle of humanitarian
law is the result of a compromise between opposing concepts: humanity and
necessity." This fundamental principle can very well be applied to economic
sanctions.

and physical harm, then they might well be appropriate in evaluating another instrument that can produce similar effects."[304] Therefore, sanctions should be necessary, proportionate, and maximize discrimination[305] between combatants and non-combatants.[306] Applying international humanitarian law standards to the enforcement actions of the Security Council also poses certain limits on the powers of the Council.

Necessity and Proportionality

The concept of necessity deals with the following question: "How much, if any, collateral damage is permissible in a particular case?"[307] Necessity has been defined as the minimum collateral damage necessary to achieve the objective of the action. "Yet," as Reisman and Stevick point out, "the concept of necessity must be elastic enough to allow for substantial collateral damage when the dangers to public order warrant it."[308] Reisman and Stevick suggest that the natural law criteria of necessity and proportionality should be applied when implementing economic sanctions: "[T]he tolerance for lawful violence, with the corresponding level of collateral damage that will ensue, varies in part, according to the degree of injury that is posed to public order and the degree of irreparability of injuries if they occur."[309] Accordingly, whatever the instrument for enforcement measures (military, economic, or propaganda),

---

[304] A.C. Pierce, "Just War Principle and Economic Sanctions" (1996) 10 Ethics and Int'l Affairs 99 at 100. And, in words of Pictet, "[t]he belief is gaining ground that it is the functions of international law to ensure minimum safeguards and humane treatment for all, whether in time of peace or in time of war, whether the individual is in conflict with a foreign nation or with his own community" (Pictet, *supra* note 303 at 31).

[305] In terms of international humanitarian law, necessity and proportionality are principles of *jus ad bellum*. "The aim of *jus ad bellum* is to avert and restrain resort to armed force in the conduct of international relations." Discrimination between combatants and non-combatants is a principle of *jus in bello* which "is vested with the secondary, but vital, office of mitigating the impact and consequences of those armed conflicts which occur despite the *jus ad bellum*." McCoubrey, *supra* note 234 at 1-2.

[306] Reisman and Stevick, *supra* note 198 at 128-40.

[307] *Ibid.* at 128.

[308] *Ibid.*

[309] *Ibid.* at 129. As an example, they compare the cases of sanctions against Saddam Hussein and Fidel Castro and conclude that a higher level of collateral damage should be legally tolerable for Saddam than for Castro.

the resulting collateral damage should be assessed through "comparative projections" of the costs to the non-combatants and the non-responsible parties.[310] The result of the principle of necessity is that, in dealing with a situation of potential implementation of economic sanctions, alternative strategies should be evaluated. The instrument that accomplishes the necessary objective with the least potential harm should be preferred.[311]

The principle of proportionality adds another condition to that of necessity. This principle requires that a "sanction programme cannot exceed the somewhat broadly construed bounds of proportionality."[312] In other words, the damage to be inflicted and the costs incurred must be proportionate to the good expected to result from the action.[313] Proportionality, as a condition for unilateral sanctions, is recognized in international law.[314] Extending this condition to collective sanctions is possible either through an analogy with unilateral sanctions or by applying principles of international humanitarian law. It is, however, very difficult to measure the intangible goals of sanctions against "tangibles like hunger, illness, and other physical deprivation."[315] It should be noted that this problem does not only arise in association with economic sanctions. The problem arises whenever the proportionality criterion is applied to a state's action, including the use of force.[316]

[310] See *ibid.* at 130. In addition, the implications for the environment should also be taken into account.

[311] *Ibid.* at 130.

[312] *Ibid.* at 131.

[313] Pierce, *supra* note 304 at 105.

[314] See the discussion in note 9 in this article.

[315] Pierce, *supra* note 304 at 106. However, A. de Hoogh, *Obligations* Erga Omnes *and International Crimes* (The Hague: Kluwer Law International, 1996) at 268, claims that

> [t]o the extent that it concerns itself with the enforcement of prohibitions of the use of force, slavery, genocide and racial discrimination, denial of self-determination, breaches of basic human rights, the criteria for judging proportionality between wrongful acts and responses thereto seem to provide more than enough leeway to justify even the imposition on a State of a complete trade embargo.

[316] According to Pierce, *supra* note 304 at 106:

> [t]he sanctions case poses no special conceptual problems in applying the proportionality criterion, which already incorporates many kinds of human suffering to be inflicted and many kinds of human values to be protected and advanced. Thus severe hunger, illness, and other forms of deprivation found in cases of sanctions are included in the traditional concept, which need no basic modification here.

Discrimination between Combatants and Non-Combatants

Since economic sanctions can, in some cases, be more destructive than military instruments, it is only logical and falls into line with "the fundamental goals of international law that are expressed in the prescribed law of armed conflict" to implement sanctions in such a way that they will have the least effect on civil populations.[317] According to *General Comment 8* of the Committee on Economic, Social and Cultural Rights,

[i]t is essential to distinguish between the basic objective of applying political and economic pressure upon the governing elite of a country to persuade them to conform to international law, and the collateral infliction of suffering upon the most vulnerable groups within the targeted country.[318]

It is, thus, preferable to implement sanctions in such a manner as to deprive the target state of a war arsenal, to change the political program, or to target those who can influence the policies of the target state. Furthermore, "more collateral damage may be permitted when the target is democratic, for more adults may be deemed to support and be implicated in the comportment that is the target of international condemnation and sanction."[319]

General embargoes can be highly destructive and, therefore, they should not be implemented. According to Reisman and Stevick, neither the Security Council nor the Council of the League of Nations has ever studied the collateral damage likely to be caused by economic sanctions before imposing such sanctions.[320] It is, thus, proposed that every implementation of economic sanctions should be preceded by a preliminary study of the impact that the sanctions will have on different sections of the economy and on

---

[317] See Reisman and Stevick, *supra* note 198 at 131. In terms of international humanitarian law, the means of warfare should discriminate between combatants and non-combatants. This leads, then, to the problem of definition of "combatants" and "non-combatants." See generally R.R. Baxter, "The Privy Council on the Qualifications of Belligerents" (1969) 63 A.J.I.L. 290; B. Brungs, "The Distinction between Combatants and Non-Combatants" (1964) Military Law Review 76; A.M. De Zayas, "Combatants," in R. Bernhardt, ed., *Encyclopedia of Public International Law*, vol. 3 (Amsterdam: North-Holland Publishing Company, 1982) 152.

[318] *General Comment 8, supra* note 215 at para. 4. The ILC has also taken note of this subject in its commentary to Article 50 of the *Draft Articles of State Responsibility. ILC's Report on Fifty-Third Session, supra* note 6 at 335, para. 7.

[319] Reisman and Stevick, *supra* note 198 at 132.

[320] *Ibid.*

the civil population of the target state. Of course, due to the nature of economic activities and the relation of different sectors of the economy to each other, absolute precision in using such economic weapons is impossible. However, some techniques should be developed to reduce the harm:

A policy-effective sanctions programme is one that accomplishes the objective of changing an external or internal policy while minimizing collateral damage. A policy-effective programme minimizes collateral damage by reducing the duration of economic suffering, concentrating harm on those who have material influence in policy-making, and targeting resources that are not essential for civilian survival or bodily integrity but whose neutralization is likely to lead to desirable adjustments in the target's policies.[321]

Policy-effectiveness or, in terms of international humanitarian law, "probability of success," cannot be easily estimated, but past experiences and techniques of contemporary social inquiry may provide important insights into prospective effectiveness.[322] In order to increase the probability of the success of sanction programs, different economic and political factors should be taken into account. Economic factors include the nature of commercial relations between the sanctioner and the target state and the economic structure of the target state. Another important political factor that must be taken into account is the fact that the target state must be given room to change its policy without enduring a "critical value loss." In other words, the target state must be allowed to save face.[323] This goal can be achieved, in some circumstances, by proposing a package deal, in which there appears to be concessions on both sides. With an effective application of the aforementioned humanitarian norms and policy-effectiveness techniques, economic sanction programs will be less likely to cause controversy.

Taking the Long-Term Effect of Sanctions into Account:
Applying Article 55 of the Charter

Article 55 of the Charter should also be considered in application of economic sanctions because — even though the article is not directly relevant — its consideration is in line with humanitarian concerns.[324] Article 55, which is the opening article of the

---

[321] *Ibid.* at 133.

[322] See Pierce, *supra* note 304 at 108; and Reisman and Stevick, *supra* note 198 at 133.

[323] Reisman and Stevick, *supra* note 198 at 136.

[324] Swindells, *supra* note 202 at 1955.

chapter on international economic and social cooperation, states that the United Nations shall promote, *inter alia*, "higher standards of living, conditions of economic and social progress and development, [and] observance of human rights." This article "delineates elementary standards and the United Nations should take them into consideration before applying sanctions ... The organization would have to first assess the socio-economic status of the target and determine what type of sanctions would cause the least damage to the target's development."[325] The Committee on Economic, Social and Cultural Rights has also taken note of this problem:

> [W]hatever the circumstances, [economic sanctions] should always take full account of the provisions of the International Covenant on Economic, Social and Cultural Rights. The Committee does not in any way call into question the necessity for the imposition of sanctions in appropriate cases in accordance with Chapter VII of the Charter of the United Nations or other applicable international law. But those provisions of the Charter that relate to human rights (Articles 1, 55 and 56) must still be considered to be fully applicable in such case.[326]

Some of the proposals that have been submitted for the effective assessment of sanctions by UN bodies have addressed the issue of the application of Article 55 to economic sanctions. They will be discussed in the following section. Accordingly, in addition to taking the long-term effects of sanctions into account, the sanctioning state(s) or the Security Council should vigorously apply principles of international humanitarian law, including necessity, proportionality, and discrimination between combatants and non-combatants. Creating certain bodies in charge of economic sanctions and further institutionalizing the practice of implementing sanctions can be helpful in avoiding humanitarian disasters caused by economic sanctions.[327]

INSTITUTIONALIZING SANCTIONS FOR BREACHES OF THE *ERGA OMNES* OBLIGATIONS OF STATES

I have already argued for the collective use of economic sanctions in the case of violations of *erga onmes* obligations and breaches of *jus cogens* norms. However, in order for economic sanctions to be regarded as legitimate in these cases, "an international representative body must have pronounced authoritatively on the illegal

---

[325] *Ibid.*

[326] *General Comment 8, supra* note 215 at 119.

[327] See also *Draft Report of the Working Group on Sanctions, supra* note 278.

acts which originally provoked them."[328] The same rule applies for unilateral economic sanctions in cases of breaches of *erga omnes* obligations. The United Nations may be a desirable forum for orchestrating international reactions against breaches of *erga omnes* obligations. However, at the same time, the Charter, which was drafted more than half a century ago, does not reflect the realities of contemporary international law. The Charter's mechanisms are inadequate for the imposition of sanctions in cases of *erga omnes* obligations. An eventual revision of the Charter should consider the question of enforcing *erga omnes* obligations and institutionalizing the use of sanctions in such cases.

One proposal calls for the creation of a new UN Council on Economic Sanctions.[329] This proposal addresses both the general issue of the legitimacy of economic sanctions and the specific issue of sanctions imposed in response to breaches of *erga omnes* obligations. According to this proposal, a Council on Economic Sanctions should be created for the following reasons: first, it would be more inclusive than the Security Council; second, there would be no veto power for five permanent members; and, third, "the task of imposing, monitoring, and enforcing sanctions is large and complex enough to justify creating an entity wholly focused on doing these important functions well."[330] In my view, this proposal would not attract sufficient support, for practical reasons, in the event of a reform of the Charter.[331] Ideally, the creation of a separate council, with a large membership and no veto power, would increase the legitimacy of the decisions of the Security Council and would

---

[328] Cassese, *supra* note 201 at 244. According to Cassese, this pronouncement can be in the form of a Security Council resolution designating a situation as a breach of the peace (for example, Resolution 502 (1983) to the effect that Argentina committed a "breach of the peace" in the case of the Falklands/Malvinas), a decision of the competent body of a regional organization (for example, EEC Council of Ministers decision in the same case), or a resolution adopted by a very large majority in the General Assembly (for example, Resolution ES-6/2 on January 14, 1980 deploring the arm intervention in Afghanistan as contrary to the fundamental principles of respect for sovereignty) (*ibid.*).

[329] See L. Dumas, "A Proposal for a New United Nations Council on Economic Sanctions," in Cortright and Lopez, supra note 7 at 187.

[330] *Ibid.* at 191.

[331] Even though Dumas who has presented this proposal describes it as "far from utopian," there is no doubt that reaching an agreement on such a broad range of issues especially involving veto power of the permanent member of the Security Council is impossible. In fact, it is very utopian!

encourage participation in sanctions programs. However, realistically, the adoption of such a proposal would result in inefficiency.[332] Strengthening the sanctions committee, effective monitoring, the constant evaluation of sanctions programs and their human consequences, and the inclusion of provisions regarding enforcement action in response to breaches of *erga omnes* obligations in the Charter are more feasible solutions. Compiling a list of sanctionable violations, addressing the problem of how sanctions should be terminated, and adopting a uniform policy for the imposition of sanctions are other steps that would lead to the institutionalized implementation of economic sanctions.

Another proposal for institutionalizing the implementation of economic sanctions concentrates on the application of Article 55 of the Charter to economic sanctions. According to this proposal, the specialized agencies of the United Nations could "form a mechanism to assess the impact of sanctions prior to their implementation, to monitor application of the sanctions, minimize sanctions' collateral damage, and ensure delivery of humanitarian assistance."[333] The role of the specialized agencies in assessing the impact of sanctions is especially important because of the agencies' presence in target states and their links with non-governmental organization experts and local authorities.[334] In order to avoid amending the Charter, it is proposed that "ECOSOC could establish the mechanism to monitor the targeted state by creating a sub-commission pursuant to Article 68 of the U.N. Charter."[335] Of

---

[332] In the past, there have been similar proposals for increasing the efficiency of the enforcement of economic sanctions. In the case of sanctions against Rhodesia, the African delegations advanced proposals for the appointment of a commissioner for United Nations sanctions against Rhodesia, who would be responsible to the Security Council and with a broad mandate to coordinate all existing actions under the Security Council sanctions resolutions. This proposal failed (see R. Zacklin, *The United Nations and Rhodesia, a Study in International Law* (New York: Praeger Publishers, 1974) at 99).

[333] Swindells, *supra* note 202 at 1955, 1956.

[334] In the case of Haiti, agencies and organizations working in Haiti proved to be the most useful in helping to monitor the impact of sanctions on the target's population by the information, constructive comments, relevant input that they provided (*ibid.* at 1956).

[335] Article 68 states that "[t]he Economic and Social Council may make suitable arrangements for consultation with non-governmental organizations which are concerned with matters within its competence. Such arrangements may be made with international organizations and, where appropriate, with national organizations after consultation with the Member of the United Nations concerned."

course, in this case, the constant cooperation between the Economic and Social Council (ECOSOC) and the Security Council to transmit the result of the assessments would be necessary.

PROTECTING THIRD STATES

Third states or individuals often suffer the consequences of economic sanctions. The effects of sanctions on third parties should be considered in the planning stage. In imposing sanctions, the sanctioning states may violate the rights of their own nationals. Violations of these rights, and the remedies available to individuals in cases of violations, are issues related to the domestic constitutional law of states. Suffice it to say that the basic human rights of nationals should be protected in any event. Proposals to reduce the negative effects of collective sanctions on the economies of third states are relevant to the present discussion. In his report, *An Agenda for Peace; Preventive Diplomacy, Peacemaking and Peace-keeping*, Boutros Boutros-Ghali proposes, in response to the problem of collateral damages of sanctions, that the injured states "should be entitled not only to consult the Security Council but also to have a realistic possibility of having their difficulty addressed."[336] He elaborates on this proposal and recommends that "the Security Council devise a set of measures involving the international financial institutions and other components of the United Nations system that could be put in place to address the problem."[337] Following up on this idea, in the *Supplement to an Agenda for Peace*, Boutros-Ghali reports that he sought the opinion of the heads of the international financial institutions.[338] They acknowledged the collateral effects of sanctions but proposed that injured states should be helped in the framework of "existing mandates for support of countries facing negative external shocks and consequent balance-of-payment difficulties" and that no special provisions should be made for that purpose.[339] In the *Supplement to an Agenda for Peace*, he proposes a mechanism to, *inter alia*, "explore ways of assisting Member States that are suffering collateral damage and to evaluate claims

[336] *An Agenda for Peace; Preventive Diplomacy, Peacemaking and Peace-keeping, Report of the Secretary-General pursuant to the Statement Adopted by the Summit Meeting of the Security Council on 31 January 1992*, UN Doc. A/47/277; S/24111 (1992) at 75, reprinted in 31 I.L.M. 956 [hereinafter *An Agenda for Peace*].

[337] *Ibid.*

[338] Doxey, *supra* note 6 at 80.

[339] *Supplement to an Agenda for Peace, supra* note 131 at para. 74.

submitted by such States under Article 50."[340] The fact that the former secretary-general of the United Nations acknowledges the problem of the effects of sanctions on third parties indicates that the mechanisms that are now in place are not sufficient. Implementing the proposals of Boutros-Ghali is the least that can be done to address the problem.

To summarize, the proposals presented in this part concentrated on the following: rendering the Security Council's decisions more legitimate by creating more encompassing consultative bodies and possibly reforming the veto; addressing the problem of the reverse veto by incorporating different voting procedures for the termination of sanctions or providing for sunset provisions; applying international humanitarian law standards of necessity, proportionality, and discrimination between combatants and non-combatants to economic sanctions; in accordance with Article 55 of the Charter, taking into account the long-term effects of sanctions; institutionalizing sanctions for breaches of *erga omnes* obligations; creating effective mechanisms for protecting third party interests; and, finally, creating a United Nations mechanism for anticipating and tracking sanctions impacts and developing the administration and procedural law of sanctions.

CONCLUSION

The growth in the use of collective sanctions in the post-Cold War epoch calls for a re-examination of the legal basis and restraints on the implementation of sanctions. Fortunately, in the past few years, sanctions have increasingly been the centre of focus in academic as well as in diplomatic circles.[341] In the words of Kofi Annan, "the 'Sanctions Decade' provides a number of critical lessons" on the

---

[340] *Ibid.* at para. 75. This mechanism would have to be located in the UN Secretariat and should be empowered to utilize the expertise available through the UN system, in particular, that of the Bretton Woods institutions (*ibid.* at para. 76).

[341] In addition to various academic studies at universities, conferences, and roundtables and policy think-tank projects on the subject of sanctions, the Security Council has been preoccupied with improved implementation of sanctions. Several notes by the president of the Council and creation of the working group on sanctions are witnesses to new trend in the Council. See also *We the Peoples: The Role of the United Nations in the 21st Century, Millennium Report of the Secretary General,* UN Doc. A/54/2000, paras. 229-233, in which the secretary-general recalls some of the problems of imposing economic sanctions discussed in this article and "invite[s] the Security Council, in particular, to bear them in mind when designing and applying sanctions regimes" (*ibid.* at para. 233).

effect of sanctions.[342] Due to the developments in international law of the past century and the emergence of *erga omnes* obligations, traditional doctrines are no longer sufficient for justifying enforcement actions — including economic sanctions — that are taken by states. Even the open-textured quality of Article 39 of the Charter is not a sufficient legal basis. There is a lacuna in the field of the enforcement of international law and especially of *erga omnes* obligations, and the Security Council has tried to fill that lacuna by using its powers and discretion.

In cases of a breach of *erga omnes* obligations, the Council is expected to intervene. However, in certain cases, it is impossible to justify such sanctions within Chapter VII. Yet interventions can be justified under international law. The proper framework and procedure for implementation in these cases has yet to be created. Notwithstanding this legal limitation, there are other reasons to prefer collective sanctions over unilateral ones.[343] As the world economy has become increasingly interconnected, unilateral economic sanctions are less likely to be successfully implemented.[344] Target states can always satisfy their needs from alternate markets. Furthermore, collective actions are generally cheaper, more able to neutralize domestic political opposition, better at offering opportunities to acquire useful political allies, more able to reassure the

---

[342] *Opening Remarks of Secretary-General Kofi Annan to the International Peace Academy Seminar on Sanctions, in New York,* April 17, 2000, UN Press Release SG/SM/7360, text can be accessed online <http://www.un.org/News/Press/docs/2000/20000417.sgsm7360.doc.html> (date accessed: October 14, 2001).

[343] It is becoming more difficult for states to impose unilateral economic sanctions due to the regulation of trade and new state obligations that have resulted from the *General Agreement on Tariffs and Trade* (October 30, 1947, 58 U.N.T.S. 187, Can. T.S. 1947 No.27 (entered into force January 1, 1948) and agreements in the framework of the World Trade Organization [hereinafter WTO], established according to Agreement Establishing the Multilateral Trade Organization, December 15, 1993, 33 I.L.M. 13. Considering the limitations placed on the use of unilateral economic sanctions by provisions of the WTO agreements, the likelihood that unilateral sanctions will be used in the near future is slight (See Reisman and Stevick, *supra* note 198 at 95). Even the United States, which, traditionally, has frequently been using sanctions as a policy tool, seems to have reached the conclusion that priority should be given to collective sanctions in comparison with unilateral sanctions. In April 1999, in the context of a broader attempt at comprehensive sanctions reform, it was announced that the goal is to resort to unilateral sanctions only after all other options, including diplomacy and multilateral sanctions have been exhausted ("U.S. Eases Policy on Some Sanctions," *New York Times* (April 21, 1999) A1 and A12).

[344] Dumas, *supra* note 329 at 190.

international community that operations have limited and legitimate goals, and better at reducing the risk of large-scale force being used by rival powers.[345]

As far as collective sanctions are concerned, they are one of the only means of international enforcement; and, in the absence of suitable alternatives, their application is inevitable. The emphasis, thus, should be on refining sanction programs. The cases of implementation of sanctions in the past have been subject to valid criticisms. Even when the classical conditions of legality of sanctions were observed, it was argued that sanctions were still subject to restrictions and their application raised problems related to broader constitutional issues within the United Nations as well as within the structure and functioning of the Security Council. Limits should be set on the Security Council's absolute discretion, and it should not be conceived to be an agency *legibus solutus.*[346]

The solution to problems relating to the structure of the Security Council, the veto, and constitutional control lies, in part, in reform proposals. These questions are very complicated and subject to political concerns. They relate to a delicate balance between effective security and legitimacy.[347] In the meantime, there are interim solutions. There is, undoubtedly, room for improving the legitimacy of the Security Council's decision-making procedure. In the absence of an agreement on UN reforms, heavy emphasis should be placed on process "not because ... justice is merely procedural, but because ... our diverse global community is more likely to find its vision of substantive justice through a process involving debate."[348] In order to reduce the effect of the veto, non-permanent members of the Security Council can at least ask for the inclusion of modified voting clauses or sunset clauses.[349] It is also suggested that while the obligations created by the implementation of Chapter VII sanctions trump other state's obligations,[350] the sanctions law or sanctions

---

[345] A. Roberts, "The United Nations and International Security" (1995) 35:2 Survival 3 at 6.

[346] See B. Conforti, "Non-Coercive Sanctions in the United Nations Charter: Some Lessons from the Gulf War" (1991) 2 European J. Int'l L. 110 at 112.

[347] See Reisman, *supra* note 130 at 98.

[348] Caron, *supra* note 129 at 588.

[349] *Ibid.* at 587

[350] Article 103 of the Charter, *supra* note 5. For example in Resolution 841 (imposing sanctions on Haiti) at paragraph 9 stated that "[the Security Council] calls upon all states, and all international organizations, to act strictly in accordance

administration and procedural law are among the least-developed areas of international law.[351] Establishing a proper mechanism for the implementation and institutionalization of sanctions — especially in cases of implementation in response to breaches of *erga omnes* obligations — will ameliorate the current situation and diminish the criticism of the Security Council actions.[352]

A major concern regarding the implementation of sanctions in the recent years relates to their human impact. Contrary to the traditional view that sanctions are "perceived as a non-violent alternative to the use of force," recent cases have proved that, sometimes, "sanctions may have a more devastating impact on the general population than a limited but directed use of force."[353] It has been argued that to address this concern, sanctions should be subject to the principles of international humanitarian law. Sanctions must be applied more discriminately in order to hit their intended target.

A rigorous assessment of the collateral damages caused by sanctions is, thus, very important. The assessment of sanctions should be done on a case-by-case basis, taking into account different circumstances. The decision regarding the appropriateness of sanctions should be based on an understanding of the environment targeted by the sanction and the price of achieving the desired objectives through sanctions. It is even suggested that "sometimes a precise use of the military strategy will more efficiently achieve the international objective and more closely approximate the tests of lawful international coercion than would an undefined economic sanctions programme."[354] This conclusion has broader repercussions in terms of international law. A few decades ago, H.L.A. Hart claimed that in disputed matters in international law, "often no

---

with the provisions of the present resolution, notwithstanding the existence of any rights or obligations conferred or imposed by any international agreement or any contract entered into or any license or permit granted prior to 23 June 1993."

[351] See Conlon, *supra* note 301 at 664-65.

[352] In line with such proposals it is suggested that under Article 55 of the Charter, the United Nations is required to create a sustainable development policy and the sanctions applied under Article 41 of the Charter should not undermine that duty (see Swindells, *supra* note 202 at 1961).

[353] J. Boulden, *The Application of Sanctions under Chapter VII of the United Nations Charter: A Contemporary Assessment* (Ottawa: Canadian Centre for Global Security, 1994).

[354] Reisman and Stevick, *supra* note 198 at 141.

mention is made of moral right or wrong, good or bad."[355] Conversely, it is evident that there is no room nor tolerance for immoral behaviour today. International law and international public opinion will simply not allow it. The fact that in recent cases, the international community did endeavour to act with wisdom and prudence and to learn from past mistakes renders the questions of human impact and moral repercussions of imposing sanctions even more difficult.[356]

Finally, as Damrosch states,

[s]electivity in the adoption of sanctions may be inevitable for the foreseeable future, as key international actors set the agenda in accordance with their own perceptions of interests and resource constraints ... but over the longer term, as the international community matures, elaboration of normative criteria for the application of sanctions will be a critical step, leading to the eventual goal of treating like cases alike.[357]

The lawyer's ideal of promoting the rule of law in international relations necessitates that a social order in which law is enforced by organized and regularized procedures be put into place.[358] Economic sanctions are one of the only such social orders available in international relations. In installing this system of social order, in the words of Lon Fuller, "ends and means cannot be divorced."[359] The proposals in this article are intended to reinforce this ideal. Of course, power and the politics of present-day international relations complicate matters immensely.

---

[355] Hart, *supra* note 162 at 228.

[356] Damrosch, *supra* note 200 at 275.

[357] *Ibid.* at 277.

[358] I.L. Claude, Jr., "Sanctions and Enforcement: An Introduction," in J.M. Paxman and T.G. Boggs, eds., *The United Nations: A Reassessment; Sanctions, Peacekeeping, and Humanitarian Assistance* (Charlottesville: University Press of Virginia, 1973) 21.

[359] L. Fuller, *The Morality of Law*, rev. ed. (New Haven: Yale University Press, 1969), cited in S.J. Toope, "Confronting Indeterminacy: Challenges to International Legal Theory" (29th Annual Conference of Canadian Council on International Law, Ottawa, October 18-20, 1990) (1990) 19 Can. Council Int'l L. Proc. 209.

Sommaire

Le recours aux sanctions économiques en droit international: regard contemporain

Le recours croissant aux sanctions économiques collectives dans la période de l'après-guerre froide invite à revoir les fondements juridiques et les contraintes de la mise en œuvre de telles sanctions. Cet article examine, dans une perspective juridique, les problèmes et les restrictions associés à ces sanctions, suggérant certains moyens de les rendre plus légitimes eu égard aux exigences juridiques internationales. Bien que les sanctions obéissent en règle générale aux principes issus des traités internationaux, l'inexécution d'une obligation erga omnes *justifie également une telle mesure. Outre les considérations économiques traditionnelles, il y aurait lieu de tenir compte d'autres limitations, comme le respect des principes du droit international humanitaire. Une fois déterminées les restrictions nécessaires à la mise en œuvre des sanctions internationales, certaines avenues sont proposées afin de raffiner la pratique actuelle en matière des sanctions économiques. En conclusion, il appert possible de recourir aux sanctions collectives d'une manière plus humaine et institutionnellement plus cohérente.*

Summary

Use of Economic Sanctions under International Law: A Contemporary Assessment

The growth in the use of collective economic sanctions in the post-Cold War epoch calls for a re-examination of the legal basis and constraints on the implementation of sanctions. This article is an attempt to explore, from a legal point of view, the problems and restrictions associated with sanctions, and to suggest the ways in which economic sanctions can be rendered more legitimate in terms of international legal requirements. It is argued that, in addition to the traditional treaty basis of collective sanctions, a breach of an erga omnes *obligation is also a legitimate legal basis for economic sanctions. It is also contended that, in addition to traditional economic considerations, sanctions should be subject to other limitations such as respect for principles of international humanitarian law. After determining the restrictions on the implementation of sanctions, the author makes proposals for refining current practices in imposing economic sanctions. In conclusion, it is argued that collective sanctions have the potential of being used in a more humane and institutionally coherent way.*

Feature Article / Article vedette

Interpreting Intervention

CRAIG SCOTT

INTRODUCTION

Since the North American Treaty Organization's (NATO) intervention in Yugoslavia during the Kosovo crisis, a number of
leading actors have been pushing for the general recognition of the
lawfulness of "humanitarian intervention" in certain circumstances
and in the absence of express authorization from the United Nations
Security Council. Various normative phenomena have begun to
emerge in the 1990s, which suggest that the practice of some actors
(both state and non-state, including the United Nations Secretary-
General) and the relative acquiescence of others have combined to

Craig Scott, Associate Professor of Law and Associate Dean of Research and
Graduate Studies, Osgoode Hall Law School, York University, Toronto. The present
article is an elaboration of an address delivered to the "Think Canada" Conference
on Issues for the Twenty-First Century: Think Peace and Security, Tokyo, Japan,
April 17, 2001. It was written in May 2001 and has deliberately not been substan-
tively revised since then in light of either the events of September 11, 2001, or of
the report released in December 2001 by the International Commission on Intervention and State Sovereignty [hereinafter ICISS]. See ICISS, *The Responsibility
to Protect* (Ottawa: International Development Research Centre, 2001), which can
also be found at <http://www.iciss.gc.ca/report-e.asp> (last visited April 1, 2002).
Indeed, the author has refrained from reading any of the report until after the edit-
ing process for the present article has ended. It was felt by both the author and the
Yearbook editors that the analysis and approach of the present article, as written in
the spring of 2001, should stand on their own as contributions to the debates that
have taken on a new meaning since the article was written, notably the intercon-
necting normative debates on humanitarian intervention flowing from the ICISS
report and the debates on security-related intervention in the aftermath of September 11. Thank you to Graham Boswell for his able research assistance, to Stella
Harmantas for her critical proofing, and to Shedrack Agbakwa for help with the
final revisions.

produce a widening and deepening view that a Security Council consensus sufficient to produce a binding resolution explicitly authorizing the use of force is, while desirable, not in all contexts necessary for an intervention to be considered lawful. The primary contexts in which these phenomena have played themselves out have been: the use of military force against Iraq as a means of enforcing compliance with the United Nations weapons inspection regime for that country as well as a means of enforcing no-fly zones over areas of northern and southern Iraq; the intervention of a regional organization known as the Economic Community of West African States (ECOWAS) into Liberia; and the war launched by NATO against Yugoslavia as a result of the crisis in Kosovo. One irony of these developments is that they have occurred in tandem with a quantum leap in Security Council activities in the 1990s — an evolution of international governance in the peace and security field that one might have expected would have led to even less acceptance of any freedom of states to circumvent the Council. In the face of this irony, the mounting sense of the acceptability of either threatening or using force without express authorization of the Security Council seems, in part, explicable because of the fact that some protagonists have begun to settle on a series of justifications that manage to present interventions not as acts of blatant side-stepping but rather as acts that have been undertaken in some form of collaboration with the Council. Alongside these intertwined political and moral discourses, we are also witnessing the rising influence of various legal theories of *implied* authorization and strong purposive arguments that contend that legal validity can be generated through decision-making processes that fulfill the collectivist spirit of the Security Council's scheme, even as they depart from the letter of the Charter of the United Nations (Charter) text.[1]

Receptivity to the aforementioned emergent justifications has arguably been bolstered by four developments that sometimes complement, but also sometimes exist in tension with, the apparent resurgence of Security Council authority since the end of the Cold War. First of all, there has been a rise in the discursive influence of various actors in "transnational civil society," and the successful adoption (many would say appropriation) by state and interstate actors of humanitarianism is a powerful normative language in transnational relations. Second, a certain triumphalism and

---

[1] Charter of the United Nations, June 26, 1945, Can. T.S. 1945 No. 7, 59 Stat. 1031, 145 U.K.F.S. 805. art/ 2(7) [hereinafter Charter].

resurgent messianism has fuelled the impatience of the world's hegemon, the United States, and its in-law, the United Kingdom, with any "obstructionism" by other P-5 powers (notably China and Russia but also France) as well as positions taken by states such as India, which are dismissed as self-serving and/or illiberal. Third, the economic levers available to the more affluent states, in particular, the United States, and the formal criteria for participation in the global economic order (notably, admission to the World Trade Organization) have made many states much more likely to accede to "lobbying" from affluent states. Fourth, non-formalist, open-textured theories of international law have come into their own, such as the contextual and process-oriented approaches associated with the "New Haven School."[2] The congeniality of such theories of international law has developed partly for reasons that are internal to discourse in the scholarly community of international law and international relations and partly because these theories fit better with the agendas of the actors described in the above sentences.

Against this backdrop, the purpose of this article is to relate this evolution of an implicit-authorization rationale to comments recently made in a keynote speech by Lloyd Axworthy about the decision-making process in which he participated as then-Minister for Foreign Affairs for Canada during the Kosovo crisis.[3] Axworthy noted how Canada's Department of Foreign Affairs and International Trade (DFAIT) considered whether, at the point at which NATO military intervention was imminent, authority to intervene could be interpretively distilled from the existing body of Kosovo-related Security Council resolutions. He noted that he and his advisors considered that these resolutions were indeed not sufficient. Accordingly, Canada gave its consent to the military initiatives of NATO, having arrived at the view that such use of force was illegal under the current state of international law. I agree with this conclusion and also respect the fact that Canada more or less decided that the issue of intervention over Kosovo was, therefore, one of compelling moral justification for acting unlawfully. The tragic choice faced by former Foreign Minister Axworthy has

[2] For a classic and accessible introduction to this approach, see Michael Reisman, "International Lawmaking: A Process of Communication" (1981) 75 Proceedings of the American Society of International Law 101.

[3] Lloyd Axworthy, "Keynote Speech" ("Think Canada" Conference on Issues for the Twenty-First Century: Think Peace and Security, Tokyo, Japan, April 17, 2001) [unpublished].

clearly contributed to a real concern on his part, as well as on the part of other leading politicians, such as the minister of foreign affairs of the Netherlands, to see the legal framework changed so as to eventually secure recognition of the power, even the duty, to intervene in situations of extreme humanitarian necessity.[4]

What I would like to suggest is that the Canadian government's inquiry — as to whether authority could be read into the existing complex of Security Council resolutions — is itself significant because of its apparent willingness to entertain the possibility that express authorization may not in all circumstances be necessary. Despite the highly dangerous dimensions of such a theory — a theory that, I would note, is embraced by the United States and to some extent by the United Kingdom — it is worth considering whether *evolving re-interpretation* may not be the preferable way to think about accommodating humanitarian intervention to the greatest extent possible within the UN Charter itself, by resolutely insisting lawfulness *does* require Security Council authorization and, at the same time, being more flexible in determining what constitutes authorization. In other words, can and should the complex of words and conduct of Security Council members and closely related actors, such as the Secretary-General, sometimes be reasonably interpreted as clearly welcoming and, to that extent, authorizing intervention despite the failure to adopt a binding resolution that explicitly says so?

Before moving to the heart of my argument, I feel compelled to say that I do have profound misgivings about the process of Charter re-interpretation as it is currently evolving due to the overbearing role of the United States, and of the West in general, and due to the relative lack of critical self-awareness of many states that their silence and pragmatic acquiescence is feeding into a normative realignment of Charter peace and security law. Greater transparency and less manipulation is needed in order for the process I am about to describe to be something that I would feel comfortable treating as a legitimate form of evolutionary constitutional reform. However, that said, I do see what is starting to happen as being a more sophisticated way of understanding the relationship

---

[4] See Lloyd Axworthy, Minister of Foreign Affairs of Canada, "Human Rights and Humanitarian Intervention: Notes for an Address (2000/29)" (Washington, DC, June 16, 2000) [unpublished]; Jozias van Aartsen, Foreign Minister of the Netherlands, "Opening Remarks," in International Peace Academy, "*Humanitarian Action: International Peace Academy Report*," report of a Conference (New York: International Peace Academy, 2000), Annex II, at 12.

of legality and morality in global governance on peace and security issues than an approach that views things in either one of two other ways: (1) an approach that sees legality as a static question of reading the Charter text textually and, as a corollary, formal Charter amendment as the only way to create greater responsiveness of the international community to humanitarian crises around the world; or (2) an approach that pushes us to view the ethics of intervention as being about either moral breaches of constitutional (Charter) law or as being about the endorsement of a theory of exceptionalism whereby the world's leading military power simply asserts the power to advance the purposes of a "just" world order as it sees fit when it sees fit, while denying that this power is a general legal permission for other states, notably regional powers such as India, Brazil, Russia, China, Indonesia, or Nigeria, to do the same.[5]

Having lodged this major caveat, I nonetheless view the justificatory process surrounding Kosovo and also Iraq as a process that can be provisionally embraced as an opportunity to channel our energies towards a more *collectivist* process of re-interpreting the Charter in a way that stands a chance of attracting a sufficiently general consensus — a consensus that is far from existing at the moment. In this respect, while I will not have time to elaborate, it is worth outlining at this stage how a variety of kinds of collaborations might provide a process-oriented basis for harmonizing law, politics, and morality. Such collaborative processes, first of all, help to get us as close to legality as possible by promoting overarching legal values through engagement in collective decision-making, which may not satisfy the precise legal-formal requirements of the Charter but which, nonetheless, adheres quite closely to its spirit. Second, quite apart from rubbing shoulders with legality, collectivist consensus-seeking processes necessarily involve putting a premium on persuasion and a corresponding merger of self-interest with a broader consensus on the general interest to be served by advocated courses of action. Related to this moral benefit, such processes also help to mitigate the potential for abuse and thus help increase the legitimacy portion of a course of action to the extent that external observers can feel reasonably confident that a decision was not taken as a pure assertion of power. Third, the foregoing benefits interact with questions of political effectiveness.

[5] On US normative exceptionalism, see, on the academic front, Michael Glennon, "American Hegemony in an Unplanned World Order" (2000) 5 Journal of Conflict and Security Law 3; and, on the journalistic front, Christopher Hitchens, "Rogue Nation U.S.A.," *Mother Jones*, May/June 2001, at 32.

Widespread support enhances the credibility of collective resolve to act forcefully, which enhances individual diplomatic efforts — for example, by allowing diplomatic actors (including the Secretary-General) to *warn* offending regimes about the need to change their conduct without directly *threatening* them. Credibility of the resolve to act at the international level is further enhanced to the extent that the collective processes of decision-making help deepen political will at the domestic level and lessen the chances that electorally sensitive governments will be fickle in the strength and longevity of their support for forceful measures as a result of the waxing and waning of the tolerance of the domestic electorate for an involvement in foreign military action.

These introductory comments in mind, I now proceed to a core example of the process of Charter interpretation as it has occurred during the 1990s with respect to Iraq. It is not claimed that the use of military force in the Iraq context has been an example of compelling humanitarian necessity (indeed, concomitant use of economic sanctions on Iraq has contributed significantly to a humanitarian disaster in that country) but, rather, that it is an example of more traditional perceptions of necessity because of an extreme security threat.[6]

IRAQ AS PRECURSOR TO KOSOVO

Security Council Resolution 678 authorized states cooperating with Kuwait to use "all necessary means" to force Iraq's withdrawal from Kuwait and also to "restore international peace and security in the area."[7] After Operation Desert Storm succeeded in ousting Iraqi forces from Kuwait, the Security Council adopted Resolution 687.[8] It imposed a cease-fire on all combatants and also established the United Nations Special Commission (UNSCOM), which was

---

[6] I do not wish to deny that the concerns about the production and possible re-use of some weapons of mass destruction by the current, or a future, Iraqi regime does not have a humanitarian component. It clearly does. The goal of preventing a capacity to use such weapons as chemical and bacteriological warheads is clearly a legitimate humanitarian concern from a preventative perspective. The use of the term "weapons of mass destruction" includes mass death.

[7] UN Security Council Resolution 678 (1990), November 29, 1990, text can be accessed online at <http://www.un.org/Docs/scres/1990/678e.pdf> (last visited March 28, 2002).

[8] UN Security Council Resolution 687 (1991), April 3, 1991, text can be accessed online at <http://www.un.org/Docs/scres/1991/687e.pdf> (last visited March 28, 2002).

the United Nations's most ambitious and sophisticated monitoring regime to date. UNSCOM was charged with the mandate of discerning Iraq's continuing weapons of mass destruction (WMD) programs and verifying that its weaponry and weapon-making capacity had been destroyed by Iraq. A comprehensive sanctions regime was also associated with the weapons-inspection regime. The removal of sanctions was the intended prize for Iraq once it had complied with all requirements to eliminate its WMD capacity. In relatively short order, Iraq resisted the UNSCOM inspections regime, employing a gamut of tactics to do so. These tactics included engaging in periodic games of brinkmanship with the United States and the United Kingdom whenever the latter states made clear that they were willing to employ military force as a response to Iraq's non-compliance with Resolution 687. Starting with the United States, a number of states, including Japan, began to advance or quietly accept an interpretive theory that contended that if the inspection requirements of Resolution 687 were "materially breached," then the cease-fire mandated by Resolution 687 could reciprocally be considered by states that had been cooperating with Kuwait as having been suspended.[9] The consequence of this suspension of the requirement to respect the cease-fire would be, according to this theory, that the original Resolution 678 would become applicable again, including, in particular, the authorization to use "all necessary means ... to restore international peace and security in the area." There are all kinds of problems with the plausibility of this interpretive theory of the relationship between Resolutions 687 and 678, not least being the chronological problems of Resolution 678 having envisioned a *restoration* of peace and security. Such a mandate, quite clearly, did not contemplate the *revision* of the *status quo ante* through a comprehensive disarmament program aimed at Iraq.

There is clearly a crucial issue as to whether (and, if so, how) an evolutionary interpretive meaning can be accorded to Resolution 678 so as to render it capable of bouncing back into shape as a consequence of any serious non-compliance with Resolution 687 by Iraq. However, my focus will be on a less-straightforward interpretive evolution within Security Council practice, which has (arguably) transpired despite what initially seemed to be the vocal

[9] This is an argument by analogy with the provisions on material breach of treaties: see Article 60 of the Vienna Convention on the Law of Treaties, January 27, 1969, 1155 U.N.T.S. 331.

resistance of a permanent member of the Security Council to the interpretation in question. My narrative looks at the effect of warnings from the Security Council about the future "serious" or "severest" consequences of continuing non-compliance with Council resolutions. Although the immediate purpose of this upcoming discussion is more sociological than normative, the normative issue raised by my account is profound and warrants highlighting at this point: should the international legal community accept warnings of unspecified consequences from unspecified quarters as being sufficient to authorize states to act militarily in order to force compliance, without having first received any further instructions from the Council? Answering this question will be part of what animates the discussion later in this article when I seek to present a framework for thinking about the role the General Assembly must play in validating claims that implicit authorizations have emerged from the Security Council.

Before proceeding, two preliminary points must be made in order to prepare the reader for the nuanced nature of the normative signalling games in which states engage in the context of negotiating the space between the Charter's multilateral monopoly over the use of force other than in self-defence and the reality of unilateral or oligopolistic judgments being made by states wishing, or simply being willing, to use force to secure (what are presented) as the ends of the international community as a whole. First of all, central to my narrative will be the linguistic acts of two actors — the President of the Security Council and the Secretary-General — who are not expressly accorded an authoritative role with respect to interpreting the meaning of Security Council resolutions, let alone a central one. A key part of the signalling game at stake in the Iraq context has been the relationship between their statements and the formally binding collective acts of the Security Council in the form of resolutions. Second, I have been using the term "warning" to describe the statements emanating from the Security Council, and I will continue to use this term. However, I do so advisedly, because a significant part of the ambiguity surrounding the import of these statements is precisely whether or not they are best characterized as warnings or, instead, as threats. The difference hinges on the relationship between the actor(s) uttering the threat or warning and the actor(s) that are meant to be understood as being prepared to act on that threat or warning should the triggering conditions (indicated in the threat or warning) be met. The actor who utters a threat will be the actor that will make good on the threat, whereas the actor acting on a warning will be different from the actor issuing the warning. If it is tolerably clear that the members of the Security Council at any given time intend the expressions "serious consequences" or "severest consequences" to refer to, or at least to include, military measures (in a manner not dissimilar to how "all necessary means," as used in Resolution 678, is now understood as a term of art for an express authorization to use force), it is by no means clear in which of at least three possible ways the Security Council wishes to be understood. The options are (1) as a threat that the Security Council, seized of the matter, will return to it and subsequently expressly authorize military measures; (2) as a warning that there are some states that will take matters into their own hands and adopt the military option (leaving this as a factual statement with no normative stance being taken towards this eventuality one way or the other); or (3) as a hybrid in which threat and warning join hands in such a way that the signal is that some states will adopt this option *and* that, if this happens, the Council will treat this conduct as lawful. It is the third validating signal that transmits a warning simultaneously as a threat — and, put differently, as an implicit authorization of the Council for states to act as its agent. I now turn to how it is that the combined role — even tag-team performance — of the Security Council president and the Secretary-General may have helped convert a threat of future action by the Security Council (the first signal) and a warning of future action by unspecified states (the second signal) into this third hybrid signal.

In early 1998, Secretary-General Kofi Annan went, on his own initiative, to Baghdad in order to seek concessions from Iraq that would have the effect of avoiding military strikes that were being threatened by the United States in particular. After Annan's return to New York in March 1998 with the United Nations-Iraq Memorandum of Understanding (MOU), many in the United States' foreign policy apparatus were incensed at his intervention, which had made it politically impossible at that time for the United States to go ahead with its military strikes — strikes that were viewed as being necessary in light of a persistent pattern of bad faith noncompliance by Iraq with the UNSCOM regime.[10] To soften the sting, the Security Council adopted Resolution 1154, in which it was stated that the "severest consequences" would result should Iraq

[10] United Nations — Iraq Memorandum of Understanding, February 23, 1998, (1998) 37 I.L.M. 501.

not live up to the MOU that it had just entered into with Secretary-General Annan.[11] The employment of this phrase seemed designed to tap into a discursive precedent that seems to have become instantiated as a linguistic convention in prior Security Council practice *vis-à-vis* Iraq, albeit not within, but rather parallel to, Security Council resolutions — in the form of statements of the president of the Council. Note that, in this regard, the presidency of the Security Council rotates amongst the different member states of the Council, with the president's statements being issued, by commonly accepted practice, only where the president of the Security Council of the time is confident that the statement in question reflects the consensus of the Security Council members.

On at least two occasions prior to 1998, in 1993 and then again in 1997, the Security Council president used similar, while not identical, language when Iraq was warned of "serious consequences" should it continue to fail to comply with Security Council demands for cooperation with UNSCOM.[12] Following the 1993 warning (indeed, only two days later), the United Kingdom, the United States, and France went on to bomb Iraqi targets in southern Iraq.[13] Whether or not any firm consensus had evolved by 1998 amongst the permanent members of the Security Council with respect to at least a *de facto* acquiescence in recourse to military action following a presidential warning of "serious consequences," the aforementioned 1998 warning did seem to represent a qualitative shift in the Council's linguistic signalling practice, since it differed in two significant respects from those of 1993 and 1997 — in both form and content. In terms of form, the 1998 warning was inserted within Security Council Resolution 1154 itself, rather than being articulated at one step removed through the formally non-binding vehicle of presidential notes or statements. As for the

[11] See, UN Security Council Resolution 1154 (1998), March 2, 1998, at para. 3, text can be accessed online at <http://www.un.org/Docs/scres/1998/sres1154.htm> (last visited March 28, 2002): "The Security Council ... [s]tresses that compliance ... is necessary for the implementation of resolution 687 (1991), but that any violation would have severest consequences for Iraq."

[12] *Note by the President of the Security Council*, UN Doc. S/25091 (1993). In 1997, the president said: "The Security Council warns of the serious consequences of Iraq's failure to comply immediately and fully." *Statement of the President of the Security Council*, UN Doc. S/PRST/1997/49, October 29, 1997, text can be accessed online at <http://www.un.org/Docs/sc/statements/1997/prst9749.htm> (last visited 28 March 2002).

[13] See Christine Gray, "After the Ceasefire: Iraq, the Security Council and the Use of Force" (1994) 65 British Yearbook of International Law 135 at 154, 167.

content of the warning, the expression "severest consequences" is obviously an order of magnitude beyond "serious consequences." Combining form and substance, an external observer would be forgiven for interpreting there to have been a deeper level of collective resolve in 1998: if warnings of "serious consequences" outside the body of a Security Council resolution could be understood (that is, in the 1993 and 1997 precedents) as an implicit signal by the Security Council that force may be used, then "severest" consequences warned — or threatened — within a resolution must *a fortiori* be an even clearer signal: an implicit authorization.

However, in 1998, matters had changed, it would seem. During the debate over the terms of Resolution 1154, China stated emphatically that the warning of "severest consequences" in that resolution would, in China's words, not lead to "automatic authorization of the use of force against Iraq."[14] On the surface of things, it would seem that China knew full well what normative stakes were involved in Resolution 1154's terminology in light of the signalling games of 1993 and 1997, in which it, China, had participated. At this point, the role of soloist in the concerto, which had previously been that of the president, was now taken up by Secretary-General Annan himself. His solo performance in the interpretive tug-of-war over what Resolution 1154 was permitting involved a United States television news appearance. Should Iraq not comply with the MOU he had brokered in early 1998, Annan was asked, would the use of military force require a new Security Council resolution or would Resolution 1154's language be sufficient to allow willing states to take military measures against Iraq? In what were obviously very closely constructed sentences, Annan noted that the United States had consulted broadly throughout the crisis, and this action had resulted in Annan going to Baghdad to seek the MOU. Then, he added the following: "The Russians, the French and Chinese ... resisted [the] idea of automaticity. And therefore, if the United States had to strike, I think some sort of *consultations*

---

[14] For the summary records of China's remarks, see UN Doc. S/PV.3858, 1998, at 14. With respect to the fact that China was reported to have the support of two other permanent members, see John Goshko, "Three on Security Council Oppose 'Automatic Trigger' on Iraq," *Washington Post,* February 28, 1998, at A20: "Diplomatic sources said that France, Russia, China and council members belonging to the Non-Aligned Movement, all of which have opposed military strikes, are insisting that any resolution require further council consideration before force is authorized. The sources said these countries are agreeable to warning Iraq of potential consequences but, as of now, refuse to accede to the idea of an automatic trigger."

with the other members would be required."[15] Some eight months later, in November 1998, the United States, the United Kingdom, and France eventually did decide to use military force on the basis that Iraq had continued to fail to comply with both Resolution 687 and the March 1998 MOU.

For the purposes of the present discussion, what is significant (and needing of more study) is the extent to which these states engaged in consultations with other Security Council members before unleashing their bombing campaign in November 1998. Recall China's own carefully chosen words in the debate over the language of Resolution 1154 — China had objected to an interpretation of the words "severest consequences" that would permit an *automatic* recourse to force — and Secretary-General Annan had glossed over that objection by seemingly suggesting that "consultations" would satisfy China's concerns with automaticity. To the extent that the United States, the United Kingdom, and France did consult prior to their strike in November 1998, did they do so in the belief that at some level China had sent a normative signal that it understood that force could result without a subsequent, fresh resolution by virtue of its own careful choice of words during the debates over Resolution 1154 and its subsequent lack of objection — or, at least, objection on the public record — to the Secretary-General's interpretive spin broadcast on US television, which was widely reported thereafter?

What, precisely, is the relevance of the foregoing narrative? At least four points can be made. First of all, as I hope has emerged with some clarity from the discussion itself, a Security Council-oriented practice of engaging in layered signalling games blurs with the creation of real-world, shared understandings on how to go about interpreting Security Council resolutions in which the implicit authorization of the use of force (for example, in Resolution 1154) is at stake. Second, as a corollary to the first point, the handling of Iraq suggests how the frames of reference within which Security Council resolutions are drafted are constantly evolving. Another way of putting this point is to say that baseline understandings evolve in such a way that formulations that are initially viewed as being opaque by external viewers and as being coded by internal

---

[15] See "Annan: U.S. Must Consult before Attacking Iraq," remarks of the Secretary-General, which can be accessed online at <http://www.cnn.com/WORLD/9803/08/iraq.wrap/index.html> (last visited March 28, 2002) [emphasis added]. The remarks of the Secretary-General were made on ABC News, *This Week* (ABC television broadcast, March 8, 1998).

participants come to take on a clarity. For example, the search for implicit authorization of the use of force can evolve from a broad contextual inquiry into a simple semantic exercise of identifying a key phrase that has been invested with particular meaning at some point in time. So, just as "all necessary means" (recall Resolution 678) is now an accepted code for Security Council authorization of military force and, as such, is virtually an "express" authorization within the language community in question, the practice of warning of "serious consequences" is perhaps becoming generally understood by the permanent members of the Security Council to be a warning — or, in line with the earlier discussion, a hybrid warning-threat — that future military action may occur without a subsequent Security Council resolution expressly authorizing this action. Measured against the conventions of drafting legal instruments, the lawyer concludes that, when the Security Council goes on to use the same language again, this use is intentional and interpreters are meant to understand the words in the new case as they have come to be understood in light of previous practice.

Third, Security Council resolutions are framed not only by the Council's own practice but also by the Charter itself and by all of the presumptions of interpretation that one can infer from it. For example, two American scholars in a recently co-authored article conclude that the interaction of the Charter's text and overarching policy considerations yield an interpretive rule that Security Council authorizations of force must be explicit (or, at the very least, clear) and not implicit.[16] Jules Lobel and Michael Ratner start with two fundamental Charter values, the peaceful settlement of disputes and the principle that force is to be used "in the interest of and under the control of the international community." From these twin values, they argue that an overriding policy must be viewed as being part of Chapter VII, namely that the Security Council must retain "strict control" over the initiation, duration, and objectives of force. If the argument for this policy is indeed a sound one, then specific consequences follow with respect to interpreting the meaning of Security Council resolutions and, what amounts to the same thing, with respect to the language that the drafters of the Security Council resolution must use if they seek to secure certain results. Two such consequences, from Lobel and Ratner's perspective, are,

---

[16] Jules Lobel and Michael Ratner, "Bypassing the Security Council: Ambiguous Authorizations to Use Force, Cease-Fires and the Iraqi Inspection Regime" (1999) 93 American Journal of International Law 124.

again, that there is a requirement of explicit Security Council authorization of force and also that, in some grey zone between the explicit and the implicit, ambiguous aspects of authorization should be narrowly construed.[17] The broader point that emerges is that there is a symbiotic link between the premises and conventions governing the interpretation of Security Council resolutions and the interpretation of the Charter itself. As such, what we may be witnessing with the various levels of collaboration in coded silences and half-hearted resistance is a simultaneous re-interpretation of the Charter's premises through a Security Council practice that has begun to condone, even embrace, the possibility of treating Security Council resolutions as containing implicit authorizations to use force.

The fourth and final point of relevance that emerges from the Iraq example is that it helps us understand why a focus on customary international law as a locus for new law on humanitarian intervention may make little sense. Given its special "constitutional" status, the Charter cannot be contradicted by customary international law, unless the customary norm is of that very special kind known as *jus cogens*. At most, custom can develop in a subject area covered by the Charter only in a way that complements the Charter or, conceivably, in a way that conflicts with some Charter values if the Charter can be reasonably understood as having created a permissive gap in the text within which custom is to be permitted to develop.[18] The essential point is that the Charter and custom exist in the shadow of each other, each conditioning the other, such that references to the customary law on humanitarian intervention should be more self-consciously understood as being really about interpretive practice that is related to the Charter.[19] It makes little

---

[17] *Ibid.* at 219.

[18] It is this latter move that some scholars and states attempt to make when they argue that Article 51 of the Charter should be viewed as permissive and not preclusionary in terms of the circumstances that generate a right of self-defence. Article 51 states that self-defence is triggered if "an armed attack occurs." There are those who make the point that this language should not be read as if it says "if and only if an armed attack occurs." In this way, these jurists seek to find open space in the customary realm for the law of self-defence to develop as custom.

[19] While being at pains to emphasize custom exists apart from the Charter, the International Court of Justice could, nonetheless, be read as having said something similar in *Military Activities in and against Nicaragua Case (Nicaragua v. United States of America)*, [1986] I.C.J. Rep. 14 at para. 181: "However, so far from having constituted a marked departure from a customary international law which still exists unmodified, the Charter gave expression in this field to principles

sense *conceptually* to say that custom evolves separately from an interpretation of powers and duties within the Charter itself. Yet also, from a *policy perspective,* one must prefer evolutionary interpretations of a constitutional instrument to an approach that effectively creates a gap in the applicability of the constitution precisely in the fields in which one would expect it to apply with full force. Thus, humanitarian intervention is best seen either as something condemned to be morality's rebuke to legality in situations where necessary action is not forthcoming because of Security Council reticence or internal blockage or, instead, as a practice in quest of lawfulness through the complex interpretive interaction of words and conduct with the Charter text — not as something that exists in a Charter-separate "customary" world. Given that it is extremely unlikely that a formal Charter amendment can occur any time soon, the pressure to embrace intervention interpretively as part of an evolution of the meaning of the Charter itself is understandably great. The burden of my account of some of the interpretive controversies concerning the Iraq situation and the discussion of the normative significance of those narratives has been to demonstrate that there is good evidence that the interpretive re-fashioning of the Charter's law on peace and security is being pursued with some vigour by key actors, who are not only states such as the United States and the United Kingdom but also a particularly charismatic and influential Secretary-General.

UN Charter and Evolutions in Meaning

It is by now trite law that evolutionary meanings *are* possible both as a matter of general international treaty law and also as an accepted way of viewing the capacity of the UN Charter to have prevailing meanings revised in light of some form of moving consensus. Let us speak of "interpretive evolutions" as the general category for meanings that evolve either simply by clarification (where there is an initial period in which ambiguity produces disagreement and, thus, no consensus meaning, but where consensus on meaning eventually clarifies) or by a radical re-reading of the text.

---

already present in customary international law, and that law has in the subsequent four decades developed under the influence of the Charter, to such an extent that a number of rules contained in the Charter have acquired a status independent of it. The essential consideration is that both the Charter and the customary international law flow from a common fundamental principle outlawing the use of force in international relations."

By way of contrast, let us use the term "legislative interpretations" to refer to interpretive evolutions in meaning that are closer to the latter end of the spectrum — that is, interpretations in which there is an element of re-writing the text under the formal guise of re-reading it (either by implying rules and principles into the text or by consciously reading words in a way that accords neither with their ordinary meaning nor with what is commonly understood to have been their original meaning at the time of adoption of the text).

However radical an interpretive evolution in meaning may be, the key point is that the evolution is inextricably connected to the practice of argument in which text is brought to bear on concrete situations in such a way that, with time, certain interpretive arguments prevail. An oft-given example of interpretive evolution arising through argumentative practice in the Charter context is that of Article 27(3).[20] This provision sets out the voting requirements for a Security Council resolution to be adopted; such adoption is in turn necessary for the Security Council to bind states to its will. One of the conditions for a resolution to be adopted is that nine "affirmative" votes are needed and also that the "concurring" votes of all five permanent members are required. Two issues have arisen. First of all, can an abstention by a permanent member count as a "concurring vote"? Second and more radically, can the requirement of the "concurring votes of the permanent members" be satisfied when a permanent member is absent from the vote and, thus, casts no vote at all?

With respect to the abstention-as-concurring issue, interpretive controversy has been relatively mild. With some fits and starts, ambiguities in both the text and the negotiating record of Article 27(3) were resolved through consistent practice beginning as early as 1946.[21] Certainly, abstentions are now universally understood

---

[20] "Decisions of the Security Council on all other [non-procedural] matters shall be made by an affirmative vote of nine members including concurring votes of the permanent members; provided that, in decisions under Chapter VI, and under paragraph 3 of Article 52, a party to a dispute shall abstain from voting." Article 27(3) of the Charter, *supra* note 1.

[21] Lobel and Ratner, *supra* note 16 at 135, note 42. See also Constantin Stavropoulos, "The Practice of Voluntary Abstentions by Permanent Members of the Security Council under Article 27, Paragraph 3, of the Charter of the United Nations" (1967) 61 American Journal of International Law 737, notably at the article's final sentence at 752: "That practice [of voluntary abstentions counting as concurring votes] has been acquiesced in by other Members of the Organization, and can now be considered a firm part of the constitutional law of the United Nations."

to count as concurring votes. Indeed, China has, throughout the 1990s, quite consistently practised a policy of abstaining in many contexts in which it is uncomfortable with the military interventionism being proposed by the Security Council.[22] In this way, China's concur-but-do-not-affirm policy has permitted a form of consensus to develop that has permitted the Security Council to become exceptionally active in a number of crises during the 1990s.

With respect to the absence-as-concurring issue, one crisis — the Korean peninsula crisis of 1950 — has come to be taken as interpretively constitutive by many commentators and most, if not all, states. In protest of the recognition of the nationalist Taiwan-based regime, which was being treated as the government of China for purposes of representation in the United Nations, the Soviet Union had been boycotting the Council for some five months when North Korea invaded South Korea.[23] In the absence of the Soviet delegate, the Security Council adopted a series of four recommendatory resolutions that, in effect, counselled states to assist South Korea in its self-defence and, then, for such states wishing to give such assistance, to place their forces and equipment under the unified command of the United States. On one account, a large percentage of the members of the United Nations of the day (some 53 per cent) sent messages of support for the Security Council initiative.[24] The Soviet Union's position was that these resolutions were *ultra vires* because of the Soviet Union's failure to concur due to its absence. This view was *de facto* overridden by the generality of support for the Council combined with the passage of time, such that this general interpretation took on a *de jure* life as the governing interpretation on the question of absence within Article 27(3). I say "the generality of support" because the mechanism by which this interpretation was validated should be viewed as one of a general, as opposed to universal, recognition of the interpretive evolution in question. In

---

[22] "On April 4, 1946, Australia was the first non-permanent member, and on April 9, 1947, the United Kingdom was the first permanent member, not to take part in a vote of the Security Council. This practice, which has been followed by other permanent members of the Security Council, has been used most frequently by the People's Republic of China." Bruno Simma and Stefan Brunner, "Article 27," in Bruno Simma, ed., *The Charter of the United Nations: A Commentary* (New York: Oxford University Press, 1994) 433 at 453.

[23] Myres McDougal and Richard N. Gardner, "The Veto and the Charter: An Interpretation for Survival?" (1951) 60 Yale Law Journal 258 at 259.

[24] *Ibid.*

contrast to the abstention-as-concurring issue, it would be obfuscation in the absence-as-concurring context to speak of the acquiescence of states as having been the validating mechanism without
specifying that one key interested actor did not acquiesce. Thus, an
interpretation evolved rather as customary norms evolve — with
general and widespread support but without the need for all interested actors to be participating in the practice that produces the
normative shift (even a key actor in the context, which in this
case was a permanent member on an issue crucial to its special
place in the UN system).

The Article 27(3) example falls closer to the end of interpretive
evolution (that is, the clarification of an ambiguity in the Charter
text) than it does to the end of what I have called legislative interpretations. This fact partly accounts for how it is that with time the
Soviet Union's lack of participation in the initial forging of the
interpretation on the absence question has not generally been
treated as being fatal to that interpretation. There is, however,
another major example of interpretive evolution of the Charter
that is significant for our discussion because it involves a clearly
"legislative" interpretation — indeed, some would say it came very
close to an interpretive amendment of the Charter or, less provo-
catively, to an interpretive modification — and it occurred in the
face of vocal resistance from powerful states. The example in question is that of the re-interpretation of the meeting of Chapter XI of
the UN Charter, which is entitled the Declaration Regarding Non-
Self-Governing Territories.

This term — non-self-governing territories — is amongst the
baldest of euphemisms in international legal history, in that it
has served as a code for "colonies." The key point is precisely that
Chapter XI of the Charter makes no express reference to colonization.[25] Apart from the semantic avoidance of calling colonization
for what it is, the text also contains no duty to de-colonize or any
right of a "non-self-governing" people, as a collectivity, to take that
course, including through independence if it wishes. Rather, the
paternalistic and, indeed, racist notion of a sacred trust became
the governing concept according to which the only duty expressly
placed by the Charter on the administering power (the colonizer)
was to attend to the well-being of the populace and to foster the

---

[25] Chapter XI consists of two articles, Articles 73 and 74, neither of which use the
word "colony" or any derivative.

movement of the non-self-governing population towards a capacity for "self-government."[26]

Yet, despite the hurdles of text and power, anti-colonial states (including "pre-states" such as India) and especially newly decolonized states began to use the UN General Assembly as the locus for a normative battle against colonization in which the right of peoples to self-determination was the battle standard. Despite the lack of receptivity in Chapter XI of the Charter to a duty to decolonize — and, indeed, a complete failure to even acknowledge that colonization existed — this coalition of states, with support from civil society, succeeded in having a high-normative resolution of the General Assembly passed that affirmed the right of all peoples to self-determination and listed the right of a people to organize itself into an independent state as one of the choices such a people could make whatever the will of the colonizing power.[27] The 1960 Declaration on Granting Independence to Colonial Countries and Peoples (Colonial Declaration) was increasingly invoked as the authoritative interpretation of the meaning of Chapter XI of the Charter to the point that, in relatively short order, the right of colonized peoples to self-determination and the associated right to become independent were read into the Charter despite the lack of any express recognition of either concept in the text itself.[28]

[26] It is only with respect to a special kind of colony called the "trust territory," which, in effect, were/are colonies of losing powers in both the First and Second World Wars, that the Charter specifically refers to the independence of the peoples of trust territories as a goal, however much it is a hedged goal. The specific mention of independence with respect to this form of territory and its stark absence in relation to the broader category of Chapter XI non-self-governing territories reinforced the textual and background assumptions that the Charter did not intend that colonizing powers be under a duty to de-colonize. See Chapter XII, entitled "International Trusteeship System," Articles 75-85 and notably Article 76, of the Charter, *supra* note 1.

[27] Declaration on Granting Independence to Colonial Countries and Peoples, UN GA Res. 1514 (XV), December 14, 1960 [colloquially known as the Colonial Declaration].

[28] See, for example, W. Ofuatey-Kodjoe, "Chapter Seven: Self-Determination," in Oscar Schachter and Christopher Joyner, eds., *United Nations Legal Order*, vol. 2 (New York: Cambridge University Press, 1995) 349 at 350: "Still others have argued that the principle of self-determination has evolved into a legal right by virtue of UN practice. For instance, considering the Declaration on the Granting of Independence to Colonial Countries and Peoples, Rosalyn Higgins arrived at the conclusion that 'that Declaration, taken together with seventeen years of evolving practice by the United Nations organs, provide ample evidence that there now exists a legal right of self-determination.'"

Institutions evolved to push this normative understanding and to put colonizing states under a spotlight. Most notable was the Decolonization Committee, which was (and, indeed, continues to be) in charge of identifying those peoples who are to be considered non-self-governing and to oversee the process of decolonization, usually through a UN-supervised vote on political status. Thus, we see an example of a virtual constitutional amendment to the Charter in an area of high political salience and against the wishes of very powerful actors — a phenomenon that occurred by way of an interpretive strategy that harnessed the normative force of the General Assembly by way of its capacity to adopt special resolutions called declarations. An important element of the story is that the interaction between the General Assemby's initial and subsequent pronouncements on the decolonization question and the Charter text occurred in a context in which the Charter itself expressly states that, other than for certain matters internal to the workings of the UN, General Assembly resolutions are recommendatory only. That being the case, the way in which Chapter XI came to be rewritten highlights the sterility of thinking that embraces a rigid dichotomy between binding and non-binding legal effect and obscures the reality that legality operates as much in degrees as in an off/on fashion, especially in international relations.

The decolonization example further gives rise to the following important points. First of all, the initial resistance of colonizing states to some kind of duty to decolonize did not last all that long once the anti-colonial coalition had succeeded in having the Colonial Declaration adopted in the face of resistance from a clutch of states. As such, we can see that interpretive change need not be initiated with all parties onboard. Nor, however, can it be imposed by some interested parties without having eventually achieved some threshold of acquiescence on the part of those inclined to object to the legal development. In tandem with the notion of acquiescence, it is helpful to think in terms of some kind of requirement of sufficiently general recognition by the international community as a whole as a way to think about legal development occurring in a "legislative" fashion — that is, in a fashion that binds all members of the community.

In this respect, the interpretive change to the Charter's law on colonized peoples would seem to have similarities to the way we think about the evolution of customary norms. However, there may be important differences between the extent of acquiescence, or the comprehensiveness of general recognition, with respect to treaty texts compared with customary norms. Whatever the epistemological problems may be, we tend to view these texts as having a certain "objective" existence. We speak of their meaning being "in" that text in light of its purposes and context(s). Of course, we do realize that meaning is something generated by interpretive communities creating shared understandings. In that sense, we are not naïve: texts do not generate their own meaning. So, by "objective," I mean the *idea* of something chronologically prior to the act of interpretation, something legislated through a legitimate process that requires us to imagine it — the text — as having its own integrity and, thus, standing apart from any given state's or societal sector's understanding of it.

All of this discussion suggests the potential for authoritative new interpretations that are not necessarily consensus ones and that, indeed, can be argued to be legally correct in the face of resistance by powerful actors — at least to the extent that other important actors share the same interests as the resisters and have begun to embrace the new legal development (against interest) in such a way that increases the confidence with which we can understand the legal development as reflecting the common interest. In domestic law we are used to interpretations through the courts as creating, through decision, meanings that are accepted as law even if incredibly powerful social and political interests have been resisting such an interpretation. There is no such court-like actor in the international system; the International Court of Justice certainly does not play a parallel role. However, the decolonization example suggests that *political* institutions, most notably the General Assembly, can play a very special role in interpretively rewriting texts even in the face of serious resistance.

From Kosovo to the General Assembly

Having set the scene with some discussion of the normative politics in the Security Council over Iraq and in the General Assembly over decolonization, we now turn to the Kosovo crisis. It is common ground that there was no explicit authorization for NATO's use of force against Yugoslavia in late March 1999. As well, no one would argue that there was any *explicit* retroactive endorsement of NATO's decision to go to war when the terms of the peace settlement with Yugoslavia were incorporated into Security Council Resolution

1244.[29] Yet, the idea of *implicit* authorization in some kind of mutually supportive relationship with *implicit* retroactive validation has

[29] The lack of explicit retroactive endorsement is in considerable contrast to the retroactive response by the Security Council to ECOWAS's 1990 intervention into Liberia. In that context, the Security Council did not go so far as to expressly say that what was an illegal intervention was to be treated as retroactively validated as lawful, but the language of "commend[ing]" the intervention was used. See UN Security Council Resolution 788 (1992), November 19, 1992, text can be accessed online at <http://www.un.org/documents/sc/res/1992/s92r788e.pdf> (last visited March 28, 2002), in which, in operative paragraph 1, the Security Council "[c]ommends ECOWAS for its efforts to restore peace, security and stability in Liberia." In addition, in paragraph 4, the Council uses more implicit, but still significant, language when it "[c]ondemn[ed] the continuing armed attacks against *the peace-keeping forces* of ECOWAS in Liberia" [emphasis added]. There is also an indirect form of "support and endorsement," albeit in the preamble only, when the Council welcomes *the Organization of African Unity's* "endorsement and support" of ECOWAS. By such a double reference to a pan-continental regional organization and a sub-regional organization, the Council may well have wanted to signal that the retroactive validation found in paragraph 1 (recall "commends ECOWAS ...") had something to do with the depth of legitimacy created by two regional organizations acting in concert, a signal even more strongly hinted at by another preambular paragraph "[r]ecalling the provisions of Chapter VIII [Regional Arrangements] of the Charter." As Resolution 788 occurred a full two years after the ECOWAS intervention, evidence of ongoing acquiescence by the Security Council during those two years would help bolster an interpretation that paragraph 1 of Resolution 788 amounts to a retroactive validation removing any unlawfulness that might have otherwise attached to the act of intervention. In this respect, the following observations by Christine Gray in "Chapter Six: Regional Arrangements and the United Nations Collective Security System," in Hazel Fox, ed., *The Changing Constitution of the United Nations* (London: British Institute of International and Comparative Law, 1997) 91 at 104-5, are of interest: "In this [Liberia/ ECOWAS] instance ... it is striking that not much attention was paid in the Security Council even to the question of the legality of the operation under the UN Charter. States in the Security Council debates simply assumed that ECOWAS had legally established peacekeeping forces. The ECOWAS communiqués to the Security Council made no express reference to Chapter VIII but Nigeria spoke of 'ECOMOG as holding the fort for the UN in accordance with Chapter VIII.' The USA and China spoke simply of the peacekeeping forces set up by ECOWAS and appeared to assume their legality."

Some commentators addressing the Kosovo intervention have considered Resolution 788's treatment of the Liberia situation to be a precedent for the possibility of the Security Council sanctioning an intervention after the fact. See, for example, Christopher Greenwood, "International Law and the NATO Intervention in Kosovo" (2000) 49 International and Comparative Law Quarterly 926 at 929. This point is fine as far as it goes — and indeed this is an important benchmark against which future Security Council resolutions do indeed need to be interpreted — but the simple fact of a post-intervention Security Council

some support as the way that we might think about the possible lawfulness of the NATO action. However, those individuals making such an argument have an uphill battle. No single provision in any single Security Council resolution can be pointed to as the textual location for inferring either a prior authorization or an *ex-post facto* validation. Rather, any lawfulness such as may exist can only be "located" in the Security Council texts taken as a whole and viewed over time, not as isolated snapshots.

Now, I would note that I adhere to a set of views about law, including (if not especially) international law, which understands both the identification of law and its articulation in concrete decision-making contexts in terms of a rhetorical enterprise. Rhetorical theories of law and justification emphasize that lawfulness need not be seen as an either/or matter and, even less, as one in which formal textual sources may be invoked to the exclusion of other relevant considerations that possess various degrees of normative weight in argument. Legal justification becomes a matter of the degree of persuasiveness of an overall argument, in which a multiplicity of interconnected individual arguments are composed into some harmonious whole and in which the cumulative persuasive force of the totality of arguments is assessed in terms of the aesthetics of the ensemble. Such an assessment includes both formal properties of coherence in argument and the receptivity of particular audiences to particular kinds of arguments or combinations thereof. From this standpoint, shared, or at least compatible, premises play a crucial role in linking diverse arguments and contributing to their combined force.[30]

---

resolution seeking to deal with the results of an intervention does not in itself amount to the support and endorsement of the intervention itself. Absent something explicit along the lines of what the Security Council said about the Liberia context, the Council must be taken only to be dealing with the aftermath of a war in the best fashion that it can, as it would deal with any war, however illegally initiated.

[30] The kind of premises to which I refer include understandings about the *prima facie* legal standards in play, about the facts, about the nature and function of the law, and of the particular decision-making institution called upon to act, about systemic background values that cocoon legal reasoning, about the balance between textual, contextual, and instrumental arguments in one's approach to interpretation, and so on. For an account of how political and moral discourses can insinuate themselves into the realm of legal rhetoric in the use of force context, see Craig Scott, "Grenada, Nicaragua, and Panama: Tracking Force-for-Democracy Discourse in the 1980s," in Yves LeBouthillier, Donald McRae, and Donat Pharand, eds., *Selected Papers in International Law: Contribution*

What, then, have been the main arguments that some advocates of the lawfulness of the NATO intervention have put forward — albeit with each advocate emphasizing specific arguments more than others and combining them in different ways?[31] First of all, many start with the fact that the Security Council had indeed taken cognisance of the escalating humanitarian crisis in Kosovo and had adopted Chapter VII resolutions that made clear that Yugoslavia was under a legal duty to remedy the situation. Second, prior to March 1999, a strategy of threatening force had already been used by NATO. Most notably, the United States diplomatic envoy, Richard Holbrooke, had gone to Belgrade in the fall of 1998 in order to threaten Slobodan Milosevic with military force should he fail to agree to a cessation of violence in Kosovo. Milosevic did indeed agree to such cessation and also to the insertion of observers from the Organization for Security and Cooperation in Europe. Security Council Resolution 1203 of October 1998 did not condemn the threat of force that had produced this agreement but, rather, welcomed the agreement secured with the assistance of threats by "endorsing and supporting" the agreement.[32] This

---

of the Canadian Council of International Law (The Hague, London, Boston: Kluwer Law International, 1999) 169 at 195-200.

[31] These have been distilled and amalgamated from, *inter alia*, the accounts in the following articles: Bruno Simma, "NATO, the UN and the Use of Force: Legal Aspects" (1999) 10 European Journal of International Law 1; Ian Brownlie and C.J. Apperley, "Kosovo Crisis Inquiry: Memorandum on the International Law Aspects" (2000) 49 International and Comparative Law Quarterly 878 and 910; Christine Chinkin, "The Legality of NATO's Action in the Former Republic of Yugoslavia (FRY) under International Law" (2000) 49 International and Comparative Law Quarterly 345; Greenwood, *supra* note 29; Vaughan Lowe, "International Legal Issues Arising in the Kosovo Crisis" (2000) 49 International and Comparative Law Quarterly 358; Ruth Wedgwood, "NATO's Campaign in Yugoslavia" (1999) 93 American Journal of International Law 828; Louis Henkin, "Kosovo and the Law of 'Humanitarian Intervention'" (1999) 93 American Journal of International Law 389; Richard Falk, "Kosovo, World Order, and the Future of International Law" (1999) 93 American Journal of International Law 412; and Michael Reisman, "Kosovo's Antinomies" (1999) 93 American Journal of International Law 425; Foreign Affairs Committee, House of Commons, United Kingdom, *Fourth Report of the House of Commons Foreign Affairs Committee* (June 7, 2000), Doc. HC28-I, text can be accessed online at <http://www.fas.org/man/dod-101/ops/2000/2802/index.html> (last visited March 28, 2002).

[32] UN Security Council Resolution 1203 (1998), October 24, 1998 at para. 1, text can be accessed online at <http://www.un.org/Docs/scres/1998/sres1203. htm> (last visited March 28, 2002): "Endorses and supports the agreements

technique was, of course, was the exact formulation used in 1991 with respect to actual, as opposed to threatened, military intrusion into Liberia by ECOWAS. So, while it remains common ground that the Security Council did not repeat this formulation once NATO had actually intervened and Yugoslavia had then surrendered in the summer of 1999, the Security Council had indeed been willing to adopt a resolution in the fall of 1998 that stood for some kind of acceptance that threats of force may well be tolerated at a certain level by an enthusiastic embrace of results that appear to have only been achievable through such threats. This fact alone suggests a significant potential legislative reinterpretation of the Charter, given that Article 2(4) prohibits, on its face, threats of force and not only the use of force.[33]

Third, as the NATO action against Yugoslavia was underway, Russia tabled a motion before the Security Council that sought to have the NATO states condemned for an illegal initiation of a war. It appears that Russia may have radically miscalculated because that motion was voted down twelve to three. Only China and Namibia joined Russia in voting for its motion. While it is a completely disingenuous argument (that some, especially the United States, have nonetheless attempted) to suggest that this vote alone amounted to a validation of NATO's action, it remains the case that, from a perspective where normativity is a matter of weight, the view of the large majority of the Security Council was not without

---

signed in Belgrade on October 16, 1998 between the Federal Republic of Yugoslavia and the Organization for Security and Cooperation in Europe, and on October 15, 1998 between the Federal Republic of Yugoslavia and NATO, concerning the verification of compliance by the Federal Republic of Yugoslavia and all others concerned in Kosovo with the requirements of its resolution 1199 (1998), and demands the full and prompt implementation of these agreements by the Federal Republic of Yugoslavia."

[33] All of that said, Resolution 1203 does not expressly refer to the means adopted to achieve the agreement with Yugoslavia, so there is still some room to say that the Security Council simply did not address the question of the unlawfulness of any actions by the North Atlantic Treaty Organization [hereinafter NATO] in the lead-up to that October 1998 agreement. As well, some might be inclined to say that the loosening of tolerance for the rule against threatening force in international relations — assuming Resolution 1203 is an example of that loosening — does not in and of itself mean that the same agreement produced as a result of the actual use of force in the same circumstances would have been welcomed in the same fashion. However much diplomats wish for threats of force to be understood as credible threats, there is a qualitative difference between threatening and actually carrying out military action.

significance in the overall calculus of whether there were sufficient reasons to adjudge NATO to have acted lawfully.[34]

Fourth, Secretary-General Kofi Annan once again stepped up to play an important discursive role. On at least one occasion, he as much as said that his view was that the Charter must be sufficiently flexible to allow for the properly motivated uses of force in certain humanitarian crises. In Annan's words, "[i]t is indeed tragic that diplomacy has failed, but there are times when the use of force may be legitimate in the pursuit of peace."[35] While Annan has not exactly been a reticent figure in making public pronouncements on various matters during his tenure as Secretary-General (recall the Iraq example), it is decidedly the case that, when he does, the terms of his public comments are very carefully chosen and formulated. This fact makes the preceding quotation all the more important to take seriously and to parse.

Fifth, the existence of UN Charter Article 53 on regional enforcement may have some relevance in the overall structure of argument. What Article 53 makes clear is that regional organizations are specifically contemplated as a legitimate agency of the United

---

[34] It is important to note here that NATO states may have thought that they had Russia's quasi-consent to use force. Tim Judah in his book *Kosovo, War and Revenge* (New Haven: Yale University Press, 2000) 183-85, describes how the foreign minister of Russia, Igor Ivanov, had said at a meeting with NATO foreign ministers that Russia would veto any resolution brought to the Security Council seeking permission to use force (that is, of the "all necessary means" kind), but that, if the Security Council was avoided entirely, all that Russia would do would be to "make a lot of noise" through a public protest. NATO's legal strategy may have assumed that Russia would not bring the matter to a vote in the way that it actually did and, thus, that there would be no voting record of P-5 opposition. This is all to say that, even as the failed motion by Russia indicates that a majority of the Security Council were opposed to the condemnation of NATO, it simultaneously is an important official record that the intervention did not have the support of two permanent members, China and Russia. It should also be noted in passing that there are several reasons why it was unacceptable for the NATO states to have invested so much meaning — that is, if they sincerely did — in the statements made by Foreign Minister Ivanov on that one occasion; however, elaboration of this point will have to wait until another occasion. See also the discussion in note 40 in this article.

[35] In Judith Miller, "Conflict in the Balkans: The U.N.; The Secretary General Offers Implicit Endorsement of Raids," *New York Times,* March 25, 1999, at A13, Secretary-General Anan is quoted as saying: "I deeply regret that, in spite of all the efforts made by the international community, the Yugoslav authorities have persisted in their rejection of a political settlement, which would have halted the bloodshed in Kosovo and secured an equitable peace for the population there. It is indeed tragic that diplomacy has failed, but there are times when the use of force may be legitimate in the pursuit of peace."

Nations for using force in collective security contexts.[36] Of course, the fact that regional organizations may use force does not mean that they may use force based on their own appreciation of the situation and judgment. As a textual matter, Article 53 is clear that any regional enforcement action requires authorization of the Security Council, unless of course it involves not collective security as such but, rather, an act of collective self-defence. All of that said, however, the presence of Article 53 may suggest that the consensus necessary to produce regional enforcement of the kind carried out by NATO in the Yugoslavia context *may* be an area where *implicit* authorization is more justifiable, such that Security Council resolutions may be construed more flexibly in this context than, for example, if it is a situation of a single hegemonic state (with an ally or two) intervening on its own into another country.[37]

Sixth and finally, the Security Council resolution that inserted KFOR forces into Kosovo after the brokering of the peace agreement with Yugoslavia did not aver to the means by which peace came about, and the aforementioned "support and endorsement" that had occurred with respect to the temporary cease-fire agreement in the fall of 1998 was not repeated.[38] Nonetheless, some

---

[36] Article 53 reads in part: "The Security Council shall, where appropriate, utilize such regional arrangements or agencies for enforcement action under its authority. But no enforcement action shall be taken under regional arrangements or by regional agencies without the authorization of the Security Council." Here, it must of course be noticed that NATO has consistently resisted characterizing itself as a regional organization precisely in order to avoid an overly onerous degree of accountability to the United Nations. To the extent that this is formally the case even if, in substance, NATO is indeed a regional organization, the remaining points to be made with respect to Article 53 should probably be approached more in terms of a close analogy than in terms of a directly applicable argument.

[37] Recall the linkage of the ECOWAS/Liberia precedent to regional enforcement, which is dicussed in note 29 in this article. This loosening of the standard for the interpretive importing of authorization into a Security Council resolution, of course, makes most sense where the intervention at issue is into a member state of the regional organization. This was not the case with respect to the NATO intervention, as Yugoslavia was out of area with respect to NATO's membership. Note also the Cuban missile crisis and the arguments relating to implicit authorization used by the United States, which were widely accepted in the Western Hemisphere at that time. See Abram Chayes, *The Cuban Missile Crisis: International Crises and the Role of Law* (Oxford: Oxford University Press, 1974); Roger K. Smith, "The Legality of Coercive Arms Control" (1994) 19 Yale Journal of International Law 455 at 491-93.

[38] Security Council Resolution 1244 (1999), June 10, 1999, text can be accessed online at <http://www.un.org/Docs/scres/1999/99sc1244.htm> (last visited March 28, 2002).

would contend that the failure to expressly condemn the means used in March 1999 and onward amounts to a form of Security Council acquiescence. As the argument might go, an endorsement of an outcome produced through the use of force triggers a responsibility to expressly condemn the use of force leading to that outcome or to have it understood that the use of force has been accepted. For many obvious reasons, this is a particularly weak argument from a rule-of-law perspective. It amounts to saying that those engaging in unlawful military activity can validate their own behaviour if they happen to be permanent members of the Security Council, by blocking any attempt to have that behaviour condemned when the Security Council attempts to deal with the aftermath of their military incursions. The perversions of this line of reasoning hardly need to be elaborated other than to note that, within the current framework of the Security Council, the failure to achieve the explicit "support and endorsement" of China and Russia is of greater significance for the (un)lawfulness of NATO's action than is the failure of the United States, the United Kingdom, and France to condemn their own actions through the Security Council. It should also be noted that this is a particularly weak form of argument in light of the ECOWAS/Liberia precedent. In that case, an actual military incursion had occurred, and the Security Council *did* use language particularly conducive to validating the incursion and not simply the state of affairs produced by it. So, while the ECOWAS intervention suggests that retroactive validation of some kind does fall within the jurisdictional purview of the Security Council, it undermines, at the same time, the case that any such validation took place in the Kosovo context.

I have already indicated that I am sympathetic to a theory of legal analysis that permits more flexible argumentation than is allowed by a traditional legalistic point of view. However, it is not as if anything goes. The phrase, "it is a matter of interpretation," cannot become shorthand for saying that any interpretation is valid as long as it is put forward with a straight face. Acknowledging that the legal enterprise is more complex than is accepted by many conventional approaches does indeed open up serious dangers — notably that, in a decentralized world order (especially one with a single hyper-power), the powerful may simply come to expect that their assertions carry with them the kernel of their only legality. The emphasis in rhetorical theory on the persuasiveness of an overall argument based on the arrangement of interacting and cumulative reasons cannot be allowed to generate into a crude listing of supporting reasons in the place of sophisticated argumentation, or even a listing of reasons accompanied by some attempt to invoke a quantitative metaphor according to which it is argued that, on balance, the arguments in favour (of legality or illegality) outweigh the arguments against. There must be a web of coherence that, in ideal terms, is persuasive to reasonable observers. And where no arm's-length reasonable observers have a determinative role in pronouncing upon legality, the degree of support for a position from the significant majority of interested actors — and especially from those actors that the legal system has already designated as having a special importance, notably the permanent five members of the Security Council — must be viewed as an important surrogate in terms of identifying which interpretive community must accept an overall argument as being persuasive for this argument also to be recognized as legally valid. A justificatory narrative cannot simply dismiss such factors as what the text appears to say or what counter-interpretations are advanced by non-supportive states. Rather than being seen as an on/off switch, legal authority is indeed best approached as a matter of degree, where neither received understandings of texts' meanings, on the one hand, nor a lack of wide consensus, on the other hand, are absolutely dispositive, *but* where both are still essential factors that have to be accounted for in such a way that a compelling case is made as to why they do not, ultimately, govern the result. For example, the text must at least continue to mean that implicit authorizations based on holistic readings of Security Council resolutions in their discursive context cannot be lightly presumed and that the community at large must at least be persuaded that, as Richard Falk has put it, "diplomatic alternatives to war have ... been fully explored in a sincere and convincing manner."[39] In Kosovo, many states — including many states looking at the matter in good faith — are not convinced that this was the case.[40]

---

[39] Falk, *supra* note 31 at 856.

[40] Here I would draw attention to the significance of one point made by Axworthy in his April 2001 Tokyo speech, *supra* note 3, when he revealed that Canada, during the Kosovo crisis, considered various different ways of trying to engage Russia so as to try to secure Russian agreement on *a different resolution* from one that would simply have authorized NATO states to use "all necessary means" based on NATO's judgment of necessity. Mention was made of the possibility that an economic forum such as the G-8 might have been an avenue to explore, had the right conditions been in place for such an initiative. In this regard, I would note that it does not take great imagination to conclude that Russia may

However, for present purposes, I will leave one counterfactual (that of whether or not Russia could have been successfully engaged) in order to turn to another counterfactual, namely whether we would now be faced with a different interpretive terrain if NATO had gone to the General Assembly in order to attempt to secure a Uniting for Peace Resolution.[41] The best consideration of this issue is probably found in the detailed report of the United Kingdom Parliament's Foreign Affairs Committee.[42] In this report, it is stated that the Foreign and Commonwealth Office (FCO) of the United Kingdom had done a sounding and felt that they would not have been able to get the two-thirds majority needed for the adoption of a Uniting for Peace Resolution. As I will soon refer to the Uniting for Peace Resolution as part of the way forward, it is important at this juncture to understand that I am not assuming that the General Assembly has authority by virtue of the Uniting for Peace Resolution to authorize a military intervention that is not otherwise lawful on a legal basis, such as the right of self-defence or the consent of the relevant state parties.[43] However, I am assuming that the

---

well have accepted that some intervention could be justified if it was centred on providing significant military support to the on-site Organization for Security and Cooperation in Europe observers on the ground in Kosovo as a result of the Fall 1998 agreement between NATO and Slobodan Milosevic. If Russia also had been content with some arrangement that would have involved itself in the military contingents, it is not at all unlikely that China would have followed its consistent practice of abstaining. In this way, a very different resolution might have gone forward in the Security Council as compared to the sort that Russian Foreign Minister Ivanov warned would be vetoed by Russia if brought before the council — in other words, a resolution that would indeed have authorized the use of force against Yugoslavia's will but in a way far different from the full-blown air campaign that NATO opted for. I have strong views on the failure to have fully pursued what might be called "the Russia option," but, as with the earlier footnoted discussion of the significance of Ivanov's role, elaboration of these views will need to be put aside for another occasion; see discussion in note 34 in this article.

[41] Uniting for Peace Resolution, UN GA Res/337A, UNGAOR, 5th Sess., Supp. No. 20, at 10, UN Doc. A/1775, 1951.

[42] Foreign Affairs Committee, *supra* note 31.

[43] Note that, because the Uniting for Peace Resolution foresees only a *recommendation* of action by the General Assembly, consistent with its powers under Article 10 of the Charter, it is misleading to say the General Assembly authorizes the intervention itself; rather, what it authorizes to binding legal effect are the expenses associated with a military operation that it has recommended come into being. In terms of the observation, this "authorization" is limited to interventions that would otherwise be lawful if states organized themselves outside the auspices of the United Nations. The International Court of Justice in *Certain*

General Assembly may *recommend* enforcement action going beyond self-defence or invitation situations even if it could not go on to authorize expenses to support such action (were states to act on the recommendation).[44] Only if other bases for intervention evolve,

---

Expenses of the United Nations, [1962] I.C.J. Rep. 151 (Advisory Opinion) determined that financial levies on UN members to cover UN expenses arising from two peacekeeping operations (one in the Congo and one in the Middle East) were within the General Assembly jurisdiction. However, these missions were within the purview of states to have organized on their own due to the consent of the relevant actors. Similarly, once the Soviet Union returned to the Security Council and began to veto further Council resolutions on the Korean conflict, the General Assembly called on states to aid the UN Supreme Command, but, in this case, the title for intervention was one that states, again, could have invoked without UN authorization, namely, collective self-defence. (It was the Korean conflict that led both to the adoption of the Uniting for Peace Resolution and its first invocation.) This is all to say that, quite apart from the binding force of any Uniting for Peace initiative, the General Assembly has never, to the knowledge of this writer, purported to use the resolution as a way to authorize or order what the Charter assigns as the Security Council's function: enforcement action that cannot be justified by either self-defence or invitation.

[44] Kay Hailbronner and Ekhart Klein, "Article 10," in Bruno Simma, ed., *The Charter of the United Nations: A Commentary* (Oxford: Oxford, University Press, 1994) 227, share this view:

From [the reasoning of the ICJ in *Certain Expenses of the United Nations*] ... it remains unclear whether recommendations of the GA can also include the adoption of enforcement measures. Consideration of the fundamental division of functions between the SC and the GA, and also the practice of the organization, support the interpretation that the authority of the GA is only limited ... when the GA is of the opinion that binding enforcement measures according to Chapter VII of the Charter, for which the SC alone is responsible, are to be decided upon.

There is a decisive difference between the recommendation of enforcement actions, and the actual taking of such measures. This is illustrated by the formal definition of the term "enforcement," according to which the existence of an "enforcement action" is not determined by the character of the action itself but by the binding nature of the measure taken. Therefore a non-binding recommendation is not to be considered "action," so that the GA is not prevented ... from recommending coercive measures. This norm only recalls the fact that the GA shall not take any enforcement measures binding on all member states (at 233).

Such valid recommendations of "coercive measures" would function in effect as recommendations to the Security Council because states would not be able to invoke General Assembly authority as a ground of lawfulness should they act on the General Assembly's recommendation. To the extent that the General Assembly recommends intervention to states outside the self-defence and consent bases for intervention, then it is recommending unlawful conduct. Any subsequent levies to pay for UN expenses related to unlawful uses of force would have to be seen as *ultra vires* the General Assembly.

which do not require Security Council approval (for example, a free-standing power of humanitarian intervention), could the General Assembly piggyback on that lawfulness to both recommend such action and to go on to authorize expenses to support a UN operation that would result from states acting on the recommendation.

So, what is the significance of going to the General Assembly if the starting point is that the Security Council currently retains the only legal power to authorize humanitarian intervention and if Uniting for Peace Resolutions of the General Assembly are, in formal terms, simply recommendations? The starting point must be open acknowledgment that it is a form of interpretive amendment of the Charter that is at stake in seeking to make it lawful for states to intervene in other countries for humanitarian reasons, in limited circumstances, and without express Security Council authorization. As such, the General Assembly is surely as important a forum as any in terms of helping to nudge along a new authoritative consensus about what its governing text — the Charter — should mean. This, after all, was exactly the role that the General Assembly played with respect to the previously described interpretive amendments to the Charter with respect to decolonization, to which I will return again shortly.

Hence, putting aside the question of the degree of bindingness of General Assembly resolutions, the central issue is one of finding *implicit* Security Council authorization by seeking far wider and representative consensus through General Assembly pronouncements than occurs when all of the interpretive analysis focuses on the words and conduct of fifteen Security Council members — and, most notably, the five permanent members — that take place as some kind of shadow dance with the UN Secretary-General and whomever, and whichever state, happens to be the president of the Council. With respect to the question of the degree of legal force attached to the envisaged General Assembly pronouncements, bindingness is not the pivotal question in a more open-ended framework in which what matters is the cumulative persuasiveness of multiple arguments. The normative value of a specific argument must be appreciated differently where any given argument is not being relied upon as the single and sole source of legal validity. In this respect, it is telling, if only in terms of the language used, that the FCO official testifying to the United Kingdom's Parliamentary Foreign Affairs Committee did acknowledge that "a resolution of the General Assembly would have been *particularly persuasive* [even though] the U.N. Charter still specified that military action required

Security Council endorsement."[45] That said, it also bears remarking that the same FCO official went on to tell the committee that the voting pattern of fifteen Security Council members may have been more significant than a two-thirds General Assembly vote would have been. He said: "[But] in some ways a bare two-thirds majority would have been less persuasive than the majority (of twelve to three) actually secured in the Security Council on 26 March 1999," when Russia unsuccessfully proposed a resolution condemning the start of the NATO bombing.[46]

The contrast drawn by the FCO official warrants further comment. It reveals just how problematic is any conclusion that we can interpret the Security Council to have implicitly authorized or endorsed NATO intervention in the Kosovo context. Was the FCO official engaging in a crude quantitative comparison and concluding that the defeat of the Russia motion by 80 per cent in a vote of fifteen states was normatively more significant than a vote of 67 per cent of approximately 190 states would have been? Keep in mind that the issue in this case is one that goes to the heart of a structural reinterpretation of the central constitutional text of the global legal order. It also points to a broader issue of legitimacy in the evolving process of reinterpreting the Charter. In this regard, I return now to the example of the 1960 Colonial Declaration.

The resistance of colonial states and their allies to this declaration did not stop those states who were wishing for the abolition of the inhumanity of colonialism from adopting the resolution by a significant majority. It then became the normative magnet around which a deeper and broader consensus first emerged, then discursively marginalized the remaining western colonial powers, and eventually produced the earlier-described reinterpretation of Chapter XI of the Charter. My argument is that a process of this nature is far more legitimate — and ultimately more effective in terms of taking root in the general consciousness — than a strategy that remains content with the ad hoc, less-than-transparent signalling game that is represented by the Iraq and Kosovo examples. Lloyd Axworthy in his Tokyo speech referred to the emergence of a sophisticated and passionate transnational civil society capable of allying with progressive state positions and shaming states as a

---

[45] Foreign Affairs Committee, *supra* note 31 at para. 128 [emphasis added].

[46] *Ibid.* It is, of course, not surprising, given the United Kingdom's position in the Kosovo crisis, that this Foreign and Commonwealth Office official would have taken this position.

whole into doing the right thing, such as on the land mines issue.[47] Can such a "new power bloc," as referred to by Axworthy, be marshalled to help achieve a declaration on legitimate humanitarian intervention, which would draw inspiration from the Colonial Declaration?

It has not been my purpose to arrive at a point where I would suggest what the substantive content of such a resolution should be. However, consistently (I hope) with the general positions that I have advanced to this point, my tentative view is that such a humanitarian intervention declaration is best directed towards the Security Council or, viewed from a different perspective, towards the states who happen to be the members of the Security Council at a given time. The declaration would not be framed as a set of criteria for *unilateral* intervention — that is, intervention that cannot be justified by reference to a Security Council mandate. That is to say, the principles that would be stated in such a declaration should be framed in such a way that the declaration serves as the basis for the collective consideration of when and how intervention should occur *with* Security Council backing. The substantive criteria, the decision-making processes, and any institutional innovations that would be "recommended" to the Security Council by the General Assembly in the envisaged standing resolution would be designed to shine a global spotlight on Security Council politics so as to mobilize the power of shame on a timely basis and create something resembling a much more transparent process than currently exists.

By constructing the General Assembly declaration as a recommendation with respect to an international *duty* to intervene, we would simultaneously be constructing a framework that the General Assembly could draw upon in specific crises to assess whether or not the Security Council had acted reasonably with respect to any given crisis in terms of either failing to authorize intervention when needed or, conversely, failing to "fully explore" diplomatic alternatives "in a sincere and convincing manner" (to invoke again Richard Falk's language on the last-resort principle) or authorizing the wrong kind of intervention. In those instances when the General Assembly can achieve a significant majority in favour either of an express call for intervention or an express view that humanitarian intervention is not justified by the facts at hand, such an express statement can then become an interpretive baseline against which one interprets Security Council resolutions that do not contain

---

[47] Axworthy, *supra* note 3.

express authorizations or clear retroactive validations. In terms of a crisis-by-crisis role of the General Assembly, I am envisaging a normative document that would resemble the Colonial Declaration in terms of its statements of general principle but also have an operational element that would resemble an updated Uniting for Peace Resolution. Let us call the resolution the Declaration on Interventions for Human Security (DIHS). The DIHS could create a streamlined process involving a special committee of the General Assembly that meets in informal session to parallel all Security Council activity dealing with humanitarian crises that are on an alert list drawn up by the committee, so as to be prepared to pass judgment should the Security Council fail to act in accordance with the criteria set out in the overarching substantive principles of the DIHS.[48]

I have no illusions about the fact that many will react to this concrete proposal by dismissing it as not just abstract but also naive. All that I can say at this stage is that international politics have had a way of embracing so-called naivety in recent years — whether we are talking about the Convention on the Prohibition of the Use, Stockpiling, Production and Transfer of Anti-Personnel Mines and on Their Destruction,[49] or about the successful adoption of the Statute of the International Criminal Court,[50] or about the successful targeting and delaying of the adoption of a multilateral agreement on investment as a result of a concentrated civil society campaign, or about the flourishing attempt to reset the global economic agenda through street protest. I do not envisage that such a declaration, as in the hypothetical DIHS, would be one that most, if any, of the permanent five members of the Security Council would support.

---

[48] It would be evident to scholars of UN law that such a declaration would probably also need to reorient the balance of powers between the General Assembly and the Security Council beyond that endorsed in the *Certain Expenses of the United Nations* judgment of the ICJ, *supra* note 43, to the relatively limited extent of allowing the General Assembly to consider crises that are under active consideration by the Security Council while they are under such consideration. This is why I have taken care to indicate that the General Assembly would be in an *informal* session.

[49] Convention on the Prohibition of the Use, Stockpiling, Production and Transfer of Anti-Personnel Mines and on Their Destruction, September 18, 1997, Conference on Disarmament CD/1478, text can be accessed online at <www.mines. gc.ca/VII_AA_I-en.asp> (date accessed: September 2, 2002).

[50] Statute of the International Criminal Court, July 17, 1998, UN Doc. A/Conf. 183/9, text can be accessed online at <www.un.org/law/icc/statute/romefra. htm> (date accessed: September 2, 2002).

However, it is possible that a creative combination of humanitarianism and multilateralism could build a momentum that would eventually pressure the major players to reconcile themselves with this process.

Very savvy organizing would undoubtedly be needed to build state coalitions and alliances with key actors in civil society. For example, it seems to me that the early and central involvement of the Organization of African Unity in a DIHS initiative would be crucial given that Africa is the continent that currently hosts the widest and most serious range of humanitarian crises and that has seen a host of failures of the international community to intervene, either preventively or reactively. My own — highly anecdotally informed — sense is that there tends to be, in Africa, a sophisticated approach to the question of the balance between concerns of imperialism and imperatives of humanitarianism in light of the Rwanda experience and ongoing horrors such as the multi-state war in central Africa. While very few people are starry-eyed about the dangers of an intervention model, at the same time there does seem to be widespread resentment in many African countries over Western indifference (if not callousness and racism), which is reflected by Western unwillingness to save African lives, especially after the Somalia syndrome had passed on its contagion to those who ended up handling the looming Rwanda genocide in the corridors of the United Nations and the capitols of powerful states. Finally, we might consider how China might be engaged in the initiative by elevating its policy of abstention throughout the 1990s as a model to be emulated by other members of the Security Council in situations where a large majority of Council members representing a significant cross-section of states are in favour of a particular resolution.

Sommaire

Intervention et interprétation

L'auteur considère le bien-fondé de justifications pour l'intervention humanitaire faute d'autorisation expresse du Conseil de sécurité. Partant de l'affirmation par l'ancien ministre des affaires étrangères, Lloyd Axworthy, que le Canada a participé dans l'intervention au Kosovo sachant que celle-ci n'était pas entièrement justifiée en droit mais considérant qu'elle était néanmoins justifée moralement, l'auteur pèse la possibilité d'une acceptation générale que l'autorisation explicite du Conseil de sécurité n'est pas obligatoire. Il prétend qu'une interprétation évolutive de la Charte est justifiable. Par conséquent, bien que l'autorisation du Conseil de sécurité demeure obligatoire pour toute intervention humanitaire, une approche flexible à ce que constitue l'autorisation devient nécessaire. À cet égard, l'auteur prévoit qu'une déclaration de l'Assemblée générale sur la légitime intervention humanitaire serait important pour établir un point de repère pour l'interprétation d'une résolution donnée du Conseil de sécurité.

Summary

Interpreting Intervention

The author considers whether humanitarian intervention can be justified even without express Security Council authorization. Starting with the statement of former Canadian Minister of Foreign Affairs Lloyd Axworthy that Canada intervened in Kosovo knowing that it did not have full legal justification, but feeling that such intervention was nevertheless morally justified, the author explores whether there is an evolving acceptance that explicit Security Council authorization is not necessary. He argues that an evolving reinterpretation of the Charter is appropriate such that, while Security Council authorization remains necessary for humanitarian intervention, there has to be flexibility in determining what constitutes authorization. In this respect, it would be important for a General Assembly declaration on legitimate humanitarian intervention to be in place in order to provide a baseline for interpreting a given Security Council resolution.

Notes and Comments /
Notes et commentaires

The Problems and Promise of
Spraytech v. *Hudson*

I N 1991, THE TOWN OF Hudson, Québec, adopted a by-law restricting the use of pesticides within the town perimeter. The
town purported to act under two sections of Québec's Cities and
Towns Act.[1] Section 410(1) grants the town, through its council, the
power to make by-laws to "secure peace, order, good government,
health and general welfare in the territory of the municipality."
Section 412(32) authorizes the council to "regulate or prohibit the
... use of ... combustible, explosive, corrosive, toxic, radioactive or
other materials that are harmful to public health and safety." The
appellants, who are landscaping and lawn care companies operating in the greater Montreal region, challenged the validity of the
by-law upon being charged under it in 1992. They sought relief in
the form of a declaration that the by-law was *ultra vires* the town
council. The Superior Court denied the motion, a decision that was
upheld in the Court of Appeal.

In *114957 Canada Ltée (Spraytech, Société d'arrosage)* v. *Hudson
(Town)*,[2] the Supreme Court of Canada, sitting as a seven-person
bench, unanimously dismissed the appeal. Madame Justice
L'Heureux-Dubé, for the majority, held that pesticides were not
toxic materials for the purposes of section 412(32) of the act but
that the town had authority to adopt the by-law under the "health"
component of section 410(1). L'Heureux-Dubé J. rejected the
appellants' argument that the by-law was an absolute ban on pesticide use not authorized by the enabling act, pointing to the by-law's
implicit distinction between essential and non-essential uses as

---

[1] Cities and Towns Act, R.S.Q., c. C-19.

[2] *Canada Ltée (Spraytech, Société d'arrosage)* v. *Hudson (Town)*, 2001 S.C.C. 40 at paras.
24-27 [hereinafter *Spraytech*].

evidence that the town acted to promote the health of its inhabitants. L'Heureux-Dubé J. also rejected the appellants' argument that the by-law drew discriminatory distinctions between pesticide uses, holding that while these distinctions were not specifically authorized by the act, they were necessarily incidental to the exercise of the town's power to safeguard the health of its residents.[3] It was at this point in her judgment that L'Heureux-Dubé J. made the observations that are the subject of this comment. "To conclude this section on statutory authority," she wrote, "I note that reading s. 410(1) to permit the Town to regulate pesticide use is consistent with the principles of international law and policy." Quoting from her judgment in *Baker* v. *Canada*[4] and from *Driedger on the Construction of Statutes,*[5] the learned judge observed:

The interpretation of By-law 270 contained in these reasons respects international law's "precautionary principle," which is defined as follows at para. 7 of the *Bergen Ministerial Declaration on Sustainable Development* (1990):

> In order to achieve sustainable development, policies must be based on the precautionary principle. Environmental measures must anticipate, prevent and attack the causes of environmental degradation. Where there are threats of serious or irreversible damage, lack of full scientific certainty should not be used as a reason for postponing measures to prevent environmental degradation.

Canada "advocated inclusion of the precautionary principle" during the Bergen Conference negotiations ... The principle is codified in several items of domestic legislation ...

Scholars have documented the precautionary principle's inclusion "in virtually every recently adopted treaty and policy document related to the protection and preservation of the environment" ... As a result, there may be "currently sufficient state practice to allow a good argument that the precautionary principle is a principle of customary international law" ... The Supreme Court of India considers the precautionary principle to be "part of the Customary International Law" ... In the context of the

---

[3] *Ibid.* at paras. 28-29.

[4] *Baker* v. *Canada,* [1999] 2 S.C.R. 817 [hereinafter *Baker*].

[5] R. Sullivan, *Driedger on the Construction of Statutes,* 3rd ed. (Toronto: Butterworth, 1994) at 330: "[T]he legislature is presumed to respect the values and principles enshrined in international law, both customary and conventional. These constitute a part of the legal context in which legislation is enacted and read. In so far as possible, therefore, interpretations that reflect these values and principles are preferred."

precautionary principle's tenets, the Town's concerns about pesticides fit well under their[6] rubric of preventive action.[7]

L'Heureux-Dubé J. concluded her reasons by dismissing the appellants' claims that the impugned by-law was rendered inoperative by conflict with federal and provincial legislation.

Mr. Justice Le Bel concurred in the result but differed from the majority on the relevance of international law to the disposition of the appeal. Le Bel J. wrote:

> The appellants assert that no provision of the *Cities and Towns Act* authorizes By-law 270. If such legislative authority exists, the by-law is nevertheless void, because of its discriminatory and prohibitory nature. A solution is to be found in the principles governing the interpretation and application of the laws governing cities and towns like the respondent in the Province of Quebec. Interesting as they may be, references to international sources have little relevance. They confirm the general importance placed in modern society and shared by most citizens of this country on the environment and the need to protect it. Nevertheless, no matter how laudable the purpose of the by-law may be, and although it may express the will of the members of the community to protect their local environment, the means to do it must be found somewhere in the law.

The reasons of Le Bel J. were concurred in by Justices Major and Iacobucci — the latter of whom wrote the partial dissent in *Baker* rejecting the use of treaties to control the exercise of statutory discretion.

SPRAYTECH AND THE PRECAUTIONARY PRINCIPLE

The majority in *Spraytech* comes very close to pronouncing upon the status of the precautionary principle in international law.

---

[6] The word "their" appears to be a mistake. "The" is probably the intended word. The French version reads: "Dans le contexte des postulats du principe de précaution, les craintes de la Ville au sujet des pesticides s'inscrivent confortablement sous *la* rubrique de l'action préventive" (emphasis added).

[7] *Spraytech, supra* note 2 at paras. 31-32. I have omitted, for the sake of clarity, the several international, statutory, case law, and secondary sources quoted or cited in this passage. These include: the Bergen Ministerial Declaration on Sustainable Development in the ECE Region 1990, reprinted in (1990) 20 Env. Policy and Law 100; the judgment of the Supreme Court of India in *A.P. Pollution Control Board* v. *Nayudu*, (1999) S.O.L. Case no. 53; D. Freestone and E. Hey, "Origins and Development of the Precautionary Principle," in D. Freestone and E. Hey, eds., *The Precautionary Principle and International Law: The Challenge of Implementation* (The Hague: Kluwer Law International, 1996); J. Cameron and J. Abouchar, "The Status of the Precautionary Principle in International Law," in Freestone and Hey, *Precautionary Principle, supra* note 7; O. McIntyre and T. Mosedale, "The Precautionary Principle as a Norm of Customary International Law" (1997) 9 J. Env. L. 221.

L'Heureux-Dubé J. declares that there "may be" sufficient state practice to support, in the words of J. Cameron and J. Abouchar, "a good argument that the precautionary principle is a principle of customary international law."[8] L'Heureux-Dubé J. also quotes the stronger words of O. McIntyre and T. Mosedale: "[T]he precautionary principle has indeed crystallized into a norm of customary international law."[9] Finally, she quotes, seemingly with approval, the Supreme Court of India's pronouncement that the precautionary principle is part of customary international law. Although L'Heureux-Dubé J.'s careful words do not say outright that the precautionary principle has entered the corpus of customary international law, future cases may show that they amount to that. Her pronouncements are bold affirmations of the precautionary principle, not simply as a matter of policy but as elements of international and Canadian law.

The strength of these pronouncements is to be contrasted with the faint methodology employed to support them. The test for the existence of a rule of customary international law is well known.[10] The purported customary rule must be supported by consistent state practice[11] motivated by *opinio juris* (the belief that the practice is required by law).[12] This test is a demanding one, and rightly

---

[8] Cameron and Abouchar, *supra* note 7 at 52.

[9] McIntyre and Mosedale, *supra* note 7 at 241.

[10] On international custom generally, see Sir Robert Jennings and Sir Arthur Watts, eds., *Oppenheim's International Law*, 9th ed., vol. 1 (Harlow, UK: Longman, 1992), section 10; I. Brownlie, *Principles of Public International Law*, 5th ed. (Oxford: Clarendon Press, 1998) at 4-11; P. Sands, *Principles of International Environmental Law I: Frameworks, Standards and Implementation* (Manchester: Manchester University Press, 1995) at 118-22. For discussions by Canadian writers, see C. Emanuelli, *Droit international public: contribution à l'étude du droit international selon une perspective canadienne* (Montréal: Wilson and Lafleur, 1998) at 41-61; H. Kindred et al., *International Law Chiefly as Interpreted and Applied in Canada*, 6th ed. (Toronto: Emond Montgomery, 2000) at 129-48.

[11] The state practice need not be universal, but it must be general: *North Sea Continental Shelf Cases (Federal Republic of Germany v. Denmark; Federal Republic of Germany v. The Netherlands)*, [1969] I.C.J. Rep. 3 at para. 73 [hereinafter *North Sea Continental Shelf*]; *Fisheries Jurisdiction Case (United Kingdom v. Iceland) (Merits)*, [1974] I.C.J. Rep. 3 at 23-26; *Case Concerning Military and Paramilitary Activities in and against Nicaragua (Nicaragua v. United States of America)*, [1986] I.C.J. Rep. 14 at para. 186. Likewise, the state practice need not be unbroken, but breaks with it must be viewed as breaches of the rule rather than as indications of a new rule (at 98).

[12] *Opinio juris* serves to differentiate state practice motivated by courtesy or morality (which amounts only to international usage) from that motivated by a sense

so, for once a rule is found to be customary international law it becomes binding upon all states.[13] One might have expected the court to apply the test for customary international law or, at least, to acknowledge it before pronouncing upon the status of the precautionary principle. Rather than examine the questions of state practice and *opinio juris* for itself, however, the majority relied on academic works submitted by counsel for a group of intervenors.[14] The written submissions of these intervenors included only a brief analysis of state practice and no discussion of *opinio juris*. Instead, these submissions relied heavily on the academic works later adopted by L'Heureux-Dubé J. in her reasons.[15] No other intervenor or party made submissions on the precautionary principle. In sum, the court heard little argument on the status of the precautionary principle in international law, and what it did hear came entirely from one side of the debate. It was on the basis of these limited submissions that the majority made its pronouncement.[16]

All of this is not necessarily to say that the court got it wrong. Recent academic writings on the status of the precautionary principle in international law, some of which were cited by the majority, reveal a significant body of state practice espousing the

---

of legal obligation (which evidences customary international law). Often international courts and tribunals are willing to presume that state practice is motivated by *opinio juris* unless the contrary is proven. This approach was advocated by Sir Hersch Lauterpacht, *The Development of International Law by the International Court* (London: Stevens, 1958) at 380. In at least three leading cases, however, the International Court of Justice has insisted upon stricter proof: *Case of the S.S. Lotus (France v. Turkey)* (1927), P.C.I.J. (Ser. A) no. 10 at 33; *North Sea Continental Shelf, supra* note 11 at 43-45; and *Case Concerning Military and Paramilitary Activities in and against Nicaragua, supra* note 11 at para. 207. See the discussion in Brownlie, *supra* note 10 at 7-9.

[13] There are two exceptions. First, a rule of customary international law is not binding on those states that have persistently objected to it during its formation. Proving persistent objection is almost as difficult as proving custom. Second, where the custom is regional, only states within the region and which have not persistently objected to the custom during its formation, are bound by it: *Asylum Case (Columbia v. Peru)*, [1950] I.C.J. Rep. 266.

[14] The intervenors, the Federation of Canadian Municipalities, Nature-Action Québec Incorporated, and the World Wildlife Fund Canada, were jointly represented by the Sierra Legal Defence Fund.

[15] Factum of the Intervenors, Federation of Canadian Municipalities et al. (on file with the author) at paras. 22-25.

[16] As we have seen, the minority disapproved of reliance on international law in the first place. They made no criticism, however, of the majority's method.

precautionary principle. In the last fifteen years or so, the precautionary principle has been expressed and advocated in numerous international conventions,[17] non-binding declarations,[18] judicial pronouncements,[19] and domestic laws.[20] Proving *opinio juris* is, of

[17] Some leading instruments include: 1987 Montreal Protocol on Substances That Deplete the Ozone Layer (1987) 26 I.L.M. 154, preamble; 1992 Paris Convention for the Protection of the Marine Environment of the North-East Atlantic (1993) 32 I.L.M. 1068, art. 2(2)(a); 1992 UN Framework Convention on Climate Change (1993) 31 I.L.M. 849, art. 3(3); 1992 Convention on Biological Diversity (1992) 31 I.L.M. 874; 1992 Treaty on European Union (1992) 31 I.L.M. 247, art. 130R(2); 1992 Convention on the Protection of the Marine Environment of the Baltic Sea Area, available online at <http://www.helcom.fi/helcom/convention.html>, art. 3(2); 1995 Agreement for the Implementation of the Provisions of the United Nations Convention on the Law of the Sea Relating to the Conservation and Management of Straddling Fish Stocks and Highly Migratory Fish Stocks, available online at <http://www.un.org/Depts/los/convention_agreements/texts/fish_stocks_agreement/CONF164_37.htm>, arts. 5(c), 6. All websites visited August 6, 2002.

[18] Major declarations include: 1984 Bremen Ministerial Declaration of the International Conference on the Protection of the North Sea, preamble; 1987 London Ministerial Declaration of the Second International Conference on the Protection of the North Sea; 1990 Hague Declaration of the Third International Conference on the Protection of the North Sea; 1995 Esbjerg Ministerial Declaration of the Fourth International Conference on the Protection of the North Sea (all declarations available online at <http://odin.dep.no/md/nsc/declaration/index-b-n-a.html>); 1990 Bergen Ministerial Declaration on Sustainable Development in the ECE Region, *supra* note 7 at para. 7; 1992 Rio Declaration on the Environment and Development (1992) 31 I.L.M. 874, principle 15; 1994 Fort Lauderdale Resolution (on amendments to the 1973 Convention on International Trade in Endangered Species), available online at <http://www.cites.org/eng/resols/9/9_24.shtml>. All websites visited August 6, 2002.

[19] See the opinion of the International Court of Justice in Request for an Examination of the Situation in Accordance with Paragraph 63 of the Court's Judgment of 20 December 1974 in the *Nuclear Tests (New Zealand v. France)*, [1995] I.C.J. Rep. 288 at 290, where the court describes the precautionary principle as "very widely accepted in contemporary international law." See also the dissenting opinion of Judge Weeramantry, in which the learned judge explains (at 342):

> Where a party complains to the Court of possible environmental damage of an irreversible nature which another party is committing or threatening to commit, the proof or disproof of the matter alleged may present difficulty to the claimant as the necessary information may be largely in the hands of the party causing or threatening the damage.
>
> The law cannot function in protection of the environment unless a legal principle is evolved to meet this evidentiary difficulty, and environmental law has responded with what has come to be described as the precautionary principle — a principle which is gaining increasing support as part of the international law of the environment.

course, the difficult part, but this may have been an appropriate occasion on which to apply the lower standard of proof advocated by Lauterpacht, whereby state practice is presumptively motivated by *opinio juris* unless a contrary intent can be shown.[21] In short, there is, as Philippe Sands puts it, "a good argument to be made" that the precautionary principle represents customary international law.[22]

See also the dissenting opinion of Judge Palmer (at 412), who observes that "the norm involved in the precautionary principle has developed rapidly and may now be a principle of customary international law relating to the environment."

[20] See, for example, the following enactments and secondary works. For Canada, see Oceans Act, S.C. 1996, c. 31, preamble; Canadian Environmental Protection Act, S.C. 1999, c. 33 ("CEPA"), s. 2(1)(a); and the Endangered Species Act, S.N.S. 1998, c. 11, ss. 2(1)(h) and 11(1). See also the non-binding Agreement on Internal Trade, available online at <http://strategis.ic.gc.ca/SSG/il00021e.html> (visited August 8, 2002), at art. 1505(8). See also D. Vander-Zwaag, "The Precautionary Principle in Environmental Law and Policy: Elusive Rhetoric and First Embraces" (1998) 8 J. Env. L. and Pr. 355 at 369-72. For Australia, see C. Barton, "The Status of the Precautionary Principle in Australia: Its Emergence in Legislation and as a Common Law Doctrine" (1998) 22 Harv. Env. L. R. 509. For Germany, the United Kingdom, and Hungary, see Cameron and Abouchar, *supra* note 7 at 38-40. For the origins of the precautionary principle in German municipal law, see K. von Moltke, "The Vorsorgeprinzip in West German Environmental Policy," in Royal Commission on Environmental Pollution, *Twelfth Report* (London: HMSO, 1988), appendix 3. In a recent Organization for Economic Co-operation and Development [hereinafter OECD] publication, a panel of experts observed that "[r]eference to precaution is now a standard feature in food and health legislation and increasingly also in environmental regulation": OECD, *Trade and Environment: Report on a Meeting of Management Experts Held under the OECD Labour/Management Programme,* Doc. PAC/AFF/LMP(2001)6, July 19, 2001.

[21] See Lauterpacht, *supra* note 12.

[22] Sands, *supra* note 10 at 212-13. There is also a good counter-argument, founded particularly in the treaties and jurisprudence of the World Trade Organization [hereinafter WTO]. The leading case is *EC Measures Concerning Meat and Meat Products (Hormones)* (1998) WTO Doc. AB-1997-4. Canada and the United States filed a complaint against the European Communities [hereinafter EC] relating to an EC prohibition of imports of meat and meat products derived from cattle to which certain natural and synthetic hormones had been administered. Two WTO panels found against the EC. On appeal to the Appellate Body, the EC defended its prohibition by invoking certain provisions of the Agreement on the Application of Sanitary and Phytosanitary Measures [hereinafter SPS Agreement], arguing, *inter alia,* that the panels erred on the issue of burden of proof under the agreement by failing to defer to the EC's application of the precautionary principle. The EC submitted that the precautionary principle was a general rule of customary international law or, at least, a general principle of

Even if the majority is right in suggesting that the precautionary principle now represents customary international law, the methodology employed to arrive at this conclusion is worrisome. Reflecting upon the court's use of treaties, Stephen Toope has complained that,

> [a]lthough the [Supreme] Court often invokes international treaties as an aid to interpretation, particularly of the Charter, it does so in a fluid, not to say unprincipled, manner. Treaty norms are alluded to but simply to provide context for the specific interpretations promoted by the various Justices ... Treaty obligations are not so much "relevant and persuasive" as instrumentally useful or merely interesting.[23]

The majority's invocation of the precautionary principle in *Spraytech* v. *Hudson* is, I fear, a customary law instance of this same phenomenon. Rather than apply the established criteria for the recognition of new international customary rules, the majority was content to rely on secondary sources. Rather than declining to pronounce upon the status of the precautionary principle in a case in which it was unnecessary for the determination of the dispute, the majority made its observations as *obiter dicta* in a case in which the issue was not even argued by the disputing parties but presented only by intervenors. This lackadaisical approach to international law gives one the sense that the court does not consider it to be "real" law at all, but simply a well into which it is free to dip as it sees fit. As William Schabas has put it in the context of the court's treatment of international human rights law, the message seems to be that

---

law applicable to the assessment of risk under the SPS Agreement. The United States responded by denying that the precautionary principle was a matter of international law, saying that it represented only an "approach" and, furthermore, that it was an approach not recognized in the SPS Agreement. Similarly, Canada argued that the precautionary principle could not override the express provisions of the SPS Agreement, though Canada did characterize the "precautionary approach" as an emerging principle of international law which may in future crystallize into one of the "general principles of law recognized by civilized nations" within the meaning of Article 38(1)(c) of the 1945 Statute of the International Court of Justice, [1945] Can. T.S. No. 7. In upholding the panels, the Appellate Body noted the development of the precautionary principle but declined to rule on its status in international law. Instead, it found that while the principle is reflected in certain provisions of the SPS Agreement, it is not reflected in, and could not override, Articles 5.1 and 5.2, which were the subject of the dispute.

23 S. Toope, "Keynote Address: Canada and International Law," in *The Impact of International Law on the Practice of Law in Canada: Proceedings of the 27th Annual Conference of the Canadian Council on International Law, Ottawa, October 15-17, 1998* (The Hague: Kluwer Law International, 1999) 33 at 36.

international law "never binds the courts, that its sources are eclectic, contradictory and confusing, that erudite judges are of course welcome to invoke it, but that at the end of the day its significance is secondary and marginal."[24]

SPRAYTECH AND BAKER

Although there is cause for concern about the methodology in *Spraytech* v. *Hudson*, there is also reason to applaud the result. Environmentalists will surely be pleased to see the precautionary principle so strongly affirmed in the country's highest court. What is also pleasing about *Spraytech* is the further light it sheds on the court's important judgment in *Baker* v. *Canada*.

Baker established for the first time in Canadian law that Canada's obligations under international treaties may be invoked to control the exercise of statutory discretion.[25] Whether the rule in *Baker* applies in cases outside the human rights field was, until *Spraytech*, uncertain. Although it was not decided on the grounds of the Canadian Charter of Rights and Freedoms,[26] *Baker* was very much a human rights case (among other things). The appellant was an illegal immigrant fighting her imminent deportation after residing in Canada since 1981. She argued that the minister's decision in her case should be set aside because, *inter alia*, the minister had unreasonably failed to give sufficient weight to the interests of Baker's Canadian-born children as required by the 1989 Convention on the Rights of the Child, a leading international human rights instrument.[27] The court's reasoning in allowing Baker's appeal was open to the interpretation that international treaties could be invoked in this way only when the subject matter of the decision touched on human rights or where the treaty relied upon was a human rights instrument.[28] *Spraytech* shows this narrow reading of

---

[24] W. Schabas, "International Human Rights Law and the Canadian Courts," in T.A. Cromwell et al., *Human Rights in the Twenty-First Century: Prospects, Institutions and Processes* (Montréal: Thémis, 1996) 21 at 44.

[25] See G. van Ert, "Using Treaties in Canadian Courts" (2000) 38 C.Y.I.L. 3 at 42-61.

[26] Canadian Charter of Rights and Freedoms, Part 1 of the Constitution Act 1982, being Schedule B to the Canada Act 1982 (U.K.), 1982, c. 11.

[27] Convention on the Rights of the Child, [1992] Can. T.S. No. 3.

[28] L'Heureux-Dubé J.'s phrase in *Baker*, quoted in *Spraytech*, was "the values reflected in *international human rights law* may help inform the contextual approach to statutory interpretation and judicial review": *Baker*, *supra* note 4 at 861 (emphasis added).

Baker to be mistaken, for, in *Spraytech*, L'Heureux-Dubé J. cites *Baker* as an authority for the proposition that a matter of international environmental law (the precautionary principle) may be invoked in determining the validity of delegated legislation concerning a matter that is only indirectly related to human rights (community health). Nor does *Spraytech* suggest any new limits to the use of treaties by judicial review applicants. Any international law, whatever its subject-matter, may seemingly be invoked to impugn the validity of administrative decisions. This is as it should be.

Spraytech also confirms that the rule in *Baker* is not limited to international treaties but also encompasses rules of international custom. This comes as no surprise, since it is difficult to imagine how international custom might justifiably be excluded from the scope of matters properly considered by those exercising statutory discretion. Just as the legislation conferring administrative decision-making power is presumptively consistent with Canada's treaty obligations, so too is it presumptively consistent with Canada's obligations under customary international law.

Spraytech is also of interest (particularly to administrative lawyers) as an example of how international law may be used to broaden, rather than narrow, the powers of an administrative decision-maker or secondary law-maker. In *Baker*, international law was raised as a means of impugning the minister's decision. The holding in *Baker* was, in effect, that an administrative decision-maker acted unreasonably and, therefore, *ultra vires*, by failing to consider the requirements of international law. The use of international law in *Spraytech* was quite different. Here, the intervenor relied on international law to support the validity of the delegate's act. L'Heureux-Dubé J., for the majority, accepted this use of international law and suggested that the presumption of international legality ought to be applied to the delegate's authorizing statute.[29] "I note," said L'Heureux-Dubé J., "that reading s. 410(1) to permit the Town to regulate pesticide use is consistent with principles of international law and policy." She went on to cite *Baker* and quote *Driedger's* formulation of the presumption of international legality: "[T]he legislature is presumed to respect the values and principles enshrined in international law."[30] The implication in this case is

[29] On the presumption of international legality, see van Ert, *supra* note 25 and G. van Ert, *Using International Law in Canadian Courts* (The Hague: Kluwer Law International, 2002) at 99-136.

[30] *Spraytech*, *supra* note 2 at para. 30.

that the town's by-law powers can be shored up — some might say expanded — by resort to the presumption that the town's authorizing act is consistent with international law. It was on this point that the majority and minority parted ways. Le Bel J. disapproved of this use of international law, saying that "references to international sources have little relevance ... [T]he means to do it must be found somewhere in the law."[31] By "the law," Le Bel J. apparently did not mean "Canadian and international law" but only the enabling act under which the town adopted its by-law.[32] In my respectful view, the minority's approach is mistaken. The presumption of international legality applies to all statutes, including those such as the Cities and Towns Act, which delegate law- or decision-making power. If one accepts that the precautionary principle is a rule of customary international law, one must presume that Canadian legislation is consistent with this rule, unless that presumption is rebutted by the clear words of the enabling act or some other convincing indication of the legislature's intent.

Spraytech and the Internationalization of Canadian Law

The majority's decision in *Spraytech* is not immune from criticism. I have taken issue with the court's approach to the existence of customary international law. Others might challenge the majority's substantive finding that the precautionary principle has developed into customary international law. Nevertheless, the great strength of *Spraytech* is that it reaffirms the court's enthusiasm for submissions founded in customary and conventional international law. What is clear from *Baker* and *Spraytech* is that the Supreme Court of Canada has committed itself to seeing international law enforced through Canadian courts. This commitment is long overdue, for the common law has always looked on international law as an aspect of itself.[33] In the Supreme Court of Canada's

---

[31] *Ibid.* at para. 48.

[32] It is helpful to consider the French text (given here in full): "Si intéressants soient-ils, les renvois aux sources internationales ne sont guère pertinents. Ils confirment l'importance que la société moderne accorde généralement à l'environnement et à la nécessité de le protéger, position que partagent la plupart des citoyens de ce pays. Cependant, aussi louable que soit l'objet du règlement et même si celui-ci exprime la volonté des membres de la collectivité de protéger son environnement local, les moyens pour ce faire doivent être tirés de la loi."

[33] See, generally, van Ert, *supra* note 29.

much-neglected 1958 judgment *Saint John* v. *Fraser-Brace Overseas*,[34] Rand J. eloquently articulated the internationally minded position of Canadian law, saying:

> It is obvious that the life of every state is, under the swift transformations of these days, becoming deeply implicated with that of the others in a *de facto* society of nations. If in 1767 Lord Mansfield, as in *Heathfield* v. *Chilton*, ... could say, "The law of nations will be carried as far in England, as any where," in this country, in the 20th century, in the presence of the United Nations and the multiplicity of impacts with which technical developments have entwined the entire globe, we cannot say anything less.[35]

Baker and *Spraytech* are cause to hope that the Supreme Court of Canada is poised to renew the common law's ancient commitment to an internationalized jurisprudence.

If so, counsel appearing before the Supreme Court of Canada, and before lower courts too, will be unwise to neglect international law in their submissions. The difficulty, of course, is that most Canadian lawyers are unfamiliar with international law. Just as *Spraytech* illustrates the promise of an internationalized Canadian jurisprudence, it also underscores the precarious position of international law in Canada today — its use by litigants and judges is encouraged on the highest authority, yet its operation and substance remain elusive to much of the bench and bar. In the short run, then, *Baker* and *Spraytech* may portend some bad international law judgments. Yet they may also spark a new interest in international law among Canadian lawyers, which will translate, in the long run, into a more internationally conversant profession.

POSTSCRIPT: CUSTOMARY INTERNATIONAL LAW IN
SURESH V. *CANADA (MINISTER OF CITIZENSHIP AND IMMIGRATION)*[36]

Since this comment was written, the Supreme Court of Canada has released an unsigned judgment in *Suresh*. There is neither time nor space to discuss *Suresh* in full in this comment, but a few brief points are in order. Like *Spraytech*, *Suresh* asked the court to consider customary international law and, more specifically, the alleged *jus*

---

[34]   *Saint John* v. *Fraser-Brace Overseas*, [1958] S.C.R. 263.

[35]   *Ibid.* at 268-69.

[36]   *Suresh* v. *Canada (Minister of Citizenship and Immigration)*, 2002 S.C.C. 1 [hereinafter *Suresh*].

cogens, or peremptory norm, against torture. Article 53 of the 1969 Vienna Convention on the Law of Treaties[37] provides that a treaty is void "if, at the time of its conclusion, it conflicts with a peremptory norm of general international law." Article 53 goes on to define such norms as those which are "accepted and recognized by the international community of States as a whole as a norm from which no derogation is permitted and which can be modified only by a subsequent norm of general international law having the same character." It follows that rules of *jus cogens* must begin life as customary international law. For if state practice motivated by *opinio juris* is lacking, the alleged peremptory norm cannot be one "accepted and recognized by the international community." The test for *jus cogens* is therefore the same as the test for custom (namely, state practice and *opinio juris*) with the added element that the norm in question is considered by states as non-derogable — that is, impossible to displace by treaty or acquiescence.

As in *Spraytech,* the Supreme Court of Canada in *Suresh* did not set out in any clear way the test for customary or peremptory international law. The court said only that peremptory norms "develop over time and by general consensus of the international community."[38] In considering whether the prohibition of torture is such a peremptory norm, the court identified "three compelling indicia": the great number of treaties outlawing torture; the fact that no state has ever legalized torture and that governments accused of it regularly deny the accusation; and the many international authorities declaring the prohibition to be a rule of *jus cogens.*[39] Each of these "indicia" can be understood as forms of state practice, manifestations of *opinio juris,* or both. The court was certainly not mistaken in considering these factors. It would have been preferable, however, for the court to explain at the outset that they were examining these factors for evidence of the state practice and *opinio juris* needed to prove the existence of a customary international law prohibition of torture and a further acceptance of the non-derogable nature of this prohibition.

---

[37] Vienna Convention on the Law of Treaties, [1980] Can. T.S. No. 37 [hereinafter VCLT].

[38] *Suresh, supra* note 36 at para. 61. This formulation itself may understate the degree of recognition a norm must have to constitute a rule of *jus cogens.* Article 53 says such norms must be "accepted and recognized by the international community of States *as a whole*" (emphasis added).

[39] *Suresh, supra* note 36 at paras. 62-64.

More disappointing than the form of the court's analysis is its substantive conclusion. The court declared that, while it was not being asked to pronounce on the status of the prohibition of torture in international law, the three indicia given earlier suggest that the prohibition "cannot be easily derogated from."[40] This conclusion is frankly nonsensical: while the category of *jus cogens* norms is now established in international law, there is certainly no category of "not-easily-derogated-from norms." The prohibition on torture is either a *jus cogens* norm or it is not; there is no midway point. The question may be put quite simply: may states or may they not contract out of the customary international law prohibition of torture by making treaties or developing local custom? The answer is, to my mind at least, obvious: there may be no derogation from the customary prohibition of torture.[41] The court's classification of the prohibition of torture as hard-to-derogate-from has no foundation in international law. Where, then, did it come from? The answer, it seems, may be found in the court's analysis of whether deporting someone who faces torture at home is contrary to section 7 of the Charter. The court held that "in exceptional circumstances, deportation to face torture might be justified" under the Charter.[42] The court's conclusion based on the Charter finds a convenient parallel in its conclusion on the status of torture in international law. Just as torture is said to be hard but not impossible to derogate from at international law, deporting to torture is said to be usually, but not necessarily, unconstitutional in Canadian law. The implausibility of this assessment as a matter of international law, and its curious parallel in the court's conclusion on section 7, suggest that the court has again resorted to the instrumental approach to international law complained of by Toope.[43] *Suresh* is, in too many ways, just the sort of bad international law judgment I feared *Baker* and *Spraytech* might, in the short run, bring. I remain hopeful, however, that these cases signal the beginning of a development in Canadian

---

[40] *Ibid.* at para. 65.

[41] This conclusion was accepted by the parties in *R. v. Bow Street Metropolitan Stipendiary Magistrate et al., ex parte Pinochet Ugarte (No. 3)*, [1999] 2 W.L.R. 827 at para. 28, per Lord Browne-Wilkinson, approving the judgment of the International Criminal Tribunal for the Former Yugoslavia in *Prosecutor v. Furundzija*, Case no. 17-95-17/1-T at para. 153.

[42] *Suresh, supra* note 36 at para. 78.

[43] There remains much more to be said about *Suresh*. I refer the reader to the book by van Ert, *supra* note 29 at 28-29, 165-70, 248-49, and 263.

law that will allow us eventually to say, with Lord Mansfield and Rand J., that the law of nations is the law of Canada.

GIBRAN VAN ERT
Law Clerk, Court of Appeal for British Columbia

Sommaire

Spraytech c. *Hudson*: problématique mais prometteur

Dans Spraytech *c.* Hudson, *la Cour suprême du Canada s'est prononcée audacieusement sur le statut du principe de précaution en droit international. Bien que le raisonnement du jugement majoritaire laisse place à la critique, l'arrêt clarifie la portée de la décision novatrice de la Cour dans* Baker *c.* Canada. *Se basant sur cette dernière,* Spraytech *c.* Hudson *suggère la possibilité d'une jurisprudence canadienne véritablement internationalisée. Dans un post-scriptum à ce commentaire, l'arrêt* Suresh *c.* Canada *de la Cour suprême du Canada est discuté brièvement.*

Summary

The Problems and Promise of *Spraytech* v. *Hudson*

In Spraytech *v.* Hudson, *the Supreme Court of Canada made a bold declaration on the status of the precautionary principle in international law. While the methodology of the majority is open to criticism, the judgment is a welcome clarification of the court's groundbreaking decision in* Baker *v.* Canada *and, building on that case, offers the prospect of a truly internationalized Canadian jurisprudence. In a postscript to this comment, the judgment of the Supreme Court of Canada in* Suresh *v.* Canada *is briefly considered.*

The *Aircraft* Cases: Canada and Brazil

INTRODUCTION

The disputes between Canada and Brazil over subsidies to the regional aircraft industry, *Brazil — Export Financing Programme for Aircraft* and *Canada — Measures Affecting the Export of Civilian Aircraft* (*Aircraft* cases)[1] involved two highly important (both politically and economically) interests in each of the disputing countries (the aircraft manufacturers Embraer of Brazil and Bombardier of Canada). In addition to these considerations, at least three legal factors further complicated the conduct of the cases. First, these cases were the first to be tried under Part II (covering prohibited subsidies) of the Agreement on Subsidies and Countervailing Measures (SCM Agreement)[2] of the World Trade Organization (WTO). Accordingly, there was no WTO "jurisprudence" guiding the interpretation of the applicable provisions. Second, some of the

The author, Rambod Behboodi, is deputy director of the Trade Law Bureau, the Department of Foreign Affairs and International Trade of Canada, and has served as counsel for Canada in the cases before the panel and the Appellate Body. The views expressed in this comment are those of the author only and do not necessarily reflect the views of the Government of Canada.

[1] *Brazil — Export Financing Programme for Aircraft*, Report of the Panel, WTO Doc. WT/DS46/R, August 20, 1999 [hereinafter *Brazil — Aircraft* Panel Report] and Report of the Appellate Body, WTO Doc. WT/DS46/AB/RW, July 7, 2000 [hereinafter *Brazil — Aircraft* Appellate Body Report]; *Canada — Measures Affecting the Export of Civilian Aircraft — Recourse by Brazil to Article 21.5 of the DSU*, Report of the Panel, WTO Doc. WT/DS70/RW, May 9, 2000 [hereinafter *Canada — Aircraft* Panel Report] and Report of the Appellate Body, WTO Doc. WT/DS70/AB/RW, July 21 2000 [*Canada — Aircraft* Appellate Body Report].

[2] Agreement on Subsidies and Countervailing Measures, April 15, 1994, WTO Doc. LT/UR/A-1A/9 [hereinafter SCM Agreement].

provisions in question (for example, Annex I of the SCM Agreement) were remnants of the old Tokyo Round codes, which had been negotiated under a completely different legal arrangement. Third, some of the relevant provisions referred to semi-legal documents negotiated and maintained by other international organizations (for example, the Organization for Economic Co-operation and Development (OECD) Consensus[3] in Item (k) of the annex).

The regional aircraft market (commercial aircraft with twenty to ninety seats) is served by both turboprop and jet aircraft. Turboprop aircraft are produced by Embraer, the Brazilian manufacturer of regional and military aircraft,[4] Bombardier of Canada,[5] the German-American company Fairchild-Dornier, and ATR, a joint venture between Alenia of Italy and Aerospatiale of France. Saab of Sweden and British Aerospace of the United Kingdom also produced some turboprop aircraft in the past, but they have either left the field or announced that they are exiting the business.

A discrete market for regional *jet* aircraft did not exist before the introduction of the Canadair regional jet (CRJ) aircraft by the Canadian manufacturer Bombardier in 1993. Although small jet aircraft aimed at short-haul routes had been in operation for some time, what has become known as the "twinjet" regional jet (RJ) "revolutionized the industry."[6] It opened up new opportunities on long routes, which did not have enough traffic to justify a larger jet. It allowed smaller markets that were not served by major carriers to be hooked up, through regional airlines, to "hubs," which were the centres of operations for such carriers. It was also successfully used to replace larger jets on more heavily travelled routes during off-peak hours. Finally, the regional jet replaced turboprops on some, generally longer (300 miles or more) routes.[7] In fact, it was so successful that in just over five years since the introduction of the fifty-seat CRJ-100, two other manufacturers, Embraer and

---

[3] *Arrangement on Guidelines for Officially Supported Export Credits* (known as the OECD Consensus), text can be accessed at <http://www.oecd.org/pdf/M00029000/M00029130.pdf>.

[4] "Embraer Update," this text can be accessed online at <http://www.embraer.com/ing/embhoje.htm> (date accessed: October 16, 1998).

[5] "Bombardier Aerospace Profile," text can be accessed online at <http:// www.aerospace.bombardier.com/htmen/6_0.htm> (date accessed: October 16, 1998).

[6] "The Ubiquitous Turboprop" (May 1998) 35(5) Air Transport World 53 at 10.

[7] The "cachement" area, which is the area from which passengers could be drawn, has been increased to 1,000 nautical miles for regional airlines, allowing carriers to offer routes in new markets and non-stop service to other areas. *Ibid.*

Fairchild-Dornier, entered the market. In this same period, the three manufacturers introduced five new regional jets,[8] and well over 1,000 regional jets have already been ordered.[9]

Embraer entered the regional jet market with the certification of the EMB-145 (which is now the ERJ-145) in 1996, followed by the launch of the thirty-seven-seat ERJ-135 in 1997. In this period, Embraer captured over half of the regional jet aircraft market. Embraer recently announced that it would increase its production of regional jets to twelve per month,[10] which will be enough to satisfy, on its own, the demand for regional jet aircraft in this market segment for the foreseeable future.[11]

Canada requested consultations on Brazil's export financing program (PROEX),[12] as it applied to the export sales of its regional aircraft, the ERJ-145, on June 18, 1996. The first set of consultations took place on July 22 and 25, 1996, in Geneva. Following the high-level representations made by the Brazilian minister of foreign affairs to his Canadian counterpart, Canada agreed to another set of consultations, which were held on November 4, 1996.[13] At these consultations, the two sides agreed to enter into negotiations outside the precise confines of the WTO dispute settlement process in order to allow them more flexibility in devising

[8] The seventy-seat CRJ-700 by Bombardier; the fifty-seat ERJ-145 and the thirty-seven-seat ERJ-135 by Embraer; and the thirty-five-seat 328JET and the forty-two-seat 428JET by Fairchild-Dornier.

[9] "Regional Fleet Forecast Predicts Continuing Move to Jets" (June 1998) 16(23) Commuter Regional Airline News at 3.

[10] "Embraer Steps up Production to Meet Demand," *Gazeta Mercantil* (June 8, 1998) at C-8.

[11] Market analysts Warburg Dillon Read notes that "[f]our manufacturers are positioned to serve specific niches in what we believe is a 125+ unit per year industry." "Regional Jets: Making Props Passe," industry report, August 10, 1998, at 4 (on file with author).

[12] The government of Brazil created PROEX on June 1, 1991, by Law no. 8187/91, which was entitled "Authorizing the Granting of Financing to the Export of Brazilian Goods and Services."

[13] Canada had, in the meantime, placed two requests for the establishment of panels before the Dispute Settlement Body [hereinafter DSB]. The first was withdrawn because of the strenuous procedural objections of Brazil concerning certain aspects of the request; the second, dated October 23, was withdrawn following a high-level meeting in Ottawa. Brazil's later complaint, in its preliminary motion before the PROEX panel, that Canada took two years to bring its case before the World Trade Organization [hereinafter WTO] should therefore be seen in the light of its own early attempts, by whatever means, to delay the proceedings.

a solution to their ongoing difficulties. Further negotiations ensued, but on March 10, 1997, Brazil requested consultations on a range of Canadian programs and practices. Consultations held on April 30, 1997, failed to resolve this dispute. After many more months of bilateral discussions between officials and ministers, as well as the appointment of personal representatives by heads of government, Canada and Brazil agreed to let the matter go to dispute settlement. Panels were established on October 23, 1998.

Brazil admitted that PROEX constituted export subsidies, but it argued that the subsidies in question benefited from an exception in Annex I of the SCM Agreement. Thus, it was that the *Canada — Aircraft* case had to, for the first time, interpret and apply two critical provisions of the SCM Agreement: Article 1,[14] which defines what practices constitute a subsidy, and Article 3,[15] which prohibits

---

[14] Article 1 provides that:

For the purpose of this Agreement, a subsidy shall be deemed to exist if:

(a)(1) there is a financial contribution by a government or any public body within the territory of a Member (referred to in this Agreement as "government"), i.e. where:

(i) a government practice involves a direct transfer of funds (e.g. grants, loans, and equity infusion), potential direct transfers of funds or liabilities (e.g. loan guarantees);

(ii) government revenue that is otherwise due is foregone or not collected (e.g. fiscal incentives such as tax credits);

(iii) a government provides goods or services other than general infrastructure, or purchases goods;

(iv) a government makes payments to a funding mechanism, or entrusts or directs a private body to carry out one or more of the type of functions illustrated in (i) to (iii) above which would normally be vested in the government and the practice, in no real sense, differs from practices normally followed by governments;

or

(a)(2) there is any form of income or price support in the sense of Article XVI of GATT 1994;

and

(b) a benefit is thereby conferred [footnote omitted].

[15] Article 3 provides that:

Except as provided in the Agreement on Agriculture, the following subsidies, within the meaning of Article 1, shall be prohibited:

(a) subsidies contingent, in law or in fact,[4] whether solely or as one of several other conditions, upon export performance, including those illustrated in Annex I.[5]

[4] This standard is met when the facts demonstrate that the granting of a subsidy, without having been made legally contingent upon export performance,

subsidies "contingent, in law or in fact, upon export performance." As if these challenges were not enough, given the nature of the case and some of the information and evidence in question, the case also led to one of the more remarkable findings of the Appellate Body with respect to the rights and obligations of WTO members in dispute settlement proceedings.[16]

PROEX: Canada's Challenge of the Brazilian Interest Rate Buy-Down Scheme for Regional Aircraft

PROEX, Brazil's export financing program had two components:

1. PROEX Financing: under which the Brazilian National Treasury provided *direct financing* for exports of Brazilian goods and services at "rates lower than the cost to the Government of Brazil of raising the funds necessary for such financing";[17] and
2. PROEX Interest Rate Equalization: whereby the National Treasury granted to the financing party (usually a bank) a payment "to cover, at most, the difference between the interest charges contracted with the buyer and the cost to the financing party of raising the required funds."[18]

At issue in the dispute was the PROEX's "interest equalization" program. According to BankBoston, an agent bank of PROEX, PROEX Interest Equalization worked "by reducing the interest rate paid by the foreign importer in respect of its financing costs for the transaction. The extent of interest rate support is determined by the tenor [term] of the financing approved by PROEX for the transaction."[19] The terms, determined by the product to be exported,

---

is in fact tied to actual or anticipated exportation or export earnings. The mere fact that a subsidy is granted to enterprises which export shall not for that reason alone be considered to be an export subsidy within the meaning of this provision.

[5] Measures referred to in Annex I as not constituting export subsidies shall not be prohibited under this or any other provision of this Agreement.

[16] Many issues were re-litigated in the Article 21.5 challenge against Canada. See *Canada— Aircraft* Panel Report and Appellate Body Report, *supra* note 1.

[17] Law no. 8187/91, June 1, 1991, Article 1.

[18] Resolution 2380/97 of the Brazilian Congress.

[19] "Financing Program Offers Incentives for Importers of Brazilian Goods," text can be accessed online at <http://www.bankboston.com/today/enews/trade trends/tt%5Ffinancing.html (date accessed January 22, 1998).

varied normally from one year to ten years.[20] In special circumstances, the term could be extended to fifteen years (for regional
jet aircraft, this extended term is now common practice).[21] The
length of the financing term, in turn, determined the interest rate
reduction: the reduction ranged from two percentage points for a
one-year term to 3.8 percentage points for a term of ten years or
more.[22] Thus, PROEX payments reduced the effective interest rate
for the financing of Brazilian aircraft by up to 3.8 percentage
points per year.[23] Alternatively, the purchasing airline could elect
to receive PROEX payments in the form of a lump-sum payment
equal to the net present value of the stream of payments underwritten by Brazilian long-term treasury bonds. In this example,
the lump-sum payment would be US $2.45 million The net cost
of acquisition of the aircraft would thereby be reduced to US
$12.8 million — a 16 per cent reduction in the cost of the aircraft
to the airline.

THE FINDINGS OF THE PANEL

Preliminary Jurisdictional Motions

Canada and Brazil requested a range of preliminary rulings
from the panels, and Canada asked the panel to establish a procedure for the protection of business confidential information. Brazil
argued that certain legislative instruments listed in Canada's request for the establishment of a panel were not properly before the
panel. These instruments, according to Brazil, had been enacted
after consultation had been held and so had not been "subject
to consultations." The panel dismissed the preliminary motions

---

[20] The goods are listed in the annex to the Order (Portaria) of the Minister of State
for Industry, Trade and Tourism (MICT) 53/97, dated May 7, 1997 (on file with
the author).

[21] Presentation by Paulo Cesar, director of finance of Embraer, to a conference of
appraisers of regional jets on May 28, 1998, at 15-16. See also interview with
Mauricio Botelho, president of Embraer, who noted that "[i]n special circumstances [interest rate equalization] can be extended to 15 years." "Willing to
Win," *Airfinance Journal* (December 1996) at 4.

[22] Circular letter of the Central Bank of Brazil, Doc. No. 2601/95, November 29,
1995. PROEX subsidies are *de facto* available for fifteen-year terms (for aircraft),
while for the purpose of establishing the permitted rate reduction, the maximum term is still ten years.

[23] The agent bank may charge an agency fee of 12-15 bps, which would be deducted
from the 3.8 percentage point subsidy.

signifying its displeasure at the parties' reliance on technical argumentation to remove large parts of the dispute from its jurisdiction.

Substantive Issues

Arguments of the parties

Brazil relieved the panel from interpreting Articles 1[24] and 3[25] of the SCM Agreement by an early admission that PROEX payments constituted export subsidies.[26] Brazil argued, however, that these export subsidies were not prohibited on two independent grounds.[27] First, Brazil was entitled to "Special and Differential Treatment" under Article 27 of the SCM Agreement. Article 27 provides that Article 3 of the SCM Agreement does not apply to developing countries for a period of eight years if certain conditions are met. Second, Brazil argued that PROEX's export subsidies did not "secure a material advantage in the field of export credit terms," as set out in the first paragraph of Item (k) of the Illustrative List of Export Subsidies, which is set out in Annex I to the SCM Agreement. Brazil argued that this was so because PROEX's payments "equalized" for "Brazil cost" and also because they merely matched an "extensive array of subsidies," domestic and export, WTO-consistent and -inconsistent, that were allegedly given by Canada to Embraer's competitor, Bombardier. By *a contrario* implication, Brazil argued, PROEX export subsidies were not prohibited.[28]

Canada argued that Brazil did not meet the conditions set out in Article 27. First, Brazil had indeed increased the "level of export subsidies" since there had been, between 1994 (the benchmark year, according to Canada) and 1998, a 100 per cent increase in expenditures on all export subsidies by Brazil.[29] Second, Brazil was not "phasing out" its export subsidies, as it had entered into commitments to "grant" subsidies past the eight-year phase-out period set out in Article 27.[30] Third, Brazil had to phase out its subsidies in less than eight years as they were not in conformity with its development needs.[31]

---

[24] For the text of Article 1, see note 14.

[25] For the text of Article 3, see note 15.

[26] *Brazil — Aircraft* Panel Report, *supra* note 1 at para. 7.12.

[27] *Ibid.* at paras. 7.15 and 7.38.

[28] *Ibid.* at para. 7.15.

[29] *Ibid.* at para. 4.161-2.

[30] *Ibid.* at para. 200.

[31] *Ibid.* at para. 210.

With respect to Item (k), Canada pointed out that, first, exceptions to Article 3 may exist only by virtue of footnote 5.[32] Neither this footnote nor the scheme of Annex 1 permit exceptions by *a contrario* implication. Second, PROEX export subsidies were not "payments" of the kind referred to in Item (k), as they were made to the purchaser and not to an exporter or a financial institution to cover the "cost of obtaining funds." Third, Canada argued that "field of export credit terms" did not mean all subsidies allegedly granted to a particular competitor. Finally, Canada demonstrated that PROEX export subsidies did in fact "secure a material advantage" to the extent that they brought the interest rate paid by a purchaser by up to 3.8 percentage points, or the result of a 15 per cent cash discount to the purchaser.

Panel's findings and conclusions

(i) Item (k)

The panel first tackled Item (k). It observed that in order to find for Brazil on this ground, it would have to make a finding with respect to three questions related to Item (k). It would have to find that Item (k) does give rise to an *a contrario* exception, that PROEX subsidies were "payments" of the kind referred to in Item (k), and that PROEX's export subsidies did not secure a material advantage in the field of export credit terms. Though expressing deep skepticism,[33] the panel did not make findings with respect to the first two

---

[32] Footnote 5 to the SCM Agreement, *supra* note 2, provides that "[m]easures referred to in Annex I as not constituting export subsidies shall not be prohibited under this or any other provision of this Agreement."

[33] At paragraph 7.18, *Brazil — Aircraft* Panel Report, *supra* note 1, the panel notes: "It is by no means clear to us that it is permissible to use the first paragraph of item (k) as the basis for an *a contrario* argument as asserted by Brazil,[197] or that PROEX payments in fact constitute the 'payment by [governments] of all or part of the costs incurred by exporters or financial institutions in obtaining credits.'"[198]

In footnote 197, the panel observes:

Footnote 5 to the SCM Agreement states that "[m]easures referred to in Annex I as not constituting export subsidies shall not be prohibited under [Article 3.1(a)] or any other provision of this Agreement." The only measures in the Illustrative List that are explicitly 'referred to ... as not constituting export subsidies' are export credit practices in conformity with the interest rate provisions of the Arrangement under the second paragraph of item (k). There are also a number of other cases, cited by Canada, where the Illustrative List affirmatively provides that a measure is not prohibited — at least by that item — or is permissible. The first paragraph of item (k),

questions. The panel considered, and rejected, Brazil's reliance on the "material advantage" clause on substantive grounds.

Brazil had proposed two benchmarks for the "field of export credit terms": "Brazil risk" and Canada's subsidies to Bombardier. On the basis of either benchmark, Brazil argued, PROEX provided no material advantage." The panel rejected Brazil's benchmarks. It held that

> however, does not contain any such affirmative language, and would not appear to fall within the scope of footnote 5. Thus, a strong argument can be made that footnote 5 — together with footnote 1 — define the extent to which the Illustrative List can be used to establish that a measure is a 'permitted' subsidy or, in the case of footnote 1, is not a subsidy at all. In light of our findings with respect to "material advantage," however, we need not decide this question.

The analysis contained in this footnote was picked up, albeit implicitly, by the panel in *United States – Tax Treatment for "Foreign Sales Coprorations"* (*FSC*), WTO Doc. WT/DS108/R, October 8, 1999, Report of the Panel. At para. 7.118 of this case, the panel observes:

> several provisions of footnote 59 itself could be considered to "qualify" item (e). Thus, the first sentence of footnote 59 could be considered to "qualify" item (e) in providing that "deferral need not amount to an export subsidy where, for example, appropriate interest charges are collected," while the last sentence of footnote 50 could be construed to have the same effect in providing that "[p]aragraph (e) is not intended to limit a Member from taking measures to avoid the double taxation of foreign-source income earned by its enterprises or the enterprises of another Member."

In footnote 198, the panel adds:

> PROEX payments relating to export of Brazilian regional aircraft are provided in support of buyers' credits, i.e., export credits are extended to the foreign purchaser rather than to EMBRAER. Brazil's theory appears to be that lenders providing export credits must borrow funds in order to finance their lending, that the export credits so funded are provided at below the lenders' cost of borrowing, and that PROEX payments are provided to compensate the lenders for this difference. In Brazil's view, this difference between the lender's cost of borrowing and the rate it charges for the export credits extended to purchasers therefore represents a "cost incurred by ... financial institutions in obtaining credits." In addition, Brazil seeks to demonstrate that, although EMBRAER itself does not extend export credits to its customers, EMBRAER incurred certain costs in relation to the provision of buyer's credits to purchasers of Brazilian regional aircraft. Because our findings on the issue of "material advantage" dispose of Brazil's item (k) defense, we need not decide whether Brazil's view on this issue is correct. We note in passing, however, that — assuming lenders providing export credits supported by PROEX payments are in fact providing export credits at below their cost of funds — it is highly questionable whether that represents a cost for the lenders in *"obtaining* credits" as opposed to a cost incurred in *providing* credits.

an item (k) payment is "used to secure a material advantage" where the payment has resulted in the availability of export credit on terms which are more favourable than *the terms that would otherwise be available in the market-place to the purchaser with respect to the transaction in question.*[34]

In particular, and significantly, the panel, examining the SCM Agreement as a whole, found that "[i]n no case is it suggested that whether or not a benefit exists would depend upon a comparison with advantages available to a competing product from another Member."[35] Indeed, the panel considered that Brazil's approach (when compared with Canada's subsidies)

would effectively allow a Member to raise the provision of export subsidies — or indeed of any subsidy — by the complaining Member as a defense justifying its own provision of export subsidies. This would entail a race to the bottom, as each WTO Member sought to justify the provision of export subsidies on the grounds that other Members were doing the same.[36]

The panel rejected such an approach.[37] The panel also dismissed Brazil's use of its developing country status as a shield under Item (k). It noted that nothing in Item (k) identified it as a developing country provision and considered the evidence of the negotiating history put forward by Brazil as inconclusive.[38]

---

[34] *Brazil — Aircraft* Panel Report, *supra* note 1 at para. 7.23 [emphasis added].

[35] *Ibid.* at para. 7.24.

[36] *Ibid.* at para. 7.26.

[37] The panel also rejected Brazil's interpretation of "field of export credit terms." It held that:

> Even if we were to agree with Brazil — which we do not — that in order to ascertain whether an item (k) payment secures a material advantage it is necessary to examine the export credit terms available with respect to competing products exported from other Members, we still could not agree with Brazil's interpretation of the clause "in the field of export credit terms." It will be recalled that Brazil's interpretation of that clause would include as an export credit term the price at which a product was sold, and would therefore allow Brazil to offset through item (k) payments all subsidies provided to Bombardier that could reduce the price at which regional aircraft exported by that manufacturer could be sold and thus reduce the amount of the transaction to be financed. In our view, this interpretation stretches far beyond the ordinary meaning of the phrase in question. In its ordinary meaning, the field of export credit terms would refer to items directly related to export credits, such as interest rates, grace periods, transaction costs, maturities and the like. We consider that this interpretation is supported contextually by item (k) itself, which refers to a loan's "maturity and other credit terms." We see nothing in the ordinary meaning of the phrase to suggest that "the field of export credit terms" generally encompasses the price at which a product is sold (*ibid.* at para. 7.28).

[38] *Ibid.* at para. 7.30. Significantly, the panel observed that "the first paragraph of

The panel then turned to the facts of the case. It noted Brazil's own characterization of the PROEX scheme and its responses to the questions of the panel. Relying on these, as well as on the extensive evidence put forward by Canada, the panel considered

> it evident that PROEX payments result in the availability of export credit for Brazilian regional aircraft on terms which are more favourable than the terms that would otherwise be available with respect to the transaction in question.[39]

The panel thus rejected Brazil's affirmative defence.[40]

(ii) Article 27

The panel then considered Brazil's invocation of Article 27. The panel first held that Article 27, providing for "Special Differential Treatment for Developing Countries," was a right and not an exception and that it constituted an element of Article 3. As such, it had to be established by the complaining party where the

---

item (k) could — as noted in paragraph 7.26 above — be used by developed country Members as a justification to match, with export subsidies that would otherwise be prohibited, export subsidies provided by developing countries consistent with Article 27" (*ibid.* at para. 7.32).

[39] *Ibid.* at para. 7.34. The panel noted Brazil's admission that "Brazil's PROEX programme, applied to support exports of regional aircraft, acts to reduce the cost of export financing for the aircraft buyer" (*ibid.* at para. 7.35). It found that "as a factual matter Brazil does not argue that PROEX payments do not confer a 'material advantage' as that term has been interpreted by this Panel." The panel went on to observe that

> [n]either has Brazil asserted, much less submitted evidence supporting an assertion, that any specific transactions relating to the export of Brazilian regional aircraft supported by PROEX payments have not resulted in export credit terms that are more favourable than the terms that would otherwise have been available to the purchaser in the market with respect to those transactions. In fact, Brazil has not submitted any significant evidence regarding the specific terms and conditions, such as the interest rate, at which export credits supported by PROEX payments were provided, much less information regarding the export credit terms that would otherwise have been available with respect to the transaction in the market. Brazil did assert that, 'in transactions when the lender was inside Brazil, the actual interest rate was always above LIBOR or the OECD rate in practice.' But even with respect to this assertion, which in any event is not relevant in our view to the proper application of the "material advantage" clause, Brazil has not provided any supporting evidence *(ibid.* at para. 7.36).

[40] *Ibid.* at para. 7.37.

defending party is a developing country.[41] The panel agreed with Canada, however, that a developing country must meet each of three requirements to obtain the benefit of the Article 27 eight-year exception to Article 3.[42] According to Article 27.4, a developing country must not increase its level of export subsidies, it must phase out its export subsidies, and it must do so in a shorter time than eight years if the subsidies in question are inconsistent with its development needs.[43]

The panel decided that the "level of export subsidies" in Article 27.4 could be the aggregate level of subsidies for each country,[44] but it did not determine this to be the *only* method.[45] Brazil had argued that "budgeted amounts, rather than expenditures, are the proper basis of comparison because they are the responsibility of the Member governments of the WTO."[46] The panel was not persuaded. It pointed out that

> an increase in the level of export subsidies budgeted, which increase is not in fact actually realized, represents no more than a failed attempt by the subsidizing Member to increase the level of its export subsidies. That failed attempt in itself does not affect the interests of other Members.[47]

Brazil then argued that the benchmark year against which changes in the expenditure or budgetary allocations should be measured was 1991 (the year in which PROEX was established) or, alternatively, a weighted average of several years before the entry into force of the *Marrakech Agreement Establishing the World Trade Organization*

---

[41] *Ibid.* at paras. 7.49-57. The panel rejected Brazil's more outlandish argument that Article 27 was *lex specialis* to Article 3 and supplanted it altogether. See paras. 7.39-41.

[42] *Ibid.* at para. 7.57.

[43] *Ibid.* at para. 7.42.

[44] *Ibid.* at para 7.59.

[45] The parties had disagreed as to whether agricultural subsidies could be part of this "aggregate total." The panel did not make a finding on this issue as the two Brazilian programs in question did not include such subsidies. *Ibid.* at para. 7.60.

[46] Budgeted amounts for PROEX export subsidies had remained more or less steady over the years, although the level of expenditure had fluctuated widely (and increased significantly) since the entry into force of the Marrakech Agreement Establishing the World Trade Organization, *infra* note 48. *Ibid.* at para. 7.66.

[47] *Ibid.*

(WTO Agreement).[48] The panel disagreed. It pointed out that the WTO Agreement was signed in 1994 and entered into force in 1995. It was logical to conclude that the benchmark year against which the expectations of the members were to be measured to determine whether there had been an increase in distorting subsidies was 1994. In view of these determinations, the panel found that Brazil had, indeed, increased its level of export subsidies, contrary to the first requirement of Article 27.4.[49]

With respect to the phase-out requirement, Canada had argued that phase out and elimination were different concepts: the one denoted a gradual bringing out of use, while the other included an abrupt termination. Since the former and not the latter term had been used, a developing country member should show that it was bringing its export subsidies out of use through a program of phased elimination. The panel disagreed but did not consider that it had to resolve the issue.[50] It noted that Brazil had indeed entered into commitments to grant PROEX export subsidies well past the end of the eight-year phase-out period.[51] These commitments indicated an intention not to phase out the subsidies, as required by the SCM Agreement. Brazil was, therefore, in breach of the second requirement of Article 27.4.[52]

The panel then turned to the last requirement — early phase out in the event that export subsidies did not meet the development needs of the developing country in question — and dismissed Canada's claim. However, since Brazil had not complied with two of the requirements of Article 27 and since compliance with all three was required to benefit from the Article 27 exception, Brazil could not benefit from this exception. PROEX export subsidies were therefore prohibited under Article 3 of the SCM Agreement.

THE FINDINGS OF THE APPELLATE BODY

With the exception of three points, the Appellate Body confirmed the findings and the reasoning of the panel in the *Aircraft*

---

[48] Marrakech Agreement Establishing the World Trade Organization, Annex 2, in Results of the Uruguay Round of Multilateral Trade Negotiations — The Legal Texts 404 (1994), reprinted in 33 ILM 1226 (1994).

[49] *Brazil — Aircraft* Panel Report, *supra* note 1 at para. 7.76.

[50] *Ibid.* at para. 7.81.

[51] *Ibid.* at para. 7.84.

[52] *Ibid.* at para. 7.85.

cases. The first question with which the Appellate Body took issue was the decision of the panel to tackle Brazil's Item (k) defence before going on to consider Article 27. The Appellate Body noted that Article 27 is a threshold article. Thus, if a developing country member is not shown to be in violation of its terms, Article 3 of the SCM Agreement does not apply at all. Accordingly, the first step is to determine whether a developing country member may benefit from the coverage of Article 27. Only if it does not, should the panel proceed to determine whether the subsidy in question is in conformity with the other provisions of the SCM Agreement.[53]

The Appellate Body inexplicably ignored Brazil's own line of argument. Brazil had argued before the panel that PROEX export subsidies were not, by virtue of the application of the first paragraph of Item (k) of Annex I, subsidies *prohibited* by Article 3. Brazil had little interest in Article 27 — it was only too clearly in breach of the requirements of that article and had therefore to establish that PROEX export subsidies were practices that were not covered by Article 3 to begin with. The panel appropriately established that contrary to Brazil's arguments, PROEX export subsidies were indeed subsidies that came within the scope of the prohibition of Article 3. Only *then* was it, as a matter of logic, required to determine whether the prohibition *applied* and to what conditions it was subject.

The Appellate Body then turned to the panel's interpretation of Item (k). It determined that the panel erred in interpreting "field of export credit terms" as referring to the market. It noted that "benefit" already did refer to the market and that the panel's interpretation rendered the "material advantage" clause of Item (k) redundant.[54] Examining the context, the Appellate Body held that "field of export credit terms" must mean the interest rate provisions of the OECD Consensus, which is referred to in the second paragraph of Item (k).[55]

The Appellate Body did not, however, examine the issue that an illustrative list is, almost by definition, redundant. The definition and prohibition are set out in Articles 1 and 3. Annex I sets out practices that necessarily meet the definitions of these articles. To define "field of export credit terms" as "the market" renders Item (k) no more and certainly no less redundant than, for example,

---

[53] *Brazil — Aircraft* Appellate Body Report, *supra* note 1 at para. 143.

[54] *Ibid.* at para. 179.

[55] *Ibid.* at para. 181.

Item (a) of the same annex, which refers to "direct subsidies contingent upon export performance." More importantly, to interpret the "field of export credit terms" as the interest rate provisions of the OECD Consensus threatens to make the *second* paragraph of Item (k) redundant. This point is problematic because this paragraph, by common consent, *is*, in fact, an exception to Article 3. Its substantive integrity is therefore far more significant than that of the first paragraph of Item (k). However, the Appellate Body was not overly troubled by this difficulty.

The third issue (in terms of importance) on which the Appellate Body took the panel to task was the confusion of the point at which a subsidy is "granted" for the purposes of Article 27 and the point at which it may be said to "exist" for the purposes of Article 1. The Appellate Body determined that a subsidy might be *granted* without examining the type of financial contribution it constituted or the point at which the financial contribution in question conferred a benefit.[56] It is not clear how a panel may determine that a subsidy is "granted" without first finding that it "exists" or, indeed, whether, as a matter of logic, a panel can find that a subsidy "exists" but is not granted.

CONCLUSION

The parties to the dispute were to litigate more or less the same issues — and, in particular, the interpretation of Item (k) of the annex — in three Article 21.5 cases. However — not surprisingly for a dispute of this kind (and economic magnitude) — the findings of the panel and the Appellate Body (both in the original case and in the subsequent Article 21.5 proceedings) have yet to lead to a resolution of the dispute. So far, Canada has been awarded US $1.4 billion in retaliation rights against Brazil's failure to implement the original rulings of the Dispute Settlement Body (DSB). However, these rights, if exercised, would at most affect Brazilian imports of certain commodities into Canada and would have little impact on the actual issue at hand — the sale of subsidized Brazilian regional aircraft to international carriers. In other words, the legal win, conclusive though it might have been, has not resulted in the termination of the most egregious of the subsidies at issue.

The Article 21.5 reports did shed additional light on the interpretation and application of Item (k), second paragraph, of the

---

[56] *Ibid.* at para. 157.

annex. It might be argued that this fact only highlighted the difficulties with the Appellate Body's original approach to the interpretation of this provision. Indeed, as a result of the many logical somersaults of the Appellate Body in the original case and the first Article 21.5 appeal, the panel in Canada's second recourse to Article 21.5 was effectively forced to conclude that the new PROEX was not necessarily a *subsidy* program. The panel arrived at this conclusion even though the basic elements of the new program were hardly different from the original. In any event, it was not clear what purpose the program would serve or how it could function if it were *not* to result in the grant of a subsidy.

AIRCRAFT CASES: BRAZIL'S CHALLENGE OF CERTAIN CANADIAN PROGRAMS RELATING TO REGIONAL AIRCRAFT

Brazil challenged a number of disparate Canadian programs and practices. They were:

1. Technology Partnerships Canada (TPC), a program of the Canadian Department of Industry, under which contributions are made for research and development projects with respect to *enabling technologies* (technological developments cutting across manufacturing sectors to increase productivity), *environmental technologies* (technologies developed, in any industrial or agricultural sector, for the protection of the environment), and *aerospace and defence*. Brazil challenged contributions in the civil aircraft sector;

2. the sale of de Havilland by the Government of Ontario on January 28, 1997, under which the Government of Ontario exercised its option, agreed to by Ontario and Bombardier in 1992, to sell its 50 per cent interest in de Havilland, a manufacturer of turboprops and aircraft parts, for Cdn $49 million. Bombardier agreed, in return, to maintain de Havilland, which would operate as a manufacturer of aircraft and aircraft parts in accordance with commercial considerations;

3. the Canada-Québec Subsidiary Agreement on Industrial Development (Subsidiary Agreement), which entered into force on March 31, 1992 by the Governments of Canada and Québec for a period of five years, subject to a one-year extension. It expired on March 31, 1998. Contributions under the Subsidiary Agreement were intended to increase the competitiveness of Québec's economy and were available for domestic as well as export projects;

4. the Société de Développement Industriel du Québec (SDI), a generally available program of the government of Québec, which is aimed at improving the competitiveness of Québec's economy. Loans, loan guarantees, and repayable contributions are available for domestic projects as well as projects related to exportation out of the province of Québec (to the other provinces of Canada as well as to other countries); and

5. financing, residual value guarantees, loan guarantees, and "equity infusions" by the Export Development Corporation (EDC) in the civil aircraft sector, both on its own account and on the accounts of the government of Canada (Canada Account).

FINDINGS OF THE PANEL

Preliminary Rulings

Jurisdictional motions

Canada first asked the panel to establish a procedure for the protection of business confidential information. It also asked the panel to dismiss a number of Brazil's allegations on the grounds that Brazil had not requested consultations with respect to the financing activities of the EDC and that Brazil's request for the establishment of a panel did not have the level of specificity required by Article 6.2 of the Dispute Settlement Understanding (DSU). The panel dismissed the preliminary motion concerning the request for the establishment of the panel.

Confidentiality procedures

Of more interest for the purposes of this comment is the decision of the panel with respect to the confidentiality procedure requested by Canada. This decision was to have far-reaching consequences for Canada's conduct of its defence and the eventual outcome of the case before the Appellate Body. The inadequacy of the protections provided in these procedures for Canada's confidential business proprietary information was one of the reasons for Canada's later refusal to submit documents to the panel. This, in turn, was the basis for the Appellate Body's procedural findings in respect of Article 13.1 of the DSU.

Canada's motion was motivated by a single consideration: much of the information needed to exonerate the impugned Canadian programs or to rebut "evidence" adduced by Brazil would by its very nature be highly sensitive.[57] Some of these documents went to the core of the commercial activities of private interests not party to the dispute. Others related to the internal operations, including pricing practices, of the EDC. Still others were cabinet or ministerial documents, traditionally subject to strict controls as to distribution.

The EDC, for example, operates as a commercial bank — indeed, this is precisely what the panel later found. It is in a strict confidentiality relationship with its customers, and the slightest breach of this confidentiality could open the EDC and, indeed, its customers, to legal action.[58] In addition, some TPC documents relate to extremely sensitive work programs of private interests developing new products. These documents would be highly valuable to the competitors of the companies involved, of which one, Embraer, was actively involved in the dispute. Finally, although such information is well protected in municipal law, there are no sanctions under the WTO in the event of a breach.

In light of these considerations, Canada proposed the establishment of confidentiality procedures. These procedures were inspired by domestic safeguards employed in anti-dumping and countervailing duty investigations. They protected both the commercial and confidentiality concerns of the parties involved and the right of Brazil to view such documents. The essence of Canada's proposed procedures was control — control over the documents, in Canada's submission, should not be given to Brazil. The proposed procedures thus provided for copies to be deposited at the WTO Secretariat so that Brazil and the members of the panel could view these documents. The documents were not to be copied and distributed further. They were to be destroyed or returned to the party depositing them at the end of the process. It should be underlined that at the time Canada proposed the procedure, it had every intention of submitting highly confidential documents to the panel. Otherwise, there would have been no need for it to make

---

[57] As Canada noted in its submission to the panel on October 23, 1998: "If Brazil meets its *prima facie* burden, Canada cannot afford the luxury of not adducing the evidence necessary to defend its impugned programmes, and may have to rely upon confidential proprietary business information."

[58] Some clients, for example, negotiate "most favoured client" clauses into their purchase contracts. If they become aware of circumstances where other clients have received better treatment, the seller would be open to lawsuits for contractual breach. The banker, in turn, would be liable for the damages arising out of *both* the breach of confidentiality *and* the seller's contractual liabilities, which would not arise if the bank protects the confidential information adequately.

the motion. For Canada, in fact, Brazil's later objections were puzzling. If Brazil had needed to see the documents, it could have accepted Canada's procedures, which would have enabled it to have access to all the documents.

The panel initially made additional changes to the procedures that, in Canada's view, constituted a significant improvement. The most important of these revisions was the requirement that each party deposit a copy of its confidential documents at any of its embassies or missions selected by the other party. This requirement allowed both parties — whose lawyers and officials were spread around the world — to have a guarantee of access to documents without having to travel to the WTO Secretariat in Geneva.

Brazil, however, objected. It asked that a copy of the documents be deposited at its Mission in Geneva to allow it to have better access for review and analysis. The panels granted this request. Canada objected strenuously, noting that this request did not give Canada the requisite confidence in the procedure to deposit documents of the highest sensitivity. Canada also observed, even before the first written submission of the complainant was due, that Canada would not be in a position to submit confidential business information to the panel.[59] Canada deeply regretted having

---

[59] Letter to the panel, November 13, 1999 (on file with the author). Canada stated that,

> [i]n Canada's view, the modified procedures do not provide the requisite level of protection for business confidential information. At present, Canada does not know whether it would be necessary to submit such information into evidence. Should a situation arise where it would be necessary, Canada's defence could be seriously compromised because Canada would not be in a position to submit such evidence under the modified procedures ...
>
> We note Brazil's concern that the proposals initially made by the Panel would unduly restrict the ability of the parties to deal effectively with business confidential information during the course of this very rapid proceeding. These potential difficulties could be overcome by making special arrangements for 24-hour access to the documents at the WTO, if required. Similarly, each Party could allow access to the documents at its mission by the other Party, on request, at any time. Required access need in no way be limited to working hours.
>
> In Canada's view, the working procedures originally issued on 3 November 1998 struck a reasonable balance between the interests of the Parties to have access to evidence submitted to the Panel and to provide protection for confidential business information. Canada further submits that the interests of private parties not Party to this dispute in the protection of commercially sensitive information through the control of access by a neutral third party outweighs any inconvenience that may be caused to either Party as a result of such procedure.

to make this decision and noted that if the panel was to revert to its original ruling, it would make such information as may be necessary in its defence available to the panel. The panel rejected Canada's request.

Brazil's motion for documentary discovery

(i) Brazil's motion

The most remarkable of the preliminary motions was Brazil's request for wide-ranging documentary discovery at the very outset of the case — that is, even before it had submitted its first submission. In a letter dated October 23, 1998, Brazil requested that the panel engage in "additional fact-finding" with respect to

> the complete details of all operations of the Export Development Corporation, the Canada Account, the Technology Partnerships Canada and its predecessor programs, the Canada-Québec Subsidiary Agreement on Industrial Development, and the Société de Développement Industriel du Québec with regard to the civil aircraft industry, including all grants, loans, equity infusions, and loan guarantees, or any other direct or indirect financial contribution of any kind.[60]

(ii) Canada's reply

Canada argued that "Brazil has ... embarked on a fishing expedition and cast a drift-net — and has asked the Panel to pilot the ship."[61] Brazil's request was, according to Canada, unprecedented both in breadth and timing. First, Brazil sought information on "all operations" of the impugned programs or organizations, whether or not those operations fit within its request for the establishment of a panel. Second, Brazil sought this information even before it had submitted a single piece of evidence or argument demonstrating that it had a case at all. It was in effect asking the panel to investigate the programs and practices in question merely on the basis of a suspicion — and inflated allegations of "secret" accounts and "vast arrays of subsidies."

Canada pointed out that throughout the consultations, Brazil had asked for transaction-specific information concerning all the activities of the organs mentioned, without identifying which activities

---

[60] Letter from the government of Brazil to Mr. David de Pury, chairman of the Panel, October 23, 1998 (on file with the author).

[61] Reply Submission of Canada, October 30, 1998, at para. 3, appended to the *Canada — Aircraft* Panel Report, *supra* note 1 [hereinafter Reply Submission of Canada].

and what aspect of those activities had caused it concern. Canada had, accordingly, refused to respond to a "shot-gun" request for information.[62] This concern was further complicated by the fact that the information requested was confidential proprietary business information, and Canada had a duty to protect the interests of private individuals or entities not party to the dispute.[63]

Finally, Canada noted that there was no precedent

in the DSU, WTO practice, or international law and practice for turning the panel process into something akin to a commission of inquiry;[64] there is, more important, no provision in the DSU and no precedent in GATT or WTO jurisprudence for subjecting a responding party to a discovery process.[65]

In particular, relying on the Report of the Appellate Body in *United States — Measures Affecting Imports of Woven Wool Shirts and Blouses from India*,[66] Canada observed that it was the responsibility of Brazil to present its case and adduce evidence sufficient to raise a presumption that its claims have merit. If no such evidence were adduced, Canada did not consider itself under an obligation to provide *additional* information. Canada concluded by noting that it was

difficult to see how the WTO dispute settlement mechanism could work if even before a complainant has shown that it has a *prima facie* case, it could force the responding party to furnish it with evidence in the course of a wide-ranging and apparently limitless fishing expedition.[67]

---

[62] *Ibid.* at para. 6.

[63] *Ibid.* at para. 7.

[64] J.G. Merrills states that "inquiry" can be defined as: "a specific institutional arrangement which states may select *in preference to arbitration or other techniques,* because they desire to have some disputed issue *independently investigated*" [emphasis added]. See J.G. Merrills, *International Dispute Settlement,* 2nd ed. (Cambridge: Grotius Publications, 1991), at 43. Commissions of inquiry were introduced by the Hague Convention for the Pacific Settlement of International Disputes, July 29, 1899, entered into force September 4, 1900. Among the limitations on their mandate was that they should handle only questions of fact and not of law and that their findings should not be seen as obligatory. See Merrills, *supra* note 64 at 44. This is manifestly at odds with the objectives and the nature of WTO dispute settlement.

[65] Reply Submission of Canada, *supra* note 61 at para. 12.

[66] *United States — Measures Affecting Imports of Woven Wool Shirts and Blouses from India,* May 27, 1995, WTO Doc. WT/DS33/5.

[67] Reply Submission of Canada, *supra* note 61 at para. 17.

(iii) The panel's disposition of the motion

The response of the panel to Canada's submission was curious. It formally declined Brazil's motion.[68] However, the panel did engage in "additional fact-finding" and quite aggressively so. The panel characterized its first set of questions to the parties as seeking clarification on the issues raised in the first written submissions and at the first substantive meeting with the panel and insisted that it was not intended to elicit the detailed information referred to in Brazil's motion for discovery.[69] And yet, the panel did not limit itself to matters on which Canada had adduced evidence. Rather, it sought information in respect of defences that Canada had not even raised. In its second set of questions to Canada, dated December 10, 1998, the panel asked in question 7: "Please provide details, including terms and conditions, of any loan guarantees issued by EDC for transactions concerning the civil aircraft sector since 1 January 1995."

In this question, the panel was not seeking details of transactions "identified on the record." Rather, it was asking Canada to identify transactions and provide detailed information regarding these transactions. This point strains the panel's assertion that it "did not consider it appropriate to seek detailed information in respect of transactions (if any) *not identified in the record.*"[70] Indeed, in one

---

[68] *Canada —Aircraft* Panel Report, *supra* note 1 at para. 9.53.

[69] *Ibid.* at para. 9.51.

[70] [emphasis added]. Even when Canada responded regarding the purported transactions identified on the record, the panel seemed not to take notice of Canada's answers. Again, with respect to Export Development Corporation [hereinafter EDC] loan guarantees, on December 13, 1998, the panel asked in question 29: "At para. 4.6 of its first submission, Brazil refers to 'long-term loan guarantees' allegedly granted by EDC to Comair in 1995. Could Canada please provide details of any loan guarantees provided by EDC to Comair in 1995. Please include copies of all relevant loan guarantee agreements."

In Canada's answers of December 21, 1998, Canada replied to question 7 as follows:

It is Canada's position that Brazil has not made a *prima facie* case against EDC loan guarantees. Canada also notes the lack of adequate procedures to protect business confidential information. In this context, Canada provides to the Panel non-business confidential details of the two loan guarantees for export transactions provided by the EDC in the civil aircraft sector since January 1, 1995.

The first transaction was in support of the sale of two used de Havilland Twin Otters and two used de Havilland Dash 8-102s to an airline operating in the South Pacific. The guarantee was provided at commercial rates.

instance, the panel asked for "details of the terms and conditions of this financing, and a copy of the relevant finance agreement" with respect to a transaction to which Brazil merely "refers" in its submission.[71]

Canada refused to provide the information requested for two reasons. First, as a matter of principle, Canada did not consider it appropriate to provide evidence when no *specific* allegation about a transaction had been made or, indeed, where no credible evidence had been put forward by the party with the burden of establishing its case. Second, as noted earlier in this comment, the information in question was highly sensitive and the confidentiality procedures inadequate. The panel "regretted" Canada's decision — a phrase that was repeated *ad nauseum* by Brazil in its appeal.

The panel also found that

[i]n adducing evidence regarding the ASA transaction, Brazil does not assert, much less provide evidence to show, that EDC provided ASA with debt financing at below-market rates ... Brazil makes no attempt to specify what these rates are, or how they are calculated, or that the rates referred to are below-market. Accordingly, we find that Brazil's arguments concerning ASA provide no basis for finding that either this specific instance of EDC debt financing, or EDC debt financing in the regional aircraft sector generally, confers a "benefit" within the meaning of Article 1.1(b) of the SCM Agreement.[72]

The panel does not explain on what basis Canada was required to have provided "additional information" with respect to an "assertion" not made, evidence not adduced, and a claim not established.

The second transaction was in support of pre-shipment financing of a flight inspection system sold to a sovereign Latin American buyer. The guarantee was provided at commercial rates.

On the same date, Canada replied to question 29 as follows: "EDC provided no such loan guarantees to Comair in 1995. EDC's loan guarantee activity in the civil aircraft sector since 1 January 1995 has been described in answer to Question 7 of the Panel."

The *Canada — Aircraft* panel reposed question 29 to Canada on January 11, 1999, changing the date from 1995 to 1997. Yet, Canada had already provided a complete description of the EDC's loan guarantee activity in Canada's answer to question 7 on December 21, 1998. Nonetheless, Canada replied again to the reposed question 29, indicating that no such guarantees had been provided to Comair in 1997. Canada had identified all the applicable EDC loan guarantees in the record in its answer to question 7. There were no more.

[71] Questions of December 13, 1998 by the *Canada — Aircraft* panel.

[72] *Canada — Aircraft* Panel Report, *supra* note 1 at para. 9.179.

Substantive Findings

Brazil challenged a range of Canadian programs and practices. For practical reasons, Canada decided early on to defend itself selectively. For all but the financing activities of the EDC, Canada defended the impugned programs and practices on the ground that they were not contingent upon export performance. With respect to the EDC, Canada argued that it did not engage in subsidization. In addition, in light of its ongoing concerns about the protection of the confidentiality of proprietary business information, Canada determined, as a matter of legal strategy, to produce only such evidence as was necessary to rebut the evidence and allegations put forward by Brazil. For this reason, after receiving Brazil's first written submission, Canada asked the panel for an early ruling on whether Brazil had indeed made out a *prima facie* case. If Brazil did not have a case, Canada did not consider itself bound to respond to a case not made. If it did, Canada would produce such documents as the panel considered necessary to rebut Brazil's case.[73] Given that Brazil, as the complainant, bore the burden of proof, "it is enough for Canada to show, in respect of each impugned programme, activity or transaction, that Brazil has failed to demonstrate inconsistency with either one or the other condition."[74] At no point did either the panel or Brazil challenge this basic proposition on which Canada's refusal to adduce additional evidence was founded.

Brazil's challenge began with an unprecedented request for broad documentary discovery. Its first submission was accompanied by 1,600 pages of evidence recovered from a variety of public and private sources, including information and documents obtained by a Canadian member of the parliamentary official opposition, the Reform Party of Canada, through the Library of Parliament.[75]

---

[73] Canada's legal defence was also constrained by conventional domestic requirements relating to the confidentiality of cabinet documents, in that certain key documents, no matter how exculpatory, could not be produced. To the extent, therefore, that Brazil could establish a *prima facie* case in respect of matters subject to cabinet confidences, Canada would be barred by its domestic constitutional arrangement to defend itself and would have to "take its lumps," as it were.

[74] *Canada — Measures Affecting the Export of Civilian Aircraft — Recourse by Brazil to Article 21.5 of the DSU,* Canada's First Written Submission, at para. 4, appended to the *Canada — Aircraft* Panel Report, *supra* note 1 [hereinafter *Canada — Aircraft* Canada's First Written Submission].

[75] Despite the physical weight of the evidence, it was sufficiently light in substance (and Brazil's submission was sufficiently strong in rhetoric) for Canada to

Brazil alleged that certain financing and related activities (including loan guarantees and residual value guarantees) constituted subsidies that were contingent upon export performance. It also alleged that contributions in the civil aircraft sector under a range of research and development, as well as regional development, programs were subsidies that were, in fact, contingent upon export performance. Brazil's case relied on statements from Canadian officials praising the international competitiveness of the Canadian civil aircraft industry, the heavy export orientation of the industry, the requirements for export market reporting in application forms, and, finally, the fact that some of the programs in question provided contributions for "near market" projects.

Financing and related activities of the EDC

Brazil alleged that the EDC provided financing at "concessionary" rates. In support of this allegation, it relied on various statements by EDC officials to the effect that the "EDC complements the banks and other financial intermediaries, but cannot substitute for them."[76] It alleged that the EDC's "goal is to help absorb the risk on behalf of Canadian exporters, beyond what is possible by other financial intermediaries."[77] It then asserted that

EDC funding may be structured as direct financing at concessionary rates for up to 90 percent of the cost of an aircraft. EDC itself acknowledges the concessionary nature of its export assistance. In testimony before Parliament, Paul Labbé, President and Chief Executive Officer of EDC, noted that EDC strives to "mak[e] at least the rate of inflation," which he recognized was well below the return "that would be required to survive in the private sector."[78]

---

suspect that Brazil might be "splitting" its case. In its reply submission, Canada asked for a ruling on whether Brazil had made out a *prima facie* case and requested that the panel require Brazil to submit all available evidence so that Canada might be made aware of the case against it. As the panel refused to make a ruling, and given that there was, in fact, no more evidence, Canada determined, for the most part, to let Brazil's evidence (and Brazil's puzzling distortion of it) speak for itself.

[76] *Canada — Measures Affecting the Export of Civilian Aircraft — Recourse by Brazil to Article 21.5 of the DSU*, Brazil's First Submission, at para. 4.3 appended to the *Canada — Aircraft* Panel Report, *supra* note 1.

[77] *Ibid.*

[78] *Ibid.* at para. 4.4 [footnotes omitted].

Canada observed, however, that Brazil's case rested on evidence "presented out of context or in incomplete form so as to convey a different impression or meaning than that intended by the author of the material cited."[79]

Brazil had also initially relied on the EDC's "net interest margin" in an attempt to demonstrate that the EDC's activities amounted to subsidies. However, after an effective rebuttal by Canada it returned to the various statements made by EDC officials as support for its allegations. Finally, having failed to adduce transaction-specific evidence in support of its own broad allegations, Brazil asked the panel to draw adverse inferences from Canada's refusal to submit to the panel's request for documentary production.

Turning its attention first to the definition of "subsidy" in Article 1 of the SCM Agreement, the panel held that "the ordinary meaning of 'benefit' clearly encompasses some form of advantage."[80] The panel observed that "the only logical basis for determining [the existence of an advantage] is the market."[81] Accordingly, the panel concluded, a financial contribution would confer a benefit and constitute a subsidy "if it is provided on terms that are more

---

[79] *Canada – Aircraft* Canada's First Written Submission, *supra* note 74 at para. 4. In respect of the quotes noted earlier, for example, Canada pointed out that

[t]he ... quotation concerning the absorption of risk by the EDC, is repeated later in paragraph 6.4 to support the allegation that "[n]o private financial institution or investor would provide this degree of *financing on concessionary terms.*" The quotation is also used to allege, in paragraph 6.1, that "every move [EDC] makes" is in support of this "risk absorption" goal. The quotation is the basis for Brazil's claim that "EDC is precisely what Article 3 of the SCM Agreement was intended to prohibit."

Brazil has, however, omitted the qualifying subordinate clause of this sentence. The full sentence, placed in context, is set out in Brazil's Exhibit 7, second page:

In addition to the shift from sovereign to commercial loans, the complexity, scale and duration of financing are changing, and thereby changing the *risks* associated with insuring and financing Canadian exports.

To reinforce its capacity to manage these changing risks, EDC has established a new Financial Services Office and procedures for evaluating loan portfolios on an industry, geographic, and individual transaction basis. Our goal is to help absorb risk on behalf of Canadian exporters, beyond what is possible by other financial intermediaries, *by diversifying the Corporation's business both on a country and sectoral basis.* We are determined *to achieve this goal through growth in both emerging and established markets*" [emphasis added throughout] (*ibid.* at para. 35.)

[80] *Canada — Aircraft* Panel Report, *supra* note 1 at para. 9.112.

[81] *Ibid.*

advantageous than those that would have been available to the recipient on the market."[82]

The panel then examined the evidence put forward by Brazil. The panel first reviewed the statements on which Brazil had relied. It agreed with Canada's observations that read *in context* none of the statements supported Brazil's assertion that the EDC engaged in subsidized financing. The panel then analyzed the EDC's financial performance. Canada had demonstrated that the EDC's net interest margin compared favourably with that of commercial banks[83] — a fact that Brazil had not disputed. Brazil had, in response, attempted to undermine the usefulness of the net interest margin figures.[84] The panel noted, however, that,

> [b]y way of preliminary remark, we recall that Brazil itself initially referred to EDC's net interest margin ("a mere 2.82 percent in 1997, and 3.03 percent in 1996") to indicate the poor financial performance of EDC. We find unconvincing, therefore, that Brazil subsequently seeks to indicate that in fact EDC's net interest margin does not constitute a sufficient basis for comparison.[85]

The panel found that the net interest margin did, in fact, constitute a sufficient basis for comparison and determined that the EDC did not provide financing at concessionary rates.[86] In arriving at this

---

[82] *Ibid.*

[83] Brazil's argument in its first written submission was an interesting, but ultimately self-defeating, exercise in sleight-of-hand drafting. At para. 4.19 of its submission, Brazil said:

> Regardless of the form in which export financing is offered, EDC has itself acknowledged the concessionary nature of its subsidies, noting that in order to avoid "los[ing] money, [EDC] should be making at least the rate of inflation on [its] capital base which is [its] aim. That goal is a long cry from the 15 per cent or 20 per cent return on equity that would be required to survive in the private sector." EDC's annual reports underscore its shortcoming in this regard; its net interest margin was a mere 2.82 percent in 1997, and 3.03 percent in 1996 [footnotes omitted].

Brazil casually juxtaposed *return on equity* and *net interest margin*, implying that the far lower numbers of the latter were somehow meaningful in regard to the former. Canada demonstrated, however, that for commercial banks the net interest margin is a better indicator of financial performance than a return on equity and that the EDC in fact had a better net interest margin than many major commercial banks. Brazil's too-clever-by-half drafting did not, however, serve it well in the end.

[84] *Canada – Aircraft* Panel Report, *supra* note 1 at para. 9.166.

[85] *Ibid.* at para. 9.167.

[86] *Ibid.* at para. 9.168.

determination, the panel considered and rejected a series of arguments and assertions by Brazil, some of which were more serious than others.[87]

The panel then turned to the ASA transaction, noting that "Brazil has *referred* to the EDC debt financing provided to ASA in April 1997, in support of its claim that EDC debt financing is provided on concessionary, and therefore subsidized, terms."[88] It stated that on the basis of "information on the record," the panel asked for "details of the terms and conditions of the alleged EDC debt financing to ASA."[89] Canada refused to provide this information, and Brazil asked the panel to draw an adverse inference from Canada's refusal.

The panel recalled its "rejection of Canada's criticism of the Panel's Procedures Governing Business Confidential Information" and noted deep "regret" regarding Canada's refusal to provide the information.[90] The panel went on to state that

[w]ith regard to Canada's assertion that Brazil failed to make any specific allegation concerning the ASA transaction, we understand Brazil's claim against EDC debt financing to cover all instances of EDC debt financing in the Canadian regional aircraft sector. We therefore reject Canada's assertion that Brazil has made no allegation concerning the ASA transaction.[91]

And yet, in the very next paragraph, the panel made the following finding:

---

[87] One argument was dismissed by the rather simple, but effective, observation that "assertions based on *unsecured* bonds provide no guidance in reviewing returns on *secured* lending" (*ibid.* at para. 9.169). Another elicited the following comment from the panel:

> We are not persuaded that our analysis of Brazil's arguments concerning EDC's debt financing performance should be influenced by indemnification payments from the Government of Canada to EDC following the writing-off of sovereign debt pursuant to Canada's Paris Club commitments. We do not consider that EDC action in response Canada's Paris Club commitments is indicative of whether or not EDC debt financing in the Canadian regional aircraft sector confers a "benefit" (*ibid.* at para. 9.172).

Other allegations liberally thrown about by Brazil merited no more than "Brazil makes no attempt to suggest" and "Brazil has made no attempt to establish" for ready dismissal by the panel (*ibid.* at para. 9.173).

[88] *Ibid.* at para. 9.175.

[89] *Ibid.* at para. 9.176.

[90] *Ibid.* at para. 9.178.

[91] *Ibid.*

In adducing evidence regarding the ASA transaction, Brazil *does not assert,* much less provide evidence to show, that EDC provided ASA with debt financing at below-market rates. The only information adduced by Brazil concerning the financing terms for this transaction is contained in ASA's 1997 annual report. At pages 15/16 of the annual report, reference is made to loans or leases "with interest payable at various interest rate options determined by reference to either U.S. treasury rates or LIBOR." *Brazil makes no attempt to specify* what these rates are, or how they are calculated, or that the rates referred to are below-market. Accordingly, we find that Brazil's arguments concerning ASA provide no basis for finding that either this specific instance of EDC debt financing, or EDC debt financing in the regional aircraft sector generally, confers a "benefit" within the meaning of Article 1.1 (b) of the SCM Agreement.[92]

The panel added that "Brazil has made *no attempt to demonstrate* that EDC debt financing was provided to ASA on below-market terms."[93] The panel also systematically dismissed, for lack of evidence, Brazil's allegations concerning subsidies allegedly granted through loan guarantees,[94] residual value guarantees,[95] and equity infusions.[96]

---

[92] *Ibid.* at para. 9.179.

[93] *Ibid.* at para. 9.181 [emphasis added].

[94] The panel observed: "The only evidence adduced by Brazil in support of its claim that EDC grants subsidies in the form of loan guarantees to purchasers or lessors of Canadian regional aircraft has been fully rebutted by Canada" (*ibid.* at para. 9.190).

[95] In response to Brazil's ongoing request for drawing adverse inferences, the panel noted:

We note that the *only* evidence adduced by Brazil to support its claim that EDC provides residual value guarantees to lessors of regional aircraft is a *1994 press article* containing the '*suggestion*' that residual value guarantees *may* have been granted in 1992. In light of Canada's express denial that EDC provides residual value guarantees to lessors of regional aircraft, we find that there is *no factual basis* to Brazil's claim that the EDC has provided prohibited export subsidies in the form of residual value guarantees to lessors of regional aircraft (*ibid.* at para. 9.195) [emphasis added].

[96] The panel found that

there is no factual basis on which to establish a *prima facie* case that EDC has made equity infusions into CRJ Capital that have facilitated CRJ Capital's ability to lease or sell Canadian regional aircraft at a reduced price. We therefore reject Brazil's claim that EDC has granted prohibited export subsidies to the Canadian regional aircraft industry in the form of equity infusions into CRJ Capital (*ibid.,* at para. 9.200).

Provincial programs and activities in question

(i) Subsidiary Agreement

With respect to the Subsidiary Agreement, Brazil's allegations rested on Canada's Article 25 notification to the Subsidies and Countervailing Measures Committee as well as a study prepared by the Reform Party of Canada, the Official Opposition in the Canadian House of Commons. Canada had decided not to defend the program at all on the grounds that it was a subsidy, limiting itself instead to the proposition that the SCM Agreement was not contingent upon export performance.

In its questions to Canada, the panel nevertheless asked for extensive information and documentation with respect to various contributions made under the SCM Agreement. Subject to its on-going concerns about the protection of confidential business proprietary information and in view of its express statement that it would not defend itself against allegations relating to whether these contributions amounted to subsidies, Canada provided some documents and full responses to the panel. The panel found that Brazil's case had no merit.

Referring to Canada's Article 25 notification, the panel noted that

Article 25.7 of the SCM Agreement effectively precludes us from finding a *prima facie* case that Subsidiary Agreement assistance is provided in the form of non-repayable contributions simply on the basis of Canada's notification of that programme.[97]

Turning to the Reform Party study, the panel observed that the only contribution mentioned in the study dated back to 1989, and found that it "lends no support to Brazil's claim concerning non-repayable Subsidiary Agreement contributions to the Canadian regional aircraft industry."[98] The panel concluded that

Brazil has adduced no other evidence to demonstrate that Subsidiary Agreement assistance generally is provided in the form of non-repayable contributions, or that non-repayable contributions are provided to the Canadian regional aircraft industry in particular.[99]

Brazil's failure to adduce "other" evidence had not stopped the panel from submitting a request for documents and information

[97]   *Ibid.* at para. 9.256.

[98]   *Ibid.* at para. 9.257.

[99]   *Ibid.* at para. 9.258.

with respect to a host of other contributions. Two of these contributions Brazil conceded to have not been in the regional aircraft sector.[100] With respect to the others, the panel observed that "Brazil fails to demonstrate that any of the five instances of alleged Subsidiary Agreement assistance concerns the regional aircraft industry."[101] The panel also noted that "none of the five instances of Subsidiary Agreement assistance identified in the study is described as being 'conditionally repayable,' as alleged by Brazil."[102] With respect to one contribution to Bombardier, the panel found that

Brazil fails to *provide any evidence, or even to argue,* that the relevant contribution confers a "benefit" within the meaning of Article 1.1 (b) of the SCM Agreement ... Brazil *makes no attempt to establish* that this particular contribution is either non-repayable, or that it is conditionally repayable and the rate of return is such that the lender is not compensated for either the risk that it would have received no payment or the extended repayment period during which neither principal nor interest is due. In such circumstances, the evidence adduced by Brazil concerning the Subsidiary Agreement contribution to Bombardier provides no support for Brazil's claim that Subsidiary Agreement assistance to the Canadian regional aircraft industry takes the form of "subsidies."[103]

Inexplicably, the panel did not ask *itself* the simple question of why it would request information and document in respect of matters that Brazil had failed even to argue or even to attempt to establish.

(ii) Société de développement industriel du Québec (SDI)

Brazil's case against the successor to the SDI, Investissement Québec, relied exclusively (and impermissibly) on the Trade Policy Review of Canada, conducted by the WTO Secretariat. Canada did not defend itself with respect to whether the SDI provided subsidies. The panel found correctly that

section A(i) of the WTO Trade Policy Review Mechanism provides that the review mechanism "is not, however, intended to serve as a basis for the enforcement of specific obligations under the Agreements or for dispute settlement procedures." Accordingly, we attach no importance to the Trade Policy Review of Canada in considering Brazil's arguments concerning IQ assistance to the regional aircraft industry. Brazil has failed to adduce any evidence of IQ assistance to the Canadian regional aircraft sector.[104]

[100] *Ibid.* at para. 9.259.
[101] *Ibid.* at para. 9.260.
[102] *Ibid.*
[103] *Ibid.* at para. 9.261 [emphasis added].
[104] *Ibid.* at para. 9.274-5.

Brazil's case against the SDI was based entirely on the SDI's annual report. It made no assertions in respect of specific contributions. Indeed, as the panel noted, "[i]n its first submission, Brazil expressly cites SDI documentation that refers to 'loan[s] at the market rate.'"[105] The panel nevertheless took it upon itself to investigate the matter[106] and requested information and documents, with which request Canada partially complied. Not surprisingly, the panel concluded that "there is no *prima facie* case that SDI assistance has been provided to the regional aircraft industry in the form of subsidies within the meaning of Article 1 of the SCM Agreement."[107]

(iii) The sale of de Havilland by the government of Ontario

Brazil's most ambitious argument was that the privatization by the government of Ontario of its share of de Havilland constituted an *export* subsidy. The essence of Brazil's argument was that before privatization, the government of Ontario had allegedly paid subsidies to de Havilland. The sale price of Ontario's share of the company, Brazil argued, did not reflect the net present value of these alleged subsidies, which had been paid in the five years before privatization. The company was heavily export-oriented, and Brazil argued that the sale and, therefore, the alleged "net present value" subsidy took place in "anticipation" of future exports and were, accordingly, contingent upon export performance.

Canada did not defend the sale on the basis of Article 1 — that is, it did not argue whether the sale had constituted a subsidy.[108] However, Canada did rebut some of Brazil's more egregious allegations, such as the unfounded assertion that a loan to Bombardier by the government of Ontario had been forgiven or had been provided on other than commercial rates. Canada stated that it did not wish to defend itself under Article 1. However, the panel "asked Canada to specify the total value of de Havilland's equity on the date of the

---

[105] *Ibid.*

[106] The panel observed: "The SDI Annual Report 1997-1998 refers to three contributions under the Aerospace Industry Development Fund. We consider that these contributions are covered by Brazil's claim, since its claim effectively covers all SDI assistance to the regional aircraft industry" (*ibid.* at para. 9.277).

[107] *Ibid.* at para. 9.279.

[108] The decision to privatize de Havilland had been a political one, taken by a newly elected provincial government pursuant to a neo-conservative electoral platform. The analyses done in advance of the sale were either not available or not complete and could therefore not be relied upon to rebut an Article 1 allegation.

sale of Ontario Aerospace Corporation's 49 per cent share to Bombardier."[109] Canada furnished the panel with information indicating that the equity value of de Havilland was *negative* at the time of its sale to Bombardier. Brazil had offered no evidence as to the equity value of de Havilland and offered no evidence to contradict the information provided by Canada. And yet, the panel requested the audited statements of de Havilland, which by now was a privately owned corporation. Again, Canada noted that it had specifically determined not to defend itself on this issue, that Brazil had provided no evidence that required Canada to offer rebuttal evidence of its own and that, in any event, the confidentiality procedures were defective.

The panel determined that,

[i]n light of *the unrebutted evidence* of a decrease in the value of OAC's 49 percent equity share in de Havilland between 1992 and 1997 ... we find that there is no *prima facie* case that the sale by the OAC of its 49 percent share in de Havilland to Bombardier in 1997 constitutes an export subsidy contrary to Article 3.1(a) and 3.2 of the SCM Agreement, and we reject Brazil's claim accordingly.[110]

The panel does not explain on what authority it requested that Canada furnish it with the audited statements of a private company to support what it accepts as unrebutted evidence. Nor does the panel clearly spell out why it would "regret" the failure of Canada to provide additional information, when the party advancing the claim had shown so little respect to the WTO dispute settlement mechanism as to litigate an unsupported and indeed unsupportable case.

TPC program

Brazil's case rested on two broad evidentiary pillars. First, a report asserted that all regional jet aircraft produced by Canada

---

[109] *Canada —Aircraft* Panel Report, *supra* note 1 at para. 9.237.

[110] *Ibid.* at para. 9.246 [emphasis added]. Brazil, having failed to offer any credible evidence of subsidization — as there was none — now claimed that the sale of *negative* equity for US $49 million was a subsidy because absent the previous, unchallenged subsidies, the equity would have been even more negative (*ibid.* at para. 9.240). The panel rejected this argument and correctly determined that, "in the absence of any evidence to the contrary, we have no basis for rejecting Canada's assertion, based on a signed statement from a de Havilland executive, that de Havilland had a negative equity value at the time of the January 1997 sale" (*ibid.* at para. 9.244).

had been exported — including some twenty-four jets that had been sold and were being operated by Air Canada. Second, Canadian ministers and officials had publicly applauded the international competitiveness and, hence, the strong export orientation of some of the enterprises that received contributions under the TPC program. These elements, according to Brazil, indicated that the contributions in question had been made to the regional aircraft sector *because* of the strong export propensity of the companies involved.

Canada argued, however, that Article 3 prohibited subsidies contingent upon export performance — that is, subsidies granted on condition that exports take place. The fact that the recipients of contributions in some of the sectors supported by the TPC had a high export propensity was a reflection of the market rather than a requirement or a condition of the program. There was no evidence that stronger exports would result in more subsidies or that a failure to export resulted in less subsidies or a reimbursement of the subsidies already paid.

The panel found for Brazil. Citing sixteen different pieces of evidence, the panel determined that the TPC contributions would not have been made but for the expectation that the products in question would be exported. The panel also noted that the contributions in question were development subsidies for near-market projects. Such subsidies were more likely to be found to be contingent upon export performance than upon research-related subsidies.

Canada Account

The panel also found in favour of Brazil with respect to its allegation that financing activities on the government of Canada's accounts (and administered by the EDC) constituted subsidies contingent upon export performance. Canada had initially invoked the coverage of the OECD Consensus under Item (k) of Annex I to the SCM Agreement. However, in its second written submission, Canada observed the lack of any evidence supporting Brazil's allegations and withdrew its defence, relying instead on the basic defence of absence of a *prima facie* case.

Brazil's sole piece of evidence with respect to whether *specific* Canada Account transactions were subsidies[111] arrived in the midst

---

[111] With respect to whether Canada Account activity in itself constitutes subsidies, the panel made the following observation:

of the dispute. It consisted of a press report dated November 1998, which quoted a senior Bombardier official as acknowledging that the company had used the Canada Account for "a very small number of transactions under terms of financing described as 'close to commercial.'"[112] Canada pointed out that the official was referring to the Commercial Interest Reference Rate of the OECD Consensus, for which rates "may be above or below the market for a particular credit." The panel concluded therefore that,

> by stating that OECD Consensus CIRRs "may be above or below the market for a particular credit," we consider that Canada is *implicitly* acknowledging that the "close to commercial rates" referred to by Dr. Allaire *could themselves have been* "below the market." For this reason, we find a *prima facie* case that the Canada Account debt financing in issue confers a "benefit," and therefore constitutes a "subsidy" within the meaning of Article 1 of the SCM Agreement.[113]

The panel did not explain this simple conundrum: how something that *could* constitute a subsidy can be said to *be* a subsidy without further evidence. Having thus erased the semantic distinction between an *implied* "could be" and a "be" (Article 1 refers to subsidies deemed to "exist" when certain conditions are met), the panel found the Canada Account transactions in question inconsistent with Article 3. This finding of the panel was not appealed.

FINDINGS OF THE APPELLATE BODY

Substantive Findings

The Appellate Body upheld the panel's substantive findings, with two minor "cautions" in respect of the panel's interpretation and application of Article 3. First, the Appellate Body mildly rejected the panel's implicit argument that the "nearness to the market" of a subsidy would give rise to a "legal presumption" that it was

---

[W]e understand Brazil to argue that Canada Account assistance is, as a matter of law, granted in the form of subsidies. However, we find nothing in Brazil's various submissions in support of this argument. As Brazil itself notes, "Canada Account funds are used to support export transactions which the federal government deems to be in the national interest but which, for reasons of size or risk, the Export Development Corporation (EDC) cannot support through regular export credits." Brazil has failed to demonstrate that such "support" necessarily involves subsidization (*ibid.* at para. 9.211) [footnote omitted].

[112] *Ibid.* at para. 9.216 [footnote omitted].

[113] *Ibid.* at para. 9.224 [emphasis added].

contingent upon export performance.[114] It suggests simply that, "[i]f a panel takes this factor into account, it should treat it with considerable caution."[115] And yet, the Appellate Body does not at any point assess the extent to which the panel's error in establishing a legal presumption might have affected the final conclusion of the panel. It simply notes that the panel did not err in taking the factor into consideration.[116] As a matter of logic, however, a "presumption" is either legally significant, or it is not. The Appellate Body decided that the nearness to the market factor should be treated with "considerable caution." Curiously, it does not determine whether the panel's turning the factor into a presumption amounted to "considerable caution." As well, a presumption turns the burden of proof onto the defending party; but the Appellate Body does not address this crucial point.

Second, the Appellate Body cautions the panel that there is a difference between the expectations of the granting authority and whether the granting of a subsidy was *tied to* export performance.[117] The Appellate Body notes that the two should not be confused. However, the Appellate Body does not consider that a number of statements and pieces of evidence relied on by the panel went to those very expectations. As Canada noted before the Appellate Body in response to a direct question, the question was not whether the panel did or did not correctly assess the evidence before it. Rather, Canada referred to the evidence relied on by the panel to underline the legal error of the panel in substituting "expectations" for "tied to." The Appellate Body does not address this issue. It is not clear, therefore, whether the expectations of the granting authority — without more evidence as to the existence of a *condition* — can turn a domestic subsidy into a prohibited export subsidy.

Documentary Discovery, Adverse Inference, and Article 13 of the DSU

We now turn to the analysis that lies at the core of the Appellate Body's findings and conclusions in the *Canada — Aircraft* case — the right of a panel to compel the production of documentary evidence by a party to the dispute.[118] The questions at issue were deceptively

---

[114] *Canada — Aircraft* Appellate Body Report, *supra* note 1 at para. 174.

[115] *Ibid.*

[116] *Ibid.* at para. 177.

[117] *Ibid.* at para. 172.

[118] See also Rambod Behboodi, "'Should' Means 'Shall': The Procedural Rulings of the Appellate Body in the Aircraft Subsidies Cases" (2000) 3 J.I.E.L. 563.

simple: first, was there an obligation on the disputing parties to produce evidence to an arbitral tribunal, and, second, did the panel err in not drawing an adverse inference from Canada's refusal to provide the panel with all the documents for which it had asked. The Appellate Body responded "yes" to the first question and an enigmatic "no" to the second.

Is there a "duty to collaborate"?

Brazil argued that Canada was under a legal obligation to divulge whatever information it was asked to produce by the panel. For this proposition, Brazil relied upon Article 3.10 of the DSU, which requires Members to enter into dispute settlement in good faith. Brazil also referred to previous findings by the Appellate Body with respect to the "duty" of the parties to be "fully forthcoming" throughout the dispute settlement process. Finally, Brazil pointed to jurisprudence in international law holding that parties to a dispute were under a legal obligation to "collaborate" with the arbitral tribunal sitting in judgment of their actions. This "exceptional burden," as Brazil put it,[119] stemmed from two shortcomings of international tribunals. First, "the duty of collaboration is imposed upon a respondent to counter the obstacles facing a complainant in gathering evidence peculiarly within the control of an uncooperative respondent."[120] Second, international tribunals have no power to compel the production of evidence.[121] As a corollary to this duty, Brazil asserted, arbitral tribunals had the right and the obligation to draw "adverse inferences" when documents are not produced.

Brazil argued that Canada had not satisfied its burden of producing the documents for which it was asked by the panel. The panel had been under an obligation to draw the adverse inference that the measure in question was inconsistent with the SCM Agreement. Since it had not done so, the panel had made a legal error, which Brazil asked the Appellate Body to remedy.

---

[119] *Canada — Measures Affecting the Export of Civilian Aircraft — Recourse by Brazil to Article 21.5 of the DSU,* Brazil's Appellant's Submission, at para. 51, available by request from most governments.

[120] *Ibid.* at para. 53.

[121] *Ibid.* at para. 55.

Limits to the duty of collaboration in international law and practice

Canada agreed that in international practice there was generally a duty to collaborate.[122] After exhaustively canvassing the cases relied on by Brazil, Canada noted that

[t]he international jurisprudence and teachings of publicists demonstrate that there are carefully drawn limits on both the duty to collaborate and rule of adverse inference ... In particular, the duty to collaborate and the authority to draw adverse inferences do not arise until the claimant has made out a *prima facie* case.[123]

Indeed, Canada stated:

With the greatest of respect for the Panel in its role as fact-finder, Canada further submits that the Panel misapplied and misinterpreted both DSU Article 13.1 and the principle of the burden of proof when it requested information and evidence on the ASA transaction. The request for additional information in the absence of a *prima facie* case and in the face of not even an assertion by Brazil appeared to Canada as an effort by the Panel (even if not so intended) to collect evidence to advance Brazil's case.[124]

Canada then pointed out that the *Argentina — Measures Affecting Imports of Footwear, Textiles, Apparel and Other Items* [125] panel report, in which the duty to collaborate was first discussed, had relied heavily on the work of M. Kazazi for its analysis. According to Kazazi, given the requirement that the claimant is responsible for establishing its case,

not only should the claimant initiate the production of evidence but the evidence it provides should be of some value. The minimum standard of proof known in many municipal jurisdictions is *prima facie* evidence. Therefore it is fair to conclude that the respondent should not be expected to provide any evidence before the claimant presents at least *prima facie* evidence in favour of its case.[126]

---

[122] *Canada — Measures Affecting the Export of Civilian Aircraft — Recourse by Brazil to Article 21.5 of the DSU*, Canada's Appellee Submission, at para. 103, available by request from most governments [hereinafter *Canada — Aircraft* Canada's Appellee Submission].

[123] *Ibid.* at para. 94.

[124] *Ibid.* at para. 95.

[125] *Argentina — Measures Affecting Imports of Footwear, Textiles, Apparel and Other Items*, Doc. WT/DS121/R, Report of the Panel, circulated on June 25, 1999.

[126] M. Kazazi, *Burden of Proof and Related Issues: A Study on Evidence before International Tribunals* (The Hague: Kluwer Law International, 1996), at 137-8.

The reason was simple. If the claimant had the burden of proof, this meant, by definition, that unless this burden was discharged, the responding party did not have to do anything — it did not need to make a submission or adduce evidence, because no case existed. The task of a panel was to "objectively assess the facts of the case" and not any other facts or arguments. If the claimant had failed to put the facts before it, its case must fail. There was, in this circumstance, *ipso facto,* no reason for the responding party to adduce evidence.

More importantly, Canada referred the Appellate Body to Article 13 of the DSU. In particular, Canada pointed out that, as the Appellate Body had also found in a recent case, the panel was not to engage in fact-finding for the purpose of establishing the case of the claimant.[127] Accordingly, Canada argued:

> [W]here no *prima facie* case has been established, a panel may not embark upon a fact-finding mission, may not launch a process of discovery and may not assume the role of a commission of inquiry denied it expressly and implicitly by the DSU.[128]

---

[127] As the Appellate Body recently stated:

> Article 13 of the DSU and Article 11.2 of the SPS Agreement suggest that panels have a significant investigative authority. However, this authority cannot be used by a panel to rule in favour of a complaining party which has not established a prima facie case of inconsistency based on specific legal claims asserted by it. A panel is entitled to seek information and advice from experts and from any other relevant source it chooses, pursuant to Article 13 of the DSU and, in an SPS case, Article 11.2 of the SPS Agreement, to help it to understand and evaluate the evidence submitted and the arguments made by the parties, but not to make the case for a complaining party.
>
> In the present case, the Panel was correct to seek information and advice from experts to help it to understand and evaluate the evidence submitted and the arguments made by the United States and Japan with regard to the alleged violation of Article 5.6. The Panel erred, however, when it used that expert information and advice as the basis for a finding of inconsistency with Article 5.6, since the United States did not establish a *prima facie* case of inconsistency with Article 5.6 based on claims relating to the "determination of sorption levels." The United States did not even argue that the "determination of sorption levels" is an alternative measure which meets the three elements under Article 5.6 [emphasis added].

Japan — Measures Affecting Agricultural Products (Japan — Agricultural Products), Report of the Appellate Body, WTO Doc. WT/DS76/AB/R, March 19, 1999, at paras. 129-30.

[128] *Canada — Aircraft* Canada's Appellee Submission, *supra* note 122 at para. 112.

With respect to when the panel might draw adverse inferences, Canada noted that unlike the Statute of the International Court of Justice, the DSU did not provide panels or the Appellate Body with the authority to draw adverse inferences. And, to the extent that international tribunals had such authority, it was subject to severe limitations. In essence, in the absence of a *prima facie* case and, therefore, in the absence of a duty to collaborate, a respondent's decision not to provide information and evidence should not be perceived adversely. Canada then stated that the panel had correctly decided not to draw adverse inferences with respect to a case not established by Brazil.

"Should" means "shall": The procedural findings of the Appellate Body

(i) A member's duty to "respond fully and promptly"

Approaching the issue of the duty of a WTO member to respond fully and promptly to a request of a panel for information, the Appellate Body carefully and exhaustively examined its own decisions on the matter. It stated that

[i]n *Argentina – Measures Affecting Imports of Footwear, Textiles, Apparel and Other Items,* we ruled that Article 13 of the DSU made "a grant of *discretionary authority*" to panels enabling them to seek information from any relevant source. In *European Communities — Hormones,* we observed that Article 13 of the DSU "enable[s] panels to seek information and advice *as they deem appropriate in a particular case.*" And, in *United States — Shrimp,* we underscored "*the comprehensive nature*" of the authority of a panel to seek information and technical advice from "any individual or body" it may consider appropriate, or from "any relevant source."[129]

The Appellate Body quoted extensively from its own decision in *United States — Prohibition of Shrimps and Certain Shrimp Products,*[130] to the effect that

[t]he thrust of Articles 12 and 13, taken together, is that the DSU accords to a panel established by the DSB, and engaged in a dispute settlement proceeding, ample and extensive authority to undertake and to control the process by which it informs itself both of the relevant facts of the dispute and of the legal norms and principles applicable to such facts.[131]

---

129 *Canada — Aircraft* Appellate Body Report, *supra* note 1 at para. 184 [footnotes omitted] [emphasis added].

130 *United States — Prohibition of Shrimps and Certain Shrimp Products,* WTO Doc. WT/DS58/AB/R (98-000); *United States — Import Prohibition of Certain Shrimp and Shrimp Products,* WTO Doc. WT/DS58/R, May 15, 1998.

131 *Canada — Aircraft* Appellate Body Report, *supra* note 1 at para. 184 [emphasis in the original].

The Appellate Body then observed:

> It is clear from the language of Article 13 that the discretionary authority of a panel may be exercised to request and obtain information, not just "from any individual or body" within the jurisdiction of a Member of the WTO, but also from *any Member,* including *a fortiori* a Member who is a party to a dispute before a panel. This is made crystal clear by the third sentence of Article 13.1, which states: "*A Member* should respond promptly and fully to *any request by a panel for such information as the panel considers necessary and appropriate*" [emphasis added]. It is equally important to stress that this discretionary authority to seek and obtain information is *not* made conditional by this, or any other provision, of the DSU upon the other party to the dispute having previously established, on a *prima facie* basis, such other party's claim or defence. Indeed, Article 13.1 imposes *no conditions* on the exercise of this discretionary authority.[132]

Turning to the duties of WTO members under the DSU, the Appellate Body held that

> Article 13.1 of the DSU provides that "A Member *should* respond promptly and fully to any request by a panel for such information as the panel considers necessary and appropriate." Although the word "should" is often used colloquially to imply an exhortation, or to state a preference, it is not always used in those ways. It can also be used "to express a duty [or] obligation." The word "should" has, for instance, previously been interpreted by us as expressing a "duty" of panels in the context of Article 11 of the DSU. Similarly, we are of the view that the word "should" in the third sentence of Article 13.1 is, in the context of the whole of Article 13, used in a normative, rather than a merely exhortative, sense. Members are, in other words, under a duty and an obligation to "respond promptly and fully" to requests made by panels for information under Article 13.1 of the DSU.[133]

But, of course, there was more. If WTO members could withhold information from a panel, the panels' "undoubted right to seek" information would be rendered "meaningless."[134] A "Member could ... prevent a panel from carrying out its task of finding the facts constituting the dispute before it."[135] The Appellate Body referred to Article 12.7, which requires that "the report of a panel shall set out the findings of fact, the applicability of relevant provisions and the basic rationale behind any findings and recommendations that it makes." It then held that

---

[132] *Ibid.* at para. 185 [emphasis in the original].

[133] *Ibid.* at para. 187 [footnotes omitted] [emphasis added].

[134] *Ibid.* at para. 188.

[135] *Ibid.*

[i]f a panel is prevented from ascertaining the real or relevant facts of a dispute, it will not be in a position to determine the applicability of the pertinent treaty provisions to those facts, and, therefore, it will be unable to make any principled findings and recommendations to the DSB.[136]

The consequences of accepting "should" as "should" did not end there. The Appellate Body warned that

[t]o hold that a Member party to a dispute is not legally bound to comply with a panel's request for information relating to that dispute, is, in effect, to declare that Member legally free to preclude a panel from carrying out its mandate and responsibility under the DSU. So to rule would be to reduce to an illusion and a vanity the fundamental right of Members to have disputes arising between them resolved through the system and proceedings for which they bargained in concluding the DSU. We are bound to reject an interpretation that promises such consequences.[137]

Then, turning to Canada's arguments for refusing to provide the requested information to the panel, the Appellate Body stated that

a refusal to provide information requested on the basis that a *prima facie* case has not been made implies that the Member concerned believes that it is able to judge for itself whether the other party has made a *prima facie* case. However, no Member is free to determine for itself whether a *prima facie* case or defence has been established by the other party.[138]

The Appellate Body was not persuaded by this argument; nor was it moved by Canada's concerns about the protection of confidential commercial proprietary information, recalling that

Canada, jointly with Brazil, asked the Appellate Body to adopt *mutatis mutandis* the BCI Procedures in the course of proceedings before the Appellate Body. If Canada truly considered those procedures so inadequate as to compel it to reject the Panel's requests for information that Canada regarded as business confidential, then Canada's request that we adopt those very procedures on appeal appears to us a curious one.[139]

(ii) A panel's right to draw adverse inferences

The Appellate Body observed that the drawing of inferences of facts is part and parcel of the task of a panel. It then held that

[t]he facts must, of course, rationally support the inferences made, but inferences may be drawn whether or not the facts already on the record

---

[136] *Ibid.*

[137] *Ibid.* at para. 189.

[138] *Ibid.* at para. 192.

[139] *Ibid.* at para. 196.

deserve the qualification of a *prima facie* case. The drawing of inferences is, in other words, an inherent and unavoidable aspect of a panel's basic task of finding and characterizing the facts making up a dispute. In contrast, the burden of proof is a procedural concept which speaks to the fair and orderly management and disposition of a dispute. The burden of proof is distinct from, and is not to be confused with, the drawing of inferences from facts.[140]

The Appellate Body pointed out that Annex V of the SCM Agreement sets out in "impressive detail" circumstances under which adverse inferences may be drawn in regard to *actionable subsidies*.[141] The Appellate Body concluded:

There is no logical reason why the Members of the WTO would, in conceiving and concluding the *SCM Agreement*, have granted panels the authority to draw inferences in cases involving actionable subsidies that *may* be illegal *if* they have certain trade effects, but not in cases that involve prohibited export subsidies for which the adverse effects are presumed. To the contrary, the appropriate inference is that the authority to draw adverse inferences from a Member's refusal to provide information belongs *a fortiori* also to panels examining claims of prohibited export subsidies. Indeed, that authority seems to us an ordinary aspect of the task of all panels to determine the relevant facts of any dispute involving any covered agreement: a view supported by the general practice and usage of international tribunals.[142]

Turning to the facts of the case, the Appellate Body noted:

This appears to us to be precisely the type of situation in which a panel should examine very closely indeed whether the full *ensemble* of the facts on the record reasonably permits the inference urged by one of the parties to be drawn, because a party's refusal to collaborate has the potential to undermine the functioning of the dispute settlement system. The continued viability of that system depends, in substantial measure, on the willingness of panels to take all steps open to them to induce the parties to the dispute to comply with their duty to provide information deemed necessary for dispute settlement. In particular, a panel should be willing expressly to remind parties — during the course of dispute settlement proceedings — that a refusal to provide information requested by the panel may lead to inferences being drawn about the inculpatory character of the information withheld.[143]

Of course, the Appellate Body had held before that this "willingness of the panel" to "induce" the parties to provide it with information

---

[140] *Ibid.* at para. 198.

[141] *Ibid.* at para. 201.

[142] *Ibid.* at para. 202.

[143] *Ibid.* at para. 204.

should not be considered a *punitive* power. Rather, "[i]t is merely an inference which in certain circumstances could be logically or reasonably derived by a panel from the facts before it."[144] Finally, the Appellate Body stated that under the same circumstances, it "might well have" drawn the adverse inferences requested by Brazil. However, it noted that the panel had not erred in having not done so.[145] As it dismissed Brazil's appeal, the Appellate Body reminded Brazil that it could always bring another challenge.[146]

CONCLUSION

The significance of this case rests on two substantive and two procedural findings by the panel and the Appellate Body. The principal substantive findings in this case are the Appellate Body's interpretation and application of Articles 1 and 3 of the SCM Agreement. Procedurally, the Appellate Body expanded the jurisdiction of panels to engage in documentary discovery and granted them the authority to draw "adverse inferences" should the parties to a dispute not adduce the evidence requested.

After the end of the implementation period, Brazil launched a challenge against Canada under Article 21.5 of the DSU. The Article 21.5 panel and the Appellate Body found that Canada's changes to the TPC program brought it into compliance with Canada's obligations under Article 3 of the SCM Agreement. At the same time, following an exhaustive analysis of the scope of the "safe haven" under Item (k) of Annex I of the SCM Agreement, the Article 21.5 panel determined that Canada had failed to bring the Canada Account into compliance with the rulings and recommendations of the Dispute Settlement Body. Canada did not appeal this finding.

RAMBOD BEHBOODI
Department of Foreign Affairs and International Trade, Ottawa

---

[144] *Ibid.* at para. 200.

[145] *Ibid.* at para. 205.

[146] *Ibid.* at para. 206.

Sommaire

Affaires des aéronefs: Brésil et Canada

Les différends opposant le Canada et le Brésil en matière des subventions dans le secteur des aéronefs de transport régional sont les premiers présentés en application de la partie II (subventions prohibées) de l'Accord sur les subventions et les mesures compensatoires (Accord sur les subventions) de l'Organisation mondiale du commerce. Dans l'affaire PROEX, il s'agissait de déterminer la portée de la notion de "traitement spécial et différenciel" au sens de l'article 27 de l'Accord sur les subventions et d'interpréter le premier paragraphe de l'alinéa k de la Liste exemplative de subventions à l'exportation, apparaissant à l'Annexe I de l'Accord sur les subventions. L'affaire Canada, dossier des aéronefs, invoque pour la première fois l'article premier de l'Accord sur les subventions qui définit la pratique qui constitue une subvention et l'article 3 qui prohibe les "subventions subordonnées, en droit ou en fait ... aux résultats à l'exportation." L'affaire soulève en outre d'importantes questions en matière de la procédure de règlement des différents de l'OMC. L'auteur examine ces décisions d'un oeil critique, tant sur le fond que sous l'angle procédural.

Summary

The *Aircraft* Cases: Brazil and Canada

The disputes between Canada and Brazil over subsidies to the regional aircraft industry were the first cases under Part II (covering prohibited subsidies) of the Agreement on Subsidies and Countervailing Duties (SCM Agreement) of the World Trade Organization (WTO). The PROEX case, involved the scope of the concept of "special and differential treatment" under Article 27 of the SCM Agreement, and the interpretation of the first paragraph of Item (k) of the Illustrative List of Export Subsidies as set out in Annex I to the SCM Agreement. The Canada — Aircraft case involved, for the first time, Article 1 of the SCM Agreement, which defines what practices constitute a subsidy, and Article 3, which prohibits subsidies "contingent, in law or in fact, upon export performance." The case also dealt with important procedural issues relating to WTO dispute settlement. The author reviews critically these decisions with respect to both substantive and procedural issues.

In Memoriam: Gordon W. Smith
(1918 – 2000)

THE PASSING OF GORDON W. SMITH (B.A., M.A, Ph.D.) a little over a year ago represents a great loss to the scholarly community interested in the Arctic regions. For those who knew him, which was my privilege for some thirty-five years, Gordon will be remembered as a man of exceptional qualities, both as a person and as a scholar. Gordon was a profoundly good human being, with the greatest respect for others, even if he disagreed with their views. In expressing a different opinion, he usually prefaced his remarks by saying "I am not sure that I can completely agree with you" and would then go on to express his disagreement with such a choice of words (he had a mastery of the English language) and politeness that one practically regretted having expressed a different opinion.

As a scholar, Gordon began his contribution with his doctoral dissertation at Columbia University in 1952 on "The Historical and Legal Background of Canada's Arctic Claims." It is a masterpiece of research totalling some 496 pages with a thirty-page bibliography. For a period of about seventeen years following his doctoral degree, Gordon taught history (mainly British) in various universities and countries, but he maintained his interest in the Arctic during that time. Indeed, in 1966, he contributed to a collective work in the form of a sixty-page paper entitled "Sovereignty in the North: The Canadian Aspect of an International Problem."[1] The thoroughness of research, which has always been the hallmark of Gordon's work, is evidenced by the 270 footnotes. His conclusion that "Canada's legal right to her northern territories, in

---

[1] See R. St. J. Macdonald, ed., *The Arctic Frontier* (Toronto: University of Toronto Press, 1966), at 194-255.

particular the islands, has been well established at least since the early 1930's"[2] has never been seriously challenged.

The year 1966 was far from representing the end of his research on the Arctic. With the crossing of the Northwest Passage by the ice-breaking oil tanker *U.S.S. Manhattan* in 1969, Gordon began work on a research project, which he continued on a full-time basis until his death in October 2000. When I say "full time," I mean an average of about ten hours a day, five days a week. During those thirty years, Gordon pursued his research in the files and libraries of the government departments concerned (Indian Affairs and Northern Development, National Defence, Foreign Affairs and International Trade and Transport), the National Archives, and the Law Library of the University of Ottawa. Unfortunately, he was such a perfectionist that he did not want to bring his research to a close — in spite of my urging on many occasions — until he had reached the objective he had set for himself. This objective was to study the historical and legal aspects of Canada's sovereignty claim over the lands and waters of the Arctic and to trace the developments of the applicable law of the sea up to the signing of the 1982 Convention on the Law of the Sea.

Gordon's dedication to scholarship was such that he did all of this research, except for a period of four years when he was under contract with the Canadian government (1969-1973), completely on his own. Having lived a very frugal life on a meagre pension, his relatives and friends firmly believe that they owed it to his memory to do their utmost to make the fruits of his labour available to the public. Hopefully, this determination will prove possible. In the meantime, the note which follows describes the scope and value of his work. Jeannette Tramhel, a long-time friend of Gordon's and his family as well as a lawyer of considerable experience in international law, kindly consented to prepare it.

May the memory of Gordon W. Smith be a motivation towards excellence for us all.

DONAT PHARAND
Board of Editors

---

[2] *Ibid.* at 254.

Gordon W. Smith: A Historical and Legal Study of Sovereignty in the Canadian North and Related Law of the Sea Problems

THE TITLE OF THIS MANUSCRIPT might astonish readers, but it will certainly not mislead them, for this is indeed a serious and involved *magnum opus* of considerable length on a topic of considerable complexity. It was painstakingly researched and carefully written by Gordon W. Smith over a period of about thirty years. Recognizing the value of what was largely this man's life's work, his executors have undertaken to realize the dream that was behind the manuscript, namely, to enable its availability for the benefit of all Canadians, particularly those interested in history and international law as these subjects pertain to the Arctic. The original hand-written manuscript, which numbers several thousand pages of text, has been preserved in accordance with archival standards. The content has been reproduced in electronic format on CD ROM and amounts to over two million words. The executors hope to release this valuable and important piece of work for publication.[1]

From personal discussions that several persons had with him and upon reviewing his personal writings, it is evident that Smith was disappointed at the lack of thorough reference materials on this critically important subject. His ambition, therefore, was to create such a resource himself. A major opportunity in this regard availed itself shortly after the crossing of the *U.S.S. Manhattan* through the Northwest Passage in 1969. Overnight, concerns over Canada's sovereignty in the Arctic became an immediate priority, and Smith was retained by the government of Canada to undertake "(a) study

[1] Gordon W. Smith had access to certain classified government materials during the course of his research. Most of these materials have since been declassified. However, in keeping with his exceptionally high standards of personal and professional integrity, his executors are taking steps to ensure any necessary approvals are obtained prior to publication.

that should be in the nature of a historical, political and economic survey ... (and that) should record all activities of the Canadian Government that could have a bearing on the assertion of Canadian sovereignty in the Arctic."[2] A daunting task for any one individual! Smith took this overwhelming task to heart. Long after the immediacy of the project had passed and his report was satisfactorily received, he continued his own research simply out of his sense of calling. It was a project that he needed to see completed in accordance with his own high standards of academic research.

The intention, as much as it was to uncover original and previously unearthed source material, was to compile a comprehensive reference work for those individuals interested in this subject. Consequently, the study is heavily footnoted with extensive references, both to original sources and to secondary materials. Smith approaches the subject as a historian in somewhat of an interdisciplinary fashion, but he does not overstep unduly the boundaries of his own field. His study might be described as the historian's background brief that carefully leads the reader through every factual aspect of a particular topic and gently leaves that reader before the door to the only conclusion that could possibly be reached. The material is presented objectively, in a fair and balanced manner, with interpretation left largely to the reader. It is, as the title so accurately states, a *study*, rather than a reflection of his own personal views. Where Smith does draw his conclusions, they are usually by way of a careful summation of an ample set of prior evidentiary materials.

The manuscript was written in two parts. Part A is concerned with sovereignty over land in the Canadian North and Part B concerns sovereignty over northern waters. Part A is a comprehensive examination of activities and topics that would have relevance to Canada's sovereignty over the *lands* in the Canadian North. It covers the period from earliest recorded history until the early 1990s, although Smith did not have time to study the period after the Second World War quite as thoroughly as he studies the earlier period. Some examples of topics covered in this part include the transfers of the northern territories to Canada in 1870 and in 1880 as well as the early organization and administration of these territories; the Canadian expeditions led by Gordon, Wakeham, Low, Bernier, and Stefansson; the causes for Canadian concern over the status of the northern territories during those early years, such as the *Bering*

---

[2] Personal files of Dr. Smith.

Sea Fur-Seals Dispute,[3] the Yukon gold rush, the Alaska boundary dispute, foreign whalers in the north, and foreign explorers in the north during the period from about 1870 through 1918; the background of Canada's sector claim as it evolved at that time; and Danish sovereignty over Greenland and its relation to Canadian interests. Other topics studied are the Wrangel Island affair (early 1920s); the Krueger expedition (1930); significant government activities, such as those of the Eastern Arctic Patrol, the Royal Canadian Mounted Police, and other Canadian government expeditions; and the question of sovereignty over the Sverdrup Islands, the Labrador boundary dispute, and the Eastern Greenland case (1933),[4] together with its implications for Canada. Also described are the activities of American explorers in the Canadian North from 1918 to 1939 and certain miscellaneous aspects of sovereignty problems in the north during this period.

Another large portion of Part A is concerned with the years during the Second World War, including a review of the Permanent Joint Board on Defence and its activities; Canadian and American fears of attack from the north; and an extensive description of various war projects and initiatives in the north, including the defence of the northeastern approaches to North America, the Canadian/American involvement in the defence of Iceland and Greenland, the northeastern ferry and staging routes, the northwest staging route, efforts to build the Alaska Highway and the Canol Project. Other miscellaneous events and topics during the Second World War, which are considered in relation to the question of sovereignty in the north, include the following: the question of closing Craig Harbour and other northern posts; government and administration in the Northwest Territories and Yukon during the war; the Arctic Manual; the Northeast Planning Project, plans for a railway and an air route to Alaska, the North Pacific Planning Project; the Arctic Islands Game Preserve; and the voyages of the Royal Canadian Military Police schooner *St. Roch* through the Northwest Passage in 1940-42 and 1944.

The period after the Second World War begins with a review of the American withdrawal from the Canadian North at the end of the war. It looks at the basic factors accounting for the onset of the cold war and the return of the Americans to the North and then

---

[3] *Fur Seals Arbitration (Gr. Brit. v. U.S.),* Proceedings of the Tribunal of Arbitration, 16 volumes (Washington: Government Printing Office, 1895).

[4] *Legal Status of Eastern Greenland,* (1933) P.C.I.J. Reports.

examines early American and Canadian reaction to this new threat. Other topics include the various plans and projects for northern defence, in particular, the weather stations; the Canadian, American, and joint exercises; the Advisory Committee on Northern Development and its activities from its establishment in 1947 through to 1971; and the evolution of the structure and organization of Canada's defence forces as well as several committees that have been concerned with post-Second World War defence, including both Canadian and joint Canada-United States committees. The final subjects that are examined are certain aspects of Canada's basic defence organization and structure from 1945 to 1990, including the demobilization and reduction of forces; the Defence Research Board and its demise; the post-war reorganization of the Department of Northern Defence and the services' commands; and significant papers on defence policy.

Part B reviews and analyzes any activities and topics relevant to Canada's claim of sovereignty over the *waters* in the Canadian North. It extends from ancient times until the early 1970s, tracing the historical development of the law of the sea, and provides a summary of state practice on maritime jurisdiction, mainly in the nineteenth and early twentieth centuries. It reviews relevant treaties, conventions, conferences, arbitrations, and judgments, in particular, the *North Atlantic Coast Fisheries Arbitration (1910)*;[5] the Hague Conference of 1930 and Canada's role in it; the *Anglo-Norwegian Fisheries Case (1951)*;[6] and the *Minquiers and Ecrehos Case* (1953).[7] This part examines as well the legal status of Hudson Bay and Hudson Strait, the status of ice islands in the Arctic waters, and various aspects of submarine traffic in the Arctic waters. The jewel in this part is probably Smith's complete review of the Northwest Passage. He describes the explorations in search of it, compiles the transits, and considers the attitudes of Canadians and others towards it. He concludes with a review of its historical use and its future potential, all of which provide the background for a detailed examination of the status of the passage under international law.

Part B concludes with a study of the waters of the Canadian Arctic archipelago and recent developments in the applicable law, largely as a result of the UN Conferences on the Law of the Sea in

---

[5] *North Atlantic Coast Fisheries Arbitration,* (1910), 12 volumes (Washington: Government Printing Office, 1909-1913).

[6] *Anglo-Norwegian Fisheries Case,* (1951) I.C.J. Reports.

[7] *Minquiers and Ecrehos Case (U.K. v. France),* (1953) I.C.J. Reports.

1958, 1960, and 1973. It describes the archipelago and the physical characteristics of its waters, the various uses of these waters by the Inuit, European explorers, and church missionaries as well as the commercial uses of the waters made by the Hudson Bay Company and whalers. An important section is devoted to icebreaking in Canadian Arctic waters by the Canadian Coast Guard, along with an account of Canadian hydrography and oceanography. This discussion is followed by a review of the evolution in Canadian attitudes and policies regarding sovereignty over the waters of the Canadian Arctic archipelago. It offers an extensive analysis of the legal and international aspects of the waters of the Canadian Arctic archipelago, tracing concepts regarding archipelago waters and the effect on these concepts of the Hague Codification Conference of 1930 and of the Law of the Sea conferences. In addition, Smith wrote a special and important piece on the relocation of the Inuit in 1953 from Hudson Bay and Baffin Island to the High Arctic, a subject on which he made a presentation to the Royal Commission on Aboriginal Peoples in June 1993.[8]

By its sheer size and volume, it is clear that the manuscript was never intended as a work that one could ever hope to read and digest in one sitting. Rather, it was intended to act as something like an encyclopedia for persons interested in one or more aspects of the subject matter. With this in mind, each chapter has been written so that it may stand alone. Unfortunately, Smith was not able to fulfill his intention, once he had completed his work, to review the manuscript in its entirety and bring it up to date. Besides his manuscript, Smith maintained an extensive set of research notes and index cards that, in large measure, correspond to the manuscript. These materials have also been preserved, together with the original handwritten manuscript, as was noted earlier.

The subject of Canadian sovereignty in the Arctic is somewhat akin to the Arctic itself: mysterious, unknown, vast, and forbidding. Like the Arctic itself, however, the subject will not remain ignored for long. Two reasons, in particular, which were identified by Smith himself, suggest that the subject of Arctic sovereignty will assume

---

[8] Donat Pharand also made a presentation that same evening and expressed his admiration for Smith's talent as follows: "I knew Gordon had an extraordinary memory, but not to the extent he demonstrated that evening: he made a half-hour presentation without any notes whatever, recalling events in minute details with names and dates, all in a well-structured, logical and convincing manner. It was obvious that the members of the Commission, in particular Madam Justice Bertha Wilson (by then retired from the Supreme Court) were most impressed."

greater importance in the years ahead: "The first of these is the steady and unremitting progress in technology, which continues to make use of arctic waters easier and more feasible ... The (second) steady continuous phenomenon is the gradual warming process that is taking place in the Arctic, with accompanying receding and disappearance of arctic ice, and, as a result, steadily improving navigability. Put these two phenomena together, and it is easy to visualize a not-very-distant day when commercial and other traffic in arctic waters will become (much more feasible)."[9] The need for a comprehensive study of a topic that holds such importance for Canada is clearly evident. The manuscript, A Historical and Legal Study of Sovereignty in the Canadian North and Related Law of the Sea Problems, by Gordon W. Smith may be considered the most definitive discourse on the nature and importance of the Canadian North in existence. It deserves special recognition as a resource for today and for future generations of Canadians.

JEANNETTE TRAMHEL
Calgary, Alberta

[9] Personal papers of Gordon Smith.

Chronique de Droit international économique en 2000 / Digest of International Economic Law in 2000

I Commerce

préparé par
SOPHIE DUFOUR

I INTRODUCTION

Sur la scène commerciale internationale, l'année 2000 s'est amorcée dans un climat de morosité. Il importe en effet de se rappeler que les gouvernements des États membres de l'Organisation mondiale du commerce (OMC) n'ont pas réussi, lors de la troisième Conférence ministérielle tenue à Seattle (États-Unis) au mois de décembre 1999, à lancer un nouveau cycle de négociations commerciales multilatérales. Tout au plus se sont-ils engagés à amorcer, à compter du mois de mars 2000, deux négociations sectorielles dans les domaines de l'agriculture et du commerce des services. Cette morosité n'a cependant pas empêché les trente-quatre ministres des Finances des gouvernements des États participant à la création de la future zone de libre-échange des Amériques de poursuivre leurs pourparlers à Cancun (Mexique) le 3 février 2000 et de s'entendre sur une série de mesures en vue de lutter contre la corruption, le blanchiment d'argent et l'évasion fiscale à travers le continent américain. Elle n'a pas non plus freiné la volonté du Canada et du Costa Rica d'entreprendre des négociations bilatérales, le 11 juillet 2000, en vue de conclure un accord de libre-échange en matière de commerce des produits et des services de

Sophie Dufour, Avocate, professeure à la Faculté de droit de l'Université de Sherbrooke (LL.B., Université Laval, Québec; LL.M., Osgoode Hall Law School, Toronto; LL.M., University of Cambridge, Angleterre; LL.D., Université Laval, Québec).

même que des accords parallèles en matière de travail et d'environnement, en s'inspirant des ententes nord-américaines de 1994 en cette matière.

Cet échec des gouvernements des États membres de l'OMC quant à l'amorce d'un nouveau cycle de négociations commerciales multilatérales aurait pu avoir pour effet de ternir l'image de l'Organisation et d'affaiblir l'efficacité des accords du cycle d'Uruguay dont le *Mémorandum d'accord sur les règles et procédures régissant le règlement des différends* (*Mémorandum d'accord*). Ce sombre scénario ne s'est toutefois pas concrétisé. En effet, un examen de la procédure de règlement des différends de l'OMC — l'un des baromètres de la confiance des États membres à l'endroit du système commercial multilatéral — au cours de l'année 2000 révèle une activité habituelle à celle observée au cours des années précédentes. Ainsi, trente et une nouvelles plaintes ont été soumises à l'OMC en 2000, soit une de moins qu'en 1999, pour un total de 215 différends depuis la création de l'Organisation au mois de janvier 1995.

Parmi ces différends, un peu moins d'une dizaine doivent retenir notre attention: impliquant le Canada à titre (a) de plaignant, (b) de mis en cause, ou (c) des deux à la fois, ils ont connu des développements importants en 2000.

II   Le Canada à titre de plaignant

A   AUSTRALIE — MESURES VISANT LES IMPORTATIONS DE SAUMONS

Le Canada et l'Australie ont d'abord réussi, au printemps 2000, à mettre un terme à leur différend relatif à certaines mesures sanitaires et phytosanitaires imposées par l'Australie à l'égard de l'importation de saumons canadiens. Rappelons-nous à cet égard qu'en 1998, un Groupe spécial et, par la suite, l'Organe d'appel de l'OMC, avaient conclu que la prohibition imposée par l'Australie à l'importation de saumons provenant du Canada sur la base d'une réglementation nationale relative à la quarantaine en vigueur depuis 1975 était incompatible avec les termes de l'*Accord sur les mesures sanitaires et phytosanitaires* de l'OMC (*Accord SPS*). L'Australie avait donc dû procéder à certaines modifications réglementaires afin de rendre sa politique d'importation de poissons conforme aux prescriptions de ladite entente. Insatisfait de ces nouvelles mesures, le Canada a toutefois demandé à ce que la nouvelle politique australienne soit examinée par le même groupe spécial formé en 1997 pour entendre la plainte initiale canadienne. Dans son rapport du

18 février 2000, le Groupe spécial donne raison au Canada, concluant que les changements apportés à la politique australienne ne suffisent pas pour assurer la conformité de cette dernière avec les règles de l'*Accord SPS*. Plutôt que de demander à l'Organe de règlement des différends de l'OMC (ORD), conformément à l'article 22.2 du *Mémorandum d'accord*, l'autorisation de suspendre, à l'égard de l'Australie, l'application de concessions tarifaires et d'obligations connexes au titre du GATT de 1994, comme il aurait été en droit de le faire à la suite de l'adoption du rapport du Groupe spécial du 18 février 2000, le Canada a cherché à négocier une solution de compromis avec l'Australie. Ainsi, moins de trois mois plus tard, le 16 mai 2000, les gouvernements des deux pays annoncent la conclusion d'un accord mettant un terme au différend canado-australien.

B ÉTATS-UNIS — MESURES TRAITANT LES RESTRICTIONS
   À L'EXPORTATION COMME DES SUBVENTIONS

Le 24 juillet 2000, le Canada a par ailleurs demandé à ce que soit établi un groupe spécial en vue de déterminer si les États-Unis pouvaient traiter les restrictions imposées à l'exportation des billes de bois canadiennes comme une subvention à l'exportation donnant ouverture à l'imposition de droits compensateurs sur le bois d'œuvre résineux canadien exporté sur le marché américain. Selon le Canada, les États-Unis considèrent en effet que ces restrictions procurent un avantage aux producteurs canadiens de bois d'œuvre lors de l'achat des billes de bois, dès lors qu'elles ont pour effet d'accroître l'offre des billes de bois et d'en faire baisser le prix sur le marché canadien. Or, de l'avis du Canada, ce traitement par les États-Unis des restrictions à l'exportation en tant que subventions à l'exportation est contraire à l'*Accord sur les subventions et les mesures compensatoires* (*Accord SMC*) de l'OMC. La position canadienne sera confirmée moins d'un an plus tard par le Groupe spécial constitué aux fins d'étudier la plainte canadienne.

C COMMUNAUTÉS EUROPÉENNES — MESURES AFFECTANT
   L'AMIANTE ET LES PRODUITS EN CONTENANT

Le Canada n'a toutefois pas eu gain de cause dans l'affaire relative à l'interdiction de l'amiante chrysotile décrétée par la France depuis 1997. Constitué en 1998 à la demande du Canada en vue d'examiner la compatibilité de l'interdiction française avec les règles de l'OMC, le Groupe spécial a conclu, dans son rapport rendu public le 18 septembre 2000, que le Décret français en cause contrevenait à l'article III:4 du *GATT de 1994* en appliquant à l'égard de l'amiante chrysotile un traitement moins favorable qu'aux fibres d'APV, de cellulose ou de verre. Le Groupe spécial a toutefois jugé que ce traitement discriminatoire imposé par la France à l'endroit de l'amiante chrysotile était justifié en vertu de l'exception de protection de santé publique prévue à l'article XXb) du *GATT de 1994*. L'appel soumis par le Canada le 23 octobre 2000 ne produira pas les fruits escomptés. Tout en renversant certains points de droit en faveur du Canada dans son rapport du 12 mars 2001, l'Organe d'appel maintiendra la conclusion du Groupe spécial selon laquelle la politique française d'interdiction de l'amiante chrysotile entre dans la catégorie des politiques destinées à protéger la santé et la vie des personnes, au sens de l'article XXb) du *GATT de 1994*.

III   Le Canada à titre de mis en cause

A   canada — certaines mesures affectant
    l'industrie automobile

Le Canada a subi une autre défaite le 11 février 2000 alors qu'un Groupe spécial de l'OMC a conclu à l'incompatibilité des dispositions de l'*Accord entre le Gouvernement canadien et le Gouvernement des États-Unis d'Amérique concernant les produits de l'industrie automobile de 1965* (*Pacte de l'automobile*) avec les disciplines de l'OMC. Le Groupe spécial avait été établi en février 1999 afin d'examiner les plaintes de l'Union européenne et du Japon selon lesquelles la législation canadienne mettant en œuvre les dispositions du *Pacte de l'automobile* favoriserait injustement les fabricants américains d'automobile — Ford, Daimler Chrysler et General Motors — en les exemptant du droit de douane de 6,1 % autrement applicable aux véhicules importés au Canada. Le Groupe spécial a notamment conclu que le Canada avait contrevenu à ses obligations relatives au traitement de la nation la plus favorisée et au traitement national contenues aux articles I:1 et III:4 du *GATT de 1994* de même qu'à l'article II:1 de l'*Accord général sur le commerce des services*. Bien que l'Organe d'appel ait, dans son rapport du 31 mai 2000, renversé certaines des conclusions émises par le Groupe spécial, il a néanmoins maintenu celle selon laquelle le Canada avait agi de manière incompatible avec l'article I:1 du *GATT de 1994* en accordant le régime de l'importation en franchise aux seuls véhicules fabriqués par les trois grands constructeurs américains alors que cet avantage aurait dû être accordé immédiatement et sans condition aux produits similaires originaires du territoire de tous les autres États membres de l'OMC. Afin d'honorer ses engagements auprès de l'OMC, le Canada a mis fin au *Pacte de l'automobile* le 19 février 2001.

B   CANADA — PROTECTION CONFÉRÉE PAR UN BREVET
    POUR LES PRODUITS PHARMACEUTIQUES

La politique canadienne sur les brevets pharmaceutiques a pour sa part connu un meilleur sort au terme de son examen par le Groupe spécial établi en février 1999 à la demande de l'Union européenne. Celle-ci contestait la validité de deux exceptions contenues dans la *Loi sur les brevets* du Canada, alléguant la non conformité de ces dernières à la règle de l'exclusivité des droits des titulaires de brevet de produits pharmaceutiques énoncée à l'article 28 de l'*Accord sur les aspects des droits de propriété intellectuelle qui touchent au commerce* (*Accord sur les ADPIC*). Contenue à l'article 55.2(1) de la *Loi sur les brevets*, la première exception — communément appelée l'exception pour l'examen réglementaire — vise à permettre aux concurrents potentiels du titulaire d'un brevet sur un produit pharmaceutique d'origine d'obtenir des pouvoirs publics l'approbation de commercialisation pendant la durée du brevet de manière à ce que lesdits concurrents détiennent l'autorisation réglementaire de vendre le produit générique sur le marché dès l'expiration du brevet. Prévue à l'article 55.2(2) de la *Loi,* la seconde exception vient pour sa part reconnaître aux concurrents du titulaire du brevet le droit de fabriquer et de stocker des produits brevetés pendant la période de validité du brevet. Ces marchandises ne peuvent cependant pas être vendues tant que le brevet n'est pas échu. Tout en refusant de reconnaître la légitimité de cette seconde exception canadienne, le Groupe spécial a, dans son rapport rendu public le 17 mars 2000, conclu que l'exception pour l'examen réglementaire se justifiait en vertu de l'article 30 de l'*Accord sur les ADPIC* en ce qu'elle satisfait aux trois critères énoncés dans ce dernier. En effet, l'exception de l'article 55.2(1) de la *Loi* est: 1) limitée; 2) elle ne porte pas atteinte de manière injustifiée à l'exploitation normale du brevet; et 3) elle ne cause pas un préjudice injustifié aux intérêts légitimes du titulaire du brevet compte tenu des intérêts légitimes des tiers. Le Canada s'est déclaré satisfait

de la décision du Groupe spécial, l'exception pour l'examen réglementaire étant considérée particulièrement importante pour l'industrie pharmaceutique puisque, sans elle, un laps de temps devrait
nécessairement s'écouler entre l'expiration du brevet et la commercialisation des médicaments génériques. En ce qui a trait à la
seconde exception relative au stockage des versions génériques
d'un médicament, le Canada a procédé à son abrogation en respectant le délai du 7 octobre 2000 qui lui avait été imposé par un arbitre agissant au titre de l'article 21.3c) du *Mémorandum d'accord.*

C   CANADA — DURÉE DE LA PROTECTION CONFÉRÉE
    PAR UN BREVET

Dans le cadre d'un autre différend impliquant à nouveau le
régime des brevets canadiens, les États-Unis ont demandé, en 1999,
à ce que soit établi un Groupe spécial en vue de déterminer de la
compatibilité de l'article 45 de la *Loi sur les brevets* du Canada relatif
à la durée de protection accordée par le brevet avec les obligations
du Canada aux termes de l'*Accord sur les ADPIC.*

Tant le Groupe spécial, dans son rapport du 5 mai 2000, que
l'Organe d'appel, dans son rapport du 18 septembre 2000, ont
conclu que l'article 45 de la loi canadienne contrevient aux articles
33 et 70 de l'*Accord sur les ADPIC* en raison du fait que la durée de la
protection conférée par le brevet, qui est de dix-sept ans à compter
de la date de délivrance pour les demandes de brevet qui ont été
déposées avant le 1er octobre 1989, prend souvent fin avant l'expiration d'une période de vingt ans à compter de la date du dépôt.
Or, selon eux, le Canada est tenu, conformément aux articles 33 et
70.2 de l'*Accord sur les ADPIC,* d'offrir une protection ne prenant
pas fin avant l'expiration d'une période de vingt ans à compter de
la date du dépôt de la demande de brevet et ce, pour toutes les
inventions protégées par un brevet le 1er janvier 1996. Cela inclut
les inventions protégées par des brevets délivrés au titre de l'article
45, puisque toutes les inventions brevetées sont des "objets existants
... qui sont protégés" au sens où cette expression est employée à
l'article 70:2 de l'*Accord sur les ADPIC.*

Afin d'assurer la mise en œuvre des constatations et conclusions
du Groupe spécial et de l'Organe d'appel dont les rapports furent
adoptés par l'ORD le 12 octobre 2000, le Canada a apporté des
modifications aux articles 45, 78.1, 78.2, 78.4 et 78.5 de la *Loi sur
les brevets* par l'entremise de l'adoption de la *Loi modifiant la Loi sur
les brevets* de 2001.

IV   Le Canada à titre de plaignant et de mis en cause
     dans le cadre du différend canado-brésilien sur
     les aéronefs civils

La saga des aéronefs civils canadiens et brésiliens s'est poursuivie
au cours de l'année 2000 alors que le Canada et le Brésil ont tour
à tour cherché à démanteler la position adverse et à préserver
les intérêts de leur industrie aéronautique nationale auprès des
instances arbitrales de l'OMC.

Ainsi, le 9 mai 2000, deux groupes spéciaux de l'OMC constitués
en vue d'examiner la conformité des nouvelles mesures adoptées
par le Canada et le Brésil respectivement en vue d'honorer leurs
obligations commerciales internationales dans le secteur des aéronefs civils ont rendu publics leurs rapports. Le Groupe spécial
responsable de l'examen des politiques brésiliennes a conclu que le
Brésil continuait de subventionner son industrie aéronautique au
détriment des exportateurs canadiens par le biais du programme
PROEX et que les changements apportés à ce dernier n'étaient
nullement suffisants pour le rendre conforme aux disciplines de
l'OMC. De son côté, le Groupe spécial chargé du dossier canadien
a adopté une position mitoyenne: tout en donnant son aval aux
modifications effectuées par le Canada au programme fédéral
Partenariat technologique Canada, il a émis certaines réserves à l'endroit des changements apportés au *Compte du Canada* et indiqué le
type de modifications requises afin de le rendre pleinement conforme aux règles de l'OMC.

Le 10 mai 2000, le Canada annonce à bon droit son intention de
demander à l'ORD l'autorisation de prendre des contre-mesures à
l'encontre de différents produits brésiliens, conformément à l'article 4.10 de l'*Accord SCM* et à l'article 22.2 du *Mémorandum d'accord*
pour une valeur de 700 millions de dollars canadiens par an. Selon
le Canada, cette valeur correspond au niveau des avantages con-
sentis à l'industrie brésilienne des aéronefs civils du fait de l'octroi
de subventions gouvernementales illégales au titre du PROEX.

À l'occasion de la réunion de l'ORD du 22 mai 2000, le Brésil
indique toutefois son intention de contester, par voie arbitrale,
cette valeur de 700 millions de dollars par année revendiquée par
le Canada à titre de contre-mesures, considérant que cette valeur
est totalement arbitraire puisqu'établie par le Canada en l'absence
de détermination juridique d'annulation ou de réduction éven-
tuelle d'avantages qu'aurait subie le Canada en conséquence du
programme brésilien de subventions PROEX. Lors de cette même

réunion, le Brésil notifie à l'ORD son intention d'interjeter appel de certaines questions de droit ainsi que de certaines interprétations du droit adoptées par les groupes spéciaux dans leurs rapports du 9 mai 2000.

Le 21 juillet 2000, l'Organe d'appel de l'OMC rend public ses constatations et conclusions relatives à la légalité des rapports des groupes spéciaux du 9 mai 2000. L'Organe d'appel confirme d'abord la non compatibilité du programme brésilien de subventions aux exportations d'aéronefs PROEX avec les disciplines de l'OMC: PROEX représente toujours une forme de subvention illégale des pouvoirs publics. L'Organe d'appel maintient par ailleurs la conclusion de conformité émise le 9 mai 2000 par le Groupe spécial à l'égard du programme canadien, *Partenariat technologique Canada,* et note qu'aucune autre modification n'est requise aux fins de permettre au Canada d'honorer ses obligations commerciales internationales.

À peine un mois plus tard, le 28 août 2000, le Brésil subit un autre revers alors qu'un groupe spécial d'arbitrage de l'OMC autorise le Canada à appliquer des contre-mesures d'une valeur de 344 millions de dollars canadiens par an contre le Brésil. Bien qu'inférieur au niveau de 700 millions de dollars annuels initialement revendiqués par le Canada, il s'agit néanmoins du niveau de rétorsion le plus élevé établi à ce jour à l'OMC ce qui, indéniablement, révèle la gravité du préjudice causé à l'industrie canadienne des aéronefs civils du fait de l'existence et du maintien du programme PROEX par le Brésil. Le Canada a toutefois choisi de remettre à plus tard l'exercice de son droit de représailles contre le Brésil, sachant pertinemment que sa mise en œuvre pourrait se traduire par une guerre commerciale sans précédent.

V CONCLUSION

L'année 2000 a marqué le cinquième anniversaire du *Mémorandum d'accord sur les règles et procédures régissant le règlement des différends.* L'intérêt et la confiance des États membres de l'OMC envers ce mécanisme d'arbitrage international *sui generis* ne semble pas démordre et ce, malgré certaines failles fondamentales telles que la lenteur du mécanisme, le langage trop souvent boîteux des règles qui le gouvernent, la nature parfois inappropriée des mesures susceptibles d'être imposées par un État à titre de représailles à l'encontre d'un autre État membre, l'incapacité de l'ORD à limiter la multiplicité des recours, etc. Le différend canado-brésilien relatif aux aéronefs civils illustre certaines de ces failles avec acuité. Certes, ces failles affectent la crédibilité de la procédure de règlement des différends de l'OMC. Toutefois, le nombre sans cesse croissant de différends soumis auprès de l'ORD depuis 1995 témoigne de la confiance que lui accordent l'ensemble des États membres de l'OMC, quel que soit leur niveau de développement économique.

Ainsi, en attendant de pouvoir négocier des engagements additionnels de libéralisation des échanges dans le cadre d'un nouveau cycle de négociations commerciales multilatérales, les États membres de l'OMC sont à tout le moins en mesure de clarifier la nature de leurs droits et de leurs obligations internationales existantes par l'entremise de cette procédure de règlement des différends qui demeure, somme toute, l'un des instruments les plus performants du système commercial multilatéral de l'OMC.

II   Le Canada et le système financier international en 2000

préparé par
BERNARD COLAS

OUTRE LE PASSAGE SANS LES EFFETS appréhendés du bogue de l'an 2000, cette année a été marquée par la poursuite de la consolidation du système financier international et l'intensification de la lutte contre le blanchiment d'argent. La consolidation du système financier international est apparue plus que nécessaire suite au ralentissement de l'économie mondiale et à la crise financière de l'Argentine et de la Turquie, la première étant confrontée à des dépassements budgétaires chroniques, la seconde aux problèmes structurels de son secteur bancaire.[1] Cette consolidation a été menée de concert par le Groupe des vingt (I), les institutions internationales (II) et les organismes de contrôle des établissements financiers (III). La lutte contre le blanchiment d'argent s'est quant à elle intensifiée au cours de l'année principalement sous l'impulsion du Groupe d'action financière (IV).

I   LE GROUPE DES VINGT

Réuni à Montréal les 24 et 25 octobre 2000, le Groupe des vingt (G-20) a consacré sa rencontre à la mise en place d'une stratégie

---

Bernard Colas, Avocat de l'étude Gottlieb & Pearson (Montréal), Docteur en droit, Président de la Société de droit international économique (SDIE). L'auteur remercie Xavier Mageau, LL.M., de la même étude pour son importante contribution à la préparation de cet article.

[1] Ces deux pays ont même reçu le soutien financier du Fonds monétaire international (ci-après FMI). Pour l'Argentine, l'aide mise en place a atteint 39,7 milliards de dollars américains alors qu'elle s'est élevée à 7,5 milliards de dollars américains pour la Turquie, *Rapport sur les opérations effectuées en vertu de la Loi sur les accords de Bretton Woods et des accords connexes 2000* aux pp. 11–12 (ci-après *Bretton Woods*).

pour renforcer le système financier international. Les ministres des finances, gouverneurs des banques centrales des pays du G-7 et leurs homologues de pays en développement[2] ont identifié les facteurs de vulnérabilité de certains pays face aux crises financières et décidé de mettre en œuvre des solutions propres à prévenir les crises et à en limiter la propagation. L'Union européenne, le FMI et la Banque mondiale ont également participé à cette rencontre du G-20.

Parmi les facteurs de vulnérabilité des pays face aux crises financières, les membres ont identifié la subite dévaluation des monnaies, la mauvaise gestion de la dette publique des États en crise, la faiblesse de la réglementation et de la surveillance des banques ainsi qu'une communication inadéquate des informations économiques aux investisseurs étrangers.[3]

Outre l'identification de ces facteurs, les membres se sont attachés à trouver les solutions permettant de prévenir et de résoudre les crises financières.[4] D'abord, les membres ont convenu de l'importance des normes et codes internationaux pour la réduction de la vulnérabilité des pays aux crises financières. Dans ce contexte, les pays membres participeront au Programme d'évaluation du secteur financier et à la production de rapports sur l'observation des normes et codes.[5]

Les membres ont également porté leur attention sur le renforcement de la transparence et de la stabilité du système financier.[6] Désormais, les politiques et des données économiques seront publiées régulièrement pour assurer la transparence de l'information. Les membres se sont entendus pour améliorer leurs politiques monétaires, financières et budgétaires. Cet engagement est d'autant plus important que ce sont ces politiques intérieures solides, crédibles et uniformes qui servent de base aux membres pour fixer leur régime de taux de change. Sur le plan de l'endettement,

---

[2] Les pays en développement participant au Groupe des vingt sont l'Afrique du Sud, l'Arabie saoudite, l'Argentine, le Brésil, la Chine, la Corée du Sud, l'Inde, l'Indonésie, le Mexique, la Russie et la Turquie.

[3] Ayant mal évalués leurs risques, les investisseurs ont, durant la crise asiatique, pris panique et retiré rapidement les capitaux qu'ils avaient investis dans certains pays d'Asie.

[4] *Communiqué des Ministres des Finances et gouverneurs des banques centrales des pays du G-20*, 25 octobre 2000 (ci-après *Communiqué du G-20*).

[5] B. Colas, "Le Canada et le système financier international en 1999," A.C.D.I., 2000.

[6] *Communiqué du G-20, op. cit.* note 4.

les membres ont rappelé la nécessité de gérer efficacement et de façon prudente la dette du secteur public et la faveur qui doit être accordée aux emprunts à long terme en monnaie intérieure. En effet, ces derniers ont comme avantage de réduire considérablement la dépendance des pays vis à vis des financements extérieurs à court terme.

Les membres ont également insisté sur la nécessité de renforcer les systèmes financiers nationaux et de responsabiliser tous les acteurs financiers (e.g. gouvernements, institutions financières, organismes de contrôle et prêteurs étrangers).

Le G-20 a enfin invité le Fonds Monétaire International (FMI) à continuer d'assister ces pays dans la mise en œuvre de réformes qui, comme certains exemples le montrent, nécessitent des ajustements de grande ampleur.

II   Les institutions internationales

A   fonds monétaire international (fmi)

Cet appel lancé par le G-20 en direction du FMI constitue le prolongement de la publication, en juillet 2000 à Fukuoka, du rapport des ministres des Finances du G7 aux chefs d'États et de gouvernement sur le renforcement de l'architecture financière internationale.[7] Le rapport propose une série de mesures pour encadrer la poursuite des travaux sur la réforme du FMI en matière de renforcement de la surveillance, de mise en œuvre des normes et des codes internationaux, des mécanismes du FMI et du renforcement de la régie du FMI.

Suite à ce rapport, le FMI a adopté un certain nombre de mesures de nature à accroître la transparence du système. Ainsi, le FMI a créé en l'an 2000, pour compléter la norme spéciale de diffusion des données (NSDD) de 1996, une nouvelle catégorie de données sur les dettes extérieures.[8] La NSDD a pour objet de mieux informer les marchés au sujet de l'évolution financière et économique et de renforcer les activités de surveillance. La nouvelle catégorie sur les dettes extérieures, dont la diffusion sera trimestrielle, doit être intégrée par les pays participant au plus tard fin mars 2003. Cette idée de transparence, sous-jacente à la

---

[7] *Rapport des ministres des Finances du G7 aux chefs d'État et de gouvernement sur le renforcement de l'architecture financière internationale présenté au Sommet économique de Fukuoka,* juillet 2000.

[8] *Bretton Woods, op. cit.* note 1 à la p. 16 et *Rapport annuel 2000 du FMI* à la p. 41.

création de cette nouvelle catégorie de données, se révèle d'ailleurs être le fil conducteur de l'action du FMI en cette année 2000. La mise en place par le FMI de mécanismes pour assurer une meilleure utilisation des ressources du FMI n'est ni plus ni moins que la traduction concrète de cette transparence. Parmi ces mécanismes, citons l'obligation faite aux banques centrales utilisatrices des ressources du FMI de publier des états financiers annuels vérifiés selon les normes internationales de vérification.[9]

Toujours dans le même esprit, le FMI a entrepris une réforme de ses mécanismes de prêt non concessionnel.[10] Cette réforme a entraîné l'élimination de plusieurs mécanismes peu utilisés et désuets ainsi que la rationalisation de la Facilité de financement compensatoire. Le FMI a également envisagé les possibles changements en vue de garantir l'utilisation plus efficace des ressources du FMI et de réorienter les activités de prêt du FMI vers la prévention des crises.[11] Suite à cette réflexion, le FMI a décidé de mettre en place une structure rationalisée de mécanismes de prêt destinée à encourager les pays à solliciter des capitaux privés et à décourager l'utilisation excessivement prolongée ou importante des ressources du FMI.[12]

C'est cette même volonté d'encourager l'utilisation de capitaux privés qui a conduit le FMI à se pencher sur la question de la participation du secteur privé dans la gestion des crises.[13] Le Canada, favorable à une participation accrue du secteur privé, s'est d'ailleurs situé en première ligne sur cette question.[14] Les propositions canadiennes ont trouvé écho dans le communiqué du Comité monétaire et financier international publié le 20 avril 2000.[15]

Le Canada s'est également distingué en matière d'aide au développement des pays pauvres très endettés (PPTE). Le Canada a, en effet, effacé la totalité de la dette des pays les plus pauvres, lors de la présentation du Budget en février 2000. Cet effacement a même

---

[9] Cette nouvelle politique découle de la multiplication des déclarations inexactes et aux mauvaises utilisations des ressources du FMI.

[10] *Bretton Woods, op. cit.* note 1 à la p. 17.

[11] *Bretton Woods, op. cit.* note 1 à la p. 17.

[12] *Bretton Woods, op. cit.* note 1 à la p. 17.

[13] *Rapport annuel du FMI* à la p. 50 (ci-après *FMI*).

[14] *Bretton Woods, op. cit.* note 1 à la p. 21.

[15] *Bretton Woods, op. cit.* note 1 à la p. 22 et *Communiqué du Comité monétaire et financier international du Conseil des gouverneurs du Fonds monétaire international*, 20 avril 2000.

été étendu à tous les PPTE à condition qu'ils se soient engagés à faire de réels efforts pour améliorer le bien-être de leurs citoyens. Cette mesure complète utilement l'initiative du FMI et de la Banque mondiale en faveur des PPTE renforcée pour porter à vingt le nombre de pays bénéficiant d'un allègement de leur dette. À la fin de l'année 2000, leur nombre était même de vingt-deux. Cette mesure représente une réduction de 34 milliards de dollars américains de frais de services de la dette.[16]

B   BANQUE MONDIALE

La Banque mondiale a consacré une part de ses activités à l'amélioration de la qualité de la vie des populations tant en matière de santé que d'environnement. La Banque mondiale a consacré une autre part de ses activités à fournir un soutien économique aux pays en développement.

C   SANTÉ ET ENVIRONNEMENT

Pendant l'exercice 2000, la Banque mondiale a mis sur pied nombre de programmes liés au VIH/SIDA dont le programme multinational de lutte contre le VIH/SIDA en Afrique de l'IDA. Ce programme prend la forme de prêts dont le montant avoisine les 500 millions de dollars américains. Ces fonds seront dirigés vers la prévention et le traitement de la maladie sur l'ensemble du continent africain.[17]

Au titre de la protection de l'environnement, la Banque mondiale a créé un fonds en fiducie pour les polluants organiques persistants. Ce fonds auquel participent l'Agence canadienne de développement international (ACDI) et la Banque mondiale est doté d'un budget de 20 millions de dollars.[18] L'objet de ce fonds est le renforcement des capacités des économies en développement et en transition, dans la réduction et l'élimination des émissions de ces polluants. La Banque mondiale a également créé le Fonds prototype pour le carbone.[19] Ce fonds, qui constitue le premier mécanisme d'échange commercial des émissions de carbone, finance plusieurs projets destinés à réduire de manière substantielle les

---

[16] *Bretton Woods, op. cit.* note 1 à la p. 77.

[17] *Rapport annuel 2000 de la Banque mondiale* à la p. 87 (ci-après *Banque mondiale*).

[18] *Bretton Woods, op. cit.* note 1 à la p. 39.

[19] *Bretton Woods, op. cit.* note 1 aux pp. 58–59 et *Banque mondiale, op. cit.* note 17 à la p. 94.

émissions de gaz à effet de serre. Le Canada a annoncé cette année qu'il contribuerait à ce fonds jusqu'à hauteur de 10 millions de dollars américains.[20]

La dernière initiative d'importance de la Banque mondiale pour accroître la qualité de vie des populations est le lancement de l'alliance pour l'avenir des villes. Cette initiative a pour objectif principal la promotion des stratégies de développement urbain au profit des personnes démunies. Financée à hauteur de 800 000 $ par l'ACDI, l'initiative a vu le jour grâce au Centre des Nations Unies pour les Établissements Humains, aux donateurs bilatéraux, aux organisations non gouvernementales et la communauté des affaires. En matière de développement humain, on ne peut passer sous silence la publication du rapport de la Banque mondiale sur le développement dans le monde.[21] L'intérêt de ces mesures réside essentiellement dans les diverses mesures proposées pour promouvoir le développement économique des pays les plus pauvres.

D   SOUTIEN ÉCONOMIQUE AUX PAYS EN DÉVELOPPEMENT

La contribution de la Banque mondiale au développement économique des pays les plus pauvres a porté sur trois points: la transparence des marchés, les nouvelles formes de soutien à ces pays, et l'adaptation au secteur privé.

En matière de transparence des marchés, la Banque mondiale a dressé un bilan des actions menées depuis 1997 pour aider les pays en développement à combattre les pratiques de corruption. Ce bilan a conduit la Banque mondiale à réformer ses directives en matière d'adjudication des marchés pour exclure les entreprises soumissionnaires impliquées dans des activités de corruption.[22]

En matière de nouvelles formes de soutien, la nouveauté réside dans la fourniture par la Banque mondiale de services de conseil, d'analyse, de formation et de perfectionnement des connaissances à l'appui du renforcement des capacités intérieures.[23]

Quant à l'adaptation au privé, cette dernière a engendré une profonde restructuration de la Banque mondiale. Les deux objectifs

---

[20] *Bretton Woods, op.cit.* note 1 à la p. 59.

[21] *Rapport sur le développement dans le monde, 2000–2001: lutter contre la pauvreté,* Banque mondiale, 2000.

[22] *Bretton Woods, op. cit.* note 1 aux pp. 56–57.

[23] *Bretton Woods, op. cit.* note 1 à la p. 31 et *Banque mondiale, op. cit.* note 17 à la p. 103.

principaux poursuivis par cette restructuration sont l'instauration d'un climat favorable aux affaires et la mise en place d'une contribution au financement des petites et moyennes entreprises. Une nouvelle structure sera créée à l'issue de la restructuration. Les liens entre les travaux de la Banque mondiale et ceux de la Société Financière Internationale dans le secteur privé seront également renforcés.[24]

Outre l'intérêt qu'il porte à cette question du recours au secteur privé comme outil de développement économique, le Canada est resté très attentif aux intérêts des Petits États.[25] Cet intérêt s'est manifesté à l'occasion du premier forum des petits États tenu au siège de la Banque mondiale en septembre 2000. Ce forum a été l'occasion pour la Banque mondiale et cinq autres institutions multilatérales de renouveler leur engagement de travailler avec les petits États et de mettre en œuvre le programme décrit dans le rapport final "Petits États: relever les défis de la mondialisation"[26] du Groupe d'intervention créé en 1998 par la Banque mondiale et le secrétariat du Commonwealth.

III   ORGANISMES DE CONTRÔLE DES ÉSTABLISSEMENTS FINANCIERS

L'action complémentaire du Comité de Bâle sur le contrôle bancaire et de l'Organisation internationale des commissions de valeur (OICV) pour le développement et la mise en œuvre de normes prudentielles joue également un important rôle dans la consolidation du système financier international.

A   COMITÉ DE BÂLE SUR LE CONTRÔLE BANCAIRE

Le Comité de Bâle sur le contrôle bancaire s'est principalement consacré, en 2000, à la révision de l'Accord de Bâle sur les fonds propres[27] qui sert maintenant de fondement à la réglementation d'une centaine de pays. Cette révision a pour objet de définir des exigences de solvabilité correspondant mieux au profil de risque réel des établissements de crédit. La révision menée en vue d'un

---

[24] *Bretton Woods, op. cit.* note 1 à la p. 54 et *Banque mondiale, op. cit.* note 17 aux pp. 99–100.

[25] Le Canada représente 11 petits États des Caraïbes auprès de la Banque mondiale.

[26] *Petits États: relever les défis de la mondialisation, avril 2000.*

[27] *Rapport de gestion Commission fédérale des banques 2000* aux pp. 249–58 (ci-après *Commission fédérale*).

nouvel Accord prend appui sur trois piliers à savoir le ratio minimal de fonds propres, le processus de surveillance prudentielle et les exigences en matière de communication financière.[28] Le premier pilier répond à deux considérations. Il s'agit d'abord de couvrir les risques de crédit et les autres risques pour ensuite définir une méthode d'évaluation appropriée de ces risques. Le second pilier relatif à la surveillance prudentielle et individualisée tend à imposer aux établissements de crédit une évaluation permanente de leurs besoins en fonds propres à la lumière de leur profil de risque actuel et la définition d'une véritable stratégie en matière de solvabilité. Les autorités de contrôle assureront, quant à elles, le suivi de ces évaluations internes et pourront, le cas échéant, imposer des normes de solvabilité plus strictes à un établissement de crédit au vu des risques spécifiques de celui-ci. Quant au troisième pilier, il consiste à imposer à l'établissement de crédit l'obligation de fournir des informations qualitatives et quantitatives suffisantes pour que le public ait une idée exacte de la structure des fonds propres, du profil de risque et de la solvabilité de l'établissement de crédit. Le nouvel Accord vient donc renforcer la sûreté et la solidité du système financier en insistant davantage qu'auparavant, (i) sur le contrôle interne et la gestion exercés par les établissements de crédit sur eux-même, (ii) sur les examens de surveillance, et (iii) sur la discipline du marché.[29]

Le développement d'Internet pose en matière bancaire un certain nombre de questions telles que l'ouverture d'un compte en ligne ou l'identification du client. Ce sont ces préoccupations[30] qui ont conduit à la mise en place de l'"Electronic Banking Group" du Comité de Bâle sur le "E-Banking."[31] Le premier rapport intermédiaire[32] publié en 2000 définit le projet relatif aux standards minimaux de diligence en matière d'identification et de surveillance des clients. Ce rapport ne vise qu'à faciliter l'analyse et l'échange d'informations et d'expériences entre les différentes autorités de

---

[28] *Rapport annuel 1999–2000 Commission bancaire et financière* aux pp. 135 et s. (ci-après *Commission bancaire et financière*).

[29] *Rapport annuel 2000–2001 du Bureau du Surintendant des institutions financières* à la p. 38.

[30] Ces préoccupations sont partagées par l'OICV. En effet, l'OICV et le Comité de Bâle sur le contrôle bancaire collaborent sur ces questions.

[31] *Commission fédérale, op. cit.* note 27 aux pp. 260–61.

[32] *Electronic Banking Group and White Papers, Basel Committee on Banking Supervision,* octobre 2000.

surveillance. Le rapport final et les principes fondamentaux pour une surveillance appropriée des services bancaires électroniques sont attendus pour l'année 2001.

L'"Accounting Task force" a publié un document de consultation intitulé "Internal audit in banking organisations and the relationship of the supervisory authorities with internal and external auditors."[33] Ce document, qui contient dix-huit principes, traite essentiellement des questions liées à l'externalisation en matière bancaire, à la mise en place de comités d'audit, aux relations entre auditeurs internes, externes et autorités de surveillance. Le document définitif devrait être publié en 2001.

Le Comité de Bâle a émis de nombreuses recommandations de saine pratique à l'usage des établissements de crédits et de leurs autorités de contrôle ont été émises au cours de l'année.[34] Ces recommandations portent principalement sur l'obligation de diligence à l'égard de la clientèle, le risque de règlement dans les opérations de change, la communication financière, les institutions à fort levier et l'évaluation du risque de crédit.

B   ORGANISATION INTERNATIONALE DES COMMISSIONS
    DE VALEURS (OICV)

L'OICV regroupe les organismes de contrôle des sociétés d'investissement de quatre-vingt-douze pays. En 1998, elle adoptait, à l'occasion de sa réunion annuelle, un texte sur les buts et principes relatifs à la surveillance du marché des valeurs mobilières.[35] Cette année lors de sa réunion annuelle, à Sydney, l'OICV a souhaité conférer à la résolution de 1998 un caractère obligatoire et lui assurer une transposition. C'est le "Implementation Committtee" créé par l'OICV en 2000 qui assumera cette tâche.[36]

L'OICV dans une résolution du Comité des Présidents a recommandé à ses membres l'adoption et l'application des trente Principes fondamentaux du Comité des normes comptables internationales (IASC) aux émissions et cotations transfrontalières des sociétés multinationales. Cette décision est une avancée importante dans la mesure où la question était à l'étude depuis 1995.[37]

---

[33] *Commission fédérale, op. cit.* note 27 aux pp. 258–59.

[34] *71ᵉ rapport annuel de la Banque des Règlements Internationaux* à la p. 171.

[35] *Objectives and Principles of Securities Regulation*, Organisation Internationale des Commissions de Valeurs, septembre 1998.

[36] *Commission fédérale, op. cit.* note 27 à la p. 266.

[37] *Commission bancaire et financière, op. cit.* note 28 aux pp. 144–45.

À l'instar du Comité de Bâle et en collaboration avec lui, l'OICV a depuis 1998 entamé l'analyse des implications d'Internet dans le domaine des valeurs mobilières. Cette année, les travaux ont porté sur la mise au point de directives relatives à la réglementation et la surveillance du commerce des valeurs mobilières sur Internet (contenu des pages Internet, publicité, échanges d'information, protection des investisseurs).[38]

Le groupe de travail commun à l'OICV et à la Banque des Règlements Internationaux a publié un rapport sur les standards applicables aux systèmes chargés de la compensation et du règlement dans le cadre du commerce national et international des valeurs mobilières. Ce rapport dresse dix-huit recommandations concernant les bases juridiques, les confirmations des transactions, les cycles de compensations et de règlement, les contreparties centralisées, le securities lending, la livraison contre paiement, la protection du client, la communication, la transparence ainsi que la surveillance et la réglementation.[39]

IV Groupe d'action financière (GAFI)

Outre la publication en juin 2000 de la liste des pays et territoires non-coopératifs, le GAFI a décidé en 2000 d'entreprendre une révision de ses quarante Recommandations, qui sont désormais largement acceptées comme normes mondiales de lutte contre le blanchiment de capitaux. Cette révision s'imposait puisque la dernière révision remonte à 1996 et que depuis cette date les techniques et tendances du blanchiment[40] ont considérablement évolué.

Parallèlement à la révision des quarante recommandations,[41] les pays membres du GAFI[42] ont procédé à un exercice d'auto-évaluation afin de mesurer les progrès réalisés dans la mise en œuvre des

---

[38] *Commission fédérale, op. cit.* note 27 à la p. 266.

[39] *Commission fédérale, op. cit.* note 27 à la p. 267.

[40] *Rapport annuel 2000–2001 du Groupe d'action financière sur le blanchiment de capitaux* aux pp. 19–20 (ci-après *GAFI*).

[41] Le texte des 40 Recommandations peut être consulté à l'adresse suivante: http://www.oecd.org/fatf/40Recs_fr.htm.

[42] Les membres du GAFI sont: Allemagne, Argentine, Australie, Autriche, Belgique, Brésil, Canada, Danemark, Espagne, États-Unis, Finlande, France, Grèce, Hong Kong, Chine, Irlande, Islande, Italie, Japon, Luxembourg, Mexique, Norvège, Nouvelle-Zélande, Portugal, Royaume des Pays-Bas, Royaume-Uni, Singapour, Suède, Suisse et Turquie.

mesures de lutte contre le blanchiment de capitaux et surtout des vingt-huit[43] Recommandations du GAFI nécessitant des mesures spécifiques.

Aux termes de cette évaluation,[44] dix membres du GAFI ont mis en œuvre l'ensemble des vingt-huit Recommandations nécessitant des mesures spécifiques,[45] cinq autres pays les respectent toutes sauf une. Plus des trois quarts des membres du GAFI ont intégralement appliqué au moins vingt-quatre des vingt-huit Recommandations. S'agissant de certaines des juridictions présentant apparemment un faible nombre de Recommandations pleinement appliquées — le Japon, les États-Unis et le Mexique — il convient de noter que la défaillance porte sur la non-application de mesures à certaines catégories d'institutions financières non bancaires.

Quant au Canada, il respecte intégralement seize Recommandations. Il ne respecte que partiellement onze Recommandations[46] alors qu'une autre est ignorée. Dans le cadre de la lutte contre le blanchiment d'argent, le Canada a adopté en 2000 la loi sur le recyclage des produits de la criminalité qui impose des obligations de lutte contre le blanchiment à l'ensemble des institutions financières.[47]

Le GAFI conclut l'évaluation annuelle de ses membres en notant que si les États ont peu de difficultés à appliquer les Recommandations traitant des questions juridiques et des questions de coopération internationale,[48] ils rencontrent davantage de difficultés en ce qui a trait aux Recommandations financières.[49]

---

[43] Les 28 Recommandations sont décrites de manière succincte aux notes 48 et 49.

[44] Annexe D du *Rapport annuel 2000–2001 du Groupe d'action financière sur le blanchiment de capitaux.*

[45] Ces membres sont l'Allemagne, la Belgique, le Brésil, le Danemark, la Grèce, l'Irlande, l'Italie, le Luxembourg, la Norvège et la Nouvelle-Zélande.

[46] Les Recommandations que le Canada ne respecte que partiellement sont des recommandations financières au sens défini à la note 49.

[47] La *Loi sur le recyclage des produits de la criminalité* a été sanctionnée le 29 juin 2000.

[48] Ces Recommandations portent essentiellement sur la répression de la lutte contre le blanchiment de capitaux et sur la coopération internationale. S'agissant de la répression, ces recommandations affectent le champ d'application de l'infraction de blanchiment de capitaux, la confiscation et les sanctions pénales et autres du blanchiment de capitaux. Quant à la coopération internationale, il s'agit essentiellement d'améliorer l'échange d'informations au niveau étatique, d'améliorer l'entraide judiciaire.

[49] Ces Recommandations ont trait au comportement des institutions financières et des autorités de contrôle compétentes dans la lutte contre le blanchiment de

L'année 2000 aura donc été marquée par la consolidation du système financier international et par l'intensification de la lutte contre le blanchiment d'argent. Ces deux priorités de l'année 2000 concourent en réalité à la réalisation d'un seul et même objectif: la stabilité du système financier international. En dépit des réformes et des décisions adoptées au cours de cette année, l'aggravation de la situation financière de l'Argentine et de la Turquie rappelle que cette stabilité nécessite un effort continu et commun des États, des institutions internationales et des organismes de contrôles des établissements financiers.

---

capitaux. Pour ce qui est des institutions financières, les recommandations concernent en particulier l'identification des clients; la conservation des documents relatifs aux transactions nationales et internationales; la diligence des institutions financières à l'égard de transactions complexes, importantes, inhabituelles, douteuses; les procédures internes de lutte contre le blanchiment de capitaux. Pour ce qui est des autorités de contrôle, les recommandations visent essentiellement le contrôle par celles-ci de la mise en place de programmes adéquats de lutte contre le blanchiment d'argent au sein des institutions financières; l'élaboration de directives adressées aux institutions financières pour les aider à détecter les modes de comportement suspects de leurs clients; et la réglementation et la supervision des institutions financières pour éviter que les criminels ou leurs complices n'acquièrent une part significative d'institutions financières.

III Investissement

préparé par
CÉLINE LÉVESQUE

I Introduction

Au cours de l'année 2000, trois sentences arbitrales sur le fond ont été rendues sous le régime du Chapitre 11 de l'ALÉNA[1] traitant des investissements. Il s'agit là d'un développement majeur, car jusqu'à cette année, on ne comptait qu'une seule décision sur le fond.[2] Les trois sentences sont d'autant plus intéressantes que le Canada est la partie défenderesse dans deux des trois instances. La présente chronique vise donc à présenter les affaires *Pope & Talbot Inc. c. Gouvernement du Canada,*[3] *Metalclad Corporation c. Gouvernement*

Céline Lévesque, professeure à la Faculté de droit, Université d'Ottawa.

[1] *Accord de libre-échange nord-américain entre le gouvernement du Canada, le gouvernement des États-Unis d'Amérique et le gouvernement des États-Unis du Mexique, le* 17 décembre 1992, 32:3 I.L.M. 605 (entrée en vigueur: 1er janvier 1994) (ci-après ALÉNA).

[2] Voir *Robert Azinian et al. c. Mexique,* ICSID Case No. ARB(AF)/97/2 (1999), 14 I.C.S.I.D. Rev. 535 (ci-après *Azinian*). Les Tribunaux ont eu à juger de leur compétence dans quelques instances. Voir *Ethyl Corporation c. Canada,* Award on Jurisdiction (1998), 38 I.L.M. 708; *Waste Management, Inc. c. Mexique,* ICSID Case No. ARB(AF)/82/2 (2000), 15 I.C.S.I.D. Rev. 214; *Marvin Roy Feldman Karpa c. Mexique,* Interim Decision on Preliminary Jurisdictional Issues, ICSID Case No. ARB(AF)/99/1 (2001), 40 ILM 615 (6 décembre 2000). Quelques sites Internet contiennent le texte des sentences rendues sous le régime du Chapitre 11. Voir en ligne: Ministère des Affaires étrangères et du Commerce international (ci-après MAÉCI) à <http://www.dfait-maeci.gc.ca/tna-nac/NAFTA-f.asp>; U.S. Department of State à <http://www.state.gov/s/l/c3439.htm>; CIRDI à <http://www.worldbank.org/icsid/cases/awards.htm>; et T. Weiler <http://www.naftaclaims.com/> (date d'accès: 5 avril 2002).

[3] *Pope & Talbot Inc. c. Canada,* Interim Award, 26 juin 2000 et Award on the Merits of Phase II, 10 avril 2001, en ligne, respectivement: MAÉCI <http:// www.dfait-maeci.gc.ca/tna-nac/pubdoc7.pdf> et <http://www.dfait-maeci.gc.ca/tna-nac/

du Mexique,[4] et *S.D. Myers, Inc.* c. *Gouvernement du Canada,*[5] premières balises dans l'interprétation du Chapitre 11.

Cette chronique ne peut évidemment être le cadre d'une étude détaillée de tous les aspects de ces sentences.[6] En revanche, une comparaison axée sur trois des obligations substantielles des Parties révèle d'ores et déjà des contradictions significatives et des lacunes surtout en matière d'interprétation des Traités. Les débats les plus controversés ont porté sur l'article 1105 (norme minimale de traitement) (I), l'article 1110 (expropriation et indemnisation) (II), et l'article 1102 (traitement national) (III).

II   Norme minimale de traitement

Dans les trois affaires sous étude, les Tribunaux ont conclu à la violation de l'article 1105 de l'ALÉNA. Cet article, intitulé "Norme minimale de traitement", stipule que: "[c]hacune des Parties accordera aux investissements des investisseurs d'une autre Partie un traitement conforme au droit international, notamment un traitement juste et équitable ainsi qu'une protection et une sécurité intégrales." Ce résultat peut sembler surprenant compte tenu de l'évolution du concept de norme minimale en droit international.

Award_Merits-e.pdf> (date d'accès: 5 avril 2002) (ci-après *Pope & Talbot,* et *Pope & Talbot Phase II*). La sentence rendue en 2001 a tout de même été incluse dans cette chronique afin de permettre une analyse plus complète.

[4] *Metalclad Corporation* c. *Mexico,* ICSID Case No. ARB/AF/97/1 (2001), 16 I.C.S.I.D. Rev. 168 (sentence rendue le 30 août 2000) (ci-après *Metalclad*).

[5] *S.D. Myers, Inc.* c. *Canada,* Partial Award, 13 novembre 2000, en ligne: MAÉCI <http://www.dfait-maeci.gc.ca/tna-nac/myersvcanadapartialaward_final_13-1 1-00.pdf> (date d'accès: 5 avril 2002) (ci-après *S.D. Myers*).

[6] Elle ne peut pas davantage offrir une description complète du régime prévu au c. 11 de l'ALÉNA. Voir généralement D.M. Price, "An Overview of the NAFTA Investment Chapter: Substantive Rules and Investor-State Dispute Settlement" (1993) 27:3 Int'l Lawyer 727; D.M. Price, "Chapter 11—Private Party vs. Government, Investor-State Dispute Settlement: Frankenstein or Safety Valve?" (2000) 26 Can.-U.S. L.J. 107; C.D. Eklund, "A Primer on the Arbitration of NAFTA Chapter Eleven Investor-State Disputes" (1994) 11:4 J. of Int'l Arbitration 135; A.J. VanDuzer, "Investor-State Dispute Settlement under NAFTA Chapter 11: The Shape of Things to Come?" (1997) 35:2 A.C.D.I. 263; G.N. Horlick et A.L. Marti, "NAFTA Chapter 11B—A Private Right of Action to Enforce Market Access through Investments" (1997) 14:1 J. of Int'l Arbitration 43; J.C. Thomas, "Investor-State Arbitration under NAFTA Chapter 11" (1999) 37 A.C.D.I. 99; A. Lemaire, "Le nouveau visage de l'arbitrage entre État et investisseur étranger: le chapitre 11 de l'ALÉNA" (2001) 1 Rev. Arb. 43.

À l'origine, le concept de norme minimale est controversé. Les pays développés soutiennent que le droit international général contient un standard minimum de traitement des étrangers, tandis que les pays en développement s'opposent à ce que les étrangers reçoivent un traitement qui n'est pas égal à celui des nationaux.[7] Si, à l'heure actuelle, on ne peut douter de l'existence en droit international de certaines obligations de traitement à l'égard des étrangers, le contenu de ces obligations demeure difficile à identifier.[8] Une chose apparaît toutefois claire: en vertu du droit international coutumier, le seuil à partir duquel la responsabilité des États s'engage est assez élevé.[9] Avec cette évolution en toile de fond, les arbitres ont eu à déterminer l'étendue (A) ainsi que le contenu (B) de la norme minimale de traitement à l'article 1105 de l'ALÉNA.

A ÉTENDUE

La question principale qui s'est posée quant à l'étendue est de savoir si la norme de "traitement juste et équitable" s'ajoute à la norme de "traitement conforme au droit international" ou, au contraire, fait partie de cette dernière. Dans *Pope & Talbot*, le Tribunal a conclu que ces normes étaient indépendantes, tandis que dans *S.D. Myers*, explicitement, et dans *Metalclad*, implicitement, les arbitres ont considéré qu'il s'agissait d'une norme unique.

Il est tout d'abord utile de rappeler les faits dans l'affaire *Pope & Talbot*. L'investisseur, Pope & Talbot Inc., se plaint de la façon dont le Canada a mis en oeuvre l'*Accord sur le bois d'oeuvre résineux* entre le Canada et les États-Unis. En vertu de cet Accord, un système de quotas à l'exportation a été établi, en échange duquel les États-Unis se sont engagés à ne pas entreprendre certaines actions contre le Canada. Le système prévoit l'imposition de charges croissantes,

---

[7] Voir R. Preiswerk, *La protection des investissements privés dans les traités bilatéraux*, Zurich, Polygraphes S.A., 1963 aux pp. 26-29.

[8] Voir J.-P. Laviec, *Protection et promotion des investissements — Étude de droit international économique*, 1985 à la p. 86.

[9] *Ibid.* à la p. 88. Dans l'affaire *Neer*, souvent citée comme point de référence, le standard minimum a été exprimé de la façon suivante: "the treatment of an alien, in order to constitute an international delinquency, should amount to an outrage, to bad faith, to wilful neglect of duty, or to an insufficiency of gouvernemental action so far short of international standards that every reasonable and impartial man would readily recognize its insufficiency." Voir *L.F.H. Neer and Pauline Neer (U.S.A.) v. United Mexican States* (1926), 4 R.S.A.N.U. 60 aux pp. 61-62.

au-delà d'un certain seuil, imposées sur les exportations de bois aux États-Unis. Des quotas furent donc alloués aux différentes compagnies exportatrices, dont Pope & Talbot Ltd. (l'investissement au Canada de Pope & Talbot Inc.).[10]

Pope & Talbot Inc. invoque plusieurs arguments à l'effet que le système établi par le Canada et sa mise en oeuvre constituent des violations à l'article 1105 de l'ALÉNA. Le Tribunal retiendra un seul des arguments présentés, ayant trait à ce qu'il appellera le "Verification Review Episode."[11] Après avoir décrit en détails cet épisode, le Tribunal conclut, notamment que Pope & Talbot Ltd. a été l'objet de menaces en ce qui concerne l'obtention de quotas, qu'on lui a refusé des demandes raisonnables d'informations pertinentes, qu'elle a été obligée de faire des dépenses inutiles et a subi des perturbations en se pliant aux exigences du gouvernement.[12] Ce traitement, selon le Tribunal, dépasse de loin les erreurs et les accrocs auxquels on peut s'attendre d'un processus administratif et constitue "nothing less than a denial of the fair treatment required by NAFTA Article 1105."[13] Sur cette base, le Tribunal conclut que le Canada est responsable des dommages subis par l'investisseur.

Le Tribunal a atteint ce résultat au moyen d'une analyse démontrant qu'il existe une obligation de traitement juste et équitable, qui est indépendante de l'obligation de traitement conforme au droit international reconnue par l'article 1105. Cette conclusion n'est pas banale, car elle a le potentiel d'élargir considérablement la responsabilité des États, en assujettissant le comportement de ces derniers à une norme générale d'équité. Encore faut-il que l'interprétation retenue soit conforme aux règles d'interprétation des Traités.

Bien qu'il admet que les articles 31 et 32 de la *Convention de Vienne sur le droit des traités*[14] sont applicables à la question, le Tribunal les ignore dans l'interprétation qu'il propose. En premier lieu, il ne donne pas aux termes leur sens ordinaire.[15] Ensuite, il

---

[10] Voir *Pope & Talbot, supra* note 3 aux par. 1-7 et 27-40.

[11] Voir *Pope & Talbot Phase II, supra* note 3 aux par. 156-81.

[12] *Ibid.* au par. 181.

[13] *Ibid.*

[14] *Convention de Vienne sur le droit des traités*, 23 mai 1969, 8 I.L.M. 679 (entrée en vigueur: 27 janvier 1980) (ci-après Convention de Vienne).

[15] En particulier, le Tribunal interprète le mot "including" d'une façon contraire à son sens ordinaire, qui est "inclusive" (dénotant l'inclusion) et non pas "additive" (dénotant l'addition). En se fondant sur une comparaison avec les termes

impose aux Parties un renversement du fardeau de la preuve.[16] Enfin, il applique un standard de droit national plutôt que de droit international contrairement à l'article 1131.[17]

À l'opposé, l'interprétation selon laquelle le traitement juste et équitable est compris dans la référence au droit international a été retenue dans *S.D. Myers*, explicitement, et dans *Metalclad*, implicitement. Dans *S.D. Myers*, le Tribunal a considéré que l'article 1105 présentait un concept global. Ainsi, les mots "juste et équitable" et "protection et sécurité intégrales" devaient être lus, non pas isolément, mais conjointement avec la phrase introductive de l'article.[18] Dans *Metalclad*, le Tribunal, sans se prononcer explicitement, énonce que l'investissement de Metalclad "was not accorded fair and equitable treatment in accordance with international law."[19] Si cette interprétation de l'étendue de la norme minimale à l'article 1105 paraît davantage conforme à l'intention des Parties, on peut avoir des doutes quant à l'interprétation donnée par ces Tribunaux du contenu de la norme prévue.

---

généralement utilisés dans les traités bilatéraux d'investissements étrangers — qui sont "additive" — le Tribunal estime que l'art. 1105 doit être interprété conformément au libellé de ces Accords. Voir notamment *Pope & Talbot Phase II*, *supra* note 3 aux par. 109-13. Cette façon de procéder ignore non seulement le sens ordinaire des mots, mais a pour effet d'incorporer à l'article des termes qui n'y apparaissent pas. Qui plus est, l'interprétation des versions française et espagnole de l'art. 1105, contenant les mots "notamment" et "incluido" respectivement, aurait démontré que les termes utilisés dans les trois langues dénotent l'inclusion.

[16] Par exemple, lorsqu'on a souligné que les Parties à l'ALÉNA avaient peut-être justement voulu diverger de la pratique des traités bilatéraux en adoptant une formulation différente, le Tribunal a énoncé qu'aucune preuve n'avait été soumise à l'effet que "les Parties avaient l'intention de rejeter le caractère additif des BITs" (notre traduction). En d'autres mots, le Tribunal exige des Parties non pas la preuve de l'intention telle qu'elle se reflète dans les termes du Traité, mais la preuve "négative" que leur intention n'était pas d'écarter un sens découlant de termes qui n'apparaissent pas dans le texte! Voir *ibid.* aux par. 114-16.

[17] En effet, le Tribunal interprète l'art. 1105 comme exigeant un traitement juste et équitable et une protection et une sécurité intégrales selon "ordinary standards applied in the NAFTA countries, without any threshold limitation that the conduct complained of be 'egregious,' 'outrageous' or 'shocking,' or otherwise extraordinary" (notes omises). Voir *ibid.* au par. 118. Cette interprétation, qui renvoie à des standards nationaux, ignore l'art. 1131 de l'ALÉNA qui stipule que le droit applicable pour trancher les différends en vertu du Chapitre est le texte de l'ALÉNA et les règles applicables du droit international.

[18] Voir *S.D. Myers*, *supra* note 5 au par. 262.

[19] Voir *Metalclad*, *supra* note 4 au par. 74.

B   CONTENU

Le débat quant au contenu de la norme minimale, auquel on pouvait par ailleurs s'attendre, a pris une tournure inattendue dans les sentences sous étude. En effet, on s'est longuement attardé à la question de savoir si la référence au "droit international" englobait toutes les sources du droit international, telles que décrites à l'article 38 du *Statut de la Cour Internationale de Justice* (CIJ). L'argument selon lequel, *dans le contexte* de l'article 1105, la norme minimale de traitement en est une de droit international coutumier n'a pas été retenu, notamment par le Tribunal dans *Pope & Talbot*. Le résultat de l'interprétation dans *S.D. Myers* et dans *Metalclad* indique également que ces Tribunaux ne se sont pas sentis limités par les normes de droit international coutumier en la matière.

Deux questions, en particulier, ont mis en évidence cette opposition. Est-ce que l'article 1105 englobe des principes, tels que la transparence, qui ne sont pas reconnus comme tel en droit international coutumier? La violation d'une obligation du Chapitre 11 de l'ALÉNA, par exemple celle de l'article 1102 ou 1110, peut-elle constituer du fait même une violation de l'article 1105? Dans *Metalclad*, le Tribunal a répondu affirmativement à la première question. Dans *S.D. Myers*, de façon claire, et dans *Metalclad* de façon implicite, on a répondu affirmativement à la deuxième question.

Le critère utilisé par le Tribunal dans *Metalclad* pour conclure que le Mexique avait violé l'article 1105 est celui de la transparence.[20] Un rappel des faits dans cette affaire s'impose. Metalclad Corporation, une compagnie américaine, a fait l'acquisition d'une entreprise mexicaine dans le but d'exploiter un poste de transbordement et un site d'enfouissement de déchets dangereux. Ayant obtenu les permis requis notamment par l'administration fédérale, l'entreprise a procédé à la construction du site. Les autorités de l'état et de la municipalité concernés se sont toutefois opposées à ce projet, et la municipalité a ordonné la suspension des travaux au motif que l'entreprise ne possédait pas de permis municipal de construction. À cause de certaines complications, et bien qu'on eût terminé la construction par la suite, le site n'a jamais été exploité.[21] En janvier 1997, après des négociations infructueuses avec les autorités, Metalclad a déposé une plainte en vertu du Chapitre 11 de l'ALÉNA. En septembre 1997, le gouverneur de l'état décréta

---

[20]   *Ibid.* aux par. 76 et 88.

[21]   *Ibid.* généralement aux par. 28-62.

une zone écologique protégée couvrant le site d'enfouissement, décret qui a eu pour effet d'empêcher de façon permanente l'exploitation du site.[22]

Au coeur de cette affaire, selon le Tribunal, était la question de savoir si un permis municipal était véritablement requis pour la construction du site. Après avoir analysé la question, le Tribunal a conclu que:

The absence of a clear rule as to the requirement or not of a municipal construction permit, as well as the absence of any established practice or procedure as to the manner of handling applications for a municipal construction permit, amounts to a failure on the part of Mexico to ensure the transparency required by NAFTA.[23]

En définitive, le Tribunal a conclu que Metalclad n'avait pas été traité d'une manière juste et équitable et que le Mexique avait ainsi violé l'article 1105 de l'ALÉNA.

Le Tribunal a par la suite jugé que ce traitement, notamment, lui permettait de conclure que Metalclad avait aussi été victime d'une expropriation indirecte, car on l'avait empêchée illégalement d'exploiter le site d'enfouissement.[24] Le Tribunal se trouvait ainsi a répondre de façon affirmative à la question de savoir si une violation d'une autre obligation au titre du Chapitre 11 de l'ALÉNA, en l'occurrence l'article 1110, pouvait constituer au surplus une violation

---

[22] *Ibid.* au par. 59.

[23] *Ibid.* au par. 88. Selon le Tribunal, la source de l'obligation de transparence se trouve à l'art. 102(1) de l'ALÉNA qui stipule que: "Les objectifs du présent accord, définis de façon plus précise dans ses principes et ses règles, notamment le traitement national, le traitement de la nation la plus favorisée et la transparence, sont les suivants..." Aucunement gêné de ce que les principes de traitement national et de la nation la plus favorisée se trouvent au Chapitre 11 de l'ALÉNA (aux art. 1102 et 1103), tandis que le principe de transparence n'y apparaît pas, le Tribunal a interprété l'obligation de transparence de la façon suivante: "The Tribunal understands this to include the idea that all relevant legal requirements for the purpose of initiating, completing and successfully operating investments made, or intended to be made, under the Agreement should be capable of being readily known to all affected investors of another Party. There should be no room for doubt or uncertainty on such matters" (*ibid.* au par. 76).

[24] *Ibid.* aux par. 104-07. Le Mexique a demandé l'annulation de la sentence dans l'affaire *Metalclad*, demande qui a été en partie accordée par le juge Tysoe de la Cour Suprême de Colombie Britannique le 2 mai 2001. Voir *United Mexican States* v. *Metalclad Corp.* 2001 BCSC 664, [2001] B.C.J. No. 950 (QL) et Supplementary reasons for judgment, 2001 BCSC 1529, [2001] B.C.J. No. 2268 (S.C.).

de l'article 1105. Le Tribunal dans *S.D. Myers* a rendu une décision majoritaire au même effet, ayant conclu que, dans les circonstances de cette affaire, une violation de l'article 1102 établissait du même coup une violation de l'article 1105.[25]

Les Parties à l'ALÉNA, apparemment insatisfaites de l'interprétation large donnée à l'article 1105, ont choisi de clarifier et de réaffirmer la signification de cette disposition à travers la Commission du libre-échange.[26] Cette interprétation précise que l'article 1105 prescrit "la norme minimale de traitement conforme au droit international coutumier à l'égard des étrangers…" Elle précise également que: "[l]es concepts de 'traitement juste et équitable' et de 'protection et de sécurité intégrales' ne prévoient pas de traitement supplémentaire ou supérieur à celui exigé par la norme minimale de traitement conforme au droit international coutumier à l'égard des étrangers." Enfin, elle spécifie que "[l]a constatation qu'il y a eu violation d'une autre disposition de l'ALÉNA ou d'un accord international distinct ne démontre pas qu'il y ait eu violation de l'article 1105(1)."[27] Aussitôt émise, cette interprétation a elle-même fait l'objet de nombreuses critiques.[28]

---

[25] Voir *S.D. Myers, supra* note 5 au par. 266. Bien que le Tribunal dans *Metalclad* n'a pas fait d'efforts pour donner un contenu à la norme minimale au delà de l'obligation de transparence, le Tribunal dans *S.D. Myers* a précisé que: "The Tribunal considers that a breach of Article 1105 occurs only when it is shown that an investor has been treated in such an unjust or arbitrary manner that the treatment rises to the level that is unacceptable from the international perspective. That determination must be made in light of the high measure of deference that international law generally extends to the right of domestic authorities to regulate matters within their own borders. The determination must also take into account any specific rules of international law that are applicable to the case" (*ibid.* au par. 263).

[26] L'article 1131(2) de l'ALÉNA, *supra* note 1, prévoit que: "[u]ne interprétation faite par la Commission d'une disposition du présent accord liera un tribunal en vertu de la présente section."

[27] Commission du libre-échange de l'ALÉNA, *Notes d'interprétation de certaines dispositions du chapitre 11*, 31 juillet 2001, en ligne: MAÉCI <http://www.dfait-maeci.gc.ca/tna-nac/NAFTA-Interpr-f.asp> (date d'accès: 19 mars 2002). Voir aussi l'affaire *Azinian, supra* note 2 au par. 92 où le Tribunal laisse entendre qu'une violation de l'art. 1110 ne constitue pas en elle-même une violation de l'art. 1105.

[28] Notamment, elle a été critiquée par Sir R. Jennings dans une opinion soumise dans le cadre de l'Affaire *Methanex Corp.* c. *United States of America*, disponible en ligne: T. Weiler <http://www.naftaclaims.com/> (date d'accès: 5 avril 2002) (ci-après Opinion — Jennings).

III   Expropriation

Un Tribunal a conclu à la violation de l'article 1110 de l'ALÉNA
uniquement dans une des trois affaires sous étude, soit *Metalclad.*
Cet article, intitulé "Expropriation et indemnisation," stipule que:

Aucune des Parties ne pourra, directement ou indirectement, nationaliser
ou exproprier un investissement d'un investisseur d'une autre Partie sur
son territoire, ni prendre une mesure équivalant à la nationalisation ou
à l'expropriation d'un tel investissement ("expropriation"), si ce n'est:
a) pour une raison d'intérêt public; b) sur une base non-discriminatoire;
c) en conformité avec l'application régulière de la loi et le paragraphe
1105(1) [norme minimale de traitement]; et d) moyennant le versement
d'une indemnité conformément aux paragraphes 2 à 6.

L'une des difficultés d'interprétation de cet article réside dans
l'absence de définition du concept d'expropriation à l'ALÉNA. Si,
pendant longtemps, l'expropriation directe était la plus répandue,
et facilement identifiable, cette époque semble en grande partie
révolue. L'expropriation prend de nos jours des formes beaucoup plus subtiles.[29] Afin de surmonter cette difficulté, on doit s'en
remettre aux règles applicables du droit international, en plus
des règles de l'ALÉNA.[30] Les contours imprécis de l'expropriation
indirecte et rampante en droit international ne feront, par contre,
qu'ajouter au défi d'interprétation de l'article 1110 de l'ALÉNA.
Cette subtilité et cette imprécision ont engendré beaucoup d'incer-
titude quant à l'étendue (A) mais aussi au contenu (B) de la notion
d'expropriation à l'article 1110.

A   ÉTENDUE

C'est l'interprétation des termes "mesure équivalant" à l'expropriation (en anglais: measure tantamount to expropriation) qui a
soulevé la principale question quant à l'étendue de l'article 1110.
En particulier, on s'est interrogé afin de déterminer si ces termes
couvraient davantage que l'expropriation indirecte ou rampante
(en anglais: "creeping expropriation") pour englober des mesures
qui dépassent la couverture du droit international coutumier.

Dans *Pope & Talbot* comme dans *S.D. Myers*, les Tribunaux ont
conclu que non. Ils ont raisonné que "tantamount" voulait uniquement dire "équivalent," ce qui était par ailleurs confirmé dans les

---

[29] Voir généralement CNUCED, *Taking of Property,* UNCTAD Series on issues in
international investment agreement, New York, United Nations, 2000.

[30] Voir ALÉNA, *supra* note 1, art. 1131(1).

versions française et espagnole du Traité. En toute logique, ont-ils dit, ce qui est équivalent ne peut contenir davantage.[31]

Ces décisions devraient rassurer quelque peu le Canada qui, en particulier, avait émis des craintes quant à l'interprétation large de ces termes.[32] Par rapport au contenu, par contre, les positions divergentes des Tribunaux n'ont rien de très rassurant.

B   CONTENU

L'un des obstacles auxquels on est rapidement confronté est d'ordre lexical. Les arbitres utilisent des termes tels que "expropriation," "taking" "deprivation" "confiscation" sans bien expliciter leur signification. Évidemment, leur tâche serait de beaucoup facilitée s'il existait en droit international des repères plus éclairants à cet égard. Malgré tout, les arbitres dans les affaires sous étude semblent s'entendre sur quelques éléments communs. Comme on s'en doute, les points de désaccords sont tout aussi, sinon plus, importants.

Dans les trois sentences, les Tribunaux se réfèrent à la notion de "taking" pour définir l'expropriation. On s'entend aussi pour dire que cet enlèvement de la propriété[33] doit avoir pour effet une privation de droits, plus ou moins importante selon les Tribunaux. Dans le cas de l'expropriation indirecte ou rampante ("creeping"), l'ingérence dont l'État expropriant fait preuve doit avoir des conséquences équivalentes à un enlèvement de propriété.

Cette cohérence apparente se dissout rapidement. Deux sujets de désaccord attirent l'attention: quel degré d'ingérence de la part de l'État permet de conclure à l'existence d'une expropriation indirecte ou rampante et, de façon plus particulière, une mesure de réglementation peut-elle constituer une expropriation.

En ce qui concerne le degré d'ingérence, le Tribunal dans l'affaire *Metalclad* adopte l'interprétation la plus libérale. Après

---

[31] Voir *Pope & Talbot, supra* note 3 aux par. 96 et 104 et *S.D. Myers, supra* note 5 aux par. 285-86. Dans *Metalclad*, le Tribunal ne s'est pas prononcé de manière explicite sur cette question, bien qu'il ait adopté une définition large de l'expropriation.

[32] Voir C. Lévesque, "Chronique de Droit international économique en 1999 — Investissement" (2001) 38 A.C.D.I. 310 aux pp. 316-18.

[33] C'est ainsi qu'on a notamment traduit le terme anglais "taking." Voir G. Fouilloux, *La nationalisation et le droit international public*, Paris, Librairie générale de droit et de jurisprudence, 1962 à la p. 143.

avoir cité le texte de l'article 1110, et de l'article 201 (1) qui définit ce qu'est une mesure,[34] le Tribunal continue:

> *Thus*, expropriation under NAFTA includes not only open, deliberate and acknowledged takings of property, such as outright seizure or formal or obligatory transfer of title in favour of the host State, but also *covert or incidental interference* with the use of property which has the effect of depriving the owner, in whole or in significant part, of the use or reasonably-to-be-expected economic benefit of property even if not necessarily to the obvious benefit of the host State.[35]

Fait notable, par l'emploi de l'adverbe "thus" pour introduire la phrase, le Tribunal semble indiquer qu'il tire cet énoncé du texte même de l'article 1110, lu en conjonction avec la définition de mesure. Le fait que le Tribunal ne cite aucune autre source au soutien de son énoncé confirme cette inférence.

Dans les paragraphes suivant l'énoncé, le Tribunal utilise tantôt les termes "expropriation indirecte," tantôt les termes "mesures équivalant à l'expropriation," en toute apparence de façon interchangeable. En bref, le Tribunal a jugé que le Mexique avait violé l'article 1110 en prenant part, ou en acquiesçant, au "denial to Metalclad of the right to operate the landfill, notwithstanding the fact that the project was fully approved and endorsed by the federal government."[36] Le décret écologique constituait également une expropriation, car il avait pour effet d'empêcher en permanence l'exploitation du site par Metalclad.[37]

Dans *Pope & Talbot*, le Tribunal a retenu une interprétation décidément moins libérale du degré d'ingérence requis. Selon ce Tribunal, le "test" est de savoir si l'ingérence est "sufficiently restrictive to support a conclusion that the property has been 'taken' from the owner."[38] Il ajoute: "Thus, the *Harvard Draft* defines the standard as requiring interference that would 'justify an inference

---

[34] Voir ALÉNA, *supra* note 1, art. 201 (1) qui stipule que "mesure s'entend de toute législation, réglementation, procédure, prescription ou pratique."

[35] *Metalclad, supra* note 4 au par. 103 [je souligne].

[36] *Ibid.* au par. 104.

[37] Voir *ibid.* aux par. 109-11. Le Tribunal a spécifié que: "a finding of expropriation on the basis of the Ecological Decree is not essential to the Tribunal's finding of a violation of NAFTA Article 1110. However, the Tribunal considers that the implementation of the Ecological Decree would, in and of itself, constitute an act tantamount to expropriation" (*ibid.* au par. 111). La controverse liée au fait que le décret avait été adopté après le dépôt de la plainte par Metalclad s'en trouvait du même coup réduite.

[38] *Pope & Talbot, supra* note 3 au par. 102.

that the owner ... will not be able to use, enjoy, or dispose of the property..."[39] En l'espèce, le Tribunal a conclu que le degré d'ingérence n'était pas suffisamment élevé pour conclure à une expropriation. Ainsi, malgré les quotas à l'exportation, Pope & Talbot Ltd. avait continué à exporter des quantités importantes de bois aux États-Unis et à faire des profits substantiels. Notamment, la compagnie n'avait en aucun moment perdu le contrôle de son entreprise ou la direction de ses opérations.[40]

Dans le même ordre d'idées, les Tribunaux ont envisagé l'hypothèse qu'une mesure de réglementation constitue une expropriation. Sur la base des principes énoncés, l'affaire *Pope & Talbot* rend cette éventualité plus plausible que l'affaire *S.D. Myers*.

Dans *Pope & Talbot*, le Tribunal a rejeté l'argument présenté par le Canada à l'effet que des mesures de réglementation, adoptées en vertu du pouvoir de police de l'État et non discriminatoires, ne pouvaient constituer une violation de l'article 1110 de l'ALÉNA. Le Tribunal, bien que reconnaissant qu'il faille analyser ces questions avec beaucoup de soins, constate que la réglementation peut très bien être utilisée de façon à constituer une expropriation rampante. Le Tribunal conclura sur ce point en ajoutant que: "Indeed, much creeping expropriation could be conducted by regulation, and a blanket exception for regulatory measures would create a gaping loophole in international protections against expropriation."[41]

Dans *S.D. Myers*, le Tribunal adopte une approche beaucoup plus restrictive. Selon le Tribunal, l'ensemble des précédents ne

---

[39] *Ibid.* La note de bas de page réfère à la *Draft Convention on the International Responsibility of States for Injuries to Aliens*, art. 10(3).

[40] Voir *ibid.* aux par. 100-01.

[41] *Pope & Talbot, supra* note 3 au par. 99. Au soutien de sa position, le Tribunal cite un extrait du *Third Restatement of the Foreign Relations Law of the U.S.* publié par l'American Law Institute, une société savante américaine. Le *Restatement* est une "récapitulation, ordonnée et raisonnée, de l'ensemble des règles de Droit qui régissent une matière déterminée." Voir P. Juillard, "Chronique de droit international économique, Investissements" (1988) 34 AFDI aux pp. 582-83. Comme le reconnaît P. Juillard, par contre, "malgré son très grand souci de neutralité et d'objectivité, le Restatement repose sur certains soubassements idéologiques, qui sont ceux de la doctrine dominante aux États-Unis, et qui affleurent par endroits" (*ibid.* à la p. 583). Certes, on peut considérer que le *Restatement*, constituant une oeuvre de doctrine au sens de l'art. 38(1)d) du Statut de la CIJ, est une source auxiliaire de détermination des règles de droit international (*ibid.*) En revanche, le Tribunal semble donner un poids outrancier au *Restatement* lorsqu'il déclare, par exemple, que "Canada's suggestion that ... is inconsistent with the *Restatement*." Voir *Pope & Talbot, supra* note 3 à la note 73.

considèrent habituellement pas que des mesures de réglementation équivalent à l'expropriation.[42] Sans nier que cela soit une possibilité, le Tribunal affirme qu'il est improbable que la réglementation par les autorités publiques soit objet de plainte légitime en vertu de l'article 1110 de l'ALÉNA.[43]

La façon dont le Tribunal suggère de distinguer entre "réglementation" et "expropriation" est à tout le moins curieuse. En effet, le Tribunal énonce que: "Expropriations tend to involve the deprivation of ownership rights; regulations a lesser interference."[44] Dans la mesure où il est admis que la privation de droits peut être une conséquence de l'expropriation autant que de la réglementation, la première partie de cet énoncé semble vide de sens. Dans *Pope & Talbot*, on a plutôt retenu le critère de "substantial deprivation."[45] Pour ce qui est de la deuxième partie de l'énoncé, il est assurément vrai que la réglementation comporte un degré d'ingérence moindre que l'expropriation. Toutefois, la sentence fait peu pour éclaircir ces concepts, sinon que d'énoncer qu'une mesure temporaire a moins de chance de constituer une expropriation qu'une mesure permanente.[46] En l'espèce, la mesure avait un caractère temporaire.

Avant de procéder plus avant, il est utile de rappeler les faits de cette affaire. S.D. Myers Inc. est une compagnie constituée en Ohio aux États-Unis qui s'occupe entre autres de décontamination de déchets toxiques. Au début des années 1990, la compagnie a élaboré le projet d'importer aux États-Unis des BPC en provenance du Canada pour en faire l'élimination dans ses installations en Ohio.[47] L'environnement législatif et réglementaire de l'époque ne permettait pourtant pas à S.D. Myers de mettre ses plans à exécution. En effet, la frontière américaine était fermée à l'exportation et à l'importation de BPC depuis 1980. Le 26 octobre 1995, toutefois, S.D. Myers a obtenu la permission de l'agence américaine de protection de l'environnement (EPA) d'importer des BPC en provenance du Canada. Apparemment surpris par la permission accordée, le Canada a rapidement mis en place une prohibition

---

[42] Voir *S.D. Myers, supra* note 5 au par. 281.

[43] *Ibid.*

[44] *Ibid.* au par. 282.

[45] *Pope & Talbot, supra* note 3 au par. 102.

[46] Voir *S.D. Myers, supra* note 5 aux par. 283-84.

[47] Pour mener à bien ce projet, une corporation fut constituée au Canada en 1993 du nom de Myers Canada (l'investissement). *Ibid.* au par. 111.

d'exportation de BPC.[48] La frontière est demeurée fermée jusqu'en février 1997 (soit durant à peu près seize mois), moment où un amendement permit l'exportation vers les États-Unis.[49] En 1998, S.D. Myers déposait une plainte en vertu du Chapitre 11 de l'ALÉNA alléguant violation de la part du Canada de ses obligations notamment en vertu de l'article 1110. Le Tribunal est arrivé à la conclusion que la prohibition d'exportation ne constituait pas une mesure d'expropriation, mais elle constituait une violation de l'obligation de traitement national.[50]

IV Traitement national

Les Tribunaux ont conclu à la violation de l'obligation de traitement national dans l'affaire *S.D. Myers* et ont rejeté cette allégation dans *Pope & Talbot*.[51] L'article 1102(1) de l'ALÉNA stipule:

Chacune des Parties accordera aux investisseurs d'une autre Partie un traitement non moins favorable que celui qu'elle accorde, dans des circonstances similaires, à ses propres investisseurs, en ce qui concerne l'établissement, l'acquisition, l'expansion, la gestion, la direction, l'exploitation et la vente ou autre aliénation d'investissements.[52]

Selon Laviec, "[l]a norme du traitement national vise à mettre sur un pied d'égalité juridique des investissements étrangers et nationaux."[53] Fréquemment combinée dans les traités bilatéraux d'investissements étrangers avec une clause de la nation la plus favorisée (NPF), la clause de traitement national est une incarnation du

---

[48] Au Canada, la réglementation applicable prohibait l'exportation de BPC, sauf vers les États-Unis et à condition d'une approbation préalable d'EPA. *Ibid.* au par. 100. Le Canada a notamment argumenté que la prohibition d'exportation de BPC mise en place était conforme à ses obligations internationales en vertu de la *Convention de Bâle sur le contrôle des mouvements transfrontières de déchets dangereux et de leur élimination* de 1989 et de l'*Accord entre le Gouvernement du Canada et le Gouvernement des États-Unis d'Amérique concernant les déplacements transfrontières de déchets dangereux* de 1986. Voir *ibid.* aux par. 150 et 205-16.

[49] Quelques cinq mois plus tard, la frontière fut à nouveau fermée suite à une décision des Tribunaux américains. *Ibid.* au par. 128.

[50] Le Canada a demandé l'annulation de la sentence dans l'affaire *S.D. Myers* à la Cour fédérale du Canada le 8 février 2001. Au sujet de ce recours, voir en ligne: MAÉCI <http://www.dfait-maeci.gc.ca/tna-nac/NAFTA-f.asp#SDM> (date d'accès: 5 avril 2002).

[51] L'article 1102 n'a pas été l'objet de plainte dans *Metalclad*.

[52] L'article 1102(2) de l'ALÉNA, *supra* note 1, prévoit la même obligation mais au profit des "investissements des investisseurs d'une autres Partie."

[53] Laviec, *supra* note 8 à la p. 95.

principe de non-discrimination. Plusieurs seront déjà familiers avec la formulation de l'article 1102 car elle rappelle celle de l'article III du GATT.[54] C'est en effet dans les accords de commerce que le traitement national trouve ses origines conventionnelles.[55] L'une des difficultés liées à l'interprétation de l'article 1102 dans le cadre de l'ALÉNA est d'adapter le contenu de la norme au contexte des investissements, tout en respectant l'économie générale du Traité. Ce cadre de référence équivoque soulève des questions quant à l'étendue (A) mais surtout quand au contenu (B) de l'article 1102.

A   ÉTENDUE

Dans *S.D. Myers* et *Pope & Talbot*, les Tribunaux reconnaissent que l'article 1102 couvre les cas de discrimination *de jure* et *de facto*.[56] Dans *Pope & Talbot*, on s'est interrogé notamment afin de déterminer l'étendue de la prohibition de la discrimination de fait. Le Tribunal a rejeté l'argument présenté par le Canada selon lequel pour constituer une violation de l'article 1102 la discrimination devait causer un "disproportionate disadvantage" aux investisseurs étrangers. En rejetant cet argument, le Tribunal a notamment souligné qu'il n'y avait pas lieu de traiter les désavantages causés par la discrimination *de facto* d'une façon différente de ceux entraînés par la discrimination *de jure*.[57]

B   CONTENU

La question principale qui s'est posée quant au contenu de l'obligation de traitement national a été de définir les termes "dans des circonstances similaires." Cette expression constitue la clé de voûte de l'article 1102 car elle permet d'identifier les investisseurs nationaux dont le traitement sera comparé à celui des investisseurs étrangers. L'approche des Tribunaux est similaire à plusieurs égards, mais les fondements de cette dernière divergent de manière significative.

Premièrement, les Tribunaux s'entendent pour dire que la signification de l'expression est appelée à varier selon les faits de

---

[54] Voir GATT, *Résultats des négociations commerciales multilatérales du cycle d'Uruguay — Textes juridiques*, Genève, Secrétariat du GATT, 1994.

[55] Voir CNUCED, *National Treatment*, UNCTAD Series on issues in international investment agreement, New York, United Nations, 1999 à la p. 7.

[56] Voir *S.D. Myers*, *supra* note 5 au par. 252 et *Pope & Talbot Phase II*, *supra* note 3 aux par. 78-79.

[57] Voir *Pope & Talbot Phase II*, *ibid*. au par. 70.

chaque espèce.[58] Deuxièmement, ils s'entendent sur la nécessité de garder en tête "the overall legal context in which the phrase appears."[59] Dans *Pope & Talbot*, le Tribunal a estimé que le contexte incluait autant les objectifs de libéralisation de l'ALÉNA que les antécédents de la dispute de longue date entre le Canada et les États-Unis sur le bois d'oeuvre.[60] Dans *S.D. Myers*, le Tribunal a jugé que ce contexte incluait les différentes dispositions de l'ALÉNA, de l'*Accord nord-américain de coopération dans le domaine de l'environnement* (ANACE) et les principes qui sont affirmés dans cet Accord, y compris ceux de la Déclaration de Rio.[61] Troisièmement, quant aux conséquences à tirer du contexte, les Tribunaux s'entendent généralement sur les étapes de la démarche à suivre. Ainsi, lorsqu'il s'agit de comparer le traitement qui est offert aux investisseurs, il ne suffit pas d'identifier les investisseurs domestiques qui sont "dans des circonstances similaires" parce qu'ils opèrent dans le même secteur économique ou commercial que les investisseurs étrangers. Il faut poursuivre la démarche et se demander, le cas échéant, si le traitement moins favorable accordé aux étrangers résulte d'une politique rationnelle du gouvernement qui n'est pas liée à la nationalité des investisseurs. Si tel est le cas, suivant le raisonnement proposé, les investisseurs nationaux et étrangers ne sont pas "dans des circonstances similaires."

Mais, lorsqu'on dépasse les généralités et qu'on s'attarde à la façon dont les Tribunaux sont arrivés à l'adoption de cette approche, on est frappé par les divergences mais aussi par l'interprétation anémique des arbitres. Dans *Pope & Talbot*, on s'est appuyé uniquement sur l'interprétation des termes "dans les mêmes circonstances" (en anglais: "in like situations") contenus dans l'instrument de l'OCDE relatif au traitement national.[62] À cet égard, il faut noter que la Déclaration n'est pas de droit coutumier. Au

---

[58] Voir *S.D. Myers, supra* note 5 aux par. 243-44 et *Pope & Talbot Phase II, ibid.* au par. 75.

[59] *S.D. Myers, ibid.* au par. 245 et *Pope & Talbot Phase II, ibid.* au par. 76, citant *S.D. Myers.*

[60] *Pope & Talbot Phase II, ibid.* au par. 77.

[61] Voir *S.D. Myers, supra* note 5 au par. 247.

[62] Voir *Pope & Talbot Phase II, supra* note 3 à la note 73. Dans *Pope & Talbot*, l'analyse de la preuve a démontré que dans chaque cas allégué de discrimination, le Tribunal était en mesure d'identifier un objectif gouvernemental rationnel expliquant le traitement différentiel. Ainsi, les investisseurs nationaux et étrangers ne se trouvaient pas "dans des circonstances similaires" et le Canada n'avait pas violé ses obligations en vertu de l'art. 1102.

mieux, elle représente la pratique de certains États.[63] Dans *S.D. Myers*, le Tribunal a également fait mention de cette Déclaration.[64] Toutefois, son interprétation s'est inspirée de façon plus significative des dispositions du GATT et de l'interprétation donnée à l'expression "like products" dans le cadre de l'OMC.[65]

C'est ici que la question de l'adaptation de la norme commerciale au contexte des investissements se pose le plus clairement. Dans le cadre de l'OMC, l'application de l'article III du GATT sur le traitement national ne donne pas lieu à une analyse des justifications de la mesure alléguée discriminatoire. On s'en remet pour cela à l'article XX (exceptions générales). Un équilibre est ainsi établi. Or, l'article XX du GATT est incorporé dans l'ALÉNA, mais il est notamment applicable au commerce des produits et des services, et non pas à l'investissement.[66]

Les Tribunaux ayant à interpréter l'article 1102 de l'ALÉNA, et voulant reproduire l'équilibre du GATT, sont ainsi confrontés à une tâche délicate. Une approche est de mettre l'accent sur les différences entre "produits similaires" (article III du GATT) et "circonstances similaires" (article 1102 de l'ALÉNA), de façon à permettre une analyse des justifications de la mesure à même "les circonstances" qui est un concept plus large.[67] Une autre approche,

---

[63] Voir OCDE, *Traitement national des entreprises sous contrôle étranger*, Paris, OCDE, 1993 (ci-après *Traitement national des entreprises*). Ce document comporte certaines clarifications des termes utilisés dans l'instrument de l'OCDE relatif au traitement national, notamment des termes "dans les mêmes circonstances." Cette clarification est utilisée comme source de droit dans l'affaire *Pope & Talbot*. Il faut noter par ailleurs que la formulation retenue à l'art. 1102 de l'ALÉNA diffère de façon significative de la définition de traitement national dans l'instrument de l'OCDE qui prévoit que: "les pays Membres, compte tenu de la nécessité de maintenir l'ordre public, de protéger les intérêts essentiels de leur sécurité et de remplir leurs engagements concernant la paix et la sécurité internationales, devraient accorder aux entreprises ... un régime ... qui ... ne sera pas moins favorable que celui dont bénéficient dans les mêmes circonstances les entreprises nationales" (*ibid.* à la p. 14).

[64] Voir *S.D. Myers, supra* note 5 au par. 248.

[65] *Ibid.* aux par. 244-46.

[66] L'article 2101 (Exceptions générales) de l'ALÉNA incorpore l'article XX du GATT mais uniquement en ce qui a trait au commerce des produits et aux obstacles techniques au commerce (ALÉNA, *supra* note 1, art. 2101(1)). Cet article prévoit aussi une exception liée au commerce des services et aux télécommunications (*ibid.*, art. 2101(2)).

[67] On serait en mesure de cette façon d'arriver à un résultat similaire à celui visé par l'instrument de l'OCDE relatif au traitement national. Voir *Traitement national des entreprises, supra* note 63.

plus indirecte, est de remettre en question l'interprétation restrictive de "produits similaires" à l'article III du GATT, de façon à
introduire des éléments de justification à cette étape de l'analyse,
plutôt que dans le cadre de l'article XX.[68] Le Tribunal dans *S.D.
Myers* a adopté une autre approche. Il a
choisi de donner une interprétation extensive du contexte juridique de l'article 1102, lui permettant *de facto* d'appliquer les
principes contenus à l'article XX du GATT. Cette façon de procéder, cependant, n'est pas conforme aux règles d'interprétation
des Traités. Premièrement, le Tribunal confond "texte" et "contexte" en imposant aux Parties des obligations qui ne font pas
partie du Chapitre 11.[69] Deuxièmement, le Tribunal ne respecte
pas l'économie générale de l'ALÉNA. Notamment, il fait fi du
principe *expressio unius est exclusio alterius*[70] lorsqu'il incorpore *de
facto* l'article XX du GATT au Chapitre 11 de l'ALÉNA contrairement à l'intention exprimée par les Parties.[71]

À la méthode proposée pour interpréter les termes "dans des
circonstances similaires," il faut finalement ajouter la dimension
de l'intention discriminatoire. Dans *Pope & Talbot*, cette dernière
semble déterminante.[72] Dans *S.D. Myers*, le Tribunal estime que

---

[68] Pour un raisonnement analogue, consulter l'affaire de l'amiante où l'Organe
d'appel de l'OMC étudie la relation entre l'art. III:4 et l'art. XX du GATT. Voir
*Communautés européennes — Mesures affectant l'amiante et les produits en contenant.
(Plainte du Canada)* (2001), OMC Doc. WT/DS135/AB/R (Rapport de l'Organe
d'appel), notamment aux par. 113-18 et 149-54; en ligne voir: OMC <http://
www.wto.org/french/docs_f/docs_f.htm> (date d'accès: 26 mars 2002).

[69] Voir notamment *S.D. Myers, supra* note 5 au par. 250: "The Tribunal considers
that the interpretation of the phrase 'like circumstances' in Article 1102 must
take into account the general principles that emerge from the legal context of
the NAFTA, including both its concern with the environment and the need to
avoid trade distorsions that are not justified by environmental concerns."

[70] Voir I. Brownlie, *Principles of Public International Law*, 5e éd., Oxford, Oxford University Press, 1998 à la p. 634.

[71] Le Tribunal ne tient pas davantage compte de la présence d'exceptions particulières aux art. 1101(4) et 1106(6) et de la présence de l'art. 1114 (Mesures
environnementales) au Chapitre 11. Il ne s'agit pas ici de porter jugement sur le
bien fondé de permettre une comparaison entre investisseurs nationaux et
étrangers "dans des circonstances similaires" qui aille au-delà de la relation de
concurrence entre ces investisseurs, par exemple. Il s'agit plutôt de souligner les
failles dans l'interprétation que les Tribunaux futurs devraient éviter.

[72] Voir la clarification à l'instrument de l'OCDE relatif au traitement national, cité
par le Tribunal, qui indique que: "En tout état de cause, la seule façon de déterminer si une mesure discriminatoire appliquée à des entreprises sous contrôle
étranger constitue une exception au Traitement national consiste à vérifier si la

l'intention est importante, mais pas nécessairement déterminante: "protectionist intent is not necessarily decisive on its own."[73] Il doit en résulter un effet défavorable pour l'investisseur étranger. Si cet effet est présent, par contre, l'intention semble déterminante. En l'espèce, le Tribunal a accordé beaucoup de valeur à la preuve de l'intention discriminatoire de la Ministre de l'Environnement.[74]

Dans la pratique du GATT et de l'OMC, qui a par ailleurs inspiré le Tribunal dans *S.D. Myers*, on arrive à un résultat contraire. L'intention discriminatoire n'est pas déterminante dans l'interprétation de l'obligation de traitement national; ce qui compte est l'effet discriminatoire.[75] Dans l'affaire *Services transfrontières de camionnage et d'investissement*, rendue en vertu du Chapitre 20 de l'ALÉNA, le Tribunal a également estimé que l'intention discriminatoire n'était pas pertinente.[76] Ainsi se pose à nouveau la question de l'adaptation des normes au contexte des investissements; question qui en l'espèce incite à une réflexion sur la raison d'être de cette divergence entre le droit des investissements et le droit applicable au commerce des produits.

---

discrimination est motivée, au moins en partie, par le fait que les entreprises concernées sont sous contrôle étranger." Voir *Pope & Talbot, supra* note 3 à la note 73 et au par. 79.

[73] *S.D. Myers, supra* note 5 au par. 254.

[74] Voir *ibid.* au par 162. De façon générale, l'analyse du Tribunal dans cette affaire est assez décousue et parfois contradictoire, ou à tout le moins confuse. Par exemple, le Tribunal, après avoir reconnu que la mesure avait pour effet de désavantager les étrangers, juge que: "there was no legitimate environmental reason for introducing the ban" (*ibid.* aux par. 193-95). Plus tard, par contre, le Tribunal indique que si l'objectif "indirect" poursuivi par le Canada était légitime, les moyens utilisés ne l'étaient pas. Le Tribunal conclut que: "CANADA was concerned to ensure the economic strength of the Canadian industry, in part, because it wanted to maintain the ability to process PCBs within Canada in the future. This was a legitimate goal ... The indirect motive was understandable, but the method contravened CANADA's international commitments under the NAFTA" (*ibid.* au par. 255).

[75] Voir *Japon — Taxes sur les boissons alcooliques (Plaintes des Communautés européennes, du Canada et des États-Unis)* (1996) OMC Doc. WT/DS 8, 10, 11/AB/R (Rapport de l'Organe d'appel) à la p. 34; en ligne voir: OMC <http://www.wto.org/french/docs_f/docs_f.htm> (date d'accès: 26 mars 2002).

[76] Voir *Re Services transfrontières de camionnage et d'investissement (Mexico v. United States)* (2001) USA-MEX-98-2008-01 (Groupe arb. c. 20) au par. 214; en ligne: Secrétariat de l'ALÉNA <http://www.nafta-sec-alena.org/french/index.htm? decisions/decisions.htm> (date d'accès: 29 mars 2001).

V CONCLUSION

Cette chronique a souligné plusieurs contradictions entre les sentences rendues sur le fond en 2000, ainsi qu'identifié de nombreuses failles dans l'application des principes d'interprétation des Traités. La spécialisation professionnelle de certains arbitres pourrait expliquer, en partie, ce désordre. Ainsi, il est possible que trop peu d'entre eux possèdent des connaissances poussées en matière de droit international public, droit international économique ainsi qu'en droit de l'arbitrage commercial international.[77] Ces trois domaines sont par ailleurs en relation constante dans le cadre du Chapitre 11 de l'ALÉNA.

Mais la source du problème réside ailleurs. Il s'agit de la conception même du mode *ad hoc* de règlement des différends prévu au Chapitre 11. Les Parties, confrontées à des Tribunaux trop aventuriers par exemple, ont trois options principales. La première est une interprétation de la Commission du libre-échange. Selon cette méthode, les Parties sont en mesure de lier les Tribunaux futurs à l'interprétation donnée.[78] Mais, il doit uniquement s'agir d'une interprétation et non d'un amendement,[79] ce qui laisse aux Parties une marge de manoeuvre relativement limitée. La deuxième option est justement l'amendement à l'ALÉNA.[80] À moins d'une réouverture de l'Accord pour d'autres motifs, il est très peu probable que le Chapitre 11 soit modifé. La troisième option est la demande d'annulation devant les tribunaux de droit commun. Il s'agit là d'un recours exceptionnel qui devrait être manié avec le plus grand soin. Le danger qui guette les Parties est celui d'abuser de ce recours faute d'alternatives. Une telle approche pourrait

---

[77] Voir Thomas, *supra* note 6, qui soutient que la "composition of Chapter 11 tribunals will have an impact on the awards that they render." Il explique que: "There has not been a great deal of cross-fertilization between the largely separate worlds of international trade law under the ... GATT and ... WTO, private international commercial arbitration, and international investment dispute settlement under bilateral investment treaties and the ICSID Convention. Thus, in some cases, arbitrators who are experienced in one field may be presented for the first time with complex treaty concepts and legal issues from another field" (*ibid.* à la p. 102) (notes omises).

[78] Voir *supra* note 26.

[79] Voir Opinion — Jennings, *supra* note 28 et la déclaration de G.A. Alvarez, dans le cadre de l'affaire *Methanex Corp.* c. *United States of America*, publié dans *Inside US Trade*, Vol. 20, No. 1 — January 4, 2002, notamment aux pp. 23-24.

[80] Voir ALÉNA, *supra* note 1, art. 2202 (Modifications).

affaiblir les fondements mêmes de l'arbitrage international qui dépend pour sa légitimité et son efficacité de la déférence des Tribunaux de droit commun. Quelle est la solution à ce problème? Elle réside peut-être dans la création d'une instance d'appel, une quatrième option qui soulève ses propres difficultés.

Canadian Practice in International Law /
Pratique canadienne en matière de
droit international

At the Department of Foreign Affairs
in 2000-1 / Au ministère des Affaires
étrangères en 2000-1

compiled by / préparé par
MICHAEL LEIR

ENVIRONMENTAL LAW

Proposed Amendments to the Espoo Convention on the Environmental
Impact Assessment in a Transboundary Context

In a legal opinion dated February 2, 2001, the Legal Bureau wrote:

In the current proposal, the unanimity requirement (which is an exception to the provisions of the Convention that bring amendments into force
upon ¾ ratifications) is not part of the amendment to the Convention but
rather a part of the decision adopting the amendment.

In Canada's view, changes or exceptions to the legal provisions of the
Convention should be done through amendments to that legal text. In our
view the current proposal creates a legal ambiguity as to the relationship
between the unanimity exception in the decision and the ¾ ratification
rule in the legal text of the Convention.

It is an important point of treaty practice for Canada that amendments
to a treaty be undertaken in accordance with the legal provisions of the

Michael Leir, Legal Adviser, Department of Foreign Affairs and International
Trade, Ottawa. The extracts from official correspondence contained in this survey
have been made available by courtesy of the Department of Foreign Affairs and
International Trade. Some of the correspondence from which the extracts are
given was provided for the general guidance of the enquirer in relation to specific
facts that are often not described in full in the extracts within this compilation. The
statements of law and practice should not necessarily be regarded as a definitive
statement by the Department of Foreign Affairs and International Trade of that law
or practice.

treaty. The treaty is the legal framework created and agreed to and hence it is the instrument that turns sovereign "countries" into "Parties."

The current structure of the proposed text suggests that Parties to the Convention can disregard the amending provisions of the Convention and amend the text through a parallel process or stand alone agreement. In Canada's view, this would not be a desirable precedent to establish for this Convention. It would mean, in practical terms, that the first amendment to this Convention was not adopted by the "Parties to the Convention" but by a group of "sovereign states" under a "subsequent agreement." More importantly, it would also suggest that "sovereign states" could adopt any procedures that they wished to change the legal commitments of the treaty outside of the provisions of the Convention that they had negotiated.

In Canada's view, where exceptions need to be made to the provisions of a Convention, the exception should be done within the amending formula and procedures of the Convention.

Canada's Sovereignty in Changing Arctic Waters

In a paper dated March 19, 2001, the Legal Bureau wrote:

Land and Law

First of all, Canada has no "claims" of sovereignty over the Arctic Archipelago. Canadian sovereignty is an accepted fact. There is no dispute about the ownership of the lands and islands of the Canadian Arctic Archipelago ... they belong to Canada.

Without delving too deeply into the legal history, the salient points are as follows: the legal title to the Arctic islands belonging to Great Britain was formally transferred to Canada by means of an Imperial Order-in-Council in 1880. In 1895, by its own order-in-council, Canada explicitly established the boundaries of its northern possessions, which included all islands up to latitude 83¼ north, i.e., the northern-most point of Ellesmere Island. This order-in-council enclosed all the islands southward from that latitude as part of Canada.

Between the two world wars, it is true that there were nebulous claims from other countries as to the legitimacy of Canadian sovereignty in the High Arctic. About 1920 the Danes started to view Ellesmere Island as terra nullius, a no man's land, and Greenland hunters began killing musk-oxen on the island ... The Technical Advisory Board, made up of senior civil servants, was established to study the sovereignty issue. The committee concluded that greater governmental presence in the High Arctic was needed to fend off any competing claims. Starting in 1922, the Canadian government began sending annual expeditions to the area, mostly by members of the Royal Canadian Mounted Police. Another order-in-council was adopted in 1926, this one creating the Arctic Islands Preserve and which made the Arctic region a hunting preserve for the exclusive use of its aboriginal inhabitants. At the same time, the annual American expeditions to the High Arctic Islands of the mid-1920's complied with the 1925 amendment to the Northwest Territories Act that obliged foreign explorers to obtain a Canadian permit before conducting research in that area ...

From reading the history of the Department of External Affairs, one learns that important diplomatic steps were taken to affirm Canadian sovereignty over the Sverdrup Islands, which were "discovered," named and apparently claimed by the Norwegian explorer, Otto Sverdrup, in the 1880's. In a 1928 diplomatic note, Norway notified Canada that it intended to affirm its rights in international law over these islands ... Through the good offices of the Canadian Pacific Railroad agent in Oslo, there being no Canadian Embassy, a deal was worked out. Ottawa would pay an ex gratia payment of $67,000 to Mr Sverdrup in return for the formal affirmation that Norway would recognize Canada's sovereignty over the Sverdrup Islands. The quid pro quo for Norway was Ottawa's assurance that, should the Arctic Islands Preserve order-in-council ever be lifted, Canada would treat applications by Norwegian citizens to operate in the region "in most friendly manner." On this basis the deal was closed in 1930 ...

Prime Minister Trudeau could advise Parliament in May 1969 that Canada's sovereignty over the Arctic "is well established and that there is no dispute concerning this matter. No country has asserted a competing claim, no country now challenges Canada's sovereignty on any other basis; and many countries have indicated in many ways the recognition of Canada's sovereignty over these areas." In 1971 the then-Director-General of the Legal Bureau of the Department of External Affairs ... emphasized that "Canada is aware of no challenge to its sovereignty over the mainland and islands of the Canadian Arctic." This remains true today, thirty years later. Only tiny Hans Island, ... in Kennedy Channel exactly half-way between Ellesmere Island and Greenland, remains in dispute.

All this means that the land areas of Canada's Arctic Archipelago are undisputed parts of Canada. This is true whether the islands are inhabited or not. Should persons travel to the islands and, without Canada's lawful permission, take from them any wildlife, or minerals, or fresh water, or archaeological relics or if they leave their wastes and garbage, then they are breaching the laws of Canada and they can be prosecuted. Canada's legal sovereignty does not somehow evaporate simply because there are no Canadians on the island in question.

Sea, Ice and Law

There is also the question of sovereignty over the waters of the Canadian Arctic. Historically, this has not been a problem because the international law of the sea largely deals with ships and shipping. Until recently, commercial shipping in the Arctic was not feasible, so no-one was interested in contesting Canada's sovereignty. But now the Arctic's non-renewable resources have entered the picture. Beginning with the discovery of oil at Prudhoe Bay on the Beaufort Sea shore of Alaska in 1967, the potential for oil and gas in the Arctic has generated a renewed interest in the Arctic offshore. At the same time, this re-opened the jurisdictional question.

The international law of the sea is crystal clear on one point: that the "territorial sea" of a coastal state, where the state has sovereignty, extends only a short distance (three nautical miles, later extended to 12 nautical miles) from "straight baselines" that approximate the low water mark but enclose the mouths of bays, inlets, rivers and "internal waters." Internal waters are any waters on the landward side of the straight baselines. Beyond the limit of the territorial sea is the "high seas" which are international waters. The law of the sea also incorporates something called an "international strait" in which rights of transit passage apply for state surface vessels, together with the right of innocent passage for commercial vessels . . .

I do not digress when I pause to point out that the Arctic waters of Canada are unique in one obvious respect: they are not "waters" like other ocean areas. They are mostly ice-covered. The existence of permanent ice raises the question whether for legal reasons the "waters" of the Arctic Archipelago should be treated as "water," or whether the correct analogy is with land. Regardless, the Canadian government has never relied on the "ice as land" concept to support a claim at law of sovereignty . . .

The rejection of the "ice as land" concept means that, even if the ice were to melt, Canada's legal sovereignty would be unaffected. This is because Canada has consistently considered its waters in the Arctic legally as being the same as open water elsewhere. The waters of the North are coloured blue on the maps and, in terms of our sovereignty over them, they are in law "blue water."

Ice-breaking Ships

Where there is ice, there are frequently ice-breaking ships. In 1969, the ice-breaking oil tanker *Manhattan* cruised through the Northwest Passage, picked up a single symbolic barrel of oil from Prudhoe Bay, and returned to the United States . . .

Canada's view, then and now, is that since the 1880 deed transfer, the waters of the Arctic Archipelago have been Canada's internal waters by virtue of historic title. These waters have been used by Inuit, now of Canada, since time immemorial. Canada has exercised unqualified and uninterrupted sovereignty over the waters.

In accordance with its sovereignty, Canada is committed to protect the vulnerable environment of its Arctic waters and coasts. With the development of ice-breaking vessels like the Manhattan which could operate in those waters, Canada responded by adopting the Arctic Waters Pollution Prevention Act. Since the adoption of that Act, vessels planning to operate in Canada's Arctic internal waters must satisfy Canadian authorities that the voyage will not harm the environment . . .

The main purpose of the [1988 Agreement on Arctic Cooperation] is to regulate ice-breaker navigation in the Canadian Arctic. It ensured that "all navigation by US icebreakers in waters claimed by Canada to be internal will be undertaken with the consent of the Government of Canada. Article 4 sets out that nothing in the agreement, nor any practice developed thereunder, would effect the respective legal positions of the two parties, Canada and the US. Instead, it is a practical means to ensure that US icebreakers seek Canada's consent and meet all requirements of Canadian law while in the waters of the Canadian Arctic Archipelago. Recently, under the terms of the 1988 Agreement, the US Coast Guard ice-breaker *Healy* traversed the Passage during the summer of 2000 without incident after meeting all appropriate Canadian legal requirements. This voyage proved that Arctic navigation can take place without threatening Canadian sovereignty.

Interpretation of a Boundary Water under the Boundary Waters Treaty

In a legal opinion dated July 12, 2001, the Legal Bureau wrote:

The Preliminary Article begins by establishing a broad definition, followed by the specific exclusions. The broad category includes as "boundary waters" the waters from main shore to main shore of the lakes, rivers and connecting waterways along which the international boundary passes. The Preliminary Article then excludes waters tributary to the boundary waters, waters flowing from boundary waters and the waters of rivers flowing across the boundary.

To be included as a boundary water, the Preliminary Article requires only that the international boundary pass through the lake, river or connecting waterway. Then, the Preliminary Article excludes certain waters using flow as a criterion. Flow is not necessary to qualify a body of water as a boundary water, it can only be used to exclude a body of water. That said, it is the Government of Canada's position that flow does not necessarily exclude a body of water either.

It has also been suggested that a literal interpretation of the Preliminary Article could assert that the boundary must pass "along" the length of a lake, river or connecting waterway, as opposed to simply passing through the lake. Among other things, this interpretation would mean that the IJC [International Joint Commission] or a Party's right to stop a project that would pollute or affect the levels and flows on the other side of the boundary would depend upon whether or not more of the shore of that body of water runs parallel to the boundary or at a right angle to it. Since the effects on the other country in no way depend on whether the shore of the lake runs parallel to the boundary or not, this interpretation would be inappropriate and inconsistent with the intention of the drafters. This interpretation could exclude Lake Superior and the Lake of the Woods from the definition of a boundary water, which would constitute a clearly erroneous result.

Similarly, the Preliminary Article does not make the "direction of flow" of a body of water a necessary prerequisite to defining a lake as "boundary waters." Inclusion of the "direction of flow" in the definition would leave a large gap in the application of the Treaty as waters that did not have a discernible flow would not be covered by the Treaty if not classified as "boundary waters." This would be inconsistent with the purpose of the Treaty to establish a legal regime governing all waters found straddling the boundary ...

The use of the term "along" only makes sense when speaking of rivers that constitute boundary waters in order to distinguish them from waters of rivers flowing across the boundary. In the context of lakes, the phrase "along which the ... boundary ... passes" can only be reasonably interpreted as meaning "through which the ... boundary ... passes.

HUMAN RIGHTS AND HUMANITARIAN LAW

Canadian Brief with the International Criminal Tribunal for the Former Yugoslavia

On November 15, 2000, the Department of Foreign Affairs and International Trade filed a written brief with the International Criminal Tribunal for the former Yugoslavia in the case of *Prosecutor* v. *Blago Simic, Milan Simic, Miroslav Tadic, Stevan Todorovic and Simo Zaric* in the matter of Canada's application for review under Rule 108 *bis* of Trial Chamber III's interlocutory decision on motion for judicial assistance to be provided by SFOR and others dated October 18, 2000. The following are excerpts from that brief:

Principles applicable to orders made pursuant to Article 29

The Government of Canada has been and remains a strong supporter of the International Criminal Tribunal for the former Yugoslavia. Canada has cooperated with the Tribunal and fully accepts the need for a robust, independent Tribunal with the power necessary to fulfil the mandate accorded it: to bring to justice those responsible for genocide, crimes against humanity, and war crimes committed in the territory of the Former Yugoslavia since 1991. The issuance of orders to States for the production of evidence is contemplated in the unambiguous wording of Article 29 of the Statute, which requires States to "comply without undue delay with any request for assistance or an order issued by a Trial Chamber, including, but not limited to the taking of testimony and the production of evidence." The Statute of the Tribunal was adopted by the Security Council in Resolution 827, under Chapter VII of the Charter of the United Nations. Member States of the United Nations are therefore obliged to carry out that Resolution, pursuant to Articles 2, 25 and 41 of the Charter of the United Nations, and are under a binding obligation to comply with orders of the Tribunal, including orders for the production of evidence, subject only to such recognized limitations or exceptions as may be applicable ...

At the same time, Canada also supports the conclusion of the Appeals Chamber in *Prosecutor* v. *Blaskic* which indicated that the power to issue orders for the production of evidence is not unlimited, and that orders for the production of evidence may be challenged by the receiving party. Canada submits that the typical bases for such a challenge include the scope, specificity, relevance or necessity of the order, that the order does not provide for sufficient time to produce the documents, that the requested documents do not exist or are not in the possession of the receiving party, or that national interests would be at stake ...

The procedural and substantive requirements of Rule 54 *bis* reflect the different roles and obligations of States as opposed to those of the Prosecutor and Defence. Rules 54 *bis* enables the Prosecutor and Defence to seek relevant information from States; The obligation to "disclose" on the Prosecutor under Rule 68, namely "to disclose to the defence the existence of evidence known to the Prosecutor which in any way tends to suggest the innocence, or mitigate the guilt of the accused, or may affect the credibility of prosecution evidence," is clearly of a different nature than the obligation of States under Article 29 of the Statute to cooperate with the Tribunal.

As a party to the proceedings, the Prosecutor invited the Trial Chamber to make its determination as to the relief sought by the Defence on the basis of the current record viewed in the light most favourable to the Defence. The Trial Chamber has rejected this invitation. The Trial Chamber has not determined whether the issues raised and therefore the documents sought could, on the basis of any reasonable hypothetical construction, be materially relevant to the relief being sought by the Defence. The Trial Chamber appears to have adopted the position that this will depend upon what the documents that may be produced might indicate. Canada respectfully submits that such an approach, in light of the position advanced by the Prosecutor, should not be used to determine an application for an order pursuant to Article 29. Rather, Canada submits that an order may only be issued pursuant to Article 29 after there has been a preliminary determination that the issues raised by the applicant are materially relevant to a judicial determination that the Tribunal could render.

As stated by the Appeal Chamber in *Blaskic,* paragraph 28, the power of the Tribunal to issue orders for assistance from States pursuant to Article 29 of the Statute is ancillary or incidental to the Tribunal's primary function of acting in a judicial function to try persons who are allegedly responsible for the crimes defined in articles 2 to 4 of the Statute. Canada submits that the purpose of seeking an order pursuant to Article 29 of the Statute is not to conduct a discovery exercise. The purpose of seeking an order is to obtain specific documents that are relevant to the judicial functions of the Tribunal and to the discharge of its primary function of trying persons who are allegedly responsible for the crimes defined in articles 2 to 4 of the Statute.

In this case, information concerning the arrest of Mr. Todorovic is being sought by the Defence in support of a motion for his release. The information sought does not relate to any matter suggesting the innocence or mitigating the guilt of the accused and could be interpreted as an indirect attack on the validity of the arrest warrant issued by this Tribunal. The principles governing the issuance of orders to States that were set out in the *Blaskic* decision were outlined in the context of information which related to the guilt or innocence of an accused person. When, as in this case, the issue raised by the applicant is at best collateral to the guilt or innocence of the accused, extreme caution should be applied before resort is had to a power that the Appeals Chamber in *Blaskic* said should be exercised only when absolutely necessary:

The Appeals Chamber endorses the Prosecution's contention that:

[A]s a matter of policy and in order to foster good relations with States ... cooperative processes should wherever possible be used, ... they should be used first, and ... resort to mandatory compliance powers expressly given by Article 29(2) should be reserved for cases in which they are really necessary.

In the final analysis, the International Tribunal may discharge its functions only if it can count on the *bona fide* assistance and cooperation of sovereign States. It is therefore to be regarded as sound policy for the Prosecutor, as well as defence counsel, first to seek, through cooperative means, the assistance of States, and only if they decline to lend support, then to request a Judge or a Trial Chamber to have recourse to the mandatory action provided for in Article 29.

Charte mondiale de l'autonomie locale

Dans une opinion juridique rédigée en février, 2001, le Bureau juridique écrivait:

Vous avez sollicité une opinion juridique concernant certains aspects du projet de Charte mondiale de l'autonomie locale (ci-après CMAL) ...

Question 1: Comment cette Charte diffère-t-elle d'autres instruments internationaux tels le Pacte relatif aux droits civils et politiques et la Déclaration universelle des droits de l'Homme?

À la lecture des dispositions de l'ébauche de la CMAL, il ne fait aucun doute que cette instrument se veut un traité international, créateur d'obligations pour les États qui y seront parties. Ainsi, en vertu de son article 1, les Parties "s'engagent à se considérer liés" par les articles subséquents. De plus, la CMAL prévoit, comme il est d'usage dans tout traité, des dispositions concernant les moyens par lesquels les États peuvent devenir Partie au traité. L'article 18 précise que la CMAL est ouverte à la signature de tous les États et que ces derniers pourront, pour y devenir Parties, la ratifier ou y adhérer. De même, l'article 19 prévoit son entrée en vigueur trente jours suivant le dépôt auprès du Secrétaire général des Nations Unies du vingtième instrument de ratification ou d'adhésion.

On peut donc en conclure que la CMAL, une fois adoptée, constituera un traité au même titre que le Pacte international relatif aux droits civils et politiques ou encore la Charte des Nations Unies. Tout comme ces deux instruments, il s'agira d'une convention multilatérale c. à d. un instrument auquel tous les États membres de la communauté internationale peuvent devenir Parties.

De même que pour le Pacte, les États s'engagent dans la CMAL à respecter l'exercice de certains droits sur leur territoire. Toutefois, le Pacte visant la protection des individus et la CMAL celle des autorités locales, ces deux instruments diffèrent de façon significative en terme de contenu.

En sa qualité de traité, la CMAL se distingue d'autres instruments internationaux, notamment des résolutions de l'Assemblée générale (AG) des Nations Unies. Ces dernières ne sont pas juridiquement contraignantes pour les États. Il est vrai que le texte final de la CMAL est également susceptible d'être un jour adopté officiellement par l'AG à titre de convention des Nations Unies. Toutefois, à la différence d'une simple résolution, elle sera par la suite soumise à la ratification ou l'adhésion des États et, une fois en vigueur, liera ceux qui y sont devenues Parties. Par conséquent, il importe de bien distinguer la CMAL non seulement de la DUDH mais aussi de certaines autres résolutions de l'AG qui, bien que qualifiées de "Charte," n'en demeurent pas moins que des résolutions. Ainsi en est-il par exemple de la "Charte sur le nouvel ordre économique" adoptée dans les années 70 par l'AG.

Par ailleurs, comme l'a confirmé la Cour internationale de justice dans son Avis consultatif sur la légalité des armes nucléaires, quelques résolutions, parmi les milliers adoptées par l'AG, peuvent contribuer à la création d'obligation internationale d'origine coutumière. Ainsi, en considérant certains facteurs, tels le contenu d'une résolution, le support que celle-ci a reçu au moment du vote et le degré de conformité de la pratique subséquente des États avec la résolution en question, il peut être soutenu que certaines résolutions contribuent à la création d'obligations internationales pour l'ensemble des États, et ce même en l'absence d'un traité sur le sujet faisant l'objet de la résolution. Plusieurs auteurs sont notamment d'avis que l'ensemble de la DUDH constitue du droit coutumier alors que d'autres soutiennent que seulement certaines normes précises dans la DUDH lient tous les États. Quoi qu'il en soit, il est certain que la DUDH a atteint une notoriété indiscutable comme en témoigne son évocation dans le préambule de plusieurs instruments internationaux et notamment dans celui de la CMAL. Néanmoins, malgré l'impact juridique de la Déclaration, rappelons à nouveau qu'il ne s'agit pas d'un traité et, par conséquent, qu'elle constitue un instrument international différent en nature de la CMAL.

Enfin, en terme de contenu, la DUDH traite, comme la CMAL, de l'exercice de droits sur le territoire d'un État mais, tout comme le Pacte elle vise la protection des individus et non d'entité telle les autorités locales.

Question 2: Quel est le mécanisme d'adoption de la CMAL?

Pour répondre à cette question il s'avère utile, dans un premier temps de retracer les origines de la CMAL et d'indiquer où en sont les négociations concernant cet instrument.

Le concept de la CMAL tire ses origines profondes dans l'adoption par le Conseil de l'Europe en 1985 de la Charte européenne de l'autonomie locale (CEAL) et, subséquemment, dans l'adoption d'une Déclaration mondiale sur l'autonomie locale par l'Union internationale des autorités locales à Toronto en 1993. Toutefois, l'événement le plus décisif dans le développement d'un important mouvement en faveur de l'adoption d'une convention multilatérale sur l'autonomie locale a probablement été la tenue d'Habitat II à Istanbul en 1996. La Déclaration issue de cette rencontre souligne l'importance des autorités locales. Ainsi, au par. 12 de la Déclaration, les États affirment ce qui suit:

"Recognizing local authorities as our closest partners, and as essential, in the implementation of the habitat Agenda, we must, within the legal framework of each country, promote decentralization through democratic local authorities and work to strengthen their financial and institutional capacities in accordance with the conditions of countries, while ensuring their transparency, accountability and responsiveness to the needs of people, which are key requirements for governments at all levels."

De plus, dans la section intitulée Enablement and Participation, les États acceptent, parmi d'autres objectifs, le suivant: "Decentralizing authority and resources, as appropriate, as well as functions and responsabilities to the level most effective in addresssing the needs of people in their settlements.

Suite à Habitat II, le Centre des Nations Unies pour les Établissements Humains (Habitat) a conclu, en 1997, une entente avec la Coordination des Associations Mondiale des Villes et des Autorités Locales (CAMVAL), une organisation formée peu de temps avant Habitat II et dont le mandat inclut notamment la préparation d'une CMAL. En vertu de l'entente, Habitat et CAMVAL se sont engagés à travailler ensemble pour concrétiser ce projet.

En avril 1998 un comité d'experts, composé de représentants de HABITAT et de WALAC, a proposé une première ébauche de la CMAL. Ce premier jet était en très grande partie inspiré de la CEAL. Il a par la suite fait l'objet de discussions dans diverses rencontres régionales et une deuxième ébauche a été présentée à la première session du Comité préparatoire de la session extraordinaire de l'Assemblée générale consacrée à un examen et à une évaluation d'ensemble de l'application du programme pour l'Habitat (Comité préparatoire) en mai 2000. Au terme de la discussion il a été décidé que cette question serait de nouveau abordé[e] lors de la deuxième réunion du Comité préparatoire en février 2001.

En supposant qu'en février 2001 suffisamment d'États appuient le projet de CMAL en février 2001, la CMAL pourrait être soumise à ECOSOC et puis, par la suite, en juin, à l'AG pour adoption. Cette dernière pourrait alors décider de renvoyer ce dossier à un de ces organes subsidiaires existants ou de créer un groupe de travail pour examiner davantage ce projet avant de considérer s'il y a lieu de l'adopter. L'AG est toutefois libre de décider de procéder immédiatement à son adoption, auquel cas elle devra déterminer le processus le plus approprié dans le cas en espèce. Ainsi, bien que l'AG adopte normalement des conventions par consensus, elle peut également décider, exceptionnellement, de procéder par vote. Toutefois, si un vote majoritaire suffit pour l'adoption d'une convention, il reste que la manifestation d'une division au sein de la communauté internationale au moment de l'adoption peut dissuader plusieurs États de ratifier, du moins rapidement, un instrument. De plus, un vote sur la question pourrait constituer un sérieux obstacle à tout argument éventuel que l'adoption d'une telle convention constitue un indice de l'émergence d'une coutume internationale sur le droit à l'autonomie locale. Cela ne signifie pas, à l'inverse, qu'un vote unanime ou par consensus suffirait pour considérer un ou plusieurs articles de la CMAL comme de possibles normes coutumières. Notre propos vise plutôt à souligner que l'absence d'unanimité au moment de son adoption fragiliserait nécessairement l'acceptation, que ce soit par voir conventionnelle ou coutumière du contenu de la Convention.

Etant donné que le projet de CMAL n'a pas encore fait l'objet de négociations soutenues entre les États, il ne nous apparaît pas souhaitable que ce projet soit soumis à l'AG pour adoption. D'ailleurs, à en juger par les documents présentement disponibles pour la deuxième rencontre du Comité préparatoire, un tel scénario n'apparaît pas probable. D'une part, le projet de CMAL n'est pas expressément mentionné dans l'agenda. D'autre part, le paragraphe 19 de l'ébauche de Déclaration sur les Cités, déclaration qui sera vraisemblablement soumise pour adoption par l'Assemblée générale en juin, propose la poursuite des délibérations sur ce projet.

Question 3: Quelle est la force contraignante de la dite Charte sur les États signataires? Crée-t-elle des obligations juridiques?

Si la CMAL est adoptée, il appartiendra ensuite à chaque État de déterminer s'il y a lieu ou non de la signer. La fait de signer un traité emporte des conséquences juridiques. En effet, en vertu de l'article 18 de la Convention de Vienne sur le droit des traités, tout État signataire s'engage à ne pas prendre d'actions allant à l'encontre de l'objet et du but du traité jusqu'au moment où il indique clairement qu'il n'a pas l'intention de ratifier le dit traité. Par conséquent, même si un État signataire n'a pas à respecter dans le détail chacune des obligations précises d'une convention, sa marge de manoeuvre est néanmoins délimitée par les principaux objectifs de celle-ci.

Concernant la création d'obligations juridiques, il est certain, tel que nous l'avons exposé lors de notre réponse à la première question, qu'un État qui devient Partie à un traité, soit en le ratifiant ou en y adhérant, accepte toutes les obligations énoncées dans celui-ci, à moins que le traité ne lui permette d'agir autrement. À cet égard, la CMAL comporte la particularité suivante: elle permet à chaque État Partie un degré de flexibilité concernant les obligations qu'il accepte au moment de la ratifier ou d'y adhérer. Ainsi, son article 14 prévoit qu'une partie doit se considérer liée par au moins 30 des 38 paragraphes composant la Première partie de la Charte. Cette première partie, de l'article 2 à l'article 13, énonce des obligations de nature substantive. Comme certaines des obligations énumérées sont considérées plus importantes que d'autres, l'article 14 précise également qu'au moins douze des trente obligations qu'un État accepte doivent être choisis parmi une liste de 14 paragraphes identifiés à l'article 14. Par ailleurs, un État est évidemment libre d'accepter plus de 30 paragraphes au moment de ratifier ou d'adhérer à la CMAL ou encore à tout autre moment ultérieur.

Cet article, qualifié par certains d'article à la carte, a pour but d'encourager les États à devenir partie à la CMAL en leur donnant une certaine flexibilité en ce qui concernent les obligations prévues par celle-ci. Ainsi, ses rédacteurs, conscients que les arrangements constitutionnels et législatifs touchant aux autorités locales peuvent varier considérablement d'un État à l'autre, et en particulier entre un État à structure fédérale et un État centralisé, ont tenté, par l'article 14, de créer un équilibre délicat entre l'acceptation par l'ensemble des Parties des dispositions les plus fondamentales de la Charte et le besoin de reconnaître les différences législatives et institutionnelles existant entre États. Évidemment, la flexibilité de l'État sera plus ou moins grande selon la proportion de paragraphes qu'il aura à accepter. À cet égard, notons que dans la première ébauche de la CMAL l'État n'avait qu'à accepter 20 paragraphes sur les 36 alors existants et seulement 10 des 14 dispositions considérées comme fondamentales.

Certaines conventions du Conseil de l'Europe, notamment dans la Charte européenne des langues régionales ou minoritaires et dans le Code européen de sécurité social, contiennent des dispositions semblables à l'article 14. Toutefois, ce type de disposition est inusitée dans des conventions universelles. Par conséquent, le Canada devra déterminer dans quelle mesure il est souhaitable d'appuyer une telle approche dans un cadre universel.

Un État peut également limiter ses obligations en émettant des réserves à une convention au moment de la ratifier ou d'y adhérer. Certains traités prévoient expressément que des réserves sont permises à l'ensemble ou à certains des articles de la convention. D'autres traités stipulent au contraire que toute réserve est interdite. Enfin, d'autres conventions, et c'est là le cas de la CMAL, sont silencieuses sur le sujet. Dans ces conditions, la Convention de Vienne sur le droit des traités permet à chaque État d'émettre des réserves pourvu que celles-ci ne soient pas contraire à l'objet et au but du traité, ce qui nécessite un exercice d'interprétation pour chaque réserve envisagé[e]. Ainsi, il n'est pas clair qu'un État pourrait apporter une réserve à l'un des 14 paragraphes spécifiquement identifiés à l'article 14 de la CMAL. Par ailleurs, soulignons que l'approche canadienne est de généralement favoriser le développement de conventions peu susceptibles de donner lieu à des réserves.

The Concept of "Separation" in the Refugee Context

In a memorandum dated March 7, 2001, the Legal Bureau wrote:

Principles applicable to the use of separation

Entry and eligibility for protection: The principle of direct entry of Article 31 of the Convention Relating to the status of refugees 1951 (the Refugee Convention) applies and obliges States to admit asylum seekers without penalty. The act or process of separation cannot be applied in a way which hinders or prohibits entry on the part of refugees. Their movement and residence may however be restricted on grounds of public security. Separation of armed elements from refugees inside the territory of the State of origin, prior to arrival of the host State, is improper. Apart from the case of active combatants, separation must follow after a fair process of screening and respect for procedural fairness in exclusion or refusal to grant refugee status. The role of separation in the eligibility process is not definitive of any legal status, but would rather serve as interim measure from which other forms of legal status apply i.e., with respect to active armed elements, separation leads to internment.

Prohibition on subversive activities: The prohibition on subversive activities applies in particular to attempts to disturb the internal political order or security of a foreign State by slander, malicious propaganda, or violence, on the grounds that the territories of host States shall not be used as bases for subversive or terrorist activities against the people of another State. As a corollary of the prohibition on subversive activities, there is a duty on the part of refugees to obey the laws of the host State. Separation is a method to weed out from the refugee population those persons bent on using refugee protection as a base for subversive activities against other States.

Safe location: The practice of refugee protection establishes the principle of the safe location of refugees in the territories of the receiving States for reasons of their safety, protection against recruitment and for the security of the receiving States.

Restrictions on freedom of movement and residence within host States: From a human rights perspective, separation takes the form of restriction on freedom of movement and residence within States on the part of those that are separated out. Does this necessity for separation provide justification for the restriction of freedom of movement and residence on grounds of public order, public security or safety, as prescribed by Art. 26 of the Refugee Convention? Such restriction may derive from the application of Article 9 of the Refugee Convention which envisages provisional measures to be taken on grounds of war, national security or other exceptional circumstances. Article 31 of the Refugee Convention prohibits States from applying restrictions on movement, other than those which are necessary. The Executive Committee of the United Nations High Commission for Refugees has laid down certain guiding principles under art. 31 to the effect that as a minimum standard, refugees arriving en masse should not, in general, be subjected to restrictions on their movements, other than those which are necessary in the interest of public health and public order. Restrictions should, however, be clearly temporary.

Obligation of host States to separate out armed elements by interment under the Law of Neutrality: The issue of separation would also appear to be based on the application of the concept of internment by neutral States. Internment connotes separation and the principle of the safe location of internees would apply.

Need to elaborate criteria for separation: In practice, separation can be undertaken, sometimes, as a function of screening and exclusion. It should not be the case that screening, and therefore separation, has to be carried out all times where there is a mass out-flow of refugees.

Much should depend upon the nature of the refugee out-flow, but composite out-flows in which armed elements are present in the midst of refugees necessitates separation. In such cases, the legal definition of "armed elements" should provide legal criteria for the screening and separation process.

Legal Considerations Related to the Draft Program of Action to Prevent, Combat and Eradicate the Illicit Trade in Small Arms and Light Weapons Flowing from the Nature of the Instrument

In a memorandum dated May 24, 2001, the Legal Bureau wrote:

Nature of the small arms document to be elaborated at the July conference

While not legally binding on participating states, the draft Program of Action is intended to be "politically binding" on them. In other words, while participating states have no legal obligation to implement its provisions/principles and there are no sanctions for failing to do so, it is understood that they have a good faith commitment to respect and implement the provisions. It is also important to note in this regard that "politically binding" instruments (i.e. plans of action, declarations, codes of conduct) that are implemented by a large majority of states over an extended period of time, can become customary law and thus legally binding. Moreover, principles agreed upon in these sorts of documents quite often become the basis for legally binding instruments, such as conventions ... Therefore, care should be taken to ensure that each of the principles agreed upon at the conference can be implemented by the Government.

Obligations of a binding nature contained in a politically binding document

Even though the Program of Action that is to be finalized at the July conference is not a legally binding instrument, the Delegation should be alert to the possible emergence of provisions with a legally binding effect. Use of the word "shall" clearly falls within this category and words such as "ensure" and "undertake" come close to the threshold. For example, in section II, paragraph 1, states "undertake the following measures." If the word "shall" were to be added before the word "undertake," it would have the effect of transforming the list of provisions that follow into legally binding obligations. Before accepting such obligations (which includes a provision for the "criminalization of all illicit brokering activities"). Ministerial approval should be obtained.

Need for ministerial authority

The advantage of developing "politically binding" documents, as opposed to legally binding instruments (conventions, treaties), is that by obviating the need for national ratification/accession processes, it increases comfort levels for negotiators and in turn promotes consensus. However, there are also risks. While such a method skirts the national ratification/accession processes, it nevertheless constitutes a political commitment by participating states. Particular attention must be paid to ensure that there is political/ministerial support for the principles contained in these documents. There are at least three reasons for this: a) a political commitment is being assumed; b) the possibility that the principles elaborated could develop into customary law; c) the tendency to follow up "politically binding" documents with legally binding instruments (e.g. conventions) patterned closely on the principles agreed to in the former. Indeed, in the subject draft Program of Action, section IV 1; (d) recommends that the General Assembly "consider the elaboration of an international instrument to restrict the production and trade in small arms and light weapons."

Inter-American Democratic Charter and the OAS Charter:
Nature and Relationship

In a memorandum dated August 29, 2001, the Legal Bureau wrote:

The Inter-American Democratic Charter (the Democratic Charter) and the OAS Charter both constitute international instruments (regional rather than universal) that either fall within the treaty category (legally binding instrument) or the MOU category (non-legally binding instrument).

Basic principles of modern treaty law and practice

Article 2(1)(a) of the Vienna Convention on the Law of Treaties defines "treaty" as an international agreement concluded between States in written form and governed by international law, whether embodied in a single instrument or in two or more related instruments and whatever its particular designation.

For the above Charters to be considered legally binding instruments, the following elements must be considered. "Governed by international law" suggests an intention to create obligations under international law. Intention must be gathered from the terms of the instrument itself and the circumstances of its conclusion, not from what the parties say afterwards was their intention. Regarding the issue of "designation," considering the unsystematic way in which treaties are designated, it is often more a matter of the practice of international organizations or groups of states, or political preference, which determines how a treaty is named. What is decisive is whether the negotiators intended the instrument to be (or not to be) legally binding.

Although not explicitly stated in the definition, a treaty does not have to be signed, but it must be registered under article 102 of the UN Charter. There can be circumstances when the use of an unsigned instrument is preferred for political reasons.

Evidence of the intention to conclude (or not to conclude) a legally binding instrument, may be drawn from factors such as terminology, the inclusion of a clause providing for the settlement of disputes by compulsory international judicial body, express provisions as to the status of the treaty as a "political commitment" or otherwise and the existence or absence of a registration clause.

The nature of the OAS Charter and the Democratic Charter

The OAS Charter constitutes a legally binding instrument, since it was the intention of the OAS member States to create such an instrument as evidenced, inter alia, by the clear language of the instrument. The Democratic Charter, as currently drafted, does not seem to contain the elements that would lead to the conclusion that it is a legally binding instrument. The terminology used is not mandatory language, it does not seem to follow the same format, content and clauses as other OAS legally binding instruments, i.e. there is no preamble, no clause concerning the settlement of disputes, ratification, registration, the coming into force, or the common final clauses (amendment procedures).

Parliamentary Declarations in 2000-1 / Déclarations parlementaires en 2000-1

compiled by / préparé par
LYDIA BOURQUI

A   STATEMENTS MADE ON THE INTRODUCTION OF LEGISLATION /
DÉCLARATION SUR L'INTRODUCTION DE LA LÉGISLATION

*1   Bill S-17: An Act Respecting Marine Liability, and to Validate
Certain Bylaws and Regulations / Loi S-17: Loi concernant la
responsabilité en matière maritime et la validité de certains règlements*

Mr. Brent St. Denis (Parliamentary Secretary to the Minister of
Transport):

[T]he marine liability act represents a monumental step in the modernization of Canadian legislation regarding liabilities arising from shipping
activities...

I take this opportunity to bring to the attention of the House Canada's
efforts on the international scene with regard to the modernization of
two important liability regimes to better reflect the nature of modern shipping. I refer to the liability regimes for compensation for oil pollution,
cleanup and damages, and to the liability for the carriage of goods.

On oil pollution liability, Canada is a party to the 1992 protocol to the
international convention on civil liability for oil pollution damage, 1969,
and the international convention on the establishment of an international
fund for compensation for oil pollution damage, 1971. The purpose of
these conventions is to provide adequate compensation to victims of oil
pollution catastrophes.

The realization that the fund could prove to be inadequate to compensate all victims of the incident prompted calls from many of the
countries that are party to the fund for a review of the limits of available
compensation...

Lydia Bourqui is at the Faculty of Law at the University of Ottawa / Faculté de droit
à l'université d'Ottawa.

From the outset Canada has been active in the discussions that led to a proposal to increase the limit to the maximum level permitted by the provisions of the international conventions. This proposal, to be submitted next month to the International Maritime Organization, is co-sponsored by Canada and will see the limit of the fund increased to approximately $405 million Canadian. As a result of these efforts Canadians will have an improved compensation scheme available to assist them in the event of such a tragedy occurring in our waters.

Under the title of cargo liability I would like now to turn to our initiative relating to the liability of shipowners for the carriage of goods . . .

Internationally Canada has always participated in transport related initiatives to harmonize shipping standards, rules and regulations with other countries. The current legislation governing the liability of the shipowner for damage to cargo during maritime carriage is governed by the 1993 Carriage of Goods By Water Act . . .

Prior to the so-called COGWA, 1993, that is the Carriage of Goods by Water Act, Transport Canada published a discussion paper recommending the adoption of the Hamburg rules by Canada. Shippers clearly preferred the adoption of the Hamburg rules and felt that these rules were more responsive to their interests than the Hague-Visby rules, especially in terms of the new approach to carriers' defences and increased limits of liability.

Many ship owners, their insurers, cargo insurers and legal experts strongly favoured the adoption of the Hague-Visby rules because they believed the Hamburg rules would have a major impact on shipping costs and litigation costs as the new regime would need to be tested in the courts since previous case law would no longer hold . . . Eventually a compromise solution was reached with the adoption of a staged approach to both regimes.

This approach involved the immediate implementation of the Hague-Visby rules with provisions to bring the Hamburg rules into effect at a later date when a sufficient number of Canada's trading partners had ratified them. The staged approach would therefore ensure that Canadian law is always in step with that of our trading partners.

It also resulted in the adoption of a provision in the 1993 COGWA, which requires the Minister of Transport to conduct a periodic review of the act to determine whether the Hague-Visby rules should be replaced by the Hamburg rules.

This approach reflected Canada's intention to accept the Hamburg rules when it was proven that they would provide a viable basis for new liability conditions for international trade. In the intervening period the government committed itself to promote the Hamburg rules and to pursue with Canada's trading partners the possibility of a co-ordinated action that would lead to wider acceptance of the Hamburg rules at the international level.

. . . [T]o fulfil the legal requirement contained in the Carriage of Goods by Water Act, 1993, and as part of the first review period, the Minister of Transport submitted a report to parliament in December of last year in which he concluded: first, the Hague-Visby rules should be retained in the current Carriage of Goods by Water Act until the next review period ending January 1, 2005 and, second, Transport Canada should continue to make efforts in consultation with industry and in co-operation with like-minded countries with a view to developing practical options for a new international regime of liability for the carriage of goods by sea, which would achieve a greater uniformity than the Hague-Visby rules.

The outcome of this review was driven by the developments in international law on cargo liability, the stagnant position of the Hamburg rules internationally and their minimal impact on Canadian seaborne trade ...

Currently the subject of cargo liability is on the agenda of the OECD maritime transport committee. The committee recognized that there was sufficient interest internationally to consider measures that would improve the current situation.

UNCITRAL and CMI have undertaken to review current practices and laws on the international carriage of goods by sea to determine why countries cannot reach consensus in this area ...

Canada will continue to pursue, in co-operation with trading partners, the objective of a uniform international law on carriage of goods by water and will assist UNCITRAL and CMI in their current efforts. Canada will support any new initiative at the international level that would have a realistic chance at success in achieving this objective. These are just two of the things that Canada wishes to do when it comes to the matter of proving the international liability regimes for the carriage of goods around the world.

(House of Commons Debates, October 6, 2000, pp. 9028-30)
(Débats de la Chambre des Communes, le 6 octobre 2000, pp. 9028-30)

2   Bill S-2: An Act Respecting Marine Liability, and to Validate Certain
    Bylaws and Regulations / Loi S-2: Loi concernant la responsabilité
    en matière maritime et la validité de certains règlements[1]

Mr. Ovid Jackson (Bruce — Grey — Owen Sound):

The bill introduces for the first time Canadian legislation regarding ship-owners' liability for the carriage of passengers and new rules for the apportionment of liability in maritime law. At the same time, it will consolidate existing marine liability regimes, which are currently scattered throughout various statutes, into a single statute.

This important Canadian legislation will modernize the Canada Shipping Act to make sure it concurs with the legislation. Some 40 million Canadians travel by sea. There are various oil spillages. Liabilities have resulted all around the world, in Europe, in Canada and in Greece. The act will consolidate and make shipowners responsible. It will take away the fact that in the fine print on tickets and so on they can exempt themselves from looking after their liabilities to Canadians.

---

[1] Bill S-2 replaces Bill S-17 that was introduced during the 36th Parliament, 2nd Session.

(House of Commons Debates, February 23, 2001, p. 1112)
(Débats de la Chambre des Communes, le 23 février 2001, p. 1112)

3   Bill C-11: An Act Respecting Immigration to Canada and the
Granting of Refugee Protection to Persons Who Are Displaced,
Persecuted or in Danger / Loi C-11: Loi concernant l'immigration
au Canada et l'asile conféré aux personnes déplacées, persécutées ou
en danger

Hon. Elinor Caplan (Minister of Citizenship and Immigration):

[Bill C-11] is tough on criminal abuse of our immigration and refugee
protection systems. The bill creates severe new penalties for people smug-
glers and for those caught trafficking in humans ... There will be fines of
up to $1 million and sentences of up to life in prison for persons convicted
of smuggling and trafficking in humans. It will also allow our courts to
order the forfeiture of money and other property seized from traffickers.

The bill clarifies our existing grounds for detention and our criteria for
inadmissibility to Canada. It provides immigration enforcement officers
with the tools they need to see that serious criminals, threats to national
security, violators of human rights, participants in organized crime and
members of terrorist organizations are barred entry to Canada ...

Bill C-11 does not expand on the existing grounds for protection. It
simply consolidates several current protection criteria and corresponding
protection decisions into a single step. Grounds for protection will remain
the same as they are at present in keeping with Canada's international
human rights obligations ...

Finally ... the United Nations high commissioner for refugees will be
allowed to observe IRB hearings and participate as an intervener in cases
before the refugee appeal division. I believe these improvements both
strengthen the bill's integrity and protects the rights of individuals before
the immigration and refugee protection systems.

(House of Commons Debates, February 26, 2001, pp. 1170-73)
(Débats de la Chambre des Communes, le 26 février 2001, pp.
1170-73)

M. Mark Assad (secrétaire parlementaire du ministre de la Citoyen-
neté et de l'Immigration):

[E]n vertu des démarches qui ont été faites par les ONG canadiens et les
Nations Unies, nous avons incorporé dans le projet de loi un élément au
sujet de la torture, à savoir que les gens qui sont ou ont été victimes ou sont
sous la menace de torture peuvent se qualifier pour devenir citoyens canadiens, à condition que d'autres éléments soient respectés.

(House of Commons Debates, June 1, 2001, p. 4538)

(Débats de la Chambre des Communes, le 1ᵉʳ juin 2001, p. 4538)

4   *Bill C-6: An Act to Amend the International Boundary Waters Treaty Act/ Loi C-6: Loi modifiant la Loi du traité des eaux limitrophes internationales*

Hon. John Manley (Minister of Foreign Affairs):

Bill C-6 would protect boundary waters, including the critical resource of the Great Lakes, from bulk removal under federal law ...

Les modifications à la Loi du traité des eaux limitrophes internationales inscrites dans le projet de loi C-6 sont basées, en premier lieu, sur l'obligation qui incombe au Canada, en vertu du traité, de ne pas prendre chez lui des mesures modifiant des niveaux et des débits des eaux limitrophes du côté américain de la frontière. Je signale que les États-Unis ont une obligation réciproque envers le Canada.

Ces modifications ont aussi un second objectif, celui de préserver l'intégrité des écosystèmes tributaires des eaux limitrophes. Elles comportent trois volets: une disposition de prohibition, un régime de licences et, troisièmement, des peines.

The prohibition provision imposes a prohibition on the bulk removal of boundary waters from the water basins. Exceptions will be considered for ballast water, short term humanitarian purposes and water used in the production of food or beverages.

While many boundary waters along the Canada-U.S. border are affected by the prohibition, the main focus would be on the Great Lakes. This would enable Canada to stop future plans for bulk water removal from the Great Lakes.

There would be a licensing regime separate from the amendments dealing with prohibition. Licences would cover dams and other projects in Canada that obstruct boundary and transboundary waters if they affect the natural level and flow of water on the other side of the boundary. Under the treaty such projects must have the approval of the International Joint Commission and the Government of Canada ... The licensing regime would not cover bulk water removal projects. These, if proposed, would be covered by the act's prohibition provision ...

Je voudrais par ailleurs situer le projet de loi C-6 dans le contexte général de la stratégie annoncée par le Canada, le 10 février 1999, et consistant à interdire des prélèvements massifs d'eau de tous les grands bassins hydrographiques canadiens.

Il va sans dire que nous devons coopérer étroitement avec les instances américaines, tant fédérales qu'étatiques, pour que les régimes institués de part et d'autre de la frontière soient les plus cohérents et restrictifs possible. Dans les années à venir, le Traité des eaux limitrophes restera un instrument critique pour la protection des droits du Canada sur les Grands Lacs et les autres eaux limitrophes et transfrontalières ...

By adopting Bill C-6 parliament would set down in law an unambiguous prohibition on bulk water removal in waters under federal jurisdiction and especially in the Great Lakes. This is a forward looking action which places the highest priority on ensuring the security of Canada's fresh water resources. It demonstrates leadership at the federal level. It affirms an approach which is comprehensive, environmentally sound, respectful of constitutional responsibilities and consistent with Canada's international trade obligations.

Hon. David Anderson (Minister of the Environment):

The amendments to the International Boundary Waters Treaty Act would give the federal government the legislative authority needed to prohibit bulk removals from the boundary waters shared with the United States, principally in the Great Lakes, but also on the New Brunswick-Maine boundary...

The International Joint Commission concluded that international trade law does not prevent Canada and the United States from taking measures to protect their water resources and preserve the integrity of the Great Lakes...

Notre approche vise à préserver l'intégrité écologique de nos grands bassins versants. De plus, elle garantit que nous-mêmes, Canadiens, déterminions comment nos eaux sont gérées, et non les tribunaux du commerce extérieur — je le répète — non les tribunaux du commerce extérieur.

(House of Commons Debates, April 26, 2001, pp. 3204-7) (Débats de la Chambre des Communes, le 26 avril 2001, pp. 3204-7)

5 *Bill C-16: An Act Respecting the Registration of Charities and Security Information and to Amend the Income Tax Act / Loi C-16: Loi concernant l'enregistrement des organismes de bienfaisance et les renseignements de sécurité et modifiant la Loi de l'impôt sur le revenu*

Mr. Lynn Myers (Parliamentary Secretary to the Solicitor General of Canada):

Bill C-16 ... is an act designed to allow the government to use and protect classified security, criminal intelligence and information in denying or revoking the charitable status of an organization with terrorist affiliations.

Bill C-16 balances the government's need to protect classified information against the basic requirement to ensure fairness and transparency in assessing the status of registered charities or applicants for charitable status.

The objective is to prevent the abuse of the charity registration system now and in the future by those few organizations that would provide support to terrorism ...

The legislation allows the government to respond to threats to the public safety and national security of Canada and to other states stemming from front groups using charitable status to cloak in the blanket of legitimacy their activities in support of terrorism. We all know that terrorism is a global problem that ignores borders. That is why Canada is and must be committed to working globally to fight it. For this reason, Canada works in a wide range of international fora to encourage both the collective condemnation of terrorism and effective, practical action against it.

Over the last number of years a series of G-8 communiqués and declarations and United Nations conventions and resolutions have addressed the issue of terrorism and more specifically the financing of terrorism. These international statements and agreements depend on action by Canada and other partner countries to give them life.

Starting in 1995 with the Ottawa ministerial declaration on countering terrorism, G-8 countries agreed to: share intelligence and technical knowledge; share information on terrorist organizations and terrorist incidents; share expertise on the protection of public buildings; and improve procedures for tracing and tracking suspected terrorists. At the same time they agreed to pursue measures aimed at depriving terrorists of their sources of funding.

In February of last year Canada was one of the first countries, and we should be proud of this, to sign the international convention for the suppression of the financing of terrorism. Canada has been a vigorous advocate in this area . . .

Many terrorist organizations have devised unscrupulous methods of finding the money they need. This bill will put a stop to one of those methods, that being the use of charitable tax receipts to help support the use of violence in pursuit of a political objective . . .

Canada was one of the first countries to sign the UN convention last year. Our commitment is clear. We will fulfill our international obligations and will do so in accordance with Canadian values.

(House of Commons Debates, April 30, 2001, pp. 3321-23)
(Débats de la Chambre des Communes, le 30 avril 2001, pp. 3321-23)

6   *Bill C-287: An Act to Amend the Food and Drugs Act (Genetically Modified Food) / Loi C-287: Loi modifiant la Loi sur les aliments et drogues (aliments transgéniques)*

Hon. Charles Caccia (Davenport):

[Bill C-287] is in favour of mandatory labelling of genetically modified foods in Canada . . . Just last week Ottawa hosted a meeting of the Codex Alimentarius Commission's Committee on Food Labelling. Last month Canada signed a biosafety protocol to regulate the trade on living modified organisms. Finally, the European Union, Japan, Australia, New Zealand, South Korea and others are developing or implementing legislation requiring mandatory labelling on genetically modified foods. Against this background, the issue of labelling genetically modified foods requires urgent attention because Canada's domestic labelling policy has implications for people, for international trade and for Canada's compliance with international agreements . . .

There is confusion surrounding which foods should be labelled . . . The confusion arises from the fact that genetically modified foods in Canada fall under the broad definition of novel foods in the Food and Drugs Act.

By contrast, international agreements are clear on that issue. As a result, members will find in Bill C-287 that genetically modified food is defined in accordance with the Cartagena protocol on biosafety. This protocol has been signed by Canada. Consequently, the labelling would apply only to food or food ingredients that contain genetic material obtained through the use of modern biotechnology . . .

Bill C-287 would put in place a simple mandatory label stating "this food is genetically modified," or "this food contains an ingredient that is genetically modified" . . .

Mandatory labelling is necessary for trade and economic reasons. Our farmers and agribusiness have already incurred costs as the result of the loss of export markets. Without a reliable system for separating genetically modified crops from non-genetically modified crops, we continue to lose export markets in countries that have banned genetically modified foods or require the labelling of genetically modified foods.

(House of Commons Debates, May 7, 2001, pp. 3631-33)

(Débats de la Chambre des Communes, le 7 mai 2001, pp. 3631-33)

7   *Bill S-17: An Act to Amend the Patent Act / Loi S-17: Loi modifiant la Loi sur les brevets*

Hon. Brian Tobin (Minister of Industry):

The amendments contained in the bill . . . have one purpose . . . to bring Canada's Patent Act into compliance with two separate rulings of the World Trade Organization, the WTO . . .

One of the rulings dealt with a dispute with the United States . . . In September 2000, the WTO body sided with the U.S. interpretation of the dispute and ruled that Canada's patent terms for certain old act patents were inconsistent with obligations under the TRIPS agreement.

Bill S-17 complies with the ruling by establishing the term of protection for outstanding old act patents as the greater of 17 years from the date the application was granted or a minimum of 20 years from the date the application was filed in Canada as defined by the patent rules . . .

The second WTO ruling addressed by Bill S-17 is a dispute with the European Union. In the second dispute the WTO ruled in March 2000 that Canada's stockpiling exception was inconsistent with the TRIPS agreement. This exception allowed generic drug manufacturers to make and to stockpile their version of a patented product during the last six months of the patent term . . .

The government has already complied with the WTO ruling on stockpiling, by way of regulation. The repeal of the stockpiling provisions simply ensures that the Patent Act itself conforms with our TRIPS obligations.

The bill before us today deals exclusively with the issues of patent term and stockpiling. It does not attempt to go into the broader aspects of patent protection in Canada . . . it is very important that we proceed expeditiously with the amendments before us because the WTO has imposed a deadline for compliance with the patent term ruling. Canada has until

August 12, 2001 to comply. Otherwise we could face retaliatory trade action.

The amendments contained in Bill S-17 would provide extensions to certain old act patents that are still in force and that do not benefit from a minimum patent term of 20 years from the date the patent application was filed. I should point out that there are, relatively speaking, a small number of patents that will be affected by this amendment.

(House of Commons Debates, May 7, 2001, pp. 3669-70)
(Débats de la Chambre des Communes, le 7 mai 2001, pp. 3669-70)

B   STATEMENTS IN RESPONSE TO QUESTIONS / DÉCLARATIONS
    EN RÉPONSE AUX QUESTIONS

1   Environment / L'environnement

Mr. Andy Savoy (Tobique — Mactaquac):

[Y]esterday the Minister of the Environment tabled the sustainable development strategies for 28 government departments and agencies. Is the Minister of the Environment able to tell the House what these strategies will accomplish?

Hon. David Anderson (Minister of the Environment):

[T]he 28 sustainable development strategies tabled yesterday are designed to ensure that federal departments and agencies consider the environment, the economy and society in all policy and program decisions, and do so in an integrated manner. The strategies will greatly assist in achieving the commitments Canada made during the 1992 earth summit.

(House of Commons Debates, February 15, 2001, pp. 778-79)
(Débats de la Chambre des Communes, le 15 février 2001, pp. 778-79)

(a) Cartagena Protocol on Biosafety / Le Protocole de
    Cartagena sur la prévention des risques biotechnologiques

Ms. Judy Sgro (York West):

[W]hat is Canada's progress with regard to the Cartagena protocol on biosafety?

Hon. David Anderson (Minister of the Environment):

[L]ast Thursday in New York I signed the Cartagena protocol on biosafety on Canada's behalf ... This protocol is a clear reflection of the government's commitment to reconcile economic policies and trade policies with strong protection of the environment and its concerns.

(House of Commons Debates, April 24, 2001, p. 3055)
(Débats de la Chambre des Communes, le 24 avril 2001, p. 3055)

(b) Hazardous waste / Les déchets dangereux

Ms. Paddy Torsney (Burlington):

Could the Minister of the Environment tell us what actions his department is taking to ensure that there is no illegal dumping of hazardous and toxic waste in Canada?

Hon. David Anderson (Minister of the Environment):

Canada has ratified the United Nations Basel convention on the control of transboundary movements of hazardous waste, and we take it seriously. The new Canadian Environmental Protection Act, 1999 ... provides my department's enforcement officers, who incidentally have been substantially increased in numbers, with new tools to combat the illegal disposition of hazardous waste, such as new regulations to control certain waste, requirements for disposal plans by exporters and new criteria for permits.

(House of Commons Debates, February 27, 2001, p. 1248)
(Débats de la Chambre des Communes, le 27 février 2001, p. 1248)

(c) Kyoto Protocol / Le Protocole de Kyoto

Mme Monique Guay (Laurentides):

[H]ier, les États-Unis ont décidé de ne pas ratifier le Protocole de Kyoto ... le ministre de l'Environnement peut-il expliquer pourquoi il baisse les bras devant la décision américaine?

Hon. Ralph Goodale (Minister of Natural Resources and Minister responsible for the Canadian Wheat Board):

Canada is very seriously pursuing its international obligations. We negotiated with respect to the Kyoto protocol. We have been very active in the years since Kyoto in not only elaborating upon the international implementation mechanisms but taking action at home in Canada. Last year in the budget of February and the mini budget in October we committed $1.1 billion over the next five years, which will eliminate 65 megatons of carbon dioxide from our atmosphere ... We will also continue to work with all our international partners to put together an international arrangement that works. We obviously disagree with President Bush's decision and we will work very hard to obtain an international consensus to bring down greenhouse gases and mitigate the problem of climate change.

(House of Commons Debates, March 30, 2001, p. 2560)
(Débats de la Chambre des Communes, le 30 mars 2001, p. 2560)

Ms. Alexa McDonough (Halifax):

Why will Canada not act responsibly, denounce the American environmental recklessness and restore Canada's international reputation for conservation and environmental stewardship?

Right Hon. Jean Chrétien (Prime Minister):

[T]he goal of the government is to achieve the objectives that were agreed upon in Kyoto. The government has already done one-third of what has to be done to meet the level that was established in Kyoto. We intend over the period that has been allocated to meet the objectives of Kyoto. It is the environmental policy of the Canadian government.

(House of Commons Debates, May 1, 2001, p. 3392)
(Débats de la Chambre des Communes, le 1er mai 2001, p. 3392)

Mr. Joe Comartin (Windsor — St. Clair):

Will the Prime Minister ... commit to the House, to all Canadians and to the international community that Canada will ratify the Kyoto protocol as scheduled in 2002?

Right Hon. Jean Chrétien (Prime Minister):

The government, the Minister of the Environment and I are committed to implement the Kyoto agreement, but we would like to have two amendments that are extremely important for Canada. The sink is extremely important for Canada. Because we have a lot of land we could create a situation where a lot of CO_2 could be absorbed if we had a good system of trees or plants in Canada. Plus we want to have credit because we are exporting a lot of resources to the United States, such as natural gas and electricity.

(House of Commons Debates, April 4, 2001, p. 2778)
(Débats de la Chambre des Communes, le 4 avril 2001, p. 2778)

Ms. Alexa McDonough (Halifax):

[W]hat is preventing the Canadian government from ratifying the Kyoto accord before climate change talks resume in July?

Hon. David Anderson (Minister of the Environment):

The reason is that while we have accepted and agreed to targets for various countries for Kyoto, there is no agreement on how those targets will be reached. We are having further negotiations in Bonn in July and I trust they will be successful.

(House of Commons Debates, June 12, 2001, p. 4985)
(Débats de la Chambre des Communes, le 12 juin 2001, p. 4985)

(d) Persistent organic pollutants / Les polluants organiques persistants

Ms. Beth Phinney (Hamilton Mountain):

What is Canada doing to protect the environment and the health of Canadians from persistent organic pollutants?

Mrs. Karen Redman (Parliamentary Secretary to Minister of the Environment):

Canada played a pivotal role in the United Nations environment program convention on POPs, successfully completed last December in Johannesburg. This agreement will reduce significantly or eliminate foreign sources of this pollutant that impact the health and environment of Canadians, particularly in our Arctic. As well, Canada invested $20 million in budget 2000 to help developing countries reduce or eliminate the release of POPs. Canada has already banned or severely restricted production, use and release of these pollutants in our environment.

(House of Commons Debates, February 9, 2001, pp. 478-79)
(Débats de la Chambre des Communes, le 9 février 2001, pp. 478-79)

Ms. Paddy Torsney (Burlington):

[T]hree years ago the international community agreed to dramatically reduce or even eliminate persistent organic pollutants ... Could the Minister of the Environment tell the House what action Canada is taking domestically and internationally to reduce these substances?

Hon. David Anderson (Minister of the Environment):

I will be signing, on behalf of Canada, the United Nations convention on persistent organic pollutants in Stockholm next week.

(House of Commons Debates, May 14 2001, pp. 3988-89)
(Débats de la Chambre des Communes, le 14 mai 2001, pp. 3988-89)

(e) Trafficking of endangered species / Le trafic des espèces en danger de disparition

Mr. Keith Martin (Esquimalt — Juan de Fuca):

Given that Canada is the third largest conduit for the trafficking of endangered species products around the world ... will the minister work with the

Minister of Foreign Affairs and the Minister of Justice to develop a plan of action to address this serious problem?

Hon. David Anderson (Minister of the Environment):

Just as with many other smuggling issues around the world, it is extraordinarily difficult to deal with it simply at the borders. We will have to deal with it in some of the markets of Singapore or Hong Kong or elsewhere in the world. We will have to deal with it in concert with other countries. This is not simply a question of more and more heavy enforcement at border points.

(House of Commons Debates, February 2, 2001, pp. 146-47)
(Débats de la Chambre des Communes, le 2 février 2001, pp. 146-47)

2 *Foreign Affairs / Les Affaires étrangères*

(a) China / La Chine

Mr. Peter Goldring (Edmonton Centre-East):

Could the minister explain why we are now teaching winter warfare tactics to a country that is clearly not one of our allies?

Hon. Art Eggleton (Minister of National Defence):

[W]e are not cozying up and we are not training them. We are entering into a dialogue with the Chinese. The Chinese military is an important part of the elements of security and defence in the Pacific. Engaging in constructive dialogue is a good thing to do ... It also gives us the opportunity to show them how we operate in Canada and how our values of democracy work well.

(House of Commons Debates, March 16, 2001, p. 1774)
(Débats de la Chambre des Communes, le 16 mars 2001, p. 1774)

(b) Colombia / La Colombie

Ms. Alexa McDonough (Halifax):

[T]he Secretary of State for Latin America ... does not support Plan Colombia ... Could he give absolute assurances that Canada is not and will not sell any equipment to the Colombian military?

Hon. David Kilgour (Secretary of State (Latin America and Africa)):

Plan Colombia has a very large social assistance program and a number of features to it which are not military. Canada is not participating in any of the military side of Plan Colombia, as the Minister of National Defence knows. Canada will not be providing any military equipment as we would be violating our non-involvement in the war in Colombia.

(House of Commons Debates, February 27, 2001, pp. 1247-48) (Débats de la Chambre des Communes, le 27 février 2001, pp. 1247-48)

(c) Cultural policy / Les politiques culturelles

Mme Eleni Bakopanos (Ahuntsic):

[D]e plus en plus de nations réalisent que leur culture, leurs traditions et leur expression culturelle sont menacées ... étant donné la présence de la culture américaine ... Que fait ce gouvernement pour combattre ce fléau mondial?

Mme Sarmite Bulte (secrétaire parlementaire de la ministre du Patrimoine canadien):

[L]e Canada a réussi à inscrire la diversité culturelle dans le programme international. Créé à Ottawa en 1998 ... La troisième réunion du Réseau [international sur les poliques culturelles] aura lieu en Grèce à la fin de septembre. Il y a trois thèmes qui seront abordés: le patrimoine culturel, l'identité et la diversité culturelles dans le cadre de la mondialisation et les possibilités d'action nationale.

(House of Commons Debates, September 21, 2000, p. 8498) (Débats de la Chambre des Communes, le 21 septembre 2000, p. 8498)

(d) Democratic Republic of Congo / la République démocratique du Congo

Mme Carole-Marie Allard (Laval-Est):

[L]e secrétaire d'État à l'Afrique et à l'Amérique latine a rencontré, vendredi dernier, à New-York, le nouveau président de la République démocratique du Congo, M. Joseph Kabila. Peut-il nous en donner les résultats?

L'hon. David Kilgour (secrétaire d'État (Amérique latine et Afrique)):

[J]'ai fait part au président Kabila de la position canadienne, y compris de notre appui à une solution négociée au conflit s'appuyant sur l'accord d'Osaka et sur les résolutions appropriées du Conseil de sécurité. Nous donnons notre appui à un dialogue intercongolais qui mènerait à des institutions démocratiques, et à la nécessité de permettre le déploiement des forces des Nations Unies ... le Canada, comme les autres pays, recherche une solution viable au conflit afin de mettre fin aux souffrances énormes du peuple congolais.

(House of Commons Debates, February 8, 2001, pp. 428-29)
(Débats de la Chambre des Communes, le 8 février 2001, pp. 428-29)

(e) Diplomatic immunity / L'immunité diplomatique

Mr. Bill Casey (Cumberland — Colchester):

Will the Government of Canada spearhead an international initiative to change the rules of diplomatic immunity to stop protecting drunk and dangerous drivers?

Hon. John Manley (Minister of Foreign Affairs):

[I]t would be useful for us to discuss the rules of diplomatic immunity, although I do not believe they were intended to apply to a case such as this one ... It is very important that our diplomats have the protection of the Vienna Convention, particularly those serving in some countries where respect for the rule of law is not as it is in Canada.

(House of Commons Debates, February 1, 2001, p. 110)
(Débats de la Chambre des Communes, le 1er février 2001, p. 110)

Mr. Chuck Strahl (Fraser Valley):

[W]e have a copy of the letter that was sent from the Department of Foreign Affairs to the Russian embassy ... written after the arrest by the police and suspension of ... [Mr. Knyazev's] ... driver's licence for 90 days. The letter reads: The Department finds the actions of the Ottawa-Carleton Regional Police unacceptable and wishes to apologize for this incident ... The Department wishes to inform the Embassy that Mr. Knyazev's driver's licence is attached and that all the charges have been withdrawn.

Hon. John Manley (Minister of Foreign Affairs):

[T]he letter was sent in response to a diplomatic note from the Russians ... the apology did reflect the fact that a diplomat was treated not in accordance with the Vienna Convention.

(House of Commons Debates, February 2, 2001, pp. 155-56)
(Débats de la Chambre des Communes, le 2 février 2001, pp. 155-56)

(f) Ethiopia and Eritrea / L'Éthiopie et l'Érythrée

Mr. Bryon Wilfert (Oak Ridges):

Ethiopia and Eritrea reached a formal settlement to their border war on December 12, 2000 ... Would the Secretary of State for Africa give the House an update on Canada's efforts to promote peace in this region?

Hon. David Kilgour (Secretary of State (Latin America and Africa)):

Some of us will be going to Ethiopia and Eritrea next month to deal with the politicians to try to persuade them to continue to maintain the peace. There are 450 Canadians who are serving extremely well in that part of the world.

(House of Commons Debates, May 10, 2001, p. 3878)
(Débats de la Chambre des Communes, le 10 mai 2001, p. 3878)

(g) Importation of plutonium / L'importation de plutonium

Mᵐᵉ Jocelyne Girard-Bujold (Jonquière):

[L]e Canada importera ... du plutonium MOX de la Fédération russe ... Comment le premier ministre peut-il justifier l'importation du MOX?

Hon. Ralph E. Goodale (Minister of Natural Resources and Minister responsible for the Canadian Wheat Board):

[T]he rationale for the testing of MOX fuel ... is to try to make this world safer and more secure from the nuclear threat of the plutonium stockpiles in existence in the United States and Russia ... Anything that happens in this country is fully consistent with the laws of Canada, the Environmental Protection Act, the Nuclear Safety and Control Act, the Transportation of Dangerous Goods Act, the International Civil Aviation Organization and the International Atomic Energy Agency.

(House of Commons Debates, September 21, 2000, pp. 8498-99)
(Débats de la Chambre des Communes, le 21 septembre 2000, pp. 8498-99)

(h) India / L'Inde

Mr. Gurbax Malhi (Bramalea — Gore — Malton — Springdale):

[Y]esterday the Minister of Foreign Affairs announced that Canada had decided to restore formal relations with India. Why has the Government of Canada changed its policy and announced a re-engagement with India? What does the announcement mean for Canada-India relations?

Hon. Rey Pagtakhan (Secretary of State (Asia-Pacific)):

Canada's re-engagement with India recognizes the fact that a better climate now exists which allows us to pursue an effective dialogue for all aspects of our relationship. Canada is committed to pursuing the broadest political, cultural and economic relationship with India. We will continue to call upon India to renounce its nuclear weapons program. Moreover, re-engagement through full ministerial visits and full restoration of CIDA programming, as well as support for cultural exchanges, will enrich our political relationship.

(House of Commons Debates, March 21, 2001, pp 1984-85) (Débats de la Chambre des Communes, le 21 mars 2001, pp. 1984-85)

(i) International Conference on War-Affected Children / La Conférence Internationale sur les enfants touchés par la guerre

Mrs. Sue Barnes (London West):

[L]ast week in Winnipeg dozens of young people from war torn countries came ... to the international conference on war affected children ... Will the Minister of Foreign Affairs tell us the outcome of these important meetings attended by delegates from 120 countries and other multilateral organizations?

Hon. Lloyd Axworthy (Minister of Foreign Affairs):

[A] 14 point action plan was put in place that will bring together governments, NGOs and young people in a network that will begin to develop a major momentum toward a special UN session that will take place next year. One concrete way was that we were able to successfully negotiate an agreement with the governments of Sudan, Uganda and Egypt and ourselves to begin the release of abducted children who have gone into Sudan. The release actually started to take place yesterday. It is a good example of how Canada can provide real leadership in the world.

(House of Commons Debates, September 18, 2000, pp. 8245-46) (Débats de la Chambre des Communes, le 18 septembre 2000, pp. 8245-46)

(j) International loans / Les prêts internationaux

Mr. Charlie Penson (Peace River):

Does the finance minister not understand the irony of the situation of loaning money to Brazil which allowed them to subsidize their aerospace industry to the detriment of Canadian companies such as Bombardier?

Hon. Paul Martin (Minister of Finance):

The loan was not made by Canada. The loan was made by the Bank for International Settlements. What Canada did was to provide a guarantee, for which we were paid. The guarantee was never exercised ... More important, to the point about Canada's international responsibilities, we are a G7 country. As a G7 country we will exercise those responsibilities on behalf of the vast assembly of nations.

(House of Commons Debates, February 8, 2001, pp. 423-24)
(Débats de la Chambre des Communes, le 8 février 2001, pp. 423-24)

(k) Iraq / L'Irak

M. Antoine Dubé (Lévis-et-Chutes-de-la-Chaudière):

[L]a semaine dernière, le gouvernement américain autorisait des bombardements en Irak ... Le ministre est-il lui-même d'accord avec l'attitude des États-Unis?

L'hon. John Manley (ministre des Affaires étrangères)

[N]ous sommes en effet en faveur des zones d'exclusion ... pour protéger les populations civiles en Irak, les Kurdes au nord ou bien les Chiites arabes ... pour l'Irak, la meilleure chose à faire, c'est d'accepter les normes établies par les Nations Unies.

(House of Commons Debates, February 19, 2001, p. 881)
(Débats de la Chambre des Communes, le 19 février 2001, p. 881)

(1) Middle East / Le Moyen-Orient

Mme Francine Lalonde (Mercier):

[L]a Rencontre de Paris a échoué, cette semaine, sur la demande palestinienne d'une enquête internationale refusée par Israël ... Le Canada ... ne pourrait-il pas prendre l'initiative d'offrir sa contribution pour aider la région à sortir de ce conflit?

L'hon. Ronald J. Duhamel (secrétaire d'État (Diversification de l'économie de l'Ouest canadien) (Francophonie)):

[N]ous sommes prêts à faire presque n'importe quoi pour s'assurer qu'il y ait de la stabilité ... On a même fait une intervention, il y a deux jours, au Conseil de sécurité pour essayer de rapprocher les parties, essayer de trouver une solution. Nous y sommes, nous y serons et nous continuons à vouloir qu'ils trouvent une façon de s'entendre, de travailler et de vivre ensemble.

(House of Commons Debates, October 6, 2000, p. 9018)
(Débats de la Chambre des Communes, le 6 octobre 2000, p. 9018)

Mr. Svend J. Robinson (Burnaby — Douglas):

Why did Canada not support the call for a special session of the UN commission on human rights into the situation in the Middle East?

Hon. Lloyd Axworthy (Minister of Foreign Affairs):

Canada has been very active in the last several days making calls to try to support that process. The Prime Minister called his counterparts in the Middle East, along with President Clinton. I spoke yesterday to Syrian and Lebanese representatives to talk about the kidnapping of the Israeli soldiers and to see if we could have some return in those areas. We met with the Israeli envoy today to talk particularly about how we can assist as Canadians in trying to restore peace. This is the important thing.

(House of Commons Debates, October 16, 2000, p. 9080)
(Débats de la Chambre des Communes, le 16 octobre 2000, p. 9080)

(m) National Missile Defence Proposal / Le projet national de défense antimissile

Ms. Alexa McDonough (Halifax):

The NMD proposal violates the 1972 anti-ballistic missile treaty. Why will the government not ... condemn the NMD madness?

Hon. Art Eggleton (Minister of National Defence):

[W]e are concerned with global security issues. We are concerned also with the proliferation of weapons of mass destruction ... We are in dialogue with the United States ... We are in dialogue with our other allies, as is the United States ... We have made it very clear that the ABM treaty is an important treaty, that it is important to address it and that it is important to talk to the Russians, the Chinese and all our other allies.

(House of Commons Debates, February 22, 2001, p. 1041)
(Débats de la Chambre des Communes, le 22 février 2001, p. 1041)

(n) North Korea / La Corée du Nord

Mr. Bryon Wilfert (Oak Ridges):

Given the fact that North Korea's missile and nuclear program has contributed to uncertainty in the region and that it has withdrawn from the International Atomic Energy Agency, how will Canada approach engagement with this regime in terms of trade, regional security issues and the need to encourage and promote North Korea into rejoining the atomic energy agency?

Hon. John Manley (Minister of Foreign Affairs):

[E]stablishing diplomatic relations ... provides us with an increased opportunity to work with the North Koreans in advancing Canadian values, including democratic rights, human rights, economic development and trade issues. On the ... matter of the International Atomic Energy Agency, Canada annually co-ordinates a resolution before the agency at an annual meeting concerning North Korea. We will continue to do so.

(House of Commons Debates, February 14, 2001, pp. 697-98) (Débats de la Chambre des Communes, le 14 février 2001, pp. 697-98)

(o) Northern Ireland/ L'Irlande du Nord

Mr. Pat O'Brien (London — Fanshawe):

Could the parliamentary secretary explain ... the efforts that Canada has been making to the peace process in Northern Ireland?

Mr. Denis Paradis (Parliamentary Secretary to Minister of Foreign Affairs):

Canada has encouraged and participated in the peace process at all levels. Canada has contributed $1 million to the international fund for Ireland.

(House of Commons Debates, September 20, 2000, pp. 8411-12) (Débats de la Chambre des Communes, le 20 septembre 2000, pp. 8411-12)

(p) Ottawa Convention Banning Anti-Personnel Land Mines / La convention d'Ottawa sur les mines antipersonnel

Mr. David Pratt (Nepean — Carleton):

The Ottawa convention banning anti-personnel land mines has been in force for two years now. Could the minister explain ... what the government has done, is doing and will do to ensure the success of this vital international convention?

Hon. John Manley (Minister of Foreign Affairs):

Yesterday, on its second anniversary, we had the 111th country ratifying the treaty. We have seen a significant reduction in land mine problems around the world as fewer mines are going out than are being withdrawn from the minefields. The number of injuries is falling. Canada has made an important contribution to de-mining efforts in countries as disparate as Nicaragua, Jordan, Bosnia and Afghanistan. This is a credit to Canada ... This is the kind of thing we need to be doing.

(House of Commons Debates, March 1, 2001, p. 1410) (Débats de la Chambre des Communes, le 1er mars 2001, p. 1410)

(q) Pakistan / Le Pakistan

Mr. Bryon Wilfert (Oak Ridges):

There are concerns that our engagement with India will lead to further isolation of Pakistan and increase the possibility of destabilization of the sub-Indian continent. Could the Secretary of State for Asia-Pacific affairs clarify for the House Canada's current policy toward the government in Islamabad?

Hon. Rey Pagtakhan (Secretary of State (Asia-Pacific)):

Canada does not wish to isolate Pakistan. We know there is a need for political stability and the absence of nuclear proliferation in that region. In fact Canada has pursued a policy of selective engagement on a bilateral and multilateral basis since Pakistan tested its nuclear weapons in 1998 followed by a military coup in 1999. We believe that selective engagement will allow Canada to help Pakistan in the transition to a stable economy and sustainable democracy.

(House of Commons Debates, March 26, 2001, pp. 2228-29) (Débats de la Chambre des Communes, le 26 mars 2001, pp. 2228-29)

(r) Russia / La Russie

Mr. Monte Solberg (Medicine Hat, Canadian Alliance):

I would like to follow up on the recent case involving the drunken Russian diplomat who took the life of an Ottawa woman and injured another … Why has the Prime Minister not directly phoned Vladimir Putin, the president of Russia, to impress upon him the need to prosecute this case to the fullest extent of Russian law?

Hon. Herb Gray (Deputy Prime Minister):

[T]he government has taken action under our mutual legal assistance treaty with the Russian federation. All the documents have been transmitted to the Russian legal authorities. I am confident our embassy is pressing the authorities to take the appropriate action under the treaty and in light of the documents.

(House of Commons Debates, February 5, 2001, p. 226) (Débats de la Chambre des Communes, le 5 février 2001, p. 226)

(s) Sierra Leone / La Sierra Leone

Mrs. Sue Barnes (London West):

Could the foreign affairs minister tell us what Canada's position is with respect to the special court that is being set up by the United Nations in Sierra Leone.

Hon. John Manley (Minister of Foreign Affairs):

[T]he Government of Canada continues to be very concerned by what is happening in Sierra Leone. We are particularly concerned that those who are responsible for many crimes and atrocities be held accountable for their actions. However the details with respect to the organization and budget for the special court for Sierra Leone are still not finalized. The Canadian government will consider those in determining whether to make a financial contribution at the appropriate time.

(House of Commons Debates, May 18, 2001, pp. 4226-27)
(Débats de la Chambre des Communes, le 18 mai 2001, pp. 4226-27)

(t) Sri Lanka / Le Sri Lanka

Mr. John McKay (Scarborough East):

[T]he government of Sri Lanka and the Tamil tigers appear to be approaching a retrenchment primarily through the government of Norway ... could the Secretary of State for Asia-Pacific tell the House Canada's policy with respect to this important peace initiative?

Hon. Rey Pagtakhan (Secretary of State (Asia-Pacific)):

Canada supports Norway's efforts and is willing to play an active role in the peace process upon invitation by both parties.

(House of Commons Debates, April 2, 2001, p. 2621-22)
(Débats de la Chambre des Communes, le 2 avril 2001, p. 2621-22)

(u) Sudan / Le Soudan

Ms. Jean Augustine (Etobicoke — Lakeshore):

Canadians have expressed concern about the situation in Sudan. It is one year since the special adviser to DFAIT, Mr. Harker, submitted his report. Could the Secretary of State for Africa tell us what Canada's position has been in response to Mr. Harker's report?

Hon. David Kilgour (Secretary of State (Latin America and Africa)):

[S]ince the Harker report the government has done a number of things, including opening an office of the Canadian embassy in Khartoum with the mandate to promote the peace process in human rights. Second, it appointed Lois Wilson as our special envoy to the Sudan peace process. Third, we expect Talisman Energy to avoid becoming involved in actions that result in more suffering for civilians.

(House of Commons Debates, February 12, 2001, p. 535)
(Débats de la Chambre des Communes, le 12 février 2001, p. 535)

(v) Tax agreements / Les conventions fiscales

Mme Pauline Picard (Drummond):

[E]st-ce que le premier ministre ne devrait pas prendre une position claire et rassurante pour les gens que nous représentons en s'engageant à combattre les pratiques fiscales dommageables dans les trois Amériques, contrairement à la position annoncée par son ministre des Finances?

Mr. Roy Cullen (Parliamentary Secretary to Minister of Finance):

We are involved with the OECD and many countries to eliminate harmful tax competition. We have tough money laundering legislation that passed the House and the Senate. We are on the leading edge of these discussions. We want to make sure, though, that the process is transparent and fair before we list countries that are not involved in harmful tax competition. The Minister of Finance is leading this charge and we will get to the root of the problem to try to resolve it.

(House of Commons Debates, April 4, 2001, p. 2780)
(Débats de la Chambre des Communes, le 4 avril 2001, p. 2780)

(w) Terrorism / Le terrorisme

Mr. Jim Abbott (Kootenay — Columbia):

[T]errorists raise funds through welfare scams, drugs, credit cards, passport frauds and human smuggling. These are all international security issues which put all Canadians at risk.

Hon. Lloyd Axworthy (Minister of Foreign Affairs):

Canada has taken a very active role in developing an international convention against fundraising for terrorism. We chaired the committee that put the convention together. We have tabled the convention at the United Nations and we were one of the signatories. The next step is to develop legislation in consultation with the provinces, because it is a criminal matter, to set up a process of due law so that people who are considered to be under suspicion can have a full protection of the law and we can also use the instruments of the law.

(House of Commons Debates, September 28, 2000, p. 8808)
(Débats de la Chambre des Communes, le 28 septembre 2000, p. 8808)

(x) Vietnam / Le Vietnam

Mr. Monte Solberg (Medicine Hat):

[T]he government has sent tens of millions of dollars to Vietnam supposedly to improve its justice system but last spring that justice system unfairly executed a Canadian citizen ... Why are we restoring relations when there is not a shred of evidence that sort of travesty will not happen again?

Hon. Lloyd Axworthy (Minister of Foreign Affairs):

Canada did take very severe measures when the execution took place ... We insisted on a series of very clear responses, such as the return of the mother, that the Toronto police would be allowed to go and undertake proper negotiations on drug trafficking, that we would promptly have the returns placed. Those conditions have now been met. We have not restored normal relations but we have started communicating, dialoguing and engaging with the Vietnamese to make sure it does not happen again.

(House of Commons Debates, September 19, 2000, pp. 8375-76) (Débats de la Chambre des Communes, le 19 septembre 2000, pp. 8375-76)

(y) Yugoslavia / La Yougoslavie

Ms. Colleen Beaumier (Brampton West — Mississauga):

What is Canada's reaction to recent unofficial reports that the voters have elected opposition candidate Kostunica?

M. Denis Paradis (secrétaire parlementaire du ministre des Affaires étrangères):

Nous encourageons les autorités yougoslaves à reconnaître la volonté du peuple, et souhaitons voir la République fédérale de Yougoslavie réintégrer la société des nations démocratiques. As soon as a government committed to reform and reconciliation is in place we will initiate the removing of sanctions, ending the isolation of Yugoslavia and increasing assistance to support political and economic reform.

(House of Commons Debates, September 26, 2000, p. 8680) (Débats de la Chambre des Communes, le 26 septembre 2000, p. 8680)

Mr. Chuck Strahl (Fraser Valley):

Has the government been in touch with our allies to ensure that we have a common approach and a common front to assist that stable transition to what we hope will be a stable democracy?

Hon. Herb Gray (Deputy Prime Minister.):

I understand that the very questions the hon. member has raised are being discussed today at a meeting of the OSCE, the Organization for Security and Co-operation in Europe, and Canada has a representative at those meetings.

Mr. Monte Solberg (Medicine Hat):

[T]wo Canadians ... Shawn Going and Liam Hall ... have unfairly been held prisoners in a jail in Belgrade since August ... what steps have been taken to ensure their safety during this period of unrest?

Mr. Denis Paradis (Parliamentary Secretary to the Minister of Foreign Affairs):

Canada believes that there is no legitimate reason for their continued detention, which is clearly motivated by political purposes. We appreciate the efforts of the OSCE, the United Nations and our bilateral partners to help secure the release of the four men. We will continue to press the FRY authorities to secure their quick release.

M. Gilles Duceppe (Laurier — Sainte-Marie):

Je demande au vice-ministre si le gouvernement canadien a également l'intention de reconnaître que M. Kostunica a été le vainqueur des élections et qu'il est désormais en droit d'être le président de la Fédération yougoslave.

Hon. Herb Gray (Deputy Prime Minister):

[I]t is clear that opposition candidate Kostunica won a majority in the first round of presidential elections on September 24. We do not accept the validity of yesterday's ruling by the constitutional court which tried to overturn the September 24th elections and called for new ones next summer. This is clearly a political move on the part of Mr. Milosevic to retain power ... we urge Mr. Milosevic to accept the clearly expressed will of the Yugoslav people.

Mᵐᵉ Francine Lalonde (Mercier):

Est-ce que le vice-premier ministre peut nous assurer que le Canada va rester ferme dans sa volonté de traduire Milosevic devant le Tribunal pénal international de La Haye.

Hon. Herb Gray (Deputy Prime Minister):

[O]ur position on this matter remains the same as it always has been ... It is the international practice to recognize states rather than individual governments of those states, but we are demanding that Mr. Milosevic step down now.

(House of Commons Debates, October 5, 2000, p. 8966-67)
(Débats de la Chambre des Communes, le 5 octobre 2000, p. 8966-67)

(z) Zimbabwe / Le Zimbabwe

Mr. Keith Martin (Esquimalt — Juan de Fuca):

[W]ill the Minister of Foreign Affairs say to our representatives at the International Monetary Fund and the World Bank that they will push for a withholding of all grants and loans to Zimbabwe until the rule of law is once again restored?

Hon. John Manley (Minister of Foreign Affairs):

The expression of concern that arose at the Commonwealth meeting a few weeks ago was an example of that. We have been calling upon Zimbabwe to respect the norms of democratic principles, to respect the right of dissent, and to maintain the independence of the judiciary, the media and the press. All these issues have been raised in some concern by a variety of NGOs. If action is warranted, we will indeed take it.

(House of Commons Debates, May 1, 2001, p. 3398)
(Débats de la Chambre des Communes, le 1er mai 2001, p. 3398)

3   Human Rights / Les droits de la personne

(a) China / La Chine

Mr. Svend Robinson (Burnaby — Douglas):

Last week the Dutch foreign minister cancelled his ... visit to China because the Chinese government refused to allow a round table to go ahead in Hong Kong with human rights practitioners including Falun Gong ... will our government ... sponsor a similar round table during this current team Canada visit to China? Will we show we are serious about human rights?

Hon. John Manley (Minister of Foreign Affairs):

[T]he Prime Minister will have the opportunity to address the issue of human rights again during his visit. He has made Canada's position very clear. It has been our ability to engage China over the years because we have been seen by them to be their friends. This is why we have been able to make progress on a continuing dialogue on human rights, including the important contributions we have made to enhancing the judicial process in the People's Republic of China.

(House of Commons Debates, February 12, 2001, pp. 529-30)
(Débats de la Chambre des Communes, le 12 février 2001, p. 529-30)

(b) Crimes against humanity/ Les crimes contre l'humanité

Mr. Sarkis Assadourian (Brampton Centre):

April 24 marked the 86th anniversary of the Armenian genocide of 1915. What is the minister doing to promote understanding of this tragic event and its important message to mankind that crimes against humanity are society's worst scourge and must not be allowed and tolerated in a civilized world?

Hon. John Manley (Minister of Foreign Affairs):

Mr. Speaker, in 1999 the Government of Canada articulated its concern over the terrible calamity that befell the Armenian people in 1915, and today we restate that concern. Canada is actively pursuing the development of positive and extensive bilateral relations with all the countries of that region. In particular, we are working very closely to encourage the Armenian and Turkish governments to reconcile and establish a more open dialogue between them. CIDA is providing practical support to Armenia and annual assistance to a variety of Turkish non-governmental organizations.

(House of Commons Debates, May 1, 2001, p. 3395)
(Débats de la Chambre des Communes, le 1er mai 2001, p. 3395)

(c) Workers' rights / Les droits des travailleurs

Ms. Colleen Beaumier (Brampton West — Mississauga):

[O]n Monday an historic labour agreement was signed with Costa Rica. My question is for the Parliamentary Secretary to the Minister of Labour. Could she explain to the House the importance of this agreement?

Mrs. Judi Longfield (Parliamentary Secretary to the Minister of Labour):

[T]his agreement on labour co-operation with Costa Rica demonstrates Canada's commitment to promoting and protecting worker rights in the context of the trade liberalization of the Americas. Both countries have pledged to enforce their laws relating to the 1998 ILO declaration on fundamental rights and principles at work.

(House of Commons Debates, April 25, 2001, p. 3151)
(Débats de la Chambre des Communes, le 25 avril 2001, p. 3151)

4 International Aid / L'aide internationale

M. Gilles Duceppe (Laurier — Sainte-Marie):

[L]'aide canadienne aux pays en voie de développement est en chute libre. Selon les données de l'OCDE, le Canada est passé, en cinq ans, de 6e à

17ᵉ sur la liste des 22 pays qui contribuent ... Le premier ministre est-il prêt à ... consacrer 0,7 p. 100 du produit national brut à l'aide aux pays en voie de développement, comme le recommandent les Nations Unies?

Le très hon. Jean Chrétien (premier ministre) :

[A]u cours des dernières années, nous avons augmenté nos contributions et nous avons l'intention de continuer à le faire. Nous avons l'intention, au cours de l'année 2001-2002, d'augmenter nos dépenses dans ce domaine de 7 à 10 p. 100.

(House of Commons Debates, April 30, 2001, pp. 3311-12)
(Débats de la Chambre des Communes, le 30 avril 2001, pp. 3311-12)

Mᵐᵉ Sue Barnes (London-Ouest):

The United Nations has asked for international assistance ... What is Canada doing to assist Afghanistan?

Mr. Eugène Bellemare (Parliamentary Secretary to the Minister for International Cooperation):

[O]n February 8 the minister responsible for the Canadian International Development Agency announced $1.3 million in response to the current crisis, to provide immediate relief supplies to international displaced persons, including blankets, plastic sheets, clothes and tents, and to help address the most urgent humanitarian needs of Afghan refugees through various UN agencies.

(House of Commons Debates, February 9, 2001, p. 476)
(Débats de la Chambre des Communes, le 9 février 2001, p. 476)

5   *Law of the Sea / Le droit de la mer*

(a) UN Convention on the Law of the Sea / La convention des Nations Unies sur le droit de la mer

Hon. Charles Caccia (Davenport):

[M]y question ... concerns Canada's ratification of the United Nations Convention on the Law of the Sea, which is a 1993 red book promise. Given the importance of this convention ... when could Canadians expect the ratification of the law of the sea to take place?

M. Denis Paradis (secrétaire parlementaire du ministre des Affaires étrangères):

[L]e Canada tient à ratifier la Convention de l'ONU sur le droit de la mer. La seule question qu'il nous reste à déterminer, à ce moment-ci, est le moment de la ratification. Le Canada va ratifier cette Convention sur le droit de la mer dans un contexte beaucoup plus vaste de la politique canadienne sur la pêche en haute mer. Ce dont nous avons besoin, c'est d'un régime efficace d'application internationale en haute mer pour protéger les populations de poissons qui chevauchent la zone de pêche de 200 milles du Canada. C'est ce que nous voulons, c'est ce que nous allons obtenir.

(House of Commons Debates, May 30, 2001, p. 4402)
(Débats de la Chambre des Communes, le 30 mai 2001, p. 4402)

(b) Fisheries / Les pêches

Mr. Larry Bagnell (Yukon):

Could the Minister of Fisheries and Oceans update the House ... on the progress of the bilateral discussions with the United States?

Hon. Herb Dhaliwal (Minister of Fisheries and Oceans):

[A]fter 16 years of negotiation the United States and Canada have reached an agreement on Yukon salmon ... Our agreement clearly states the catch sharing agreements, the conservation and the enhancement of Yukon salmon.

(House of Commons Debates, April 5, 2001, pp. 2862-63)
(Débats de la Chambre des Communes, le 5 avril 2001, pp. 2862-63)

6 *Reproductive Technologies / Les technologies de reproduction*

M. Réal Ménard (Hochelaga — Maisonneuve):

[E]st-ce que le gouvernement entend appuyer, auprès de la communauté internationale, la proposition de nombreux scientifiques voulant que le génome humain et son séquençage soient déclarés patrimoine de l'humanité?

L'hon. Gilbert Normand (secrétaire d'État (Sciences, Recherche et Développement)):

[L]a position du Canada au sujet de la propriété des gènes est la même que celle adoptée par MM. Clinton et Blair. Nous n'accepterons pas de propriété privée en ce sens, et la réglementation qui suivra à l'échelle internationale se fera conjointement avec tous les pays du G8.

(House of Commons Debates, February 13, 2001, p. 606)
(Débats de la Chambre des Communes, le 13 février 2001, p. 606)

Mᵐᵉ Pauline Picard (Drummond):

[H]ier, le ministre de la Santé a lancé l'idée, à Genève, de rédiger une convention internationale qui interdirait les techniques de reproduction et, notamment, le clonage humain. Comment le ministre peut-il prétendre se poser en leader mondial dans le domaine des techniques de reproduction, quand on sait qu'il a ... un avant-projet de loi qui va repousser d'une autre année toute décision à ce sujet?

Hon. Robert Nault (Minister of Indian Affairs and Northern Development):

[T]he Minister of Health said that because of the importance of cloning, not only to Canada but to the rest of the world, he would be working with his colleagues across the globe to prepare and look at developing a convention among governments prohibiting this practice, one which we support as a government and I am sure all members of the House support.

(House of Commons Debates, May 16, 2001, p. 4099)
(Débats de la Chambre des Communes, le 16 mai 2001, p. 4099)

7 *Trade / Le commerce*

Ms. Judy Wasylycia-Leis (Winnipeg North Centre):

Will the trade minister ... agree to act with urgency to protect Canada's health care system in all its trade deals?

Hon. Pierre Pettigrew (Minister for International Trade):

[L]et me reaffirm ... the firm commitment of our government in the past, today and tomorrow, never to open the door to force our public health or public education systems into a challenge at the international trade level. In all our trade agreements, whether at the GATS level or at the FTAA, Canada will protect the margin of manoeuvre of our government and our provincial governments in the health and education sectors.

(House of Commons Debates, March 20, 2001, p. 1913)
(Débats de la Chambre des Communes, le 20 mars 2001, p. 1913)

(a) Aerospace industry / L'industrie aérospaciale

Mr. Charlie Penson (Peace River):

In January the industry minister said the Government of Canada would offer subsidized credit to stop Brazil's Embraer from benefiting from unfair trade practices ... When will the Liberal government learn that Canadian interests lie in a rules based policy and not an accelerated trade war with Brazil?

Right Hon. Jean Chrétien (Prime Minister):

[I]n the case of Brazil it is not respecting the decision of the World Trade Organization. We have said to them that we want to follow trade practices that are acceptable and that they cannot steal jobs away from workers in all parts of Canada who are producing a very good airplane. They should not have their jobs stolen because another country does not respect the rules of this international organization.

(House of Commons Debates, May 28, 2001, p. 4271)
(Débats de la Chambre des Communes, le 28 mai 2001, p. 4271)

(b) Agriculture / L'agriculture

Mr. Rick Borotsik (Brandon — Souris):

[Y]esterday the Prime Minister said that his first order of business when discussing business with President Bush would be the unfair American agriculture subsidies.

Right Hon. Jean Chrétien (Prime Minister):

[Y]esterday I clearly said that it was the wish of the government and the House of Commons that I express to the president of the United States that a war on subsidies between countries on agriculture is counterproductive. I will tell him that very clearly ... we cannot compete and do not have the means to compete with the Americans and the Europeans in a war like that ... We have to convince them to do the right thing and make sure that there is a possibility for everyone to compete together on a fair basis.

(House of Commons Debates, February 1, 2001, p. 107)
(Débats de la Chambre des Communes, le 1er février 2001, p. 107)

M. Pierre Paquette (Joliette):

[L]e ministre a fait état d'un questionnaire, qui serait resté sans réponse des autorités brésiliennes, pour justifier son embargo sur le boeuf brésilien. Le ministre ... peut-il nous dire s'il a trouvé quelque chose d'anormal qui justifierait ses craintes et l'embargo qu'il a imposé sur le boeuf brésilien?

Hon. Lyle Vanclief (Minister of Agriculture and Agri-Food):

[T]his questionnaire was put together by the NAFTA partners, Canada, the United States and Mexico. In 1998 those three countries decided which countries they would send the questionnaire to and that when the results were received, they would jointly assess the information that came back. Brazil did not send its information back until a week ago last Friday and at that time it was not complete. Technicians are going there today to follow up on that information.

(House of Commons Debates, February 13, 2001, pp. 600-1)
(Débats de la Chambre des Communes, le 13 février 2001, pp. 600-1)

Mr. Rick Casson (Lethbridge):

The government is currently negotiating a trade deal with Costa Rica on sugar. Canada already has the most open sugar market in the world. Any change to the present rules will be disastrous to Canada's sugar cane refineries, sugar beet processors and sugar beet producers. Why is the government ... systematically destroying our agriculture industries one at a time by poorly placed trade policies?

Mr. Pat O'Brien (Parliamentary Secretary to the Minister for International Trade):

[B]y pursuing a free trade agreement with Costa Rica the only interest the government has is in improving the trade relations of all parts of the economy of Canada with the country of Costa Rica.

(House of Commons Debates, February 28, 2001, p. 1328)
(Débats de la Chambre des Communes, le 28 février 2001, p. 1328)

Mr. Howard Hilstrom (Selkirk — Interlake):

The trade minister continues to give supplemental import licences that allow more milk products into Canada than agreed upon during the trade negotiations ... Will the minister commit to ending this practice and guarantee that future milk imports will not exceed the agreed upon quota?

Hon. Pierre Pettigrew (Minister for International Trade):

[N]o, our government of course respects its international trade obligations. It respects the quotas it has agreed to. It might happen from time to time that a consumer locally needs a particular product and some exceptions are made around it. Obviously it is not our intention to make a habit or a rule to go beyond the quotas we have actually agreed upon.

(House of Commons Debates, May 29, 2001, pp. 4354-55)
(Débats de la Chambre des Communes, le 29 mai 2001, pp. 4354-55)

(c) Asbetos industry / L'industrie de l'amiante

M. Gérard Binet (Frontenac — Mégantic):

Avec la décision de l'organe d'appel de l'OMC, cette semaine, qui a donné raison à la France en déclarant l'interdiction de l'amiante chrysotile conforme aux accords commerciaux multilatéraux, quelles sont les conséquences de cette décision, à court et à long terme, pour le Canada sur les marchés internationaux?

L'hon. Pierre Pettigrew (ministre du Commerce international):

[N]ous sommes très déçus de la décision finale de l'Organisation mondiale du commerce, bien que notre appel ait servi à gagner des points très importants sur la jurisprudence pour les dossiers à venir. Nous croyons toujours que l'utilisation sécuritaire du chrysotile est une approche beaucoup plus appropriée que son interdiction totale. L'industrie de l'amiante doit maintenant poursuivre les démarches avec encore plus d'ardeur dans l'avenir afin de faire la promotion de l'utilisation sécuritaire du chrysotile chez d'autres partenaires, à l'étranger, et notre gouvernement sera auprès d'eux pour le faire.

(House of Commons Debates, March 15, 2001, p. 1723)
(Débats de la Chambre des Communes, le 15 mars 2001, p. 1723)

(d) Auto industry / L'industrie automobile

Mr. Bill Blaikie (Winnipeg — Transcona):

[T]he WTO has ruled against the auto pact and will be making further regulations as to how Canada can comply with that ruling ... What is the minister going to do to protect those jobs in the auto industry?

Hon. Pierre S. Pettigrew (Minister for International Trade):

[W]e are absolutely confident that the industry will continue on its very healthy progress of the last few years. As for the WTO decision, we had asked for ten and a half months to implement the decision. We were very pleased that we were given eight months. We will respect that international commitment to the WTO that protects Canadian interests around the world all the time because we need a rules based system.

(House of Commons Debates, October 4, 2000, p. 8858)
(Débats de la Chambre des Communes, le 4 octobre 2000, p. 8858)

(e) Drug patents / Les brevets pharmaceutiques

Mr. Deepak Obhrai (Calgary East):

[T]he WTO drug patent ruling is yet another example of the government wasting valuable time and money on a senseless dispute before the WTO ... the minister went ahead with an appeal that he knew would be lost ... Why?

Hon. Pierre S. Pettigrew (Minister for International Trade):

[W]e received the answer from the WTO panel and did not particularly like it. I am very relieved, however, that that particular decision will not force Canada to change substantially the overall balance of our present legislation.

(House of Commons Debates, September 20, 2000, p. 8412)
(Débats de la Chambre des Communes, le 20 septembre 2000, p. 8412)

(f) Chapter 11 of the NAFTA Agreement / Le chapitre 11 de l'ALENA

Mr. Bill Blaikie (Winnipeg — Transcona):

[T]he Canadian firm Methanex has launched a $1 billion lawsuit against the U.S. under chapter 11 of NAFTA ... The International Institute for Sustainable Development in Winnipeg has made a request to be involved in the hearing, along with other NGOs, so that their concerns can be made known. The panel has reserved judgment on this and has given Canada until next Friday to make its position known ... what is the position of the Canadian government on this?

Hon. Pierre S. Pettigrew (Minister for International Trade):

Our officials are in discussions with people at justice. We also have to see, along with the government of Mexico and the government of the United States, what sort of precedent it would create. I certainly commend the contribution IISD has been making on that file. We will advise the House on what our government will decide after consultations with our trade partners.

(House of Commons Debates, October 5, 2000, p. 8974)
(Débats de la Chambre des Communes, le 5 octobre 2000, p. 8974)

M. Yvan Loubier (Saint-Hyacinthe — Bagot):

Comment le premier ministre peut-il expliquer la contradiction entre sa déclaration sur le chapitre 11 et celle de son ministre du Commerce international, qui affirmait encore récemment qu'il ne signerait pas une ZLEA contenant un tel mécanisme?

L'hon. Pierre Pettigrew (ministre du Commerce international):

Ce que j'ai toujours dit, c'est que les protections des investissements étaient absolument nécessaires. Nous avons des investisseurs canadiens partout à travers le monde, partout à travers les Amériques, et ces investissements doivent être protégés. Ce que nous avons dit cependant, c'est que nous souhaitions clarifier, non pas rouvrir, non pas renégocier le chapitre 11 — nous l'avons signé — mais nous souhaitons clarifier certains aspects du chapitre 11, parce que nous croyons qu'il y a eu certaines interprétations ou qu'il y aurait certaines interprétations qui, manifestement, ne reflètent pas les intentions des trois pays signataires, au moment où nous l'avons signé.

(House of Commons Debates, April 23, 2001, pp. 2966-67)
(Débats de la Chambre des Communes, le 23 avril 2001, pp. 2966-67)

Ms. Alexa McDonough (Halifax):

The promise was to get rid of chapter 11 in NAFTA and not sign on to any other trade deals that repeat the same mistake ... Why has the government changed its position?

Right Hon. Jean Chrétien (Prime Minister):

[W]e have not changed our position. We have signed an agreement on chapter 11. We have explained that when there is $1.3 billion of trade on a daily basis in American dollars with the United States, the number of cases under chapter 11 is not extravagant. In most cases the government has won. We will always look at it and improve it if it is in the interest of all partners to do so, but chapter 11 has been there for the past seven years. At this moment there is no likelihood that it will be changed within the next few months.

(House of Commons Debates, April 24, 2001, pp. 3052-53)
(Débats de la Chambre des Communes, le 24 avril 2001, pp. 3052-53)

(g) Free Trade Area of the Americas / La zone de libre-échange des Amériques

M. Richard Marceau (Charlesbourg — Jacques-Cartier):

Le secrétaire parlementaire réalise-t-il que ni la population du Québec, ni le gouvernement du Québec n'a mandaté le gouvernement fédéral pour négocier, en son nom, quoi que ce soit dans les champs de compétence du Québec?

L'hon. Stéphane Dion (président du Conseil privé de la Reine pour le Canada et ministre des Affaires intergouvernementales):

D'après la Constitution canadienne, le gouvernement est mandaté pour négocier des traités. Mais dans les compétences exclusives des provinces, une province qui n'aime pas le traité, peut ne pas l'appliquer.

(House of Commons Debates, March 1, 2001, pp. 1402-3)
(Débats de la Chambre des Communes, le 1ᵉʳ mars 2001, pp. 1402-3)

Mme Francine Lalonde (Mercier):

[L]orsque nous avons questionné le gouvernement sur le respect des droits humains et la démocratie en Chine, le premier ministre a répondu en disant que le gouvernement pensait que c'est en intensifiant les liens avec ce pays que nous pourrons le mieux promouvoir ces valeurs auprès du gouvernement chinois. Comment le gouvernement peut-il justifier que dans le cas de Cuba, il adopte une position opposée et qu'il refuse la présence de ce pays au Sommet des Amériques?

L'hon. Pierre Pettigrew (ministre du Commerce international):

Sur le plan bilatéral, nous sommes engagés à l'endroit de la Chine et nous sommes engagés également à l'endroit de Cuba. La différence, c'est que, lorsque nous créons un Sommet des Amériques pour promouvoir la démocratie, et que c'est ce Sommet qui crée une Zone de libre-échange des Amériques pour consolider la démocratie, il s'agit là d'une relation beaucoup plus étroite et nous sommes parfaitement justifiés, comme hôte du Sommet, d'agir comme nous le faisons à l'heure actuelle.

(House of Commons Debates, March 19, 2001, pp.1830-31)
(Débats de la Chambre des Communes, le 19 mars 2001, pp. 1830-31)

(h) Lumber industry/ Le bois d'œuvre

Mme Francine Lalonde (Mercier, BQ):

Le premier ministre peut-il nous confirmer que la position qu'il a défendue sur la question du bois d'oeuvre devant le président américain, c'est le retour intégral au libre-échange?

Le très hon. Jean Chrétien (premier ministre):

[C]'est la position que le gouvernement a toujours préconisée. Cependant, il faut également tenir compte, dans cette discussion, du fait que les Américains ont une certaine part de responsabilité.

Mme Francine Lalonde (Mercier):

[E]st-ce que le premier ministre ... a obtenu la garantie du président américain que les États-Unis n'imposeront pas de droits compensateurs aux exportations québécoises de bois d'oeuvre, comme cela s'est fait auparavant?

Le très hon. Jean Chrétien (premier ministre):

[J]e n'ai reçu aucune indication en ce sens. Nous avons entrepris un dialogue avec eux et nous espérons trouver une solution d'ici le 31 mars de cette année. Mais nous, nous savons très bien qu'en vertu de l'Accord de libre-échange, le gouvernement canadien ne donne absolument aucun subside à aucun producteur de bois et que les produits canadiens peuvent entrer sans frais, suivant l'Accord de libre-échange, dans toutes les parties des États-Unis.

(House of Commons Debates, February 6, 2001, p. 306)
(Débats de la Chambre des Communes, le 6 février 2001, p. 306)

M. Pierre Paquette (Joliette):

Alors qu'on est à trois semaines de la fin de l'accord, comment le gouvernement entend-il éviter une guerre commerciale avec les Américains dans le dossier du bois d'oeuvre?

L'hon. Pierre Pettigrew (ministre du Commerce international):

Puisque nous n'aurons plus d'accord ... cela veut dire que nous allons avoir, du côté des États-Unis, la possibilité de recourir à leurs lois nationales et aux panels de libre-échange.

(House of Commons Debates, March 12, 2001, p. 1520)
(Débats de la Chambre des Communes, le 12 mars 2001, p. 1520)

Mr. Gary Lunn (Saanich — Gulf Islands):

[I]n 11 days the softwood lumber agreement will expire ... Will the minister agree that going back to court for four more years is not the answer while Canadians lose their jobs?

Hon. Pierre Pettigrew (Minister for International Trade):

Moving toward free trade means that every country can have some recourse to its legal tools that we have in the kit ... Canada has initiated a WTO challenge against the United States legislation regarding export restraints of Canadian logs.

(House of Commons Debates, March 20, 2001, pp. 1912-13)
(Débats de la Chambre des Communes, le 20 mars 2001, pp. 1912-13)

(i) Water / L'eau

Mr. Loyola Hearn (St. John's West):

[T]he premier of Newfoundland has reintroduced the bulk export of water issue ... how does the government plan to ... protect our valuable water resource?

Mr. Denis Paradis (Parliamentary Secretary to the Minister of Foreign Affairs):

The Canadian government has full sovereignty over the management of water when it is in its natural state. What is important is that the NAFTA parties confirmed in 1993 that water in its natural state was not a good. We strongly urge Newfoundland to stand by its original decision and actions to prohibit bulk water removal. Everyone needs to be on board to protect this environmental resource.

(House of Commons Debates, March 30, 2001, pp. 1914-15)
(Débats de la Chambre des Communes, le 30 mars 2001, pp. 1914-15)

Ms. Cheryl Gallant (Renfrew — Nipissing — Pembroke):

Bill C-6 provides that the minister can license federally the sale of bulk water exports. Canadians are concerned about bulk water sales. Why is the government intent on ignoring our abundant water heritage and sponsoring legislation that will allow bulk water exports?

Hon. John Manley (Minister of Foreign Affairs):

Bill C-6 creates a legal regime that will prevent the removal of bulk water from the drainage systems in Canada, thereby prohibiting the exportation of water in bulk, which we view is not a good that can be subject to exportation. It is not permitted under Bill C-6.

(House of Commons Debates, May 15 2001, p. 4075)
(Débats de la Chambre des Communes, le 15 mai 2001, p. 4075)

(j) Wine industry / L'industrie du vin

Mr. Tony Tirabassi (Niagara Centre):

Would the Minister of Agriculture and Agri-Food explain to the House when Canadian ice wines will be granted access to the very important European market?

Hon. Lyle Vanclief (Minister of Agriculture and Agri-Food):

[Y]esterday the European Union adapted the regulations which will allow our very fine wine, the best ice wine in the world, to now go into the European market. This is another step forward in the wine and spirit industry around the world, and we will now open that market for ice wine in the European Union.

(House of Commons Debates, April 26, 2001, p. 3216)
(Débats de la Chambre des Communes, le 26 avril 2001, p. 3216)

Treaty Action Taken by Canada in 2000 / Mesures prises par le Canada en matière de traités en 2000

compiled by / préparé par
ANDRÉ BERGERON

I BILATERAL

Algeria
Convention between the Government of Canada and the Government of the People's Democratic Republic of Algeria for the Avoidance of Double Taxation and the Prevention of Fiscal Evasion with respect to Taxes on Income (with Protocol). Algiers, February 28, 1999. *Entered into force* December 26, 2000, *with effect from* January 1, 2001. CTS 2000/29.

Argentina
Treaty between the Government of Canada and the Government of the Argentine Republic on Mutual Assistance in Criminal Matters. Buenos Aires, January 12, 2000.

Agreement between the Government of Canada and the Government of the Argentine Republic Concerning the Provision of Satellite Facilities and the Transmission and Reception of Signals to and from Satellites for the Provision of Satellite Services to Users in Canada and the Argentine Republic (with Protocol). Buenos Aires, October 17, 2000. *Entered into force* October 17, 2000. CTS 2000/27.

Austria
Treaty on Extradition between the Government of Canada and the Government of the Republic of Austria. Ottawa, October 5, 1998. *Entered into force* October 1, 2000. CTS 2000/15.

Belgium
Exchange of Notes amending the Agreement between the Government of Canada and the Government of Belgium on Air Transport, done at Brussels on May 13, 1986. Brussels, May 23, 2000.

Chile
First Additional Protocol to the Free Trade Agreement between the Government of Canada and the Government of the Republic of Chile, done in Santiago on December 4, 1996 (with Annex). Toronto, November 4, 1999. Entered into force January 1, 2000. CTS 2000/2.

Czech Republic
Treaty between Canada and the Czech Republic on Mutual Assistance in Criminal Matters. Ottawa, November 3, 1997. *Entered into force* November 1, 2000. CTS 2000/19.

André Bergeron, Treaty Registrar, Legal Advisory Division, Department of Foreign Affairs / Greffier des Traités, Direction des consultations juridiques, Ministère des Affaires étrangères.

European Community
Agreement between the Government of Canada and the European Community Renewing the Cooperation Programme in Higher Education and Training (with Annex). Ottawa, December 19, 2000.

European Space Agency
Cooperation Agreement between the Government of Canada and the European Space Agency. Paris, June 21, 2000. *Entered into force* June 21, 2000, *with effect from* January 1, 2000. CTS 2000/13

France
Exchange of Notes between the Government of Canada and the Government of the Republic of France constituting an Agreement modifying: the Agreement concerning Cinematographic Relations done in Ottawa, on May 30, 1983, as amended by Exchanges of Notes done in Ottawa, on February 8, 1989, and on April 11, 1991, and September 8, 1992; the Agreement concerning the Promotion of Film and Video Co-production Projects in the Field of Animation, done in Paris on January 10, 1985, as amended by an Exchange of Notes done in Ottawa, April 11, 1991, and September 8, 1992; the Agreement on Television Relations, done in Paris, on July 11, 1983, as amended by Exchanges of Notes done in Ottawa, on February 8, 1989, and on April 11, 1991, and September 8, 1992; and the Agreement regarding the development of French language audiovisual co-production projects for television, done in Ottawa, on March 14, 1990. Ottawa, January 21 and March 22, 2000. *Entered into* force March 22, 2000. CTS 2000/7.

Greece
Audio-visual Co-production Agreement between the Government of Canada and the Government of the Hellenic Republic. Athens, December 15, 1997. *Entered into force* February 3, 2000. CTS 2000/4.

Treaty between the Government of Canada and the Government of the Hellenic Republic on Mutual Legal Assistance in Criminal Matters. Athens, July 14, 1998. *Entered into force* January 28, 2000. CTS 2000/3.

Jordan
Convention between the Government of Canada and the Hashemite Kingdom of Jordan for the Avoidance of Double Taxation and the Prevention of Fiscal Evasion with Respect to Taxes on Income (with Protocol). Amman, September 6, 1999. *Entered into force* December 24, 2000, with effect from January 1, 2001. CTS 2000/33.

Kyrgyzstan
Convention between the Government of Canada and the Government of the Kyrgyzstan Republic for the Avoidance of Double Taxation and the Prevention of Fiscal Evasion with Respect to Taxes on Income and on Capital (with Protocol). Ottawa, June 4, 1998. *Entered into force* December 4, 2000. CTS 2000/36.

Lebanon
Air Transport Agreement between the Government of Canada and the Government of the Lebanese Republic. Beirut, May 18, 2000. *Applied provisionally* from May 18, 2000.

Agreement regarding Cooperation on Consular Matters of a Humanitarian Nature between the Government of Canada and the Government of the Lebanese Republic. Beirut, April 13, 2000.

Luxembourg
Convention between the Government of Canada and the Government of the Grand Duchy of Luxembourg for the Avoidance of Double Taxation and the Prevention of Fiscal Evasion with respect to Taxes on Income and on Capital. Brussels, September 10, 1999. *Entered into force* October 17, 2000, *with effect from* January 1, 2001. *Note:* This terminates the January 17, 1989 Agreement. CTS 2000.

Convention between the Government of Canada and the Government of the Grand Duchy of Luxembourg for the Avoidance of Double Taxation and the Prevention of Fiscal Evasion with respect to Taxes on Income and on Capital. Luxembourg, January 17, 1989. *Entered into force* July 8, 1991. CTS 1991/21. *Terminated* January 1, 2001.

Mexico
Exchange of Notes amending the Air Transport Agreement between the Government of Canada and the Government of the United Mexican States, done at Mexico on December 21, 1961. Mexico, April 9, 1999. *Entered into force* September 22, 2000. CTS 2000/20.

Agreement between the Government of Canada and the Government of the United Mexican States Concerning the Provision of Satellite Services. Mexico, April 9, 1999. *Entered into force* November 21, 2000. CTS 2000/35.

Peru
Treaty between the Government of Canada and the Government of the Republic of Peru on Mutual Legal Assistance in Criminal Matters. Ottawa, October 27, 1998. *Entered into force* January 25, 2000. CTS 2000/5.

Portugal
Treaty between Canada and the Republic of Portugal on Mutual Legal Assistance in Criminal Matters. Lisbon, June 24, 1997. *Entered into force* May 1, 2000. CTS 2000/8.

Russia
Air Services Agreement between the Government of Canada and the Government of the Russian Federation. Ottawa, December 18, 2000.

Agreement between the Government of Canada and the Government of the Russian Federation on the principles and basis for cooperation between the Provinces and Territories of Canada and the Subjects of the Russian Federation. Ottawa, December 18, 2000. *Entered into force* December 18, 2000. CTS 2000/25.

Treaty between Canada and the Russian Federation on Mutual Legal Assistance in Criminal Matters. Moscow, October 20, 1997. *Entered into force* December 18, 2000. CTS 2000/24.

Senegal
Audio-visual Co-production Agreement between the Government of Canada and the Government of the Republic of Senegal. Santorini, September 27, 2000.

Slovenia
Convention between the Government of Canada and the Government of the Republic of Slovenia for the Avoidance of Double Taxation and the Prevention of Fiscal Evasion with respect to Taxes on Income. Ljubljana, September 15, 2000.

Sweden
Treaty on Extradition between the Government of Canada and the Government of Sweden. Stockholm, February 15, 2000.

Treaty between the Government of Canada and the Government of Sweden on Mutual Assistance in Criminal Matters. Stockholm, February 15, 2000.

Thailand
Exchange of Notes amending the Air Transport Agreement between the Government of Canada and the Government of the Kingdom of Thailand, done at Bangkok on May 24, 1989. Bangkok, May 28 1999 and April 11, 2000. *Entered into force* April 11, 2000. CTS 2000/17.

United States of America
Agreement between the Government of Canada and the Government of the United States of America for the Promotion of Aviation Safety. Toronto, June 12, 2000. *Entered into force* June 12, 2000. CTS 2000/10.

Exchange of Notes amending the Air Transport Agreement between the Government of Canada and the Government of the United States of America, done at Ottawa on February 24, 1995. Ottawa, January 20, 2000 and Toronto, June 12, 2000. *Entered into force* June 12, 2000. CTS 2000/12.

Exchange of Letters amending the Softwood Lumber Agreement between the Government of Canada and the Government of the United States of America, done at Washington May 29, 1996. Washington, October 24, 2000. *Entered into force* October 24, 2000. CTS 2000/30.

Exchange of Notes constituting an Agreement Extending the Agreement between the Government of Canada and the Government of the United States of America on the Organization and Operation of the North American Aerospace Defence Command (NORAD), done at Washington on 12 May 1958, as amended. Washington, June 16, 2000. *Entered into force* June 16, 2000, *with effect* from May 12, 2001. CTS 2001/11.

Protocol between the Government of Canada and the Government of the United States of America amending the Agreement between the Government of Canada and the Government of the United States of America on Air Quality, done at Ottawa on March 13, 1991. Washington, December 7, 2000. *Entered into force* December 7, 2000. CTS 2000/26.

Exchange of Notes between the Government of Canada and the Government of the United States of America constituting an Agreement amending their Agreement for Water Supply and Flood Control in the Souris River Basin, signed at Washington on October 26, 1989. Ottawa, December 20 and 22, 2000. *Entered into force* December 22, 2000. CTS 2000/28.

Exchange of Notes between the Government of Canada and the Government of the United States of America constituting an Agreement extending the Agreement between the Government of Canada and the Government

of the United States of America Providing for Coordination of the Icebreaking Activities of Canada and the United States on the Great Lakes, done at Ottawa on December 5, 1980, as amended. Washington, December 4 and 5, 2000. *Entered into force* December 5, 2000. CTS 2000/32.

Agreement between the Government of Canada and the Government of the United States of America concerning the Operation of Commercial Remote Sensing Satellite Systems. Washington, June 16, 2000. *Entered into force* June 16, 2000. CTS 2000/14.

Protocol Amending the Agreement for Cooperation in the Boreal Ecosystem Atmosphere Study (BOREAS) between the Government of Canada and the Government of the United States of America, done at Washington, D.C., on April 18, 1994. Washington, November 30, 1999. *Entered into force* November 30, 1999. CTS 1999/47. *Terminated* November 2, 2000.

Uzbekistan

Convention between the Government of Canada and the Government of the Republic of Uzbekistan for the Avoidance of Double Taxation and the Prevention of Fiscal Evasion with respect to Taxes on Income (with Protocol). Ottawa, June 17, 1999. *Entered into force* September 14, 2000. CTS 2000/18.

II   MULTILATERAL

Agriculture

International Agreement for Creating a New International Potato Centre. Lima, November 26, 1999. *Entered into force* November 26, 1999. *Signed* by Canada December 16, 1999. *Entered into force* for Canada January 1, 2000. CTS 2000/40.

Atomic Energy

Acceptance of the Amendments to Article VI and Article XIV of the Statute of the International Atomic Energy Agency. Vienna, October 1, 1999. *Accepted* by Canada September 15, 2000.

Business Ethics (OECD Guidelines)
Decision of the Council of the Organization for Economic Cooperation and Development on the Guidelines for Multinational Enterprises. Paris, June 27, 2000. *Entered into force* June 27, 2000. *Entered into force* for Canada June 27, 2000. CTS 2000/16.

Conformity Assessment
Mutual Recognition Agreement on Conformity Assessment between the Government of Canada and the Governments of the Republic of Iceland, the Principality of Liechtenstein and the Kingdom of Norway. Brussels, July 4, 2000. *Signed* by Canada, July 4, 2000. *Ratified* by Canada November 23, 2000.

Corruption
Inter-American Convention against Corruption. Caracas, March 29, 1996. *Entered into force* March 6, 1997. *Signed* by Canada on June 8, 1999. *Ratified* by Canada June 6, 2000 (with a Statement of Understanding). *Entered into force* for Canada July 6, 2000.

Customs
Accession to the Protocol of Amendment to the International Convention on the Simplification and Harmonization of Customs Procedures, done at Kyoto on 18 May 1973. Brussels, June 26, 1999. *Accession* by Canada November 9, 2000.

Environment
1996 Protocol to the Convention on the Prevention of Marine Pollution by Dumping of Wastes and Other Matter, 1972. London, November 7, 1996. *Accession* by Canada April 15, 2000.

Adjustments to the Montreal Protocol on Substances that Deplete the Ozone Layer, done at Beijing 3 December 1999. *Entered into force* July 28, 2000. *Entered into force* for Canada July 28, 2000. CTS 2000/37.

Human Rights
Acceptance of the Amendment to Article 43, paragraph 2, of the Convention on the Rights of the Child, adopted at the Conference of the States Parties on December 12, 1995, and approved by the United Nations General Assembly on December 21, 1995 (Convention adopted by the United Nations General Assembly on November 20, 1989. It entered into force on September 2, 1990. Convention signed by Canada on May 28, 1990 and ratified on December 13, 1991). New York, December 21, 1995. *Acceptance* by Canada September 17, 1997. *Entered into force* June 28, 2000. *Entered into force* for Canada June 28, 2000.

Optional Protocol to the Convention on the Rights of the Child on Involvement of Children in Armed Conflicts (with Declaration). New York, 25 May 2000. *Signed* by Canada June 5, 2000. *Ratified* by Canada July 7, 2000.

Intellectual Property
Acceptance of the Amendment to Article 9 (3) of the Convention Establishing the World Intellectual Property Organization, done at Stockholm on July 14, 1967, as amended on September 28, 1979, with Declaration. Geneva, September 24, 1999. *Accepted* by Canada August 11, 2000.

International Criminal Law
Rome Statute of the International Criminal Court, 1998. Rome, July 17, 1998. *Signed* by Canada December 18, 1998. *Ratified* by Canada July 7, 2000.

Labour
Ratification of the International Labour Organization Convention Concerning the Prohibition and Immediate Action for the Elimination of the Worst Forms of Child Labour. Geneva, June 17, 1999. *Ratified* by Canada June 6, 2000.

Outer Space
Agreement among the Government of Canada, Governments of Member States of the European Space Agency, the Government of Japan, the Government of the Russian Federation, and the Government of the United States of America Concerning Cooperation on the Civil International Space Station.

Washington, D.C., January 29, 1998. *Signed* by Canada January 29, 1998. *Ratified* by Canada July 24, 2000. *Note:* This Agreement, on entry into force, will terminate the 1988 Agreement.

Telecommunications
Final Acts of the Conference of the International Telecommunication Union, Minneapolis (1998). Minneapolis, November 6, 1998. *Signed* by Canada November 6, 1998. *Ratified* by Canada February 8, 2000.

Final Acts of the World Radiocommunication Conference of the International Telecommunication Union, Istanbul (WRC-2000). Istanbul, June 2, 2000. *Signed* by Canada June 2, 2000. *Ratified* by Canada October 9, 2000.

Terrorism
International Convention for the Suppression of the Financing of Terrorism. New York, December 9, 1999. *Signed* by Canada February 10, 2000.

Trade — NAFTA
Exchange of Letters between the Government of Canada, the Government of the United States of America and the Government of the United Mexican States rectifying Annex 401 and Annex 403.1 of the Free Trade Agreement between the Government of Canada, the Government of the United States of America and the Government of the United Mexican States, done at Ottawa on 4 December and 17 December 1992, at Mexico, D.F. on 14 December and 17 December 1992 and at Washington, D.C. on 8 December and 17 December 1992. *Signed* in Mexico on February 3, 2000, in Ottawa on February 18, 2000 and in Washington on February 22, 2000. *Entered into force* March 1, 2000. *Entered into force* for Canada March 1, 2000. CTS 2000/38.

Exchange of Letters constituting an Agreement amending the tariff schedules to Annex 302.2 of the North American Free Trade Agreement between the Government of Canada, the Government of the United Mexican States

and the Government of the United States of America (with Annex). *Signed* in Mexico on December 20, 2000 and in Ottawa on December 28, 2000.

Transport
Agreement Concerning the Establishing of Global Technical Regulations for Wheeled Vehicles, Equipment and Parts which can be Fitted and/or be Used on Wheeled Vehicles, done at Geneva on June 25, 1998. *Signed* by Canada June 22, 1999 without reservation as to ratification, acceptance or approval. *Entered into force* August 25, 2000. *Entered into force* for Canada August 25, 2000. CTS 2000/34.

I   BILATÉRAUX

Agence Spatiale Européenne
Accord de coopération entre le Gouvernement du Canada et l'Agence spatiale européenne. Paris, le 21 juin 2000. *En vigueur* le 21 juin 2000, *avec effet* à compter du 1er janvier 2000. RTC 2000/13.

Algérie
Convention entre le Gouvernement du Canada et le Gouvernement de la République algérienne démocratique et populaire en vue d'éviter les doubles impositions et de prévenir l'évasion fiscale en matière d'impôts sur le revenu (avec Protocole). Alger, le 28 février 1999. *En vigueur* le 26 décembre 2000, *avec effet* à compter du 1er janvier 2001. RTC 2000/29.

Argentine
Traité d'entraide judiciaire en matière pénale entre le Gouvernement du Canada et le Gouvernement de la République argentine. Buenos Aires, le 12 janvier 2000.

Accord entre le Gouvernement du Canada et le Gouvernement de la République argentine concernant la fourniture d'installations de satellite de même que la transmission et la réception de signaux à destination et en provenance de satellites pour la fourniture de services par satellite aux utilisateurs du Canada et de la République argentine (avec Protocole). Buenos Aires, le 17 octobre 2000. *En vigueur* le 17 octobre 2000. RTC 2000/27.

Autriche
Traité d'extradition entre le Gouvernement du Canada et le Gouvernement de la République d'Autriche. Ottawa, le 5 octobre 1998. *En vigueur* le 1er octobre 2000. RTC 2000/15.

Belgique
Échange de Notes modifiant l'Accord sur le transport aérien entre le Gouvernement du Canada et le Gouvernement de la Belgique, fait à Bruxelles le 13 mai 1986. Bruxelles, le 23 mai 2000.

Chili
Premier protocole supplémentaire de l'Accord de libre échange entre le Gouvernement du Canada et le Gouvernement de la République du Chili, fait à Santiago le 4 décembre 1996 (avec Annexe). Toronto, le 4 novembre 1999. *En vigueur* le 1er janvier 2000. RTC 2000/2.

Communauté Européenne
Accord entre le Gouvernement du Canada et la Communauté européenne renouvelant le Programme de coopération dans le domaine de l'enseignement supérieur et de la formation. Ottawa, le 19 décembre 2000.

États-Unis d'Amérique
Accord entre le Gouvernement du Canada et le Gouvernement des États-Unis d'Amérique concernant la promotion de la sécurité aérienne. Toronto, le 12 juin 2000. *En vigueur* le 12 juin 2000. RTC 2000/10.

Échange de Notes modifiant l'Accord relatif aux transports aériens entre le Gouvernement du Canada et le Gouvernement des États-Unis d'Amérique, fait à Ottawa le 24 février 1995. Ottawa, le 20 janvier 2000 et Toronto, le 12 juin 2000. *En vigueur* le 12 juin 2000. RTC 2000/12.

Échange de Lettres entre le Gouvernement du Canada et le Gouvernement des États-Unis d'Amérique modifiant l'Accord sur le bois d'oeuvre résineux, fait à Washington le 29 mai 1996. Washington, le 24 octobre 2000. *En vigueur* le 24 octobre 2000. RTC 2000/30.

Échange de Notes constituant un Accord prolongeant l'Accord entre le Gouvernement du Canada et le Gouvernement des États-Unis d'Amérique concernant l'organisation et le fonctionnement du Commandement de la défense aérospatiale de l'Amérique du Nord (NORAD), fait à Washington le 12 mai 1958, tel que modifié. Washington, le 16 juin 2000. *En vigueur* le 16 juin 2000 *avec effet* à compter du 12 mai 2001. RTC 2000/11.

Protocole entre le Gouvernement du Canada et le Gouvernement des États-Unis d'Amérique modifiant l'Accord entre le Gouvernement du Canada et le Gouvernement des États-Unis d'Amérique sur la qualité de l'air, fait à Ottawa le 13 mars 1991. Washington, le 7 décembre 2000. *En vigueur* le 7 décembre 2000. RTC 2000/26.

Échange de Notes entre le gouvernement du Canada et le gouvernement des États-Unis d'Amérique constituant un Accord modifiant leur Accord sur l'approvisionnement en eau et la protection contre les crues dans le bassin de la rivière Souris, signé à Washington le 26 octobre 1989. Ottawa, le 20 et le 22 décembre 2000. *En vigueur* le 22 décembre 2000. RTC 2000/28.

Accord entre le Gouvernement du Canada et le Gouvernement des États-Unis d'Amérique concernant l'exploitation de systèmes commerciaux de télédétection par satellite. Washington, le 16 juin 2000. *En vigueur* le 16 juin 2000. RTC 2000/14.

Échange de Notes entre le Gouvernement du Canada et le Gouvernement des États-Unis d'Amérique constituant un Accord prolongeant l'Accord entre le Gouvernement du Canada et le

Gouvernement des États-Unis d'Amérique prévoyant la coordination des activités canado-américaines de brisage des glaces dans les Grands Lacs, fait à Ottawa le 5 décembre 1980, tel que modifié. Washington, le 4 et 5 décembre 2000. *En vigueur* le 5 décembre 2000. RTC 2000/32.

Protocole modifiant l'Accord entre le Gouvernement du Canada et le Gouvernement des États-Unis d'Amérique concernant la coopération dans le cadre de l'étude de l'atmosphère et des écosystèmes boréaux (BOREAS), fait à Washington, D.C., le 18 avril 1994. Washington, le 30 novembre 1999. *En vigueur* le 30 novembre 1999. RTC 1999/47. *Résilié* le 2 novembre 2000.

France
Échange de Notes entre le Gouvernement du Canada et le Gouvernement de la République française constituant un Accord modifiant: l'Accord sur les relations cinématographiques fait à Ottawa, le 30 mai 1983, tel que modifié par des Échanges de Notes faits à Ottawa, le 8 février 1989, et le 11 avril 1991 et le 8 septembre 1992; l'Accord relatif à la promotion de projets de coproduction cinématographique ou audio-visuelle dans le domaine de l'animation, fait à Paris, le 10 janvier 1985, tel que modifié par un Échange de Notes fait à Ottawa, le 11 avril 1991 et le 8 septembre 1992; l'Accord sur les relations dans le domaine de la télévision, fait à Paris, le 11 juillet 1983, tel que modifié par des Échanges de Notes faits à Ottawa, le 8 février 1989, et le 11 avril 1991 et le 8 septembre 1992; et l'Accord relatif au développement de projets de coproduction audiovisuelle télévisée de langue française, fait à Ottawa, le 14 mars 1990. Ottawa, le 21 janvier et le 22 mars 2000. *En vigueur* le 22 mars 2000. RTC 2000/7.

Grèce
Accord de coproduction audiovisuelle entre le Gouvernement du Canada et le Gouvernement de la République hellénique. Athènes, le 15 décembre 1997. *En vigueur* le 3 février 2000. RTC 2000/4.

Traité d'entraide judiciaire en matière pénale entre le Gouvernement du Canada et le Gouvernement de la République hellénique. Athènes, le 14 juillet 1998. *En vigueur* le 28 janvier 2000. RTC 2000/3.

Jordanie
Convention entre le Gouvernement du Canada et le Royaume hachémite de Jordanie en vue d'éviter les doubles impositions et de prévenir l'évasion fiscale en matière d'impôts sur le revenu (avec Protocole). Amman, le 6 septembre 1999. *En vigueur* le 24 décembre 2000, *avec effet* à compter du 1ᵉʳ janvier 2001. RTC 2000/33.

Kirghizistan
Convention entre le Gouvernement du Canada et le Gouvernement de la République kirghize en vue d'éviter les doubles impositions et de prévenir la fraude fiscale en matière d'impôts sur le revenu et sur la fortune (avec Protocole). Ottawa, le 4 juin 1998. *En vigueur* le 4 décembre 2000. RTC 2000/36.

Liban
Accord relatif aux transports aériens entre le Gouvernement du Canada et le Gouvernement de la République libanaise. Beyrouth, le 18 mai 2000. *Appliqué provisoirement* à compter du 18 mai 2000.

Accord concernant la coopération en certaines matières consulaires à caractère humanitaire entre le Gouvernement du Canada et le Gouvernement de la République libanaise. Beyrouth, le 13 avril, 2000.

Luxembourg
Convention entre le Gouvernement du Canada et le Gouvernement du Grand-Duché de Luxembourg en vue d'éviter les doubles impositions et de prévenir la fraude fiscale en matière d'impôts sur le revenu et sur la fortune. Bruxelles, le 10 septembre 1999. *En*

vigueur le 17 octobre 2000, *avec effet* à compter du 1ᵉʳ janvier 2001. L'Accord du 17 janvier 1989 est résilié. RTC 2000/22.

Convention entre le Gouvernement du Canada et le Gouvernement du Grand-Duché de Luxembourg en vue d'éviter les doubles impositions et de prévenir l'évasion fiscale en matière d'impôts sur le revenu et sur la fortune. Luxembourg, le 17 janvier 1989. *En vigueur* le 8 juillet 1991. RTC 1991/21. *Résiliée* le 1ᵉʳ janvier 2001.

Mexique
Accord entre le Gouvernement du Canada et le Gouvernement des États-Unis du Mexique concernant la fourniture de services par satellite. Mexico, le 9 avril 1999. *En vigueur* le 21 novembre 2000. RTC 2000/35.

Échange de Notes modifiant l'Accord relatif aux transports aériens entre le Gouvernement du Canada et le Gouvernement des États-Unis du Mexique, fait à Mexico le 21 décembre 1961. Mexico, le 9 avril 1999. *En vigueur* le 22 septembre 2000. RTC 2000/20.

Ouzbékistan
Convention entre le Gouvernement du Canada et le Gouvernement de la République d'Ouzbékistan en vue d'éviter les doubles impositions et de prévenir l'évasion fiscale en matière d'impôts sur le revenu (avec Protocole). Ottawa, le 17 juin 1999. *En vigueur* le 14 septembre 2000. RTC 2000/18.

Pérou
Traité d'entraide judiciaire en matière pénale entre le Gouvernement du Canada et le Gouvernement de la République du Pérou. Ottawa, le 27 octobre 1998. *En vigueur* le 25 janvier 2000. RTC 2000/5.

Portugal
Traité d'entraide judiciaire en matière pénale entre le Canada et la République portugaise. Lisbonne, le 24 juin 1997. *En vigueur* le 1ᵉʳ mai 2000. RTC 2000/8.

Russie
Accord relatif aux services aériens entre le Gouvernement du Canada et le Gouvernement de la Fédération de la Russie. Ottawa, le 18 décembre 2000.

Accord entre le Gouvernement du Canada et le Gouvernement de la Fédération de la Russie concernant les principes et la base de la coopération entre les Provinces et Territoires du Canada et les Membres de la Fédération de la Russie. Ottawa, le 18 décembre 2000. *En vigueur* le 18 décembre 2000. RTC 2000/25.

Traité d'entraide judiciaire en matière pénale entre le Canada et la Fédération de Russie. Moscou, le 20 octobre 1997. *En vigueur* le 18 décembre 2000. RTC 2000/24.

Sénégal
Accord de coproduction audiovisuelle entre le Gouvernement du Canada et le Gouvernement de la République du Sénégal. Santorin, le 27 septembre 2000.

Slovénie
Convention entre le Gouvernement du Canada et le Gouvernement de la République de Slovénie en vue d'éviter les doubles impositions et de prévenir l'évasion fiscale en matière d'impôts sur le revenu. Ljubljana, le 15 septembre 2000.

Suède
Traité d'entraide judiciaire en matière pénale entre le Gouvernement du Canada et le Gouvernement de la Suède. Stockholm, le 15 février 2000.

Traité d'extradition entre le Gouvernement du Canada et le Gouvernement de la Suède. Stockholm, le 15 février 2000.

Tchèque (République)
Traité d'entraide judiciaire en matière pénale entre le Canada et la République Tchèque. Ottawa, le 3 novembre 1997. *En vigueur* le 1ᵉʳ novembre 2000. RTC 2000/19.

Thaïlande
Échange de Notes modifiant l'Accord sur les services aériens entre le Gouvernement du Canada et le Gouvernement du Royaume de Thaïlande, fait à Bangkok le 24 mai 1989. Bangkok, le 28 mai 1999 et le 11 avril 2000. *En vigueur* le 11 avril 2000. RTC 2000/17.

II MULTILATÉRAUX

Agriculture
Accord international portant création d'un nouveau Centre international de la pomme de terre. Lima, le 26 novembre 1999. *En vigueur* le 26 novembre 1999. *Signé* par le Canada le 16 décembre 1999. *En vigueur* pour le Canada le 1er janvier 2000. RTC 2000/40.

Commerce —ALÉNA
Échange de Lettres entre le Gouvernement du Canada, le Gouvernement des États-Unis d'Amérique et le Gouvernement des États-Unis du Mexique rectifiant l'Annexe 401 et l'Annexe 403.1 de l'Accord de libre-échange entre le Gouvernement du Canada, le Gouvernement des États-Unis d'Amérique et le Gouvernement des États-Unis du Mexique, fait à Ottawa les 4 décembre et 17 décembre 1992, à Mexico, D.F. les 14 décembre et 17 décembre 1992 et à Washington, D.C., les 8 décembre et 17 décembre 1992. *Signé* à Mexico le 3 février 2000, à Ottawa le 18 février 2000 et à Washington le 22 février 2000. *En vigueur* le 1er mars 2000. *En vigueur* pour le Canada le 1er mars 2000. RTC 2000/38.

Échange de Lettres constituant un Accord modifiant les listes tarifaires de l'Annexe 302.2 de l'Accord de libre-échange nord-américain entre le Gouvernement du Canada, le Gouvernement des États-Unis du Mexique et le Gouvernement des États-Unis d'Amérique (avec Annexe). *Signé* à Mexico le 20 décembre 2000 et à Ottawa le 28 décembre 2000.

Corruption
Convention interaméricaine contre la corruption. Caracas, le 29 mars 1996. *En vigueur* le 6 mars 1997. *Signée* par le Canada le 8 juin 1999. *Ratifiée* par le Canada le 6 juin 2000 (avec un Énoncé d'interprétation). *En vigueur* pour le Canada le 6 juillet 2000.

Douanes
Adhésion au Protocole d'amendement à la Convention internationale pour la simplification et l'harmonisation des régimes douaniers, fait à Kyoto le 18 mai 1973. Bruxelles, le 26 juin 1999. *Adhésion* du Canada le 9 novembre 2000.

Droit international pénal
Statut de Rome de la Cour pénale internationale, 1998. Rome, le 17 juillet 1998. *Signé* par le Canada le 18 décembre 1998. *Ratifié* par le Canada le 7 juillet 2000.

Droits de la personne
Acceptation de l'amendement au paragraphe 2 de l'article 43 de la Convention relative aux droits de l'enfant, adopté à la Conférence des États parties le 12 décembre 1995, et approuvé par l'Assemblée générale de l'Organisation des Nations Unies le 21 décembre 1995 (Convention adoptée par l'Assemblée générale de l'Organisation des Nations Unies le 20 novembre 1989. Elle est entrée en vigueur le 2 septembre 1990. La Convention a été signée par le Canada le 28 mai 1990 et ratifiée le 13 décembre 1991). New York, le 21 décembre 1995. *Acceptation* par le Canada le 17 septembre 1997. *En vigueur* le 28 juin 2000. *En vigueur* pour le Canada le 28 juin 2000.

Protocole facultatif à la Convention relative aux droits de l'enfant, concernant l'implication d'enfants dans les conflits armés. New York, le 25 mai 2000. *Signé* par le Canada le 5 juin 2000. *Ratifié* par le Canada le 7 juillet 2000.

Énergie atomique
Acceptation des modifications à l'article VI et à l'article XIV du Statut de l'Agence internationale de l'énergie

atomique. Vienne, le 1ᵉʳ octobre 1999. *Acceptation* par le Canada le 15 septembre 2000.

Environnement
Protocole de 1996 à la Convention de 1972 sur la prévention de la pollution des mers résultant de l'immersion de déchets. Londres, le 7 novembre 1996. *Adhésion* du Canada le 15 avril 2000.

Ajustements au Protocole de Montréal relatif à des substances qui appauvrissent la couche d'ozone, fait à Beijing le 3 décembre 1999. *En vigueur* le 28 juillet 2000. *En vigueur* pour le Canada le 28 juillet 2000. RTC 2000/37.

Évaluation de la conformité
Accord de reconnaissance mutuelle sur la conformité entre le Gouvernement du Canada et les Gouvernements de la République d'Islande, de la Principauté du Lichtenstein et du Royaume de Norvège. Bruxelles, le 4 juillet 2000. *Signé* par le Canada le 4 juillet 2000. *Ratification* du Canada le 23 novembre 2000.

Espace extra-atmosphérique
Accord entre le Gouvernement du Canada, les Gouvernements d'États Membres de l'Agence spatiale européenne, le Gouvernement du Japon, le Gouvernement de la Fédération de la Russie et le Gouvernement des États-Unis d'Amérique sur la coopération relative à la station spatiale internationale civile. Washington, D.C., le 29 janvier 1998. *Signé* par le Canada le 29 janvier 1998. *Ratifié* par le Canada le 24 juillet 2000. Le traité de 1988 sera résilié à l'entrée en vigueur du traité de 1998.

Éthique de travail (Principes Directeurs de l'OCDE)
Décision du Conseil de l'Organisation de Coopération et de Développement économiques concernant les Principes directeurs à l'intention des entreprises multinationales. Paris, le 27 juin 2000. *En vigueur* le 27 juin 2000. *En vigueur* pour le Canada le 27 juin 2000. RTC 2000/16.

Propriété intellectuelle
Acceptation de la modification à l'article 9(3) de la Convention instituant l'Organisation mondiale de la propriété intellectuelle, faite à Stockholm le 14 juillet 1967, et modifiée le 28 septembre 1979, avec Déclaration. Genève, le 24 septembre 1999. *Acceptée* par le Canada le 11 août 2000.

Télécommunications
Actes finals de la Conférence de l'Union internationale des télécommunications, Minneapolis (1998). Minneapolis, le 6 novembre 1988. *Signés* par le Canada le 6 novembre 1998. *Ratifiée* par le Canada le 8 février 2000.

Actes finals de la Conférence Mondiale de Radiocommunication de l'Union internationale des télécommunications, Istanbul (CMR-2000). Istanbul, le 2 juin 2000. *Signés* par le Canada le 2 juin 2000. *Ratifiée* par le Canada le 9 octobre 2000.

Terrorisme
Convention internationale pour la répression du financement du terrorisme. New York, le 9 décembre 1999. *Signée* par le Canada le 10 février 2000.

Travail
Ratification de la Convention de l'Organisation internationale du Travail sur l'interdiction des pires formes de travail des enfants et l'action immédiate en vue de leur élimination. Genève, le 17 juin 1999. *Ratifiée* par le Canada le 6 juin 2000.

Transport
Accord concernant l'établissement de règlements techniques mondiaux applicables aux véhicules à roues, ainsi qu'aux équipements et pièces qui peuvent être montés et/ou utilisés sur les véhicules à roues, fait à Genève le 25 juin 1998. *Signé* par le Canada le 22 juin 1999 sans réserve quant à la ratification, acceptation ou approbation. *En vigueur* le 25 août 2000. *En vigueur* pour le Canada le 25 août 2000. RTC 2000/34.

Cases / Jurisprudence

Canadian Cases in Public International Law in 2000-1 / Jurisprudence canadienne en matière de droit international public en 2000-1

compiled by / préparé par
KARIN MICKELSON

Arbitration — judicial review of arbitral decisions under the North American Free Trade Agreement

United Mexican States v. *Metalclad Corporation* (2001), 89 B.C.L.R. (3d) 359. British Columbia Supreme Court.

This involved a challenge by Mexico of an arbitration award issued by a tribunal constituted under Chapter 11 of the North American Free Trade Agreement. In the award, the tribunal granted damages against Mexico in favour of the respondent, Metalclad Corporation, an American corporation. The matter came before the British Columbia Supreme Court because the place of the arbitration was designated to be Vancouver, BC.

Through its subsidiaries, Metalclad owned a site in the State of San Luis Potosi that it had planned to operate as a hazardous waste landfill. Although it received the necessary permits from the federal and state governments, it commenced construction activities at the site without a municipal construction permit. The municipality issued a stop work order due to the absence of a municipal permit. The municipal permit was applied for late in 1994. The municipality officially denied this application over a year later, in December 1995. In the meantime, the landfill facility had already been completed by March 1995. Due to a variety of circumstances,

Karin Mickelson is at the Faculty of Law at the University of British Columbia.

including local protests, the landfill facility was not actually opened, and it has not subsequently been operated. Following unsuccessful attempts to resolve the matter through negotiations, Metalclad gave notice and commenced an arbitration proceeding. After the arbitration proceeding was underway, but before the hearing in the arbitration was held, the governor of the State of San Luis Potosi issued an ecological decree on September 20, 1997. The Ecological Decree declared an area of 188,758 hectares within the municipality, which included the site, to be an ecological preserve for the stated purpose of protecting species of cacti. The arbitral tribunal rendered the award on August 30, 2000.

In discussing the award, Tysoe J. begins by summarizing the law that the Tribunal considered to apply to the arbitration. The two central provisions that Metalclad asserted that Mexico had violated were Article 1105, which provides that each party shall accord to investments of investors of another party treatment in accordance with international law, including fair and equitable treatment and full protection and security ("fair and equitable treatment"), and Article 1110, which provides that no party may directly or indirectly nationalize or expropriate an investment of an investor of another party in its territory or take a measure tantamount to nationalization or expropriation of such an investment ("expropriation.") except in accordance with certain specified conditions. The term "measure" is defined in Article 201 to include "any law, regulation, procedure, requirement or practice."

After quoting Article 1105, the tribunal stated that an underlying objective of NAFTA is to promote and increase cross-border investment opportunities and ensure the successful implementation of investment initiatives. It referred to "transparency" as being prominent in the statement of the principles and rules that introduce NAFTA. The tribunal understood "transparency" to include the idea that all relevant legal requirements for the purpose of initiating, completing, and successfully operating investments should be capable of being readily known to all affected investors of a party and that there should be no room for doubt or uncertainty. The tribunal held that, if the authorities of the central government of a party become aware of any scope for misunderstanding or confusion in this connection, it is their duty to ensure that the correct position is promptly determined and clearly stated.

The tribunal considered that a central point in the case was whether a municipal permit for the construction of a hazardous waste landfill was required. It briefly reviewed the opposing views of the expert opinions presented by Metalclad and Mexico, and found that if a municipal construction permit was required, the federal authority's jurisdiction was controlling and the authority of the municipality only extended to appropriate construction considerations (that is, those related to the physical construction or defects in the site). The tribunal found that Metalclad had been led to believe by federal authorities that the federal and state permits issued allowed for the construction and operation of the landfill, and it made reference to Metalclad's position (which the tribunal appeared to have implicitly accepted) that it was also told by federal officials that if it submitted an application for a municipal construction permit, the municipality would have no legal basis for denying the permit. The tribunal found that the municipality's denial of the construction permit was improper because it did not have reference to construction aspects or flaws of the physical facility.

The tribunal went on to hold that Mexico failed to ensure a transparent and predictable framework for Metalclad's business planning and investment. It said that the totality of the circumstances demonstrated a lack of orderly process and timely disposition in relation to an investor acting in the expectation that it would be treated fairly and justly in accordance with NAFTA. The tribunal stated that, moreover, the acts of the State of San Luis Potosi and the municipality (which were attributable to Mexico) failed to comply with or adhere to the requirements of Article 1105. Accordingly, the tribunal held that Metalclad had not been treated fairly or equitably under NAFTA and had succeeded on its claim under Article 1105.

The tribunal then dealt with the claim of expropriation prior to the Ecological Decree. The tribunal defined expropriation under Article 1110 of the NAFTA as the open, deliberate, and acknowledged taking of property, as well as covert or incidental interference with the use of property which has the effect of depriving the owner, in whole or in significant part, of the use or reasonably-to-be-expected economic benefit of property even if it is not necessarily to the obvious benefit of the host state. The tribunal held that Mexico took a measure tantamount to expropriation in violation of Article 1110 by permitting or tolerating the conduct of the municipality in relation to Metalclad (which the tribunal had already held was unfair and inequitable treatment) and by thus participating or acquiescing in the denial to Metalclad of the right to operate the landfill.

The tribunal next turned to the issue of expropriation after the Ecological Decree. Earlier in its decision, the tribunal held that it could consider issues relating to the Ecological Decree. It went on to hold that the Ecological Decree was a further ground for a finding of expropriation, but stated that it was not strictly necessary for its conclusion. The tribunal found that the Ecological Decree had the effect of barring forever the operation of Metalclad's landfill. It rejected Mexico's representations to the contrary by making reference to provisions of the Decree. The tribunal stated that it considered that the implementation of the Decree would, in and of itself, constitute an act tantamount to expropriation.

Having provided an overview of the applicable NAFTA provisions and the award, Tysoe J. notes that a threshold issue for the challenge to the award is the determination of which of two statutes governs this Court in its review of the award. The two potentially applicable statutes are both British Columbia Acts, the International Commercial Arbitration Act, R.S.B.C.1996, c. 233 (International CAA) and the Commercial Arbitration Act, R.S.B.C. 1996, c. 55 (CAA). The choice between the statutes depends, not on the interpretation of the word "international" as one might expect from the difference in the names of the two statutes, but on the meaning of the word "commercial." The most important distinction between the two statutes, for the purposes of this proceeding, is that the CAA allows the court to review points of law decided by the arbitral body, while the International CAA is more restrictive.

In the definition of "arbitration agreement" in the CAA, an agreement to which the International CAA applies is specifically excluded. This means that it is first necessary to consider whether the International CAA applies to the arbitration agreement in this case. If it is found to apply, its provisions will govern and the CAA need not be considered. If the International CAA is not found to apply, the provisions of the CAA will govern by default.

As its name indicates, the International CAA applies to international commercial arbitrations. There is no dispute that the arbitration between Mexico and Metalclad was an international arbitration. Whether the arbitration was a commercial arbitration depends on section 1(6) of the International CAA, which provides in part that an arbitration is commercial if it arises out of a relationship of a commercial nature including, but not limited to, investing. In its definition of the term "arbitration agreement," section 7 of the International CAA confirms that the relationship need not be contractual in nature.

Tysoe J. notes that the International CAA is based on a model law for international commercial arbitrations developed by the United Nations Commission on International Trade Law (UNCITRAL). He cites UNCITRAL commentary, which section 6 of the International CAA specifically authorizes the court to refer to in construing the legislation, in support of the view that the term "commercial" should be given a wide interpretation. Tysoe J. notes that he does not agree with the submission on behalf of Mexico that the relationship between Mexico and Metalclad was not commercial but regulatory. Clause (p) of section 1(6) of the International CAA requires that the phrase "a relationship of a commercial nature" be interpreted to include a relationship of investing, and the arbitration in this matter arose out of a relationship of investing. Tysoe J. finds further support for this conclusion in the fact that Chapter 11 itself deals with investment and investment disputes. It is true that the dispute between Metalclad and the municipality arose because the municipality was purporting to exercise a regulatory function. However, the primary relationship between Metalclad and Mexico was one of investing and the exercise of a regulatory function by the municipality was incidental to that primary relationship. The arbitration did not arise under an agreement between Metalclad and the municipality in connection with regulatory matters. Rather, the arbitration was between Metalclad and Mexico pursuant to an agreement dealing with the treatment of investors. In addition, it must be remembered that Metalclad qualified to make a claim against Mexico by way of arbitration under Chapter 11 because it was an investor of Mexico. If Metalclad was not considered to be an investor of Mexico, the arbitration could not have taken place.

Having determined that the review of the award is governed by the provisions of the International CAA, Tysoe J. turns to a consideration of the standard of review. He notes that the extent to which the Court may interfere with an international commercial arbitral award is limited by the provisions of International CAA. Subsection 34(1) of the act states that recourse to a court against an arbitral award may only be made in accordance with subsections (2) and (3). The pertinent portions of subsection 34(2) provides that an arbitral award may be set aside by the Supreme Court only if the party making the application furnishes proof that the arbitral award deals with a dispute not contemplated by or not falling within the terms of the submission to arbitration, or it contains decisions on matters beyond the scope of the submission to arbitration.

Tysoe J. notes that counsel for Mexico and for the intervenor attorney general of Canada had urged the Court to utilize a "pragmatic and functional approach" to determine the appropriate standard of review, based on domestic jurisprudence dealing with decision of administrative tribunals. However, the standard of review is set out in the International CAA, and it would be an error to import into that act an approach that has been developed as a branch of statutory interpretation in respect of domestic tribunals created by statute.

As the scope of the submission to arbitration is critical to a consideration of section 34(2)(a)(iv), it is appropriate to set out the question put to the tribunal. Article 1122 of the NAFTA provides that each party (in this case, Mexico) consents to the submission of a claim to arbitration under the NAFTA. The question that Metalclad posed was whether Mexico had breached its obligations under Chapter 11 of the NAFTA "guaranteeing national treatment; most favoured nation treatment; minimum treatment in accord with international law, fair and equitable treatment, and full protection and security, prohibiting performance requirements; and, depriving [Metalclad] of its investment through [Mexico's] actions that directly and indirectly resulted in, and were tantamount to, expropriation of that investment without due process and full compensation." Metalclad relied on the events which had occurred up to the time of the commencement of the arbitration proceeding and, as noted above, it also relied on the Ecological Decree, which was announced after the arbitration process had been initiated by Metalclad.

Tysoe J. then turns to the various holdings of the tribunal. In dealing with Article 1105, Tysoe J. expresses agreement with the reasoning of the Arbitral Tribunal in *SD. Myers v. Government of Canada*, which in order to qualify as a breach of Article 1105, the treatment in question must fail to accord to international law. For instance, treatment may be perceived to be unfair or inequitable, but it will not constitute a breach of Article 1105 unless it is treatment that is not in accordance with international law. In using the words "international law," Article 1105 is referring to customary international law that is developed by common practices of countries. It is to be distinguished from conventional international law, which is comprised in treaties entered into by countries (including provisions contained in the NAFTA other than Article 1105 and other provisions of Chapter 11).

Tysoe J. notes that he is unable to agree with the reasoning in *Pope*

& Talbot v. *Canada*, in which the Arbitral Tribunal concluded that investors under NAFTA are entitled to the international law minimum, plus the fairness elements. That tribunal interpreted the word "including" in Article 1105 to mean "plus," which has a virtually opposite meaning. Its interpretation is contrary to Article 31(1) of the Vienna Convention, which requires that terms of treaties be given their ordinary meaning. The evidence that the NAFTA parties intended to reject the "additive" character of bilateral investment treaties is found in the fact that they chose not to adopt the language used in such treaties; it is surprising that the tribunal considered that other evidence was required.

In the framework of the International CAA, the issue is whether the tribunal made decisions on matters beyond the scope of the submission to arbitration by deciding upon matters outside Chapter 11. Tysoe J. holds that the tribunal did make decisions on matters beyond the scope of Chapter 11. The tribunal did not simply interpret Article 1105 to include a minimum standard of transparency. No authority was cited or evidence introduced to establish that transparency has become part of customary international law. The tribunal did not simply interpret the wording of Article 1105. Rather, it misstated the applicable law to include transparency obligations and it then made its decision on the basis of the concept of transparency.

In addition to specifically quoting from Article 1802 in the section of the award outlining the applicable law, the tribunal incorrectly stated that transparency was one of the objectives of NAFTA. In that regard, the tribunal was referring to Article 102(1), which sets out the objectives of NAFTA in clauses (a) through (f). Transparency is mentioned in Article 102(1), but it is listed as one of the principles and rules contained in NAFTA through which the objectives are elaborated. The other two principles and rules mentioned in Article 102, national treatment and most-favoured nation treatment, are contained in Chapter 11. The principle of transparency is implemented through the provisions of Chapter 18, not Chapter 11. Article 102(2) provides that the NAFTA is to be interpreted and applied in light of the objectives set out in Article 102(1), but it does not require that all of the provisions of the NAFTA are to be interpreted in light of the principles and rules mentioned in Article 102(1).

In its reasoning, the tribunal discussed the concept of transparency after quoting Article 1105 and making reference to Article 102. It set out its understanding of transparency, and it then reviewed the relevant facts. After discussing the facts and concluding that the municipality's denial of the construction permit was improper, the tribunal stated its conclusion which formed the basis of its finding of a breach of Article 1105; namely, Mexico had failed to ensure a transparent and predictable framework for Metalclad's business planning and investment. Hence, the tribunal made its decision on the basis of transparency. This was a matter beyond the scope of the submission to arbitration because there are no transparency obligations contained in Chapter 11.

Tysoe J. next turns to a consideration of Article 1110. He notes that prior to its consideration of the Ecological Decree, the tribunal concluded that the actions of Mexico constituted a measure tantamount to expropriation in violation of Article 1110. The tribunal based this conclusion on its view that Mexico permitted or tolerated the conduct of the municipality, which amounted to unfair and inequitable treatment breaching Article 1105 and that Mexico therefore participated or acquiesced in the denial to Metalclad of the right to operate the landfill. The tribunal subsequently made reference to the representations by the Mexican federal authorities and the absence of a timely, orderly, or substantive basis for the denial of the construction permit by the municipality in concluding that there had been indirect expropriation. It is unclear whether the tribunal equated a "measure tantamount to expropriation" with "indirect expropriation" or whether it made two separate findings of expropriation.

Tysoe J. expresses agreement with the submission of counsel for Mexico that the tribunal's analysis of Article 1105 infected its analysis of Article 1110. The tribunal's statement that Mexico took a measure tantamount to expropriation was directly connected to its finding of a breach of Article 1105. The statement that Mexico permitted or tolerated the conduct of the municipality is a clear reference to the tribunal's view that Mexico failed to ensure a transparent and predictable framework for Metalclad's business planning and investment. Similarly, the tribunal relied on the absence of a timely, orderly, and substantive basis for the denial of the construction permit by the municipality in making its statement that there had been indirect expropriation. This is also a reference to a lack of transparency. Thus, the tribunal based its conclusion that there had been a measure tantamount to expropriation/indirect expropriation, at least in part, on the concept of transparency. In finding a breach of Article 1105 on the basis of a lack of transparency, the tribunal decided a matter beyond the scope of the submission to arbitration. In relying on the concept of transparency, at least in part, to conclude that there had been an expropriation within the meaning of Article 1110, the tribunal also decided a matter beyond the scope of the submission to arbitration.

Tysoe J. then considers the situation with regard to the application of Article 1110 after the ecological decree. Tysoe J. notes that he cannot agree with the submission on behalf of Mexico that the tribunal improperly considered the ecological decree but that, in any event, it did not base its decision on the decree. It is true that the tribunal stated that it did not attach controlling importance to the Ecological Decree and that a finding of expropriation on the basis of the Decree was not strictly necessary or essential to its finding of a violation of Article 1110. However, the tribunal made these statements because it also made a finding of expropriation on the basis of the events preceding the announcement of the decree. It now becomes potentially important because I have held that the tribunal decided a matter beyond the scope of the submission to arbitration in finding that the events preceding the announcement of the Decree amounted to an expropriation.

Although the tribunal used an incorrect tense in the award when it stated that it considered that the implementation of the Ecological Decree would, in and of itself, constitute an act tantamount to expropriation, it is clear from another passage of the award that the tribunal considered that the implementation of the decree did constitute expropriation. While the comments of the tribunal with respect to the Ecological Decree were *obiter dicta* in view of the tribunal's conclusion that the events preceding the announcement of the decree constituted an expropriation of the site, that does not detract from the fact that the *obiter dicta* comments of tribunal represent an alternative finding of expropriation on the basis of the decree, which alternative finding becomes the governing finding in the event that the primary finding is set aside.

Having concluded that the tribunal did find that the Ecological Decree amounted to an expropriation of the site, Tysoe J. goes on to decide that the tribunal was correct in its conclusion that it could consider the Ecological Decree. Furthermore, he determines that it did not decide a matter beyond the scope of the submission to arbitration when it concluded that the announcement of the Ecological Decree constituted an act tantamount to expropriation. This conclusion stands on its own and is not based on a lack of transparency or on the tribunal's findings of a breach of Article 1105. He finds it unnecessary to decide whether a patently unreasonable decision is a ground for setting aside an arbitral award pursuant to the International CAA, as he find that the tribunal did not make a patently unreasonable error. Tysoe J. notes that the tribunal gave an extremely broad definition of expropriation for the purposes of Article 1110. In addition to the more conventional notion of expropriation involving a taking of property, the tribunal held that expropriation under NAFTA includes covert or incidental interference with the use of property, which has the effect of depriving the owner, in whole or in significant part, of the use or reasonably-to-be-expected economic benefit of property. This definition is sufficiently broad to include a legitimate rezoning of property by a municipality or other zoning authority. However, the definition of expropriation is a question of law with which this Court is not entitled to interfere under the International CAA. The tribunal reviewed the terms of the Ecological Decree and concluded that it had the effect of barring forever the operation of Metalclad's landfill and constituted an act tantamount to expropriation. This conclusion is not patently unreasonable. Tysoe J. concludes that there is no ground under section 34 of the International CAA to set aside the award as it relates to the conclusion of the tribunal that the issuance of the ecological decree amounted to an expropriation of the site without compensation.

Tysoe J. then deals with the submission on behalf of Mexico that there were two categories of improper acts on the part of Metalclad, which were not explicitly addressed by the tribunal and which render the award in conflict with the public policy in British Columbia such that the award should be set aside pursuant to section 34(2)(b)(ii) of the International CAA. Tysoe J. notes that the matters in question were canvassed extensively during the arbitration and concludes that it has not been established that there were any improper acts on behalf of Metalclad that put the award in conflict with the public policy in British Columbia.

Tysoe J. then considers the final basis on which Mexico seeks to set aside the award: that the tribunal failed to answer all questions raised by it which could have affected the result. Tysoe J. observes that the tribunal must answer the questions that have been submitted to it and give its reasons for its answers. In other words, the tribunal must deal fully with the dispute between the parties and give reasons for its decision. It is not reasonable to require the tribunal to answer each and every argument that is made in connection with the questions that the tribunal must decide. In the present case, the questions submitted to the tribunal were essentially whether Article

1105 or Article 1110 had been breached and, if so, what measure of damages would compensate Metalclad for the breach or breaches. The tribunal answered these questions and gave reasons for its answers in the award. In answering the questions, the tribunal explicitly or implicitly dealt with each argument that had been made. Tysoe J. concludes that the tribunal adequately dealt with the principal issues before it and the failure of the tribunal to explicitly deal with all of Mexico's arguments is not sufficiently serious to justify the exercise of this Court's discretion to set aside the award.

Tysoe J. concludes by noting that in order to have the Court set aside the award in its entirety, Mexico was required to successfully establish that all three of the tribunal's findings of breaches of Articles 1105 and 1110 of the NAFTA involved decisions beyond the scope of the submission to arbitration or that the award should be set aside in view of Metalclad's allegedly improper acts or the tribunal's alleged failure to answer all questions submitted to it. Although Mexico succeeded in challenging the first two of the tribunal's findings of breaches of Articles 1105 and 1110, it was not successful on the remaining points. Accordingly, the award should only be set aside in its entirety, but only to the extent necessary to reflect that the only finding of a breach in respect of which there is no basis to set it aside is expropriation through the issuance of the Ecological Decree.

Tysoe J. notes that although he has concluded that the tribunal made decisions on matters outside the scope of the submission to arbitration when it found the first two breaches of Articles 1105 and 1110, he should not be taken as holding that there was no breach of Article 1105 and no breach of Article 1110 until the issuance of the Ecological Decree. The function of the Court is limited to setting aside arbitral awards if the criteria set out in section 34 of the International CAA are shown to exist. Tysoe J. therefore expresses no opinion on whether there was a breach of Article 1105 or a breach of Article 1110 prior to the issuance of the Decree on grounds other than those relied upon by the tribunal.

Immunity of international organizations

Miller v. *Canada,* [2001] 1 S.C.R. 407. Supreme Court of Canada.

Miller had been employed by the International Civil Aviation Organization (ICAO), and had worked in the ICAO head office in Montreal, the premises of which the Crown was responsible for leasing. Miller alleged that he had suffered health problems because of the inadequate air quality in the building, and that the Crown was aware of the air quality problem and failed to warn him or other employees about the danger to their health. Miller brought an action against the Crown as well as the owner of the building, seeking damages. At trial, the Crown brought a motion to dismiss for lack of jurisdiction, based on Article 33(b) of the Headquarters Agreement between the Government of Canada and the International Civil Aviation Organization. The Superior Court dismissed the motion, and that decision was upheld by a majority of the Court of Appeal.

In dismissing the appeal, Bastarache J., writing for the Court, notes that the Crown had argued that Miller's claim fell within working conditions and, therefore, within the area of labour relations. As such, it is governed by the ICAO Service Code, and, pursuant to international agreements between ICAO and the Canadian government, the administrative regime in the Service Code must be followed. Thus, the Superior Court does not have jurisdiction to hear the claim.

There is no basis for the claim that Miller's status as a civil servant of an international organization should impinge on his ability to bring an action against the Crown. His status as an international civil servant is irrelevant since he is not bringing an action in that capacity. Immunity pursuant to Article 33(b) only transfers to an employee of ICAO when the employee is a defendant in a court action and not when he or she is a plaintiff. This interpretation is consistent with the international agreements and conventions upon which Article 33 is based.

The mere fact that Miller's damages were stated to have arisen from working conditions and were stated to be "entirely work-related" cannot change the true nature of the claim into one of labour relations. Miller has not made a claim against ICAO in the Superior Court. If he had, it is clear from the Headquarters Agreement, the ICAO Staff Rules, and the ICAO Service Code that the action would have been disallowed. Miller is not attempting to gain employee benefits from this action but rather compensation for the alleged wrongful acts of the Crown, which are not based on the breach of an employment contract but which are rather extra-contractual.

Although the Crown states that it is not arguing that the ICAO immunity is transferred to the Crown, in essence, it is arguing that the immunity of the organization extends to the location of work and, because the respondent's injuries were incurred therein, all those who may be responsible for the alleged damages are protected by such immunity. In stating that the nature of the actions giving rise to the claim determine if they are "sovereign" actions, the Crown is in fact saying that anything occurring at the place of employment, where that location results from an international agreement between an international organization and the Crown, is a sovereign act and, therefore, that no matter how remote, this act is protected by the immunity. This is incorrect. The immunity of ICAO and its employees is for the protection of the organization. This is clearly stated in Article 21 of the Headquarters Agreement. One must not simply look at the activities involved and the place in which these occurred but also at the effect that these claims may have on the organization. Therefore, the actual parties to any court action are important and must be considered, as well as the nature of the claim.

There will be some instances where dealing with events that occur during someone's employment may lead to intrusion into sovereign activities of an international body. The present case is not one of them. The Superior Court is only being asked to determine if the Crown had knowledge of the environmental conditions in the building, if it or its representatives failed to exercise their duty to warn those who work within it, and if this caused the respondent's damages. Within this analysis, a consideration of the ICAO's internal functions and procedures is neither relevant nor necessary.

Treaties and principles of international law — Domestic application

114957 Canada Ltée (Spraytech, Société d'arrosage) v. *Town of Hudson,* [2001] 2 S.C.R. 241. Supreme Court of Canada.

This case concerned the statutory authority of the respondent Town of Hudson to enact a by-law restricting use of pesticides within its perimeter to specified locations and enumerated activities. The appellants were landscaping and lawn care companies operating in the region of greater Montreal that make regular use of pesticides.

Writing for four members of the court, L'Heureux-Dubé J. begins by emphasizing that the context of this appeal includes the realization that the common future of every Canadian community depends on a healthy environment. She notes that the case arises in an era in which matters of governance are often examined through the lens of the principle of subsidiarity: the proposition that law-making and implementation are often best achieved at a level of government that is not only effective, but also closest to the citizens affected and thus most responsive to their needs, to local distinctiveness, and to population diversity. She also notes that in *Our Common Future*, the report produced in 1987 by the World Commission on the Environment and Development, the commission recommended that local governments should be empowered to exceed national norms.

L'Heureux-Dubé J. then proceeds to consider whether the Town had the statutory authority to enact the provision in question. Having discussed the relevant Canadian law, she notes that an interpretation of domestic law that permits the Town to regulate pesticide use is consistent with principles of international law and policy and, in particular, with international law's "precautionary principle," as defined in paragraph 7 of the 1990 Bergen Ministerial Declaration on Sustainable Development:

> In order to achieve sustainable development, policies must be based on the precautionary principle. Environmental measures must anticipate, prevent and attack the causes of environmental degradation. Where there are threats of serious or irreversible damage, lack of full scientific certainty should not be used as a reason for postponing measures to prevent environmental degradation.

She notes that Canada supported the inclusion of the precautionary principle during the Bergen Conference negotiations and that the principle is codified in several items of domestic legislation. She also notes that scholars have documented the precautionary principle's inclusion in nearly all recent international environmental treaties and policy documents, and quotes the views of several commentators that the precautionary principle is a principle of customary international law. She concludes that in the context of the precautionary principle's tenets, the Town's concerns about pesticides fit well under their rubric of preventive action.

United States v. *Burns*, [2001] 1 S.C.R. 283. Supreme Court of Canada.

The respondents Burns and Rafay, both Canadian citizens, were each wanted on three counts of aggravated first degree murder in the State of Washington. If found guilty, they would face either the death penalty or life in prison without the possibility of parole. Both respondents were eighteen years old at the time when the crimes, which they were alleged to have committed, occurred. They returned to Canada where, as a result of investigative work by undercover RCMP officers, they were eventually arrested. The attorney general of British Columbia decided against a prosecution in that province. United States authorities commenced proceedings to extradite the respondents to the State of Washington for trial pursuant to the Extradition Treaty between Canada and the United States of America. The minister of justice at the time, after evaluating the respondents' particular circumstances, including their age and their Canadian nationality, ordered their extradition pursuant to section 25 of the Extradition Act, R.S.C. 1985, c. E-23, without seeking assurances from the United States under Article 6 of the treaty that the death penalty would not be imposed, or, if imposed, would not be carried out. The minister declined to seek such assurances because of his policy that assurances should only be sought in exceptional circumstances, which he decided did not exist in this case. The British Columbia Court of Appeal, in a majority decision, ruled that the unconditional extradition order would violate the mobility rights of the respondents under section 6(1) of the Canadian Charter of Rights and Freedoms. The Court of Appeal therefore set aside the minister's decision and directed him to seek assurances as a condition of surrender.

Having provided an overview of the background of the case, the Court begins with an analysis of the minister's powers and responsibilities under the Extradition Act. The Court notes that the Act confers a broad statutory discretion on the minister. In *Kindler v. Canada (Minister of Justice)*, [1991] 2 S.C.R. 779, the Court had recognized that the minister's discretion was limited by the Charter, and that the Charter required a balancing on the facts of each case of the applicable principles of fundamental justice. The Court affirms the correctness of the balancing test. The Charter does not give the Court a general mandate to set Canada's foreign policy on extradition, and the Court notes that it has historically exercised restraint in the judicial review of extradition decisions. The customary deference to the minister's extradition decisions is rooted in the recognition of Canada's strong interest in international law enforcement activities. The Court affirms that it is generally for the minister, not the Court, to assess the weight of competing considerations in extradition policy, but the availability of the death penalty, like death itself, opens up a different dimension. The Court is the guardian of the constitution, and death penalty cases are uniquely bound up with basic constitutional values. The difficulties and occasional miscarriages of the criminal law are located in an area of human experience that falls squarely within the inherent domain of the judiciary.

The Court then turns to the mobility rights argument under section 6(1) of the Charter. Traditionally, nationality has afforded no defence to extradition from Canada. The Court affirms that extradition is a *prima facie* infringement of the section 6(1) right of every Canadian citizen to "remain in" Canada, and that the forcible removal of the respondents would have to be justified under section 1 of the Charter. However, the Court takes the view that efforts to stretch mobility rights to cover the death penalty controversy are misplaced. The real issue here is the death penalty. The death penalty is overwhelmingly a justice issue and only marginally a mobility rights issue. The death penalty issue should be confronted directly, and it should be confronted under section 7 of the Charter. Similarly, in relation to the argument under section 12, the Court asserts that the degree of causal remoteness between the extradition order to face trial and the potential imposition of capital punishment as one of many possible outcomes to this prosecution make this a case more appropriately reviewed under section 7 than under section 12.

In relation to section 7, the Court begins by noting that it has recognized that the punishment or treatment reasonably anticipated in the requesting country is clearly relevant. Section 7 is concerned not only with the act of extraditing, but also the potential consequences of the act of extradition. In *Kindler*, La Forest J., at p. 833, referred to a section 7 "balancing process" in which "the global context must be kept squarely in mind." It is inherent in the balancing process set out in *Kindler* and *Reference Re Ng Extradition,* [1991] 2 S.C.R. 858, that the outcome may well vary from case to case depending on the mix of contextual factors put into the balance. Some of these factors will be very specific, such as the mental condition of a particular fugitive. Other factors will be more general, such as the difficulties, both practical and philosophic, associated with the death penalty. Some of these factors will be unchanging; others will evolve over time. The outcome of this appeal turns more on the practical and philosophic difficulties associated with the death penalty that have increasingly preoccupied the courts and legislators in Canada, the United States, and elsewhere rather than on the specific circumstances of the respondents in this case. This analysis will lead to the conclusion that in the absence of exceptional circumstances, assurances in death penalty cases are always constitutionally required.

The minister approached this extradition decision on the basis of the law laid down in *Kindler* and *Ng* and related cases. Having regard to some of the expressions used in the case law, he concluded that the possibility of the death penalty does not pose a situation that is "simply unacceptable," nor would surrender of the respondents without assurances "shock the conscience" of Canadians or violate "the Canadian sense of what is fair and right."

While affirming that the "balancing process" set out in *Kindler* and *Ng* is the correct approach, the Court emphasizes that the phrase "shocks the conscience" and equivalent expressions are not to be taken out of context or equated to opinion polls. The words were intended to underline the very exceptional nature of circumstances that would constitutionally limit the minister's decision in extradition cases. The words were not intended to signal an abdication by judges of their constitutional responsibilities in matters involving fundamental principles of justice. Use of the "shocks the conscience" terminology was intended to convey the exceptional weight of a factor such as the youth, insanity, mental retardation, or pregnancy of a fugitive, which, because of its paramount importance, may control the outcome of the *Kindler* balancing test on the facts of a particular case. The terminology should not be allowed to obscure the ultimate assessment that is required: namely whether or not the extradition is in accordance with the principles of fundamental justice. The rule is not that departures from fundamental justice are to be tolerated unless in a particular case it shocks the conscience. An extradition that violates the principles of fundamental justice will always shock the conscience. The important inquiry is to determine what constitutes the applicable principles of fundamental justice in the extradition context.

The "shocks the conscience" language signals the possibility that even though the rights of the fugitive are to be considered in the context of other applicable principles of fundamental justice, which are normally of sufficient importance to uphold the extradition, a particular treatment or punishment may sufficiently violate our sense of fundamental justice as to tilt the balance against extradition. Examples might include stoning to death individuals taken in adultery or lopping off the hands of a thief. The punishment is so extreme that it becomes the controlling issue in the extradition and overwhelms the rest of the analysis.

The principles of fundamental justice are to be found in the basic tenets of our legal system. They do not lie in the realm of general public policy but in the inherent domain of the judiciary as guardian of the justice system. The distinction between "general public policy," on the one hand, and "the inherent domain of the judiciary as guardian of the justice system," on the other, is of particular importance in a death penalty case. The broader aspects of the death penalty controversy, including the role of retribution and deterrence in society and the view that capital punishment is inconsistent with the sanctity of human life, are embedded in the basic tenets of our legal system, but they also reflect philosophic positions informed by beliefs and social science evidence outside "the inherent domain of the judiciary." The narrower aspects of the controversy are concerned with the investigation, prosecution, defence, appeal, and sentencing of a person within the framework of the criminal law. They bear on the protection of the innocent, the avoidance of miscarriages of justice, and the rectification of miscarriages of justice where they are found to exist. These considerations are central to the preoccupation of the courts and directly engage the responsibility of judges "as guardian[s] of the justice system." The present controversy in Canada and the United States over possible miscarriages of justice in murder convictions must be regarded as falling within the second category, and therefore as engaging the special responsibility of the judiciary for the protection of the innocent.

There are a number of factors that might be said to favour extradition without assurances: that individuals accused of a crime should be brought to trial to determine the truth of the charges, the concern being that if assurances are sought and refused, the Canadian government could face the possibility that the respondents might avoid a trial altogether; that justice is best served by a trial in the jurisdiction where the crime was allegedly committed and the harmful impact felt; that individuals who choose to leave Canada leave behind Canadian law and procedures and must generally accept the local law, procedure, and punishments that the foreign state applies to its own residents; and that extradition is based on the principles of comity and fairness to other cooperating states in rendering mutual assistance in bringing fugitives to justice. A state seeking Canadian cooperation today may be asked to yield up a fugitive tomorrow. The extradition treaty is part of an international network of mutual assistance that enables states to deal both with crimes in their own jurisdiction and transnational crimes with elements that occur in more than one jurisdiction. Given the ease of movement of people and things from state to state, Canada needs the help of the international community to fight serious crime within our own borders. Some of the states from whom we seek cooperation may not share our constitutional values.

Their cooperation is nevertheless important. The minister points out that Canada satisfies itself that certain minimum standards of criminal justice exist in the foreign state before it makes an extradition treaty in the first place.

On the other hand, a number of other factors appear to weigh against extradition without assurances that the death penalty will not be imposed. First, the Court considers the principles of criminal justice as applied in Canada. The death penalty has been rejected as an acceptable element of criminal justice by the Canadian people, speaking through their elected federal representatives, after years of protracted debate. Second, the Court considers the international context. Although this particular appeal arises in the context of Canada's bilateral extradition arrangements with the United States, it is properly considered in the broader context of international relations generally, including Canada's multilateral efforts to bring about change in extradition arrangements where fugitives may face the death penalty, and Canada's advocacy at the international level of the abolition of the death penalty itself. A provision for assurances is found in the extradition arrangements of many countries other than Canada and the United States. Concerns about the death penalty have been expressed in a number of international instruments. The Court notes that the examples it mentions do not establish an international law norm against the death penalty, or against extradition to face the death penalty. It does show, however, significant movement towards acceptance internationally of a principle of fundamental justice that Canada has already adopted internally, namely the abolition of capital punishment.

Since *Kindler* and *Ng* were decided in 1991, a greater number of countries have become abolitionist. This trend against the death penalty supports some relevant conclusions. First, criminal justice, according to international standards, is moving in the direction of abolition of the death penalty. Second, the trend is more pronounced among democratic states with systems of criminal justice comparable to our own. The United States (or those parts of it that have retained the death penalty) is the exception, although, of course, it is an important exception. Third, the trend to abolition in the democracies, particularly the Western democracies, mirrors and perhaps corroborates the principles of fundamental justice that led to the rejection of the death penalty in Canada.

A third factor that appears to weigh against extradition without assurances is that almost all jurisdictions treat some personal characteristics of the fugitive as mitigating factors in death penalty cases. Examples of potential mitigating factors include youth, insanity, mental retardation, and pregnancy. In this case, the respondents rely on the fact that at the time of the crime they were eighteen. The Court canvasses a number of international instruments as well as the provisions of the new Extradition Act and concludes that the relative youth of the respondents at the time of the offence does constitute a mitigating circumstance in this case, albeit a factor of limited weight.

Other factors that weigh against extradition without assurances include the growing awareness of the rate of wrongful convictions in murder cases and concerns about the "death row phenomenon." The Court deals at length with the former, noting that while the possibility of miscarriages of justice in murder cases has long been recognized as a legitimate objection to the death penalty, our state of knowledge of the scope of this potential problem has grown to unanticipated and unprecedented proportions in the years since *Kindler* and *Ng* were decided. This expanding awareness compels increased recognition of the fact that the extradition decision of a Canadian minister could pave the way, however unintentionally, to sending an innocent individual to his or her death in a foreign jurisdiction. Similarly, while the death row phenomenon is not a controlling factor in the section 7 balance, even many of those who regard its horrors as self-inflicted concede that it is a relevant consideration. To that extent, it is a factor that weighs in the balance against extradition without assurances.

Having reviewed the factors for and against unconditional extradition, the Court concludes that to order extradition of the respondents without obtaining assurances that the death penalty will not be imposed would violate the principles of fundamental justice. The minister has not pointed to any public purpose that would be served by extradition without assurances that is not substantially served by extradition with assurances, carrying as it does in this case the prospect on conviction of life imprisonment without release or parole. International experience confirms the validity of concerns expressed in the Canadian Parliament about capital punishment. It also shows that a rule requiring that assurances be obtained prior to extradition in death penalty cases not only accords with Canada's principled advocacy on the international level, but is also consistent with the practice of other countries with whom Canada generally invites comparison, apart from the retentionist jurisdictions in the United States.

The "balancing process" mandated by *Kindler* and *Ng* remains a flexible instrument. The difficulty in this case is that the minister proposes to send the respondents without assurances into the death penalty controversy at a time when the legal system of the requesting country is under such sustained and authoritative internal attack. Although rumblings of this controversy in Canada, the United States and the United Kingdom pre-dated *Kindler* and *Ng*, the concern has grown greatly in depth and detailed proof in the intervening years. The arguments in favour of extradition without assurances would be as well served by extradition with assurances. There was no convincing argument that exposure of the respondents to death in prison by execution advances Canada's public interest in a way that the alternative, eventual death in prison by natural causes, would not. This is perhaps corroborated by the fact that other abolitionist countries do not, in general, extradite without assurances.

The arguments against extradition without assurances have grown stronger since this Court decided *Kindler* and *Ng* in 1991. Canada is now abolitionist for all crimes. The international trend against the death penalty has become clearer. The death penalty controversies in the requesting state, the United States, are based on pragmatic, hard-headed concerns about wrongful convictions. None of these factors is conclusive, but taken together they tilt the section 7 balance against extradition without assurances. Accordingly, the minister's decision to decline to request the assurances of the State of Washington that the death penalty will not be imposed on the respondents as a condition of their extradition violates their rights under section 7 of the Charter.

The final issue is whether the minister has shown that the violation of the respondents' section 7 rights that would occur if they were extradited to face the death penalty can be upheld under section 1 of the Charter as reasonable and demonstrably justifiable in a free and democratic society. The Court does not foreclose the possibility that there may be situations where the minister's objectives are so pressing and where there is no other way to achieve those objectives other than through extradition without assurances, that a violation might be justified. In this case, there is no such justification. While the government objective of advancing mutual assistance in the fight against crime is entirely legitimate, the minister has not shown that extraditing the respondents to face the death penalty without assurances is necessary to achieve that objective.

The minister cites two important policies that are integral to Canada's mutual assistance objectives, namely (1) maintenance of comity with cooperating states; and (2) avoiding an influx to Canada of persons charged with murder in retentionist states for the purpose of avoiding the death penalty. With respect to the argument on comity, there is no doubt that it is important for Canada to maintain good relations with other states. However, the minister has not shown that the means chosen to further that objective in this case — the refusal to ask for assurances that the death penalty will not be exacted — is necessary to further that objective. There is no suggestion in the evidence that asking for assurances would undermine Canada's international obligations or good relations with neighbouring states. The extradition treaty between Canada and the United States explicitly provides for a request for assurances and Canada would be in full compliance with its international obligations by making it. More and more states are becoming abolitionist and reserving to themselves the right to refuse to extradite unconditionally, as already mentioned.

The argument that Canada must avoid becoming a "safe haven" for persons who commit crimes sanctioned by the death penalty in other states might qualify as a pressing and substantial objective, and it was accepted as such in *Kindler.* However, whether fugitives are returned to a foreign country to face the death penalty or to face eventual death in prison from natural causes, they are equally prevented from using Canada as a safe haven. Elimination of a "safe haven" depends on vigorous law enforcement rather than on infliction of the death penalty once the fugitive has been removed from the country.

The infringement of the respondents' rights under section 7 of the Charter cannot be justified under section 1 in this case. The minister is constitutionally bound to ask for and obtain an assurance that the death penalty will not be imposed as a condition of extradition.

Rasa v. *Canada (Minister of Citizenship and Immigration)* (2001), 191 F.T.R. 129. Federal Court Trial Division.

This was an application for judicial review of the decision that, pursuant to subsection 70(5) and paragraph 53(1)(d) of the Immigration Act, R.S.C., c. I-2, as amended, the applicant constituted a danger to the public in Canada. The applicant had arrived in Canada in 1989 and was found to be a convention refugee in

1991. He became a permanent resident of Canada in 1992. In 1998, the applicant pled guilty to three offences under the Criminal Code, R.S.C. 1985, c. C-46. In March of that year, the applicant was sentenced for those offences. The wiretap evidence that had led to the applicant's arrest disclosed that there were two organized criminal groups within the Tamil community in the greater Toronto area. The evidence indicated that the applicant was a member of one of the criminal groups and that he held a position of some authority in that criminal group. In August 1998, the applicant was found to constitute a danger to the public in Canada.

Among the issues raised by the applicant was the question of whether the delegate of the minister of citizenship and immigration breached the principles of fundamental justice under section 7 of the Canadian Charter of Rights and Freedoms. This, in turn, raised a number of sub-issues, the first of which was whether the minister breached her obligation under the International Covenant on Civil and Political Rights, the Convention against Torture, or the Convention Relating to the Status of Refugees, thus causing a breach of section 7.

The applicant argues that the minister's decision to return the applicant to Sri Lanka, a country where he may likely face harsh or inhuman treatment violates the terms of the international agreement to which Canada is a party. This, the applicant argues, causes a breach of either section 7 or section 12 of the Charter. O'Keefe J. notes that he has read the reasons of Robertson J.A., writing on behalf of the Federal Court of Appeal in *Suresh* v. *Canada*, [2000] 2 F.C. 592 (noted at (2000) 38 Canadian Yearbook of International Law 433) and adopts his conclusions. Part of those conclusions are that the International Covenant on Civil and Political Rights does not deal with the issue of the *refoulement* and, in particular, it does not cover whether a prohibition against the *refoulement* of a convention refugee is a non-derogable right; and that the torture prohibited by Article 7 is torture or other unacceptable conduct that occurs within a geographic area over which the party has control. That is not the case here as Canada has no jurisdiction over Sri Lanka. Thus, there is no breach of the Covenant.

Similarly, the Convention against Torture deals only with acts of torture that may be carried out in a territory within the state's jurisdiction. Article 16(2) states that the provisions of the convention are "without prejudice to the provisions of any other international instrument ... which relates to extradition or expulsion." This qualification is important because Canada is a signatory to the Convention Relating to the Status of Refugees, Article 32(2) of which would allow the minister, in appropriate cases, to order the *refoulement* of a refugee when that person's life or freedom would be threatened. The minister did not, by her exercise of discretion in the present case, breach any of the three named conventions. The minister, by issuing an order pursuant to section 53(1)(d) of the Immigration Act, was acting in a situation contemplated by Article 33(2) of the Convention Relating to the Status of Refugees. O'Keefe J. also adopts the reasoning of Robertson J.A. in *Suresh* with respect to that part of the decision, which states that principles of customary international law may be recognized and applied in Canada only to the extent that these principles do not conflict with Canada's domestic law. The customary international law urged upon the Court in this case would conflict with section 53(1) of the Immigration Act.

Cangene Corp. v. *Octopharma AG*, [2000] 9 W.W.R. 606. Manitoba Queen's Bench.

The case concerned the interpretation of Article 8(1) of the Model Law on International Commercial Arbitration, which was adopted by the United Nations Commission on International Trade Law on June 21, 1985, as set out in Schedule B to the International Commercial Arbitration Act, S.M. 1986-87, c. 32, Cap. C151. The act makes the Model Law applicable in Manitoba. Article 8(1) provides that "a court before which an action is brought in a matter which is the subject of an arbitration agreement shall, if a party so requests not later than when submitting his first statement on the substance of the dispute, refer the parties to arbitration unless it finds that the agreement is null and void, inoperative or incapable of being performed." Morse J. reviews a number of cases from other Canadian jurisdictions and concludes that the imperative "shall" in Article 8(1) require the court to refer the parties to arbitration once that is requested by a party with respect to a matter subject to an arbitration agreement, provided the agreement is not null and void, inoperative, or incapable of being performed. In this case, the agreement is not "inoperative" and there is no suggestion that Octapharma submitted any "first statement on the substance of the dispute" before filing its motion to refer the parties to arbitration. The parties are bound by their agreement to have their dispute settled by arbitration.

Mack v. *Canada (Attorney General)* (2002), 55 O.R. (3d) 113. Ontario Superior Court of Justice.

The plaintiffs seek a public apology, damages, and other remedies arising out of the moneys paid to the government of Canada in respect of the so-called "Head Tax" and other effects of the Chinese Immigration Acts, enacted between 1885 and 1923. They bring the action on their own behalf and on behalf of a class comprising the surviving payers of the Head Tax and their surviving spouses and descendants. The defendant, the attorney general of Canada, moves to strike out the plaintiffs' statement of claim pursuant to the Rules of Civil Procedure, R.R.O. 1990, Reg. 194, on the ground that it discloses no reasonable cause of action or on the ground that it is frivolous, vexatious, or an abuse of process.

The plaintiffs ground their claim in domestic constitutional and international law, specifically, the Canadian Charter of Rights and Freedoms and various international human rights instruments. Cumming J. notes that the Charter cannot apply retroactively or retrospectively. Cumming J. rejects the plaintiffs' argument that they are not asking the court to apply the Charter in this fashion, but rather that their present Charter rights are infringed as a result of the government's refusal to provide redress relating to the Head Tax. This claim seeks redress for events that took place over fifty years ago. Accepting all the facts as pleaded by the plaintiffs, the proposed application of the Charter is retrospective.

In relation to the argument that the claim can be grounded in international law norms, Cumming J. canvasses a number of international human rights treaties and documents, but notes that international treaties and conventions do not form part of Canadian law unless they have been expressly implemented by statute. While it is true that international law norms can act as an aid to interpreting domestic law, the plaintiffs have pointed to no domestic law apart from the Charter that could apply to their claim. International law norms can also properly inform the development of common law. The contemporary application of a common law doctrine, that by international standards is unjustly discriminatory, demands reconsideration by a court. However, the situation at hand does not involve the common law, but rather federal statutes. Moreover, the legal regime created by those repealed statutes expired over half a century ago.

Even accepting that the instruments cited by the plaintiffs could be applied domestically, it is unclear that there currently exists a principle of accepted international law such that governments owe a positive legal duty to provide redress for wrongs involving violations of international norms respecting human rights, although there may now be an embryonic international norm in this regard. The international instruments and treaties cited by the plaintiffs evince a norm prohibiting racial discrimination. They may also demonstrate that states owe a positive legal duty to redress wrongs by states in this regard. However, this is different from showing a positive legal duty to provide redress for historical wrongs that occurred prior to the development of the international norm.

Cumming J. notes that none of these international norms existed when the final Chinese Immigration Act was repealed in 1947, and many of the treaties cited by the plaintiffs were not ratified by Canada until after 1970. The plaintiffs' proposed analysis of this issue would necessarily involve the application of norms and principles that did not exist at the material times. Even if the international instruments referred to were to have been incorporated into domestic law, they would have no retroactive effect unless, by their terms, they so provided. Cumming J. cites Article 28 of the Vienna Convention of the Law of Treaties in support of this conclusion.

Cumming J. also considers international law in relation to the plaintiffs' argument regarding unjust enrichment. The plaintiffs contend that international law norms provide evidence that the Chinese Immigration Act could not constitute a juristic reason so as to defeat the claim of unjust enrichment. For the purposes of this argument, it is accepted that principles of equality and non-discrimination may have taken on the status of international law norms in the relevant time period, being 1885 to 1947. However, it is problematic that such norms could supersede the operation of validly enacted, albeit racist, domestic legislation. Even today, international law norms and conventions can ground an argument in domestic law in the face of an offending domestic statute, constitutionally enacted, only where such norms and conventions have been expressly incorporated into domestic legislation. Cumming J. concludes that it is plain and obvious that the plaintiffs' claim cannot succeed and grants the defendant's motion to strike out the statement of claim in its entirety.

Note: See also *Gal* v. *Northern Mountain Helicopters* (2000), 72 B.C.L.R. (3d) 374 (British Columbia Court of Appeal). The appeal concerned the interpretation of Article 29 of the Warsaw

Convention for the Unification of Certain Rules Relating to International Carriage by Air, which has the force of law in Canada by reason of the Carriage by Air Act, R.S.C. 1985, Chap. C-26. Article 29 provides that the right to damages shall be extinguished if an action is not brought within two years, reckoned from the date of arrival at the destination, or from the date on which the aircraft ought to have arrived. Case authority in the United States, the United Kingdom, and elsewhere in Canada supports the view that a passenger who does not bring an action against the carrier under the convention within two years is without a remedy. The appellant had asserted that Article 29 is an ambiguous provision that has been subject to conflicting interpretations. Writing for the Court, Huddart J.A. notes that she did not find in any of the materials presented by the appellant reason for concluding Article 29 is a limitation provision capable of bearing more than one interpretation, such that it must be interpreted narrowly and made subject to local equitable or statutory modification.

Note: See also *R. v. Sharpe*, [2001] 1 S.C.R. 45 (Supreme Court of Canada), a case involving child pornography in which L'Heureux-Dubé, Gonthier, and Bastarache JJ., undertaking an analysis under section 1 of the Canadian Charter of Rights and Freedoms, note that the protection of children from harm is a universally accepted goal, that there is a wide array of international instruments that emphasize the protection of children, and that a number of international bodies have recognized that possession must be targeted to effectively address the harms of child pornography.

Sovereign immunity

Schreiber v. *Federal Republic of Germany* (2001), 196 D.L.R. (4th) 281. Ontario Court of Appeal.

This was an appeal from a decision of Nordheimer J. of the Ontario Superior Court of Justice (noted at (2000) 38 Canadian Yearbook of International Law 423), in which an action was dismissed on the ground that the Federal Republic of Germany enjoys sovereign immunity, as codified by the State Immunity Act, R.S.C. 1985, c.S-18. The Federal Republic of Germany had sought the extradition of the plaintiff. The plaintiff then commenced an action claiming, *inter alia*, damages for personal injuries suffered as a result of his arrest and detention prior to being released on bail.

Writing for the court, Doherty J.A. begins by addressing the submission that Nordheimer J. applied an improper test in dismissing the motion. Nordheimer J. interpreted the relevant statutory provisions and concluded that none of the allegations came within those provisions as he interpreted them. He decided the motion based on his determination of the correct interpretation to be given to the exemptions set out in the State Immunity Act. Counsel for Schreiber submits that the motion judge should not have decided the ultimate question as to the meaning of the statutory provisions but should only have decided whether it was "plain and obvious" and "beyond doubt" that Germany was entitled to claim sovereign immunity in relation to the allegations made in the Statement of Claim. In making this submission, counsel relies on the well-established principle that pre-trial motions to strike claims or dismiss actions on the basis that they do not reveal a cause of action should only succeed in the clearest of cases.

There are strong and well-recognized policy reasons that preclude the pre-emptive striking of claims or dismissal of lawsuits on the basis that they do not disclose a cause of action. However, the "plain and obvious" approach cannot be applied to a motion to dismiss founded on a claim of sovereign immunity. That claim challenges the obligation of the foreign state to submit to the court's jurisdiction. Until that challenge is decided, the action cannot proceed. Unlike a court faced with an allegation that a claim does not disclose a cause of action, a court faced with an immunity claim cannot withhold its decision until the end of the trial. There can be no trial until the court decides whether the foreign state is subject to the court's jurisdiction.

The State Immunity Act clearly contemplates that any claim of sovereign immunity will be decided on its merits before the action proceeds any further. Section 4(2)(c) provides that a state submits to the jurisdiction of a court where it "takes any step in the proceedings before the court." Section 4(3)(b), however, permits the foreign state to appear in the proceedings strictly for the purpose of asserting sovereign immunity without thereby submitting to the court's jurisdiction. Participation beyond a claim of immunity may, however, result in the loss of any immunity to which the foreign state might otherwise have been entitled.

If, on a motion to dismiss based on a sovereign immunity claim, a court were to conclude that it was not "plain and obvious" that the claim should succeed and direct that the matter proceed to trial, the foreign state would be in the untenable position of either not participating in the trial and risking an adverse result or participating in the trial and thereby losing its immunity claim. The scheme set out in the State Immunity Act is workable only if immunity claims are decided on their merits before any further step is taken in the action.

Having concluded that Nordheimer J. properly approached the motion by deciding whether Germany was entitled to immunity, Doherty J.A. then considers the correctness of that decision. First, Doherty J.A. addresses the argument that Germany had submitted to the jurisdiction of Ontario. This is premised on the contention that the extradition proceedings initiated by Canada in the Superior Court on behalf of Germany are the same proceedings as the lawsuit initiated by Schreiber in the Superior Court after his arrest and detention on the extradition warrant. However, there is no merit to this argument. The extradition proceedings are separate and distinct from Schreiber's lawsuit. Extradition proceedings are part of the process through which Canada honours its obligations to other nations. Schreiber's claim is a private action for damages. The fact that Schreiber's claim is based on conduct that occurred during the extradition process does not in any way make the extradition proceedings and Schreiber's lawsuit one and the same proceeding. Even if it could be said that Germany initiated the judicial proceedings under the Extradition Act (a characterization that is hard to accept since it was Canada that sought the warrant for Schreiber's arrest), those proceedings are entirely distinct from a lawsuit that Schreiber initiated.

The statutory provisions relied on by Schreiber are clear and leave no room for the argument that Germany submitted to the jurisdiction of Ontario. However, this argument ought to be rejected even if one could look beyond the clear words of the statute to policy considerations. It is entirely contrary to concepts of comity and mutual respect as between nations to hold that a country that calls upon Canada to adhere to its treaty obligations and to assist in extradition to that country does so only at the expense of submitting to the domestic jurisdiction of Canadian courts in matters connected to the extradition request. Extradition is fundamentally a matter between sovereign nations, each exercising its sovereign authority. As a matter of policy, there is no reason why the exercise of that sovereign authority by a foreign state should somehow cost that foreign state its right to claim sovereign immunity in Canadian domestic courts.

Doherty J.A. then addresses the argument that Schreiber's claim falls under section 6(a) of the State Immunity Act, which provides that a foreign state is not immune from the jurisdiction of a court in any proceedings that relate to any death or personal injury that occurs in Canada. Doherty J.A. notes that apart from *Walker* v. *Bank of New York* (1994), 16 O.R. (3d) 504, and *United States* v. *Friedland*, (1999), 182 D.L.R. (4th) 614, noted at (2000) 38 Canadian Yearbook of International Law 419, there is little on the Canadian legal landscape that assists in determining the meaning of "personal injury" in section 6(a). Unlike the "commercial activity" exception to state immunity in section 5 of the State Immunity Act, the exception in section 6(a) was created by the statute and has no common law ancestry to inform the meaning of the statutory exception. The section attracted virtually no attention in the Parliamentary debates and committee proceedings leading to the enactment of the State Immunity Act. Subsequent commentaries on the act do not consider the section in any depth, and Doherty J.A. notes that the Court was not referred to by any other provincial appellate authority that has addressed the section.

In *Walker*, McKinlay J.A., for the Court, had expressed agreement with the position taken by counsel for Walker that the scope of personal injury covered by section 6 is not merely physical, but could include mental distress, emotional upset, and restriction of liberty. However, in *Friedland*, in which the plaintiff had attempted to rely on the personal injury exception to immunity in relation to damage to his reputation, emotional upset, and personal embarrassment, McKinlay J.A's statement was characterized as *obiter* that should not be taken to mean that section 6 extends to mental distress or emotional upset in all cases. Instead, the Court took the position that the personal injury exception refers primarily to physical injury and that section 6(a) extends to mental distress and emotional upset only in so far as such harm arises from or is linked to a physical injury. That interpretation of section 6(a) was essential to the court's decision that Friedland's claim must fail.

Doherty J.A. addresses the submission by counsel for Schreiber that while the court in *Friedland* held that claims for mental distress or upset were not "personal injury" claims absent some physical injury, it did not advert to claims based exclusively on the restriction of personal liberty. While it is true that *Friedland* does not refer to restraint of liberty when explaining the passage from *Walker*, there is no basis upon which to read personal injury as requiring physical injury for some types of harm but not others. It is particularly difficult to draw a distinction between allegations of mental distress and allegations of interference with personal liberty. The two allegations will almost inevitably go together. The latter brings about the former. To say that an allegation of interference with personal liberty is a "personal injury" absent any physical injury is in effect to say that at least some claims for mental distress are personal injury claims even without any physical harm. That position is foreclosed by *Friedland*.

Thus, *Friedland* is dispositive of Schreiber's submission that his claim falls within the section 6(a) exemption to state immunity, unless the court were to choose to depart from *Friedland*. Doherty J.A. acknowledges that the Court is not strictly bound by its earlier decisions, but that the mere fact that a panel might decide a matter differently than a previous panel is no reason to depart from that prior authority. Doherty J.A. then notes that a review of Canadian, English, and American case law does not give cause to depart from *Friedland*. Similarly, the scope of the "personal injury" exception to state immunity as understood by international lawyers is consistent with the conclusion arrived at in *Friedland*. Doherty J.A. refers, *inter alia*, to the International Law Commission's treatment of immunity, and its conclusion that the "personal injury" exception to sovereign immunity contemplated physical injury.

Doherty J.A. also finds support for the interpretation of "personal injury" adopted in *Friedland* in the French version of section 6(a), which provides that the foreign state enjoys no sovereign immunity in claims related to "dommages corporels." "Corporel" has been interpreted to mean physical injury to the body. The English and French versions of a federal statute are equally authoritative. Where the meaning of the words in one version of a statute is broader than the meaning that can be given to the words in the other version of the statute, the task is to find a meaning that is shared by both versions. The phrase "personal injury" is broader and more ambiguous than the phrase "dommages corporels." While "personal injury" might mean non-physical injuries, "dommages corporels" speaks more clearly to physical injury. Thus, physical injury is the shared meaning of the two versions of the statute.

Finally, Doherty J.A. also finds some support for interpreting "personal injury" as meaning physical injury by its combination in section 6(a) with the word "death." The two read in combination connote physical harm to the person.

Note: See also *Athabasca Chipewyan First Nation* v. *British Columbia* (2001), 281 A.R. 38 (Alberta Court of Appeal): the principle of sovereign immunity does not apply between Canadian provinces. To the extent that the rationale underlying sovereign immunity has any importance in a federal state, that function is fulfilled by the doctrine of Crown immunity.

Cook v. *Wade,* [2001] B.C.C.A. 285 British Columbia Court of Appeal.

This was an appeal of an order of a judge in chambers that a five-year-old girl be returned to the State of Alaska. The parties had been granted joint legal and physical custody of the child but had become embroiled in a series of disputes about access, involving, *inter alia,* allegations of abuse. The mother left Alaska with the child without informing the father. The father was later granted sole custody of the child; the mother was to have supervised access. The father then learned that the respondent was residing with the child in Vancouver and sought to have her returned to Alaska.

The appeal turned on the interpretation of provisions of the Hague Convention on Civil Aspects of International Child Abduction. Low J.A. notes that the chambers judge took what she refers to as a practical approach. She determined that the issue of custody of the child was properly before the court in Alaska, and she simply ordered that the child be returned to that jurisdiction. She did not consider the issues raised by the parties under the Hague Convention. In this, she was in error. She was bound to determine whether the child should be returned to Alaska under the convention, under other international law of comity or under the provisions of the Family Relations Act of British Columbia. It therefore falls to the Court of Appeal to determine whether the order was proper under the Hague Convention. Low J.A. concludes that it was. Article 3 of the convention provides that the removal or the retention of a child is to be considered wrongful where it is in breach of rights of custody attributed to a person, either jointly or alone, under the law of the state in which the child was habitually resident immediately before the removal or retention. Article 5 clarifies that rights of custody shall include rights relating to the care of the person of the child and, in particular, the right to determine the child's place of residence. Low J.A. acknowledges that the convention deals only with custodial rights and not with access rights. The court should not return a child to a jurisdiction in which she habitually resided to address access rights interfered with by the removal. However, Low J.A. does not accept the argument that the Alaskan orders, in reality, gave the father no more than access rights. The regime put in place by the court in Alaska clearly involved shared custody. Removal of the child from Alaska amounted to interference with the father's custodial rights as contemplated by the Hague Convention. The convention provisions should be applied to uphold the order appealed from.

Canadian Cases in Private International Law in 2000-1 / Jurisprudence canadienne en matière de droit international privé en 2000-1

compiled by / préparé par
JOOST BLOM

A   *Jurisdiction / Compétence des tribunaux*

1   Common Law and Federal

(a)   Jurisdiction *in personam*

Constitutionally valid jurisdiction (jurisdiction simpliciter*) — real and substantial connection — non-resident defendant*

Pacific International Securities Inc. v. *Drake Capital Securities Inc.* (2000), 194 D.L.R. (4th) 716, 82 B.C.L.R. (3d) 329. British Columbia Court of Appeal.

The plaintiff, a securities dealer in British Columbia, brought an action for damages against the defendant, a securities dealer in California, for breach of a contract to sell shares to the plaintiff. The contract between the plaintiff and the defendant had been made by telephone and confirmed by exchange of faxes. The damages claimed were the added amount that the plaintiff had had to pay in order to acquire the shares for its client in the open market. The plaintiff alleged that the British Columbia securities regulator had directed it to acquire the shares in this manner. The plaintiff claimed the right to serve the defendant *ex juris* without leave under Rule 13(1)(g) of the British Columbia Rules of Court, which refers to a breach of contract committed in British Columbia. Alternatively, the plaintiff sought leave to do so under Rule 13(3), which gives the court the discretion to give such leave in any case in which the claim does not fall under any of the categories in which the

---

Joost Blom is at the Faculty of Law at the University of British Columbia.

plaintiff is not entitled to serve *ex juris* without leave. The chambers judge held that the alleged breach of contract had been committed in California, not British Columbia, but granted leave under Rule 13(3). The defendant appealed, arguing that leave should not have been given. The defendant argued that the court lacked jurisdiction *simpliciter* because the case had no real and substantial connection with British Columbia or the British Columbia court was *forum non conveniens.*

The Court of Appeal, by a majority, upheld the decision to give leave to serve *ex juris.* The discretion granted by Rule 13(3) incorporated the real and substantial connection test for jurisdiction *simpliciter.* Although — unlike Rule 25(1)(h) in Ontario — damage sustained within the jurisdiction from a tort or breach of contract committed elsewhere is not a specific ground for asserting jurisdiction under Rule 13(1), there is no reason why it cannot be relied upon as a real and substantial connection "in any other case" under Rule 13(3). Here the plaintiff claimed that its damage was sustained in complying with British Columbia regulatory obligations. It might be that the rules of other jurisdictions would ultimately also be held to apply, but the British Columbia rules would be engaged at least on questions of mitigation of damages. In the context of this dispute, that was a real and substantial connection of the cause of action to British Columbia.

On the *forum non conveniens* issue, the chambers judge had been right in placing the onus on the defendant to show that the plaintiff should be denied its choice of forum because there was a clearly more appropriate forum in California. There was no reversible error in the judge's conclusion that the defendant had not met the onus, since the plaintiff did business here, the alleged damage was suffered here, and the cost of witnesses was a minor factor since under the British Columbia summary trial procedure the matter could be decided on affidavit evidence. If United States securities laws proved to be applicable, it could fairly be interpreted and applied by the British Columbia court.

The dissenting judge would have held that since the defendant had no presence in British Columbia, it did no business there, and the cause of action arose outside British Columbia, the mere impact of the breach on the British Columbia firm was not a real and substantial connection with the province. Nor was the role played by British Columbia regulatory rules; this is an era of intense regulation and California regulatory bodies might also be involved.

Easthaven Ltd. v. *Nutrisystem.com Inc.* (2001), 202 D.L.R. (4th) 560, 55 O.R. (3d) 334. Ontario Superior Court of Justice.

The plaintiff, a Barbados corporation, had registered the domain name "sweetsucces.com." The registering authority was Tucows, a Delaware corporation with its head office in Toronto, Ontario. The defendant, a Delaware corporation with its principal place of business in Pennsylvania, owned the trade mark SWEET SUCCESS, which it used in association with weight loss products that it marketed in the United States and in Canada. The defendant had approached the plaintiff about buying the domain name, but the plaintiff demanded a high price for it. The defendant sued the plaintiff in Pennsylvania claiming that the plaintiff's domain name infringed its trade mark rights and also contravened the Anticybersquatting Consumer Protection Act, P.L. 106-113 (1999), enacting 15 U.S.C. § 1125(d).

The Pennsylvania court issued a preliminary injunction against the plaintiff without having heard the plaintiff on the merits of the dispute. On the strength of this order, the defendant requested Tucows to transfer the domain name to it, which Tucows did. The next day, the plaintiff brought the present action, claiming damages against the defendant, a declaration that it, the plaintiff, owned the domain name, and an order that Tucows transfer the domain name back to it. Tucows responded by placing the domain name on "Registrar hold," which meant that nobody could register it. The plaintiff consequently discontinued the action against Tucows. The defendant now brought a motion to dismiss or stay the plaintiff's action against it, on the ground that it was *res judicata* given the Pennsylvania proceeding; that it was an abuse of process; and that the court lacked jurisdiction or should decline jurisdiction.

Nordheimer J. held against the defendant on the first two grounds. The Pennsylvania judgment had not been given on the merits and so could not be *res judicata*, and the plaintiff's action in Ontario could not be said to be an abuse of process. However, the Ontario court lacked jurisdiction because of the absence of a real and substantial connection between the litigation and Ontario. This was an issue distinct from *forum non conveniens*.

The court referred to an American decision on jurisdiction in Internet matters, *Panavision International* v. *Toeppen*, 141 F. 3d 1316 (9th Cir. 1998), for its analysis in terms of general and specific jurisdiction. There was no general jurisdiction over the defendant because it was not domiciled in Ontario, nor was there any evidence that it had engaged in activities in Ontario that were substantial or continuous and systematic. Specific jurisdiction depended upon three factors. First, the (*ex hypothesi*) non-resident defendant must have done an act or consummated some transaction in Ontario or purposefully availed itself of the privilege of conducting activities in Ontario, thereby invoking the benefits and protection of its laws. Here, the defendant had done nothing in Ontario. Second, the claim must be one that arises out of, or results from, the defendant's forum-related activities, which for the same reason was not the case here. Third, the exercise of jurisdiction must be reasonable. Here it would be unreasonable, given that the defendant was a Pennsylvania corporation that was being sued by a Barbados corporation. The sole connection to Ontario was the registering authority Tucows, but once the plaintiff discontinued its action against Tucows, the connection was removed.

Had it been necessary to consider the question of *forum non conveniens*, the judge would have held that Pennsylvania was clearly the more convenient forum for the determination of the issues in the action. Among other factors, the judge referred to the lack of any juridical advantage to the plaintiff from suing in Ontario, compared with the possible loss of juridical advantage to the defendant if the action were heard there, given the defendant's reliance on the anticybersquatting statute of the United States.

Note. The *Easthaven* case presented the comparatively rare situation where neither of the principal parties to the ligitagion had a presence in the province, and this made the decision on jurisdiction *simpliciter*, the constitutionally required minimum connection with the forum, relatively easy to resolve. More difficult are cases in which the plaintiff resides in the province but most of the facts giving rise to the action occurred elsewhere. As the division of opinion in the *Pacific International* case shows, it may not be easy to say whether the mere adverse effect of the alleged wrong on a resident plaintiff is a real and substantial connection with the forum province. This issue has arisen frequently in Ontario, where Rule 25 (1) (h), referred to in *Pacific*, allows service *ex juris* without leave if the plaintiff's claim is for damage sustained in Ontario from a tort or breach of contract wherever committed (Manitoba R. 17.02 (h) is similar). Is such damage *per se* a real and substantial connection? Practically always, seems to be the view taken in *Duncan (Litigation*

Guardian of) v. *Neptunia Corp.* (2001), 199 D.L.R. (4th) 354, 53
O.R. (3d) 754 (Ont. S.C.J.). The Ontario court was held to have
jurisdiction *simpliciter* in an action brought for the wrongful death
of an Ontario resident against the foreign corporation that had
employed him in China and provided an apartment for him there.
His injuries allegedly stemmed from a gas leak in the apartment.
The deceased's illness had lasted for years, for most of which time
he was back in Ontario. The aftermath of the wrong having been
suffered in Ontario was held to be a sufficient connection. The
court favoured a liberal interpretation of "real and substantial
connection" so as to minimize disputes about jurisdiction *simpliciter*
and decide jurisdictional issues primarily on the basis of a *forum
conveniens* analysis. A factor in that analysis was that the plaintiffs
had limited resources to pursue their claim in China, whereas the
defendants were multinational corporations.

A similar case is the wrongful dismissal claim in *Strukoff* v. *Syn-
crude Canada Ltd.* (2000), 80 B.C.L.R. (3d) 294 (C.A.). Although
the plaintiff's employment was in Alberta and his former employer
had no presence in British Columbia, the real and substantial
connection was supplied by the fact that the employer acquiesced
in the plaintiff's taking his disability leave in British Columbia,
where his condition deteriorated until he was dismissed allegedly
for cause, namely, maintaining that he was disabled when he was
not. The medical circumstances relating to the issue of cause were
mostly connected with British Columbia.

Where the alleged tort caused physical harm in the province,
jurisdiction *simpliciter* is readily established because the tort is usually treated as committed where the damage is foreseeably done:
see *Gariepy* v. *Shell Oil Co.* (2000), 51 O.R. (3d) 181 (Ont. S.C.J.), a
class action by Canadian consumers of polybutylene piping against
United States manufacturers of the resin that was used to manu-
facture the piping, and *Moellenbeck* v. *Ford Motor Co. of Canada*
(2000), 13 C.P.C. (5th) 287, 145 B.C.A.C. 183 (B.C.C.A.), an
action against the American manufacturer of an automobile seat
belt that broke in a road accident in British Columbia. The same is
true of financial harm if the alleged wrongful act can be seen as
specifically directed against business activities in Canada: *1248671
Ontario Inc.* v. *Michael Foods Inc.* (2000), 51 O.R. (3d) 789 (S.C.J.)
(Canadian importer alleging that an American manufacturer
lured away clients by using confidential information supplied by
the importer).

Declining jurisdiction — exclusive choice of forum clause

Note. In *Barber* v. *Height of Excellence Financial Planning Group Inc.* (2001), 106 Sask. R. 141 (Q.B.), Saskatchewan-resident investors sued a number of parties, about half with a presence in Saskatchewan and the others resident in British Columbia, who they said had wrongfully induced them into buying shares in a British Columbia limited partnership that did business in Nevada. The subscription agreements and the partnership agreement contained clauses that any action by the investors "will be brought" in British Columbia or "will be referred to the courts" of that province. The Saskatchewan judge read these clauses as providing for concurrent rather than exclusive jurisdiction, and so refused to stay the action.

Declining jurisdiction — forum non conveniens

Note. Actions brought against a defendant that is resident in the province are seldom stayed on *forum non conveniens* grounds, for obvious reasons: see *Agra Foundations Ltd.* v. *Konkrete Const. Ltd.* (2001), 205 Sask. R. 298 (Q.B.) (Saskatchewan firm sued for concrete supplied to the plaintiffs' plant in Alberta). The defendant's residence is less significant if the defendant does business in other jurisdictions and the litigation arises out of the extra-provincial business. Thus, in *Lan Associates XVIII L.P.* v. *Bank of Nova Scotia* (2000), 138 O.A.C. 114 (Ont. C.A.), the defendant was a Canadian bank with its main office in Toronto, but the claims were brought by Connecticut-based companies that had borrowed money from the bank to finance a hotel and casino project in the Turks and Caicos Islands (TCI). The claims were based on misrepresentation, breach of fiduciary duty, and other causes of action. The loan agreements were negotiated at least partly in TCI, they were governed by TCI law, and the loans were administered through the bank's TCI branch. Even though some of the alleged wrongful acts by bank officials had taken place in Ontario, the court held that TCI were overwhelmingly the more appropriate forum.

The presence of a vessel in Canadian waters, although it founds jurisdiction as of right in Admiralty cases, is a less compelling connection than the personal connection of the defendant, and a *forum non conveniens* argument may well succeed: *Nissho Iwai Co.* v. *Shanghai Ocean Shipping Co.* (2000), 185 F.T.R. 314 (T.D.) (cargo shipped on Chinese vessel from Vancouver to Japan was lost when the ship ran aground on one of the Kurile Islands north of Japan;

action by Japanese cargo owner stayed, conditional on the Chinese shipowners' waiving the limitation period in the Chinese court).

In contract actions, the fact that the plaintiff is a resident, and a non-resident defendant dealt with the plaintiff knowing that, is often by itself enough to make the province *forum conveniens* for a claim against the non-resident. In *Shercom Industries Inc.* v. *Pelletier Equitpment Ltée/Ltd.* (2001), 205 Sask. R. 95 (Q.B.), Saskatchewan was held the *forum conveniens* for an action by the Saskatchewan purchaser of an allegedly defective machine sold by a New Brunswick seller. By contrast, in *Progressive Holdings Inc.* v. *Crown Life Ins. Co.*, [2000] 7 W.W.R. 79, 147 Man. R. (2d) 175 (Q.B.), the litigation centred around a Manitoba corporation's contract to acquire, from a Saskatchewan-based insurance company, shares in a group of Alberta companies. None of the defendants in the action, which was in contract, tort and breach of fiduciary duty, was connected with Manitoba except the insurance company, which did business there. The main contracts in question were governed by the law of Alberta or Saskatchewan, and the alleged torts were all committed outside Manitoba. Alberta was held clearly to be the more appropriate forum for the litigation.

Declining jurisdiction — lis alibi pendens

Western Union Insurance Co. v. *Re-Con Building Products Inc.* (2001), 205 D.L.R. (4th) 184, application for leave to appeal dismissed, 9 May 2002 (S.C.C.). British Columbia Court of Appeal.

Re-Con, a British Columbia building materials business that exported most of its products to the United States, had a class action brought against it in California. It was not authorized to conduct intra-state business in that state and had no office or employees there. It brought an action in California against its liability insurers, Canadian corporations that did no business in California, for a declaration that they were obliged to defend the class action. The insurers then brought the present action in British Columbia for a declaration that the insurance policies issued to Re-Con were void *ab initio*. Re-Con applied for a declaration that the British Columbia court had no jurisdiction in the matter or should decline jurisdiction. The chambers judge held that the court had jurisdiction and that British Columbia was the *forum conveniens* for the dispute about the insurance policies, notwithstanding that the California proceeding had been commenced first. The judge refused to reconsider his denial of a stay when, subsequently, the California court also refused a stay of the proceeding there.

The Court of Appeal dismissed Re-Con's appeal. The test for *forum non conveniens* when there are parallel proceedings in two appropriate jurisdictions is, which jurisdiction has the closest real and substantial connection to the litigation and the parties. There was ample evidence to support the judge's finding that British Columbia was that jurisdiction. The judge was also correct in holding that the California action's being first in time was not determinative. The refusal of a stay by the California court was not a ground for reopening the chambers judge's decision. If such a reconsideration was essential every time that a foreign court took a step subsequent to the local court's decision on *forum non conveniens*, no litigation would ever be final.

Note. This case should be compared with *Westec Aerospace Inc. v. Raytheon Aircraft Co.* (1999), 173 D.L.R. (4th) 498, 67 B.C.L.R. (3d) 278 (noted in (1999) 37 Canadian Yearbook of International Law 435), in which the same court stayed a British Columbia proceeding because a parallel proceeding had been commenced in Kansas before the British Columbia one. The critical difference was that, in that case, the American court was seen as an equally appropriate forum for the dispute, which was between a British Columbia party and a Kansas party. The Court of Appeal responded to the argument that a "first to commence" approach might lead to a "race to the courthouse" by observing that the alternative approach would encourage a "race to judgment," since, if both forums are appropriate, it is likely that each will recognize a final judgment given in the other. This remark was given point when in January 2001, at the hearing of the appeal from the *Westec* decision, (2001), 197 D.L.R. (4th) 211*n.*, before the Supreme Court of Canada, the chief justice announced that the court had just learned that the Kansas court had in the meantime given judgment, which altered the issues in the case. The parties chose not to proceed and the appeal was dismissed.

(b)   Class proceedings

Class including non-residents

Note. Wilson v. Servier Canada Inc. (2000), 52 O.R. (3d) 20 (Div. Ct.), application for leave to appeal dismissed, Sept. 6, 2001 (S.C.C.), was a class action by those who had taken a prescription weight-loss drug, which had harmful side-effects, against the French manufacturer and the Canadian distributor of the drug. Some 155,000 potential claimants in Canada had taken the drug, of which about 56,000 lived in Ontario. Earlier cases had upheld the inclusion of non-residents of Ontario in the class of plaintiffs, but the defendants argued that those cases involved defendants who were connected with Ontario, whereas here the defendants were not. It was said that the combination of non-resident plaintiffs and non-resident defendants exceeded the proper limits of the Ontario court's jurisdiction. The court rejected this argument. It was in the interests of the efficient administration of justice that Canadians resident elsewhere in Canada should have the option of having their claims resolved in a single action together with the Ontario plaintiffs. They were not bound to do so because they could opt out of the class. It is still an unresolved question whether a final judgment in the Ontario class action would bind, in their own provinces' courts, non-residents of Ontario who had failed to opt out of the national class. It is likewise unresolved whether Ontario has the constitutional power to authorize, in its class action statute, a national class in which non-residents are required to opt out rather than opt in.

(c)   Actions relating to property

Bankruptcy and insolvency

   Note. Knai v. *Steen Contractors Ltd.* (2001), 22 C.B.R. (4th) 223 (Ont. S.C.J.), involved simulatenous bankruptcy proceedings in Québec, for two companies, and in Ontario, for their subsidiary. Two former officers of the Ontario subsidiary, one of whom had also had employment agreements with the two parent companies, sought to have their breach of contract claims against the three companies all adjudicated in the Québec proceedings. Both claimants were resident in Québec. The Ontario judge held that it would be more much convenient to have the validity of their claims against all three companies dealt with together in the Québec proceedings and, therefore, declined jurisdiction in respect of the claims against the Ontario firm.

(d)   Matrimonial proceedings

Divorce and corollary relief

   Note. See *Wlodarczyk* v. *Spriggs* (2000), 12 R.F.L. (5th) 241, 200 Sask. R. 129 (Q.B.), which held that a court cannot give corollary relief under the Divorce Act, R.S.C. 1985, c. 3 (2nd Supp.), where the parties have been divorced in a foreign court. Federal jurisdiction in the matter of corollary relief is tied to its jurisdiction in divorce.

(e)   Infants and children

Custody — grounds for jurisdiction

Note. See *Chan* v. *Chow,* noted later under the heading "Child Abduction — Hague Convention on the Civil Aspects of International Child Abduction."

Custody — declining jurisdiction

Note. If custody is dealt with by way of corollary proceedings under the Divorce Act, R.S.C. 1985, c. 3 (2nd Supp.), section 6 of the act gives the court discretion to transfer the proceedings to another province if the child is more substantially connected with that province. In *Shields* v. *Shields* (2001), 281 A.R. 320 (C.A.), the Court of Appeal held that the trial judge, in the circumstances of the case, was obliged to order the transfer of custody proceedings to Ontario because of the very limited connections of the children with Alberta.

Custody proceedings other than corollary to a divorce are subject to jurisdictional rules that are statutory in some provinces and common-law in others, but *forum conveniens* considerations play a key role in both schemes. In *Cheema* v. *Cheema,* [2001] 3 W.W.R. 629, 85 B.C.L.R. (3d) 222 (C.A.), the court refused to decline jurisdiction in favour of a court in India, where the father had commenced divorce proceedings, because the British Columbia forum was much better placed to decide on the interests of the child, who was born in British Columbia and had lived most of his life there with his mother. The facts were similar in *Krisko* v. *Krisko* (2000), 11 R.F.L. (5th) 324 (Ont. C.A.), in which the Ontario court refused to stay custody proceedings in favour of a court in Dubai, where the father lived, partly out of a concern about whether a court in Dubai would resolve the dispute on the basis of the best interests of the children.

Custody — enforcement of extraprovincial custody order

Note. See *S.(J.)* v. *K.(L.)* (2001), 192 N.S.R. (2d) 388 (S.C.), in which the court refused to exercise its *parens patriae* jurisdiction to enforce a Québec custody order in favour of the father, which was in conflict with orders made in the mother's favour in Nova Scotia. Québec had not enacted the uniform Reciprocal Enforcement of Custody Orders legislation, so that mechanism for enforcement was unavailable. The proper procedure was to appeal the Nova Scotia order.

Child Abduction — Hague Convention on the Civil Aspects of International Child Abduction

Chan v. *Chow* (2001), 199 D.L.R. (4th) 478, [2001] 8 W.W.R. 63. British Columbia Court of Appeal.

The father, a citizen of Hong Kong, and the mother, an Australian citizen, had married in Alberta in 1993. Their daughter was born there and they lived there until they separated for the first time in 1995. Later they reconciled and lived together with the daughter for a short time in Hong Kong. After another period of separation, and a divorce granted by the court in Alberta in 1997, they reconciled again and the family lived in Ontario and British Columbia. The parents separated for the last time in 1999, shortly after they moved back to Hong Kong. For a year after that, the child lived with each of them in Hong Kong for approximately an equal time. As part of the divorce proceeding, the Alberta court had, by consent, awarded them joint custody.

In March 2000, the father brought the child without the mother's consent to Vancouver. In November of that year, the mother commenced proceedings in British Columbia to have the daughter returned to Hong Kong pursuant to the Hague Convention on Civil Aspects of International Child Abduction, implemented in British Columbia by section 55 of the Family Relations Act, R.S.B.C. 1996, c. 128. The father cross-applied for custody. He had withdrawn his sponsorship of the mother and daughter for immigration to Hong Kong, and the permit for the child to remain in Hong Kong was to expire at the end of June 2001.

The chambers judge held that the Hague Convention's requirements had not been met because the child had not been habitually resident in Hong Kong at the time of the father's removal of her and, even if she had been, there was no evidence that the removal was in violation of the mother's custody rights. He therefore ordered that the custody proceeding should continue. Subsequently, but before the hearing of the present appeal, the father was convicted of a criminal offence and his conditional sentence required him to reside in Alberta until January 2003.

The Court of Appeal affirmed the decision that the child should not be returned to Hong Kong, but on different grounds. She had been habitually resident in Hong Kong at the time of her removal because her residence was with her parents and, at the time, both of them were habitually resident there because they had a settled intention for an appreciable period of time to make Hong Kong their home. Her removal by the father was in violation of the mother's custody rights because, applying the presumption that Hong Kong law was the same as British Columbia's, the joint custody order made in the Alberta divorce decree meant that neither of them could change the child's residence without the consent of the other. However, the Court of Appeal invoked the exception in Article 13 of the convention, which permits the court to refuse to order a child's return if "there is a grave risk that his or her return would expose the child to physical or psychological harm or otherwise place the child in an intolerable situation." The child had no right to remain in Hong Kong after June 2001, and so would have to move again if she were returned to the mother there. Second, the mother had a very unstable living pattern and thus a return to her custody might lead to further instability in the daughter's life. Third, there was a risk that the mother, as she had done before, would hide the child from the father if the child returned to Hong Kong. Finally, the father could not travel outside Canada for the next two years to protect his or the daughter's interest in any foreign custody proceeding.

Given the determination that the child should not be returned, Article 16 of the convention permitted the British Columbia court to proceed to determine custody. Moreover, section 44 of the Family Relations Act provided that a child who was not habitually resident in British Columbia was subject to the court's jurisdiction in custody if six conditions were fulfilled, and all of these were met here, including that, on the balance of convenience, it was appropriate for the British Columbia court to exercise jurisdiction.

Note. The "grave risk" exception was argued, but rejected, in *C.(D.M.)* v. *W.(D.L.)* (2001), 15 R.F.L. (5th) 35 (B.C.C.A.), and *New Brunswick (Attorney General)* v. *Majeau-Prasad* (2000), 10 R.F.L. (5th) 389 (N.B.Q.B.). In both cases, the removal or retention from the jurisdiction of habitual residence (Alaska and New Zealand, respectively) was wrongful because the applicant parent had had joint custody there. Another exception in Article 13 of the convention, which applies if the applicant parent has consented to, or acquiesced in, the removal or retention of the child, was rejected on the facts in *Katsigiannis* v. *Kottick-Katsigiannis* (2001), 203 D.L.R. (4th) 386 (Ont. C.A.) (child ordered to be returned to Greece). In *S.(J.R.)* v. *S.(P.R.)*, [2001] 9 W.W.R. 581, 208 Sask. R. 243 (Q.B.), the child was ordered to be returned to Pennsylvania and the mother's argument, that to do so violated his constitutional right as a Canadian citizen to live in Canada, was held to be without merit.

Adoption

Note. In *L.(T.I.)* v. *F.(J.L.)* (2001), 197 D.L.R. (4th) 721, [2001] 4 W.W.R. 455 (Man. C.A.), the court reversed the first instance judge's refusal to hear an adoption proceeding, which had been based on a finding that the adoptive parents, residents of Manitoba, and the child's mother, a resident of North Dakota, had conspired to circumvent the act's provisions on intercountry adoptions. There was no evidence to support such a finding, and in any event it did not go to the issue of jurisdiction, which under the act is based solely on the residence of the child and the adoptive parents in the province. The child's father had not established that North Dakota, where he also lived, was clearly the more convenient forum for the hearing of the adoption application, since all those who had significant insight into the child's life, and the child himself, resided in Manitoba.

2   Québec

(a)   Action personnelle

Compétence internationale — article 3148 C.C.Q. — faute commise au Québec — fait dommageable s'est produit au Québec

Conserviera S.p.A. c. *Paesana Import-Export Inc.*, [2001] R.J.Q. 1458. Cour d'appel du Québec.

Les appelantes sont des sociétés italiennes qui ont conclu un contrat de vente de conserves de tomates avec la société québécoise défenderesse. Comme les boîtes de conserves devaient être livrées au Canada, les appelantes ont obtenu de l'État italien et de la communauté européenne de substantielles primes à l'exportation, primes qui n'étaient toutefois pas offertes si les tomates étaient exportées aux États-Unis. Afin de prouver que les tomates avaient bel et bien été livrées au Canada, la société québécoise a fourni des documents douaniers canadiens attestant le dédouanage de la marchandise. Par la suite, les autorités italiennes ont appris que ces documents étaient des faux et que la marchandise avait pris le chemin des États-Unis. Elles ont réclamé aux appelantes les primes à l'exportation qu'elles leur avaient versées.

S'estimant fraudées, les appelantes ont alors intenté, en Italie, un recours en dommages-intérêts contre deux sociétés italiennes mandatées pour transporter les marchandises, contre la société québécoise et contre un résident des États-Unis qui aurait orchestré l'ensemble de l'opération frauduleuse.

Elles ont par la suite intenté au Québec une action en dommages-intérêts contre la société québécoise et son administrateur ainsi que contre le résident américain et la société dont il est l'administrateur. Elles leur réclament, dans un premier temps, le remboursement des primes à l'exportation qui leur ont été réclamées et, dans un deuxième temps, le prix des tomates vendues et livrées. Elles poursuivent également les deux signataires des chèques sans provision, qui sont des résidents américains. Les intimés ont présenté une exception déclinatoire, alléguant l'incompétence des tribunaux québécois. Le premier juge a accueilli l'exception déclinatoire des quatre intimés américains.

La Cour d'appel a accueilli l'appel en partie. D'une part, une requête pour soustraire le litige au régime de la procédure allégée constitue, en principe, une reconnaissance implicite de compétence, mais ce caractère implicite disparaît lorsque, comme en l'espèce, la requête contient une réserve expresse à l'effet contraire. D'autre part, l'exercice auquel le tribunal doit se livrer dans l'application de l'article 3148 C.C.Q. relève d'un examen de la situation individuelle de chacun des intimés.

À cet égard, si le résident américain à l'origine de la fraude est l'*alter ego* de la société québécoise, tous les gestes fautifs que celle-ci aurait commis au Québec à son instigation de même que tous les faits dommageables qui peuvent lui être attribués constituent des facteurs de rattachement qui confèrent compétence aux tribunaux québécois à l'endroit de cet intimé. De plus, comme participante de première ligne aux gestes fautifs attribués au résidant américain et aux faits dommageables qui se sont produits au Québec, la compagnie américaine se trouve aussi soumise à la compétence des tribunaux québécois.

Quant aux signataires des chèques sans provision souscrits à l'étranger, il n'y a aucun facteur de rattachement qui donnerait compétence aux tribunaux québécois. L'article 159(1) de la Loi sur les lettres de change, L.R.C. 1985, c. B-4, est de peu de secours dans les circonstances. Par conséquent, le pourvoi doit être rejeté contre les deux intimés signataires des chèques.

Par ailleurs, les tribunaux québécois étant compétents contre deux des intimés, doivent-ils décliner compétence en vertu de la règle du *forum non conveniens* prévue à l'article 3135 C.C.Q.? En l'espèce, ni les tribunaux italiens ni les tribunaux américains n'apparaissent clairement favorisés pour trancher sans encombre le litige. Le tribunal saisi, peu importe sa nationalité, devra faire face à des contraintes sur le plan de la détermination de la loi applicable, de la langue d'usage des témoins ou de leur éloignement relatif ou, enfin, de l'exécution du jugement à intervenir. Finalement, il n'y a pas litispendance entre l'action introduite au Québec et celle instituée en Italie. De plus, un sursis n'est pas souhaitable en l'espèce en raison de la différence dans les enjeux, de l'approche plus globale de l'action intentée au Québec et du stade apparemment peu avancé des procédures italiennes.

Compétence internationale — article 3148 C.C.Q. — préjudice subi au Québec

Quebecor Printing Memphis Inc. c. *Regenair Inc.*, [2001] R.J.Q. 966, demande d'autorisation d'appel rejetée, 14 février 2002 (C.S.C.). Cour d'appel du Québec.

Regenair, une société québécoise, a vendu à Quebecor Memphis, une société américaine, un système de récupération, qu'elle a installé aux Etats-Unis. Impayée, Regenair a intenté au Québec une action sur compte contre Quebecor Memphis. Celle-ci a soulevé l'incompétence des tribunaux québécois et, subsidiairement, elle a demandé l'application de la règle du *forum non conveniens*, prévue à l'article 3135 C.C.Q. Le premier juge a conclu que le contrat de vente était intervenu au Québec et il a appliqué l'article 68.3 C.P.C., qui permet d'intenter une action dans le lieu où le contrat a été conclu.

La Cour d'appel a accueilli (avec dissidence) l'appel de Quebecor Memphis. M. le juge Beauregard a expliqué que l'obligation de Regenair ne devait pas être exécutée en partie au Québec et en partie à Memphis, mais totalement à Memphis. Qu'à cette fin Regenair ait eu à fabriquer cette machinerie au Québec n'a pas de pertinence. D'autre part, le refus par Quebecor d'exécuter son obligation de payer à Memphis ne peut être tenu comme un fait dommageable survenu au Québec, et le fait que Regenair, dont le siège social est au Québec, ne reçoit pas le paiement de sa créance, laquelle est payable à Memphis, ne fait pas qu'un préjudice a été subi au Québec. Si Regenair avait raison, la compétence des tribunaux au Québec serait automatique dans le cas où le demandeur est un résident du Québec et les autres chefs de compétence visés à l'article 3148 C.C.Q. seraient inutiles. Il n'y a pas lieu d'interpréter d'une façon large l'article 3148 du fait de l'existence de l'article 3135 C.C.Q. Ce dernier article trouve application une fois qu'on a constaté que, interprété d'une façon raisonnable, l'article 3148 confère juridiction au tribunal québécois.

M. le juge Philippon, dissident, était d'avis que le défaut de paiement constitue une atteinte au patrimoine de Regenair qui s'est produite au lieu du domicile de Regenair, au Québec. Les critères attributifs de compétence énumérés à l'article 3148 C.C.Q. sont nombreux, distincts et indépendants les uns des autres. L'existence de l'un d'entre eux suffit. Quant au *forum non conveniens*, il ne se dégage pas en l'espèce une impression nette tendant vers l'instance étrangère.

(b)   Famille

Enfants — garde d'enfant — compétence

L.F. c. N.T., [2001] R.J.Q. 300. Cour d'appel du Québec.

Les parties se sont mariées en Côte d'Ivoire et leurs deux enfants y sont nés. En 1992, l'épouse a intenté une action en divorce devant le tribunal ivoirien. Un jugement provisoire lui a confié la garde des enfants et a accordé des droits d'accès au père. En 1992 aussi, la mère a obtenu l'autorisation de quitter le pays avec les enfants pour rendre visite à sa famille au Canada. Elle a décidé de s'y établir. Par la suite, la Cour d'appel de la Côte d'Ivoire a infirmé l'ordonnance de garde et a confié la garde provisoire des enfants au père. Il a alors été convenu que les enfants termineraient leur année scolaire au Québec et ce n'est qu'à l'été 1993 que leur père est venu les voir au Canada. À cette même époque, la mère s'est désistée de sa demande de divorce en Côte d'Ivoire et en a intenté une au Québec. À la demande du père, la procédure de divorce a été remise au rôle du tribunal ivoirien.

À l'été 1994, le père est revenu rendre visite aux enfants au Canada et les a ramenés en Côte d'Ivoire à l'insu de la mère. Au mois d'octobre 1994, la Cour supérieure a prononcé un jugement de divorce mais a déterminé que le tribunal compétent pour se prononcer sur la garde des enfants était celui de la Côte d'Ivoire.

En 1995, le tribunal ivoirien a prononcé le divorce des parties et a confié la garde des enfants au père. Par la suite, la mère s'est installée provisoirement en Côte d'Ivoire pour rendre visite aux enfants et a interjeté appel du jugement de divorce. La Cour d'appel de ce pays a rejeté son pourvoi mais, en 1998, la Cour suprême lui a donné raison au motif que la garde des enfants lui avait été déjà accordée par un tribunal canadien au moment du divorce. La demande de divorce du père a été rejetée, ainsi que celle visant à obtenir la garde des enfants. La mère est alors revenue avec les enfants au Québec, où elle a demandé la garde. Cette requête a été accueillie provisoirement, sous réserve de la compétence des tribunaux québécois, qui devait être déterminée dans le cadre de la requête pour exception déclinatoire introduite par le père. Celle-ci a fait l'objet du jugement dont appel. Le premier juge a conclu qu'avant l'arrêt de la Cour suprême de la Côte d'Ivoire de 1998 les enfants avaient leur domicile dans ce pays, malgré leur séjour au Canada. Selon lui, après ce jugement, aucun des parents n'avait obtenu la garde des enfants et ne pouvait exercer seul l'autorité parentale. La mère devait donc obtenir le consentement du père avant d'amener les enfants au Canada.

Entre-temps, la Cour suprême de la Côte d'Ivoire a suspendu l'exécution provisoire du jugement de 1998 et a décidé que les parties se trouvaient dans un vide juridique quant à la garde des enfants.

La Cour d'appel du Québec a rejeté l'appel du jugement de la Cour supérieure. La Convention sur les aspects civils de l'enlèvement international d'enfants et la Loi sur les aspects civils de l'enlèvement international et interprovincial d'enfants, L.R.Q., c. A-23.01, n'ayant pas été ratifiées par la Côte d'Ivoire, ce sont les articles du Code civil du Québec qui s'appliquent pour décider de la compétence des tribunaux québécois à statuer sur la garde des enfants. Suivant l'article 3142 C.C.Q., ceux-ci sont compétents si les enfants sont domiciliés au Québec. Or, en vertu de l'article 80 C.C.Q., le domicile d'un enfant dont les parents n'ont pas de domicile commun est déterminé par sa résidence habituelle. En l'espèce, avant le jugement de la Cour suprême de la Côte d'Ivoire de 1998, le domicile des enfants était donc dans ce pays puisque leur déplacement au Canada résultait d'un acte unilatéral de la mère. Après le jugement de 1998, la mère ne pouvait, à l'insu du père, ramener les enfants au Canada puisque, conformément au Code Civil de la Côte d'Ivoire, les deux parents continuaient d'exercer conjointement l'autorité parentale, aucun d'eux n'ayant obtenu la garde des enfants. C'est donc à bon droit que le premier juge a conclu que la Côte d'Ivoire était la résidence habituelle des enfants.

L'application immédiate du critère de l'intérêt de l'enfant au stade de la détermination de la compétence matérielle du tribunal apparaît prématurée. Quant aux exceptions prévues aux articles 3136 et 3140 C.C.Q. et susceptibles de conférer compétence aux tribunaux québécois dans des situations exceptionnelles, la demande de la mère de réserver ses recours à cet égard étant donné l'instabilité politique qui sévit en Côte d'Ivoire est accueillie.

B   Procedure / Procédure

1   Common Law and Federal

(a)   Remedies

Damages — foreign currency — conversion

Stevenson Estate v. *Siewert* (2001), 202 D.L.R. (4th) 295 (Alta CA).

The Alberta Court of Appeal had earlier held that a lawyer, his secretary, and a bank were liable in conversion for having permitted a US $100,000 bank draft, belonging to a trustee on behalf of a legally incompetent party, to find its way into the hands of a third party who had misappropriated the funds (see the note in (2000) 38 Canadian Yearbook of International Law 471). In the present proceeding, the court agreed to rehear the case on the issue of the exchange rate that should be applied in calculating the damages.

In its earlier decision, the court had held it was free to apply the rate as of either the date of the conversion, which was July 1990, or the date of its own judgment in August 2000. The court had applied the date of conversion. Now, after further argument, the court held that, as between the two dates, the date of its own judgment was the fairest and most equitable to choose. Between July 1990 and August 2000, the Canadian dollar value of US $100,000 had risen from C $116,500 to C $149,000. The basic principle of tort damages was that the victim should be put in the same position, as far as possible, as if the tort had not occurred. The tortfeasors knew they were dealing with US dollars, the value of which was subject to fluctuation. The use of prejudgment interest would not, contrary to what the court had said in its earlier reasons, serve to mitigate the currency exchange loss of the plaintiff, since it would likely have been awarded in any event. It could not be expected that either of the two dates would result in perfect fairness to both parties. That being so, if any equities must fall unequally on the parties, they should fall more heavily on the wrongdoer than on the victim.

The plaintiff therefore should have judgment for US $100,000 converted into Canadian funds as at the date of the present judgment. Prejudgment interest should be awarded at the rates prescribed under the Judgment Interest Act, S.A. 1984, c. J-0.5, as calculated on US $100,000 and converted to Canadian dollars according to the exchange rate in effect for the purchase of Canadian dollars on the first of January of each year with respect to which interest was calculated.

Note. One can imagine circumstances in which the plaintiff would be most fairly compensated by using a conversion date that is neither the date of breach nor the date of judgment. If, for instance, the defendant can show that the plaintiff himself would at some point have converted the foreign currency into Canadian funds, the fairest way to calculate damages would be to use the exchange rate as of the time when the plaintiff would have held his asset in Canadian currency in any event. The legally incompetent party who beneficially owned the funds in this case had died before trial of the conversion action, and the defendants argued in the present proceeding that the court should use the date on which the person's estate was first distributed, presumably because the US funds, if the trustee had still had them, would have been changed to Canadian funds at that time. The court held that there was insufficient evidence before it to provide adequate justification for choosing a date other than the two — breach date and judgment date — that were canvassed. It did, however, indicate (at para. 4) that in the future a court might see fit to expand the range of possible conversion dates beyond those two. If the plaintiff would hold its funds in the foreign currency at all times, the theoretically most appropriate date is when the judgment is actually paid, which is the date laid down in the uniform Foreign Money Claims Act, which has (or provisions similar to which have) been enacted in British Columbia, Ontario and Prince Edward Island. See, for instance, Foreign Money Claims Act, R.S.B.C. 1996, c. 155. The Ontario equivalent, the Courts of Justice Act, R.S.O. 1990, c. C.43, s. 121, gives the court a discretion to choose another date instead of the date of payment.

If interest rates differ from one currency to another, the court should choose the one that is appropriate to the currency in which the plaintiff's claim is denominated at the time in question. This, again, is the solution adopted in the uniform Foreign Money Claims Act. Thus the theoretically fairest prejudgment interest in this case would be the rate on US dollar accounts, not Canadian dollar accounts, from the date of the tort until the date of judgment. Whether a court is free to adjust the rate by reference to the currency of the claim depends on the prejudgment interest legislation, the relevant terms of which vary from province to province. Section 2(3) of the Alberta statute permits the court to award a rate of interest other than the prescribed rate "if it considers it just to do so having regard to . . . the circumstances of the case."

See also *Skaggs Companies* v. *Mega Technical Holdings* (2000), [2001] 1 W.W.R. 359, 85 Alta. L.R. (3d) 181 (Alta. Q.B. (Master)), an action on a Utah judgment, in which the court ordered the judgment debt to be converted into Canadian currency using the exchange rate on the effective date of the Alberta judgment.

C   Foreign Judgments / Jugements étrangers

1   Common Law and Federal

(a)   Conditions applicable to enforcement by action or registration

Jurisdiction of original court — attornment to the jurisdiction

Note. The debtor under an Alberta judgment was held in *Auger* v. *Smith* (2000), 73 B.C.L.R. (3d) 248 (C.A.), to have attorned to the jurisdiction of the Alberta court. He had defended the action, although his counsel had left the proceeding when the judge refused to grant an adjournment on the ground of the defendant's illness. Registration of the judgment under the Court Order Enforcement Act, R.S.B.C. 1996, c. 78, was therefore proper.

Jurisdiction of original court — agreement to submit to the jurisdiction

Note. Skaggs Companies v. *Mega Technical Holdings* (2000), [2001] 1 W.W.R. 359, 85 Alta. L.R. (3d) 181 (Alta. Q.B. (Master)), enforced a Utah default judgment on the basis that the contract in question provided that the parties agreed to submit to the jurisdiction of the Utah court. It was immaterial that activities under the contract were carried out mainly in Alberta.

(b)   Defences applicable to enforcement by action or registration

Public policy

Society of Lloyd's v. *Meinzer* (2001), 210 D.L.R. (4th) 519, 55 O.R. (3d) 688, application for leave to appeal dismissed, June 13, 2002 (S.C.C.). Ontario Court of Appeal.

The defendants were Canadian-resident "Names," that is, members of underwriting syndicates at Lloyd's. The contracts by which they had engaged in this business were entered into in England and were expressly governed by English law. The contracts empowered Lloyd's to regulate the underwriting business of the syndicates to which the Names belonged. To deal with the financial crisis in the insurance market in the early 1990s, Lloyd's made cash calls on all the Names. When many of them refused to pay, the resulting mass of litigation was dealt with by Lloyd's adopting in 1996 a restructuring plan. Many Names accepted the offer of settlement included in this plan, but Lloyd's exercised its regulatory power to compel even those who refused the offer of settlement, to have their liabilities mandatorily reinsured with a group of companies called Equitas. Under the terms of the reinsurance contract the Names were obliged to pay the premiums for the reinsurance free and clear from any set-off, counterclaim, or other deduction, including in respect of claims against Lloyd's. Lloyd's brought an action in England to recover the Equitas premiums from the non-settling Names, including the Canadian residents who were defendants in the present case.

Some years earlier, a group of Canadian Names had brought an action against Lloyd's in Ontario on claims of fraud as well as contravention of Ontario securities legislation by marketing securities without a prospectus. The Ontario courts stayed this action on the ground that England was the *forum conveniens* for dealing with these claims, especially given the express choice of forum clause in the Names' contracts with Lloyd's (*Ash* v. *Corp. of Lloyd's* (1992), 9 O.R. (3d) 755 (Ont. C.A.), application for leave to appeal dismissed, Oct. 8, 1992 (S.C.C.)).

The present case was brought by Lloyd's to enforce the judgments by which the English court held the Names liable to pay the premiums. The English judge had rejected the defence of fraud on the part of Lloyd's on the ground that, even assuming the allegations of fraud were true, it did not relieve the Names of their obligation to pay the Equitas premiums. Rescission of their contracts with Lloyd's was impossible because, *inter alia*, it would retroactively invalidate the insurance business that each Name, through the relevant Lloyd's syndicate, had done since entering into the agreement with Lloyd's. Because of the terms of the reinsurance contract imposed on the Names, any damages for fraud could not be set off against the liability for the premiums. The English court also rejected the arguments based on Lloyd's having failed to comply with Ontario securities laws, on the ground that this breach, assuming it had taken place, was not a defence in an action in England.

Lloyd's applied to register the English judgments in Ontario under the Reciprocal Enforcement of Judgments (U.K.) Act, R.S.O 1990, c. R.6, incorporating the Canada-United Kingdom Convention for the Reciprocal Recognition and Enforcement of Judgments in Civil and Commercial Matters. The judgment debtors invoked, *inter alia*, the defences of natural justice and public policy. The trial judge (whose decision is noted in (2000) 38 Canadian Yearbook of International Law 473, *sub nom. Society of Lloyd's* v. *Saunders*) held that the judgments were registrable under the convention. The Court of Appeal dismissed the judgment debtors' appeal.

For the purposes of the analysis, the Court of Appeal, whose judgment was given by Feldman J.A., assumed that breach of natural justice, although not specifically mentioned, is comprised in the public policy defence in article IV(1)(e) of the convention. The Names argued that natural justice had been denied them because they were not permitted a trial on the merits of their claims of fraud. This argument, held the Court of Appeal, was misconceived. The Names were not deprived of the legal effect of a full hearing on the merits because the fraud was assumed to be proved. The substantive complaint was based on the "pay now, sue later" policy that was imposed on the Names and was upheld by the English courts. Had those courts not proceeded on the basis that the fraud claims, if proved, would not have provided a defence to the judgments because the remedy of rescission was not available, the other procedural safeguards might well not have overcome the failure to provide the Names with an opportunity to present the fraud defence.

A second alleged breach of natural justice was that the English court had made findings of fact on contested issues without a trial, which would be contrary to Ontario procedures on summary judgment or motions on issues of law. The Court of Appeal rejected this argument because the Names had not shown, in the record of the English proceedings, that any purely factual issues were in dispute. It was the English court's conclusions of law, rather than any specific issue of fact, that the Names contested.

The Names' public policy argument was founded on Lloyd's failure to file a prospectus, as required by Ontario securities legislation, before trading in securities with Ontario Names. The breach of Ontario securities laws was assumed for the purposes of the present application and appeal. The Court of Appeal reviewed all the important Canadian case law on the meaning of public policy as a defence to the enforcement of a foreign judgment or to the application of foreign law in Canadian proceedings. The exemption was narrow and had seldom been applied. This was consistent with the trend expressed in *Morguard Investments Ltd.* v. *De Savoye*, [1990] 3 S.C.R. 1077, 76 D.L.R. (4th) 256, a foreign judgment case, and *Tolofson* v. *Jensen*, [1994] 3 S.C.R. 1022, 120 D.L.R. (4th) 289, a choice of law case. That trend was to emphasize the concept of comity among nations and particularly among provinces of Canada when addressing the issue of enforcement of judgments and choice of law.

Public policy had been universally described as "fundamental values" and "essential principles of justice." It was appropriate at this stage in the development of our society to characterize the protection of our capital markets and of the public who invest in and depend on the confident and consistent operation of those markets as such a fundamental value. However, to determine whether enforcement of the particular judgment would be contrary to the public policy of Ontario, the court must consider the historical and factual context of the proceedings that led to the granting of the judgment and, where there are competing policy imperatives, whether, overall, registration would be contrary to public policy.

In many circumstances, the enforcement of a foreign judgment upholding a securities transaction that would have been unenforceable in an action brought in Ontario would be contrary to the public policy of Ontario. In this case, however, there were two factors that outweighed the breach of the Securities Act. One was the Court of Appeal's own earlier decision in *Ash* v. *Corporation of Lloyd's*. The court had held that England was the more appropriate forum for the litigation of Lloyd's claims against the Ontario Names, being well aware of the possibility that the English courts would not find Ontario law to be the proper law of the contracts and, therefore, would not hold the Ontario Names entitled to the protection of the Securities Act. It was implicit in the earlier decision that a refusal by the English courts to give effect to the Securities Act would not prevent enforcement of the English judgments in Ontario. To now conclude that the English judgments were unenforceable in Ontario as contrary to public policy would undermine the credibility of the earlier decisions of Ontario's courts and of its judicial system.

The other factor militating against the public policy argument was international comity. The Lloyd's contracts were international contracts, involving an English insurance and investment system where the participant members or Names were located worldwide. All Names entered into the same agreements wherein they agreed to litigate their disputes in England under English law. Names were solicited in their home jurisdictions, many of which had securities legislation with provisions similar to those in Ontario requiring disclosure of material information to investors. The US courts that had faced the same public policy argument made by the Names had almost uniformly rejected it on the basis of international comity principles. All had been satisfied that to grant rescission to some Names, when the insurance policies that they had underwritten remained outstanding, would create a situation of economic chaos as well as unfairness. The result reached by the English courts, that the Names must pursue their damages remedy for fraud after paying their premiums and participating in the scheme necessary to retain the viability of this very important worldwide insurance market, was a sensible one. In that context, Ontario's public policy of enforcing the rules of comity where justice, necessity, and convenience all favoured enforcement, outweighed the concerns that the court might otherwise have where there has been a breach of the prospectus requirements of the Ontario Securities Act.

Note. The court's treatment of the public policy defence is the fullest and most carefully nuanced discussion of this topic in any Canadian case so far. Especially valuable is the insight that a court must put into the scales not only the fundamental values that would be impaired if the judgment were enforced but also the fundamental values that would be impaired if it were not enforced.

Fraud

Beals v. *Saldanha* (2001), 202 D.L.R. (4th) 630, 54 O.R. (3d) 641, leave to appeal granted, 16 May 2002 (S.C.C.). Ontario Court of Appeal.

The defendants, two couples resident in Ontario, sold a parcel of land in a Florida subdivision to the plaintiffs, two couples resident in Florida, for a price of US $8,000. The plaintiffs later sued the defendants in Florida for rescission of the contract of purchase and sale and damages for fraud. The plaintiffs alleged that the defendants had fraudulently led them to believe that they were purchasing another lot rather than the lot that was actually conveyed. The pleadings said only that the damages claimed were "in excess of [US]$5,000." The defendants received notice of the Florida action but, on the advice of their lawyer that a default judgment would be unenforceable in Ontario, did not defend the action. Under Florida law, the defendants' default entitled the plaintiffs to judgment but damages had to be assessed by a jury. On the basis of evidence, the plaintiffs put before them, the jury awarded US $210,000 compensatory and $50,000 punitive damages. The bulk of the compensatory damages were for loss of profits that the plaintiffs said they would have made if they had been able to complete construction of the model home on the lot in question and thus initiate an extensive development on other property nearby. The defendants took no step to set aside the Florida default judgment or to appeal it because, again, their lawyer advised them that the judgment was not enforceable against them in Ontario.

The plaintiffs brought an action in Ontario on the Florida judgment. The amount claimed, including interest, was roughly C $800,000. The trial judge held ((1998), 42 O.R. (3d) 127 (Gen. Div.), noted in (1999) 37 Canadian Yearbook of International Law 457) that the judgment was unenforceable on the grounds of the plaintiffs' fraud, failure of natural justice, and public policy. The judge found fraud in several aspects of the case that the plaintiffs had advanced before the jury on the issue of damages. One was that the claim for lost profits related to profits that would have been made, not by them, but by a corporate vehicle that had ceased to exist before they commenced their action. Another was that they had concealed from the jury the fact that the construction of the model home had been stopped because the plaintiffs had had a falling-out, which had nothing to do with the identity of the lot and so meant that the defendants' alleged wrong had not caused the loss of the profits being claimed. The judge added that if required to do so he would also have found that enforcement of the judgment would violate public policy. He said that the great expansion of the Canadian rules for recognition of foreign default judgments in *Morguard Investments Ltd.* v. *De Savoye*, [1990] 3 S.C.R. 1077, 76 D.L.R. (4th) 256, implied the need to apply a broader notion of public policy, "some sort of judicial sniff test in considering foreign judgments" (at para. 69). This judgment failed the sniff test, apparently because the defendants had no warning that the damages would be so disproportionately high in relation to the value of the lot that the defendants had bought.

The Ontario Court of Appeal held two to one that neither fraud, nor violation of public policy, nor failure of natural justice had been made out and the judgment was accordingly enforceable. Doherty J.A., Catzman J.A. concurring, adopted the view, originally advanced in *Jacobs* v. *Beaver* (1908), 17 O.L.R. 496 (C.A.), that the defence of fraud, when raised against the enforcement of a foreign judgment, requires proof of the same elements as the setting aside of a domestic judgment for fraud. The defendant must demonstrate that the fraud is revealed by newly discovered facts, that is, facts that could not have been discovered by the exercise of due diligence prior to the obtaining of the judgment whose enforcement the defendant seeks to prevent. The trial judge had erred in failing to limit "newly discovered facts" to those facts that could not have been discovered prior to the Florida judgment by the exercise of reasonable diligence. All the facts relied upon by the trial judge as evidence of fraud would easily have been ascertainable by the defendants had they chosen to participate in the Florida proceeding.

Moreover, the evidence the judge relied upon, even if it had been relevant, did not support his conclusion that the plaintiffs were guilty of fraud. The point that the claim for lost profits belonged, not to the plaintiffs, but to their corporation, might or might not be correct under Florida law but there was no evidence that the jury was misled in any way as to the corporation's role in the transactions. The plaintiffs' having stopped construction because they fell out with each other was not inconsistent with the plaintiffs' claim that their money had been wasted as a result of the defendant's alleged fraud, and the lost future profits could still be a legitimate claim by the two plaintiffs who, it appeared, had intended to continue with the project even if the other two backed out. The award for lost profits was the main reason for the disproportion between the modest sale price of the land and the very large size of the judgment, but there was no evidence as to the factual material placed before the jury in support of the lost profit claim. Without such evidence, it was impossible to conclude that the jury was somehow misled or that the award was determined in a manner that offended principles of fairness and fundamental justice.

Doherty J.A. also disagreed with the trial judge's view that the "substantial connection" approach to jurisdiction taken by *Morguard* compelled a broader public policy defence to the enforcement of foreign judgments. To the contrary, the rationale underlying *Morguard* was entirely consistent with the narrow application of the public policy defence in previous Canadian decisions. Even if "some sort of judicial sniff test" were applied, there was no reason not to enforce this judgment. The plaintiffs had brought their allegations in the proper forum, followed the proper procedures, and were immensely successful in no small measure because the defendants chose not to participate in the proceedings.

Weiler J.A., dissenting, thought that the defence of fraud had been made out. She disagreed that the same standard should be applied to applications to set aside a local judgment on the ground of fraud, and defending against the enforcement of foreign judgments on that ground. To do so was to ignore the distinction between setting aside a defended judgment and a default judgment. The "newly discovered facts" rule applied to defended judgments. An application to set aside a local default judgment would be based, not upon fraud, but upon a full examination of the merits. That remedy was not available in enforcement proceedings relating to a foreign default judgment. Where fraud was raised as a defence to enforcement of a foreign default judgment, a flexible approach was appropriate, and should take into account the reasons why the defendants let judgment go against them by default and whether it was now possible or practicable to seek a remedy before the foreign court. The defendants here did not appreciate the extent of their jeopardy as a result of the plaintiffs' pleading, were not in a position to make an informed decision to defend, and were advised that the Florida judgment could not be enforced against them. The fraud was not apparent on the face of the judgment but became known only when enforcement of the judgment was sought in Ontario. Hence, the defendants should be entitled to raise the defence of fraud even on facts that were known or available to them at the time of the Florida proceeding. The judge was justified in finding that plaintiffs' presentation of their corporation's lost future profits as their own, and their suppression of the reason why construction of the house was abandoned, had fraudulently caused the jury to make an erroneous award of damages.

Note. The Canadian view of the defence of fraud, which is usually taken to be the one set forth in *Jacobs* v. *Beaver* and adopted by the majority in this case, is narrower than the English rule, which allows the judgment debtor to rely upon a fraud that the debtor could have countered, or even did counter, before the foreign court: *Abouloff* v. *Oppenheimer* (1882), 10 Q.B.D. 295 (C.A.); *Vadala* v. *Lawes* (1890), 25 Q.B.D. 310 (C.A.). Weiler J.A.'s proposed rule would fall between the two. The recent evolution of Canadian jurisprudence has thrown the issue into higher relief. The *Morguard* case rendered foreign judgments enforceable in Canada on the basis that the action had a real and substantial connection with the foreign country. This has opened the way to enforcing many more foreign default judgments than was formerly possible. The proper scope of the defence of fraud has therefore acquired greatly enhanced significance, as this case illustrates vividly.

Natural justice

Note. See *Society of Lloyd's* v. *Meinzer* and *Beals* v. *Saldanha*, which is noted immediately above, both of which included defences based on natural justice. See also *Oyj* v. *Reinikka* (2000), 133 O.A.C. 1 (Ont. C.A.), which held that the judgment debtor under a Finnish judgment could not say that natural justice had been violated just because, owing to procedural irregularities, he had not received notice of the original action. He had received notice of the default judgment and of his right to a trial on the merits in Finland if he applied in thirty days, which for inadequate reasons he did not do.

(c)   Registration under uniform reciprocal enforcement of judgments legislation or an international convention

Defences unique to registration statutes

Note. See *Auger* v. *Smith* (2000), 73 B.C.L.R. (3d) 248 (C.A.), which, in upholding registration of an Aberta judgment under the Court Order Enforcement Act, R.S.B.C. 1996, c. 78, denied that the judgment debtor could avail himself of the defence in section 29(6)(g) of the act that he "would have a good defence if an action were brought on the judgment." He had no defence to an action on the judgment, as distinct from a defence to the original cause of action. That latter, contrary to the chambers judge's view, was not opened up by this provision.

See also *Niles* v. *Bahadoorsingh* (2000), denying registration because the original court lacked jurisdiction as required by the Reciprocal Enforcement of Foreign Judgments Act, R.S.N.B. 1973, c. R-3, and as defined by the Foreign Judgments Act, R.S.N.B. 1973, c. F-19. The court noted that the "real and substantial connection" ground for the recognition of an extra-provincial judgment was not part of the law of New Brunswick because of the Foreign Judgments Act, but will become so if the Canadian Judgments Act, R.S.N.B. 1973, c. C-0.1, is proclaimed in force.

(d)   Registration under uniform reciprocal enforcement of maintenance orders legislation

Provisional order — applicable law

Note. *Penner* v. *Lee,* [2001] 6 W.W.R. 285, 201 Sask. R. 114 (U.F.C.), includes an extensive discussion of the problem of the applicable law when a Saskatchewan resident claims under the uniform Reciprocal Enforcement of Maintenance Orders Act, S.S. 1996, c. R-4.2, for a provisional order for support from a former common law spouse resident in another province. In that case, the parties' cohabitation had been in Manitoba and the respondent now lived in British Columbia. The claim was out of time by the law of the other provinces but not by the law of Saskatchewan. The scheme of the act is that the court making the provisional order applies its own law, and the confirming court can only entertain defences based on that law. The problem is that the *lex fori* for the provisional order, as in this case, may have little connection with the facts out of which the support claim arises. However, the issue did not need to be determined because the claim was for a lump sum payment, not for periodic maintenance, and thus could not be entertained in any event.

Confirmation of provisional order — evidence required

Note. In *F.(L.P.)* v. *Ontario (Director, Family Responsibility Office)* (2001), 15 R.F.L. (5th) 52 (Ont. S.C.J.), a Manitoba order for monthly child and spousal support had been made against the respondent twelve years earlier. He had moved to Ontario at about that time and had not received notice of the order until now, his driver's licence was suspended for non-payment of support, pursuant to the Family Responsibility and Support Arrears Enforcement Act, S.O. 1996, c. 31. The Ontario court held that the Manitoba order could only be considered at best a provisional order, which could not be enforced in Ontario until confirmed under the Reciprocal Enforcement of Support Orders Act, R.S.O. 1990, c. R-7. Confirmation was not possible because of a lack of evidence as to the claimant's household standard of living, which was needed to assess the appropriate amount of support. The matter was remitted to the Manitoba court to obtain the evidence. See also *Kearney (Guardian ad litem)* v. *Willis* (2001), 15 R.F.L. (5th) 96 (Nfld. U.F.C.), in which a provisional order was made, applying Newfoundland law to the obligation of a father, resident in Nova Scotia, to support the mother and their child, who had been conceived in Nova Scotia but born in Newfoundland. The most substantial connection of mother and child was held to be with Newfoundland.

(e)   Recognition of foreign judgment as *res judicata*

Issue estoppel

Banque National de Paris (Canada) v. *Canadian Imperial Bank of Commerce* (2001), 195 D.L.R. (4th) 308, 52 O.R. (3d) 161, application for leave to appeal dismissed, Nov. 1, 2001 (S.C.C.). Ontario Court of Appeal.

The plaintiffs brought an action in Ontario for a declaration that the defendant's security interest in the assets of a company that had filed for bankruptcy was void as against them. Some months later an unsecured creditor of the bankrupt firm commenced proceedings in Québec against the defendant bank, also contesting the validity of its security and claiming damages for wrongful conduct in respect of a "soft receivership" that preceded the bankruptcy and in respect of the realization of assets. The bank applied to have the plaintiffs added to the proceedings as *mis-en-cause*. The plaintiffs agreed to a standstill of the Ontario proceedings pending the outcome of the Québec action. After a forty-two-day trial and an appeal to the Québec Court of Appeal by the bank and by the plaintiffs, the bank's security was held invalid in part and the bank was held liable to pay $500,000 damages to the creditors. The plaintiffs resumed their Ontario action and now sought to amend their statement of claim to include allegations of misconduct in the receivership and in the realization of assets. The bank objected that these claims were *res judicata*. The judge at first instance held that the latter claim was *res judicata*, but not the former.

The Court of Appeal held that both claims were *res judicata* by virtue of issue estoppel. Issue estoppel had three elements. First, the same issue must have been decided in the earlier proceeding, which was the case here. Second, the earlier decision must be final, which this one was. And, third, the parties to the earlier decision or their privies must be the same as the parties to the present proceedings. The plaintiffs actively supported the unsecured creditor's claims in the Québec proceeding. They were privies to that party because they had privity of interest with it. Privity of interest existed because there was a sufficient degree of identification between the plaintiffs and the unsecured creditor that it was just to hold them bound to the proceedings in which the latter was a party. They were intervenors to the Québec proceedings to a limited extent and they could have broadened the scope of their intervention had they sought to do so. They had allowed the unsecured creditor to carry the battle in which they had a practical and legal concern. Justice and common sense compelled the conclusion that they abide by the decision and there was no unfairness or policy basis for not holding them bound.

D   *Choice of Law (including Status of Persons) / Conflits de lois (y compris statut personnel)*

1   Common Law and Federal

(a)   Characterization

Substance and procedure

   Note. Tolofson v. *Jensen,* [1994] 3 S.C.R. 1022, 120 D.L.R. (4th) 289, changed the law to hold that statutes of limitation are not procedural but substantive in nature. Claims are therefore governed by the limitation law of the jurisdiction whose law governs the cause of action. In Alberta, section 12 of the Limitations Act, S.A. 1996, c. L-15.1 (as am.), reverses this position. It provides that "[t]he limitations law of the Province shall be applied whenever a remedial order is sought in this Province, notwithstanding that, in accordance with conflict of law rules, the claim will be adjudicated under the substantive law of another jurisdiction." It was held in *DiPalma* v. *Smart* (2000), 90 Alta. L.R. (3d) 171, 280 A.L.R. 1 (Q.B.), that the provision was not retroactive and so claims arising out of an automobile accident in Saskatchewan that took place before the date on which the act came into force (March 15, 1999) were statute barred by virtue of the law of Saskatchewan.

(b)   Contracts

Proper law — no agreed choice

   Note. A contract of sale of transport trailers by an Iowa seller to a Saskatchewan buyer was held governed by Iowa law, as the law with the closest and most real connection to the transaction: *Hawkeye Tanks & Equipment Inc.* v. *Farr-Mor Fertilizer Services Ltd.* (2000), 198 Sask. R. 161 (Q.B.), affd., 2002 SKCA 44.

(c) Torts

Applicable law

Note. Tolofson v. *Jensen*, [1994] 3 S.C.R. 1022, 120 D.L.R. (4th) 289, decided that tort claims arising out of automobile accidents are governed strictly by the *lex loci delicti*, but it left the door slightly ajar to applying the *lex fori* if the accident took place outside Canada and the connections with Canada were exceptionally strong. Three first instance decisions in Ontario have applied the suggested exception. All of them involved single car accidents in which an injured passenger sought to claim against the driver's insurance. In all of them, the automobile was registered and insured in Ontario and all the parties were from Ontario. In *Lebert* v. *Skinner Estate* (2001), 53 O.R. 93d) 559, 31 C.C.L.I. (3d) 61 (S.C.J.), and *Wong* v. *Lee* (2000), 50 O.R. (3d) 419 (S.C.J.), revd. (2002), 211 D.L.R. (4th) 69 (Ont. C.A.), the accident took place in the United States; in *Lau* v. *Li* (2001), 53 O.R. (3d) 727, 26 C.C.L.I. (3d) 94 (S.C.J.), in Québec. Since the reversal of *Wong* v. *Lee,* to be noted in next year's *Yearbook,* the exception must be taken to be severely narrowed.

(d) Corporations and partnerships

Partnerships — status of foreign partnership for purposes of Canadian taxation law

Note. In *Backman* v. *Canada,* [2001] 1 S.C.R. 367, 196 D.L.R. (4th) 193, Canadian investors had acquired interests in a limited partnership organized under Texas law to operate an apartment building there. They immediately disposed of the apartment building. They sought to deduct their respective shares of the accumulated losses of the partnership. The Supreme Court denied the deductions because the partnership, whatever its status under the law of Texas, lacked — once the Canadians acquired it — an essential characteristic of a partnership under Canadian law, namely, an intention by the supposed partners to carry on business together for profit.

(e)   Husband and wife

Recognition of foreign divorce

Note. In *Wlodarczyk* v. *Spriggs* (2000), 12 R.F.L. (5th) 241, 200 Sask. R. 129 (Q.B.), the last seventeen years of the parties' married life had been spent in Saskatchewan. When the marriage broke up the husband returned to Australia, where he had lived for fifteen years before he married, and obtained a divorce there almost immediately after returning. The divorce was recognized on the basis of his real and substantial connection with Australia. Although section 22(1) of the Divorce Act, R.S.C. 1986, c. 3 (2nd Supp.), enacts a statutory ground of one year's ordinary residence by either party in the foreign jurisdiction, section 22(3) preserves common law grounds of recognition, of which the real and substantial connection test is one. Another common law ground that would appear to have applied is the husband's domicile of choice in Australia, which he would have reacquired as soon as he arrived there, provided that he had a fixed and settled intention to remain there (it was not his domicile of origin).

2   Québec

(a)   Classification

Effets du mariage — patrimoine familial

G.B. c. *C.C.*, [2001] R.J.Q. 1435, [2001] R.D.F. 435. Cour d'appel du Québec.

Après avoir fait vie commune pendant sept ans en Ontario, les parties s'y sont mariées en 1998. Aucune convention matrimoniale n'a précédé leur mariage. La séparation du couple est survenue en 1994 et l'épouse a alors déménagé au Québec. En 1996, le mari, qui n'a jamais cessé d'être domicilié en Ontario, a intenté une action en divorce dans le district de Hull, lieu de résidence de l'épouse. Celle-ci a tenté d'obtenir le renvoi du dossier devant les tribunaux ontariens, mais sans succès. Avant l'audience, les parties ont présenté une requête conjointe en adjudication sur un point de droit afin que soit déterminé si c'est la loi québécoise ou la loi ontarienne Family Law Act qui s'applique au partage de leur patrimoine familial. Le premier juge a d'abord estimé que le patrimoine familial était un effet du mariage. Il a ensuite fait référence à la règle de conflit prévue à l'article 3089 C.C.Q., qui se lit : "[alinéa 1] Les effets du mariage, notamment ceux qui s imposent à tous les époux quel soit leur régime matrimonial, sont soumis à la loi de leur domicile. [alinéa 2] Lorsque les époux sont domiciliés dans des États différents, la loi du lieu de leur résidence commune s'applique ou, à défaut, la loi de leur dernière résidence commune ou, à défaut, la loi du lieu de la célébration du mariage." Comme la dernière résidence commune des parties était en Ontario, le juge a conclu que les lois de cette province s'appliquaient.

La Cour d'appel a rejeté l'appel. Il est bien établi par la jurisprudence québécoise que le patrimoine familial est, en droit interne, un effet du mariage. Pour qualifier le patrimoine familial en droit international privé, il faut procéder à la sélection de la règle de conflit applicable. Par l'article 3089 C.C.Q., le législateur québécois a voulu que tous les effets du mariage, notamment ceux qui s'appliquent à tous les époux quel que soit leur régime matrimonial, soient soumis à la loi du domicile des époux. Il a ainsi manifesté clairement sa volonté d'inclure le patrimoine familial dans la catégorie des effets du mariage. Le régime matrimonial est constitué de l'ensemble des règles que les époux ont adoptées, tandis que tout le reste relève du domaine de la loi des effets du mariage. Le patrimoine familial est donc aussi qualifié d'effet du mariage en droit international privé.

Il n'y a pas lieu d'appliquer l'article 3076 C.C.Q., qui permet au juge de mettre de côté la règle de conflit normalement applicable au profit d'une disposition interne lorsque son application s'impose en vertu de son but particulier. Or, même si les dispositions relatives au patrimoine familial sont d'ordre public, elles ne sont pas d'application nécessaire. En effet, elles n'ont pas un caractère vital pour la société et ne mettent pas en péril l'existence même de la société. Les règles de conflit particulières prévues quant aux effets du mariage et quant aux régimes matrimoniaux renvoient dans l'un et l'autre cas aux règles de la dernière résidence commune (article 3089 C.C.Q.) ou de la première résidence commune (article 3123 C.C.Q.) lorsque les époux sont domiciliés dans des États différents. Le fait que le législateur n'ait pas imposé la loi du for est une indication significative que la règle n'est pas d'un intérêt vital. C'est donc à bon droit que le premier juge a conclu que les lois ontariennes s'appliquaient pour effectuer le partage des biens des parties.

Note. Veuillez voir *J.S.H.* c. *B.B.F.*, [2001] R.J.Q. 1262 (C.S.), et *C.B.* c. *H.O.*, [2001] R.D.F. 293 (C.S.), qui soulevaient aussi la question de la qualification du patrimoine familial en droit international privé et qui sont décidés avant la décision de la Cour d'appel.

Book Reviews / Recensions de livres

*The International Legal System in Quest of Equity and Universality /
L'ordre juridique international, un système en quête d'équité et universalité : liber amicorum Georges Abi-Saab.* Edited by Laurence Boisson
de Chazournes and Vera Gowlland-Debbas. The Hague, The
Netherlands: Martinus Nijhoff Publishers (co-publication with
the Graduate Institute of International Studies, Geneva, March
2001). 849 pp. Euros 235.00 / US $205.00 / GB £143.00

It is rather unusual to review a *"liber amicorum,"* however, I believe
that an exception to the rule should be made in view of Georges
Abi-Saab's enormous contribution to the development of international law.[1] His *opus magnus*, which could be considered "international law in a nutshell,"[2] because he has used his versatile skills
in many branches of international law, leaving, as various contributors to this book have acknowledged, a lasting imprint on the
thoughts of future generations of international lawyers.

Although I have never been a student of Abi-Saab's, in the strict
sense of the word, there was an immediate affinity when I first met
him about twenty years ago, due to my expertise on the Israeli-
Palestinian question.[3] In addition, a striking feature of Georges's

[1] Laurence Boisson de Chazournes and Vera Gowlland-Debbas, eds., *The International Legal System in Quest of Equity and Universality / L'ordre juridique international,
un système en quête d'équité et universalité : liber amicorum Georges Abi-Saab* (The
Hague, The Netherlands: Martinus Nijhoff Publishers (co-publication with the
Graduate Institute of International Studies, Geneva), March 2001).

[2] Nicholas Chambers, "International Law in a Nutshell" (London: Sweet and
Maxwell, 1966).

[3] See my article, Johannes van Aggelen, "Protection of Human Rights in the Israeli
Held Territories in the Light of the Fourth Geneva Convention" (1976) 32 Rev.
E.D.I. 83.

warm personality, which runs as a continuous thread through the contributions, is what one long-standing Egyptian friend called his "unattainable simplicity."[4]

The book under review[5] synthesizes many ideas taken from his general course, which was given at the Hague Academy of International Law in French in 1987.[6] This course had such an impact on the legal community that it became the subject of a review article by Jean-Marc Sorel in the *Journal du droit international*[7] and by the newly elected member of the International Law Commission (ILC), Martii Koskenniemi, under the title "Repetition as Reform."[8] These short comments show that, unlike many other lecturers in these prestigious courses, Abi-Saab never shies away from concealing his national and cultural background. The same holds true for the collection under review in that it brings to the fore his multi-faceted background.

Despite his official retirement, Abi-Saab continues to publish, and a total of six publications from his pen are mentioned in the *Revue suisse de droit international et de droit européen.*[9]

The book is divided into five parts, comprising twenty-two articles in English and twenty-one in French, in addition to two short introductory notes in French. The first part is entitled "Georges Abi-Saab and the Concept of the International Legal System." It traces in a rather theoretical and philosophical way some fundamental legal principles that have guided Abi-Saab with conviction throughout his life, such as social justice, the legitimate struggle of a people for independence, and, as far as the codification of international law is concerned, the need to recognize the relativity of the formal sources of international law, which cautions against the danger of the fragmentation of international law. The relevance of this concern is demonstrated by a study on the risks that have ensued from the fragmentation of international law in 2000 within the long-term program of work of the ILC. In this connection,

---

[4] (Alsahlu almomtanei); Boisson de Chazournes and Gowland-Debbas, eds., *supra* note 1 at 229.

[5] *Ibid.*

[6] G. Abi-Saab, "Cours général de droit international public," in *Collected Courses of the Hague Academy of International Law,* vol. 207 (The Hague: Martinus Nijhoff Publishers, 1987), which was belatedly published in 1996.

[7] Jean-Marc Sorel, "L'enlacement du droit international" (1997) 124 J.D.I. 963.

[8] M. Koskenniemi, "Repetition as Reform" (1998) 9:2 Eur. J. Int'l L. 405.

[9] (2001) 3 Revue suisse de droit international et de droit européen 427.

Sorel notes that a rule does not become legal because it is sanctioned; rather it is sanctioned because it is legal.[10] It is clear that Abi-Saab wholeheartedly agrees with this affirmation when one considers his views on more pragmatic topics such as wars of national liberation and international humanitarian law.

The second part[11] of the book is entitled "Foundations of the International Legal System: The Quest for Expansion." In this large segment of the book, the reader is provided with seventeen different topics, ranging from a philosophical reflection on "The Idea of Justice in the Works of Early Scholars in International Law," by Emmanuel Roucounas, to a contemporary interpretation of Shakespeare entitled "Race, Liberty, Equality: An International Lawyer's Post-Colonial Perspective on Shakespeare's Tempest," by Theodore Meron.[12] It also contains an article that ties in with Abi-Saab's new function as a judge in the Appellate Body of the World Trade Organization, which is entitled "Developing Countries and the Multilateral Trade Rules: The Continuing Quest for an Equitable Playing Field," by A.A. Yusuf.

It is a pleasure to reveal that the article "Manifeste pour le droit international du XXè siècle" was written by M.G. Kohen, one of Georges's brightest former doctoral students, who is currently teaching at the Graduate Institute of International Studies. It is one of the clearest examples of the master passing on his knowledge to the student when Kohen observes that the turn of the century has witnessed a remarkable phenomenon, namely that international society has structurally changed while the legal system on which it is based has until now remained unchanged.[13] It is indeed this reviewer's opinion that until this gap is closed, society will have to live with a system of corrective justice, while Abi-Saab's craving for a system of distributive justice will remain until then a "utopian concept in the making."[14]

The article by Richard Falk, "Humanitarian Intervention after Kosovo" reminds us in retrospect that the concept of humanitarian intervention changed on March 24, 1999. The gravamen of his argument is that "genocidal behaviour cannot be shielded by claims

[10] Sorel, *supra* note 7 at 59.

[11] Boisson de Chazournes and Gowlland-Debbas, eds., *supra* note 1 at 77-426.

[12] For an analogous article, see Theodore Meron "Crimes and Accountability in Shakespeare" (1998) 92 A.J.I.L. 1.

[13] Boisson de Chazournes and Gowlland-Debbas, eds., *supra* note 1 at 130.

[14] *Ibid.* at 96.

of sovereignty, but neither can these claims be overridden by an unauthorized use of force delivered in an excessive and inappropriate manner."[15] This postulate shows that we are currently facing a dialectic political system with poly-interpretational legal norms reducing traditional international norms to a hybrid form. In addition, it once more underscores the danger of the fragmentation of international law.[16]

The second article on the Kosovo crisis by Daniel Warner, which is entitled, "Ethics, Law and Unethical Compassion in the Kosovo Intervention," shows us to what extent political expediency is able to upset our juridical foundations and moral convictions. This article has even led to the first exchange of legal arguments in cyberspace between Bruno Simma and Antonio Cassese, which has subsequently been published in the *European Journal of International Law*.[17] How thin the dividing line was between the presumed legality and illegality of the North Atlantic Treaty Organization (NATO) intervention in Kosovo is evidenced by the wealth of literature it has generated.[18] However, it is this reviewer's opinion that Warner is incorrect to interpret Simma's reading of the NATO intervention

---

[15] *Ibid.* at 179.

[16] *Ibid.* at 186.

[17] Brunno Simma, "NATO, the UN and the Use of Force: Legal Aspects" (1999) 10:1 Eur. J.I.L. 1; Antonio Cassese, "*Ex iniuria ius oritur:* Are We Moving towards International Legitimation of Forcible Humanitarian Countermeasures in the World Community?" (1999) 10:1 Eur. J. I. L 23; Antonio Cassese, "A Follow-up: Forcible Humanitarian Countermeasures and Opinio Necessitatis" (1999) 10:4 Eur. J. I. L. 791.

[18] See, for example, the articles by H. McCoubrey, "Kosovo, NATO and International Law" (1999) 14:5 International Relations 29; Kohen, "L'emploi de la force et la crise du Kosovo: vers un nouveau désordre juridique international" (1999) 32 Revue belge de droit international 122; Duursma, "Justifiying NATO's use of Force in Kosovo?" (1999) 12 Leiden J. Int'l L. 287; Tsagourias, "Humanitarian Intervention after Kosovo and Legal Discourse: Self-Deception or Self-Consciousness" (2000) 13 Leiden J. Int'l L. 11; Philip Allott, "Kosovo and the Responsibility of Power" (2000) 13 Leiden J. Int'l L. 83; Eric Suy, "NATO's Intervention in the Federal Republic of Yugoslavia" (2000) 13 Leiden J. Int'l L. 193; Vera Gowlland-Debbas, "The Limits of Unilateral Enforcement of Community Objectives in the Framework of UN Peace Maintenance" (2000) 11:2 Eur. J. Int'l L. 361; Alain Pellet, "Brief Remarks on the Unilateral Use of Force" (2000) 11:2 Eur. J. Int'l L. 385; Mary Ellen O'Connell, "The UN, NATO and International Law after Kosovo" (2000) 22 Hum. Rts. Q. 57; Kritsiotis, "The Kosovo Crisis and NATO's Application of Armed Force against the Federal Republic of Yugoslavia" (2000) 49 I.C.L.Q. 330; and Abraham D. Sofaer, "International Law and Kosovo" (2000) 36 Stan. J. Int'l L. 1.

as being legal.[19] It was rather Cassese who was inclined to view the intervention as legal, although he admitted that no consensus nor *opinio iuris* existed at the time on the matter.

His compatriot, Mohammed Gomaa, provides us with an article on "Non-Binding Agreements in International Law." This topic is very relevant since the conclusion of non-binding agreements, such as the Oslo Agreements,[20] which were signed on September 13, 1993 and which are, in effect, declarations of intent, are becoming standard practice on the international political scene. He is correct in observing that the more parties that are party to an instrument, the more general the content will be in order to reach consensus.[21] The protracted negotiations on the final declaration and program of action of the Durban Conference on Racism, which took place in early September 2001, even led to a deferral of the fifty-sixth session of the General Assembly. A glaring, positive exception to this practice was the adoption of the International Convention on the Rights of the Child on November 20, 1989,[22] which had reached almost universal ratification after only a few years.

Chapters 14 and 15 on "Sociabilité et droit du commerce international" and "Alternatives to Cash in International Law and Practice" are of a rather private law nature. The examples given in Chapter 14[23] with respect to normative commercial conventions concluded by international organizations testify to the usefulness of the analysis on non-binding instruments, which is included in the previous chapter by Gomaa, and give the examples provided by Jean-Michel Jacquet a deeper dimension. Chapter 15 covers a very interesting, but rather unexplored, field of international law. The author regrets that there is a severe lack of case law on this issue.[24]

---

[19] Boisson de Chazournes and Gowlland-Debbas, eds., *supra* note 1 at 209.

[20] Israel-Palestine Liberation Organisation: Declaration of Principles of Interim-Government Arrangements, 32 I.L.M.1527 (1993), containing the establishment of the Palestinian civil authority (Oslo 1 and the Gaza-Jericho Agreement) as well as the interim agreement on methods of implementation of those principles (Oslo 2). See in general: G.R. Watson, *The Oslo Accords: International Law and the Israeli-Palestinian Peace Agreements* (Oxford: Oxford University Press, 2000), reviewed in (2001) 14 Leiden J.Int'l.Law 485.

[21] Boisson de Chazournes and Gowlland-Debbas, eds., *supra* note 1 at 235.

[22] International Convention on the Rights of the Child, November 20, 1989, GA Res. 44/25.

[23] Boisson de Chazournes and Gowlland-Debbas, eds., *supra* note 1 at 257.

[24] *Ibid.* at 278.

On page 283, in the last paragraph, the word "developed" should read "developing."

Chapters 16-19 touch on issues of state responsibility — a topic selected for codification by the ILC as early as 1949 and approved by the General Assembly in Resolution 799 (VIII) on December 7, 1953. The article by Alain Pellet gives a cursory overview of the history of its codification, highlighting the imprints of the successive special rapporteurs, Garcia-Amador, Ago, Riphagen, Arangio-Ruiz, and Crawford. His final observations[25] are a reflection of the debate that took place after Crawford had presented his fourth and final report during the fifty-third session in 2001.[26]

Julio Barboza's reflection on Article 19 of the ILC 1996 draft on state responsibility concerning "state crimes" in international law (Chapter 19)[27] is very timely and borne out by, *inter alia*, the jurisprudence of the International Criminal Tribunal for the Former Yugoslavia (ICTFY) in the *Prosecutor* v. *Blaskic* case.[28] Indeed, under the current international legal system states cannot be the subject of criminal sanctions akin to those provided in national criminal systems. Special Rapporteur Crawford also took this view in his first report in 1998,[29] although it took many "mini-debates " during the 2001 session until the article was finally deleted in the second reading. The aforementioned article on "Developing Countries and the Multilateral Trade Rules" provides the reader with a serious, well-founded criticism of the implementation of the so-called "Marrakech" Agreement Establishing the World Trade Organization[30] as well as a look at its prospective risks. I wonder whether the secretary-general's Global Compact, which was announced in Davos in January 1999, and the increasing human rights concern

---

[25] *Ibid.* at 302-4

[26] *Fourth Report on State Responsibility,* April 2, 2001, UN Doc. A/CN.4/517, in combination with the comments received from governments, *State Responsibility: Comments and Observations Received from Governments,* March 16, 2001, UN Doc. A/CN.4/515.

[27] Draft Articles on State Responsibility, *Report of the ILC on the Work of the Forty-Eighth Session,* General Assembly, Official Records, 51st Session, Supplement no.10, Doc. A/51/10,125 at 131.

[28] *Prosecutor* v. *Blaskic ,* Case no. IT-95-14-PT.

[29] *First Report on State Responsibility,* April 24, 1998, UN Doc. A/CN.4/490/Add.2, pp. 2-6.

[30] Marrakech Agreement Establishing the World Trade Organization, April 15, 1994, 33 I.L.M. 15 (1994).

regarding trade-related issues,[31] will, in due time, be able to narrow existing gaps. Measuring compliance against economic, social, and cultural rights is far less tangible and more complicated as the procrastination in the discussion on a future optional protocol to the International Covenant on Economic, Social and Cultural Rights[32] shows. The appointment of an independent expert on this issue by the Commission on Human Rights in 2001 may be a positive step in the right direction. The special report on human rights in 2000 by the United Nations Development Programme and the change in the mandate of the Working Group on the Right to Development by the Commission on Human Rights after the adoption of the Declaration on the Right to Development in 1986[33] are further examples of the many problems that have occurred.

With respect to this subject, I refer to an article entitled "Perceptions of the Rule of Law in Transitional Societies," which was presented at a global conference sponsored by the World Bank in June 2000 by Mamphela Ramphele, in which he observes that nowadays "domestic and international law are deeply intertwined, and in small and weak states, international law and best practices, whether economic or human rights law, have a strong impact on the character of states and hence civil society. It is in recognition of this impact, that donor countries tie liberal democratic development — whether it is political, economic, or legal-to aid."[34]

Part III of the book under study is entitled "Promoting Values in the International Legal System: The Quest for Humanization." It contains six articles related to aspects of international human rights law, criminal law, and international humanitarian law. The first article, which is written by the *primus inter pares* among the

[31] Sub-Commission on the Promotion and Protection of Human Rights, "Globalization and Its Impact on the Enjoyment of Human Rights," 53rd Sess., August 2, 2001, UN Doc. E/CN 4/Sub.2/2001/10 (currently being undertaken by two members of the Sub Commission on the Promotion and Protection of Human Rights) and Sub-Commission on the Promotion and Protection of Human Rights, "Intellectual Property Rights and Human Rights," 52nd Sess., June 14, 200, UN Doc. E/CN 4/Sub.2/2001/12.

[32] International Covenant on Economic, Social and Cultural Rights, G.A. Res. 2200A (XXI), 21 U.N. GAOR Supp. (No. 16) at 49, UN Doc. A/6316, 1966, 993 U.N.T.S. 3, entered into force Jan. 3, 1976.

[33] Declaration on the Right to Development, G.A. Res. 41/128, Annex 41, U.N. GAOR Supp. (No. 53) at 186, UN Doc. A/41/53, 1986.

[34] Cited in Rudolf van Puymbroek, ed., "Comprehensive Legal and Judicial Development: Towards an Agenda for a Just and Equitable Society in the 21st Century" (Washington, DC: World Bank, 2001) at 431.

international criminalists Antonio Cassese, is entitled "Crimes against Humanity: Comments on Some Problematical Aspects." This article has obtained a particular relevance due to the attacks on the United States on September 11, 2001, which have been denounced as crimes against humanity. The author questions whether organs or agents of a state must perpetrate the offence or whether individuals not acting in an official capacity can also commit such crimes.[35] He provides a prudent reply, in which he presupposes that for the offence to be characterized as a crime against humanity, the governmental authorities should approve of, or condone, the offence or the crime should fit into a general pattern of official misconduct.[36] Indeed, the polemic has already started in the legal community, and John Cerone comments on it in "Acts of War and State Responsibility in Muddy Waters: The Non-state Actor Dilemma."[37]

Cassese rightly questions the narrow scope of crimes against humanity in the statutes of the ad hoc criminal tribunals, in so far as it limits its victims to any civilian population, and he alerts the reader to the fact that the International Criminal Court (ICC) will also judge crimes against humanity in times of peace.[38] Nevertheless, the ICTFY, in its judgment on appeal in the *Prosecutor* v. *Dusko Tadic* case,[39] which was handed down on July 15, 1999, broadened the scope of its application. It removed the linkage between crimes against humanity and armed conflict, excluded isolated attacks against civilians, and made personal motives of defendants irrelevant.[40] The last part of Cassese's article touches on one of the most controversial issues, namely whether there exists an obligation for the national courts to try alleged authors of these crimes under the principle of universal jurisdiction. Former US secretary of state Henry Kissinger recently reflected on this issue in the periodical *Foreign Affairs*.[41] Although he called the ICC an indiscriminate

---

[35] Boisson de Chazournes and Gowlland-Debbas, eds., *supra* note 1 at 435.

[36] *Ibid.* at 444.

[37] See American Society of International Law Insights, which can be viewed online at <http://www.srdi.ws/Asil.htm> at 3.

[38] Boisson de Chazournes and Gowlland-Debbas, eds., *supra* note 1 at 444-45.

[39] *Prosecutor* v. *Dusko Tadic,* Case no. IT-94-1-A.

[40] Yoram Dinstein, "Crimes against Humanity after Tadic" (2000) 13 Leiden J. Int'l L. 373.

[41] Henry Kissinger, "The Pitfalls of Universal Jurisdiction" (2001) 80 Foreign Affairs 86; see also P. Kirsch and V. Oosterveld, "Diplomacy and the ICC" (2001) 46 McGill L. J. 1142.

court,[42] he admitted that it replaces the claims of national judges to universal jurisdiction and, therefore, would greatly improve the state of international law. He prophesied that it entails a fundamental change in US constitutional practice, which could only be brought about with the full participation of Congress and that, in its present form "of assigning the ultimate dilemmas of international politics to unelected jurists and to an international judiciary," the United States was not ready for such a change.[43]

Chapter 24, entitled "A UN Constabulary to Enforce the Law on Genocide and Crimes against Humanity," links the idea of a new, permanent transnational institution to the evolving regime of international criminal law as embodied in the Rome Statute for the International Criminal Court.[44] This innovative idea is based on the premise that law enforcement mechanisms will subsequently be required after the United Nations has taken action under Chapter VII of the Charter of the United Nations.[45] Although it is a laudable conception, because its members would be individually recruited international civil servants who are directly employed by the United Nations rather than by their national military authorities, the experience of the past decade has shown that contributing countries to peace-building or peace-enforcement activities still prefer national military contingents to be provided on a voluntary basis. The authors acknowledge that their plan faces substantial political obstacles[46] because states fear that an international police force could erode their (that is, state) sovereignty. In addition, the fact that its presumed mandate should be limited to the charges of genocide and crimes against humanity severely limits its scope and efficiency. The ideas advanced in this article come close to some recommendations made in the *Report of the Panel on United Nations Peace Operations* — the so-called *Brahimi Report* — which was published on August 23, 2001. In this report, the panel on United Nations Peace Operations recommended "a doctrinal shift in the use of civilian police, other rule of law elements and human rights experts in complex peace operations to reflect an increased focus

[42] *Kissinger, supra* note 41 at 92.

[43] *Ibid.* at 83.

[44] Rome Statute for the International Criminal Court, UN Doc. A/CONF.183/9 (1998), reprinted in 37 I.L.M. 999 (1998).

[45] Charter of the United Nations, June 26, 1945, Can. T.S. 1945, No. 7, 59 Stat. 1031, 145 U.K.F.S. 805.

[46] Boisson de Chazournes and Gowlland-Debbas, eds., *supra* note 1 at 459.

on strengthening rule of law institutions and improving respect for human rights in post-conflict environments."[47] In addition, "Member States are encouraged to each establish a national pool of civilian police officers that would be ready for deployment to United Nations peace operations on short notice, within the context of the United Nations Standby Arrangements System."[48] However, the Afghanistan peace negotiations, which have been led by the same Lakhdar Brahimi, have shown that an international "stabilization force," as conceived by the contributors, falls far short of the idea launched in this article. The article nevertheless underscores the importance of human rights components in many peace agreements.[49] The short article by Victor Yves Ghebali, which is entitled: "Remarques politico-historiques sur l'étiologie des guerres civiles" (Chapter 25) could also have been placed after Chapter 6 because the origins of civil wars form part of the foundations of the international legal system. Luigi Condorelli's article on the 1999 circular issued by the United Nations secretary-general on the *Observance by United Nations Forces of International Humanitarian Law*[50] is a welcome reflection on the relationship between international humanitarian law and peacekeeping operations. The author correctly observes that international humanitarian law nowadays develops through "instant custom," which is influenced by the application of its norms to peacekeeping operations. In particular, Section 4 on the violations of international humanitarian law is unfortunately borne out by experiences in Somalia and the territories of ex-Yugoslavia. It was therefore necessary for the Sub-Commission on the Promotion and Protection of Human Rights to recently entrust one of its members with the responsibility of completing a study on this subject.[51] This development confirms what Abi-Saab predicted almost two decades ago in a *liber amicorum* for Jean Pictet,

---

[47] *Report of the Panel on United Nations Peace Operations,* 55th Sess., UN Doc. A/55/305-S/2000/809, August 21, 2000, Annex III, recommendation 2(b), p. 54 [hereinafter *Brahimi Report*].

[48] *Ibid.* at recommendation 10(a), p. 55.

[49] See, in this connection, C. Bell, *Peace Agreements and Human Rights* (Oxford: Oxford University Press, 2000), especially Chapters 1 and 10, including the very useful table on the sequencing of human rights issues at 296, which is reviewed in (2001) 19:4 Netherl. Q. of H.R. 510.

[50] *Observance by United Nations Forces of International Humanitarian Law,* bulletin of the secretary-general, August 6, 1999, UN Doc. ST/SGB/1999/13.

[51] Sub-Commission on Human Rights, Decision 2001/105, UN Doc. E/CN.4/ SUB.2 DEC/2001/105, August 10, 2001.

when he stated: "[E]xpress the conviction that for the protective rules of humanitarian law to remain effective, they have constantly to expand their scope and tighten their requirements in response to the evolution of war technology on the one hand and that of the ever-increasing requirements of civilisation on the other."[52]

The last article in this section, entitled "La Palestine et les Conventions de Genève du 12 août 1949 ou l'histoire d'une adhésion avortée," is still a burning issue as the meeting of state parties to the Geneva Conventions on December 5, 2001 has shown.[53] It traces the history of this area since the self-declared independence of Palestine on November 15, 1988, followed by the instant recognition of its statehood by over ninety states and the Palestinian request to become party to the Geneva Conventions on June 14, 1989. The article intends to show that by refusing to recognize the Palestinian correspondence as an instrument of adhesion in the formal sense, the Swiss authorities in fact acted *ultra vires* — their powers as depositary of the Geneva Conventions. Despite the fact that it remained an abortive attempt in the formal sense, the international community, with a few notable exceptions, has for several decades reaffirmed that the Geneva Conventions apply to the Palestinian territories occupied by Israel.[54] The underlying legal question is, of course, whether the unilateral proclamation of Palestinian statehood may be considered an act of a state within the framework of adherence to these conventions. As a reviewer, one should mention that the citations in footnote 14 are incorrect and would lead the reader astray. Document 1985/5 does not exist. What is meant is Sub-Commission Resolution 1989/5.

The fourth part of the book considers the judicial function in the international legal system with the subtitle "The Quest for Justice." It contains, *inter alia*, articles by judges and former judges of the

---

[52] G. Abi-Saab, "The Specificities of Humanitarian Law," in C. Swinarski, ed., *Etudes et essais sur le droit international humanitaire et sur les principes de la Croix-Rouge* (The Hague: Martinus Nijhoff, 1984) at 265. See also the article by Theodore Meron with the enticing title: "The Humanization of Humanitarian Law" (2000) 94:2 A.J.I.L 239; M. Zwanenburg, "Compromise or Commitment: Human Rights and International Humanitarian Law Obligations for UN Peace Forces" (1998) 11 Leiden J. Int'l L. 229; and P. Benvenuti, "Le Respect du Droit International Humanitaire par les Forces des Nations Unies: La Circulaire du Secrétaire Général" (2001) 105:2 Rev. D.I.P. 355 ff.

[53] The article deals with all four Geneva Conventions, UN Treaty Series, vol. 75, 1950, nos. 970-73.

[54] van Aggelen, *supra* note 3.

International Court of Justice (ICJ) on several procedural and sub-stantive legal questions facing international and municipal courts. The article by former Judge Bedjaoui on "L'opportunité dans les décisions de la Cour internationale de justice" provides a teleo-logical interpretation of international law, which purports that the international law "corpus" is *ipso facto* incomplete and that the judge assists through his vision, using discretionary powers and expedi-ency as tools, to further its development.

A clear example of such a development is that the ICJ has been seized recently with questions touching on international human rights law and international humanitarian law.[55]

In view of the enormous increase of cases before the court, the ICJ changed its working methods in 1998, which has affected both the judges (in preliminary phases of the proceedings on the merits, deliberations would take place, albeit on an experimental basis, without written notes) as well as the parties (request to decrease the number of pleadings and the length of oral arguments as well as shortening the periods for preliminary objections and counter claims). This change has led to a revision of Articles 79 and 80 of the Rules of Court.[56]

The last two articles consider legal issues ensuing from the *R. v. Bow Street Metropolitan Stipendiary Magistrate and Others ex parte Pinochet Ugarte* case.[57] Chapter 36 provides the reader with insights by Sir Robert Jennings, former president of the ICJ, under the title "The Pinochet Extradition Case in the English Courts." He consid-ers the nature of *jus cogens*, its place in international law, its relation to the act of torture and the Convention against Torture and Other Cruel, Inhuman or Degrading Treatment or Punishment,[58] the re-quirement of "double criminality" in extradition cases, and the implication of another rule of international law that confers sover-eign immunity from third state domestic jurisdictions on heads

---

[55] See J. Gardam, "The Contribution of the International Court of Justice to Inter-national Humanitarian Law" (2001) 14 Leiden J. Int'l L. 349.

[56] See Rules of Court, UN Doc. A/56/4, para. 368-70; and S. Rosenne: "The Inter-national Court of Justice: Revision of Articles 79 and 80 of the Rules of Court" (2001) 14 Leiden J. Int'l L. 77.

[57] *R. v. Bow Street Metropolitan Stipendiary Magistrate and others ex parte Pinochet Ugarte,* [1998] All E. R. 897 [hereinafter *Pinochet*].

[58] Convention against Torture and Other Cruel, Inhuman or Degrading Treat-ment or Punishment, 1984, 1465 U.N.T.S. 85.

of state with respect to acts committed in their capacity as heads of state. In his conclusion, he criticizes the House of Lords for having accepted a simplistic view of the nature and effect of the doctrine of *jus cogens,* which, in his opinion, is one of the most controversial and under-developed concepts of modern international law. However, he also lashes out against the idea that only by punishing individuals can the rules of international law be enforced.

This argument is so forceful that it is worthwhile quoting in full. The author states:

One sees today the fruits of this flight of erroneous fancy from the Nuremberg Tribunal in the eagerness with which international lawyers and others seek to establish war crimes tribunals for the punishment of a necessarily small band of unfortunate factotums, believing that thereby they are developing international law; and yet by contrast put relatively little thought and energy into the establishment of international governmental machinery for preventing the development of the sort of situations which inevitably breed lawless behaviour by the wretch individuals caught up in the mess which has been allowed to come about through the patent inadequacy of the international legal system.[59]

The article by Philippe Sands, entitled "After Pinochet: The Proper Relationship between National and International Courts," cautions against the proliferation of international tribunals[60] and discusses the impact of their decisions on national courts triggered by Lord Slynn's dissenting judgment in the first phase of the *Pinochet* trilogy before the English courts, where he denied that there was any state practice or general consensus that all crimes against international law should be justiciable in national courts on the basis of universality of jurisdiction. The learned lordship even went so far as to say that if the international community already had an international criminal court, then the English courts would not have to be grappling with these issues.[61] The author also dwells upon the issue of provisional measures or, in human rights jargon, interim measures of protection, which have become increasingly relevant in international adjudication as the *Case Concerning the Vienna Convention on Consular Relations (Paraguay v. United States of*

---

[59] Boisson de Chazournes and Gowlland-Debbas, eds., *supra* note 1 at 693.

[60] *Ibid.* at 703-4. See also, in this connection, T. Buergenthal, "Proliferation of International Courts and Tribunals: Is It Good or Bad?" (2001) 14:2 Leiden J. Int'l L. 267.

[61] *Pinochet, supra* note 57.

America)[62] and *LaGrand Case (Germany* v. *United States of America)*[63] show.[64]

However, Sands admits that the legal effect of provisional measures by the ICJ, which are necessary to preserve the respective rights of the parties, remains a hotly debated issue following the judgment of June 27, 2001 in the *LaGrand* case.[65] The court was left to decide by thirteen to two votes that the United States had violated its Order of March 3, 1999[66] by failing to take all measures at its disposal to ensure that Karl LaGrand was not executed during the proceedings before the court. Sands seems encouraged that provisional measures adopted by the International Tribunal for the Law of the Sea, in accordance with Article 290, para. 6, of the Convention on the Law of the Sea,[67] are legally binding[68] when he compares the power to prescribe provisional measures in the two courts. In his final analysis, the author confronts the reader with some very interesting hypothetical questions. He argues:

[W]hat would have happened if Chile had taken Spain to the International Court of Justice maintaining that Spain had no jurisdiction over Pinochet, and that even if it did, the 1984 Torture Convention did not, as nine lords ruled, remove any immunity from the jurisdiction of national courts ... if the majority view by the House of Lords had not prevailed before the I.C.J., what repercussions would it have on the decision in English courts, the next time they were confronted with an immunity question?[69]

[62] *Case Concerning the Vienna Convention on Consular Relations (Paraguay* v. *United States of America)*, Order of April 9, 1998, [1998] I.C.J. 248.

[63] *LaGrand Case (Germany* v. *United States of America)*, June 27, 2001, [2001] I.C.J., para. 115 [hereinafter *LaGrand*].

[64] See R. St. J. Macdonald, "Interim Measures in International Law, with Special Reference to the European System for the Protection of Human Rights" (1992) 52 Zaö R. V. 703; R. Higgins, "Interim Measures for the Protection of Human Rights" (1997) 36 Colum. J. of Transnat'l L. 91; E. Rieter, "Interim Measures by the World Court to Suspend the Execution of an Individual: The Breard Case" (1998) 16:4 Netherl. Q. of H.R. 475; "Agora: Breard" (1998) 92 A.J.I.L. 666.

[65] *LaGrand, supra* note 63 at paras. 44, 92-116.

[66] *LaGrand Case (Germany v. United States of America)*, Request for the Indication of Provisional Measures, [1999] I.C.J. 9.

[67] Convention on the Law of the Sea, UN Doc. A/CONF.62/122, reprinted in (1982) 21 I.L.M. 1261.

[68] See, for example, the Separate Opinion by Judge ad hoc Shearer in the so-called *Southern Bluefin Tuna Case (New Zealand/Australia* v. *Japan)*, Request for Provisional Measures, August 27, 1999, 177 I.L.R. 148 at 181-89.

[69] Boisson de Chazournes and Gowlland-Debbas, eds., *supra* note 1 at 714.

This decision by the English House of Lords also spurred a number of international commentaries.[70]

The fifth and last part of the book is entitled "International Organisations as Vehicles for Change: The Quest for Social Order." It contains eight contributions on current problems faced by international organizations. The article by former Judge Valticos is a philosophical reflection on the "crisis" in the actual state of international law in relation to recourse to force and the problems of globalization that are at the heart of international relations in the beginning of the new millennium.[71] The author traces some trends in the evolution of international organizations and proposes a reduction of the activities of specialized institutions or an alternative development of their activities. He hits the nail on the head when he states that the world should turn to a real globalization, namely a political and social one rather than a narrowly conceived economic globalization. It is indeed true that for decades different international organizations have often tried to carry out opposite priorities, which have not led to the required results.[72] This reviewer comes to the conclusion that the article by Tunguru Huaraka on "The Southern African Development Community" (Chapter 43)

---

[70] See, for instance, H. Fox, "The First Pinochet Case: Immunity of a Former Head of State" (1999) 48 I.C.L.Q. 207; A. Bianchi, "Immunity versus Rights" (1999) 10:2 Eur. J.Int'l L. 237; R. Wedgwood, "International Criminal Law and Augusto Pinochet" (2000) 40 Va. J. of Int'l L. 829; R. van Alebeek, "The Pinochet Case: International Human Rights Law on Trial" (2000) 71 B.Y.I.L. 29; D. Woodhouse, ed., "The Pinochet Case: A Legal and Constitutional Analysis" (Oxford: Hart Publishing, 2000); D. Sugarman, "The Pinochet Case: International Criminal Justice in the Gothic Style?"(2001) 64 Mod. L. Rev. 933; J. Sears: "Confronting the Culture of Impunity: Immunity of Heads of State from Nuremberg to *ex parte* Pinochet" (1999) 42 G.Y.I.L 125; J. Bröhmer, "Immunity of a Former Head of State General Pinochet and the House of Lords: Part Three" (2000) 13 Leiden J. Int'l L. 229; C. Nicholls (leading counsel for Pinochet), "Reflections on Pinochet"(2000) 41 Va. J. Int'l L. 140; C. Blakesley, "Autumn of the Patriarch: The Pinochet Extradition Debacle and Beyond — Human Rights Clauses Compared to Traditional Derivative Protections Such as Double Criminality" (2000) 91 J. of Crim. L. & Criminology 1.

[71] See, for example, R. Moore, "Globalization and the Future of US Human Rights Policy" (1998) 21 Washington Quarterly 193; A. Anghie, "Time Present and Time Past: Globalization, International Financial Institutions, and the Third World" (2000) 32 N.Y. U. J. Int'l L. & Pol. 243; P. Spiro, "Globalization, International Law, and the Academy" (2000) 32 N.Y.U.J. Int'l L. & Pol. 567; and Sub-Commission on the Promotion and Protection of Human Rights, "Globalization and its Impact," *supra* note 31.

[72] Boisson de Chazournes and Gowlland-Debbas, eds., *supra* note 1 at 728.

reveals an example of a community that, at the regional level, seems to have its priorities set right.

Chapter 39 by Christian Dominicé on "Organisations Internationales et Démocratie" explores the emerging right to democratic governance or a right to democracy and even infers that it could develop into *jus cogens*.[73] This article could also restart the debate on the so-called "third generation" rights, which is a concept developed by Karl Vasak in the 1970s that is close to the United Nations Educational, Scientific and Cultural Organization (UNESCO) philosophy. Although severely criticized by P. Alston,[74] the concept is still considered relevant as the Sub-Commission on the Promotion and Protection of Human Rights currently devotes a study to it.[75] The attempt to enlarge the membership of the Security Council shows just how difficult it is to democratize international organizations. With respect to the contribution to democracy, the real challenge for the international community, and for international organizations, in particular, is the manner in which Afghanistan will be rebuilt.

The article by Shin-ichi Ago, entitled "Clash of Operational and Normative Activities," may be considered the executive arm of Valticos's reflections. In his conclusions, Ago correctly observes that thus far little has been written on the international responsibility of international institutions and, in particular, the status of international institutions under general international law.[76] The article by Alston is the only article devoted entirely to human rights issues, namely "The Historical Origins of General Comments in International Human Rights Law." It traces the evolution of international human rights law against the background of political

[73] *Ibid.* at 733.

[74] P. Alston, "A Third Generation of Solidarity Rights: Progressive Development or Obfuscation of International Human Rights Law" (1982) 29:3 Netherl. Int'l L. Rev. 307.

[75] See Sub-Commission on the Promotion and Protection of Human Rights, *Working Paper by Mr. Manuel Rodriguez Cuadros,* July 5, 2001, 53rd Sess., UN Doc. E/CN.4/Sub.2/2001/32; and B. Boutros Ghali, "Le Droit international à la Recherche de ses Valeurs: Paix, Développement, Démocratisation," in *Collected Courses of the Hague Academy of International Law,* vol. 286 (The Hague: Martinus Nijhoff Publishers, 2000) at 17.

[76] Boisson de Chazournes and Gowlland-Debbas, eds. *supra* note 1 at 761; See, however, A.M. Slaughter, "International Law and International Relations," in *Collected Courses of the Hague Academy of International Law,* vol. 285 (The Hague: Martinus Nijhoff Publishers, 2000) at 9, where this question is considered in Chapter V.

realities. It reveals that general comments on the human rights situation historically have been general and only in the early 1990s were the human rights committees able to draft country-specific concluding observations, parallel to another form of general comments that were hammered out by the Human Rights Committee in October 1980 and subsequently followed by all other treaty bodies, namely the practice of interpreting a specific article of a human rights convention.[77]

Chapter 42 on "La métamorphose des Opérations de Maintien de la Paix des Nations Unies" shows how necessary it has been to conduct a serious study on the operation of the United Nations Department of Peacekeeping Operations, which has led to serious criticism and reform proposals by a panel headed by Brahimi, who is mentioned earlier in this review.[78] The penultimate article on the impossible reform of the League of Arab States is a true account of realities. It would, in my humble opinion, nevertheless be a great asset in the very-needed search for a solution to the Israeli-Palestinian conflict if the individual countries constituting the League of Arab States were to act in a more coherent way.

In conclusion, the reader will discern from the first section of the book an evolution towards the need for a just social order, which is so desperately needed in today's world. The chapters and sections of the book are well organized, despite the apparent lack of time for the preparation of this *liber amicorum*. Although the last chapter recounts Abi-Saab's suggestion to go for a walk in the park in order to reflect better on academic ideas, this remainder of this monumental book incites those who read it to reflect on the whole panacea of current international law. The outstanding contributions of Abi-Saab to international law have left their mark on the science of international law as well as on those who serve this science. It is our sincere hope that he may still contribute to the development of international law in various capacities for many years to come.

JOHANNES VAN AGGELEN
Geneva

---

[77] See Compilation of General Comments and General Recommendations adopted by the Human Rights Treaty Bodies, UN Doc. HR/GEN/1/Rev. 5 of April 26, 2001.

[78] *Brahimi Report, supra* note 47.

V.V. Pustogarov, *Fedor Fedorovich Martens-yurist, diplomat,* 2d ed. (Moscow: «Mezhdunarodnye otnosheniya», 1999). xiv and 290 pages. ISBN 5-7133-0975-4, US $11.95.

Aficionados of late imperial Russia's international legal scholarship know V.V. Pustogarov as the Russian Federation's pre-eminent authority on the contributions of Fedor Fedorovich Martens (1845-1909). His *S pal'movoy vetv'yu mira: F.F. Martens-yurist, diplomat, publitsist (With the Palm Branch of Peace: F.F. Martens — Jurist, Diplomat, Publicist)* (Moscow: «Mezhdunarodnye otnosheniya», 1993) is the most comprehensive biography of Martens in any language, and it has received generally admirable translations into English and French.[1] The work under review suggests that Pustogarov's insights of 1993 are still topical, and while Christophe Swinarski's introductory treatment of Martens's contributions to the evolution of contemporary international humanitarian law represents a helpful innovation.

Martens made his most celebrated contribution to international law at the 1899 Hague Peace Conference. At his behest, the so-called Martens clause was inserted into Convention (II) with Respect to the Laws and Customs of War on Land,[2] which codified the law of land warfare. The Martens clause provided that in unforeseen circumstances, "populations and belligerents remain under the protection and empire of the principles of international law, as they result from the usages established between civilized nations, from the laws of humanity, and the requirements of the public conscience." It comprised a landmark in international humanitarian law, although its precise significance has evoked scholarly debate.[3] As recently as 1996, the International Court of Justice affirmed that it remains a valid principle of international law.[4]

The views advanced in the foregoing review are solely the author's views and should not be taken as expressing any view of the Department of Justice, Canada.

[1] V.V. Pustogarov, *Our Martens: F.F. Martens: -International Lawyer and Architect of Peace,* ed. and trans. W.E. Butler (The Hague: Kluwer, 2000); V.V. Pustogarov, *Au service de la paix : Frédéric de Martens et les conférences internationales de la paix de 1899 et 1907. Biographie d'un juriste et diplomate russe,* ed. and trans. M. Mabillard et al. (Geneva: Université de Genève, 1999).

[2] D. Schindler and J. Toman, eds., *The Law of Armed Conflicts: A Collection of Conventions, Resolutions and Other Documents* (Leiden: A.W. Sijthoff, 1973) at 64.

[3] The scholarly debate is ably recapitulated in A. Cassese, "The Martens Clause: Half a Loaf or Simply Pie in the Sky?" (2000) 11 Eur. J.Intl L. 187 at 189-92.

[4] *Legality of the Use by a State of Nuclear Weapons in Armed Conflict, Advisory Opinion,* I.C.J. Reports 1996, 66 at 260.

Yet Martens's contributions ran considerably further, marking him as one who occupied a distinctive place amidst the late imperial Russian international legal scholars. On the one hand, he published copiously on public international law, Russia's relations with other realms, and so forth. Not only was his *Sovremennoe mezhdunarodnoe pravo tsivilizovannykh narodov* (*Contemporary International Law of Civilized Peoples*)[5] a classic within Russia; it underwent translations into seven languages, thereby enabling him — which is exceptional for an international legal scholar of his time — to win a following outside his own country. On the other hand, he served repeatedly as a Russian diplomat in meetings with foreign representatives, and he was sufficiently renowned as an arbiter that he won the appellation "the chief judge of the Christian world."[6] No other Russian legal scholar of the late imperial era combined as adroitly as did he scholarly enquiry into international law with the practical experience of international relations.

Pustogarov looks beyond Martens's best-known publications on public international law and international relations for evidence illuminating his varied career. Most important, he refers repeatedly to Martens's diary, which was located in the Archive of the Foreign Policy of Russia after a lengthy hiatus. He alludes additionally to various largely unfamiliar articles that Martens published in prerevolutionary journals. His detailed knowledge of Martens's works, unpublished and published alike, arguably gives the biography its strongest claim to supersede the earlier Martens scholarship.

The evidence that Pustogarov adduces not only helps to clarify the facts of Martens's career but also illuminates his attitudes towards the environment in which he lived and worked. Pustogarov's analysis is probably most successful in probing these attitudes and their implications for scholars' broader appreciation of Martens. To take a noteworthy example, Pustogarov dissents from Arthur Nussbaum's view that Martens's attempts to secure international peace flowed primarily from "a desire to serve his sovereign."[7] The entries in Martens's diary do not depict him as being

---

[5] Fedor Fedorovich Martens, *Sovremennoe mezhdunarodnoe pravo tsivilizovannykh narodov* (*Contemporary International Law of Civilized Peoples*) 2 vols. (St. Petersburg: Izdatel'stvo Ministerstva putey soobshcheniya, 1882-1883).

[6] V.V. Pustogarov, Fedor Fedorovich Martens-yurist, diplomat, 2d ed. (Moscow: «Mezhdunarodnye otnosheniya», 1999) at 202.

[7] A. Nussbaum, "Frederic de Martens, representative tsarist writer on international law" (1952) 22:2-3 Acta scandinavica juris gentium 51 at 62.

highly esteeming of Nicholas II and his leading courtiers.[8] On the contrary, Pustogarov opines that Martens saw the promotion of peace amongst nations as the foremost purpose of international law and advocated universal peace many times in his publicizing works.[9]

Pustogarov pays less heed to the reactions that Martens elicited within his environment. Admittedly Pustogarov does not ignore the issue altogether, observing that Martens's address of March 26, 1887, to St. Petersburg University students gained him a display of respect that he found moving.[10] This episode is all the more noteworthy because archival materials throw little light on the attitudes that Martens, as a professor at St. Petersburg University, encountered.[11] Yet, Pustogarov refers only spasmodically to documentation where late imperial Russia's leading governmental figures expressed candidly how they reacted to Martens. Perhaps additional archival research would have yielded more such documentation and, with it, answers to the various questions connected with Martens's career. Why, for instance, was Martens — to his deep chagrin — not appointed head of the Russian delegation to the 1899 Hague Peace Conference?[12] Ideally, Pustogarov would have struck a balance between recording Martens's disappointment and probing the considerations that caused him to be passed over.

On balance, though, Pustogarov's biography creates a generally favourable impression. Clearly expounded, well documented, and balanced in its conclusions, it advances significantly the scholarly understanding of Martens's career and legacy. May Russian legal historians bear it in mind as they strive better to acquaint themselves with late imperial Russia's distinguished tradition of international legal scholarship.

ERIC MYLES
Department of Justice Canada, Toronto

---

[8] Pustogarov, *supra* note 6 at 141.

[9] *Ibid.* at 146.

[10] *Ibid.* at 39-40.

[11] *Ibid.* at 39.

[12] *Ibid.* at 155

Analytical Index / Index analytique

THE CANADIAN YEARBOOK OF
INTERNATIONAL LAW

2001

ANNUAIRE CANADIEN
DE DROIT INTERNATIONAL

(A) Article; (NC) Notes and Comments; (Ch) Chronique;
(P) Practice; (C) Cases; (BR) Book Review
(A) Article; (NC) Notes et commentaires; (Ch) Chronique;
(P) Pratique; (C) Jurisprudence; (BR) Recension de livre

economic sanctions, use of, under
international law, 253-330
constraints, 279-305
effects on third states, 305-8
introduction, 253-55
legal basis of collective sanctions,
255-79
politicization, selectivity, and double
standards, 308-10
proposals for modifying and refining sanction practices, 310-26
endangered species, trafficking
parliamentary declarations, 512-13
environmental law
Department of Foreign Affairs
practice, 485-89
parliamentary declarations
Cartagena Protocol on Biosafety,
509-10
hazardous waste, 510
Kyoto Protocol, 510-12
persistent organic pollutants, 512
sustainable development strategies, 509
trafficking of endangered species,
512-13
Eritrea
parliamentary declarations, 515-16
Espoo Convention
Department of Foreign Affairs practice, 485-86
Ethiopia
parliamentary declarations, 515-16

Fedor Fedorovich Martens-yurist, diplomat,
V.V. Pustogarov, reviewed by
Eric Myles (BR), 638-40
Fonds Monétaire Internationales
(FMI)
et le Canada, 453-55
Food and Drugs Act
parliamentary declarations, 507-8
foreign affairs
parliamentary declarations, 513-26
free trade. *See* libre-échange

General Agreement on Tariffs and
Trade (GATT)
commerce, 443, 444-45
genetically modified food
parliamentary declarations, 507-8
"Gordon W. Smith: A Historical and
Legal Study of Sovereignty in

the Canadian North and
Related Law of the Sea Prob-
lems," by Jeannette Tramhel
(NC), 435-40
Gowlland-Debbas, Vera and Laurence
Boisson de Chazournes, editors,
*The International Legal System in
Quest of Equity and Universality,*
reviewed by Johannes van
Aggelen (BR), 621-37
Groupe d'Action Financière (GAFI),
460-62
Le Groupe des vingt (G-20), 451-53
"La 'guerre contre le terrorisme,' le
droit international humanitaire
et le statut de prisonnier de
guerre," by Marco Sassòli (A),
211-52

Hague Convention on the Civil
Aspects of International Child
Abduction, 597-99
hazardous waste
parliamentary declarations, 510
human rights. *See also* humanitarian
law
in *Baker* case, 379-81
Department of Foreign Affairs practice, 490-99
impact of economic sanctions, 267,
295-305
Internet violations, 28-29
parliamentary declarations, 526-27
humanitarian intervention
implicit Security Council authorizations, 333-69
humanitarian law. *See also* human
rights
Department of Foreign Affairs practice, 490-99
"La 'guerre contre le terrorisme,' le
droit international humanitaire
et le statut de prisonnier de
guerre," by Marco Sassòli (A),
211-51
impact of economic sanctions, 295-
305, 317-22
principes généraux, 108-9

ICC. *See* International Criminal Court
(ICC)
immigration
parliamentary declarations, 504-5

Index of Cases /
Index de la jurisprudence